THE SHINING STRANGER

THE SHINING STRANGER

We have seen his glory . . .
seen it to be full of grace and reality

An Unorthodox Interpretation of Jesus
and His Mission

(not just Paul's words but the Gospels)

by Preston Harold

*Introductions by Gerald Heard and
Winifred Babcock*

A Harold Institute Book

DISTRIBUTED BY DODD, MEAD & COMPANY

NEW YORK

In deepest appreciation this book is dedicated to those whose words are quoted. These authors are drawn from many disciplines and in many cases their statements were not posed as part of a dialogue between their disciplines and religion, as the quotations are posed in this book. Thus, it must be emphasized that in no sense does this dedication imply that any of these individuals have embraced the whole or any part of the concept presented in this study—nor that the author of this study necessarily embraces the whole of the work of those he has quoted.

First Edition—1967
Second Edition—1968
Third Edition—1973
Copyright © 1967, 1973 by Harold Institute
All rights reserved
No part of this book may be reproduced in any form
without permission in writing from the publisher
ISBN: 0-396-06932-0
Library of Congress Catalog Card Number: 73-19480

Printed in the United States of America

ABOUT THE AUTHOR

Preston Harold is a pen name. Neither Mr. Heard, Mr. Barrie, myself, nor anyone else connected with publishing the Harold manuscript knows who or what the author was. They know only that he is deceased, and they are confident his identity can never be made known. The anonymous author was convinced that truth makes its own way, because it enlists the aid of those whose hearts resound accord as they are presented with it. To him, **THE SHINING STRANGER** must and could withstand this test.

Winifred Babcock
President
Harold Institute

P.O. Box 11024
Winston-Salem, N.C. 27106
U.S.A.

No man can reveal to you aught but that which already
lies half asleep in the dawning of your knowledge.

—Kahlil Gibran
The Prophet

Contents

INTRODUCTION BY GERALD HEARD		ix
INTRODUCTION TO THE THIRD EDITION BY WINIFRED BABCOCK		xix
Chapter 1.	The Problem, the Objective, the Crucial Questions	1
Chapter 2.	The Messianic Mission of Jesus	16
Chapter 3.	Man's Archaic Heritage	46
Chapter 4.	The Legendary Chain of Life	61
Chapter 5.	Original Sin and Saving Grace	96
Chapter 6.	Nature's Supreme Law	124
Chapter 7.	One, Itself, Is Teacher	146
Chapter 8.	The Dilemma and the Pearl	175
Chapter 9.	What Has Been Hidden	194
Chapter 10.	All Is Natural	214
Chapter 11.	Jesus' Healing Ministry	228
Chapter 12.	The Social Miracles	246
Chapter 13.	Jesus' Demonstrations of Extrasensory Perception and the Psychic Power	259
Chapter 14.	The Illusory Miracles	284
Chapter 15.	The Resurrection	311
Chapter 16.	Returning to This World	333
Chapter 17.	The Economic Doctrine of Jesus	337
Chapter 18.	Truth—What Is Truth?	374
Chapter 19.	In Conclusion	389
APPENDICES		395

CONTENTS

REFERENCES 413
BIBLIOGRAPHY 448
INDEX 457

Introduction

Today, Christianity is faced with its worst crisis and, indeed, could be in grave peril. Such questioning of orthodox Christian doctrine as is evidenced in the sensational query Is God Dead? indicates that the crisis is culminating in an effort to re-examine the teachings of Jesus to see if, in the light of today's knowledge, a new interpretation of his meaning is to be discerned. Such an effort is made in THE SHINING STRANGER.

Preston Harold takes as premise that St. Paul's interpretation of Jesus as Messiah, and the miracles Jesus is reported to have worked, estrange the Christian in today's world. He is convinced that no amount of pruning traditional Christian theology will restore modern man's faith in it, nor will the religious dilemma be resolved by making the Christian Churches more effective or more liberal social organs. Among the questions he sees Christianity to be facing are these:

Was Jesus as far removed from reality as those who expected the end of the world and the second coming of the Christ before the death of the disciple John?

Is the ethic of Jesus corrupted by the taint of a vainglorious concept of himself?

Are the Gospels corrupted by reports of miracles that did not, could not, happen?

In Harold's view, Western civilization rests so heavily upon Christianity that the questions must be answered and the integrity of Jesus' revelation must be established, or Western man confronts the prospect of having built the edifice of his culture upon a foundation of sand.

The author has a widely ranging mind with a great power of speculative and imaginative correlation. He views the life and words of Jesus with a poet's eye, but he sees in Jesus' words a grasp of reality in all its depths, and an understanding that could be conveyed to posterity only through poetic means: parable, enigmatic statements, dramatizations, because the language to couch his realization did not exist. He believes that Jesus took his stand upon the ground of nature itself, revealing the operation of natural law in the physical universe and in man, letting truth direct his actions and express itself through his voice, by which he means that Jesus saw truth to be the possession of every person able to tap its fount in his own unconscious mind. In Harold's view, Jesus' concept of man's "inner kingdom" is equivalent to psychology's concept of man's *unconscious;* and Jesus realized that the seat of the Logos, which he saw as one and the same measure of "God-being" in every human being, is in this psychic realm.

Consequently, the author presents Jesus as only one among history's great men who were truth bearers, Jesus' revelation as a development in the expression of truth; but because of the Western world's familiarity with Christianity he believes that Western man's best hope of elucidating true religion rests upon a better understanding of Jesus' own religion as opposed to Pauline doctrine.

In Harold's view, the crucial question facing Christianity today and orthodox Christianity's answer to it that is no longer creditable is the question of Jesus' Messianic role and his concept of himself. THE SHINING STRANGER is based upon a revolutionary and, insofar as I am aware, unprecedented interpretation of Jesus' Messianic mission which Harold develops as the discourse progresses, drawing upon Jesus' own words and actions to support his thesis. This interpretation involves the following points:

1. Jesus recognized the Messianic hope to be valid and universal, but misdirected when man looked beyond his individual being to find the Christ (Logos, God-Son) which Jesus saw to be incarnate in every person, revealed through humankind's unique power of speech and expression of the Word, God, One, *I*.

2. Jesus realized that until the ancient Messianic doctrines were superseded by a valid, ethical concept of the Christ, of God, and of man, the individual and society would suffer the ravages of Messianic pretension, as well as the curse of Messianic delusion which Jesus suffered but from which he recovered before beginning his ministry, recognizing himself to be no more, no less, than any other human being.

3. Jesus was convinced that until man ceased to look for a Messiah to come and solve all problems, the development of human consciousness would be arrested because man would not seek his "inner kingdom" to find the Christ of himself, the Authority that governs his life and inevitably leads him to become responsible to and for himself as well as a responsible member of society in which *truth* alone actually governs and reigns, in time destroying whatever is false, spurious, and incompatible with man's true nature and need.

4. Therefore, Jesus' purpose was *to complete and thereby destroy the Judaic Messianic tradition together with any Messianic concept akin to it through a withering of this idea as the Messianic idea he espoused, the idea of the Christ in everyone, took root and flowered to overshadow prevailing Messianic expectation.* He knew exactly what he was doing and was in no sense victimized.

5. Jesus' mission was to destroy Messianic tradition *creatively* by making "Israel" and its history a *symbol* of human personality or consciousness, while making himself a *symbol* of the Christ in every person which insures his eternal life and the evolution of his consciousness through dealing with his own forces of good and evil which Jesus saw to be equally essential to life and satisfaction in it, but he saw also that each force was in process of regeneration; Jesus made himself a symbol of the Logos in humankind to establish the pattern of the operation of the Christ in Homo sapiens' evolution from *child* to *man* free of destructive impulses by virtue of being fully conscious and completely empathetic, with dominion over himself, his flesh, and his life.

6. The Bible, one body of words encompassing the limits of *human consciousness*, truth bearer that can dwell always with men and which Jesus knew must be brought into being as a result of his words and his command to his disciples, is itself *historical Judaic Messiah*.

The implications deriving from these ideas are indeed far-reaching, but in the author's view through them Jesus' message is given logic, intelligibility, and the seemingly hopeless contradictions in his life and words are reconciled.

Harold does not believe this interpretation of Jesus' mission diminishes the importance of the Christian Church or its history because he recognizes the necessity the Church labored under to pursue the course it took, just as he recognizes the necessity for it to move beyond Pauline theology and reinterpret Jesus' message in accordance with the *Gospel reports* of his life, words, and works. He acknowledges that the answer he offers to the mystery of Jesus' Messianic role is one that St. Paul could not give. Only time could reveal it. St. Paul's place in the history of Christianity remains unshaken despite the author's rejection of the Pauline interpretation of Jesus. The book is not an attack upon the Church, but Harold separates Jesus' own words from the dogmas that attach to his life and teaching and poses these words against the "given data" of science and human experience.

The miracles, including the Resurrection, are examined and are brought into new perspective when viewed against the contradictory reports of them in the Gospels and against what is known today of the phenomena arising from hypnosis. In the author's words, Jesus showed through his works "the limits of the extrasensory and psychic power in man—*its ability to delude as well as to illuminate*—and He demonstrated the release of the body's healing power in hypnotic trance."

Harold deals with every aspect of the teachings of Jesus, and with every aspect of life upon which the words of Jesus touch. The "worldly philosophy" of Jesus, his economic doctrine, ethics, and regard for government and law, for war and peace, for the patterns of daily life are examined, and the flow of history along the paths Jesus projected is briefly traced.

Seeing Jesus' revelation as an expression of the Logos in man, complete in understanding, Harold sees Jesus' doctrine as completely valid and Jesus' integrity vindicated by today's knowledge in a way and at a depth impossible to comprehend until employment of the scientific method had revealed nature in greater depth. It follows, therefore, that a person must have some understanding of the major laws of the physical sciences and of psychology before he can appreciate the depth and breadth of Jesus' message.

Although Harold believes that religion must be congruent with scientific knowledge, if its tenets are to be valid and creditable, he does not believe religion should be limited by scientific knowledge because such knowledge is indeed limited today. He believes that a complete interpretation of Jesus' message cannot yet be given, and that the interpretation he offers could not be discerned until the many disciplines of science had reached their present level of development and science itself had suffered the revolution that it has undergone in the twentieth century. As Harold develops his concept of Jesus' revelation, it becomes an invitation to Christianity to evolve into a psychologically based religion compatible with all others and congruent with the data, aims, and destiny of modern science.

Underlying every postulation is the outline of a new psychology, a psychology that is both existential and religious, a psychology that pays more than lip service to the idea of the Christ in man, giving this idea an immediacy, a universality, a practicality that goes far beyond the transcendentalized and vicarious acceptance generally accorded these words in Christian circles. The dynamics of this new psychology are detailed as the author poses Jesus' poetic words against an explanation of modern physics as given for the layman by Arthur Eddington and others such as Wolfgang Pauli and Erwin Schrödinger, and against the words of Sigmund Freud, Carl Jung, Otto Rank, Alfred Adler, and other authorities in the field of psychology. Harold draws a parallel between the psychic operation of man and the operation of the secondary laws of physics, so that there is a three-party "wedding" of science, psychology, and religion. Undoubtedly, scientists, psychologists, and the clergy will view this as an uneasy alliance if not as an "impossible marriage."

Nevertheless, such an alliance has been suggested by authorities in the fields of both physics and psychology. Harold writes, "Einstein saw that the new physics may justly call itself a theory of life, 'for the general laws . . . claim to be valid for any natural phenomenon whatsoever' . . . [Dr. Ira Progoff] looks to the new physics to open a new road, a new view, for psychology." Among others, Harold quotes Aniela Jaffe, contributor to Jung's book, MAN AND HIS SYMBOLS, who says, "The parallelism between nuclear physics and the psychology of the collective unconscious was often a subject of discussion between Jung and Wolfgang Pauli, the Nobel prizewinner in physics. The space-time continuum of physics and the collective unconscious can be seen, so to speak, as the outer and inner aspects of one and the same reality behind appearances." Harold also quotes Dr. M-L. von Franz, contributor to Jung's book. Dr. von Franz writes, "We are still far from understanding the unconscious or the archetypes—those dynamic *nuclei* of the psyche—in all their implications . . . But the most promising field for future studies seems (as Jung saw it) to have unexpectedly opened up in connection with the complex field of microphysics. At first sight, it seems most unlikely that we should find a relationship between psychology and microphysics. The most obvious aspect of such a connection lies in the fact that most of the basic concepts of physics (such as space, time, matter, energy, continuum or field, particle, etc.) were originally intuitive, semi-mythological, archetypal ideas of the old Greek philosophers—ideas that then slowly evolved and became more accurate and that today are mainly expressed in abstract mathematical terms . . . When examining nature and the universe, instead of looking for and finding objective qualities, 'man encounters himself,' in the phrase of the physicist Werner Heisenberg . . . Pauli believed that we should parallel our investigation of outer objects with a psychological investigation of the *inner origin* of our scientific concepts."

Harold recognized the difficulties theologians encounter as they attempt to reconcile science and religion: "Samuel Miller asks if a Christian can talk to people of God 'when they find God quite unimaginable in a . . . world scientifically structured in iron law.'" But in Harold's view, "Alfred North Whitehead states the case: 'When we consider what religion is for mankind, and what science is, it is no exaggeration to say that the future course of history depends upon the decision of this generation as to the relations between them. We have here the two strongest general forces . . . which influence men.'"

As Harold poses the parallels between Jesus' words and the words of physicists and psychologists, a number of telling points and provocative ideas are put forward. In the author's view, religion has something to offer science as well as vice versa. He sees the universe as he believes Jesus saw it: as an evolving but nevertheless self-conserving, self-renewing existence which will always be able to support life.

Every ramification of Harold's basic view that he discusses in his book (a number of which will no doubt startle the reader) cannot be touched upon here. Viewed as a whole, his work is a challenge to men in every discipline to participate in resolving the religious crisis generated by the universal decline of faith in old theologies which, in turn, has generated a psychological crisis that threatens to engulf man and is a part of his every other problem. For Harold is convinced that neither an increase in scientific knowledge nor a concerted effort to give equal emphasis to the humanities in this age so dedicated to science can restore meaning and purpose to life, that only a rebirth of religion compatible with fact and built upon a base man can accept as reality will give him reason for being and the courage to move purposefully into the future. To the author's ear, the din of voices crying in today's wilderness rise in chorus to sound one mighty call: make way for the religious idea to be reborn upon the plateau of consciousness man has reached. Acknowledging the limitations of THE SHINING STRANGER, he offers it as a step in that direction.

It was the author's desire to let his work speak for itself (Preston Harold is a pen-name). The manuscript was given to Michael Barrie and me. Although I do not agree with all this book has to say, I believe it should be published, and that other efforts to discover a new meaning in Jesus' teachings will be made. Mr. Barrie and I would like to thank Winifred Babcock for her help in the project of publishing the Harold manuscript.

I, too, am aware of the limitations of this book, and of the criticism that may justly be directed against it, primarily that the author has attempted too much. A work of such scope, however, is necessary to accomplish the objective Harold saw to be essential, an objective he took from Jesus' command: "Either make the tree good and his fruit good; or else make the tree corrupt, and his fruit corrupt; for the tree is known by his fruit." To accomplish this objective, Jesus' revelation must be posed against the vast body of twentieth-century knowledge, an overwhelming task for one man to undertake. At the outset, Harold says that the new view of Jesus presented in THE SHINING STRANGER is no more than a sketch, "Its incompleteness, its limited certitude, its panoramic and therefore necessarily superficial canvas is acknowledged." He calls upon the words of many writers in his effort to present a broad view of today's knowledge and philosophical climate, choosing the ones he thinks can be understood most readily by a wide audience.

In dedicating his book to the authors he quotes, Harold emphasizes that their statements "were not posed as part of a dialogue between their disciplines and religion, as the quotations are posed in this book. Thus . . . in no sense does this dedication imply that any of these individuals have embraced the whole or any part of the concept presented in this study—nor that the author of this study necessarily embraces the whole of the work of those he has quoted."

Harold's effort was not to challenge every theology and many prevailing theories so much as it was to restore man's faith in *Jesus* by presenting Jesus' idea of man, based upon the authority of his own words as reported in the Gospels. Harold believes Jesus' idea of man is valid and that humankind can accept it wholeheartedly because in his view Jesus' teaching is congruent with the "given data" of science and human experience, and through Jesus' ability to tap the fount of truth in his own unconscious, he was able to reveal the true nature and psychological operation of each human being. How near THE SHINING STRANGER comes to stating a valid interpretation of Jesus and a valid idea of man, each reader must decide for himself. Probably, the book will stir up violent controversies, but whatever the reaction of its readers, it *will* do one thing: it will force them to re-think their whole position in regard to Jesus and Christianity.

GERALD HEARD

Santa Monica, California
October 6, 1966

GERALD HEARD, Historian, Author, Lecturer and Philosopher, was born in London in 1889. He graduated from Cambridge University, taking honors in history, returning to do post-graduate work in the philosophy of religion.

For a number of years after this he worked with Sir Horace Plunkett, founder of the Irish Co-operative Movement. Subsequently, he was editor of THE REALIST, with a board of editorial advisers consisting of Aldous Huxley, Sir Julian Huxley, H. G. Wells, Rebecca West, Arnold Bennett, and others. He was Science Commentator for The British Broadcasting Corporation during the years 1930–1934. He is the author of forty-five books. One of his early books, THE ASCENT OF HUMANITY, a philosophy of history, was awarded The Henrietta Hertz Prize by The British Academy.

In 1937, Mr. Heard came to the United States, having been offered the chair of Historical Anthropology at Duke University. However, after one term there he decided to go to California where he has made his home since.

Mr. Heard has lectured at most of the major colleges and universities in the United States—Harvard, Cornell, Princeton, the Universities of California at Los Angeles and Berkeley, Mills College, Oberlin, Wabash, the University of Southern California, and many others. He has made numerous radio and television appearances. He has also made six twelve-inch long playing phonograph recordings, and continues to write. His major works include:

THE SOURCE OF CIVILIZATION
THE SOCIAL SUBSTANCE OF RELIGION
THE THIRD MORALITY
PAIN, SEX AND TIME
MAN, THE MASTER
THE CODE OF CHRIST
THE CREED OF CHRIST
IS GOD IN HISTORY?
IS GOD EVIDENT?
GABRIEL AND THE CREATURES
THE HUMAN VENTURE

THE ETERNAL GOSPEL
(given as the Ayer Foundation Lectures at Colgate Rochester University in 1945)
TRAINING FOR A LIFE GROWTH

His latest book, THE FIVE AGES OF MAN, was published in 1963.

Introduction to the Third Edition of
The Shining Stranger

The Shining Stranger by Preston Harold, with Introduction by Gerald Heard, was published in the fall of 1967. My part in the publication was to type the manuscript, prepare the references, and supervise the publication of the book. The reception accorded it led me to form Harold Institute in 1968 for the purpose of bringing Harold's work to the attention of those who seek an answer to unanswered questions in religion, science, and psychology which will satisfy the demands of reason and the desire to find meaning and purpose in life. For me, and many others, Harold offers satisfying answers because they are in harmony with the persisting intuitions of humankind *and* with the most advanced scientific knowledge, although they move beyond many current nihilistic theories.

However, there is nothing dogmatic about Harold's appraisal of his own work, nor my personal views. He invites its further development, and so do I. He says that it is not complete, not final, not the only view that is acceptable in the light of modern knowledge. In this I concur. His aim was to open new vistas of thought, and to bring to bear upon our view of ourselves the information we now have pertaining to every area of human endeavor.

Harold dedicated his book to the authors he quoted. He called upon the work of those who have "drawn together the voices of outstanding contributors in their fields." He wanted to use books that could be obtained readily and those that presented comprehensive or panoramic views of the various disciplines with which he deals. Always, he strove to present his work in such a way that laymen could understand it and, through the words of interpreters, could understand the work of scientists and scholars who have contributed so much to modern knowledge. Because of this, when preparing the references, I decided to give only the more popular secondary sources, avoiding the rather formidable primary sources. However, the growing interest of scholars in Harold's work has now made it advisable to enlarge the reference section in this edition and give the primary sources as well. A Bibliography is included, and several Appendices needed to clarify certain points as the reader goes along, because many passages had to be omitted in order to publish *The Shining Stranger* in one volume.

I welcome this opportunity to point out aspects of the book which thread their course throughout so that they do not become apparent immediately. To begin with, the title refers to no person as such. It was taken from a line in the text: "Truth is often a shining stranger."

Harold's monumental work is presented within the framework of religion because: "Stating a valid, rational, ethical, and soul-satisfying religion is the problem that confronts humankind with each enlargement of the boundaries of consciousness. Whatever else may appear on the surface to be engaging the efforts and attention of Homo sapiens, religion is the fundamental problem he deals with, for at base it concerns the problem of himself, the question of 'Who and what am I?'" Harold saw that the worldwide collapse of faith in old theologies demands a new religious concept which is *psychologically based* because only then can it be universally valid.

In focusing upon a reinterpretation of Jesus, Harold in no way attempts to present Jesus or Christianity as the one and only, or even as the superior, religious figure and concept to be embraced by humanity. He says that the restoration of religion meaningful to humankind which the whole world seeks can come only as each person *takes a new view of his own religion and the great religious figure that is most familiar to him.* Harold saw every great religious figure as a human prototype that provides a frame of reference in which the human potential may be measured. Each is a source of authority, which is essential to us to provide inner security and generate the courage we need to cope with the insecurity of life in the outer world.

But these prototypes must be seen as *symbols* of God-consciousness expressing itself in humankind, which is the way Harold saw Jesus and all of the others. He capitalizes pronouns that refer to Jesus and to all of the great religious figures—not to deify any of them, but to show the respect he accords each one. These prototypes are "mirrors" in which we may see reflected our own psychic dynamics and the reality of our being. Each prototype confirms the other.

Using the same methodology, Harold presents the authenticity and integrity of the Bible and the sacred books of *all* the peoples of the world. Each is seen to be a development in the expression of truth, revealing in often glorious poetry the paradoxical mystery of life and creation which science is now working to describe in technical language or in mathematical terms. As Harold weaves the wisdom of all religions into his presentation of Jesus against the background of modern knowledge, *The Shining Stranger* becomes a tapestry of the "light" of humankind.

Jesus' words and acts seem to be related to profound scientific concepts. Harold shows the sometimes astounding parallels between them. But in no sense does he limit Jesus' revelation to these concepts. He says that Jesus' works, words, and the concepts he presents in drama "are congruent with scientific data and with the given data of human experience," but his message leads to precepts beyond these—and he adds, "A religious idea which fails to lead beyond the measurable is not congruent with man or science." New insights into the relationship between religion, science, and psychology are presented. New concepts as to the nature of humankind and the Cosmos are offered. They are so well-founded that they must in time make a tremendous impact upon our view of ourselves and nature. Harold's theory of the living universe challenges what I think of as the "Chicken Little" cosmologies—the ones that say we are in a collapsing, dying system.

Issues are faced squarely. And Harold refuses to dodge words that in many instances may set up a "mental road block" immediately. But his use of such words as *hypnotism, reincarnation,* or the *unconscious* have a much wider connotation than is given generally. The reader should refrain from "turning off" until he has read the entire presentation of these subjects. This, of course, is true also of the thorny questions Harold deals with—particularly those confronting Judaism and Christianity.

Judaism and Christianity twist like a double helix through the past two thousand years, inseparable, yet diametrically opposed, together providing the base upon which Western civilization rests. Harold took a new look at these religions. He focused attention upon Jesus because a thousand cordial words will not erase the fact that if the Judaic interpretation is correct—that Jesus was *not* Messiah—then the Christian interpretation is wrong, and vice versa. And if either Christian or Judaic theology is correct, then every other religion suffers a downgrading in its traffic with reality. But the same is true of all religions, because each cherishes some type of Messianic ideal and, historically, has been exclusive in its approach, tending to undermine the ground the others stand upon. The religions of the world share common truths, but they also share common errors.

The major and unifying theme in Harold's work is his exploration of the Messianic complex that has expressed itself in countless ways throughout man's history, bringing in its wake such good and evil as is beyond calculation. The Messianic complex involves the compulsion to be truth-bearer, savior, judge—to play the role of God in beneficence and in exercise of power, becoming a law unto oneself. It involves giving one's life for others, and also inviting persecution to the point of martyrdom.

Today, the Messianic complex is spoken of in derisive terms, or it is recognized to be a symptom of mental illness. The desire to save the world, bear the truth, give one's life, is seen to coincide with the lust for power as well as with the compulsion to right the wrongs of the world, both ending all too often in madness. The Messianic ideal is so discredited that to millions it does not warrant discussion. To take this view is to close one's eyes to its violent expression throughout the earth, and throughout the twentieth century, ranging from Hitler's devastating Messianic delusion—he said, "Providence has ordained that I should be the greatest liberator of humanity"—to whatever evidence of it the morning paper presents. For example, the murderer, beachboy "Murf the Surf," was declared insane because psychiatrists found him to be a "self-styled savior here on earth for the purpose of righting wrongs, and he believes he has the freedom to do so."[1]

The tendency to "play God" ranges widely in degree and in the subtlety or openness of its expression. Parents, teachers, doctors, psychologists, spiritual leaders of all faiths—people in every profession and in every walk of life—are caught up in the role, although often the symptoms of their Messianic delusion or pretension are so well disguised that they themselves do not recognize them as such.

But the Messianic complex also has its constructive aspects. Dr. Abraham Maslow admitted that he was Messianic. He felt he must try to save the world, to prevent wars, hatred, and prejudice. He said that all really serious people are Messianic, having no interest in anything but their mission. And that such people are the "growing tip" of the whole human species—they are responsible for the evolution of its consciousness as well as its social systems.[2]

To greater or lesser degree, individuals, nations, ideologies are involved in the Messianic complex although few realize this or recognize its symptoms—constructive or destructive. Harold believed that until man understands the persisting Messianic dream and its compulsion that threads a course through human history, he cannot understand himself. Today, a

[1] Associated Press news release, July 3, 1968.
[2] *Psychology Today*, July 1968.

distinguished psychiatrist, Dr. Alan McGlashan of London, confirms this. He writes:

> Harold's conception of the ubiquitous presence of either Messianic delusions or Messianic pretensions, or both, in all people at all levels of society, is completely valid in my experience, and has been of immediate value in actual treatment. I believe, indeed, that it would be possible to construct a coherent system of psychotherapy springing from this one concept of Harold's ... Most analysts of experience develop in time a private world of images to convey the exact nuance of their patient's inner conflicts. And before I had read Harold's books my private term for this often encountered complex was "the Hamlet cry," based on Hamlet's agonised lament—
>
>   The time is out of joint. O cursed spite
>   That ever I was born to set it right!
>
> This "Hamlet cry" is wrung daily from a thousand hearts, and is a good image of a false dilemma—but "Messianic delusion" is a far more penetrating term, and far more effective as a therapeutic image.[3]

Harold saw that, for the Western world, the place to start dealing with the Messianic complex is in facing the question, still unanswered, of whether or not Jesus was Messiah, or believed himself to be Messiah.

Only the four Gospels, Jesus' own words, are drawn upon by Harold in developing his interpretation of Jesus' Messianic mission. He offers an answer that Judaism, Christianity, and every other religion can accept and still maintain its own integrity, as it transcends limiting dogma and enlarges the dimensions of its Messianic view. In essence, Harold's answer is as follows:

> Jesus was not, and did not believe himself to be, the long-awaited Judaic Messiah. His mission was to *destroy* the Messianic tradition of his day and *supplant it* with the idea of God indwelling every person, each expressed as Christ which means: Chalice of the life and unique power of Universal Parent Being.

Jesus rejected the Judaic Messianic expectation of his day which, I may add, differed widely as to what Messiah's role would be. Jesus saw that *truth* alone reigns and governs, freeing the individual from error. As truth comes into conscious expression among humankind, *Messiah comes into human expression*, bringing closer the golden age destined to manifest itself as truth takes over from error.

---

[3] From an unpublished paper prepared for a seminar on Harold's work, 1972.

Harold calls upon traditional Judaism to transcend its exclusiveness by *internalizing* its Messianic doctrine. In time, Messiah comes to and through every human being as surely as in time consciousness of truth, as opposed to falseness, comes to him. But Harold confirms the stand Judaism has taken. The refusal of the Jewish people to accept Jesus as their long-awaited Messiah is correct. Jesus counted upon the stubborn integrity of his people to continue to deny him, thereby keeping open the question of his Messiahship until his actual meaning came to be understood.

As for traditional Christianity, Harold acknowledges the importance of St. Paul in its history, but the Pauline interpretation of the meaning of Jesus' Messianic mission and death is rejected. He says that Christianity "can no longer ride the shoulders of St. Paul, mighty as they are. The day of dependence upon *vicarious atonement* and *vicarious acceptance* of the glory, grace, and reality of life is over." St. Paul interpreted Jesus' message as best it could be interpreted according to the consciousness of his day, and Christianity owes its life to him. But the Pauline interpretation is simply the first—not the last or only valid one.

What St. Paul realized was that no other "images of Messiah" could be cast because none would have the authenticity in terms of the authority with which Jesus played the role. What he did not understand, and what has not yet been understood, is that "Jesus, Himself, so thoroughly undermined the prevailing Messianic concept, left the question of it and His relationship to it so entangled in contradiction, so twisted and bent in every direction, that the controversy He began could not be closed, the question could not be answered, the battle He started could not cease, until the last fragment of any Messianic image was gone, and his own Messianic image, become in time a hated object of odium, had been pounded into dust."

When the significance of Jesus' own evaluation of himself is accepted, and the real meaning of Christ is understood, Harold's interpretation of Jesus' Messianic mission confirms the Pauline ideal of Christ-consciousness entering into human consciousness bringing saving grace. Jesus stated himself to be a brother-being to the least person ever born, to be the same, without reservation. Harold does not diminish the divinity of Jesus. He elevates every human being to that same level of divinity, *as Jesus himself did*.

Few indeed have realized, as Jesus and other great religious figures have, their relationship to Universal Parent Being and fellow human beings, expressing this in consciousness and behavior. But in time all will realize this relationship and express the Christ of their being as surely as Jesus did. It is in this sense that the coming of Christ-consciousness brings saving grace. And only through such grace can the human potential be realized.

But other Pauline concepts create hostility. There is aversion to the idea that through Jesus' death he "bought" humankind and made possible their salvation by taking upon himself the sin of the world, paying with his life for its atonement. And there is resentment of St. Paul's involving sexual intercourse with immorality. His attitude toward sexuality was very different from that of Jesus, who commended it as the best and natural way of life.

Sigmund Freud pointed out that anti-Semitism is at bottom hatred for Christianity. Because the Bible deals only with Jewish people, the Christians have projected upon the Jews their aversion to St. Paul's teaching. Harold acknowledged this. But he pointed out also that St. Paul's doctrine of love reconciling all mystery, of our being inseparable from the love of God no matter what we do, "transcended his redemption dogma, clothing his words in shining armor, sending them unsurpassed through the centuries to lead and comfort men." Harold in no way demeaned St. Paul, who "seized with the full force of himself the majesty of Jesus and carried Christianity forward with majesty." He saw Pauline doctrine in its historical perspective, and confronted us with the simple fact that orthodox Christianity has not as yet accepted or understood the religion of Jesus. Christianity is based largely upon the religion of St. Paul.

In Harold's view, Jesus' grasp of the reality of life that underlies appearances could not be understood until the twentieth century when science and psychology, which are still undergoing rapid change, had evolved to present levels. Jesus' mission was manifold. He did more than reverse the direction of the Messianic dream, turning it inward. In essence:

> Jesus saw that each person speaks of himself only in the name of God, which is "One, I." Speaking in this name, Jesus deliberately made himself a symbol of the God-Son in man. Using the symbolic title, Son of man, he showed how God-consciousness operates in an unknown psychological realm within each person. Jesus called this realm the "kingdom of God, or heaven," and said it is "within you." Today, psychologists call this realm the *unconscious*, and acknowledge the reality of its existence.

Jesus insisted that he spoke not of "himself." Son of man represents God and truth incarnate in equal measure in every person. Son of man is the Self of each of us that governs our lives. Harold calls this psychic factor the Authority-Ego. He believed that Jesus *symbolized it* and showed its nature and function, and that every great religious figure symbolizes and expresses this psychic factor.

Jesus' symbolical representation of psychic structures, factors, processes, and functions involves not only the drama of Son of man. It includes Israel's history, John the Baptist, Jesus' disciples—indeed, the whole spectrum of developing consciousness from Genesis through Revelation.

Jesus said that his mission was to fulfill the Scriptures. They begin with allegorical man, Adam, and a *congruent* completion of them must be realized in an allegorical Son of man. This is what Jesus made of himself. He saw that if Messiah is to "tell us all things," only a *book* spanning the last reaches of human consciousness could be Messiah. Weaving his words and work into the Scriptures, he prepared the ground for his "second coming" in the advent of the Gospels. Through his work, the Bible as we know it today came into being. It begins with the advent of God-consciousness in human expression, symbolized by Adam, which reaches its climax in one's realization of God incarnate in his being, symbolized in Jesus as Son of man, and then bears witness to the transformation in consciousness that even brief encounter with this realization evokes.

The Bible fulfills the Judaic promise to bear the body of the truth of mankind into expression. Through it, Judaic Messianic expectation has been fulfilled. In it, Christian Messianic expectation, vested in the second coming of Jesus, has been fulfilled. But truth speaks the same words in every tongue. Each great religion must rightfully treasure its own Messiah: Its sacred book, through which truth is brought into conscious expression.

At the mention of the Bible, theologians will be concerned immediately to know how Harold responded to "Form Criticism" and the "Jesus Research" that has commanded their attention almost exclusively for nearly a century. Harold does not discuss it. He says at the outset that his book is not a theological discourse. He appears to have seen that there are many scholarly points of view as to the reliability of any one passage in any Gospel as there are scholars. A good case can be made for or against the many disputed issues and for each of the Gospels. There is no consensus, no definitive conclusion. To attempt to deal with the mass of literature on the subject would require a book in itself. The result of this exhaustive research has been to so *discredit* the Gospels as a trustworthy record of Jesus' ministry that they are all but useless. Modern theology is floating upon the mass of debris that "Jesus Research" has left of *the only record of him that we have.* The only ground that Christianity has to stand upon is undermined.

The simple fact of the matter is: No one knows how or when these records were written. As helpful as Form Criticism has been in many ways, it has not provided an answer to the mystery of the Gospels. Harold offers a completely new answer as to how they were written and why they are so contradictory in many ways. Suffice it to say here that he believed Jesus understood the potential of the human mind, and how to enhance the ability to recall and respond to command or suggestion. He called upon this potential to implant in the minds of his disciples exactly what he wanted them to record of their individual experiences with him—no more, no less. Each Gospel is an honest, reliable, although personal, account. Jesus deliberately posed the contradictions in the Gospels to force examination of his teaching when Messianic expectation was spent, and to force examination of the miracles to reveal their true nature as more became known about the psychic power in humankind and the nature of mental and physical energy. In Harold's view, Jesus saw to it that the Gospels would contradict each other in many ways, on many levels, in order to *symbolize* the psychic truth that the coming of Son-consciousness to a person's conscious mind cannot be forced into a chronological pattern applicable to everyone. Nor can the operation of Son-consciousness be formalized into a given pattern.

Jesus said that the *spirit* would bring to his disciples remembrance of all he had said. In his day, there was no name for what we call psychic power. To Harold, "spirit" refers to mental, psychic energy as opposed to intellectual and physical power. Jesus' words present more than a clue. Jesus plainly stated that he called upon the untapped potential of his disciples' minds to insure that his words would not pass away, but would spring fresh from the records his disciples prepared. We know today that this can be accomplished through posthypnotic recall and response to suggestion.

The Gospels, when taken as a whole, provide as complete a pattern of the structure of the psyche and its operations as Jesus could give. He saw to it that they would appear at a time and in such a way that the likelihood of their being tampered with would be reduced to the minimum. They constitute Jesus' record as he wished to leave it. Relieved of the presuppositions theology imposes, the Jesus of the Gospels comes to life, vibrant, candid, dynamic, a living reality who presents us with paradoxes that stretch the mind and force us beyond the common ground of consciousness to explore the height, depth, and breadth of our being.

INTRODUCTION TO THE THIRD EDITION

As to the nature of our being, Jesus understood that Christ—which means Chalice of the power of God—is within each human being, and in time this power must express itself. Hence every person is susceptible to Messianic delusion and pretension, and may express the power pathologically rather than constructively until it is understood. The righteous are most susceptible: Messianic missions always begin in righteousness, but all too often end in violence or insanity. Messiahs begin to believe themselves to be masters rather than servants of the truth and power with which they are endowed. Jesus saw that until a person can recognize the Christ in another, and recognize the Christ to be in every other, he will be tempted to believe himself (or another) to be "Master," uniquely endowed by God. Such a sense of uniqueness leads him rapidly into a state of *independent existence* or "mental solitary confinement." He is apart from the human race, and fear of madness overtakes him. Harold says:

> In the history of thought there is one concept that places a man in a truly independent existence: the concept of Messiah as only Son, Himself God-incarnate, one man alone among men—the concept that, in the view of this study, Jesus gave His life to destroy, insisting that the Christ is not an independent existence, but is in every man. . . . By living the role of Messiah and dying to finish it, Jesus ransomed the righteous—those who hunger and thirst for the truth of life. That is, He relieved them of the necessity to be Messianic, to unwittingly or deliberately grasp the cruel role and drink its bitter cup; for He and the men who established His work, bringing forth the Bible of human consciousness, have completed Messiah's task.

Harold saw that Jesus revealed every facet of the Messianic complex, showing its symptoms for what they are. Jesus could not have done this with such precision unless at some time he thought himself to be Messiah. This was inevitable. Before he was born, he was confirmed in this role, and was educated to fill it, so that he could think of himself in no other terms. But came the day when he saw the "appalling horror" of madness standing in the "holy place" of his concept of himself. He realized the fallacy of the Messianic dream: that it could be fulfilled in any one person, race, nation, ideology. This psychological crisis is summarized in the temptation of Satan, to which Jesus did not succumb.

We cannot know when this realization came to Jesus, but there is no trace of Messianic delusion or pretension left when he began his ministry. He set about then to destroy Messianic expectation that encouraged Messianic pretension and delusion to express itself. In doing so, he also prepared the ground for Christ-consciousness to express itself in every human being—in terms of being *servant*, not master, of truth, so that mankind's God-given power might express itself constructively. Giving himself over to Christ-consciousness within, Jesus revealed the psychic dynamics of humankind.

When Jesus is seen as symbol of the God-Son in each of us, and the drama of Son of man is seen as a revelation of our psychic processes, the troublesome and disputed passages fall into perfect place. For example, Jesus says: "You will all see the Son of man seated at the right hand of the Power, and coming with the clouds of heaven." He makes other statements that for centuries have been taken to mean that those of his time would see him returning to earth, descending from the sky, and that this would mark the end of the world. The only reality we can ascribe with certainty to the end of the world is that *it comes for each individual as death overtakes him*. Each person to whom Jesus spoke had to die. The end of this world would come for him. At that moment, the psychic factor Jesus called Son of man "descends upon the clouds of heaven" to receive one's world of consciousness into the unknown realm of the psyche, the *unconscious*, where one's life continues although he discards his flesh. "Heaven" is within. "The clouds of heaven" indicate the subjective nature of Jesus' words. Jesus is speaking of an inner reality. By pointing to the subjective nature of the end of the world, Harold resolves the apparent contradiction between what Jesus said and his failure to reappear as expected.

Only a few face death with open eyes or are able to indicate what happens. When Stephen, the first Christian martyr, was dying, he opened his eyes and cried out, "Look, I see the heavens opened, and the Son of man standing on the right hand of God." In April 1967, when Aaron Mitchell was executed in San Quentin Prison, as he was dying he screamed, "I'm Jesus Christ." Jesus said that the least person on earth must be seen to be the same as himself. Harold believed this realization comes at death, although few are able to communicate it.

Harold believed that Jesus deliberately prohibited any description of his physical appearance. He did this so that he might become a symbol of the Self of any person and his drama might become a pattern of the psychological operation in the unknown inner kingdom. It must follow, then, that Judas, the betrayer, is to be seen as symbol of a psychic factor that acts to bring on death. Harold presents Judas as the most trusted friend of Jesus, the one he could count upon to do the most difficult job, and shows that he was commanded to his act by Jesus. Jesus did not use or misuse his unwitting disciples. Each was committed to give his life to fulfill the mission that had become their common cause. Each had an essential role to fill and filled it.

Harold deals with the miracles *as they are reported*. Over the centuries, much that is assumed has been read into them. All of them are seen to be within the realm of natural, not supranatural, phenomena. In many of them Jesus creates a pattern to show a psychic operation that is too complex to be trusted to the words of his time. Each is meaningful on many levels. Harold points out that Jesus would not "perform signs" to satisfy the curious or critical, and says: "Something in man prohibits or thwarts his efforts to use his psychic powers experimentally." Although he says that mounting evidence of psi power and ESP cannot be ignored, he also says that "in no other field are the data so prone to misinterpretation—self-deception must be guarded against."

To Harold, the importance of studying ESP was to learn more about ordinary perception. He proposed a theory that, to my knowledge, has not been suggested before: Extrasensory perception and sensory perception converge to produce normal perception and comprehension. Extrasensory perception and sensory perception operate as equal and opposite forces to produce "whole" perception and recognition of what one is perceiving. The greatest "miracle" involved is the synergistic effect that at times provides the commanding insight that allows one to see through the problem in a flash. Since Harold deals with each of the miracles in detail, no more need be said about them here.

With a thoroughness and penetration that I doubt has been equaled, Harold measures Jesus' words against the laws and findings of the sciences, showing the harmony that exists between them, drawing the parallel psychic operations. Today, scientists know that the underlying patterns in nature are similar. The gap between organic and inorganic matter narrows. Mass and energy are complementary aspects of whatever the reality is that constitutes creation, but the actual nature of this reality is still unknown. For Harold, the laws and findings of the sciences are simply developments in the expression of truth which has been intuitively grasped and poetically stated in the great religions. For example, he says: "Before the second or third century B.C., a man devised a symbol to convey his realization that life is involved in a coil and coiling action, which he named *Kundalini*, the Serpent Power lying at the base of the spine. Did he see in his mind's eye 'something' akin to DNA, the mysterious 'coil of life' that seems to be at once the mind and matter of flesh? . . . The Genesis legend also incorporates the symbol of serpent power at the base of the 'tree' of life." The spine is the "tree of life" in the body. One of the most striking parallels Harold draws between Jesus' revelation and life's hidden processes is the parallel between the operation of DNA-RNA in the cell, and the operation of Father-consciousness versus Son-consciousness as depicted in the drama of Son of man.

Harold shows that the drama of Son of man also parallels the paradoxical drama of *light*—both as particle and as wave-group. And there are many other parallels between Jesus' words and the underlying laws of nature as scientists describe them. How can one shoe fit so many "feet," ranging in "size" from Cosmic dimensions, to the nucleus of the cell, to the hidden world of the unconscious? Well, the underlying patterns are similar.

But how could so much come from the man of Nazareth? Harold believed that Jesus was as highly educated and widely traveled as his time in history would permit. But this, too, he left an open question. Did Jesus have an intellectual grasp of all that his revelation of life enfolds? No one can answer this. But Harold says:

> It is not essential to concede that Jesus understood physical phenomena and mathematics as such—it is necessary only to concede that truth preexists and inescapably imposes the path to be followed; and that the *unconscious* in man has direct access to truth; and that Jesus knew how to tap this fount within Himself, letting it express through Him and direct His drama.

Whether a person is pondering the mystery of flesh, matter, or energy, he is pondering the mystery of *mammon* which is the material, temporal realm.

Harold believed Jesus saw that God and mammon are *opposite truths* which cannot be put asunder or function apart from each other anymore than matter can function apart from space. To attempt to serve one *or* the other leads to attempting to divide the mental and physical realms which are actually indivisible. We must serve *life* in which God and mammon are met.

Jesus said that mammon is "dishonest"—in Harold's view, this is because matter and the energy surrounding it is not what either appears to be. Mammon *cannot communicate truly*—that is, it cannot communicate its true nature. Every "bit" of matter from elementary particle to the most complex atom enfolds "something" that it does not "reveal." Matter, fields, forces cannot tell "the truth, the whole truth, and nothing but the truth" of their composition and why they act as they do. In Harold's view, *space itself*—not what is in it—is, like God, truly steadfast (righteous). Time is the energy flowing through it that organizes matter which is truly volatile (unrighteous). God and mammon are, therefore, opposite truths of equal magnitude that meet in the single reality man deals with: Life. If a person serves his own life well, he will serve all life well. To do this, he must understand mammon—not despise it: Jesus said that we should make a "friend" of mammon.

Harold left an unfinished manuscript, "On the Nature of Universal Cross-Action," an hypothesis dealing with the constitution of elementary particles and the way energy communicates its forces. This work, together with notes he left outlining his theory of the living universe, has been published in *The Single Reality* (New York: Dodd, Mead and Company, 1971). In this work, Harold does, indeed, make a friend of mammon. He presents the material and mental realms as manifestations of "the single reality" that is God, or the Cosmos and all that is within it. Because this work must be seen against the background of *The Shining Stranger*, and may have been intended to be a part of it, the hypothesis only deepens the mystery of who and what Harold was.

Harold gave the name, *The Single Reality*, to all of his work. But when it was decided that the manuscripts should not be combined in one volume, we selected the title, *The Shining Stranger*, for the first book and saved his title for the second volume which contains his scientific theories. His title does not imply the ultimate, absolute, or only reality. The "single reality," as Harold saw it, is *life*. And each person's own life is the single reality he deals with—no person can merge his soul or inner world with another's. Harold saw that life cannot now express itself in absolute terms. The absolute cannot be reached in the physical or mental realms. We cannot grasp or act upon the ultimate or absolute point of truth or reality, because as we reach the penultimate point it divides into opposite truths of equal magnitude. This requires us to exercise judgment, make a free choice, and bear responsibility for that choice. Whatever the path we take, again we can reach only a penultimate point that will present us with opposite truths of equal magnitude, ad infinitum. In truth, or in reality, there is *no finality*, and that is why life, the single reality, is everlasting.

Within the single reality of life, because the absolute or ultimate cannot be expressed, each of us has our everlasting being in a single, separate reality—but not in isolation. As the opposite forces of our being operate and as we interact with others, we acquire empathy for and understanding of something of the reality of their beings, which then becomes as our own, and true communication is established. Through this process, consciousness constantly undergoes the enlargement and change that insures its evolution.

Dr. Jung Young Lee, distinguished scholar and author of *The Principle of Changes: Understanding the I Ching*, has made a careful study of Harold's work. After reading *The Single Reality*, he wrote in a paper to be included in his forthcoming book, comparing the work of Harold and the *I Ching*, as follows:

> Harold deals with the frontier thinking of our time . . . the *I Ching* is filled with ancient oracles and cryptic sayings. However, if we examine the inner or essential orientations of these great masterpieces together, we notice the amazing similarities latent between them. . . . The *I Ching* becomes the living reality in the contemporary world of the West through the work of Harold, who in return lays the foundation deep into the perennial experience of the Eastern people as enfolded in the *I Ching*.

These words again point to the scope of Harold's thought. He saw that God is all of nature and yet is apart from nature in the mind of man. He saw that mankind is a part of nature, and yet we stand apart from nature because we are vested with God-consciousness and the power of the Word. Realizing this, Harold sees God not as absolute, but as manifold:

> God is the Cosmic Whole and all it contains. But God is also "other" than this incomprehensible infinitude. God is also each person's one full measure of Primordial Parent Being—of God-life itself. This measure is to each his own loving Parent-God, "closer than breathing," entirely involved in his life, perfect in understanding, sufficient unto his every need, insuring his growth, his *humanity*, and his ability to communicate with *itself* and brother-beings through the expression of Word-power.

Harold says: "It is this Father-Son relationship that brings love to life, brings moments of joy complete, brings moments of peace that passeth understanding, brings quiet confidence in the grace of nature and of God."

Here, I would point out that Harold speaks always in terms of Father-

Son relationship, of man, mankind, using the masculine to denote the whole of the human race. But in no sense does he demean woman. He did this because he saw Homo sapiens—man and woman—to be of the *second generation* of life, in which the masculine principle is stated and Son (or second generation) consciousness is expressed.

For Harold, consciousness generates the body or structure that houses it. And in the first generation of life only "mother consciousness" or the feminine principle was expressed in the one cell organisms that reproduced through cell division. Sexuality was not a part of the procreation process. This generation of life expressed undifferentiated consciousness. There was only the sameness of the mother-cells, duplicating themselves exactly as they divided. In this generation, life was vested with its potential of endless being. Although unexpressed, "father consciousness" or the masculine principle was inherent in this first generation. In time, through cross action between the nuclei of the mother-cells, a "son" cell, capable of expressing masculine consciousness and flesh, was produced.

The second or son generation of Parent Life had come into being. This generation expressed differentiated consciousness and the masculine principle primarily, although the feminine principle remained inherent in it. Differentiated consciousness can arise only if there is something "other" to be conscious of. Sexed creatures brought "otherness" as well as "sameness" into life, because in the sexual reproductive process exact duplication cannot occur. In this generation, death entered the picture, and life was vested with the potential to evolve—as only mortal creatures can. The process of death and rebirth into ever more varied forms gave rise to ever more complex "bodies of consciousness" that generated ever more complex physical structures, culminating in Homo sapiens in so far as this planet is concerned. The evolution of consciousness initiated in this generation insures that a third generation of life will emerge in which the harmonious union and dynamic interplay of the opposite principles inherent in Parent Consciousness will be expressed fully. Just as the masculine element was submersed in life's first generation, so the feminine element is submersed in life's second generation. Homo sapiens is of the second, sexed generation in which masculine consciousness and flesh is first expressed—hence, Adam means man and wo*man*, humankind, which is *man*kind whether male or fe*male*.

Harold saw Adam as any one body of consciousness in which the masculine and feminine elements are joined in indissoluble union. This body of consciousness expresses *a body of flesh of its own*, Eve, to which it is wedded for life. All of us are as Adam, and all of us express our flesh first as Eve, the embryo, representing the "mother cell" of life. The fertilized ovum divides into two daughter cells, and they continue to divide until there is a small knot of cells called "morula." When the embryo, Eve, is about forty days old, the body acquires a recognizable human form and it is then spoken of as a fetus. By the beginning of the third month of life, the fetus has recognizable masculine genitalia. The "phallic tuberle" has formed, so that every fetus looks more like a male until it is eighty days old. Then the female form is assumed by those fetuses that will house Adam consciousness in the flesh of wo*man*. In its second generation, life gives voice to Son consciousness through man and woman. In consciousness, all of us begin as man, Adam. In the flesh all of us begin as Eve, a body expressed by Adam-consciousness to house its needs and desires. That body expresses first as Eve, undifferentiated mother-consciousness, and then gives expression in the flesh to its unmistakable masculinity, man or woman. Thereafter, according to its own or life's need, Adam-consciousness differentiates and expresses its flesh as one or the other gender, in both of which the masculine and feminine principles are operative. In Homo sapiens' generation, all of us are Sons of Parent Life.

Harold realized that there is no real distinction to be made between masculine and feminine traits as they are described ordinarily—aggression, tenderness, etc. Every human expression is shared by both sexes. These "opposites" are not simply the "absence" of the other. The masculine interpenetrates the feminine; and the feminine involves the masculine. The ancient yin-yang symbol shows us this in the black "dot" that interpenetrates the white area of the circle and the white "dot" that is enfolded in the black area.

Therefore, to Harold, the sexes represent simply *opposite arrangements of the same potentials*. If we let nature be teacher, our anatomy would tell us that when consciousness extroverts—turns outward—the masculine element is in the ascendancy; when consciousness introverts—turns inward—the feminine element is in the ascendancy. In Homo sapiens' generation, man only is represented, called man when the sexual organs are extroverted and wo*man* when they are introverted, called man when the body is organized to fertilize the ovum and wo*man* when the body is organized to bear Son-life. This is the generation in which consciousness must evolve into a more mature, human state. This can be accomplished only as we transcend the primordial introversion of the first generation of life and each of us, male and female, give expression to the Father-Son consciousness with which we are now endowed.

Woman has been conditioned to repress the expression of Son-consciousness, but this generation cannot fulfill its potential until she does. There is a startling passage in the Gospel of Thomas, attributed to Jesus, that says this. Harold did not once mention the Apocryphal Gospels. He drew only upon the four Gospels of the New Testament. But the following passage from the Gospel of Thomas is in harmony with Harold's concept that all of us must express and claim the masculine principle in this generation of life:

> Simon Peter said to them, "Let Mary go out from among us, because women are not worthy of the Life." Jesus said, "See I shall lead her so that I will make her male, that she too may become a living spirit, resembling you males. For every woman who makes herself male will enter the Kingdom of Heaven." [4]

Strange words! When will woman acknowledge that she, too, is man? Son-consciousness within will lead her to this realization. Only then can real equality between the sexes be established, freeing each to express as person in his own right, relieved of the burdensome roles society has foisted upon each sex.

Harold saw that evolution has not ceased, and that the evolution of consciousness portends a new species. A third generation of life will come into being when consciousness is complete. Complete consciousness will be incorruptible. And incorruptible consciousness will generate incorruptible flesh. No longer will we need to lay down the body in the ongoing process of life which is, even now, everlasting.

Harold took an optimistic view of humankind and its ability to deal with the problems of the day. He saw that growing empathy demands moral progress, and that "change born of the evolution of consciousness cannot be blocked."

Dr. Ira Progoff, prominent psychologist and author of many books, describes Harold as "a modern man in the best and fullest sense of the term . . . a person who has been involved in the mainstream of modern culture and has assimilated a large part of it. As a modern person, he cannot accept religious doctrines in the historical contexts out of which they arise . . . he feels the necessity of responding to any given question in a

[4] Barbara Ford, "Coptic Voices From the Past," *Science Digest:* Archeology, February 1972, p. 40.

total and encompassing frame of reference. Thus it is necessary for Harold to draw upon the formulations of physics; and upon the concepts of death psychology; and upon the study of society. As a modern person he asks himself existentially how he can place himself in the present situation of history in a meaningful way." [5]

I have thought of Dr. Progoff's words many times. They come to mind whenever I hear the passage from William Faulkner that is used by a local television station to sign off its channel. Against a winter landscape, these words are spoken:

> I have found that the greatest help in meeting any problem with decency, self-respect, and whatever courage may be required, is to know where you, yourself, stand. That is, to have in words what you believe, and are acting from.[6]

Perhaps, to Harold the most meaningful contribution he could make in the present situation of history was to put into words what he, himself, believed, and leave this statement of faith in God, nature, and man for others to share as they would, provided at least three other people felt that it was worthy of publication.

Certainly, he saw that the sickness besetting the soul of modern man cannot be healed by medical science or by social reforms: ". . . this illness is caused by loss of religion, which gives rise to a decline in one's sense of purpose and meaning in life, and to unspoken despair." He saw that beneath the problems we struggle with there is the one crucial problem of finding immortal love in ourselves, in life. I mean, finding God and a frame of reference, a source of authority, in which we can put our faith. This crucial need, disguised, is translated into countless other problems that skim the surface of our real desire like waterbugs skimming the surface of a lake.

Harold says: "To the twentieth century, Jesus' words still say, 'If thou canst believe, all things are possible to him that believeth. . . .' And like the father of the tormented child, this century cries out and says with tears: 'Lord, I believe; help thou mine unbelief.' Today, as always, 'mine unbelief' is the sickness that must first be healed." Harold tried to put a healing touch upon the mind of humanity—not to restore faith in Jesus only, but to restore *religion* and give us *reason* to believe in the grace of life and God, whatever our particular religion may be.

---

[5] Ira Progoff, "The Inner Messiah," an unpublished paper prepared for a discussion of Harold's work at Gotham Book Mart Gallery, 1968.
[6] (As quoted by the *National Observer*.)

INTRODUCTION TO THE THIRD EDITION

What is the real meaning and purpose of each life? As Harold saw it, each of us is creating through experience in the many lives we live *our own Soul*, made of all we have ever known of love and satisfaction. Jesus likened the Son of man to a Bridegroom coming toward his Bride. Self, God-Son, is the Bridegroom of our being; and is that element of *sameness* in each of us that insures the brotherhood of mankind. Soul, the Bride of our being, is that element of *otherness*, uniqueness, that each of us is generating; this factor insures our individuality and the variety that brings satisfaction to life, as we share it with others. When our Souls are fully "grown," we will be "twice glorified" by love: Self, the Bridegroom, immortal love within us, and Soul, the Bride, love of our very own, will come together in a union that will make each of us a complete and divinely human being.

Archetypal religious symbols work, whether or not they are understood. They work on subliminal levels, because they represent universal psychic facts. Peering through his "mental microscope" into the nucleus of the cell, Harold realized why the symbolic figure of Jesus has been so powerful through the centuries despite the burden of dogma it has carried: His drama parallels the operation of DNA-RNA, *so that every cell of our bodies resonates with it,* even if our intellects have not as yet comprehended the glory, grace, and reality it enfolds.

I chose the pen name for the unknown author of *The Shining Stranger:* "Preston," because it is nondescript as a given name, and "Harold," because lines from Byron's *Childe Harold's Pilgrimage* convey what the "stranger" saw to be the essence of Jesus' message, and a valid concept of humankind:

> . . . there is that within me which shall tire
> Torture and Time, and breathe when I expire;
> Something unearthly, which they deem not of.

One more thought I would share, and a comment made by a girl attending a seminar on Harold's work. She gave me an insight into Jesus' message that Harold does not mention—that had never occurred to me. She said:

The Aquarian sign in the zodiac is a man with a pitcher of water. And in the passage about the Last Supper, Jesus tells one of the disciples to go into the city and says that he will meet a man bearing a pitcher of water who will show him to the "upper room." To me, this was the "sign" leading to the "upper room of consciousness." The symbol is right there, pointing to the Aquarian age, and Jesus says it.

As she says, the sign of Aquarius is there. Perhaps Jesus indicated here that not until the dawning of this age would his message begin to be understood. But her words had other meaning also for me. I saw *The Shining Stranger*'s author as one who bears to the parched intellectualism and sometimes bemused mysticism of the Piscean age, now waning, a pitcher of sparkling clear water.

WINIFRED BABCOCK

No concept of Jesus can be definitive if it is contrived by arbitrary dealing with the Gospels, choosing to affirm certain reports that support one's theory while dismissing others as falsifications, elaborations, interpolations, or errors deriving from the disciples' loss of memory. Casting doubt upon the veracity and reliability of the Gospels renders one report and one Gospel as suspect as another, because it is possible to make a case for accepting or rejecting any part of any Gospel. Thus, a theory resting upon the unreliability of the Gospels perforce becomes as suspect and questionable as the author holds the Gospels to be.

Whatever may be said about the rest of the Bible, if a concept of Jesus is to have a firm base it must rest upon the conviction that the four Gospels are honest reports, albeit each offers a subjective view. Therefore, in THE SHINING STRANGER, concomitant with the attempt to draw a true picture of Jesus, the integrity of the four Gospels is dealt with—for example, how each could be so contradictory and different from the others, yet true, and how the memory of each disciple could have been adequate to the task of recording Jesus' actual words. Here, it may be pointed out that no one can say when the disciples recorded their reports—information as to the earliest copies in circulation is all that is available. No doubt some errors in copying and omissions occurred, but such as these do not obliterate or seriously distort the full body of the record of Jesus as given in the four versions, in which the testimony of His mother is incorporated.

It is unlikely that the disciples deliberately falsified or contrived the story of Jesus' life or His words. If this were the case, the reports would be less contradictory, certain unfavorable passages would have been omitted, and certain gaps would have been filled. It is doubtful, also, that the early Christians would have suffered martyrdom to found a religion based upon their own inventions. For these and other reasons given in the text of this book, the author accepts the four Gospels as basically honest reports, and regards every word in every Gospel as given data with which one must deal in formulating as true and complete a picture of Jesus as it is possible to obtain.

Chapter 1

THE PROBLEM, THE OBJECTIVE, THE CRUCIAL QUESTIONS

I

The central fact of modern history in the West—by which we mean the long period from the end of the Middle Ages to the present—is unquestionably the decline of religion.

—WILLIAM BARRETT [1]

The decline of Christianity, religion of the West, bespeaks the decline of faith in the Pauline interpretation of Jesus' meaning to mankind.

Today, the whole question of Jesus—His nature and His revelation—is for the most part being bypassed because, as Alfred Guillaume remarks, "Christology is such an extremely complicated and technical subject that few but professional theologians can understand the niceties of the disputes . . ." [2] This study does not engage in them. It is not a theological discourse that offers again, or in new dress, the same answers to the piercing questions that orthodox Christianity has offered in ever more obscure terms for almost two thousand years.

A new view of Jesus is presented in this book, but this portrait of Him is no more than a sketch. Its incompleteness, its limited certitude, its panoramic and therefore necessarily superficial canvas is acknowledged. Only a broad outline can be offered because an overwhelming mass of material confronts the man who attempts to take all knowledge for his province and pose it against the revelation of Jesus to determine whether a sustainable belief, congruent with the demands of both reason and intuition will emerge from a re-evaluation of His work. Subject only to the necessity of truth—in Sir Julian Huxley's words, "truth to external fact and truth of internal coherence . . ." [3]—all kinds of experience, all observable phenomena must be encompassed. And as the given data are examined they must be interpreted in such a way as to make the material comprehensible to the widest possible audience.

Questions and arguments will arise in the reader's mind as this book is read; and they cannot be answered fully at the time, but they are answered as the study unfolds. When one adds a column of figures, moving from right to left, if the column adds up to ten or more, there is a number that must be incorporated in the next column. Not until the last column is added can the sum present itself. So it is with this work, for each issue is involved with other issues, each follows its own thread of involvement, and no point to be made can be completed until the whole observation is set forth.

Because this study offers an answer that is new, it must contradict all philosophies, ideologies, theologies, and religious systems, Christian and non-Christian alike, although it partakes of each as the doctrines are examined, just as it partakes of the thought of many men in making its every summary statement. This is to say, the new answer to the mystery of Jesus offered in this study has not been received through mystic revelation. It has presented itself of its own accord as into one fold were gathered as many of Jesus' words and as much of fact and philosophy as the limited mental capacity of one man could assimilate and express in a limited number of words. Many of these words are quoted, and many quotations are from the books of men who have drawn together the voices of outstanding contributors in their field. Space permits touching upon the work and thought of only a few of those who have contributed much to twentieth-century knowledge. The most difficult task has been to select among them. Every effort has been made to present their views fairly, and again it must be said that no individual quoted in this book has endorsed any part of its postulations.

Because at first glance this effort may appear to be an attack upon Christianity and other major religions of the world, it must be stated here that this is in no sense the author's aim, as will be seen when the whole discourse is set forth. This book has been written because the time has come when a new answer to the whole question of religion must be offered—for religion itself is at the barricades.

Today the various denominations of the Christian Church boast a large number of adherents, but many of the clergy and most of the members blind themselves to the real dogma of orthodox Christian theology—else they ignore the doctrine and its affront to those of other faiths. Christians courageous enough to face the truth of the situation admit, as Samuel

Miller does, that the doctrine has become "feeble" and "unintelligible" to modern man.[4] The pace of Christianity's decline, in terms of declining belief in its tenets, accelerates. J. B. Priestley writes:

> ... if we all joined a Christian Church tomorrow the fundamental situation would be unchanged, because no Church existing today has the power—and we could not give it this power by joining it—to undo what has been done. ... the symbols no longer work, and they cannot be made to work by effort on a conscious level. ... No matter what is willed by consciousness, that which belongs to the depths can only be restored in the depths.[5]

Today, psychologists explore and interpret the depths in man, but thus far psychology serves only to present again in professional terms the notion of original sin: human ills originate in the lost Eden of history and infancy, man is victim of primordial sex drives incorporated in his being when he is expelled from the paradise of the womb. And thus:

> ... in this atomic age, sure of nothing but sex ... we are now piling on to sex the whole gigantic load of our increasing dissatisfactions, our despair, a burden far greater than it can safely take. Religion alone can carry the load, defend us against the de-humanising collectives, restore true personality.[6]

According to Dr. Carl Jung, psychology as yet is "for the most part the science of conscious contents, measured as far as possible by collective standards." [7] Thus, it cannot defend man against the dehumanizing collectives, or restore in his depths the hope that declines as religion declines —indeed, the human problem is compounded by psychologists' theories, and man must seek defense against them. Dr. J. H. van den Berg pleads this case, urges the profession to leave some act in life unsullied as it sends the child and then the man along the "road of endless regression," in the process shaking the foundations of family life:

> ... we read that the child has no enemies more dangerous than his parents .... most parents do not know how to act; they fear their children. ...[8]

They know that lack of understanding produces harmful effects, but "too much understanding is equally disastrous; too easily the child gets caught in a tie which may keep him a child for life." [9] Dr. van den Berg sees that the freedom of the child is also threatened by psychologists' early and late evaluation of him: "I should like to protect those youngsters," for there will be "very few as time goes on, who go to meet their future without a psychological examination . . . . let the child be free, let it keep away, for as long as it lives, from anything called psychology, let it *live*." [10]

But just as the sciences that brought forth the atomic age cannot and should not be abandoned, psychology, erring and insufficient though it may be, cannot and should not be abandoned. Freud and those who followed in this field opened Pandora's box, but they also presented humanity with vital knowledge, which must be dealt with now, just as nuclear power must be dealt with now—and just as the vacuum created by the decline of religion must be dealt with now, for in Priestley's words, "it is doubtful if our society can last much longer without religion . . ." [11]

Western civilization rests heavily upon Christianity. Capitalistic and communistic countries alike espouse Jesus' doctrine of the brotherhood of man. In the words of Russell Davenport:

> That which the free world has been witnessing is a kind of philosophic rape.[12]

A remark made by Nikita Khrushchev—one of several that reflect his attitude toward religion, which may have contributed to his downfall—supports Davenport's statement. Khrushchev says:

> . . . if you do look into our philosophy you will see that we have taken a lot of Christ's precepts . . .[13]

Like psychology, Marxism began as a protest against orthodoxy, but because Marxism is pseudo-Christianity it could be and was religiously embraced in spite of its profession of atheism; and thus for many it became a substitute for hollow Christian theology. But Marxism, too, is hollow insofar as its being a religion is concerned. Despite its economic and territorial gains, as a substitute for religion it is failing as rapidly as orthodox Christianity, from which so many of its ideals were drawn. Marxism has not and cannot fill the religious void. Today it is recognized for what it is: a method of government, a means to power—as in China, where traditional faiths are swept aside and militant communism forges the nation into a nuclear power.

The struggle between the capitalistic and communistic systems, East and West, serves only to divert attention from the now common threat to humankind: the universal decline of faith in old religious doctrines, for the Chinese religious traditions, Christianity, and Marxism are not the only declining religions. Jawaharlal Nehru spoke for untold numbers of men all over the world when, spurning the ideologies of both East and West, he said:

> We have to give a new direction to education and evolve a new type of humanity. Essentially, our problems are those of civilization itself. Religion gave a certain moral and spiritual discipline; it also tried to perpetuate superstition and social usages. Indeed, those superstitions and social usages enmeshed and overwhelmed the real spirit of religion. Disillusionment followed.[14]

Wherever one searches the religious question he finds that among the educated element traditional faiths are declining and as yet there is no stated doctrine to take their place.

George Bernard Shaw wrote that civilizations invariably collapse when man's power outruns his religion [15]—as man's power appears to be doing today. It is not the decline of a particular religion, but of all religions that presages catastrophe—for despite the evil that has been done in the name of religion, so much that gives meaning and purpose to life rests upon it that sanity itself may rest upon it.

Priestley suggests the answer as to what life would be without religion —*man is dehumanized*. When this happens, ethics follow suit. The universal collapsing of religions poses this threat that is glacial and moves at glacial pace. Who can stop this inching chill? What ideology can lead man out of its grinding path?

Davenport sees that the question goes far beyond any particular religion: "it is a question of our concept of man." [16] Western man cannot answer the question—who and what am I?—without first answering another—who and what was Jesus?—for upon this man the whole culture leans so heavily one merely begs the question if he will not face it. Anyone embracing Pauline doctrine must acknowledge that Jesus was Judaic Messianic expectation fulfilled, that man is His chattel, that all other religions are futile. At the risk of offending theologians, the "niceties of the dispute" will be omitted, for orthodox or Pauline Christianity is encompassed in the blunt terms of St. Paul: "You are not your own, you were bought for a price. . . ." [17] by Jesus. Broadly speaking, orthodox theology holds that Jesus, only Son of God, died for the sin of each human being, ransoming mankind with His own perfect life. God, the Father, who exacted this sacrifice of Him, may be approached only through Jesus; salvation is possible only through Him; He will come again at the end of the world to judge it, to consign the evil to hell, the good to heaven, and to begin His eternal rule over all in creation.

Far more than having to deal with the miracles in an age dominated by science, Pauline Messianic doctrine estranges the Christian in today's world. The Messianic question—who and what was Jesus, and what is His meaning with regard to the individual and to mankind at large?—is still argued today, dividing the Christian realm. Long ago this question gave rise to a split in Arab Christianity, paving the way for the advent of Muhammadanism that began with an anti-Messianic pronouncement:

> Say Praise belongs to God who has not taken a son, and has no associate in His kingdom, and [needs] no patron to defend Him from humiliation.[18]

Most of the world's great religions and philosophies appear to have begun as a protest against the prevailing Messianic concept, for, whatever its disguise, pursuit of a Messianic vision is pursuit of power, involving governmental or priestly prerogatives that rob man of his freedom. And yet in time all religions become caught up again in the renewal of the Messianic dream, as did Islam. In a broad sense, history reveals little more than man's pursuit of some sort of Messianic vision. As Davenport observes, Marxism "is the same dream, dressed in modern clothes—a messianic vision, the essence of which cannot be reduced to rational terms . . ."[19] In *Cold Friday*, Whittaker Chambers dwells upon the Messianic hue pervading both the Communist doctrine and the Russian people's concept of themselves.[20]

In calling for what amounts to a new religion, Huxley writes, "In so far as an effective new belief-system must have a religious aspect, it will doubtless need to wait for the appearance of a prophet who can cast it into compelling form and shake the world with it."[21] It may be that religions are declining throughout the world because each rests upon its own prophet, is to some degree Messianic, and in so being is an affront to all others, tacitly invalidating them, undermining the ground upon which religion itself must make its stand. Because of age old conflicting Messianic doctrines, the validity of religion itself and its bearing upon reality is today in doubt. If religion is no more than superstition perpetuated from generation to generation, can life have meaning, purpose, and real value?

Questioning religion is questioning a primary phenomenon: when Homo sapiens appeared upon earth there was no theology to be imposed upon him, and yet wherever and however man lived he expressed his innate sense of God-being. In the words of Radhakrishnan, "God-consciousness is as much an original endowment of human beings as self-consciousness."[22] In existential terms, "the truth of religion . . . must penetrate my own personal experience . . . . subjective truth is not a truth that I *have*, but a truth that I *am*." [23]

The great religious figures of history have tried to reveal the meaning inherent in man's realization of God-being, but their messages are always obscured by interpretations that pose ideological demands and create systems as fallible as the men who strive to sustain them. Thus, in time the hiatus widens between revelator and the religious doctrine expounded in his name. A wide gulf separates the words of Jesus and the tenets of Christian theology, although His fulfillment of Judaic Scriptures may appear to bridge this gulf and bring His message to rest in the Judaic Messianic eschatology of His day, which perforce estranges the Christian in today's world and shakes man's faith in His integrity. Was Jesus Himself true, or was He sadly deluded, and as far removed from reality as those who expected the end of the world and the second coming of the Christ before the death of the disciple John? Did Jesus hold a vainglorious concept of Himself? Truth comes to be with the *man* who is true:

> A good tree cannot bring forth evil fruit, neither can a corrupt tree bring forth good fruit. . . . Either make the tree good and his fruit good; or else make the tree corrupt, and his fruit corrupt: for the tree is known by his fruit.[24]

Jesus gives the command. To fulfill it is the objective of this book.

The crucial question to be settled is the nature and meaning of Jesus' Messianic role—upon this all else depends. His own words settle this question, and from them may be enunciated a concept of man that restores meaning and purpose in life whatever the path he treads. But Jesus' revelation is by no means unprecedented. As Radhakrishnan points out:

> There is no development in religious truth, though there is a development in the expression of truth.[25]

This study approaches the works and words of Jesus in this light: they are a development in the expression of truth, and insofar as men with a Western background are concerned, His message, beheld apart from the theologies clustering around it, offers still the greatest hope of true religion. Why? Because Jesus' message can be grasped more readily— His words are familiar. He is familiar as a symbol representing more of paradoxical truth than man can as yet express, and when men appear to be losing their humanity, His image appears out of the darkness to begin again to lead them onward toward light just as the Christ was seen by Alexander Blok to lead *The Twelve*.[26]

This study acknowledges, however, that the Judeo-Christian Scriptures are not the only sacred writings from which governing truth could be discerned: "The differences among religions seem prominent because we do not seem to know the basic truth of our own religions." [27] But more than the sum of knowledge, and the precepts of every religion, must be enfolded in a valid idea of man: each person to draw the breath of life represents in his being a portion to be embraced—whenever, wherever, however he lives, each figures in, contributes to reality and to the sum of the truth of Homo sapiens, even unto:

. . . one of the least of these my brethren . . .[28]

II

In orthodox theology, St. Paul's compelling interpretation of Jesus is highlighted against the background of the disciples' messages, obscuring much of their content. The pre-eminence of Pauline doctrine precludes the idea that there could be another valid concept of Jesus and His mission. But in the four Gospels another view of Him is precisely drawn, a view as natural and different from the Pauline concept as non-Euclidean geometry is natural and different from Euclid's. Since the advent of the Bible, which drew together the fragments of His picture, this answer to the question of Jesus has lain before men's eyes. It is an answer St. Paul could not give. In the early days of Christianity only a *hint of it* could be discerned, and was discerned by Saul of Tarsus—his mighty work is not to be decried. Nor could this answer have been given by those who followed and through the ages developed the Christian religion. Indeed, not until the twentieth century, when the writings of Darwin, Freud, Einstein and many other scientists had been circulated throughout the world, and science had suffered its great revolution, and mathematicians had been freed of the limitations of Greek thought, could the concept of Jesus to be offered in this study evolve as His *own* words, works, and drama are measured against the data now available.

The problems confronting man in the twentieth century are colossal, but opportunity looms equally large: ". . . the present situation is a new one, in which new facts and new knowledge are available over new fields to an unprecedented extent, and could be distilled to provide us with the truth that alone can set us free." [29] Echoed in Huxley's words is the poetry of Jesus:

> And ye shall know the truth,
> And the truth shall make you free.[30]

THE PROBLEM, THE OBJECTIVE, THE CRUCIAL QUESTIONS

Distilling the truth from such conflicting data as are given in the sciences and in the reporting of human experience depends upon grasping the synthesis that contradictory truths demand. The physicist has come to see that contradiction underlies reality: the secondary laws of physics contradict the classical laws, the two sets become compatible only as the problem is enlarged or as the numbers are increased, whereupon both sets of laws are seen to be working in truth, the microscopic contained within the macroscopic. Lawrence Durrell says, "Truth is what most contradicts itself." [31] If so, Jesus spoke the truth, for His statements appear to be so contradictory that they must, if He be true at all, converge in man's enlargement of knowledge to form a synthesis so advanced, so rich in meaning, that one must look beyond orthodoxy if he hopes to grasp it.

When a man realizes such truth as reaches beyond the current boundaries of consciousness and language, the crucial question becomes: how to express and convey it. This was Jesus' problem. Regardless of the level of His understanding, His message could be clothed only in the language of His time, and He had to *show* that for which there was no word-vehicle. But despite the advancement of His thought, He so formulated and launched His message that it began immediately to exert practical effects on the process of human transformation. To accomplish this, He worked words—which is to say, He used them poetically. *(symbols)*

Dr. Henry A. Murray writes that an "important fact not generally acknowledged is . . .":

> the Bible is poetry, in its best parts, magnificent and edifying poetry. . . . Some devout Christians overlook the fact that the stirring and sustaining power of the Book they live by depends on the wondrous emotive language, the vivid imagery and figures of speech, with which its wisdom is transmitted. . . . If the New Testament . . . had been written by a modern social scientist in the jargon of his profession, it would have died at birth. . . .[32]

As does Santayana, Dr. Murray sees that the playing down of the "crucial import of the Bible's poetry," hand in hand with the playing up of its historicity, is the great fallacy of Christianity, for thereby the scope of its traffic with and judgment of reality is severely limited.[33] Poetry does not obscure fact—it presents it in words that act as leaven in the mind to make room for fact to house there. Poetry is dazzling in its completely open and full use of words that have, as John Ciardi puts it:

> . . . far more meanings than anyone thinks about in reading factual prose. A word is not a meaning but a complex of meanings consisting

of all its possibilities: its ability to identify something, the image it releases in making that identification, its sound, its history, its associations-in-context . . .[34]

Priestley says that Johann von Herder regarded poetry "as the mother-tongue of mankind." Reaching for its definition Priestley writes, "Poetry is the break-through, the whole man addressing other whole men."[35] Arnold Toynbee says, "Each poem is like a bucketful of water drawn up from a well in which the water is 'the same yesterday and today and for ever.' At the subconscious level, from which Poetry rises, Human Nature seems to be the same always and everywhere—the same in Primitive Man as in Man in Process of Civilization; the same in different societies in process of civilization; the same in different individuals beneath their different conscious and volitional personalities."[36] If poetry can be defined, Plato defined it: "All creation or passage of non-being into being is poetry or making."[37]

Jesus spoke poetically, but if His words are true they must be a correct, albeit poetical, description of reality. That is, they cannot be true on the one hand and false on the other—true poetry is as disciplined as a true equation. In speaking of the free carry-over of words from one parallel to another, Ciardi poses the actual test of a poet: it is his "ability to do more than one thing at once and to have his choices come out equally right on all levels."[38] This is also the test of a mathematician. Sir Arthur Eddington presents both poetry and an equation concerning the generation of waves by wind:

$$\frac{p'_{vv}}{g\rho\eta} = \frac{(\alpha^2 + 2vk^2\alpha + \sigma^2)A - i(\sigma^2 + 2vkm\alpha)C}{gk(A - iC)}$$

$$\frac{p'_{xy}}{g\rho\eta} = \frac{\alpha}{gk} \cdot \frac{2ivk^2 A + (\alpha + 2vk^2)C}{(A - iC)}$$

> There are waters blown by changing winds to laughter
> And lit by the rich skies, all day. And after,
> Frost, with a gesture, stays the waves that dance
> And wandering loveliness. He leaves a white
> Unbroken glory, a gathered radiance,
> A width, a shining peace, under the night.[39]

To a mathematician, the equation might appear to be as beautiful as the poetry.

As Eddington points out, physics depends upon pointer readings of mental and mechanical devices—pointer readings that are possible only because of consciousness. He says:

> ... if the unity of a man's consciousness is not an illusion, there must be some corresponding unity in the relations of the mind-stuff which is behind the pointer readings. ... [Even the materialist] will need in the physical world something to stand for a symbolic unity of atoms associated with an individual consciousness, which does not exist for atoms not so associated .... some kind of physical substitute for the Ego ... It seems to me that the first step in a broader revelation to man must be the awakening of image-building in connection with the higher faculties of his nature, so that these are no longer blind alleys but open out into a spiritual world—a world partly of illusion no doubt, but in which he lives no less than in the world, also of illusion, revealed by the senses.[40]

Here Eddington calls for an Ego symbol.

Can art bring forth from the dark chaos of subjectivisms to which it has turned a symbol to give expression to man's psychic wholeness?—a symbol which, in existential terms, "supersedes thought, because it is richer in meaning." [41] At present, the answer would appear to be no. Artists tend to spurn symbolization, but as Jung points out: "Great art till now has always derived its fruitfulness from the myth, from the unconscious process of symbolization which continues through the ages and, as the primordial manifestation of the human spirit, will continue to be the root of all creation in the future." [42] Huxley points out that certain forms, colors, or related stimuli release certain potentials in animal or bird species and therefore play a vital part in their lives; in man, symbols can function as do recognition-markings and other releaser patterns in animals, and they can function also as vehicles of complex and multiple significance to extend the range of thought through ". . . the establishment of causal chains from mind to mind, from mental event to mental event. . . ." [43]

Three symbols predominate among those associated with Jesus: a star, a fish, the cross. Viewed as vehicles of complex and multiple significance, the star calls to mind light, the nature of it and of energy, as well as the structure and working of the universe; the fish calls to mind life arising from the waters, biological evolution; the cross (+) calls to mind the positive, the proton, the plus-factor in its every aspect affirmative. A man who must somehow convey truth that is beyond the grasp of his contemporaries can do so only through involving it with symbols that will act as recognition markers and releasers to extend the range of his thought, which can come into full flower of expression only in the minds and words of men who come after him. But before Jesus' symbols or words can be examined to elucidate an answer to the crucial question—who and what am I?—a few pertinent facts about the Gospels must be stated.

The scholar must contend with different translations of the Bible. Jesus, however, spoke with exquisite precision, and the differences in translations, if all translations are montaged, do not obliterate the truth He wished to convey. In this study, *The Holy Bible*, King James Authorized Version (1611), and James Moffatt's translation, *The Bible* (1935), are used for reference to provide both an old and new statement of Jesus' words.

The great majority of New Testament scholars agree that the first three Gospels, Matthew, Mark, and Luke, belong to a common stock, having a common root. There seems to be no doubt that Mark was written first and that the authors of Matthew and Luke had before them Mark's narrative from which they never deviate, although they add a number of discourses, parables, pithy sayings called *Logia*, as well as a number of miraculous happenings such as the virgin birth and the resurrection. There is no virgin birth story in the original account by Mark. Whether or not the author said anything about the resurrection cannot be determined, because the very last part of this account is lost. Although the men who wrote these three Gospels have the same historical view, there are considerable variations in what they stress and in what they hold to be important.

In the fourth Gospel, the Gospel of John, the miracles of turning water into wine and raising Lazarus from the dead are added. This account differs vastly from the others. The Synoptic Gospels agree that the ministry of Jesus lasts only one year, whereas in the Gospel of John it is extended to three years; it starts before history, beginning with the statement that the Logos became flesh, and presents Jesus as the creative power taking human form and character to become the instrument through whose flesh and blood man might partake of divinity and know eternal life. This Gospel is thought to be *doctrinal* rather than historical.

The Four Gospels, by Burnett H. Streeter, is considered to be the definitive work in English on the mystery of the four Gospels.[44] Because they are a mystery, this study views them one and all in the same light, taking the position that every word in each of them confronts the Christian and must be reconciled within the Christian concept—else any word in any of them may be arbitrarily dismissed. Thus, this study sees all four Gospels as both historical and doctrinal, and believes that the record of

Jesus as well as His meaning to man can be seen only as the four accounts are montaged, together presenting Jesus' portrait in as broad outline and in as much detail as can be had, each bit of the canvas as important, as true, as any other. As this study progresses, the reason for this view becomes apparent.

But whatever the view one takes of the Gospels, the scholar must contend with the contradictions and differences apparent not only as concerns the Synoptics versus the fourth Gospel, but as concerns the accounts in the first three. And at every turn the problem of the interpreter is enlarged, because Jesus presents a deeper issue to confront the questioner, thus insisting upon a digression from the point at bay. There is also the question of His meaning as meaning may be dependent upon context. In *Jesus and His Story*,[45] Ethelbert Stauffer gives as accurate a picture of His activities as can be offered, but insofar as Jesus' words are concerned, there is no possibility of arranging them chronologically and assigning them meaning drawn from order in context. Although much of the same material is used, especially in the three Synoptic Gospels, the reports vary widely at times and on other occasions the same words are blended into context so differently that the scholar must arbitrarily assume one Gospel to be correct and the others incorrect if he attempts to elicit the meaning of a statement by virtue of its placement in text. For example, Jesus says:

> . . . when the Son of man shall sit on the throne of his glory, you who have followed me shall also sit on twelve thrones to govern the twelve tribes of Israel.[46]

In Matthew, this passage appears during Jesus' ministry when He was in Judea—before He returned to Jerusalem for the final act in His drama. In Luke, this statement is made at the last supper. The passage is omitted in the Gospels of Mark and John. In Matthew, shortly after the statement is made, another incident that is included in Mark's Gospel is reported, and in it Jesus contradicts His prerogative to grant seats in the realm of heaven: when the mother of James and John, sons of Zebedaeus, asks that they sit at Jesus' right hand and left hand in "your Realm," He replies, ". . . but it is not for me to grant seats at my right and at my left; these belong to the men for whom they have been destined by my Father." [47] In Mark, not their mother, but James and John ask.[48] Jesus can offer them only the cup He is to drink. How can one reconcile such contradiction?

Until a man has grasped the full implication of Jesus' words, "the kingdom of God is within you," [49] he cannot begin to understand Him. His every word is predicated upon this revelation. It is the working of the inner kingdom He reveals. If the kingdom of heaven is within, there is no heavenly place of abode for the "redeemed" to go to—the realm of heaven is now an individual state of being, a potential mankind shall in time realize. It is inward reality as opposed to the outward illusiveness of life (and of matter, which Jesus proclaimed long before the physicists discovered it).

Because as issues are posed to trap Him Jesus poses in answer a profundity, one must follow the suggestion His poetic words give, must try to see the poetic structure that rises up around His every pronouncement, must consider His every word on any subject to grasp the synthesis His contradiction demands. All this poses still another problem: one cannot grasp the whole meaning of any of His statements unless His truth on one canvas is spread.

The objective, then, is not to present one or several new aspects, but rather a whole new concept of Jesus, for, as Albert Schweitzer points out, "What has been passing for Christianity during these nineteen centuries is merely a beginning, full of weaknesses and mistakes, not a full-grown Christianity springing from the spirit of Jesus." [50]

A new view of Jesus will be posed in this book as the four Gospels are montaged and His own words are measured against as much of the knowledge of twentieth-century man as can be touched upon. This new view cannot be briefly explained, but it can be briefly summarized:

In saying that the kingdom of God, an unknown realm, is within each person, Jesus proclaimed the existence of that psychic reality now called the *unconscious*—revealed its working and power. *He made of Himself a symbol* of the Authority within this psychic realm: the vital Self-of-selves abstracted from consciousness for which man yearns—which is unto each his own, "the Lord, your God."

Thus, Jesus made of Himself a frame of reference, to be arbitrarily chosen, in which a man could measure his conscious grasp of life. As Alfred Adler saw, such a frame of reference is necessary to man.[51] It serves as a source of authority, also indispensable to man.

Jesus saw the Ten Commandments as classical psychic law. He realized, however, that *quantum* psychic law underlies the classical law, and this secondary law governs the inner, real life of the individual—this is the law He enunciated.

Jesus moved beyond Greek philosophy. Morris Kline says of it, "the infinite is . . . frankly avoided"—the concept of a limitless process was frightening to the Greeks.[52] Jesus saw life to be infinite, saw that man's religions form one-to-one correspondences of truth, and that each man is a one-to-one correspondence with God, truth, life, and with each other man. He gave to religious expression and to humankind what Georg Cantor's transfinite mathematics gave to mathematicians late in the nineteenth century: a new freedom of thought, a grasp of the infinite.

Jesus strove to heal the breach in man's thinking upon reality, strove to rejoin the divided physical and spiritual realms, saying, poetically, that the energy which gives life to man is, potentially, in a "stone." [53] Identifying Himself and mankind with primordial energy, *light*, He dramatized and phrased in *poetic terms* the most important of the secondary laws of physics, enfolding His answer to the question of the universe in the sign positive (+). His message includes only one mathematical formula and only one mathematically-based law. These are given in word-equations that enfold basic and primary mathematical *axiomata*. How could so much come from an unlearned man—of Nazareth? Who can prove that Jesus was unlearned? But whether by design or because He knew how to tap the fount of truth in His *unconscious*, He presented in drama, symbol, and poetry the underlying physical and psychical laws that are today being revealed.

Refusing to follow the course of mystics, He gave His truth to the multitudes, expressing it in simple words, in easy parables. Just as Einstein saw that there are no absolute laws in the sense of laws independent of observers,[54] so, also, Jesus saw that no absolute actions or interventions by a supranatural force or a force external to those concerned could operate in life, and that man had only to reach and understand the power within himself to experience the miracle. Through His works He showed the limits of the extrasensory and psychic power in man—*its ability to delude as well as to illuminate*—and He demonstrated the release of the body's healing power in hypnotic trance.

For once and all, and in His every move, Jesus dealt with Messianic expectation metastasized throughout civilization, bedeviling humankind. In the following chapter as facts and theories are separated a new Messianic concept takes shape. Jesus' role is clarified. But not until the entire observation of His work is finished does this new concept of His mission emerge fully clothed and integrated into the whole of His revelation.

Chapter 2

THE MESSIANIC MISSION OF JESUS

I

As belief in Pauline doctrine waned, and Jesus began to be regarded as fallible, mortal man, the question of whether He believed Himself to be Messiah began again to be argued. Two schools of thought emerged. The first is most vividly expressed by Ernest Renan, whose devotion to Jesus seems to have come upon him in spite of all pertaining to Jesus that Renan found difficult to reconcile. On the one hand Renan saw Him as the supreme teacher, the "summit of human greatness," [1] the strongest individual force ever to come upon the earth, His words remaining steadfast as truth. On the other hand, Renan depicts Him as unlearned, save in the Judaic tradition, superstitious, vacillating, a man who stooped to the practice of thaumaturgy, working "magic miracles" against His will, in order to establish His Messianic claims. Renan paints Him as first the hesitant and then the willing victim of His age, succumbing, finally, to both the popular demands and to the prophetic conditions put upon Messiah because He, Himself, came in time to believe this was His destiny—that He was Messiah. Renan's own words, however, serve to establish that it was not Jesus who was led into Messianic delusion; rather, it was He who led His disciples through their disillusionment and confusion regarding His Messianic pretensions into dedication to truth. Renan says:

> The admirable moral which he draws from the idea of God as Father, is not that of enthusiasts who believe the world is near its end, and who prepare themselves by asceticism for a chimerical catastrophe; it is that of men who have lived, and still would live. . . . One idea . . . appears rooted in his mind, that there was no union possible between him and the ancient Jewish religion. . . . He is Son of God, but all men are . . . . he summarily destroyed the illusions of the disciples.[2]

How, then, could Jesus have been victim of the Messianic expectation of His day or coerced by His followers into the practice of magic to establish His claim to Messiah?[3] But the Messianic question cannot be dismissed, because Jesus *involved Himself in the Messianic hope by calling Himself, "Son of man."* Although in the Semitic languages, especially in the Aramean dialects, this title is simply a synonym for "man," it is directly connected with the Messianic hopes.[4]

The other school of thought holds that from the beginning Jesus was entirely committed to the Judaic Messianic concept, and that after His death the disciples and St. Paul spiritualized the idea. This concept is best presented by Albert Schweitzer. He presents Jesus as the dynamic, forceful product of Judaism who held the firm belief that He was the long-awaited Messiah and would have to suffer a martyr's death, but would return to earth at the rapidly approaching end of the world and claim it for His own kingdom, ruling over it with the twelve tribes of Israel in ascendancy, bringing about Utopia on earth:

> The question of whether Jesus thought eschatologically or not resolves itself . . . into one point, whether He held Himself to be the Messiah, or not. Anyone who admits that He did so must also admit that His ideas and expectations were of the eschatological type of late Judaism. Anyone who refuses to recognize this element in His thought must also refuse to attribute to Him any consciousness of being the Messiah. . . . it is necessary to think out all the consequences of the fact that He did actually live in the eschatological, Messianic thought world of late Judaism, and try to comprehend His resolutions and actions not by means of considerations drawn from ordinary psychology, but solely by motives provided by His eschatological expectations. . . . The mighty thought underlying the beatitudes of the Sermon on the Mount, that we come to know God and belong to Him through love, Jesus introduces into the late Jewish, Messianic expectation, without being in any way concerned to spiritualize those realistic ideas. . . . But the spirituality which lies in this religion of love must gradually, like a refiner's fire, seize upon all ideas which come into communication with it.[5]

Can Schweitzer's concept be correct in view of Jesus' insistence that true worship is worship in spirit and in truth—that heaven and earth would pass away, but not His words—and in view of the Gospel of St. John which transcends the Judaic Messianic role and places Jesus' message on a psychological level?[6] Schweitzer's own words cast doubt upon his interpretation. He says that Jesus made no claims to omniscience, "the Messianic dogma remains in the background. If He did not happen to mention it now and then, one could forget that it is presupposed all through":

> Within the Messianic hopes which His hearers carry in their hearts, He kindles the fire of an ethical faith. . . . The ethic of Reverence for Life is the ethic of Love widened into universality. It is the ethic of Jesus, now recognized as a logical consequence of thought.[7]

Schweitzer says, "The ideal would be that Jesus should have preached religious truth in a form independent of any connection with any particular period and such that it could be taken over simply and easily by each succeeding generation of man. That, however, He did not do, and there is no doubt a reason for it." [8]

A look at the world in the time of Jesus may reveal the reason, for most assuredly He did not ignore its thought patterns. The question is—how much of the world and of its prevailing beliefs did He know?

Renan states that the population of Galilee was very mixed, that even the name of the country meant "Circle of the Gentiles." In this province the inhabitants were Phoenicians, Syrians, Arabs, and Greeks. For nearly two hundred years B.C. the Jewish School of Egypt had attempted to amalgamate Hellenism and Judaism, and some Jews had embraced Hellenic culture. In close proximity were the Essenes, and Renan says: "We may believe . . . that many of the external practices of John, of the Essenes, and of the Jewish spiritual teachers of this time were derived from influences then but recently received from the far East." [9] The city of Jericho was the terminus of several important trade routes—thus, briefly, Jesus lived at the crossroads of civilization, in a place where there was ample opportunity for exchange of ideas.

Next, consider the government. Here a passage from Stauffer paints a bitter picture:

> Jesus experienced the tragic denouement in the history of the world and the beginning of the political twilight of antiquity. He was born in the triumphal year . . . of Rome and Augustus. When he was one year old, Tiberius went to Rhodes. When Jesus was two, Quintilius Varus sold the rebellious people of Sepphoris into slavery and crucified two thousand partisans before the gates of Jerusalem.[10]

While in no way overlooking the savage cruelty of Rome, consider in Renan's words its admirable qualities: "The Roman power, very stern on the one hand . . . permitted a good deal of liberty. . . . It is not recorded that Jesus was even once interfered with by the civil power.

... The Romans at this period treated all strange religions with respect...."[11] The intolerant theocracy of the Jews "disgusted that broad sentiment of justice and civil government which the humblest Roman carried everywhere with him"—Jewish law "restricted life to such a degree that it opposed all change, and all amelioration."[12]

The Jews accused Jesus of treason against the Roman government, but Renan says, "Nothing could be more unjust; for Jesus had always recognized the Roman government as the established power."[13] An interesting note from Stauffer may be injected here: he says that according to Ulla (C.A.D. 300), Jesus "stood close to the government."[14] How much did He know of Roman law? Did He realize what the Roman ideal represented in the history of man's cultural progress?

During many years of Jesus' life nothing is known of His whereabouts —thus, actually, nothing is known of His education except that He was well versed in Jewish doctrine. He read from Scriptures—He wrote on the ground.[15] But the ability to read and write would not, of course, attest to a broad education outside the Judaic tradition. There is, however, a similarity between His words and those of other philosophers. Renan attributes this to "secret channels and . . . that kind of sympathy which exists among the various portions of humanity . . . conformable to the instincts and wants of the heart in a given age."[16] Is this indicated, considering all that surrounded Jesus and His inquisitive, discerning mind? Stauffer credits Him to be a great Jewish scholar, but declares, "There can be no doubt that Jesus never read the works of Plato."[17] Would it not be more accurate to say that Jesus did not name Plato—or any other philosopher? In many ways His approach resembles that of Socrates, who, as Robert de Ropp describes him, followed the bidding of his "inner voice" endeavoring at all times "to lead men to truth by questioning. And the truth he valued most highly related not to externals but to the laws that govern man's inner being."[18] In discussing ancient Greece, Edith Hamilton points to Plato's philosophy: "Freedom is no matter of laws and constitutions; only he is free who realizes the divine order within himself, the true standard by which a man can steer and measure himself."[19] Jesus also based His teaching upon the divine order within man, the kingdom of God inherent in him. Was He unaware of Plato's teaching?

In truth there is no way to define the type and limits of Jesus' education. After the report of His visit to the temple at twelve years of age, with His parents, it is said, "And he went down with them, and came to Nazareth, and was subject unto them . . . ."[20] Here, the record breaks off and takes up again with the ministry of John the Baptist. Within the years lost to the record, Jesus could have traveled to the ends of civilization and back, studying along the way—or in neighboring cities He could have studied the cultures and philosophies of East and West. In the Gospels there is a statement that could be interpreted as indication that Jesus was away for many years: when He goes to His native place to teach and heal, people do not seem to know for sure who He is—which is to say, they ask, "Is this not the son of the joiner?" [21] Strange question to ask, even to express incredulity, had Jesus lived there since childhood and been away but a short time. Because the townspeople know His family so well, they are offended at His brilliance even though they are astounded at His teaching.

A normal appraisal of Jesus would be that such a brilliant mind would take into account all that His age represented in history. It is highly improbable that such a mind, flowering at the crossroads of civilization, would have felt only the impact of Jewish Messianic expectation, as Schweitzer surmises of Jesus, even though it had reached a new high in intensity. And in Jesus' day, a man searching for truth would have found that Israel was not alone in suffering Messianic expectation—Ranjee Shahani speaks, for instance, of India's "long and Messiah-haunted history." [22] Messianic expectation appears to be as old as man. Clyde Kluckhohn says:

> . . . one of the best established generalizations of social anthropology is that when the pressure of whites upon aborigines reaches a certain point there will be a revival of the ancient religion or a partially new cult of messianic type will arise.[23]

And Renan observes that the triumphal and often cruel entry of Greek and Roman civilization into Asia threw the people back upon their dreams, evoking their concept of Messiah as judge and avenger.[24] But what many scholars fail to emphasize is that Rome itself awaited and sought supranatural intervention. Its old religion, long since destroyed from within by Greek intellectualism, began to restate itself in Messianic terms, as may be seen in the "cycle of prophetic poems, of which the fundamental ideas were the division of the history of humanity into periods, the succession of the gods corresponding to these periods—a complete renovation of the world, and the final advent of a golden age." [25]

Thus, in Jesus' time, until man ceased to look for the advent of some one or a series of Messiahs to solve his problems, he could not realize his own potential. If Jesus realized the Judaic Messianic dream to be vainglorious, the question arises as to why He chose to inbed His work and words in Judaism, which presented itself as a perfect picture of man marking time because of the Messianic complex. And yet its Scriptures, voicing monotheism, embraced the species in its legends, and they offered the basic law of the Ten Commandments. No other one group of writings —zealously passed on from generation to generation—so concisely combined into one background a statement of Homo sapiens' consciousness and his gropings toward truth. The Scriptures begin with allegorical man and continue his line in unbroken genealogical chain, giving promise thereby of ending in allegorical fashion the story of the development of the individual to his highest potential—this is to say, a *congruent* completion of Scriptures must be allegorical in nature, effected by design: allegorical Adam's potential must be realized in an allegorical Son of man, thereby making the alpha and omega representation of humankind allegorical figures.

Jesus seized the opportunity to complete the Judaic Scriptures. This was His mission [26]—and in fulfilling it He also led men toward a high moral ethic vested in love. Why did He do it? In completing the Scriptures, He could destroy the Messianic tradition. There is no evidence that Jesus did not know what He was doing—and Schweitzer has told the twentieth century exactly what He did:

> Within the Messianic hopes which His hearers carry in their hearts, He kindles the fire of an ethical faith. Thus the Sermon on the Mount becomes the incontestable charter of Liberal Christianity. The truth that the ethical is the essence of religion is firmly established on the authority of Jesus. Further than this, the religion of love taught by Jesus has been freed from any dogmatism which clung to it by the disappearance of the late Jewish expectations of the immediate end of the world. The mold in which the casting was made has been broken.[27]

Jesus broke it. This study concludes that He knew what He was doing, knew that He was breaking the Messianic mold, and that to break it through completing the Scriptures, thus freeing mankind from the curse of Messianic expectation and Messianic delusion, was His mission. To complete may also be to destroy: William Barrett says that according to Heidegger, Nietzsche was the last metaphysician in the tradition of the West, "the thinker who at once completes and destroys that tradition." [28] Jesus completed and destroyed the Judaic Messianic tradition and any like unto it. But the destroyer may also be creative. Barrett points out that Heidegger is working within Greek tradition, "but he is also seeking to

... destroy it creatively so that it may surpass itself." [29] Jesus, too, worked within Greek tradition to destroy its restrictive patterns, as well as the restrictive patterns of Judaic tradition, for He made man come to grips with his consciousness of the infinite in his own being so that the seed of Socrates' truth might come to flower as Messianic expectation withered.

Neither Schweitzer nor those who have read his book have grasped the full implication of what he has stated: the Messianic mold is broken. The point overlooked is that Jesus, Himself, so thoroughly undermined the prevailing Messianic concept, left the question of it and His relationship to it so entangled in contradiction, so twisted and bent in every direction, that the controversy He began could not be closed, the question could not be answered, the battle He started could not cease, until the last fragment of any Messianic image was gone and His own Messianic image, become in time a hated object of odium, had been pounded into dust.

What Jesus had done was dimly, but firmly, grasped by St. Paul, who said, "The foundation is laid, namely Jesus Christ, and no one can lay any other." [30] He saw that no more images of Messiah could be cast—Stauffer points out that by A.D. 80-100 the "rabbinate had begun to avoid the apocalyptic epithet 'Son of man.' ..." [31] But St. Paul's own reaction to his overwhelming realization that Jesus had made away with the Messianic mold was to refine and enlarge the Judaic theory so that it lies at the base of his thinking. In doing this, however, he took the first step that had to be taken to preserve Christianity. He did preserve it, and time went to work to destroy Messianic expectation in any dress.

Today, men speak of the well-known Messianic complex in derisive or sympathetic terms such as are reserved for illness. The desire to save the world is seen to coincide with the lust for power as well as with the compulsion to seek persecution, both ending all too often in madness. Messianic delusion wears many guises. Later in this study they are examined. Suffice it to say here that Jesus recognized them and played through to its agonizing end the whole drama of man's Messianic-mindedness, revealing its every facet for what it is, thereby causing the eventual destruction of thought patterns in which such Messianic complex could be sustained or created anew.

But Jesus did not destroy the Messianic hope. Here, one faces the gigantic contradiction that He poses. Why not, if His mission was to break the Judaic Messiah mold? Why did He deliberately replant the Messianic seed?

Jesus appears to have seen that Greek intellectualism posed itself against the universally prevailing Messianic concepts, but superior as it was it could not destroy man's innate compulsion to search beyond his *consciousness* for saving grace, and thus alongside Greek thought, false oracular practices flourished; He saw that because Messianic hope was universal, springing eternally in man's heart, it must be a valid hope, but misdirected when man holds the concept that governing-truth or God's Messiah is foreign to his own individual being. Jesus discovered its residence in man, found the key to unlock His own *unconscious*, and said that man must seek this inner kingdom if he hopes to find God's saving grace and the sufficiency in life he craves; He then made Himself a symbol of the Authority within it, the Christ of God in man. His own words support this concept, as will be seen in the following section.

II

Thirteen scholars, grinding the Bible's marvelous poetry into staid prose, busied themselves straining at "gnats" and swallowed a "camel." [32] Without a word of explanation, the authors of *The New English Bible* substituted in the four Gospels the word *Messiah* for the word *Christ*, in forty-two of the fifty passages in which the word *Christ* appears, and in three others, deleted it. Thus, the *word* which gives Christianity its name has been virtually written out of the disciples' recounting of Jesus' story, and the word that brings to mind Judaic pretender has been written in.

As James Moffatt discusses the writing of the Gospels, he says:

> In the communities of the faithful, men had to impress upon themselves and upon others what Jesus said and did, for the more convinced they were that he was neither a Jewish pretender nor an unsubstantial deity like one of the deities of the cults, the more urgent it was for them to recall that his words were the rule of their life. . . . at least one written record of them was probably in existence by about A.D. 50. . . . Those who had been with him loved to recollect the very words he used. . . . And this from no mere pious, sentimental motive. When challenged by the Jews to justify their faith and practice, they had to fall back upon what they remembered of the instructions of their Lord. . . . in the Fourth Gospel . . . the messianic category is transcended. . . . the idea of [Jesus'] return from heaven is transmuted into the conception of his spirit entering the human spirit through faith.[33]

Henry Pitt Van Dusen sums Stauffer's *Jesus and His Story* in one line from the book: "Jesus did not refer to himself as the Messiah." [34] Stauffer goes further, "The word Messiah was not used by Jesus. . . ." And he says, "the title 'Messiah' was not sufficient for him, never was to be sufficient." [35] William Neil says that Jesus avoided this title because "It had too many ambiguous associations. To the crowd it meant the purveyor of peace and plenty, to the anti-Roman it meant political and military leadership, to the devout it meant a supernatural judge," but Jesus saw Himself as servant, calling Himself "Son of man," which Neil sees as the "deepest mystery of all." [36]

According to Moffatt's translation, only once did Jesus refer to Himself as "Messiah." According to the King James version, He did not use the word. Whichever translation may be correct, in this one instance, "Messiah" is first identified as the "Christ," and the true Messianic role, as Jesus played it, is indicated to be: to reveal the truth to man. At the well, Jesus speaks to the woman of Samaria. She says to Him:

> "Well, I know messiah, which means Christ, is coming. When he arrives he will explain it all to us."
> "I am messiah," said Jesus, "I who am talking to you."

The above is Moffatt's translation. According to the King James Bible, the woman says, "I know Messiah cometh, which is called Christ. When he is come, he will tell us all things." Jesus says to her, "I that speak unto thee am he," [37] thus, avoiding the word *Messiah*.

When Jesus asks His disciples, ". . . who do you say I am?" Peter answers, "You are the Christ, the Son of the living God." [38] Jesus names him "the rock," and says His church is to be built upon him; but the keys He gives to Peter are those to open the realm of heaven, the kingdom of God He has stated to be "within you," and thus the Christ of God in man must be there.

But whether future generations read in this passage and others the word *Messiah* where past generations have read the word *Christ*, Jesus placed the Christ, Messiah, apart from the Judaic Messianic concept:

> "Tell me," he said, "what you think about the Christ. Whose son is he?"
> They said to him, "David's."
> He said to them, "How is it then that David is inspired to call him Lord?
>
> > The Lord said to my Lord,
> > 'Sit at my right hand,
> > till I put your enemies
> > under your feet.'

If David calls him Lord, how can he be his son?"
No one could make any answer to him.[39]

In this passage, Jesus presents the issue that the Lord, the Christ, is not the Son of David, which is to say, is not as the Judaic concept holds the Christ to be, but is something other and more deeply interfused in man, something that David, too, knew within himself: MY Lord. Thus, the Christ must be Lord addressing Lord, Son addressing Son, man speaking to man.

Jesus says that He judges not the man who will not receive His word for he "hath one that judgeth him. . ."[40]—and on another occasion, He says:

> You must love the Lord your God with your whole heart, with your whole soul, and with your whole mind. This is the greatest and chief command. There is a second like it: you must love your neighbor as yourself. The whole Law and the prophets hang upon these two commands.[41]

Jesus understood that "the Lord" of which the prophets spoke reflected not an outside power, but an unknown power within, a power and authority apart from their *personalities*—and thus, He spoke not of "himself" as a *personality*:

> Were I to glorify myself, my glory would be nothing; it is my Father who glorifies me; you say "He is our God," but you do not understand him.[42]

Man pays lip service to the idea of God as Father—Jesus claimed Him literally for Himself and for all men—it is the Father within that glorifies man:

> . . . you are all brothers; you are not to call anyone "father" on earth, for One is your heavenly Father; nor must you be called "leaders" for One is your leader, *even* the Christ.[43]

Here speaks the poet, perfectly combining the truth in one word, implied, which is equally right in any of the word's meanings: *even* means "to divide perfectly in equal portions," as well as meaning "just now present." Each man must accept for himself that of God which is represented by the *name* Jesus called Himself:

> On those who have accepted him, however, he has conferred the right of being children of God, that is, on those who believe in his Name, who owe this birth of theirs to God, not to human blood, nor to any impulse of the flesh or of man.[44]

Jesus clarified the nature and equipresence of the Christ in clarifying the Reign of God which was held to be the earthly reign of Christ, Messiah. He says, "The Reign of God is not coming as you hope to catch sight of it; no one will say, 'Here it is' or 'There it is,' for the Reign of God is now in your midst." [45] Thereby, He severed His message completely from Judaic Messianic eschatology, saying in effect: the Christ is now reigning in your midst, in the kingdom of God within you. At another time, He says:

> And no man hath ascended up to heaven, but he that came down from heaven, even the Son of man which is in heaven.[46]

In these words, Jesus again presents Son of man as an inward power *presently operative within man*, "*in heaven*," the kingdom "within you."

But to accomplish His mission, He must let Messianic expectation converge around Him, even as at each step He had to reveal the Christ to be completely opposite from the concept held. On many occasions He risked losing the Messianic connection upon which His work hung.[47] Some people say Jesus is not Christ because no one will know where Christ comes from, and Jesus cries, "You know me? you know where I come from?"[48] No man fully knows himself or any other man, from whence he came, until he realizes that in the fact of his existence he is a part of the origin, a parcel of God, Son of life itself.

As the vision of Mary is reported,[49] Gabriel says the child she is to bear will be called, "Son of God," and He is so called by many, beginning with John the Baptist,[50] to whom the words meant Judaic Messiah. But as one montages the incidents wherein this term is applied to Jesus—including the accounts of deranged men He charges not to speak so or to make Him so known[51]—it appears that the Judaic Messianic term, Son of God, is what *they* call Him. Jesus uses the term objectively when He hears of Lazarus' death; and in John 5:25 He appears to call Himself "Son of God," but in the same breath He speaks of such authority granted "since he is Son of man"—that is, symbol of man, as was Adam. He uses the term only in the sense that any man, every man, may use it: the Jews accuse Him of blaspheming because, "being a man [thou] makest thyself God"—Jesus says Scripture cannot be broken and quotes, "I said, ye are gods," then asks if He blasphemes because He says, "I am the Son of God. . . ."[52] He does not make Himself God incarnate to the exclusion of all other men.

Those who would limit Jesus' concept of Himself to Judaic Messiah point to the passages in which He appears to speak freely of the coming of the Son of man at the end of the world.[53] But Jesus placed heaven *within man,* and thus it is within each man's inner world that he will see the Christ of his being coming on clouds of glory: when the Sanhedrin was trying to secure evidence against Jesus before handing Him over to Pilate, the high priest asked Him:

"Are you the Christ? . . . the Son of the Blessed?"
Jesus said, "I am. And, what is more, you will all see the Son of man seated at the right hand of the Power, and coming with the clouds of heaven." [54]

The end of the world for any man comes with death. Thus, the God-head in man must descend unto him from within when the outer world of things and time is ended for him, at his death. If a man's God-head, Son, comes to him in death, Jesus could say in truth, in fact, "Verily I say unto you, this generation shall not pass, till all these things be fulfilled" [55]—all men will live to see death, He has said that the Kingdom of God "is within you," and thus they "shall see the Son of man coming in the clouds of heaven. . . ." [56]

In the Gospel of St. Luke, it is reported that when Jesus is asked, "Art thou then the Son of God?" He answers, "Ye say that I am." [57] In the Gospel of St. Matthew, the question is put differently:

"I adjure thee by the living God, that thou tell us whether thou be the Christ, the Son of God."
Jesus answers, "Thou hast said . . ." [58]

In the Moffatt translation, the answers in these passages are given, "Certainly, I am," and "Even so!"

"Ye say that I am"—"Thou hast said"—these words imply a certainty, but they also very specifically state: *you* and not I say this. As to the answer, "Even so!" if the word, *even,* is considered fully, this answer can also mean: Yes, if you acknowledge as I do that the Christ is evenly and equally present in every person. In these two words—"Even so!"—Jesus meets the test of the poet.

When Pilate says to Jesus, "Are you the King of the Jews?" He answers, "Thou sayest it," or "Thou sayest." [59] Moffatt translates, "Certainly," but this fails to encompass the other equally valid meaning of "Thou sayest it." In the Gospel of St. John, in answer to Pilate's question, Jesus replies, "Are you saying this of your own accord, or did other people tell you about me?" When Pilate protests that he is no Jew, Jesus clarifies the issue by saying that the realm He governs is not of this world. Pilate replies, "So you are a king?" According to Moffatt, Jesus says, "Certainly I am a King"

—in the King James Bible, Jesus' answer is given, "Thou sayest that I am a king." [60] Then He reveals His mission to Pilate to be truth-bearer: "Everyone who belongs to the truth listens to my voice."

When all the answers Jesus gives to the high priest and to Pilate are considered, He appears to have said in effect: YOU call me Son of God, King of the Jews, Judaic Messiah—I do not call myself only Son of God—*thou sayest it of me*.

Over His cross was written, ". . . King of the Jews." In this drama the Judaic priesthood could sense the death knell of their Messianic concept, and they requested Pilate to modify the writing. But Pilate refused. What was written was written.[61] In the destruction of Jesus' person the Messianic mold was broken, for He played the role to the greatest degree of perfection according to the Scriptures that a man can play it, even as He made way for the light of truth to come into man's consciousness. For as He drew near His death, He left with His disciples words as to the meaning of Himself which were not ambiguous: He tells of the end of things, of the glory that is to come to Son of man; then commanding the disciples to the charitable act, He insists that He is identical to the least man on earth, that this is the *meaning* of His revelation, for "in so far as you did not do it to one of these, even the least of them, you did not do it to me." [62] As Dean Inge observed of St. Paul, he "understood what most Christians never realize, namely, that the Gospel of Christ is not *a* religion, but religion itself." [63] Or, again, in existential terms, revelation of the Christ by Jesus is not "a truth that I have, but a truth that I am."

If Jesus brought religion itself, brought "truth that I am," was He not historical Messiah? This study concludes that He was not—there was one prophecy concerning Messiah that Jesus did not and could not fulfill in its every aspect, a prophecy that no *man* can fulfill. This prophecy, to be discussed in the following section, reveals what Judaic Messiah is, how historical Messiah is to come.

III

The Gospel of St. John presents the concept that Jesus *lived* the truth, the understanding, He wished to bring to human consciousness:

So the Logos became flesh and tarried among us . . .[64]

Jesus appears to have realized that the Logos in man is man's understanding of who and what he is, the "truth that I am," and that the truth of man's being is the truth that governs men; He appears to have understood also that if Messiah is to bear the truth of man's being to humankind and dwell in a body among men, then words of truth must take a form of their own: Messiah could come only in the advent of a *Book*. By insisting that His *words* would not pass away,[65] Jesus prepared the ground for His return in the advent of the book written of Him. If one sees His second coming in the advent of the Gospels, the mystery of His statement, that the disciple, John, was to survive until He "came back," [66] is reconciled. The importance of the Gospel of St. John cannot be overemphasized. Moffatt says:

> ... the messianic category is transcended. ... In the Fourth Gospel we see Christianity facing a new era and obliged to reinterpret itself. This crisis is connected with Asia Minor, and particularly with the Ephesus, toward the close of the first century, when the faith had to translate itself into Greek terms more thoroughly than in the later epistles of Paul or in Hebrews.[67]

John lived until his record was set forth—that is, John's understanding of Jesus lived until Jesus came back and spoke again in *The Gospel According to Saint John*.

If Jesus was to fulfill His mission, the Gospels had to be as accurate an account of His words as devotion to truth could make them; the reports vary, but essentially they are congruent and serve both to validate each other and to enlarge the picture. Because Jesus interlaced His message with the Scriptures, they must be included in His story. He placed upon His disciples the missionary work recorded in the New Testament. Thus, one must conclude that He dictated the structure and, in this sense, the content of the book that would contain His work and represent in reality historical Judaic Messiah. In the view of this study, although Jesus, Himself, was not historical Messiah, through His work the Bible, itself historical Judaic Messiah, came into the world, its content delivered by the pen of the Jewish race. Moffatt points out:

> Next to the actual appearance of Jesus upon earth, as Renan observes, the issue of the gospels is the most significant phenomenon in primitive Christianity.[68]

The Bible, as Messiah, possesses glory, grace, and reality—not as THE only expression of the Logos in man, but as *an* only or *one whole* expression of it. The Bible was centuries in the writing, product of authors widely separated in time, but it has a marvelous unity of thought although it has also many contradictions—as many as man himself. It continues to be the most controversial book in the Western world because, like man, it is a supreme paradox. In sum, it contains the expression of humanity: it is Homo sapiens' complete picture of himself, from Genesis to Revelation. Beginning with the advent of man's God-consciousness, symbolized in Adam, it reaches its climax in man's realization of God *incarnate in his being,* symbolized in Jesus as Son of man, Lord, with which one's consciousness may have but brief encounter—and then it bears witness to the transformation in consciousness this encounter evokes. In the words of Henri Daniel-Rops, the Bible is "a unique and inexhaustible book in which all there is to say about God and man is said." [69] Today, the world is again witnessing its power. Ndabanningi Sithole says:

> What is the actual relevance of the Bible . . . to African nationalism? . . . The Bible is redeeming the African individual from the power of superstition, individuality-crushing tradition, witchcraft, and other forces that do not make for progress. The same Bible is helping the African individual to reassert himself above colonial powers! It is inconceivable to a logical mind that the Bible could deliver the African from traditional domination without at the same time redeeming him from colonial domination.[70]

It is inconceivable that the message of the Gospels, the brotherhood of man, could be preached for nineteen centuries and not come, finally, to flower in society—for truth will eventually prevail and of its reign there will be no end, because truth is that only which can govern, does govern, is now operative in man's midst.

But no nation, man, or race can claim to have delivered the whole of truth into the common realm. This is to say, in truth there is no competition: truth is even and evened unto all men. The Light of Asia, Lord Gautama, in denial of special divinity in His own person, said to His first disciples: "Look within, thou art the Buddha." [71] Lao-tse wrote: " . . . the sage keeps to One and becomes the standard for the world. . . . Because he does not compete no one in the world can compete with him." [72] Jesus' message reflects both these precepts and the precepts of all great religions. If He saw as a necessary development in the expression of truth the bringing forth of one whole volume encompassing Homo sapiens' consciousness, the critical challenge was how to accomplish this, for countless people had realized truth but had found the whole of it inexpressible, deranging in its magnitude, in its penetration into all things, in its boiling inversion. Jesus met the challenge because He utilized the material at hand and called upon other men to help Him. In practical effect, His words and commands placed upon an indeterminate number of men the task of writing the Bible. It was drawn from and belongs to both East and West. Its legends encompass humanity's legends.

The Bible is historical in that it represents a "Tell" upon which human beings, since the dawn of consciousness, have built edifices of truth realized, stating in the same legend-form upon a legendary spot a certain realization until a "mound" of truth and fact was raised, leaving only a telltale relic in each stratum of poetic words as countless retellings swept away the superfluous even as time buried the essentials which must be carried on generation after generation. To serve memory, as the Scriptures were retold man's realizations must have been attached to names and places, the language crystallizing finally along the path archaeologists have traced. Every civilization of the crescent of the Nile has played its part, slaves and warriors plaiting the blood and thought of men. Who were these peoples?

In 1905, Hugo Winckler "brought to the notice of the world at large the hitherto unknown Indo-Germanic Hittites and their vanished empire," which as Werner Keller points out, played a considerable part in the Old Testament.[73] Another strain also mingles in the thought of Israel: the Mitanni of Indo-Aryan stock, "their temples . . . dedicated to old Indian gods . . . "—a third of the princely correspondents from Canaan, land of Israel's nativity, have this ancestry—"the Biblical Horites were not a Semitic people. . . . at least the princely caste must be reckoned as Indo-Aryan." [74] But look further, deeper:

> The remains of Jericho have made Tell es-Sultan one of the most extraordinary scenes of discovery in the world. . . . for [in] this mound, under the strata of the Bronze age, lie traces of the Stone age that take us back to the earliest times of all, to the days when man first built himself settled habitations.[75]

One sees in this "Tell" that the Bible, as Messiah, has no nameable place to lay its head, that it is of virgin birth because its conception is both found and lost in the dawn of human consciousness and in *the* distinguishing characteristic of man—the word, his sire:

> In the beginning was the Word, and the Word was with God, and the Word was God.[76]

If God can be incarnate, He must be incarnate in Homo sapiens, empowered to speak the word, and only in words of truth and reality taken on a body of their own, *a Book*, can the whole body of truth dwell always among men. In the view of this study, however, The Bible is not the unquestionable word of God; it is the now unshakable work of men giving expression to consciousness of God in their being, bearing true witness to their realizations and to their memory of or to the traditional reporting of the words and deeds of the people whose lives are there recorded.

Jesus' insistence that His words are all important indicates that He realized Messiah must come as a book, and at least one other man before Him had related Messiah to the written word:

> Thou hast no desire for sacrifice or offering;
> it is a body thou hast prepared for me—
> in holocausts and sin-offerings thou takest no delight.
> So I said, "Here I come—in the roll of the book
> this is written of me—
> I come to do thy will, O God.[77]

In Jesus' time, a book was a roll—a scroll, but in the King James Bible the word used is "volume": "Wherefore, when he cometh into the world, he saith, Sacrifice and offering thou wouldest not, but a body hast thou prepared me: In burnt offerings and sacrifices for sin thou hast had no pleasure. Then said I, Lo, I come (in the volume of the book it is written of me) to do thy will, O God." Jesus gave this command:

> Go and learn the meaning of this word, I care for mercy, not for sacrifice.[78]

Thus, one must seek to understand His mission through the prophecy quoted above, for in the face of this command, He cannot be viewed as seeing Himself in terms of a sacrifice or sin-offering. One might say that the prophecy means: it is written that the Christ will come. True, but if Messiah is to fulfill this Scripture, the one who filled the Messiah role could not be an atoning Lamb to ransom man, a sacrifice for man's sin.

Viewed in another light, the poetic words of this prophecy also say that Messiah's advent is in the "roll of the book" written of the one who comes, a prophecy no *man* could fulfill. If Messiah is to "tell us all things," only a *book* encompassing the words spoken by countless truth-bearers to span the last reach of human consciousness could be Messiah unto all men.

The "body . . . prepared for me," for the one whose work would bring forth the book, is to be seen in the Scriptures into which Jesus wove His life and words, but it is in the volume of the book "written of me"—God, Son in man—that Messiah, the Bible, comes, comes as a roll, as a wave that surges upon the shores of the world through fulfillment of the missionary task Jesus imposed. Through the Bible, He came back.

Through it, historical Messiah comes, fulfilling the Judaic promise to bear the whole body of truth to man: the truth embodied in man's sacred writings in every language, in legends, for all these speak the same word and the Bible enfolds their like. As Heidegger sees, regardless of education or ability to articulate the reasons, an understanding rooted in existence accepts or rejects what is presented to it as true or false, so that, in Barrett's words: "We become rootless intellectually to the degree that we lose our hold upon this primary form of understanding, which is there in the act of opening our eyes upon the world." [79] Even as it was there in Adam.

It is parent understanding, this parent grasp of truth, that is revealed in the Bible—that Jesus revealed and demonstrated. Jesus speaks not of Himself as person, but of living truth, Father of being, to be identified by the same word in all mankind. He says:

> If I bear witness of myself, my witness is not true.
> My doctrine is not mine, but his that sent me.
> He that believeth on me, believeth not on me, but on him that sent me. . . . the *word* that I have spoken, the *same* shall judge him in the last day. For I have not spoken of myself . . . .[80]

And what is the *word*, the *same?* On another occasion, Jesus has said, ". . . have you not read what was said to you by God, I am the God of Abraham and the God of Isaac and the God of Jacob?" [81] Stauffer writes, "God says to Abraham: 'Seekest thou the God of Gods? . . . I am He. . . . I am before the days were'. . . ." and in another passage he speaks of the emphatic "I's" that appear in ancient Hebrew literature: "I and not an angel; I and not a seraph; I and not the envoy; I, the Lord, I am he and no other." [82] The *word*, the *same*, the *name* of God appears to be "I":

> Fear not, for I have redeemed you.
> I have called you by your name, you are mine.
> When you pass through the waters I will be with you . . .

> Before me was no God formed,
> Neither shall there be any after me.
> I, I am the Lord,
> And besides me there is no savior.

> I am the Lord your Holy one . . .

> I, I am he
> who blots out your transgressions for my own sake:

And I will not remember your sins.
See now that I, even I, am He and there is no god beside me . . .[83]

"I" appears to be the name of God declared to men by Jesus, proclaimed again just before He goes out to the Garden of Gethsemane, that men might know themselves to be "I."[84] But as one tries to explain that only through "I-being" in man can man reach the truth of his and all other men's being, he becomes object or pretender to deity, all of whom speak in terms of "I," for they can speak the truth in no other terms as they try to share it with their fellowmen. Lord Krishna says:

> There is no past when I was not,
> Nor you, nor these; and we
> Shall—none and never—cease to live
> Throughout the long to-be.[85]

The name of God in man, "I," is deeply buried in the human "tell." Jesus sought to clarify the concept, but to begin to understand His revelation one must observe that His words describing the inner kingdom parallel psychology's description of the *unconscious*, although they also reach beyond psychology's present concepts. (See Appendix I, p. 395.)

IV

Because today's psychological concepts and terminology are both confused and confusing, and because Jesus symbolized and dramatized the psychological makeup of man, a brief outline of the parallel between psychology and Jesus' teaching cannot be traced with ease and desirable clarity. But as Lancelot Law Whyte, author of *The Unconscious Before Freud*, says of his work:

> However inadequate the present study, the attempt is necessary . . . For today *faith, if it bears any relation to the natural world, implies faith in the unconscious*. If there is a God, he must speak there; if there is a healing power, it must operate there; if there is a principle of ordering in the organic realm, its most powerful manifestation must be found there.[86]

Jesus conveyed the idea that the psyche of man is divided: in the Book of Hebrews the author speaks of the Logos penetrating "to the very division of soul and spirit, joints and marrow—scrutinizing the very thoughts and conceptions of the heart. And no created thing is hidden from him; all things lie open and exposed before the eyes of him with whom we have to reckon."[87] The origin of the concept of the *unconscious* is unknown, but it was incipient in Jesus' day. Whyte writes: ". . . in a tentative and speculative manner many thinkers in different cultures had already divided the mind into two or three higher and lower parts; the Egyptians, the Hebrews, and Hindus . . ."[88] He says that in Europe after 1600 few thinkers attempted to render fertile the ancient psychic structural doctrines by introducing further principles of functional operation, but "Freud was not the first person to identify himself with the mission of enlightening man by revealing to him his own unconscious mind. In a pale manner Carus [1789–1869] experienced this task as a mission of redemption."[89]

The concept offered by this study is that Jesus identified Himself with the mission of enlightening man by revealing to him his own unconscious mind, that He saw this task as a mission of redemption, that He introduced the principles of functional psychic operations, and both symbolized and demonstrated the Authority and power in the *unconscious* versus the conscious in man. Modern psychology's beginning and what psychologists know of man's psyche appear to parallel in large measure Jesus' efforts and teaching.

Both Jesus' ministry and psychology began as a protest against the religious dogma of the day, but as Dr. Progoff says, "the net result of modern psychology has been to re-affirm man's experience of himself as a spiritual being" and its ultimate task is to re-establish man's connection to life, "not superficially in terms of slogans or therapeutic stratagems [but] in terms of experiences that "he can learn to verify by himself, within himself."[90] Jesus offered no superficialities, no stratagems. He turned man to search inwardly for the truth of himself, to experience this truth by acting upon his intuitive grasp of it, and to face it and himself in consciousness squarely if he would re-establish his connection to life.

Psychologists presented man with the staggering fact of his *unconscious* mind, and that the power of this unknown reality of himself in being cannot be fully comprehended because it enfolds a world of his being that exists apart from his conscious world of being. In Jesus' day, the staggering fact men could not accept was His proclamation of an unknown domain within, which He called the kingdom of God, or heaven, and that this realm was real, its power real, and that it must be understood in terms of the relationship between man's ego and "I."

Freud assumed that what is repressed in the *unconscious* has acquired a certain independence of the ego, the force which denies the existence of the *unconscious* and has subjected it to repressions.[91] Jesus states that the realm He refers to and its Authority have acquired a certain independence of the conscious ego, for He says, ". . . I have overcome the world," and on another occasion, ". . . I am not of this world" [92]—the world of the conscious domain known to the disciples and the egocentric hierarchy of Judaism that denied Him.

Freud came to recognize "that the unconscious does not coincide with what is repressed; it is still true that all that is repressed is Unconscious, but not . . . the whole Unconscious is repressed. A part of the ego too—and Heaven knows how important a part—may be Unconscious, undoubtedly is Unconscious," and thus he came to postulate a "third Unconscious which is not repressed," and, as Progoff says, to suspect it "to be the most important unconscious of all, the very foundation of psychic life." [93] This *very foundation of psychic life*, Jesus called the "Son of man"—man's *true Ego*, "I," his *true Authority* in life, or *Self*—and acting as its *symbol* confronted man with the fact of his inner kingdom, with the fact of its power.

The Self, or true Ego of man, is not yet defined in psychological terms. Progoff says, "The Self as conceived by Jung is the psychological potentiality that emerges in each individual personality; and the life will as conceived by Rank is the vital force with which that potentiality is expressed and fulfilled in the world"—Rank joins with Adler's "social feeling" in his concept that "no expression of the human will can be understood outside of its cultural context," although his "most basic emphasis is not on society but on the individual," for Rank "recognized only one factor of a universal scope, man's *will to immortality* . . ." [94] Jesus' new commandment, ". . . That ye love one another . . ." [95] embraces the understanding that no expression of the human will can be understood outside society, but His basic emphasis is on the individual; He recognized the universal scope of man's will to immortality, basing His message upon it. The Gospel of St. John presents the concept that Jesus symbolized the psychological potentiality each individual can realize within himself as he comes to accept for himself the *name* by which Jesus called Himself, Son of man, "I."

Psychologists agree that primary instincts start in the id, it is the older, and ego develops out of it through the influence of the outer world. In the end, Freud came to say, "What had been id must become 'I' . . ." [96] In the words, "kingdom within," Jesus enfolds man's unrealized potentials; today this kingdom is called id and *unconscious*. He presented "I" as the older or true Ego emerging from the fundamental mass of life tendencies —"Before Abraham was, I am . . ." and He said, "I am the way . . . " [97] Psychologists see the id, the *unconscious*, as "a special realm, with its own desires and modes of expression and peculiar mental mechanisms not elsewhere operative." [98] Throughout His ministry, Jesus stresses this—the "kingdom within" is a special realm apart.[99]

Psychologists agree that what the personality represses and rejects belongs to the id and obeys its mechanism, but the repressed and rejected is not born of the id, it is from the province of personality. Jesus, as symbol of the Authority in the id, opens the kingdom to all who are dispirited, hopeless, maimed, rejected, repressed, and oppressed, "Come unto me all ye that labor and are heavy laden . . ."[100]

Psychologists agree that repressions, latent in the id, reverse themselves and, disguised, may return to consciousness with a compulsiveness that overpowers logical thinking. Jesus says to the heavy laden, "I will give you rest . . ." and ". . . you will find your souls refreshed."[101] Thus, He indicates that repressions are transformed and strengthened in the domain He reveals.

Psychologists agree that the unconscious processes in the id can be raised to a conscious level just as conscious processes can travel back into the id. There is constant interplay between the psychic divisions. Jesus says, ". . . seek, and ye shall find; knock, and it shall be opened unto you."[102] He speaks of "you in me" and of "I in you."[103]

Harold McCurdy quotes Freud: the "Id is chaotic and completely devoid of morality; it is also completely indifferent to reality; and every instinct in it is clamoring for satisfaction greedily. . . ." and he says that Freud "took more and more seriously the notion that there were inborn destructive impulses as well as sexual ones."[104] Jesus described the unknown realm as a childlike world. The child fits Freud's description of the id, but there is about him an aura of innocence, of strange, primordial wisdom, and he withdraws at times as though he were going home to Self, slipping through the chaotic into another fold of being best described as certainty, mute but there.

In dealing with the concept of man's ego, one finds many definitions of the word. Philosophically, it is defined: The entire man considered as union of soul and body; the conscious and permanent subject of all experience. Psychologically, the term is defined: The self, whether considered as an organization or system of mental states, or as the consciousness of the individual's distinction from other selves. In psychoanalysis, ego is seen as: The self-assertive and self-preserving tendency. As regards ego, psychology speaks two commands: lay down your ego, cast off your self-centeredness, you may identify yourself by becoming a part of a group, by focusing your attention outside yourself—build up your ego, be an entire man, fulfill yourself by knowing, being, expressing yourself, becoming an inner-directed and not an outer-directed person. Jesus personified every aspect of ego, as the word is defined—and as it is defined, the two words, ego and life, are synonymous, so that ego must be seen as *life* to man. Jesus used the word, life. He said, simply, that man must lay down his life in order to pick it up again.¹⁰⁵ Conscious rebirth is implied, as well as rebirth into life.

Freud admitted to a sort of continuation of life in the *unconscious*. In it "are stored up vestiges of the existences led by countless former egos; and when the ego forms its superego out of the id, it may perhaps only be reviving images of egos that have passed away and be securing them a resurrection."¹⁰⁶ Freud saw this sort of immortality as a "cumulative effect in History" which gradually penetrates to "those depths of the psyche far below the ego level that actually can transmit patterns of behavior whether 'acquired' or not."¹⁰⁷ Jesus posed the concept that life continues in the inner realm of the *unconscious*. He says, "I have other sheep, too, which do not belong to this fold. . . ."—this fold of consciousness known to those He addressed—"My sheep listen to my voice, and I know them and they follow me; and I give them eternal life; they shall never perish, and no one will snatch them out of my hand."¹⁰⁸ A flock, not of the fold of consciousness, a flock to whom eternal life is given, must refer to that which is redeemed and immortal in man. In this passage, Jesus indicates that man's ego is not of the herd-instinct represented by the sheep. Ego is not motivated by the impulse to belong and follow. Ego is shepherd: the sense of *one being* as *self*, and the differentiations of personality, the sheep, follow it—or, straying from this sense of certainty in being, are lost and must be found.

Man knows himself to be a flock of selves searching always to find the Self of selves to give direction to these composite lives. Therefore, in this study the term, ego-group, will be used to designate the selves of the conscious domain and the term, Authority-Ego, will be used to designate the one governing factor of ego-group, "I" in man which has its being in the *unconscious*.

In *Man and His Symbols,* a presentation of the essential ideas of Jung, edited by him, much is said of a psychic factor at the very center of man's being called by the Naskapi Indians the "Great Man."¹⁰⁹ The Indians see this factor as an "inner companion," as "my friend." The "Great Man" dwells in the heart and is immortal. This central certainty in being, which gives meaning and order to life, is symbolized in the mandala.¹¹⁰ Jung leaned toward the concept of a collective *unconscious*, but all that he and those who contribute to his book have to say about the "Great Man" and the mandala as symbol of this inner, knowing authority tends to confirm the concept of an Authority-Ego in man, unto each his own in individual terms. The concept of an individual Authority-Ego and *unconscious* does not necessarily refute the idea of the collective *unconscious*, for the Authority-Ego must be seen as "sameness," as *one* is "sameness," in each person, thus uniting experience or providing for the correspondence between humankind in experience of the *unconscious*.

The idea of an Authority-Ego in man poses a problem for psychology, but not a new one—Freud saw that his postulation of a "third Unconscious" must pose it, but as Progoff says:

> To reinterpret the ego in terms of the Unconscious, and then to alter the conception of the Unconscious in a basic way, might totally upset the neat little system that Freud had been building in his effort to make depth psychology a precise analytical science. . . .[111]

The concept of an Authority-Ego in man, as posed by this study, is not to be confused with superego. In regard to superego, Jesus' words and drama invite another basic alteration in psychological concepts.

Superego, man's "higher nature," or the "ego-ideal," posed a knotty problem for Freud. He saw "that there is a special segment of the ego that contains the 'higher' values, the aspirations, and also the 'conscience' of the personality. . . . and he described it as speaking to the ego with the voice both of inspiration and stern commandment." [112] He saw the "closest kinship . . . between the id and the superego, the highest and lowest having the most in common by virtue of their relative lack of consciousness. . . . This 'higher nature,' however, is nothing more than the conventional moralities that traditional religions enforce." [113]

Jesus' teaching and drama draw a sharp distinction between *conscience*, or the conventional moralities that traditional religions enforce, and *superego*. He indicates that the ego-group does not form the superego from the *unconscious*, nor is the superego the ego-group as developed along the lines of self-criticism and moral conscience—nor is it the Authority-Ego, "I." In Jesus' drama, the superego is represented by the *elect*, the disciples.

Upon the disciples Jesus confers the certainty of being; and He, symbol of Authority-Ego, chooses this elect of consciousness.[114] But the call of conscience, represented by John the Baptist, must precede the formation of the superego-group, and conscience, like John the Baptist, also develops its own following of selves responding to the censuring voice or assuming the ascetic stance. Conscience prepares the way for Christ-consciousness to express itself, but the elect of Authority-Ego's choosing are not belabored by Him nor stricken by conscience to repentance. They appear to represent an element in man's consciousness that spontaneously responds to truth and accepts the invitation to do its work in this world. The following of conscience and the following of truth never merge to become one fold. Thus, he whose actions are commanded by conscience is not an acting superego, not a disciple of his Authority-Ego. Such an ego-factor is disciple of the ascetic intellect John the Baptist represented, and the "least in the kingdom of heaven is greater than he." [115] But this is not an unworthy calling, for Jesus says, "Among them that are born of women there hath not risen a greater than John the Baptist." [116] Conscience is of the conscious domain.

Jesus' drama indicates that superego is not drawn from the intellectual or learned level—it appears to be a lifting of simple consciousness to experience truth in action so that this consciousness may serve as *a bridge* between the conscious and *unconscious* domains, conveying to the ego-group the certainty of life and love. Thus, Jesus says of the elect, "They are not of the world, even as I am not of the world." [117] But He prays that they not be taken out of the world of consciousness, for here they represent "I-consciousness" in being.

Harold McCurdy does a masterly job of presenting the whole range of scientific investigation into the psychic structure of man. He refers to "I"-consciousness and writes, "The intensity of 'I'-consciousness varies through an immense range"—but once it has arrived, "the 'I' becomes a point of stability in the flux of experience." [118] He points out that Freud and others were continually being reminded of outside forces intruding on consciousness; sometimes these forces seemed to take full possession, producing unwanted, irrational desires over which the "I" had no control, so that the conscious "I" was not "master in its own house." [119] Because "I-consciousness" is not a constant as would be Lord who neither slumbers nor sleeps [120]—because it is such a variable and is not "master"—it cannot itself be the Self that man is conscious of when he experiences "I-consciousness." In the view of this study, "I-consciousness" coincides with superego. Like the disciples sleeping as Jesus agonized in the Garden, it cannot be always awake; Jesus' foretelling that Peter would deny Him dramatizes that superego is not the psychic master in man, although Peter's grasp of the Christ in man symbolizes the coming of "I-consciousness" to the superego-group. Jesus points out that the true "I-being," Son of man, has no place to lay his head,[121] neither "above" nor "below"—which is to say, this Self of selves resides not on the superconscious level nor on the subconscious level, and it is not of the preconscious ego-group.

Where, then, can it be? It is in the *unconscious*.

This brings to the discussion a vital point. Psychologists fail to draw a sharp distinction between the subconscious and the *unconscious*. The two states are not synonymous. Like a rainbow, consciousness is comprised of three primary divisions: "I-consciousness" or superconsciousness, preconsciousness, and subconsciousness. All of these levels are but colorful spans-of-knowing that may be likened to a rainbow rising up from and sinking into the horizon of the *unconscious*, an unknown world, the great promise in life, man's kingdom which has not yet "come" to him.

Preconsciousness may be readily defined: Freud conceived it to be that which is latently conscious but may be readily called to consciousness. Jesus delineated this level: eyes that see, ears that hear.[122] Subconsciousness represents a state of unconsciousness that Jesus referred to as seeing and yet unseeing, as hearing and yet unhearing.[123] The subconscious is the lowest stratum of consciousness which, paradoxically, is most aware. It contains knowledge that has not been consciously catalogued because the knowledge has been stored automatically as information is collected from the margin of awareness, but the subconscious also incorporates everything that has been consciously catalogued and stored. The answers it hands to consciousness incorporate everything that comes as stimuli, and everything that has been a part of environment or experience, for nothing escapes it. The subconscious mind is at work when man is blind and deaf to virtually all stimuli because his awareness wanes in reverie, in work, in sleep, in watching, in fixing his attention on a specific thing.

The subconscious is both as old as the man and as new as the instant, *now*, when the answer it gives represents a new analogued sum of existence, wherein the whole of one's experience has been computed, and this *sum* prompts him to specific response. The subconscious, then, is the seat of "my-being." It is "me" in terms of the sum of "my" experience. But the *unconscious* is the seat of "I-being" which is the governing factor in one's life because "I" has knowledge of what has been experienced and what has not been experienced, of what has been consciously catalogued and what has been unconsciously catalogued, of what has been repressed and must sooner or later be faced in consciousness.

Jesus says that not all who knock shall enter Authority-Ego's realm. Under certain conditions the door is closed, and there shall be "weeping and gnashing of teeth" when you see "yourselves" thrust out.[124] These words pose the concept that psychic disorder ensues when repressions, which are painful self-images, return to the conscious domain after gaining strength and undergoing a metamorphosis in the *unconscious*. Because these selves have known the *unconscious* and its Authority, they think themselves blameless and in good standing: "We have eaten and drunk in thy presence, and thou hast taught in our streets." [125] They do not recognize themselves to be pain or error incarnate. When the time comes that repressions must be faced in consciousness, the "door" to the *unconscious* must be shut, and this psychic act generates the anxiety, depression, and despair that accompany the individual's awareness of Self-estrangement.

As Whyte points out, it is not the separation of the conscious and the *unconscious* realms "but their unification as aspects of one complex continuous activity which is now held to be primary." [126] Jesus' words indicate that man's psychic division is as a cleaving, that the divided state is only "as if," that being is indivisible. He says that Son of man is:

> . . . as a man taking a far journey, who left his house, and gave authority to his servants, and to every man his work, and commanded the porter to watch.[127]

This One goes on to prepare the way, apart from consciousness, but it is not lost to its love of life: the ego-group. "Lo, I am with you alway, even unto the end of the world." [128]

The idea of Self-separation and Self-estrangement has long been voiced by man. Robert deRopp writes that the meaning of the word *yoga*, "is similar to that of the English word, to yoke. A yoke unites two beings. . . ."—the separated self, *jiva*, and the origin, *atman*, "the One seen behind the many." [129] The anxiety generated by a sense of Self-estrangement has also long been recognized. The discourse between Arjuna and Krishna heals Self-estrangement, and so do the words of the Hebrew prophets, as though consciousness speaks to the One in saying: "Whom have I in heaven but thee?" And the One speaks to consciousness in saying: ". . . and there is none upon earth that I desire besides thee." [130]

The sense of himself as both "I" and "thou" which is operative in everyone does not indicate that the unity of one's being is an illusion. As the ego-group contemplates the God-head, it must ascribe to the Authority in its life the "thou" or moving role while it remains "I" at rest. Because consciousness may center itself in or around the seat of Self in being, one may "Be still and know that I am God. . . ." that the "Lord of hosts is with us; the God of Jacob is our refuge." [131] As the ego-group calls itself by the name, "I," the Authority-Ego becomes "Thou, O Lord" because it can in no way become a part of the personality, a self-image in the group. Jesus' words with regard to the kingdom of God that are translated "within you" may also be translated, "among you"—but the difference in possible translation is of no concern when the ego-group is recognized to be myriad selves and the kingdom, seat of "I-being," is recognized to be in the midst of "you," among "you," within your pluralistic being, although it is not any one of "your" conscious selves that acts a part to make up personality.

Until man understands that he has no ego as one-entity in his conscious domain, he cannot begin to understand that the one-entity within him is Lord: Authority emanating from the *unconscious*, master of both domains, and through its work the destructive impulses are eliminated as the good and the evil of his own world are brought to face reality, truth, life as it is: all held in love. All that Jesus says of the *unconscious* indicates that it is in no way static: it is ever "coming" to consciousness and thus it insures man's "becoming" in time.

Today, existential psychotherapists tend to refute the concept of man's *unconscious* because the doctrine became a "convenient blank check on which any causal explanation can be written . . ." [132] But Dr. Rollo May writes:

> . . . this is the "cellar" view of the unconscious, and objections to it should not be permitted to cancel out the great contribution that the historical meaning of the unconscious had in Freud's terms. . . . the far-reaching enlargement of personality, which is its real meaning, should not be lost. Binswanger remarks that, for the time being, the existential therapists will not be able to dispense with the concept of the unconscious. I would propose, rather, to agree that being is at some point indivisible, that unconsciousness is part of any given being. . . . [133]

And today at least one psychiatrist begins to relate Jesus' description of the inner realm to man's *unconscious* domain. Dr. Smiley Blanton writes:

> *Trust and believe in the hidden power within you.* A psychiatrist might say, "Have faith in your unconscious." A minister might say, "Have faith in God." Personally, I see no conflict between the two ideas. Indeed, they may well be the same idea, expressed differently. After all, it was the Founder of Christianity who said that "the kingdom of heaven is within you." [134]

Dr. Blanton does not appear to grasp the implication in his statement, just as Schweitzer apparently fails to grasp the implication of his—that the Messiah mold is broken, and this as aftermath of Jesus' work. Jung, too, reveals a finding of inestimable importance, but does not appear to have realized its significance. According to Progoff, Jung saw that:

> ... some variation of the image of Jesus Christ is inevitably the center around which the symbolism of individuation is expressed. ... from a psychological point of view, the authenticity of the Christ symbol derives from the fact that it expresses the Self in a symbolic form.[135]

Clouding this discovery is the orthodox Messianic concept of Jesus which prohibits Jung's grasping the idea that *Jesus' mission was to make Himself a symbol of the Self in each man*, a physical substitute for the Ego, becoming the unifying principle that promises reunion with self-nature itself, for Progoff says that Jung does not imply that "Jesus is any the less real as Christ." [136] The Messianic question is bypassed.

How can "I" be revealed as the Christ of God in man?

> O Israel, if you would but listen to me!
> There shall be no strange god among you;
> You shall not bow down to a foreign god.
> I am the Lord your God . . .[137]

"I," the Authority-Ego is no stranger, is not an outsider or foreigner to the ego-group, "Israel," although this One is not committed to the precepts of the conscious domain upon which "Israel" operates.

Long before Jesus did, the Lord Gautama denied the efficacy of rites and sacrifices, vain prayers of consciousness and of priests and, above all, Messianic expectation—for deRopp says the great Buddha taught that: ". . . every man must depend for his liberation on his own efforts. . . . there is no god to save him or protect him or redeem him. . . . 'Hold fast to the truth as a lamp. Seek salvation alone in the truth. Look not for existence to any one beside yourself.'" [138] And the Stoics—Epictetus, in particular—attempted to turn man's search for God inward, thereby posing their teaching against the Messianic expectation and vain religious rites of their day. Harsh as their doctrine was, it postulated at the center of the universe "a benevolent God of whose divine nature man partakes. 'You are a principal work, a fragment of God himself, you have in yourself a part of him . . . and know it not. Do you think I speak of some external God of silver or gold?'" [139]

Today, psychologists, become in many ways a modern priesthood, tend to guide men around these precepts. But some protest this:

THE MESSIANIC MISSION OF JESUS

There is a fear of the unconscious, that is, of the life force itself, from which we all seem to recoil [Rank]. The apparent therapeutic effects of those methods that proceed in terms of "analytic hyperconsciousness" reveal themselves to be little more than rationalizing consolations. They seem to "work" only because they avoid the shaking contact with the depths of the psyche that is the source of their original fear, and would also be the source of a creative healing if the contact were permitted [Progoff].[140]

In the words of the Psalmist, "The fear of the Lord is the beginning of wisdom . . ."[141] He who has experienced the depths of the *unconscious* approaches with an educated respect and this is as it should be—all psychologists acknowledge the danger attendant upon probing these depths. But this does not mean that contact with the Authority within should be avoided, for: "As far as the east is from the west, so far hath he removed our transgressions from us. Like as a father pitieth his children, so the Lord pitieth them that fear him. For he knoweth our frame; he remembereth that we are dust."[142]

Rank saw that psychology does not or cannot give man the faith he needs to make him whole, that for the most part psychology is capable only of explaining, not of believing—it "was produced from the neurotic type and corresponds to it."[143] But psychology's explanations are valuable. Through them man may discover what it is that he fears and then come to understand the error, the neurosis, that is seeping through his civilization.

Jesus' real mission was not to be a messiah as such but to teach that God is within each person.

Chapter 3

MAN'S ARCHAIC HERITAGE

I

Little more than a hundred years ago, Charles Darwin's great work, *Origin of Species*, was published. Homo sapiens, outraged at first to learn of his animal ancestry, soon accepted the theory of evolution which struck a near fatal blow to Christian theology.

Within the century, Sigmund Freud began to publish his works, which also turned humanity to view its savage past: ". . . there probably exists in the mental life of the individual not only what he has experienced himself, but also what he brought with him at birth, fragments of a phylogenetic origin, an archaic heritage . . . though different in extent and character [it] corresponds to the instincts of animals."[1] According to Freud, a memory becomes part of this inheritance and penetrates consciousness in altered form and with great force when it is born of an important experience, repeated often, and has first suffered the fate of being repressed, unconscious. In expounding this theory, he, too, delivered a paralyzing blow to Christian theology, for religions of any sort he saw to be delusions containing a piece of forgotten, but historical, truth and thus imbued with psychotic symptoms.[2] In his *Moses and Monotheism*, he traces the channel of both Judaism and Christianity. Briefly stated, his thesis is:

The Egyptian Pharaoh, Ikhnaton, 1375 B.C., embraced the religion of the sun-god Aton and turned it into a strict monotheism which he imposed upon the people. Moses, a devotee, was not a Jew, but an Egyptian noble who lived during the reign of Ikhnaton, and later the legend of his birth was devised by the Jews in order to claim him as their founding father. After Ikhnaton's death and monotheism's collapse in Egypt, Moses chose the Jewish people and led them away to preserve monotheism and found a nation dedicated to it. Freud places the exodus between 1358 B.C. and 1350 B.C. The hardships and strictness of Moses' rule led the Jews to revolt and murder him. Because of the strong return of this repressed memory, they revived the figure of Moses, and tried to hide his murder by melding into the history of a later priest the history of the original Moses, calling both men by the same name and merging them into one person in their tradition. But unconsciously the Jewish race still labors under a guilt complex for this crime. Freud sees in Moses' birth legend a strange twist which supports his thesis that the original Moses was not a Jew.[3] This leads to a consideration of the part birth legends play in revealing the psychology of man.

Freud quotes from Rank: ". . . almost all important civilized peoples have early woven myths around . . . their national heros . . . . the amazing similarity, nay, literal identity, of those tales, even if they refer to different, completely independent peoples . . . has struck many an investigator."[4] Following Rank, he reconstructs the average myth:

> The hero is the son of parents of the highest station, most often the son of a king. His conception is impeded by difficulties. . . . During his mother's pregnancy or earlier an oracle or a dream warns the father of the child's birth as containing grave danger for his safety. In consequence the father (or a person representing him) gives orders for the new-born babe to be killed or exposed to extreme danger; in most cases the babe is placed in a casket and delivered to the waves. The child is then saved by animals or poor people, such as shepherds, and suckled by a female animal or a woman of humble birth. When full grown he rediscovers his noble parents after many strange adventures, wreaks vengeance on his father, and, recognized by his people, attains fame and greatness.[5]

Freud then gives the historical background he presumes provided the basis for the typical myth:

> The story is told in a very condensed way, as if what in reality took centuries to achieve, and during that long time was repeated innumerably, had happened only once. The strong male was the master and father of the whole horde, unlimited in his power, which he used brutally. All females were his property. . . . The fate of the sons was a hard one; if they excited the father's jealousy they were killed or castrated or driven out . . . . the brothers who had been driven out and lived together in community clubbed together, overcame the father, and—according to the custom of those times—all partook of his body. This cannibalism need not shock us, it survived into far later times. The essential point is, however, that we attribute to those primeval people the same feelings and emotions that we have elucidated

in the primitives of our own times, our children, by psycho-analytic research . . . . they not merely hated and feared their father, but also honoured him as an example to follow; in fact, each son wanted to place himself in his father's position. The cannibalistic act thus becomes comprehensible as an attempt to assure one's identification with the father by incorporating a part of him.[6]

In time the ritual partaking of the murdered father's body was replaced by the Totem feast in which a strong, dreaded animal was substituted. Thus Freud regards Totemism as the earliest appearance of religion, and says: ". . . more than one author has been struck by the close resemblance between the rite of Christian communion—where the believer symbolically incorporates the blood and flesh of his God—and the totem feast, whose inner meaning it reproduces."[7] To support his theory, Freud points to "the animal phobias, the fear of being eaten by the father . . . and the enormous intensity of the castration complex . . ." and says that Paul, a Roman Jew, seized upon the feeling of guilt for father murder and traced it to its primeval source:

> This he called original sin; it was a crime against God that could be expiated only through death. . . . A son of God, innocent himself, had sacrificed himself, and had thereby taken over the guilt of the world. . . . The Mosaic religion had been a Father religion; Christianity became a Son religion. The old God, the Father, took second place; Christ, the Son, stood in his stead, just as in those dark times every son had longed to do. Paul, by developing the Jewish religion further, became its destroyer.[8]

Freud says that the Jewish people continue to deny the murder of their founding father—symbolically, the murder of God—whereas the Christians, admitting it, claim themselves absolved.

Freud points out that Christianity became a cultural regression, departing from strict monotheism, re-establishing many lesser deities and the mother-goddess, a renewed triumph of the pagan priests over the God of Ikhnaton, but Christianity did mark "a progress in the history of religion . . . in regard to the return of the repressed."[9] He says that the essence of the Christian fantasy of salvation seems to be Paul's own contribution —"in any case, here lies the origin of the conception of the hero . . . who rebels against the father and kills him in some guise or other." Then Freud adds, "I have no qualms in saying that men have always known . . . that once upon a time they had a primeval father and killed him."[10] Then he suggests that the guilt attached to the murder of Moses became the stimulus of the wish phantasy for the Messiah; he says that Paul's success "was certainly mainly due to the fact that through the idea of salvation he laid the ghost of the feeling of guilt. It was also due to his giving up the idea of the chosen people and its visible sign—circumcision. That is how the new religion could become all-embracing, universal." [11] Thus, he concludes that Paul effected a "continuation of primeval history," and that both Christianity and Judaism stem from "the religion of the primeval father, and the hope of reward, distinction, and finally world sovereignty is bound up with it. The last-named wish-phantasy—relinquished long ago by the Jewish people—still survives among their enemies in their belief in the conspiracy of the 'Elders of Zion.' " [12]

Freud recognizes the jealousy the Jews evoked in maintaining that they were the first-born, chosen people of God, and takes into account the rite of circumcision that reminds humanity of the dreaded castration idea, but points out that there is a more recent motive for anti-Semitism:

> We must not forget that all the peoples who now excel in the practice of anti-Semitism became Christians only in relatively recent times . . . . under the thin veneer of Christianity they have remained what their ancestors were, barbarically polytheistic. They have not yet overcome their grudge against the new religion which was forced on them, and they have projected it on to the source. . . . The facts that the Gospels tell a story which is enacted among Jews, and in truth treats only of Jews, has facilitated such a projection. The hatred for Judaism is at bottom hatred for Christianity. . . . [13]

Freud appears to have put his finger on the neurosis of the Western world: it stems from an ambivalent acceptance of, if not outright hatred for, Pauline doctrine.

But it took Jung to see that Freud had done no more than repeat Paul's "continuation of primeval history"—for Freud reclothed the doctrine of original sin and walking the path he hacked became the hero who killed the sacred father image as he stood in its stead his doctrine of sexuality. Jung says:

> Freud, who had always made much of his irreligiosity . . . constructed a dogma; or rather, in the place of a jealous God whom he had lost, he . . . substituted another compelling image, that of sexuality. It was no less insistent, exacting, domineering, threatening, and morally ambivalent than the original one . . . . the 'sexual libido' took over the role of a deus absconditus. . . . The name alone had changed. . . . [14]

As one appraises Freud's thesis and his diagnosis that anti-Semitism is at bottom hatred for Christianity, he must consider that there is a law of history which says: error must grow until it reaches its outermost limits. Jesus revealed His understanding of this law by saying that the good seed and tares must grow together unto the harvest, and by speaking of the enlargement of conflict that must precede comprehension of the Christ in man.[15] He knew that before the Judaic Messianic mold and any like unto it could be obliterated all men would come to hate the Jew and to hate Him, His name, Son of man, and all it implies:

You will be hated by all on account of my name. . . .[16]

Thus, Jesus' own words confirm Freud's diagnosis. His words also contain a hint of Freud's theory, for on another occasion He said to the Pharisees and scribes, "you . . . have repealed the law of God to suit your own tradition," and then He quoted Isaiah, "This people honours me with their lips, but their heart is far away from me: vain is their worship of me, for the doctrines they teach are but human precepts." [17] Today, the heart of many professed Christians is far away from Jesus.

Hatred of Christianity springs from fear of Jesus, the purchaser, and from hatred of the idea of oneself *bought* at any price by anyone for any purpose. But this is St. Paul's interpretation of Jesus—His message altered to suit the tradition because in St. Paul's day the teaching of Jesus was so far beyond the grasp of man it would have been lost had not St. Paul seized with the full force of himself the majesty of Jesus and carried Christianity forward with majesty, even as error was carried forward by him into enlargement. He willingly drank the cup that Jesus drank, becoming, as Oswald Spengler saw him to be, the one prophet of Jesus.[18]

St. Paul wrestled mightily with the Freudian god, sexual libido, as is evidenced in these words: the "immoral man sins against his body . . . You are not your own, you were bought for a price; then glorify God with your body. . . . It is indeed 'an excellent thing for a man to have no intercourse with a woman'; but there is so much immorality, that every man had better have a wife of his own and every woman a husband of her own. . . ."—and then he transfers the dread of castration from the physical to the psychological level, saying that through Christ a man *is* circumcised, "in him you have been circumcised. . . ." [19]

Thus, St. Paul's beclouding of sexual encounter and turning the male into the psychologically circumcised chattel of Jesus serves only to lift the level of the fear of emasculation and makes of Him the shadowy accuser of every person who has sexual experience. In the Christian world, the circumcision rite of Judaism continues, veiled as medical practice, so that the male's castration-fear phobia is not necessarily born of race memory—for the one who has suffered circumcision, fear could be born of infant experience, and for the one who has not suffered it, circumcision becomes something denied him.

Jesus says, "Moses gave you the rite of circumcision—not that it came from Moses, it came from your ancestors," [20] which is to say, from primeval times, and then He adds, "Well, if a man gets circumcised upon the sabbath, to avoid breaking the Law of Moses, are you enraged at me for curing and not cutting, the entire body of a man upon the sabbath?"—or as the King James Bible puts it, making "a man every whit whole. . . ?" Jesus thus spurned circumcision and implied that from a psychological point of view it cuts the entire body of the male.

When one gathers Jesus' words on the subject of sex, he sees that Jesus expressed a very different attitude toward sexuality from that expressed by St. Paul. In answer to the Pharisee's question of divorce, He refers to Scripture that attests to the need, right, and desirability of male and female to engage in sexual union:

> Have ye not read, that he which made them at the beginning made them male and female, And said, For this cause shall a man leave father and mother, and shall cleave to his wife: and they twain shall be one flesh? [21]

Because God, Love, joins them, male and female are not to be put asunder—thus, in Jesus' view it is not an "excellent thing to have no intercourse with a woman." Nor are man and wife to be put asunder by a law which does not reflect the true nature of their being—He says Moses' bill of divorcement was given because of the "hardness of men's hearts, but from the beginning it was not so." The hardness of men's hearts causes them to deal inequitably with their wives—in pointing to the beginning, Jesus presents the innate bisexuality and equality of man and woman which society no longer recognized. As one turns to the beginning, he reads:

> . . . the day that God created man, in the likeness of God made he him; Male and female created he them; and blessed them, and called their name Adam, in the day when they were created.[22]

These words present the bisexual nature of Homo sapiens, the equality of man and woman; but they also suggest that, male or female, each person is as Adam: a body of consciousness through which is expressed a body of his own that he takes to wife, for Adam is joined to his *own flesh* in Eve. Thus man cannot separate himself from the desire for a body, or from the desires of his body, on the assumption that life can be divorced from physical manifestation and the need of male and female in Homo sapiens generation to express their sexuality.

But Jesus' listeners did not grasp the poetry of the Adam-Eve legend: humankind wedded each to himself in the beginning, and then each sex to the other. Nor would they accept His presentation of the equality of the sexes, and so they replied, "Better not marry at all!" Jesus answers this plaint, "True, but this truth is not practicable for everyone, it is only for those who have the gift." These words do not prohibit the indulgence of sexual desire. To the contrary, they are utterly permissive. But they are also practical, for few have the gift to live and love freely.

Jesus then lifts the discussion to another level: continence. He says that men are born eunuch, are made eunuch, or make eunuch of themselves for the sake of the realm of heaven, which is to say, in response to inner need. Such continence is to be practiced only if practicable.

Jesus named adultery for what it is—lust. ". . . I tell you, anyone who even looks with lust at a woman has committed adultery with her already in his heart." [23] He neither condemns nor condones the rescued adulteress: "Neither do I condemn thee: go, and sin no more." [24] Nor does He scorn the sinning woman, bathing His feet with her tears. He says that one who has much love will be forgiven much, and one who has not much to be forgiven, has not much love.[25]

Marriage is dealt with in the passage wherein the Sadducees confront Jesus with the concept of Homo sapiens existing forever in a place of heavenly abode: they ask, in heaven whose wife would a childless woman be had she been seven times married and to seven brothers? Jesus elevates the question in stating that when one is worthy of eternal life marriage will no longer be. Here, He presents the concept that man's nature is changing; that he will come in time to know a larger freedom than the sexual freedom marriage allows; he will be *whole*, a Self unto himself, knowing love that needs not the bonds society imposes to cope with sexuality in this generation. Then He poses the principle that although man has not yet realized his constant-being, life is, even now, a constant state: He points out that the dead are raised, saying, "God is not a God of dead people, but of living, for all live to him." [26] If all are living to God, then all will in time be worthy of eternal life, and this "adulterous generation," [27] as Jesus calls it, must be seen as only a step in the evolution of man.

In a montage of the passages, one sees that in the fullness of eternity each is a Self unto himself; but Moses' bill of divorcement admits to society's need of recognizing that in this generation there are intolerable unions; in this, Jesus acquiesces, although He points out that the law as given does not reflect the equality of the sexes to which He turns attention.

In His encounter with the Samarian woman at the well,[28] He shows that in Homo sapiens' inner world he can never be divorced from any part of his experience with another, for He numbers the men she has known, indicating that the image of every person with whom one has become one flesh lives with him as consort in his kingdom within. In the psychic sense, then, divorce is an illusion.

And one cannot be divorced by law from whatever problem it is within himself that causes his marriage to become mean bondage or contributes to its failure. Jesus' emphasis on words [29] must lead one to strive to master the problem with the person he has wed in his vow before God and man, for this vow broken divorces him from his word as his bond, creating in his human power a dichotomy he must live with.

Because one's inner world cannot be fused with the inner world of another to make of the two inner realms one world, in the last reaches of being there is but one true marriage: each person wedded to himself. Thus, any consorting with another in thought or deed adulterates one's inner world in the sense that it brings to bear upon self-union. Homo sapiens therefore represents an adulterous generation, and is dissatisfied because the Self of himself for which each person searches cannot be found in another, nor in the personality one exposes, nor in the frailty he knows his consciousness to be. Nor can the longing for this Self-absence be mitigated more than temporarily by loving or lusty union with another.

Jung saw that there is a feminine element in the male, the anima, and a masculine element in the female, the animus.[30] These elements represent the individual's relationship to the other sex: the anima is the woman within the male, the animus is the man within the female. In the view of this study, there is within each individual both animus and anima, male and female consciousness outgrown from Adam-consciousness, originally bisexual, into "Israel," a world of male and female selves. Each treats with his own sex and the other sex as he treats with his own masculine or feminine being. Humankind must become equal to itself: male and female equal and equally responsible in every sense of the word before equality among mankind can come to be—and before the individual can become equal to himself in bisexual being: man and woman, even as Adam incorporated Eve in his original being.

One's soul may be said to represent the *union* of his masculine and feminine consciousness, or to be Self as Self is being developed through conscious experience with others. The Authority-Ego may also be seen as bisexual, or as whole-being uniting within itself the masculine and feminine elements: the Self as the "us" of God, complete. In discussing Jung's concept of the archetypal symbol of Self, the "Great Man," Dr. von Franz writes:

> The many examples coming from various civilizations and different periods show the universality of the symbol of the Great Man. His image is present in the minds of men as a sort of goal or expression of the basic mystery of our life. Because this symbol represents that which is whole and complete, it is often conceived of as a bisexual being. In this form the symbol reconciles one of the most important pairs of psychological opposites—male and female. This union also appears frequently in dreams as a divine, royal, or otherwise distinguished couple.[31]

The union of the Authority-Ego and the Soul born of consciousness when the Soul is fully enunciated, appears to be the goal of man—whole-being then embraces whole-being to give rise to a *new being* more richly endowed than Homo sapiens.

More often than not the Soul is thought of as the feminine element in one's being versus the "Great Man," or masculine authority in one's being. Until an individual knows himself to be both male and female in consciousness and his Soul a union of these two aspects of being, he cannot reconcile his inner conflicts that reflect themselves in his attitudes toward other people. Nor can he view Self-union in terms of the wholeness of Authority-Ego embracing the whole of his Soul.

Jesus saw that because Homo sapiens is as yet *child*, he must approach the concept of the kingdom within and its Authority as a *child*—not in terms of sexuality. This is to say, just as a child is not and cannot be competent to understand sexuality in its actual and deepest aspects, so Homo sapiens is not competent to realize in truth or fact the meaning of the union of the feminine and masculine principles; and thus one should not approach Self-union in terms of designating a gender for Authority-Ego and the Soul unless he can see these psychic factors as man and woman, each bisexual, complete, equal, and equal to the other's needs and desires, utterly empathetic.

Not until later in this study can Jesus' revelation of love's consummate union be discussed. Suffice it to say here that He does not project Self-union to come about as consciousness abandons the flesh to remain in "spiritual state," for He projects that man shall have *life* everlasting and life depends upon physical being. Life and love embrace it, demand it, project, protect, and glorify it. Jesus projects that man shall have life and have it abundantly.[32] To this end is the coming of the kingdom of God within him. One can conclude only that the "stuff" one's own love or Soul is made of is born of his experiencing life in this world and of his love for and relationship with others—narcissism does not generate it or enrich one's sense of being. Insofar as life in this world and flesh is concerned, Jesus commanded humankind to love one another in every sense of the word, for love joined them in the beginning in sexual union and this He pointed out.

He saw bondage of any sort, however, to be hateful—be it bondage to lust's insatiable appetite, or bondage to ignorance, or to illness, or to a religious priesthood's sometimes greedy and sometimes ridiculous demands. Jesus spoke truth to free man—not to bind him to social laws that fail to reflect the truth of his nature and of the situation with which they attempt to deal. He spoke truth to free man from his own self-deceptions that lead him to circumvent social law even as he transgresses psychic law, for these transgressions take a heavier toll of him. He spoke truth to free mankind of degrading traditions that cripple the soul of male or female.

Because Jesus' words presaged such vast social reform as is still in the making, He was a threat to the corrupted power that in His day both Rome and the Judaic priesthood represented. If Christianity were to survive, St. Paul must mitigate this threat. Thus, he discouraged the amelioration of worldly conditions, as was consistent with the ancient Judaic outlook and would serve to allay the suspicions of Rome—saying, "Brothers, everyone must remain with God in the condition of life where he was called." [33]

Seeing Himself as servant, Jesus could not hold Himself to be master of servants or slaves, which St. Paul designates Him to be, saying:

> . . . a slave who is called to be in the Lord is a freedman of the Lord. Just as a free man who is called is a slave of Christ—for you were bought for a price; you must not turn slaves to any man.[34]

Ransom into slavery is St. Paul's doctrine, but as Schweitzer and others have pointed out, the Pauline redemption doctrine is not that of Jesus.[35]

Freud is wrong when he says Pauline doctrine relieves the Christian of his feeling of guilt. The Christian peoples suffer the most deep-seated guilt complex of any people in the world—they suffer guilt to some degree in the expression of their sexual appetites, and they suffer an enlarged Judaic guilt complex born of the teaching of St. Paul who restated the tradition in terms that would allow it to realize the ancient dream, world sovereignty, through the sovereignty of the Christian religion. But this was not deliberate on St. Paul's part, and neither the Jewish nor the Christian peoples are alone in pursuing this vision. Any Messianic doctrine of any time or place or people—and the world is full of them—enfolds this vainglorious aim.

In appraising Pauline doctrine, its most important contribution cannot be overlooked: love transcended his redemption dogma,[36] clothing his words in shining armor, sending them unsurpassed through the centuries to lead and comfort men who should not today forget the struggle he had with his own generation to save Christianity from premature dismissal. He transfused its feebleness with the stubborn strength of Judaism; he stands the towering figure in Christian history; his place in the Bible of man's consciousness is not to be shaken.

There is no evidence that Jesus knew it would be Saul of Tarsus who would do the tremendous job of carrying Christianity forward by compromising with Judaism, but He appears to have known that this had to happen to insure its immediate future and establish it firmly in the hands of men—and that a masterful, worldly mind would accomplish the task. This is projected in the parable of the factor facing dismissal who is praised although he bribed his Lord's debtors to provide security and welcome for himself in the houses of the people. The Lord commends him: ". . . for the children of this world look further ahead, in dealing with their own generation, than the children of Light." [37] In the parable, Jesus says in effect that he who compromises with the past in order to insure the future is, in his own generation, faithful with a large trust—for truth rests with man and all kinds of men are required to make it welcome and to carry it forward, even as they carry man's heritage forward in themselves. Or one might say that both the true and the false, the worldly and unworldly, the steadfast and the compromiser serve life's process through which man will be brought to full consciousness of himself as son of God.

There is no one to blame for the development of Christianity into an enlarged Judaism unless Homo sapiens blames himself. Certainly the Gentiles, appropriating the Scriptures and Epistles centuries ago, cannot blame their plight on the Jews, who refute Pauline doctrine wholeheartedly. The Jews are the tragic victims of the barbarism remaining in men. Theirs is an unending search for truth and mankind reaps the reward of it. They are unsurpassed in producing those scholars who have brought enlightenment and shared it freely with humanity at large. Shining brightly among them is Sigmund Freud—a man with the courage to tell the Western world what ails it. But it is time now to reappraise his doctrine.

II

Psychologists' findings indicate that there is in man an unconscious, primordial urge to belief in the existence of a higher Being he wishes to emulate—this concept of Deity and of His eternal life arose in all races. Freud states that he cannot credit the premise of the believer in God to be existing truth, but he credits it to be historical truth:

> ... I do not believe that one supreme great God "exists" today, but I believe that in primeval times there was one person who must needs appear gigantic and who, raised to the status of a deity, returned to the memory of men.[38]

If one attempts to identify this one historical, gigantic man, he must work his way back through the oft repeated murder to the murder of the first sire one can call man, and if he were murdered and eaten there is no basis for the persisting idea of his deathlessness.

Freud's analysis emerges as a natural parallel to Darwin's theory of survival of the fittest, but as theories of evolution are re-examined it is becoming evident that the conditions upon which Freud based his theory are in themselves highly questionable. Robert Ardrey writes: "That parents and sons could have at any pristine moment in the history of the human species suffered the social confinement which is a necessary premise to Freud's thesis becomes a matter of extreme improbability." [39]

Freud's contribution to knowledge cannot be denied, and the value of Darwin's work is inestimable, but together their theories do not suffice to explain Homo sapiens. From the beginning, Darwin's theory was questioned by Wallace, who could find no explanation for the sudden, unparalleled growth of brain evidenced by man. Adler added to Darwin's theory Lamarck's: that the least fit often survive and become superior.[40] But in the combination one still cannot find the germ through which was born in an animal the feeling of guilt for killing an enemy, the idea of a supranatural deity, and the concept of life after death.

And yet Freud's theory cannot be entirely dismissed. The Bible of human consciousness in some measure supports it: although the Adam legend does not follow the exact course of the typical exposure myth, most of the essential features are represented. The original paternal authority drives out his son, Adam, and later the sire drives Cain into the wilderness. The Bible is the outgrowth of this legend. In the flood sequence, the sire's anger, roused by the sons, prompts him to expose them to the waters. Again, in the Abraham drama, the Lord God sends the son away from the home of his fathers; the practice of circumcision to mark the acceptable male and remind him of his father's power to castrate is come upon. In the final act, the hero son, Jesus, rises to stand in the father's stead.

But just as a coin has two sides, so a legend contains equal and opposite truths: the Adam legend says that man was sired by an energy or spirit proceeding from a non-animal being. Although man is born into the animal world, he is of this cast only in the sense that all in creation is of the supreme Creator. It is stated that no animal creature could be found to suit man and that the female line is of the same flesh and heritage as the male. Through the outworking of the legend, love of the son and of the wife of his choice enlarges in the human father, despite his fallibility. In the final drama, Jesus personifies love of son for father and of father for son.

Although the Adam legend both parallels and refutes Freud's theory, it joins in the concept that murder is the basis of man's guilt and fear. But it is not father murder, it is *brother* murder to which this legend gives first and continuing emphasis, beginning with Cain's murder of Abel and ending with the crucifixion of Jesus, who declared Himself a brother to every man.

Humanity's legends, man's pristine and continuing concept of God, of deathlessness, and his conscience make of him a mystery that science has scarcely touched upon and psychology has served only to deepen. Freud wrote, "The moment a man questions the meaning and value of life, he is sick, since objectively neither has any existence," [41] but in truth the man who does not ask this primary question—or who does not admit that he asks—is sick, sick of his evasion of the only reality he knows: himself in being.

Ardrey observes, "Were a brotherhood of man to be formed today, then its only possible common bond would be ignorance of what man is." [42] Perhaps the question of man can never be answered to the satisfaction of scientists, but as each man seeks to answer it to his own satisfaction there is a source to which he may turn that by its very nature should inspire his confidence: humanity's legends. Psychologists have by no means exhausted their promise.

According to Samuel Miller, in primordial myths "the experience of multitudes was strained, concentrated, and objectified in archaic figures and forms." [43] Legends convey *race memory*, and because of their similarity they may be seen also as vehicles to convey man's *realizations* of inner processes, both physical and psychic, for which no adequate words existed, so that these must be stated in poetic form. The truth of a legend can become apparent only as it is compared with scientific data and observable phenomena. In this study the chain of Biblical legends is examined because they embrace so many others. Each of them must be viewed as a deeply and intricately furrowed unity enfolded into the smallest possible number of words just as the human brain is enfolded into the smallest possible space: ". . . the surface of the hemispheres began to wrinkle at an early stage. The human cortex covers the hemispheres in deep and narrow folds. If the cortex were stretched smoothly over the hemispheres, a human brain would have to be the size of a beer-barrel." [44] The "shape" of the legend follows the "shape" of the brain.

Each legend may also be likened to a canvas upon which man must repaint history, generation after generation, montaging each new picture of himself with the countenance of ancestral beings. Some turns repeat themselves, and thus their lines stand out clearly—other lines are blurred. But as with all masterpieces, any square of the picture may be enlarged to present of itself a work of art in the telling of human history.

Or one might say that a legend is like a mountain rising up from the plain of consciousness. At every moment of the day and night it is seen in a slightly different light and it casts a slightly different shadow. As one walks around it new crevices may be seen in the façade. Thus from no two points of view and at no two times will the legend present itself in exactly the same way. Its every outline upon the horizon changes, depending upon the point of view from which it is to be inspected and upon the time of the day it is viewed. Thus, each legend compresses so much, contains so much, that to observe fully and relate its every message would require volumes.

The Genesis legend may be viewed as telling the story of man from the dawn of life, retelling it through each day. It tells the story from every point of view and it is also a mound of truth enfolding the inner facts of life just as a "Tell" enfolds artifacts that reveal the lives of those who built and rebuilt upon the same spot.

A description of cataclysmic events in the outer world serves as a "parable" to describe cataclysmic psychic and physical events in the life of individual—and man must look to nature and events in the outer world to serve as "parable" to describe his evolutionary course, for only through association with visible or outward phenomena can such as this be conveyed and remembered. Evolution bespeaks "change" or "becoming"—the problem is, how to convey the passage from one state into another? Legends enfold the story. Many of them, if not all of them, are, therefore, threefold in meaning: describing in poetic terms an historical event in the "becoming" of the world to its present form, describing an inward event, psychic or physical, and describing a step in the "becoming" of consciousness which enfolds both the "inward" and "outward" history of the species and planet upon which it lives.

Only the major "artifacts" and major "folds" of some of the Biblical legends will be observed in the following chapter—but before these observations are begun it must be pointed out that in the view of this study these legends are not to be viewed as absolute dictum handed to certain men from "God on high," from an authority apart. They are mankind's own best effort to state and transmit memories of happenings and realizations that widen the boundaries of human consciousness.

Arnold Toynbee writes:

> If the Universe is a mystery, and if the key to this mystery is hidden, are not myths an indispensable means for expressing as much as we can express of the ineffable? . . . myths are the instruments through which these farthest flights of the Human Spirit are achieved. . . . A primordial element is perhaps to be found in every myth that makes its mark. Yet the stuff of which myths are fashioned is mostly local and ephemeral.[45]

It is to be hoped that the reader will remember Toynbee's words as he reads the following chapter.

Chapter 4

THE LEGENDARY CHAIN OF LIFE

I

When Darwin published his work, theologians saw in it a threat to acceptance of the Genesis legend as the truth of the origin of man. But today one may observe that each fold of the Adam-Eve drama tells a part of the story of evolution—that is, a clue is cast through the symbol used and the drama enacted. But before this study attempts to measure the Genesis legend and Jesus' words against what twentieth-century man suspects to be the story of evolution, a word of caution to the reader is necessary.

In this study, the works of several people have been selected to tell something of the story of evolution because their books were written for the layman. Today, the concept of evolution itself is virtually universally accepted, but so many individual pieces of the incomplete jigsaw puzzle are questioned that the subject is a dangerous one to write about —even the experts do not agree upon a number of particulars. Most important, it must be pointed out that because legend is poetic, only in poetic terms can the information legend offers be posed against the disputed theories and the data scientists have to work with. Thus, at the risk of offending the specialists, poetic license must be exercised. The reader must be warned of this, and informed at the outset that the purpose of the following discourse is not to question the concept of evolution itself, nor to present a complete and scientifically structured theory of evolution; it is to question certain aspects of prevailing theories, and to provoke a new train of thought upon the role of legends in telling human history.

Pierre Teilhard de Chardin postulates that consciousness is the force that raised up life from matter, and that consciousness is life's goal.[1] The Adam-Eve drama depicts life's seeking an enlarged consciousness, and it says man was raised up from the dust. The creation of cosmic dust presents as great a mystery as the creation of living matter, of how from matter came plant life in which male and female gender have their innocent being as did Adam-Eve in the garden of Eden. The legend presents them first in what might be called "plant life" or "garden-being"—other legends and symbols dealing with "Cosmic man" also indicate that he, or life, must be seen first as a *plant*.[2] Next comes the mystery of how from plant life there arose ciliated protozoa with hairlike "leaves"—which the Genesis legend names as the first garment life puts on. The mystery of life mounts until it culminates in the mystery of Homo sapiens.

To examine man in his first or original form, one must examine animal life in its first form, in the form of a one-cell creature. Thus, in his beginning, man must be seen as a one-cell creature, and one fold of the Eden legend tells of the Adam-cell—which is to say, Adam may be seen as a symbol of the simplest form of life, amoeba, for he follows amoeba's path.

There is no apparent reason why amoeba should ever die. In the course of its division a new one is not produced: there are "only fragments of the original individuals, whose life has thus been continuous back to the time when life itself was first created. . . ."[3] Like an amoeba, Adam self-divided, and there is no immediately apparent reason why Adam and Eve should ever die. But when amoebic animal life comes into the picture, innocence goes—as it does in Eden—and this is connected directly with eating. Joseph Wood Krutch explains:

> . . . all animals must eat something which is or was alive. . . . No animal, therefore, can be innocent as a plant may be. . . . And that, perhaps, is the deepest meaning of Original Sin.[4]

The Eden drama relates that loss of innocence is directly connected with eating.

The chain of life moves from the unsexed, potentially immortal amoeba to multicelled creatures engaging in sexual reproduction and subject to death—so, too, does the Eden legend. In their beginning, Adam-Eve may be seen as symbol of a multicelled individual which, like Volvox, cannot be decisively placed in the plant kingdom or in the animal kingdom. In Volvox's beginning it is more plantlike, but Leeuwenhoek, who first described it, "did not know that after a few generations have been vegetatively reproduced by the process he observed there comes a generation that will produce eggs which must be fertilized by sperm before they can develop."[5] Volvox, like Adam-Eve, brought natural death as well as sex into the world. Apparently, death is the price life must pay to become sexed. Why is it willing to do this? Krutch says:

> Offhand most of us would . . . say that sex is necessary to reproduction. . . . But as every biologist knows . . . it isn't. Its biological function is the mixing of heredities, not reproduction. Indeed, we might say that what it actually does is not permit but prevent 'reproduction'—if by that you mean complete duplication.[6]

Addressing Volvox, Krutch says, "Once you had invented the differentiation of the sexes you had started on the way to poetry as well as to rich variability . . ." for only mortal creatures evolved; and "if there had never been any such thing as sexuality evolution would have had so little variation to work with that today we might all still be protozoa—or at least some sort of very simple animal."[7] Krutch says he assumes that the biologists are right "when they tell me that Volvox, having got as far as it did, seems to have got no farther. Perhaps some other creature independently paralleled his inventions—which would make the whole thing at least twice as remarkable."[8] One senses that he feels a kindredship between this bit of life and man. His words, "we might all still be protozoa," show that man thinks of his ancestral forms in human terms—and in these terms legend tells the story.

Darwin considered natural selection to be the most important factor in organic evolution. This is a natural process that tends to cause the survival of the fittest, of those forms of animals and plants best adjusted to the conditions under which they live, and the extinction of poorly adapted forms. Although its tremendous importance is conceded, today it is suspected that other factors may be involved, for in some ways natural selection deepens the mystery of man's emergence. Krutch suggests that choice, will, consciousness may sometimes have been able to intervene in an evolutionary process, but this does not, in his words:

> . . . imply anything more than that the generally admitted ability of the human being to intervene may be assumed to have existed to some extent for a very long time—perhaps even for as long as any form of life has existed.[9]

If this be true, one is likely to assume offhand that *rational* interventions led man to the pinnacle of animal life. But to the contrary, irrationality marks the course of his triumphant evolutionary trek.

A rational evolutionary path led to creatures that grow clothing upon their bodies; only an irrational course could lead to nakedness and a body that cannot increase the density of hair covering according to climatic requirements. A rational course would not lead to retention of certain embryonic features into adult life; only an irrational course would lead to such imbalance between the development of body versus brain as man displays, ". . . compared to his brain, man's body remains at what is an embryonic phase in his closest animal relations." [10] These and many other irrational turns mark the evolutionary course of man. All other animal life behaves rationally and thus animals are predictable, will serve to confirm elegant theories. Man will not. He bedamns his irrationality—and yet the power, the freedom, to behave irrationally for no good reason may be the secret of his dominion over the animal world. Man's irrationality may free him from bondage to conditioned responses; it may prevent his automatically reacting to immediate needs and obvious force, thus preventing in him the limiting biological overspecialization seen in all other species. Aberration marks the turning points along his course.

There was a great turning point in man's evolution that came long after his ancestors had left the protozoan world, and the Eden legend depicts it in poetic terms. Dr. A. T. W. Simeons tells the scientist's side of the story:

> Just as the Ruling Reptiles were about to burst into their gargantuan evolution, one small and still primitive reptilian species broke away from the main stem. This aberrant species took to the trees of the carboniferous forests and became the first reptile to adopt an entirely tree-living mode of life.[11]

In time it developed into the one mammalian species that had never left the trees, where it began to specialize in a further evolution of its brain. This small shrewlike animal was the grandsire of all the lemurs, tarsoids, monkeys, apes, and man. Life in the treetops brought about some remarkable bodily changes, which were the rudimentary beginnings of typically mammalian features, and an entirely new trend in brain structure began to take shape.[12]

This long short story and the Eden legend coincide at the crucial points: reptile life played a leading role; the drama is centered around the *tree* in the midst of the garden and Adam knew only this "out of the world" existence; he underwent a "remarkable bodily change," but Eve's emergence was only a rudimentary beginning of typically mammalian life; Adam's naming of all creatures suggests the specialization in further evolution of the brain which culminates in aberrant Eve's act that led to a new trend in thought or brain structure, a turning point in life.

But first, "It was about fifty million years ago . . . . one species of these early carnivora . . . climbed back into the trees, and that saved it from extinction." [13] This creature, now known as *Cynodictis*, entered the treetop Eden after it had resorted to a sort of cannibalism, in the sense that the early ground-living species of reptilian ancestry began to prey upon their closest relatives until extinction overtook all but this one. "Man's timid mammalian ancestors in the trees now had a dangerous, quick and intelligent flesh-eater in their midst . . ." [14]

Cynodictis found a feast in the trees and did not die. The Eden legend says a "serpent" induced Eve to eat the fruit of the tree of knowledge of good and evil, saying, "Ye shall not surely die . . . ," and she gave of it to Adam—was this "fruit" the flesh of a sentient creature? The legend says there will be enmity between the seed of the serpent and the seed of Eve. Was *Cynodictis* the "serpent"? His descendants developed into all land-living placental carnivora, such as the dogs, cats, etc. It seems certain that some flesh-eating animal or reptile climbed into the trees of the carboniferous forests and brought to bear upon the evolution of the shrew-like ancestor of man, but whether *Cynodictis* or another creature be assigned the role of "serpent" in the drama, the important point is that neither the threat of death nor the promise of life influenced Eve—it was her "irrational" desire to *know* that led her to accept this food: the fruit was to be desired to make one wise.

The necessity for a living creature to eat something that was or is alive which gives rise to the "original sin" of amoeba—cannibalism—came to full flower not in *Cynodictis*' or some other "serpent's" progeny, but in men, some of whom became true cannibals, cracking human skulls and eating the brains. There is evidence to suggest that Peking and Neanderthal men were cannibals, but there is also evidence that tends to refute this. There is evidence that cannibalism began as a religious rite—it also may have been the last desperate resort of hungry flesh-eaters. Or primitive man may have been still trying to acquire wisdom by eating the "fruit" of the tree of knowledge of good and evil. In any event, it is a mystery why Neanderthal man became extinct in an incredibly short time, fading out as Cro-Magnon man began to thrive, unless, as Dr. Simeons suggests, "the Neanderthalers themselves contributed heavily to their own extinction." [15] If they were cannibals, perhaps this gave rise to some psychic aberration that led to their demise. There are peoples whose numbers steadily decrease for no reason anthropologists can find.[16] A psychic factor must be involved. Whatever the cause of Neanderthal man's mysterious disappearance, eventually: "Domestication provided man with a constant supply of animal food and made him independent of hunting and cannibalism. The tending of his flocks and herds changed man's life completely, because it imposed upon him work that had to be performed at regular hours." [17] In the Genesis legend, man's life changes completely as it shifts from Eden to the ground of this world wherein work, now seen to be his saving grace, has been imposed upon him. Because man can work as no other animal can, today he possesses telescopes that "enable him to see astral galaxies millions of light-years away showing him things which actually took place at a time when he himself was still a mousy, tree-living mammal." [18]

Dr. Simeons' poetic words again raise the question: did this mammal to some extent know himself—consciously intervening in the evolutionary process? The Eden legend says that ancestral-man began to be a thinking creature early in the day of his being and thought irrationally enough to risk death to gain freedom from ignorance though he was well provided for in this bondage.

Who taught him to work? Did he learn from the ants—oldest cultivators of the soil and keepers of flocks, making war and capturing slaves, suggesting human beings "more strongly than any vertebrate lower than the apes" [19]—pyramid, apartment house, and tunnel builders that they are? Man appears to possess many of their instincts, and yet he is not of them, for early in his journey he took another irrational turn—in the words of Krutch:

> If you or I had been permitted a brief moment of consciousness sometime about the middle of the Mesozoic era, when the amphibia and the insects were both flourishing, we well might have concluded that the latter were the more promising experiment. I doubt that we would have been very likely to pick out a salamander as our ancestor. Yet the evidence seems pretty definite that it is from him we come . . . . the salamander has some awareness of the world outside himself and he has, therefore, the true beginnings of a self—as we understand the term. A butterfly or a beetle does not.[20]

And then Krutch asks, "Is the ultimate answer to the question 'Why is a bungling mammal higher than an efficient wasp' simply that it is higher because it can experience parental love? Was it this, rather than mere survival, that nature was after all along?" [21]

Once upon a time Adam tended a garden into which, like an ant's underground plot, no rain had fallen; [22] and like an ant, Adam knew not parental love, although all that is necessary for survival was provided for him. Love does not come into the Genesis legend until the Abraham-Isaac sequence is told,[23] until long after a bungling mammal had entered the workaday world, and ancestral-man-cell had taken the path that would lead him to be one.

The legend says the creature that became Homo sapiens sought not survival, but wisdom and the meaning of life, of good and evil. Irrationally, man keeps on seeking more than survival; irrationally, he still thinks he would rather his species die than survive in a new type society resembling all too closely an old, old ant heap. He cannot function as a human being without love, the will o' the wisp that leads him on. Eve's act precipitated ancestral-man's expulsion from a gardener's job in a world that knew not love and hung only upon the idea of survival. In the insect kingdom subordination of all else to survival of the species leads to enthronement and enslavement of the female while manhood becomes a mockery, as with the social bees where the queen must murder if necessary to secure her throne, killing her mate in the act of fertilization.

What biological turn could work to set both sexes free of an insect's life by "making a man" of the male? Does Cro-Magnon man reveal it? "The female was much smaller than the male, and her brain was not quite as efficient." [24] Therefore, upon her shoulders the whole responsibility for the social order and survival of the species could not rest, as it does upon the queen bee and her like in the insect's world. Perhaps by evolving away from equality in physical stature ancestral female induced ancestral male to participate directly and share the responsibility that knowledge imposes, even as Eve did in Eden—Adam's participation and shared responsibility are the points upon which the drama turns.

Certainly, woman lost her physical and social equality long ago, but now the female is gaining in stature and she bids fair to gain equal status on the social level. It is difficult to believe that there has ever been a time when in actuality the female's brain was not as efficient as the male's, because woman carries the heaviest part of the load of bearing life, as the legend states Eve must do, and this responsibility must tend to sharpen her wits. The Eden legend indicates that Eve's was the questing mind. The quality of the female mind versus the male mind always has been and no doubt will be for some time to come debatable: there is the question of ways and means and opportunity for expression, the question of the female mind bringing to bear upon the male mind, and the part woman has played in bringing to life the reward of mental effort, civilization.

As ancestral primate evolved into Homo sapiens, his cultural development allowed him to adapt to widely varying environments, but this serves only to present the deeper mystery of the human mind, male and female, which led mankind in time to state the Golden Rule. Man's ability to learn returns one to the mystery of his brain which, in Arthur Koestler's words, is an "evolutionary novelty . . . quite out of proportion with the demands of his natural environment." [25] How and when he came by it is a burning question today.

II

Jesus says, "nothing is secret, that shall not be made manifest; neither any thing hid, that shall not be known and come abroad" [26]—someday man shall know the story of his evolution. In the words of Robert Ardrey, "The story of man lies hidden and awaiting revelation in the towering, orderly beds of Tanganyika's Grand Canyon of Human Evolution." He says:

> . . . hidden away in the fossil fastness are indications of Adam, and of Eden; of a Paradise lost; and of Cain, and of Abel . . .[27]

As evolutionists the world over examine their fossil finds, it is difficult for them to bypass the old, old story; Ruth Moore comments that the bones of Java and Peking man inevitably brought to mind Genesis 6:4, "There were giants in the earth in those days." [28]

But it is Ardrey who chooses the Biblical Genesis legend as a poetic backdrop against which to pose his work, and he presents Homo sapiens as *Cain's child*. Thus, his book must be examined in this study. Although his controversial *African Genesis* has not been considered seriously by some experts in the field of evolutionary theory, a number do subscribe in part to the concepts he presents, and some believe that his view is nearer the truth than any other held today. In the view of this study, his book is of great value, because it brings to the attention of a wide public some pieces of the puzzle, dramatizing the questions that engage the specialists, and it highlights one aspect of man's evolution that cannot be denied by any faction: the extraordinary turns a creature took to follow the path that led him to become man, a being "special" beyond belief. Whose child is he, and how did he evolve?

Ardrey points out that most evolutionists were committed to the theory that the large brain was "the first, not the last, of man's evolutionary endowments," [29] until the bones of the African specimens he groups as *Australopithecus africanus* (smaller) and *Australopithecus robustus* (larger) called into question this calculation. Ardrey likens these types to Cain and Abel. But more than fossil finds have upset the former calculations. In his laboratory, Dr. Sherwood L. Washburn has produced specimens that again scramble the pieces of the puzzle. By removing the jaw muscle on one side of rats' heads he caused strange creatures to grow: "On the side that had not been operated, the rats had the usual deep creases and heavy brow ridges—the same kind of ridges and creases seen in the skull of Neanderthal man and some of the other early men . . . taken as a sign of their primitiveness. On . . . the operated side, the skull of the rats was smooth, very much as the skull of modern man is smooth." [30] And studying the same species of apes and monkeys collected in Uganda at the same time, Dr. Washburn found living together creatures of which he says, "If these skulls had been found as fossils, one would have been tempted to call the first a Peking Man monkey and the other a modern type." [31]

Atomic dating has also upset the old timetable. Ruth Moore says, "Since 1950 the scientific evidence has pointed inescapably to one conclusion: man did not evolve in either the time or the way that Darwin and the modern evolutionists thought most probable." [32]

Ardrey concludes that after seventy million years of slow development, man's brain leapt to the human condition and came about when it did in an evolutionary instant as an ultimate answer to the Pleistocene's unprecedented demands.[33] His theory involves the bones of the creature he likens to Cain, *A. africanus*, discovered in 1925 by Dr. Raymond A. Dart.

Ardrey submits evidence that *A. africanus* was, as Dart held him to be, "a transitional being possessing every significant human qualification other than man's big brain" [34]—thus, he presents him as ancestor of Homo sapiens.[35] This creature was a carnivore, a killer. There is abounding evidence that he armed himself with weapons of bone which he appears to have shaped sometimes—and apparently he, too, relished the "fruit of the tree of knowledge of good and evil," brains. If he was ancestral-man, then the "human being in the most fundamental aspect of his soul and body is nature's last if temporary word on the subject of the armed predator. And human history must be read in these terms." [36] History must also be read in these terms: the remains of the South African apemen present a "positive demonstration that the first recognizably human assertion had been the capacity for murder." [37] The Cain-Abel legend reports this.

In the herbivorous *A. robustus* Abel is represented in Ardrey's drama. He says of *A. africanus* and *A. robustus*:

> Both—most significantly—have lost in equal measure the ape's fighting teeth. . . . The two have likenesses and unlikenesses. Nothing but the evolutionary experience of a common ancestor can explain the similar terrestrial specialization and the similar reduction of fighting canines. And nothing but an evolutionary parting of the ways, a very long time ago, can account for the differences. And so we must pre-

sume that their common ancestor—and ours—defeated by the ape of the forest, turned to a grubbing existence in the bush. . . . We are a mathematical improbability. . . . The emergence of the terrestrial ape cannot be regarded as logical, normal, or to any degree predetermined. It was a break with primate orthodoxy in the name of what can only be described as adventure.[38]

In the Genesis legend, Adam must represent this common ancestor who emerged in a paradise of plenty, but whose progeny "shalt eat the herb of the field," and must make their way through the terrible time of the Pliocene, indicated in the words, "cursed is the ground for thy sake. . . . Thorns and thistles shall it bring forth to thee"—such as this is all the ground could produce in that vast, mysterious, dry inferno that the Pliocene was in Africa.[39]

Ardrey, who has done so much to bring the evolutionary picture into focus, calls man a bad-weather animal, and says: "No mind can apprehend in terms of any possible human experience the duration of the Pliocene." [40] Nor can the mind apprehend in terms of any possible human experience life spans of eight to nine hundred years, as given in the generations from Adam to Noah. Each one of the names listed on man's family tree may therefore be seen to represent a step in the evolution of man, and their ages may be seen to represent the durations of each type, indicating tremendous time spans between the creatures marking evolutionary progress. One must count their days as the Biblical voices measure time—"For a thousand years in thy sight are but as yesterday when it is past, and as a watch in the night. Thou carriest them away as with a flood. . . ." [41]

Ardrey says:

> You possess a body of primitive, generalized proportions, hands of primitive, flexible simplicity, and teeth of primitive, all-purpose effectiveness. So did *Proconsul*, twenty million years ago. But sometime in the next nineteen million years before our first glimpse of the southern ape, significant changes came to your body. You gained erect carriage made possible by the development of specialized buttocks and ground-gripping feet. You became a carnivore, but strangely lost your fighting, killing teeth. Your brain increased somewhat in size, though not significantly in such a long span of time, and your snout flattened correspondingly though your jaws still protruded. . . . The human stock from *Proconsul* down through Neanderthal Man could do no better than to thicken the bone for strength. Then came your particular species in the human family, *Homo sapiens*. And at

the last evolutionary moment chance presented your jaw with a flying buttress to reinforce the V. By this single distinction, the chin, will paleontologists of far distant times . . . be enabled to classify our kind from all other primate kinds, human and prehuman, that have gone before us. There is no other final distinction.[42]

And of this creature, Homo sapiens, Ardrey says:

Were we not so evident, an impartial observer would be forced to conclude that we could not and do not exist. Man is . . . a product of circumstances special to the point of disbelief . . . . his genes . . . are marked. They are graven by luck beyond explanation. They are stamped by forces that we shall never know. . . . Never to be forgotten, to be neglected, to be derided, is the inconspicuous figure in the quiet back room. . . . He is the keeper of the kinds. . . . He is a presence, and that is all . . . . his most ancient concern is with order.[43]

But Ardrey can offer little hope to Cain's children—for "No instinct, whether physiological or cultural, that constituted a part of the original human bundle can ever in the history of the species be permanently suppressed or abandoned." [44]

The whole concept of instinct is today in a state of flux—that there is such a thing as "cultural instinct" is questioned. To explore the subject would require a lengthy discussion. Suffice it to say that Ardrey sees Homo sapiens bound to the killer instinct of *A. africanus*, his hand bound to the weapon as is his mind until in the perfection of his weapons they threaten to become his undoing. Ardrey does, however, see a possibility that man may overcome this dark heritage, but before examining the redeeming feature, two questions must be considered. Can *A. africanus* rightly be likened to Cain? Is Homo sapiens Cain's child?

Is it not a fallacy to liken a carnivorous animal to Cain who brought as offering the "fruit of the ground" indicating that he was herbivorous? The legend suggests that Abel was the carnivore, first to use tool or weapon to procure the fat of the firstlings of his flock that he offered. But the meat Abel offered was not the flesh of a brother-being, and the carnivore that must kill for food is not a murderer. *A. africanus* comes nearer to fitting the shoe that Abel wears in the legend. He must be seen as both innocent and superior. During the Pliocene, in Africa the carnivore, *A. africanus*, must have commanded more "respect" in evolution's processes than the herbivorous *A. robustus* who more nearly fits the shoe of Cain—but in that awful drought "A single commandment, unheard and unseen, overhung the birth of every infant: kill, and eat meat, or die." [45] This, perhaps, provided the extenuating circumstance—the legend says God put upon Cain a "protective mark" after he had become a killer, before he was driven out into the wilderness. Life could not, however, pass on unattenuated the genes of this creature who first of all murdered a brother-being.

If one elects to tell the story of evolution in terms of the Genesis legend, he cannot overlook Seth, meaning *compensation*, replacement seed, third son of Adam-Eve, his life paralleling Cain's in the wilderness. From Seth come the beings the legend calls truly human for "to him also there was born a son; and he called his name Enos (meaning *mortal*); then began men to call upon the name of the Lord." [46] Does Enos mark the point in the legend when ancestral-man began to identify himself as man, becoming Self-conscious, expressing his consciousness of God?

Although the Genesis legend indicates that man is Seth's child, it does indicate also that there was a crossing of Cain's progeny and Seth's: the *type* called by the name, Lamech, meaning *wild man*, is in the line of both Cain and Seth; [47] Enoch, *teacher*, appears both as son of Cain and son of Jared, descendant of Seth.[48] ". . . Enoch walked with God: and he was not, for God took him," but Lamech, father of Noah, repeated Cain's crime—he says, "I have slain a man to my wounding, and a young man to my hurt." [49] The "old, inexplicable bells" ring again in Africa—Dr. L. S. B. Leakey who discovered *Zinjanthropus* announced that "an unidentified juvenile hominid found likewise in Bed One died a probable victim of violence." [50]

Noah, meaning *rest*, may be seen to represent Cro-Magnon man, for his progeny take over the earth. The legend indicates that in the Noah type or Cro-Magnon man there was awareness of mortal error in shedding human blood, in eating human flesh, and that this type man developed into a great hunter of the beasts so beautifully depicted by some ancient Nimrod on the walls of the Cave of Lascaux.

Ardrey points out that "any mutation in a primate species making possible the digestion of meat must be a transformation of revolutionary genetic proportions." [51] If eating the fruit of the tree of knowledge of good and evil indicates partaking for the first time of the flesh or brains of a sentient creature, the Eden legend concurs and points to another revolutionary transformation that followed: nakedness. Man's nakedness is as great a mystery as all else about him—surely this was an irrational "choice" or selection. When did ancestral-man lose his coat—and why? Can fossils give the answer? Legend says this happened long ago—in

Adam's time, following a change in diet. As Adam-type hominid evolved into an omnivorous creature, he lost the ability to cover his nakedness—he must wear "coats of skins," [52] so that he must become hunter, develop weapon and tool, to provide himself with garment.

Seth, in Adam's own image and likeness, must have inherited nakedness, must have been an unspecialized omnivore, who needed tool and weapon; but to triumph in the evolutionary play, he must have a superior brain, or cortex, and a superior power such as speech is. If the Genesis legend tells evolution's story truly, and if the carnivorous *A. africanus* is Abel and the herbivorous *A. robustus* is Cain, the legend would say that *robustus* types overcame *africanus* so that he disappeared from the scene; but *robustus* himself did not make the grade and in time his get of giant men were decimated, as alongside him another primitive man evolved into Homo sapiens who embodies many characteristics similar to *robustus* and *africanus*, inherited from the common ancestor of all three and acquired through interbreeding to a limited degree with the *robustus* type, which was too brutalized in mind and body to have evolved into Homo sapiens.

Today, Dr. Leakey says that his discovery of the LLK skull "is evidence of a new heretofore undiscovered 'cousin' of modern man. The skull reaches back to about 600,000 years." [53] Thus, he postulates that "three different types of prehistoric man existed together within one hundred miles of each other in what he considers the cradle of civilization, the Olduvai Gorge in Tanzania, East Africa." [54] Dr. Leakey says that each "developed its own needs for survival . . . . various species living side by side until the weaker died out or were annihilated, leaving the stronger until eventually modern man emerged." [55] As was to be expected, his position is disputed by some, accepted at least in part by others. More time will be required to put together the whole story of man's evolution, in terms acceptable to the majority of anthropologists.

According to the legend, Seth's progeny, adulterated by Cain-type genes, came to rest in the Noah type. Man's brain and chin were there, in evolution's play compensating him for lack of a coat, and for lack of a true killer instinct which mankind at large does not unanimously possess. Man, however, has not come through the years uninvolved in Cain's crime of brother-murder. The legend says men bear Cain's trace—Cainan, meaning *acquisition*, appears on the family tree, but on it there is no trace of Abel—purely carnivorous?—whose name means *transitoriness*. The legend says that all races evolved from an ancestral type in whose genes lay the specialness man exhibits, making all humankind brothers, equals in being. This truth Jesus sought to establish. In His words, one confronts man's original endowment: the kingdom of God within him. Through his possession of this "inward kingdom" is established a sort of kindredship with Volvox, creature that is within itself "garden-being" until it moves into sexed life and death. The Eden legend may be trying to say that the garden man must tend is within himself—was so from the beginning.

If man is in bondage to his original nature, he is bound to expression in material being, for he was raised up from matter, from cosmic dust—and he is bound to immortality as is the one-cell creature. Ardrey says: "If man is a part of the natural world, then he possesses as do all other species a genetic inheritance from an ancestry as long as life itself." [56] Man can use his big brain to attenuate the errors he has acquired throughout his evolutionary journey so that in time knowledge of them will serve to innoculate him against their deadly peril. He appears to have just enough of Cain's virulent strain within him and more than enough brain power to do this. If he is bound to his original nature, he is bound to whatever it is that caused him, alone among all creatures, to speak the one original word, "I." And he is bound to that which Ardrey offers as his one redeeming feature:

> The command to love is as deeply buried in our nature as the command to hate.[57]

Through the guidance of the Self-presence that gives man the power of the word, "I," the power of speech, and the power of love, of truth, he may come in time to lay down and beat into "ploughshares" [58] his perfected weapons—a move unprecedented, save in his own history. Once, long ago, he relinquished weapons, his fighting canines, and picked up a tool. And he may again make this move, a move "irrational" in the "view" of any other creature, for "rationality" has led all others to evolve and perfect their means of offense and defense and then to utilize these means to the fullest extent.

From Ardrey's summary of man's specialness, it looks as though this one creature has possessed from his beginning a presence, or God-sense, that acts as a lamp unto his feet and a light unto his path.[59] The Genesis legend says this presence was in man's garden-being and that it has never left him. It would have required a knowing Authority within to guide ancestral-man-cell along the irrational path that led to the pinnacle. If from the beginning this presence guided ancestral-cell into and through every necessary step by blinding the creature to much in the outer world while giving it inner vision, this would make all the difference there is between man and other forms of life. This Authority would have had to insist upon selection not of more sensory, but of more mental equipment than the creature needed, as Eve is represented to have more mental equipment than she needed or could live with in paradise bound, in order that it might transcend environmental limitations, which man shows promise of doing today.

What sort of factor could truly and surely guide? This must be a factor which beforehand had known every form and being, the way into and out of each mode of life. One cannot give this factor a satisfactory name. One can say only that it is the Self-sense of the Creator, the "I-sense" of being, or "God-being" in the one-cell creature that became man, a cell resembling amoeba but different from the amoeba man knows today; for such a cell would be and would evolve into a form like unto but not identical to any other form of life, because an essential ingredient abstracted from the creature's consciousness and hidden within would chart its course.

The idea that man has incorporated in his being from one-cell creature onward a knowing Authority-Ego in an *unconscious* domain may seem fantastic. But the concept that the unconscious may have played a role in man's biological evolution from some point in the past to the present has been voiced. Dr. von Franz writes that Jung's revelation of the archetypes and his concepts opened up "new ways of looking at things in the realm of the natural sciences . . .":

> The physicist Wolfgang Pauli has pointed out that, due to new discoveries, our idea of the evolution of life requires a revision that might take into account an area of interrelation between the unconscious psyche and biological processes. Until recently it was assumed that the mutation of species happened at random and that a selection took place by means of which the "meaningful," well-adapted varieties survived, and the others disappeared. But modern evolutionists have pointed out that the selections of such mutations by pure chance would have taken much *longer* than the known age of our planet allows.[60]

God-sense voicing itself in man insists that something other than chance has brought about the housing of his soul: "Except the Lord build the house, they labour in vain that build it. . . ."[61]

Man's evolutionary journey could come of his having to *know* all being and form in order to be representative of the tree of life itself. The last and most highly developed of all life forms, man yet possesses a sense of being before creation was. This sense tells him that all he partakes of is the flesh of God, coming into being before him to prepare the way, and that everything that lives is living through God's being, even as he, himself, is. Because of this sense, man practices theophagy, making of eating a ritual that enfolds the power, glory, art, and grace of God, of life—as does the Christian communion rite. At the last supper, Jesus says:

> I am the true vine, and my Father is the husbandman. Every branch in me that beareth not fruit he taketh away: and every branch that beareth fruit, he purgeth it, that it may bring forth more fruit. . . . Abide in me, and I in you. As the branch cannot bear fruit of itself, except it abide in the vine; no more can ye, except ye abide in me. I am the vine, ye are the branches.[62]

Jesus, as symbol of Son of man—which is to say, as symbol of Adam become one with his knowing Authority within—indicates that man represents in his being the whole tree of life which his consciousness longs to know, and the vine of it is still growing—"I" go on to prepare a place from which "ye" spans of knowing may branch out higher in every direction while the *a priori* "cell of Father-being," love and truth in action within each one, acts as husbandman: truth purges and prunes, love restores and is fruitful. But toward what is the vine growing? And how is man's growth accomplished?

Lamarck believed that acquired characteristics would be inherited. Physically speaking, it would appear that they are not—as Hugo De Vries showed in bringing to light the long neglected work of Gregor Mendel and through his own experiments establishing mutation, rather than Lamarck's theory of use and disuse of physical members to be the evolutionary act that produces new species.[63] But use and disuse of various forms in a culture appear to give rise to a new species of culture—each following form related to the past with certain residual relics in evidence or on call. Today, Teilhard de Chardin questions the transmission of characteristics and points to the role education plays in social heredity and progress—suggesting that it may also play a hidden role in organic evolution. He says, "Mankind, as we find it in its present state and present functioning, is organically inseparable from that which has been slowly added to it, and which is propagated through education." [64] This study agrees, in that it postulates that the power of speech, the power of the word, with the attendant power to write, cannot be dissociated from any part of the creative or evolutionary process of individual or society or species. But this study must disagree emphatically with many other assumptions Teilhard set forth in *The Future of Man*, as will be pointed out in a later chapter.

In speaking of the creation of the social brain, Loren Eiseley writes that:

> nature, through man, has eluded the trap which has engulfed in one way or another every other form of life on the planet. Within the reasonable limits of the brain that now exists, she has placed the long continuity of civilized memory as it lies packed in the world's great libraries. The need is not really for more brains, the need is now for a gentler, a more tolerant people than those who won for us against the ice, the tiger, and the bear.[65]

Jesus, giving voice to man's Authority-Ego when the time had come that man must take an unprecedented turn, gave the commands that point the way, the only way, to bring about the transformation of man and of society that humankind seeks. The first and greatest command, "Thou shalt love the Lord, thy God, with all thy heart, and with all thy soul, and with all thy mind," [66] turns man's vision inward to grasp God-being within himself, as individual, and points him toward individualism and individual effort—the second command, He said to be like unto the first, "That ye love one another" and "thy neighbor as thyself," [67] poses the concept that cooperation, good will, decency, and the high ethic of love at work in human affairs is in the highest possible interest of individual, nation, and species. Slowly but surely realization of this fact, as the command is handed from generation to generation via the word, is creating a higher type society in which the "new command" will eventually take over from the permanent hostility animals exhibit toward territorial neighbors, their hostility reborn in each year's offspring; and in time these two commands must produce a new type man, fully conscious of himself and empathetic enough to create a satisfying society.

Jesus said this generation of man is *child*. Thus, He projects that Homo sapiens must and will change in body, mind, consciousness, awareness, and capacity to experience. Today, men tend to believe that Homo sapiens is man in very nearly finished form—that biological evolution has all but ceased—forgetting that "a thousand years in thy sight are but as yesterday. . . ." When they view life everlasting in terms of life's being forever vested in Homo sapiens' garment, they come in the end to find the prospect of it appalling. If man is child, he will outgrow his present garment, his mental and physical vesture.

Man cannot today comprehend what he will become, but he can think of himself as conscious of life and as self-conscious always—which is to say, he can think of himself as conscious of life in the form of a one-cell creature. If from ancestral-cell onwards the creature that became man had known, however dimly, the Lord, thy God, as "I" presence within, then his every legend incorporating memory of himself in being would tell a human story—as does the Genesis legend tell a human story, which parallels also the story of the amoeba, of Volvox, of a mousy mammal, of *A. africanus* and *A. robustus*. From one-cell upwards, this "I" presence would have cast off the flesh born of consciousness that had fallen from the way of truth and love, re-establishing itself in new flesh upon the ground of life that its consciousness-in-being might "Build thee more stately mansions, O my soul . . ." [68]—for, "Lo, children are an heritage of the Lord: and the fruit of the womb is his reward." [69] A short lullaby tells a long, long story:

> Rock-a-bye baby, in the treetop
> When the wind blows, the cradle will rock
> And when the bough breaks, the cradle will fall
> And down will come baby, cradle and all.

Strange song! Not at all reassuring, as one might expect a lullaby to be—unless one sees in it the mother's telling her infant that long ago a bough broke and a mousy mammal fell from his treetop Eden to the ground he had not known before, and that later a bough broke and a venturesome primate made an irrational decision to stay on the ground, and that again and again man has fallen out of some type Eden to find himself on good earth, and this is where the babe, so recently in the restricted paradise of the womb, will awaken to find himself alive. Where has he come from? If he could tell his story, he would tell of surviving an all-engulfing flood. Prenatal life is living through and emerging from a "total flood." The Noah legend tells such a story. It is a primordial myth that makes its mark—but the "stuff" of it is "mostly local."

III

Ernst Haeckel first gave an evolutionary bias to fetal development. His theory, although no longer tenable in its original form, has had tremendous influence in the study of evolution and prenatal life. The Noah legend also depicts most dramatically a "recital" of all man has known in animal life, even as it enfolds, poetically and with a surprising degree of accuracy, other aspects of birth processes, as may be seen in the following parallels:

When the ovum is pierced by the sperm, development of a very special growth called the placenta, cake, because of its shape, begins. When Noah is pierced by the word of God, he goes to work and following most explicit instructions builds a very special structure upon high ground: the ark.

Through the umbilical cord that connects the embryo and placenta, the embryo derives oxygen and food; it develops its own blood, circulatory, and digestive systems—that are at all times quite distinct from its host's. Noah was instructed to build a "window" and a "door" in the side of the ark, "and take unto thee of all food that is eaten, and thou shalt gather it to thee, and it shall be for food for thee, and for them."

The inner membrane of the ovum, or amnion (lamb), fills with a pint or more of water. In this the embryo floats. The ark (incorporating both placenta and embryo in symbolic form) is set afloat as the waters rise, Noah and his company shut within it.

As the embryo develops into fetus, soma or "body" cells multiply by division, assuming special shapes to fit them to form the tissues and organs of the body. Noah's company may be seen as a group of "body cells" there in reproductive capacity, and the company may be seen also as a sort of recital of all man has known in the realm of animal flesh, Noah and wife, his sons and their wives, representing the factors that carry the genetic code. The legend says that when the company of "body cells" comes forth, all are "after their kinds," or are "arranged in families"—as are the soma cells which form the tissues and organs.

With the spilling of the birth waters, the fetus emerges from the womb to the dry ground of life. Noah waits until the waters have drained away and then his company emerges in a body, leaving the ark behind as the placenta is "after birth." By the time the fetus is past the seventh month, its body is basically complete; but it is not uncommon for the fetus to delay until well into the tenth month before emerging. The legend says that by the seventh month, the "ark is grounded," but the story enfolds also the lengthier term—"till the tenth month the waters steadily subsided, and on the first day of the tenth month the tops of the mountains were seen."

The legend's poetic revelation of embryonic and fetal life does not end with the arrival of man on terra firma. It deals with infant being of race and individual. It says Homo sapiens must deal with his imagination, "evil from his youth," pointing to childish barbarism and man's behavior in primeval times when he resorted to cannibalism. The legend says man is given for food all plant life and creatures except his own kind—man's blood is to be held sacred, is to be strictly accounted. The most important lesson primeval man had to learn was to substitute animal flesh for human flesh to maintain himself in life—the most important lesson the infant must learn is to make this substitution, for he cannot forever feed upon his mother. The Noah story introduces a parallel to the Totem feast: Noah offers every clean beast and fowl upon an altar—man has begun to teach through ritual the realization that led him, finally, to relinquish cannibalism. Thus, this earliest religion represents enormous progress in the development of human consciousness: a forswearing of embryonic, fetal, and infantile experience wherein one must partake of human substance in order to know life—man has become as child.

The legend says that God sets a rainbow in the sky as a reminder, implying the birth of consciousness with which the legend also deals, indicating that the process is more traumatic than physical birth. It is depicted as a laying down of one ego or life and the picking up of another in differentiated consciousness. As the legend describes it, Noah lies down naked in drunken stupor and is glimpsed briefly by Ham, who is thereby cursed with "knowledge of helplessness," and reduced to servant status. His offspring becomes a mighty and cunning hunter. But Noah is covered quickly by Japeth and Shem who do not look upon the self-induced, naked helplessness of their father-consciousness. When Noah recovers, he says, "Blessed be the LORD GOD of Shem. . . . God shall enlarge Japeth and he shall dwell in the tents of Shem," through whom the line of legend continues, encompassing those who become Israel, a multitude outgrown from that which was within the ark.

Ham appears to represent a preconscious ego-sense which is one of both helplessness and cunning, subject to all other psychic factors. Having looked upon the naked parent, it is subject to the Oedipus curse—the curse so involved with the physical intermingling of person and parent, of impotence despite man's might and cunning.

Japeth appears to represent a subconscious ego-sense which is enlarged as its store of data grows through experience and learning—it becomes "a mighty one in the earth . . . the beginning of his kingdom was Babel . . ." and man's subconscious is indeed a babble of selves within him, subject to an enlarging and mighty conscience.

Shem, the blessed, appears to represent the superconscious ego-sense as it is described in this study: a natural grasp of truth, a natural responsiveness to right that needs not to be belabored by conscience or memory.

The Lord God who shuts in the ark and sets the rainbow is seen to be a visitation in man's consciousness—this, the Authority-Ego, his sense of certainty in being, dwells in the "tents" of Shem. The word, "tents," indicates that consciousness is always on the move.

Noah appears to be representative of man's sense of having been—he represents memory residue, which resides in infant consciousness long enough to ratify or to activate God-consciousness in man and then to create a schism between itself and the preconscious level before it subsides into the *unconscious*. Noah's demise coincides with infant amnesia, and his cursing of Ham indicates that every person suffers a trauma in infancy as a result of his partial glimpsing of his naked past. But the legend tells man that he cannot know himself through the exposure of his unconscious memory although it is parent of his present consciousness, for this memory spends itself in the constructive work of fetal development and birth. Thus, prior life or generation is a closed episode: the head of its household sinks into the unknown realm—a part of man's consciousness may have glimpsed it in infancy, but a part refrained from viewing the naked body of the past and this part will always cover it quickly, hiding it from curiosity's eyes. Thus, the Noah legend reveals the inner drama.

The birth legend of Moses is a symbolical representation of birth itself. As Freud points out, Moses' birth legend contradicts the typical myth—although it resembles that of Sargon of Agade, founder of Babylon. The mother of Moses exposes him to the waters when she can "hide him no longer"—but this is for the purpose of saving his life. He is taken from the Nile by a Princess of Egypt, woman of royal blood and highest culture, "and he became her son." [70] Thus, the child leaves the womb and is sent on its journey down the river of life when this becomes necessary to insure its survival, for it is precious and beautiful in the eyes of parent-host and in the eyes of the woman who draws it from the waters.

There is one crucial point stressed in all birth legends. Whether the child is born of royalty, or is rescued by royalty and brought up as their own, or whether he is born of humble people, or is rescued by them to become a king, in sum the birth legends say that man is borne down the river of life into loving *adoption* by the parents who draw him from the birth waters, and that whatever his race and upbringing, he is of royal potential, destined to be a monarch in his own right. So many legends tell of his humble upbringing, because in evolution's light the parent generation is always of more humble status, more primitive, than the child that comes to and through them, because the child is born into an environment embodying wider consciousness which he falls heir to at the moment of his birth.

But to understand fully the origin of man, one must attempt to understand what impetus drives the sperm cell into the ovum. This act, as well as fetal development and birth, is an unconscious process—one must find a birth legend related to the *unconscious* domain and the power of life within it. Jesus' birth legend, which resembles in some ways that of the Light of Asia, Lord Gautama, comes to mind.

IV

Jesus must have consented to what is written of His birth drama—to the story as Mary told it. The Gospels are an immediate account of His life and words. It is highly unlikely that His followers would so soon fabricate a baseless myth and attach it to Him. If Jesus made of Himself a symbol to convey truth, it must follow that He made, or allowed to be made, of the circumstances of His birth a legend to convey a "book of truth" compressed and refined in poetic terms—and if the man is true, the legend must stem from psychological and biological fact. Although His relationship to the House of David is drawn through Joseph, the Gospels say Jesus was born of Mary. The question is—was Jesus born of a virgin? Is this a question that may reasonably be examined in the light of today's knowledge? In legends, males are born of virgins.

In an article in *Lancet*, Dr. Helen Spurway admits to the possibility that virgin birth is a rare phenomenon. She says there are "sound reasons for biologists to look out for such births." [71] Doctors experiment with animals, but only females are produced.

Medical science confronts cases of pseudopregnancy, a psychosomatic symptom that produces the exact appearance of a true pregnancy, which progresses up to the final hour when delivery could take place and it becomes evident, if it has not been detected previously, that there is no fetus to deliver. A woman *is capable* of producing unconsciously every symptom of pregnancy short of evolvement of the fetus. Science may find someday that the further step of providing self-fertilization through cross action of ova from the woman herself can be accomplished, and that by some throw-back to primordial processes, a male child can develop. In a review of the work of Jean Rostand, *Time* reports:

> Parthenogenesis—self-fertilization, by techniques such as supplying an additional nucleus from the mother, would permit a woman to have a child that is not the child of any male.[72]

In rare cases, parthenogenesis may have been accomplished under the same unconscious compulsion that produces pseudopregnancy.

Another common fact to be considered is that exposing ovum to sperm does not necessarily produce a pregnancy—often physicians can find no reason that might prevent a couple from having children, but they remain childless until they adopt a child, and then have one of their own. Something in the unconscious workings of one or both parents must have been affected by the presence of an infant they have willingly *adopted*, and this psychic change may have affected the physical processes to permit natural pregnancy. Therefore, it appears possible that a psychological or unconscious factor of one or both parents *can* be the determining factor in conception.

Pseudopregnancy, and the strange release from sterility which so often follows the adoption of an infant give basis for believing that human birth is not a "mechanical," physical process, although it is sexually based. A psychic factor appears to be determining on the part of parents, while something altogether outside their physical or psychic capacities acts to drive the sperm into the ovum—parents cannot will this, nor can they prevent it in normal course if they engage in the sexual act. Thus, the force that drives sperm into ovum must be that of the incipient life itself, so that in this sense, every conception is miraculous. Each one's body is truly of virgin flesh, untouched save by the mind-energy that constructs of the materials at hand an embodiment for its conscious expression in life. The embryo, a symbiotical parasite, is thus a visitation, and the "X-energy" that begins the process and builds the body may finish or discard the structure it has begun.

Experiments show that there are a number of ways to manipulate the processes of birth in lower species, such as transplant of a fertilized ovum. The possibility that such techniques would produce the same results in human beings prompts Rostand to ask: "If a woman bore a child that was not genetically hers, who would be the real mother? Would it be she who carried the child or she who furnished the germ cell?" [73] Consider also artificial insemination—who would be the real father, the one who supplied the sperm or the one who cared for the pregnant mother and then raised the child as his own? The facts and theories that biologists are presenting today must turn man to question again the *real* parenthood of himself. This, Jesus tried to do two thousand years ago.

Jesus likened His body to bread. When scientists began to investigate how the genes function, Edward L. Tatum and George Wells Beadle, casting about for a simple organism needed for the study, chose Neurospora—the red mold that appears on bread in a warm climate, "for the nutritional requirements of men, molds, and all living things are essentially the same." [74] But there was another consideration. Ruth Moore writes: "If two of the lacily branching twigs of Neurospora were brought together, one of Type *A* and the other of type *a*, they would fuse sexually and form a fertile cell *Aa*. But if there was no union of the two types,

Neurospora also could reproduce non-sexually—that is, by simple cell division, as many plants do." [75] Bread mold and human kind may share more than essential nutritional requirements—reproduction on a sexual or nonsexual basis may be possible to each.

Otto Rank divided history into four eras, each defining a quest for immortality, and postulated that "Primitive man's attitude during the pre-sexual era . . . clearly indicates that sexuality meant something inner, and not something as realistic as a relation with the opposite sex," so that "Unless we can translate the language of the sexual era into that of the spiritual era, we cannot understand even the biological facts of sex." [76]

As one surveys a montage of the birth legends to find the inner meaning of sexuality, they seem to say that in sexual reproduction a psychic condition must be met: *unconsciously* both the male and female inherency in the man and woman must be willing partners of God in life itself, offering their lives and substance, as were Noah and the virgin Mary; and both the female and male inherency in the man and woman must be willing to *adopt* the child that comes to them, as the Princess of Egypt adopted Moses and Joseph adopted Jesus.

Whatever its inner meaning, sexuality involves more than is as yet accorded. The perceptive eye of Lawrence Durrell selected these words from Freud to set the stage for his investigation of modern love:

> I am accustoming myself to the idea of regarding every sexual act as a process in which four persons are involved. We shall have a lot to discuss about that. (S. Freud: *Letters*) [77]

In the view of this study, the "four persons" are four psychic factors in mankind that are symbolized in Noah, the virgin Mary, Princess of Egypt, and Joseph; and male and female, both partners of God, both willing to adopt the life that comes through use of their flesh, offer themselves with each sexual enjoining to a Son-cell, sent of God, Father, but coming also of his own accord to those who make themselves a channel into life for him, albeit this offering is made unconsciously.

There is no way for a person to acknowledge his debt to his human parents and live with it in psychic health save according them honor in life. But, in turn, the child has brought innocence into their being, has bestowed love freely, keeps God's life-covenant for and with them.

Born in the manger that cradles animal being, Jesus left as His earliest symbol a fish to provide the clue: life arises from the deeps of the world, of the body, and of the mind that is man. In His legend, the nobility involved is love and sharing of self and substance that a new embodiment in life may come into the world—such is the conscious or unconscious heritage of any human being. In this legend, the Father does not abandon His son—to the contrary, the identity He sends into the world is most precious segment of His very own being—each is as an only son with whom He has shared in one full measure His power and glory that His offspring might possess this freely and in full dominion. The child is not helpless, for the Father has wrapped this gift within him and first prepares every step of the way so that nothing can defeat the child's own chosen mission.

This study accepts that Jesus was born of Mary, and that she was a virgin—postulating that parthenogenesis, like pseudopregnancy, may be accomplished unconsciously—in rare cases producing males—and it recognizes that psychic forces within the parents as well as a force apart from parent hosts (and therefore relatable only to the child or life itself) also play a determining part in the conception of every human being, so that in this sense conception depends upon more than sexual factors.

Jesus taught that all mankind is mysteriously conceived; He insisted that each man must, as the first step toward truth, acknowledge himself to be in life through the action of God, Father, and not through the impulse of any male or female flesh.[78] Man will suffer the deep anxiety of illegitimacy and amnesia until he recognizes God as only parent, himself as God-son. Thus, Jesus perceived the psychic necessity for baptism—a ratification by parents as to the true identity of their infant, or an acknowledgment by the adult of the covenant between God and man in which he expresses his willingness to experience the miracle of life through being made channel for it. This, or for the sake of his inner kingdom he makes eunuch of himself,[79] that truth may be expressed through him. Perhaps, unconsciously, human beings render themselves sterile, or eunuch, in order that through being childless, despite their longing to bear life, their flesh may bear witness to the mystery of conception.

Jesus' legend reveals the genesis of human power: the word man speaks that sets each one apart and identifies him in the name of God, "I." In broadest sense, it is a continuation of the legend of the Tower of Babel which presents the mystery of language.

V

One has only to read C. W. Ceram's *Gods, Graves, and Scholars*[80] to see how often in human history the drama of building a Tower of Babel has been repeated. Thus, the Biblical legend must enfold many tellings of such an endeavor as it points also to the rise and fall of languages and civilizations committed to a ziggurat concept that, whatever its nature, robs one of his individuality, substituting for his God-given name, "I," a Group-ego label that "us," his personality, must wear as ball and chain upon the human soul:

> . . . let us build us a city and a tower, whose top may reach unto heaven; and let us make us a name. . .[81]

Building a tower whose top may reach unto heaven indicates a reaching beyond consciousness to the subconscious in an attempt to control man so that he will obey the dictates of his conditioners and accept their label; but those who seek through this means to build a totalitarian, utopian structure overlook the Monarch of each one's inner world, jealously guarding one's very life, utterly concerned with one's every breath. This inner Authority prevails—or so the Babel legend says: "Behold, the people is one, and they have all one language; and this they begin to do: and now nothing will be restrained from them which they have imagined to do. Go to, let us go down, and there confound their language, that they may not understand one another's speech." [82] And in the ensuing confusion, the builders disperse, the ziggurat is abandoned. What happens, psychologically speaking, to thwart this mighty effort?

Consider that each man speaks a language of his own begot of his understanding of any word. Where his understanding stops, or veers off in tangent, the babble of words falling upon his inner or outer ear serve only to confuse the issue and disperse the force of those who strive to control his thinking. Thus, he can be conditioned so far and no further—no utopian dream can permanently adjust him to Homo sapiens' insufficient lot in life: the tower cannot be finished because man, himself, is not finished. Man is only partially conscious, his body is an expression of mind power only partially in use; and powerful as it is, the subconscious is not the end of his being.

Dr. Rolf Alexander likens the subconscious to a factory that needs an over-all understanding to direct and coordinate the know-how of each laborer. But he sees that the "factory" does not *identify* the man: "Search as we will, we can never find the reality we all hunger for in the conditioned illusions of our subconscious, nor in our intellects which are oriented to these illusions. . . . we must return to the task of developing the instrument of conscious perception abandoned by us in childhood—the true personality." [83] This echoes Jesus: one must become as a child to receive his name, to enter the kingdom of God within him.[84] In these simple words, Jesus swept aside for once and for all any complicated, mechanistic practices and systems and edifices of metaphysical thought—

and above all any closed system that perforce precludes growth.

If one accepts the teaching of Jesus as revelation of the Authority-Ego in man operating from the *unconscious* domain, then one accepts the concept that the over-all understanding to direct and coordinate the subconscious is there; and that the yoke of the subconscious mind has been assumed by Self in order to enter life through nature's avenues, for nature appears to operate the animal kingdom through a subconscious, mechanistic process—that is, through converting experience into instinctive, conditioned responses.

Jesus indicates that the Authority-Ego has willingly taken this yoke upon Self because through the subconscious mind's working, the burden of accumulated knowledge is carried easily; because of it man learns rapidly; and it relieves him of the operation of his mechanistic body. As symbol of Authority-Ego, Jesus says to the ego-group:

> Take my yoke upon you, and learn of me . . .
> For my yoke is easy, and my burden is light . . .[85]

These words and the Babel legend indicate that man need not fear the hold his subconscious mind has upon consciousness, for man cannot be confined within its limitations or be enslaved by its mechanics—he is more than the "computer" that operates for him.

The Babel legend deals also with another aspect of man and the development of consciousness—it indicates the nature of the change evolutionary processes effected as man moved from his preceding state to Homo sapiens generation, and it points the way he must evolve to meet his future. The Genesis legend says man must name all that comes unto him—he must create words. But the legend also indicates that communication was established in the beginning, and in the dramas of Eden and Noah's ark there is a broader sense of communication than follows thereafter:

> In the days when the whole earth had one language and one vocabulary, there was a migration from the east . . .[86]

These words suggest an absolute means of communication, one that was effortless insofar as conscious striving was concerned. Only telepathy or clairvoyance correspond to this. The Babel legend deals with Homo sapiens' infant being, reflected today in the infant being of any man. Dr. Joan Fitzherbert, English psychiatrist, suggests that telepathy is used by the baby as a means of communication with its mother.[87] Thus, this study postulates that telepathy was and perhaps still is a prime means of communication in life.

Unrestricted as telepathy appears to be, it is insufficient to meet man's need to pass along to the next generation what he gains in knowledge and realizes to be truth. Only language, words, can meet this need. The demand to understand words and to communicate his understanding in words is put upon the child as he passes from infancy to childhood—above all, he must identify himself as man. A transition must take place within him. The Babel legend would say that some inward power speaks, and the one word it could say that would confound the babble of the childish ego-group and start it along the path of conscious striving, the one word that would make all men strangers even to themselves, is "I"—the seed of Enos, mortal, flowering in the articulated vocable, the *word*, its capacity, content, and meaning is unknown. Dr. Franz Winkler writes:

> In his second or third year, every sane child undergoes an inner experience of utmost significance, an experience which radically changes his mental life. From that moment on he ceases to refer to himself in the third person and conceives of "I." Some endowed with an unusual memory will recall this event later and will consequently not easily be swayed by philosophers and psychologists who deny the reality of selfhood.[88]

"You" or "me" are concepts a very young child can grasp; such can be telepathized or pantomimed as well as spoken. But "I," this word arising from the hidden kingdom within, this actual "calling on the name of the Lord," this *word* having come into the world of flesh, begins a new step in life. Just as it lifts the child from "me want" to the wonder of "I am," it lifts race from infant to child status, making Homo sapiens a mystery to himself, to his fellowmen, to all creatures.

The concept offered here is that when something within man and beyond his consciousness sounded through him, destroying his pre-Homo sapiens means of communication, the forces of extrasensory perception began to be dispersed, as were the tower's builders, and this drama is repeated in the life of the child today. Vestiges of ESP remained in the modern type man, but in race the force of the psychic power was turned into inward channels that led to self-exploration and the development of the mind of man as the modern type emerged. Frederick Marion, who demonstrates extraordinary ESP and works with scientists to explore psychic phenomena, does not make this same postulation, but he does say: "Everything points to the fact that humanity is not evolving towards a more universal possession of psychic powers. On the contrary, our ancestors were more greatly gifted in this respect." [89] The Babel Tower legend suggests this—it says that man moved away from his old means of communication, that he is still on the move, his development not to be arrested by any social structure he contrives.

But it must be pointed out that mental and spiritual powers rise in a spiral—ESP appears now to be returning in a form refined, for at the height of modern man's intellectual powers he is apt to experience intuitive prompting, a sort of inward clairvoyance, that vastly enhances his mental reach. Jesus, Himself, personifies the return of the power as empathy grows and intellect comes to full flower.

The Babel legend expresses a noble intellectual ideal—the fallacy is that not even Nimrod is named responsible, for it begins, "They said," so that responsibility does not come to rest anywhere, or upon anyone engaged in the gigantic group effort. The legend says that something in man prohibits the completion of any irresponsible effort to solve any problem or reach any goal. In Eden, in the beginning, man is human and is given dominion over all other life because he was made to be responsible for self and acts. Trying to *know* by eating any fruit represents a thoughtless, mechanistic effort to achieve life's goal automatically and irresponsibly. The Eden legend says such effort will fail—and the Babel legend confirms the dictum.

VI

In man's repertory of legends, exposure myths are so plentiful that they must enfold essential truth. But psychologists do not explain them by emphasizing what this study sees to be the obvious and essential message they convey: first, the child-parent relationship is one of mutual adoption; secondly, the first and last duty of the parent involves *the ejection of the child into life apart from parent host*. It is this last aspect of the legends' message that must be examined here.

The Eden drama depicts the birth and growth of consciousness. It says that each person inherently possesses male and female consciousness, that female consciousness pierces male consciousness or provides it with food to begin developing a body of knowledge, and this act precipitates expulsion from the realm of parent host. Because the fetus is a parasite, albeit symbiotic, each child expresses parasitic will. His problem is to have done with it, for it leads to an attempt to possess and feed upon another human being—mentally, emotionally, economically, and, long ago, literally.

Parent must break the parasitic bond. The mental, as well as the physical, umbilical cord must be cut. The process begins as the child is weaned and must be complete before he becomes responsible as an adult in the eyes of society, his body sufficiently mature that he may be parent himself. At best, this operation is painful for the parent, but more so for the child. Thus, psychologists have collected data to create the cruel parental image, making father, mother, or both the scapegoat upon which the child and then the man may pass off his every insufficiency and error.

Parents do err in handling their children, and the children bear these scars, sometimes for life. Many adults are themselves so committed to parasitic consciousness that they consume and enslave their children's lives. Many parents are so crippled in their souls or so immature that they spurn or neglect their young. Large numbers of parents are appallingly cruel. But the great majority of them love their children and do for them the best they can. Regardless of the type parent, however, the fact remains that the child must be cast out on his own, ejected into a life apart wherein he is responsible for himself and to society. Life demands this.

The normal ambivalence of child toward parent comes about as he is made to assume responsibility for himself and to deal with his brother generation, a barbarian horde, both a terror and delight, only partially subdued by the adult world where civility is too often thin veneer. When it becomes apparent to him that his parents, who had appeared all-powerful and able to secure him in life, cannot spare him his head-on contact with society and his peers, he sees father and mother in a new light. He turns on them, or else makes an *unconscious and therefore innocent effort to regain Eden.*

The Oedipus legend may be used as example: it symbolizes the innocent parasitic desire of child to feed upon parents. This desire extends itself in ever greater ways until parents are had by their offspring—a situation parallel to that in which the parasite so utterly consumes its host that it brings about its own downfall. This legend says that man blinds himself to this lust, which hides behind heroic front as it seeks satisfaction in devious ways. Dr. Martin Grotjahn remarks: "Today the full force of the old man's wrath is aroused when the son begins to show an undue interest in his father's business or money. The present-day King Laius fears his son Oedipus less in bed than in business." [90] Too often the son seeks only the fruits and will not labor in the field. The teen-ager's abuse of property reflects a lingering parasitical consciousness which refuses to accept responsibility commensurate with the license he demands. The young try the fiber of parental and social authority. Then suddenly, fit or not, life places responsibility upon them when their sexual development makes them potential bearers of life itself. Parents cannot withhold them from this covenant. Cruel is the parent who does not drive out the child to face the world and to become adult within himself before he becomes responsible to society and for society which sooner or later in one way or another avenges man's blood spilled by the predator or sucked by the leech. Love breaks the parasitic bond, but love also heals the wound.

The exposure myths symbolize the conscious or unconscious parent-sense that recognizes the need to drive the child out of his infantile paradise—just as God, eternal parent, drives man out when the time has come that he wants to exercise his God-given intelligence and know or experience life. The Eden legend says that man's curiosity cannot be irresponsibly expressed and idly satisfied without his doing evil, that one cannot feed upon truth irresponsibly because truth places responsibility for himself and for his acts upon him, that knowledge of life cannot be acquired within the parasitic state secured by paternalistic bonds.

There is but one enduring parental relationship in life: that between God and man, for both father and mother are of the same natural generation as the child—they are brother-beings to him. All that is enfolded in the Communion rite Jesus established cannot be elaborated at this point, but it may be pointed out that this rite dramatized the need of man to partake of the flesh and blood of brother-being to come through this into life, for Jesus stated Himself a brother to mankind. Only, however, as this food is handed him by Authority-Ego, only as he has his being in the *unconscious* primarily, is this permissible—this is to say, as embryo, fetus, and infant. Thereafter, he must become as a child, must move forward from his parasitic state, reaching forth his own hand to partake of his share in nature's realm wherein as he partakes of so much as a grain of wheat he consumes the flesh of God extended into living matter.

Man will have done with parasitic behavior when he recognizes that the one authority over him is God expressed not as Deity apart, but as the infallible law of full, free possession: what a man possesses in truth is what he holds in perfect understanding and has worked to produce. If anything be handed him on a platter, he is beholden to the host. Therefore, each must work his own way into his own kingdom.

Wherever man's condition is most deplorable, there one finds parasitic consciousness insistently and often innocently expressed by male and female at every economic level. Whatever the social system, as man tries parasitic behavior in any of its guises he is confronted by civilization's ever widening pattern of failure to meet his real and deepest needs. He suffers a growing awareness of his actual insecurity and senses that he is becoming a faceless creature in servitude to organized human frailty—society becomes his enemy and his compulsion to identify himself as an independent being is strongly reasserted. But he knows that in the end he must come to terms with society, for he is utterly dependent upon it. And so, today, psychology reduces the size of faceless terror by leading the individual to become part of a group, assuming a "group name" so to speak, so that he may cope with nebulousness in a smaller dose. Dr. van den Berg says:

> Today, acting as an adult means acting in a team. . . . The peculiarity of all work done in teams, however, is primarily the lack of responsibility of each of the participants. No one is responsible. No one is wholly mature.[91]

Thus, one sees that leaning on the team's Group-ego is but another expression of parasitic consciousness that allows the individual to escape the necessity of confronting himself in independent being, responsible to and for himself and his acts. In leading a person to use Group-ego as a crutch, the real value and need of organized effort in life is subverted.

Dependency upon the group means loss of one's individuality—this is seen by psychologists to be the growing problem. Dr. van den Berg says, "We are not ourselves; actually there is nothing we can call a 'self' anymore . . . we have as many selves as there are groups to which we belong." [92] He sees this as a sort of splintering of the psyche: "although a part of the personality always communicates, it is a different part each time; and a number of selves always remain out of communication." [93] In simple truth man does present a different self to every person, to every situation —he always has, always will, and this should not be turned into a psychic problem as religion and parenthood have been turned into problems. Psychology's whole concept of ego and superego needs revision.

Freud likened the ego to a rider, saying, "if he is not to be parted from his horse," he is often "obliged to guide it where it wants to go," and yet he saw ego in the role of a "guide for the id." [94] Nothing in psychology's explanation of ego or superego provides for man's direct correspondence with truth and joy complete—yet:

> . . . I have felt
> A presence that disturbs me with the joy
> Of elevated thoughts; a sense sublime
> Of something far more deeply interfused,
> Whose dwelling is the light of setting suns,
> And the round ocean and the living air,
> And the blue sky, and in the mind of man.[95]

Nor do psychology's concepts provide for what Dr. Alexander calls the "inner certainty of 'deathlessness.' "[96]

Man's consciousness is not expressed by an ego, but by an ego-group which includes an image that corresponds to each person he knows, sees, or thinks about. His Dr. Jekyll selves are haunted by his Mr. Hyde selves,[97] and these graduate the one into the other, standing but a step apart—but none of these selves are the man himself. Only as he tries to merge these ego-members into a Self-consistency, into a Group-ego, to replace Authority-Ego must his *identity* incorporate every degradation he has suffered, inflicted, witnessed, or read about. Attempting to be *oneself* by making of the ego-group a Group-ego causes the personality to reflect all that characterizes the group in society—no part of it is responsible for one's failure or misery, no part is wholly mature. It is because man's ego-group is a cluster of images of self and others that he may deal with his problem selves one by one, knowing that in truth Self is not differentiated as they are differentiated, is not limited as the best and worst of them are limited, is not to be identified by any one or all of them.

Today, man revolves in furious helplessness around psychologists' ideas about ego, superego, libido, complexes. He regurgitates both the inner and outer Group-ego offered by psychology, society, and theologies. In the words of De Kooning:

I don't know who I am, but I'm not THEM anymore.[98]

A governing authority, one central to man's being, appears to be necessary to him. Jesus teaches that this authority, which upholds social and moral law even as it transcends law's limitations, cannot be found in society nor in man's conscious domain where conscience operates. But such an authority is within each man: it is a certainty in being that accords with truth and turns consciousness to experience truth as it works in life. Upon this Authority's shoulders the government of one's life rests; in time it brings him to reap as he sows; it refuses much that consciousness accepts; it returns the forgotten errors the ego-group refuses to face; it will call itself only by its God-given name, "I."

Therefore, the more lost man's consciousness becomes, in the sands of humanity's ego-groups and Group-egos, the more his Authority-Ego leads him to hate his life in this world and any concept of himself or another that makes him a group-component or appendix or product even of his own family—thus, he must renounce any tie that binds him to Group-ego before he can become as One, himself, truth to his own being.[99]

"Israel," the consciousness outgrown from that which was born in

Eden, carried on in the ark, is a multitude of selves to which the Authority-Ego comes as saving grace—and "Israel's" salvation depends upon being freed of the bonds of Group-ego.

Historically, Judaism has suffered Group-ego. But Group-ego is found in all nationalities and races, expressing itself most vehemently in those most anti-Semitic. Group-ego was merely elaborated in Christianity, and was further elaborated in Nietzsche's concept of super-race, coming finally to rest in Karl Marx's mass-ego ideal wherein man in classless society must sacrifice his individuality to the State, to the super-ideology, rather than to the idea of the Chosen-race, super-religion, or super-race complex.

The Greeks and Romans suffered Group-ego. The Athenian was first a creature of the State, Athenian democracy his god, and the Roman followed in his footsteps. Therefore, both embraced ziggurat concepts, towers of Babel, the structure of their society replacing God. But in the first and "almost perfect democracy" there was no part "for women or foreigners or slaves . . ." [100] Euripides, the poet, had condemned slavery, calling it "That thing of evil," and "the Stoics denounced it." [101] But something other than slavery also worked to undermine Athenian civilization. The need of Athens was that each of her citizens take full responsibility; but in "the end, more than they wanted freedom, they wanted security, a comfortable life, and they lost all—security and comfort and freedom." [102]

Group-ego and responsibility are incompatible. Group-ego leads to the expression of parasitic consciousness.

Jesus saw that man is, first of all, in bondage to the sin and error he embraces—"Whosoever committeth sin is the servant of sin." [103] But He saw, too, that truth frees.

Truth, parent in man, will not forever allow him to embrace a false ideal. And truth, parent in man, leads the mortal parent to drive the child from parasitic bondage—both suffer the traumatic effects. But trauma also frees:

> When Pavlov's conditioned dogs were caged in a cellar that flooded one night, that single stressful exposure was so shaking that much of their conditioned learning was lost.[104]

Every human being, if he lives his normal span, suffers five traumatic events that serve to expand his consciousness and increase his need to know the truth of himself in being: the trauma of birth, of puberty, of recognizing himself to be cast out in solitary being, of losing his sexual competency, of anticipating the loss of his life. Thus, built into his nature are the stresses that periodically "flood the cellar" of his subconscious mind and free him of much of the "conditioned learning" society and Babel Tower builders have imposed upon him. Therefore, before death overtakes him, he is free of much of his spurious "conditioning."

Under hypnosis, a subject may regress in age to infancy, and then in rare cases presumably into past life. In the view of this study, the hypnotist is not then contacting a consciousness that has lived, died, and been reborn in the subconscious; he has broken through infant amnesia and is contacting an infant ego-sense symbolized in Noah's son, Ham. This ego-sense is "born" of past or "parent" consciousness and it has looked briefly upon the "body" of past or "parent" being; but it is not itself that past or "father" consciousness, and it has not yet itself experienced *death* or performed the "father" function in *rebirth of consciousness*. The secrets of these mysteries are buried in the psychic factor that Noah symbolizes which subsides in infancy and is beyond recall.

Chapter 5

ORIGINAL SIN AND SAVING GRACE

I

If one accepts the Noah legend as the "tell" describing the physical birth processes of man, placement of the story of the flood in the Genesis chain of legends *after* the Eden legend indicates that man has lived before, so that his physical birth bespeaks a re-creation of himself wherein a son-self takes the place of the father-self which subsides, as Noah does, although a part of the psyche may glimpse it. And placement of the Cain-Abel legend before the flood legend indicates that man has sinned in a prior expression of himself in conscious embodiment. The Noah legend indicates man is aware of his unclean forces.

Thus, man comes into new conscious embodiment bearing his own sin, "original" only in the sense that he, himself, committed it. His anxiety is that of an adult amnesia victim: he does not know what he has done, who he is, how he came to lose his prior consciousness, and if he presents himself to the authorities he must face the fact that he could have committed any crime, although in his new consciousness he is utterly innocent of it. Because man never recovers from infant amnesia, he fears to face his inner, knowing Authority. But the Noah legend indicates that man comes into each new birth to start life afresh with his clean forces represented sevenfold, although his unclean forces are still present in reproductive status.[1]

Together, the legends present the concept of reincarnation, or a creative process entailing rebirth into life. Dr. Alexander says, "if we accept the idea that the development of consciousness is the great purpose behind evolution, then the scrapping of each individual human mind at death of the physical body would be a most wasteful, tedious and unnecessary process."[2] He points out that: "At every stage in the development of the embryo, there is evidence that a phase of the mind directing the construction detaches itself from the processes and moves 'upstairs,' as it were, to initiate new construction on a higher level."[3] And this is what the

Authority-Ego appears to do also after birth is accomplished. As symbol of it, Jesus says:

> I go to prepare a place for you. . . . I will come again, and receive you unto myself; that where I am, there ye may be also.[4]

Jesus' acceptance of the principle of reincarnation is simple, final, and basically interwoven into His message—He says, "Ye must be born again."[5] If Jesus is true, this statement must be true as regards conscious rebirth in life and rebirth into life after death. He says:

> Except a man be born of water and of the Spirit, he cannot enter into the kingdom of God. That which is born of the flesh is flesh; and that which is born of the Spirit is spirit. Marvel not that I said unto thee, Ye must be born (or from above) again. The wind bloweth where it listeth, and thou hearest the sound thereof, but canst not tell whence it cometh, and whither it goeth: so is every one that is born of the Spirit.[6]

When Nicodemus asks, "How can these things be?" Jesus will not elaborate. He never allows the principle of rebirth to become involved in fantasy attending it—such as the transmigration concept of human soul entering animal flesh— or with the concept that the chain of births leads finally to escaping the world. To Nicodemus, Jesus simply says that eternal life is the goal.[7] Being reborn "from above" indicates a process to insure the growth and enrichment of consciousness or life through bringing to this domain the treasure of the *unconscious*. He says: "If I have told you earthly things, and ye believe not, how shall ye believe, if I tell you of heavenly things?"[8] The concept of rebirth into life is touched upon when Jesus says to the thief on the cross next to His, "Verily I say unto thee, To-day shalt thou be with me in paradise."[9] Paradise, Eden, is the womb of life as Scriptures depict it.

The concept of rebirth is also involved in this contradictory statement made by Jesus during His ministry:

> . . . for as the Father raises the dead and makes them live, so the Son makes anyone live whom he chooses. Indeed the Father passes judgment on no one; he has committed the judgment which determines life or death entirely to the Son, that all men may honour the Son as they honour the Father.[10]

Here, Jesus declares that the judgment of God on *man* is: life. The Father "makes them live." Later, He says, "And I know that [the Father's] commandment is life everlasting. . . ."[11] Yet, He says that the Son determines *who* shall live. How can the contradiction be reconciled?

The concept offered by this study is that the judgment of God is not to be made, but has been made, and that each person has been committed to eternal life. The only judgment God could in justice render is His own Self-judgment, for He is man's Creator. In justice, then, God cannot, does not judge man. He has committed man to life everlasting. This conviction has the confirming voice of Nicholas Berdyaev, who says, "Every man is made in the image of God, however indistinct that image may become, and every man is called to eternal life." [12]

Jesus indicates that the God-cell in man, his Authority-Ego, judges his own world of selves, "himself," or ego-group. Thus, Jesus says that the Son makes anyone live whom he chooses. The interpretation of these words offered by this study is that in the conscious domain man constantly creates images of others and refashions his own self-images. In sum, these images constitute his personality. Within the whole of him they are as the sands of the sea. Through rebirth, the Son within each person makes any one of these images live whom he chooses. That is, one's own Authority-Ego determines which of the faces that compose his personality are to be carried on in the *unconscious* domain and which are to return to life in the conscious domain.

Thus, only "vestiges" of former egos return to consciousness. Not all of the images of self and others in one's ego-group have loved and been loved—not all have erred, not all have learned. Those of the ego-group which have loved and been loved, those which have learned, those which have been tried and found true are of the "other fold" within. Those which have erred and those untried, ignorant, or found wanting are returned to consciousness to experience good and evil that they may become conscious of life as it operates in truth and reality. To those in the conscious domain, the superego ministers.

Man is laboring under the sum of history—his own and mankind's. The lusts of primeval times are but somewhat attenuated. Jesus perceived this. He, not Freud, introduced the murderous primeval man image, even as He presented the loving Father image, showing both sides of the coin of truth. As Jesus points to the primeval sin, He presents also the "I-Thou" relationship between ego-group and Authority-Ego—He is presenting universal psychological truth, "I seek not mine own glory . . ." in saying:

> Ye do the deeds of your father. Then they said to him, We be not born of fornication; we have one Father, even God. Jesus said unto them, If God were your Father, ye would love me: for I proceeded forth and came from God; neither came I of myself, but he sent me.

Why do ye not understand my speech? even because ye cannot hear my word. Ye are of your father the devil, and the lusts of your father ye will do: He was a murderer from the beginning, and abode not in the truth, because there is no truth in him. When he speaketh a lie, he speaketh of his own: for he is a liar, and the father of it.[13]

Here, Jesus takes man back to the first murderer, to the evasive Cain, traces of whose blood runs in the veins of Homo sapiens. But from whence did this blood come? Whatever man expresses or *is* must have its root in God, for if he received his being, his good, from the hand of God, so too he received from the same source, the only source, his evil.[14]

What makes of the murderer a liar, or vice versa, and how could such as this stem from God? The answer rests in the concept of The Absolute. Before creation was, God must be seen as The Absolute. The Absolute is now seen to be evil—in the words of Meir Ben-Horin:

> The twentieth century has seen the Absolute as the Terror. Henceforth the loyalties of enlightened mankind will go out to the religions that can help them to overcome the absolute and thus to achieve a fuller manifestation of the promise that inheres in existence, in intelligence and in love.[15]

The Cain and Abel drama presents the clue that in bringing creation as man knows it into being, the Absolute expended itself as such, having done with this evil by laying down its absolute power—which is to say, absolute power cannot now be expressed by man or God: Cain attempted to exercise ALL power, to express the absolute, to decree finality, but Abel's blood cried out from the ground, and in dealing with Cain, the Lord did not exercise ALL power, express the absolute, or decree finality. The question becomes: how does the absolute dispose of itself?

As to "The Absolute," Jesus' words appear to give this answer: God is not now absolute. God is now power thrice stated, or twice divided—The Absolute thereby becoming Father, Son, and Holy Spirit. The Son-energy is manifest. The Father-energy is unapparent. The Holy Spirit is transparent—is energy-as-such entirely spent in physical terms, as it yet remains in being, absolute unto itself only. In divesting Himself of His absolute power, God divested Himself of destructive potential, or the evil inherent in the absolute—*divested life of the power to express the absolute or to express power absolutely or finally*. Death, or the ultimate, is finished through God's laying down His absolute life and power, through His not-being in manifestation. Because death is finished in God's act, death *is not* finality for man—life *is*. That life can be absolutely destroyed is the lie, gives the lie to the murderer.

Through God's acts of creation, through His substance spent, He has established everlasting life vested in the unending, inexhaustible power of *one*, each as an only, "I," endowed with a full measure of the power, glory, and substance of life. But each one is committed to expend his one measure of destructive potential, inherent in absolute power from which he was made, even as God has expended His. And each one is committed to life everlasting, to exercise the constructive potential inherent in absolute power.

Man in image and likeness of God, *a priori*, is now *a* power absolute unto himself only, but in terms of *one*, "I," enfolding a measure of ALL, or unity. Man's *unconscious*, not manifest in life, is seat of the Father living in his being to which he returns in death and through which he is returned to life. But the Father living in man's being does not mean that the sum of mankind spells God. Creation itself, all manifestation as well as all unmanifest, is needed to spell God.

But man is made of all the powers of God, and because the Absolute, God, *a priori*, destroyed Himself-as-Absolute in giving of His life to man after He had brought forth His creation, man inherits a tendency toward self-destruction. This is to say, he expresses the need to exercise and know this God-power. Although he clings to life fiercely, the instinct to survive is by no means unopposed in him. Day after day he shows himself willing to risk death for reasons great and small. The suicide rate speaks for itself. Death is the absolute man expresses, but something within tells him that he cannot express death absolutely because life persists on the other side of this veil.

Because part of the absolute power of which man was made is evil, man must express his evil, even as God has expressed His evil so that only good, the constructive potential, remains in His being. But man cannot express the whole of his destructive potential in one act because this would be an absolute expression of power, entailing the absolute destruction of the manifest energy which he is. Evil-doing is the now limited aspect of absolute power man expresses. This is to say, he cannot express evil absolutely, finally, and thus destroy it—in parable, Jesus tells him this.[16] It would appear, then, that man must reconcile, recast, or regenerate his evil into something of value in life, laying down evil's destructive potential a measure at a time in each of the many lives he lives.

The world outgrown from Eden is any man's. It is the conscious domain which is peopled with countless images of oneself and others, images born of one's experience with them. Thus, within this domain man lives a world of lives, and each day that passes leaves a grave in the subconscious, *a* self-of-himself has expired. The "end of the world," which overtakes the many living images in the conscious domain, is subjective; it comes for any person at the day of his death. Jesus says:

> . . . the hour is coming, in which all that are in the graves shall hear his voice, And shall come forth; they that have done good, unto the resurrection of life; and they that have done evil, unto the resurrection of damnation.[17]

Jesus does not say, "shall hear MY voice." He says, "shall hear his voice," and thus He is speaking as symbol of the Son in man. His words present the concept that those of the ego-group in bondage to sin and error are returned to consciousness unto the resurrection of damnation in this domain until they spend themselves of their destructive potential and grasp truth as it works in life. Thus, the "lusts of your father ye will do." But in the process truth disciplines—it does not destroy. In the legend God does not destroy Cain. ALL that is given man is precious—even his evil. Nothing of IT is to be lost. The resurrection of good AND evil in man presages the build up of something of value to be realized in time to come as evil's destructive potential is spent.

Jesus says that the Son in man is the Self-factor that will lead him to reap in kind his sin and error. Thus, each punishes himself. But Jesus proclaims also that the power to forgive is vested in the Son, and that one's return on the bread he casts upon life's waters is hundred-fold. He saw that in reality a man cannot abuse a brother-being without in the same measure abusing himself; and that he cannot forgive a brother-being without forgiving himself a like measure of the evil he has done. As though the poet senses this, Goethe writes in *Iphigenia:*

> Life teaches us
> To be less strict with others and ourselves:
> Thou'lt learn the lesson, too.

Jesus saw that man is not chained to the sin of the past or present, prone or doomed to repeat his sins because he is bound to the wheel of rebirth; He saw that what a man has gained in *knowing*, in knowledge of good and evil, he has gained for eternity. In the words of the Psalmist, the Lord "will not suffer thy foot to be moved . . ." and he "shall preserve thy going out and thy coming in from this time forth, and even for evermore." [18] This is to say, Jesus saw that man is committed to life everlasting and thus he cannot escape it. But He saw, too, that life is becoming an ever more conscious state of being and that in time the swinging of the pendulum between life and death will move as evenly as breathing, with no loss of consciousness or sense of dying attendant upon it, that death and rebirth will be accomplished with the ease of laying down and picking up one's life again in sleep and waking.

Jesus says God is love. In the *unconscious*, the kingdom of God within, love enfolds both the tried and the true, the untried and the untrue, enfolds ALL that man is and ALL that life is. "Ye" of the conscious domain express the unattenuated lusts of prime evil which leads men to abuse themselves even as they abuse their brothers. In effect, Jesus says to the men confronting Him that only love can draw one man to another and give understanding, each of the other, and that love is not parent of the consciousness they are then expressing. Evil fathers it. But His words—"your father, the devil"—indicate that man's quota of evil is part of his very-being, and they also return one to primeval times and to Freud's concept of the "gigantic one," murdered and eaten, this act sowing the seed from which in time religion sprang.

II

Evidence that Freud's "gigantic person" did exist, and that others like him followed, may be seen in the persisting Messianic dream which indicates race memory of such towering figures—but this study postulates that the first "gigantic one" was not a cruel lust-ridden father: he was primordial *truth bearer*. He and those like him, who came after, must have attempted to reveal the nature of being that they had realized and felt compelled to express. In stating man's relationship to God to be vested only in the word, "I," they became object of deity, initiating in man's consciousness the idea of deathlessness which could have its seed in fetal experience, knowledge of this being inaccessible save through the *unconscious*. Such prototype must speak of being born again, of sowing and reaping in kind, of destruction of evil vested in himself. Such a man always brought the sword that cut the cord of infantile consciousness, posing himself an irreconcilable threat to those enjoying parasitic existence. If he penetrated their strongholds too deeply, he suffered their abuse.

The realization that prompted such men to speak with Messianic conviction must have been born of their ability to unlock the *unconscious*. They must also have had extraordinary extrasensory perception, and the ability to control self and others through the hypnotic means. The miraculous always surrounds them. How such extraordinary psychic ability happened to be released in man to give rise to the first "gigantic one" is a lost secret, but any man possesses the capacity if it can be released. This is evidenced in such cases as those of Peter Hurkos and "Hadad"—both quite ordinary men until a traumatic physical experience led to their expression of incredible psychic ability.[19] Thus, a blow from his companion's club may have produced the first "Messiah." Or meditation and control of body and mind may also have produced extraordinary psychic power, as is indicated by the great mystics of Asia. The capacity is there, apparently in every man, albeit the ability to use it may vary from not at all up to Jesus' ability to employ it to the full. Demonstrations of extrasensory perception and of healing under hypnosis must have implanted in race consciousness the concept of the supranatural being.

Homo sapiens has traveled a long way from the point in his evolution when language took over the job of communication and his psychic powers were dispersed, else Messiahs would not appear to be such "gigantic" figures as every sacred literature describes them. The number of such figures attests that time and again society has had experience of men who grasp the whole truth of life and both state and show man's power and glory, just as long ago one "gigantic person" did and thus men wish to emulate him. But true Messiah must restore to man himself the power and glory of life, freeing him in the last reaches of being from the authority of priesthood, parent, or sovereign—from all save self-governing law and the necessity to seek truth within himself.

Freud is no doubt correct in saying primeval man murdered the "gigantic one" who first said "I" am author of your being—challenging temporal authority however it was stated. And Freud is also correct in saying man repeated the primordial crime in crucifying Jesus, for the primordial crime was brother murder. In the view of this study, Jesus allowed this in order that the crime would be plainly restated for all humankind to see—the crime is against brother-being, not parent-being, or God. And He allowed it that through His death drama He could reveal again a truth seen in humanity's legends: the King's image coinciding with the Messianic concept men hold must be destroyed in order that the image of man, each monarch of a realm of his own, may rise. This is to say, as long as man fastens his mind upon any authoritarian concept, even Babel Tower building, seeing such as this to be saving grace, he will fail to seek the governing authority within himself. In society today, Kings are taking the turn Jesus gave the concept: he who would be highest is he who must be willing to spend his life in being servant to, not master of, all people.

The concept of Messiah as absolute authority in the social realm, be it an earthly or heavenly society Messiah masters, was destroyed by Jesus. When Peter posed to Jesus the worldly view of the Christ, He said, "Get thee behind me, Satan . . ." [20] In His temptation, the devil offers Him "all the kingdoms of the world"— but this He spurns.[21] After Him, the Messianic concept must be a house divided.

Jesus saw that the man who plays the role of absolute authority, or God, *a priori*, plays the same role as the man who plays Satan, for both roles veil a grasp for power. When accused by the Pharisees of casting out devils by the prince of devils,[22] He does not deny this, but answers, "And if I by Be-el-ez-bub cast out devils, by whom do your children cast them out?" Then, having spoken of the house divided if Satan casts out Satan, He adds, "But if I cast out devils by the Spirit of God, then the kingdom of God is come unto you." Jesus says *if*. He will not admit to playing either the role of the devil or of God, saying on another occasion, "Why callest thou me good? there is none good but one, that is, God." [23]

Jesus recognized that both the Satanic and Messianic concepts conceal the will to express absolute power, and that the truth bearer who loses himself in his own revelation, believing himself to be or allowing himself to become deity, poses such threat as the sanity or logic associated with Satan could never pose. He showed in His drama that the man who allows himself to be called the Son of God, God in the flesh, or Messiah, will not be tolerated, that Judaism would not in truth tolerate any *man's* fulfillment of prophecies regarding the Christ as these are set forth in the Scriptures. Judaism could not in Jesus' day, nor can it now, tolerate its own Messianic concept, if actualized, any more than Christianity can tolerate the Pauline elaboration of it.

Jesus refused to play either the role of God or of the devil. He was divinely human, and so must have been that first "gigantic one" who could not extricate himself from the role of God, intolerable, and thus was murdered only to return again and again, a promise and reminder in man's mind, as parent truth in Homo sapiens led others to speak the same words, "Ani hu." These are the words truth bearer must speak, but in Thomas Troward's words, Jesus came: ". . . not to proclaim Himself, but Man; not to tell us of His Own Divinity separating Him from the race and making Him the Great Exception, but to tell us of *our* Divinity and to show in Himself the Great Example of the I AM reaching its full personal expression in Man." [24]

III

In the view of this study, Freud is correct in saying that men murdered and then partook of the body of that first "gigantic one," for truth bearer must express himself in terms of "I" and in terms of life everlasting resting in the flesh and blood of God, God's *life*, extended into "me, myself," so that the urge to immortality could be satisfied as man partook of that life and body.

The flesh any man wears in this world is the flesh of God, is God extended into living matter, and to live man must partake of that which is or has been living. If truth speaks the same words through any truth bearer, the first "gigantic one" must have invited his murder and the partaking of his body—for "I" must also have said through his voice:

> I am that bread of life. . . . This is the bread which cometh down from heaven, that a man may eat thereof, and not die. I am the living bread which came down from heaven: if any man eat of this bread, he shall live for ever: and the bread that I will give is my flesh, which I will give for the life of the world. . . . Verily, verily, I say unto you, Except ye eat the flesh of the Son of man, and drink his blood, ye have no life in you. . . . As the living Father hath sent me, and I live by the Father; so he that eateth me, even he shall live by me. . . .[25]

Jesus speaks these words, then asks, "Doth this offend you? What and if ye shall see the Son of man ascend up where he was before? It is the Spirit that quickeneth; the flesh profiteth nothing: the words that I speak unto you, they are spirit and they are life."[26] Here, He makes plain that His strange words are not to be taken literally—that He is *sacrament* only in the sense that this word means *token* or symbol of the truth He tries to convey.

The profound mystery of life, the mystery of *sustaining* it, is wrapped up in these words and in the sacramental, symbolic enactment of them at the last supper: "Take, eat; this [bread] is my body. And he took the cup, and gave thanks, and gave it to them, saying, Drink ye all of it; For this is my blood of the new testament, which is shed for many for the remission of sins."[27]

In the view of this study, Jesus spoke profound biological truth. To do so, He unlocked His *unconscious* and let the voice of life itself, "I," speak freely through Him. His words did offend, still offend. But "doth this offend you?"—life cannot exist without something that is extracted from living or once-living tissue. That something is an enzyme.

As symbol of primordial life, giving voice to that by which all things were made, Jesus' strange words appear to enfold what is today called *biochemical* information—and from this point of view, the whole story of the Son of man as Jesus depicted it may be seen as a *parable* revealing the life of the cell. To reveal life's deepest secrets is incumbent upon truth bearer:

> That it might be fulfilled which was spoken by the prophet, saying, I will open my mouth in parables; I will utter things which have been kept secret from the foundation of the world.[28]

The psychic operation between Father, Son, and the world of man as Jesus described and depicted it parallels the biochemists' description of DNA and messenger-RNA operating in a cell. The biochemical operation may reflect the psychic operation and vice versa. Isaac Asimov does not draw the parallel between Jesus' life and the life of the cell, but he tells the fascinating story of the cell in *The Genetic Code*.[29]

One may see the cell's DNA as Father, and the cell's messenger-RNA as Son of man, which has partaken of the "life" of the Father, DNA, and is *sent* into the world of the cytoplasm to reveal the Father's, or DNA's, message. This world is a complex system containing thousands of small bodies of various sizes, shapes, and functions; these bodies are called Mitochondria and are the "powerhouses" of the cell; they may be compared to the ego-group, "Israel." But these "bodies" are not the ones messenger-RNA must impress with the Father's, DNA's, doctrine if the cell is to have life or the know-how to produce the substance it must have. In the cell, there are smaller "particulates" containing RNA; these are called Microsomes and they are the protein factories; they may be likened to the subconscious. In addition, there are tiny particles densely distributed on the network of membranes associated with the microsomal fraction in the cell; they are known as Ribosomes and may be likened to the superego or the disciples because they contain just about all of the RNA, which may be likened to "truth." But the ribosomal-RNA does not carry the genetic code; ribosomal-RNA is something like a "key-blank" which can be ground to fit any lock. Upon this "key-blank" the messenger-RNA, sometimes called template-RNA, impresses DNA's message, giving ribosomal-RNA the "keys," the secrets, of the "kingdom within," the nucleus, seat of DNA, Father.

In the world of cytoplasm the life of the Son, messenger-RNA, is short.

Once the ribosomal-RNA is "keyed in," the messenger-RNA is quickly broken down into individual nucleotides, which are put to a variety of uses in the cell. Thus, as the Son, messenger-RNA, completes its work, its "flesh and blood," or body, is given for the life of the world of cytoplasm.

In the cell, there is a "transfer" or "missionary" job to be done. This work is accomplished by small fragments of RNA, fragments so small as to be freely soluble in the cell. These are often referred to as transfer-RNA. There are a number of varieties of transfer-RNA, and each will attach itself to one particular activated amino acid and to no other: "Let us suppose that a particular variety of transfer-RNA will attach itself to activated histidine and to that alone. The transfer-RNA will then transfer the activated histidine to the messenger-RNA. . . . It will not, however, transfer to just any point on the messenger-RNA, but only to one specific point." [30] In parallel, one might say that each factor of the superego can transmit only a portion of the truth, and thus brings only its "understanding" to be "attached" to the Son, messenger-RNA, so that many prophets and apostles are necessarily involved in the whole story that the Son, sent into the world, must reveal unto it.

The world of the cytoplasm can see the Father, DNA, only in the Son, in messenger-RNA, which is somehow sent from the nucleus to give itself to "key-in" the "truth-blanks" in order that the world of the cytoplasm may partake of the Father's word and the Son's body, and thereby live. The Father, DNA, does not leave the nucleus; the "doctrine" of the messenger-RNA is not its own; it is the doctrine of the DNA that sends it. Whatever the message it gives, its judgment is true, for it gives DNA's judgment as to the particular imprint (of the particular substance) to be impressed upon the ribosomal-RNA.

In the cell, the message is expressed in a "chemical language," which may now be the only "language" left to the Father, for to the Son, man, is given the power of the word. The "chemical words" of DNA brought by messenger-RNA are life to the cells. Jesus indicates that the words of truth, sounding from the depths in man and voiced through his Authority-Ego, are life to consciousness. As it partakes of them it is partaking of that which gives it eternal being, for truth and love are the "us" of God, eternal. Thus, He says, "the words that I speak unto you, they are spirit and they are life." He insists that the spirit quickens the flesh, and thus that life itself is a nonmaterial force.

Hans Driesch came finally to believe that the edifice biochemists build is a Babel Tower; he warned that in addition to the master-plan incorporated in DNA and RNA there had to be the workman. Driesch insisted that "it is life itself, a nonmaterial force . . . that produces order and form." [31] Ruth Moore writes that this great scientist "turned increasingly to the mystical, and ultimately became deeply interested in parapsychology . . . firm in the conviction that there are explanations which go beyond the senses and beyond the mechanics of physics and chemistry. . . ." [32]

Erwin Schrödinger points out that a living organism feeds upon "negative entropy . . . to compensate the entropy increase it produces by living . . . ." and he says that living matter "while not eluding the 'laws of physics' as established up to date, is likely to involve 'other laws of physics' hitherto unknown, which, however, once they have been revealed, will form just as integral a part of this science as the former." [33]

In blood, the organic and inorganic realms are yoked. Hemoglobin, the blood protein, "can be split into two substances, *heme* and *globin*. While the latter is a simple protein, the former is not protein at all, but an iron-containing substance, with none of the properties ordinarily associated with protein. In hemoglobin, this nonprotein portion is tightly joined to the protein. Hemoglobin is, therefore, a *conjugated protein*. . . ." [34] Poetically speaking, at some point in creation, prime "stuff" that was iron-substance must command prime "stuff" that was simple protein to "partake of my substance" (or vice versa) in order to have *life*, in order for hemoglobin to be.

The word *protein* means: of first importance. Jesus' teaching points to man's psychic makeup that parallels the makeup of blood. This is to say, God is no longer a "simple protein," God is now a "conjugated protein" in the enjoinment of Father and Son, the Holy Spirit the matrix in which they have their being. Jesus' blood is shed, is given, that a new *testament*, a new statement, of this truth may come into being: God as *The Absolute* is no more, Father and Son are as a one-to-one correspondence.

Consider that the real problem of the truth bearer who has realized hidden, inner working and would share it, is how to transmit the information. Before the second or third century B.C., a man devised a symbol to convey his realization that life is involved in a coil and coiling action, which he named *Kundalini*, the Serpent Power lying at the base of the spine. Did he see in his mind's eye "something" akin to DNA, the mysterious "coil of life" that seems to be at once the mind and matter of flesh? The symbol, *Kundalini*, has inspired the Yogi to fantastic manipulations of the flesh. But Jesus said, in effect, that manipulations of the body are futile, for the flesh itself "profiteth nothing."

The Genesis legend also incorporates the symbol of serpent power at the base of the "tree" of life that invites man to partake of the fruit of the tree of knowledge of good and evil, of *sentient* being, saying "ye surely shall not die." This mysterious drama has come to be identified with "original sin," which in turn has come to be identified with life partaking of life from cell to amoeba and onward. In Jesus' words, nothing that enters a man defiles him. It is not what he eats, but the wastes of the body and the lusts of the heart that defile him.[35]

Jesus' offensive words, inviting man to partake of His body, relieve humankind of the idea that "original sin" rests with life partaking of that which is or has been living, because in His words one sees that Life commands the living to partake of it. The need to partake of life in order to live led to error; but cannibalistic men must be seen as fetal, infantile expressions of the mind that is to become man. Life has weaned them. Now, man is child. Life has taught him not to eat human flesh, but to partake instead of the flesh of God that surrounds him in whatever else is living matter.

Although Jesus saw that life itself is spirit, He saw that spirit is wedded to material being: in the beginning life separated itself from its "stuff" and separated its "stuff" into organic and inorganic matter, wed these two "stuffs" in blood, wed itself to consciousness in being, wed consciousness in being to flesh, separated this consciousness in flesh into man and woman, wed their consciousness in flesh to bring forth love in being in flesh in life. This is to say, Jesus turns the mind to consider the nature of wedded life "in the beginning" as given in the Scripture to which He wed His work.

The devil is associated always with the "serpent power." Jesus' offensive words, "your father, the devil," indicate that a "serpent power" fathers the flesh of man and its lusts, which is to say, man is involved with a powerful material factor that is resurrected in him generation after generation. (In 1928, scientists learned that a certain "coil" could be resurrected: when a batch of dead "S" bacteria were added to living "R" bacteria, the DNA of the dead "S" type somehow took over the "R" bacteria converting them to living "S" type.) [36] Jung observed that the devil is seen to be lord of matter.[37] Evil is said to be of Satan's domain which is represented as eternally burning; in this regard evil coincides with matter's oxidizing. Satan is somehow a discrete play of energy, and so is matter. God has cast Satan, evil, out of His realm; God, good, remains as spirit only, spirit with dominion over evil, matter.

But by definition the word *good* is also deeply if not completely *involved* in the material realm. Good and evil are so intermingled in creation they appear to be that which the Creator has joined, both necessary to life in manifestation. Jesus says that God is love. Love does not, apparently will not or cannot, do away with evil. Evil, too, is resurrected. Why?

Aniela Jaffé points out that Lucifer, the devil, means "light-bringer,"[38] and light is primordial energy—but Lucifer is not *himself the light he brings*. It must be that if "your father, the devil" is resurrected in man causing him to express evil, this expression brings in its wake a necessary enlightenment. If man's evil is wed to his very-being, his good, life must be recasting his evil into a measure of "something" indispensable to him, and this "something" must be flesh over which consciousness has full dominion: *flesh man can in truth call his own and keep*. To have it, man must have knowledge of evil, of matter itself, and he must have dominion over evil. That is, he must learn to live without corrupting his flesh and abusing life itself in evil doing; he must complete the task begun in Eden, which is to acquire knowledge of good *and* evil.

There is a strange twist in the Eden legend that bears examination. Eve speaks of *the* tree in the midst of the garden, but earlier in the legend this "plant" is described as *two* trees: the tree of life and the tree of knowledge of good and evil. Not until *after* Adam and Eve had partaken of the tree of knowledge of good and evil is man driven from the garden, lest he partake also of the tree of life and live forever.[39] Why was deathlessness then a danger? For life to express itself eternally in sentient flesh that could feel the extremes of pain and want, and in consciousness that could suffer intolerable boredom as want is surfeited, is a curse beyond the imagination of man. But had man partaken first of the tree of life, life must express itself eternally in a form that could not know love or a reason for being. Thus, the "fruit to be desired" was the fruit of *knowing*, so that this fruit was forbidden, thereby making it attractive.

Once man had partaken of the fruit of knowing, consciousness stood naked, until clothed in the flesh of God, in the "skins" of the animal world, and in this flesh the pain of knowing good and evil, the pain of knowing love, is borne. To know love, man must know pain. Love incorporates a degree of *agonia*. Pain, *patheia*, tends to be pathological. But pain *agonia*, or the word *agony* incorporates in its meaning: contest, celebration, violent striving, sudden delight—it involves a "wrestling" that blesses, an intensification of meaningful being that allows it to be joyfully accepted. *Patheia* is of the flesh; *agonia* is of the spirit. The spirit wears the yoke of the flesh that harnesses it to the organic and the inorganic realms in blood: hemoglobin. In terms of the Yogis' symbol, *Kundalini* is to lead to, or to be realized in, divine union of spiritual and physical realms.

The fruit of the tree of life that would give man imperishable flesh could not be partaken of, after knowledge of good and evil had been incorporated in his consciousness and being, until life had taught him the secret of these opposing forces and had attenuated through many generations the *virulence of both*. For the secret of good and evil, insofar as human experience can determine it, appears to be that good turns into evil in the maximum expression of good, and evil turns into good in the minimum expression of its force. For example, utter surfeit that gives rise to loss of appetite or desire is little if any better than hunger or extreme want. Want (evil) must be attenuated so that it cannot express beyond periodic and diversified desire; surcease from want (good) must be attenuated so that it cannot express beyond periodic and diversified satisfaction. Both good and evil must be recast in life to make everlasting life endurable and to be desired.

Up through the strange, twisted tree of knowledge that turns good to evil, and evil to good, man must grow, led by the spirit of attraction first to the one idea and then to the other, to become neither good nor evil, but divinely human—as love is. Although love and life may be corrupted as lust expresses itself, though one's "sins be as scarlet," love's returning washes them "white as snow." [40]

In rebirth, one partakes of love's spirit and of the flesh of brother beings in order that he may come into life again. He is reclothed in the flesh of God, virgin flesh, that he may live again to learn the cost of evil doing and through learning, be redeemed. In death the Authority-Ego divests man of his corrupted garment: it is this psychic factor that sheds one's blood for the remission of the many sins of his ego-group; it is this factor that determines life or death, for one may lose consciousness and sanity, but this does not mean he loses his *life* which is vested in the power of the word, "I," the Authority-Ego within him. Love itself, which is his Authority-Ego, resurrects and holds inviolate in the id those of the ego-group whose own expression of love has redeemed them; and love resurrects also those that must live again unto the resurrection of damnation until their forces of good and evil are recast into a nonmaterial responsive factor that will prevent abusive exercise of power, and into the *pure or purified evil* that matter in itself must be seen to be; and in each rebirth love brings to life something of its whole being that has yet to partake of the tree of *knowing*.

Thus, into a new world of being, the Authority-Ego brings its love of life, the ego-group restated: "He was in the world, and the world was made by him, and the world knew him not." [41] In time, as consciousness comes to the ego-group, the voice of worldly experience is heard: conscience sounds its note from one's subconscious depths. And then, the superego is formed of that element in the id that is responsive to truth and can carry a word of it to the world, as the Authority-Ego "elects" them, giving to these the "keys" to the kingdom within. Through the superego, love speaks, and makes its presence felt, in:

> . . . that blessed mood,
> In which the burthen of the mystery,
> In which the heavy and the weary weight
> Of all this unintelligible world,
> Is lightened:—that serene and blessed mood,
> In which the affections gently lead us on,—
> Until, the breath of this corporeal frame
> And even the motion of our human blood
> Almost suspended, we are laid asleep
> In body, and become a living soul . . . [42]

Why must man bear the burden of the mystery of this unintelligible world? Why cannot God, love, simply and completely reveal Himself and the nature of man's being?

By giving His power, the power of the word, to man, God destroyed His absolute power to reveal Himself and the secrets of creation. But before man appeared on the scene, the secrets had been told in mammon —in the temporal—which *reflects* them oppositely and truly, as though in a mirror, itself material, a form that is *real* is seen, albeit its "mirror-image" is not its reality in being. Thus, truth-bearer must make unto himself a friend of mammon, "unrighteous" as mammon is,[43] and he must reveal the working of the flesh, offensive and error-provoking though his words may be.

Mammon is the mirror, and perforce the mirror lies—for it, itself, is not what it reflects in its being or as its being. God, First Cause, love, life itself, is not matter as revealed in mammon; God, First Cause, love, life itself, is revealed through mammon's examination to be "spirit," or a type of "energy" unknown and unknowable in physical terms. In *Man: The Bridge Between Two Worlds,* Winkler quotes Herbert Dingle: "*All* observable physical knowledge now appears to be statistical, so that the 'real' causal world lying behind it turns out to be completely unknown. Secondly it is not only unknown, but unknowable." [44] The reality underlying the world of appearances cannot be reduced to physical terms, it is only indirectly knowable as reflected in mammon's mirror, and as it is intuitively experienced by man. Thus, "the words I speak unto you, they are spirit and they are life."

But in mammon's mirror, in evil, or in pure matter, or in life's temporal history with all its evil-doing, the image of good and its working may be beheld. This is to say, there is evidence that life is building into man a factor that will in time deliver him from evil without robbing him of its desirable aspects, and that this factor is in truth the saving grace of life.

IV

In man's struggle with good and evil, enjoining them in his every battle, he has reaped the reward of finding the key to all but unlimited power in the material realm. But this will be of no profit to him unless he also achieves self-dominion and self-control such as will prohibit his doing evil, or himself reaping its destructive force—and he must achieve this in such a way that he, himself, does not become mere "vegetable," living a life that has lost its spice, satisfactions, and meaning. Can he hope to achieve this? How might it come about universally?

Does controlled fusion of nuclei cast a clue—which is to say, is there a word to describe a psychological reaction in which passion is both loosened and controlled? Consider the word *empathy*. Ludwig Binswanger sees that it depends upon the possibility or impossibility of understanding —that it costs more, means more, than sympathy—that it is as yet beyond definition:

> In the case of "empathy" . . . we would have to examine to what degree it is a phenomenon of *warmth* . . . or a vocal or *sound* phenomenon, as when the poet Hoelderlin writes to his mother that there could not be a sound alive in her soul with which his soul would not chime in; or a phenomenon of *touch*, as when we say, "your sorrow, your joy touches me"; or a phenomenon of *sharing*, as expressed by Diotima in Hoelderlin's *Hyperion*—"He who understands you must share your greatness and your desperation"; or a phenomenon of *participation*, as in the saying, "I partake of your grief"; or, lastly, a phenomenon of *"identification,"* as when we say, "I would have done the same in your place" (in contrast to, "I don't understand how you could act that way.") All these modes of expression refer to certain phenomenal, intentional, and preintentional modes of being-together . . . and co-being . . . which would have first to be analyzed before the total phenomenon of empathy could be made comprehensive and clarifiable.[45]

When empathy exists, one experiences in his own being what is happening to another and understands that another suffers whatever is happening to oneself. Empathy is direct, involuntary. It cannot be vicariously expressed because it is borne from out the boundless deeps of a man and, to borrow words from Alfred Lord Tennyson, rises, "too full for sound or foam, but such a tide as moving seems asleep," [46] and with certainty "turns again home" whatever one does or witnesses.

Automatically, empathy turns eyes, mind, heart, and hand away from suffering, away from abuse in any of its outrages or subtleties—*unless* one will endure an enjoining upon himself of the pain he beholds that makes him re-experience all he himself has known of pain. In this sense his empathy makes of him a "medium," one who can experience another's pain. And when true empathy beholds love, happiness, fulfillment, triumph, it calls forth in the person expressing the empathy all he has known of these satisfactions—he re-experiences. This is to say, there is nothing vicarious about empathy and the reactions it produces.

Because empathy is begotten only of the wholeness of experiencing both the good and evil involved in any decision, situation, or act, it exerts an incomprehensible power—which is to say, unconsciously it is expressed and it cannot be consciously called into action. Because it is an unconsciously made automatic response, through it man gains freedom from having to make a choice between what appears to be good and what appears to be evil, for his response is both unconsciously tempered and in accord with the reality of the situation. Huxley says:

> The fullest freedom is the expression of an inner compulsion of our being, of a choice which we have come to feel as inevitably necessary . . . In general, once we manage to "see things steadily and see them whole," the choice is made for us.[47]

The effect of empathy and its meaning to life may be likened to Tao: "Tao is obscured when you fix your eye on little segments of existence only . . ." but when Tao is grasped universally, "Without law or compulsion men [will] dwell in harmony." [48] In individual terms, empathy is realizing in one's own being the Golden Rule. Empathy is Jesus' new commandment as an act in one's own soul—love one another, love the Lord your God with your whole mind, heart, and soul, and your neighbor as yourself. Only through empathy is it possible to step into another's shoes without displacing him or foisting oneself upon him or losing one's own precious identity; empathy not only makes this possible, it makes it mandatory.

When through experience all mankind has evolved complete empathy, sin will no longer be possible, for man's empathy will cause him to instinctively withdraw his mind and hand from abuse of another—his understanding will not permit him to err, for he will pay sin's wage in his own being before he commits it.

Empathy in man brings its joy or sorrow—enriches or takes its toll of him *now*, as *now* flowers into the present and plants the field of the future in reaping the harvest of past planting. Love's eternal reward and punishment is given before it is grasped—*now*. Upon that infinitely small point between the past and the future that cannot be captured or measured eternity rests, for both *now* and eternity are beyond the grasp of consciousness. Eternal punishment of sin rests with empathy, which makes a man recoil with horror at the evil he has done when he comes to understand it in his being, and thereafter he forever recoils with pain at the prospect of repeating this evil, recoils *now* as it arises in the mind to do this evil again.

Empathy is saving grace to man—it frees his past, frees his future. It is acting *now* in his midst. Homo sapiens is an empathetic "animal." He is no mistake on the part of evolution. Jesus' words say to the belabored man of the twentieth century who has come to doubt nature's wisdom in evolving his species: there is the living voice of truth, life, and love within you, and as you begin to express its power, glory, and empathy, it will say unto you, "This is my beloved Son, in whom I am well pleased." [49]

As one looks at literary expression against the background of history—sees it steadily and sees it whole—an increasing empathy appears to be guiding the pen of man, slowly reshaping the course of his thought. Empathy redefines and recasts the classic roles of Satan and Messiah—too many men have played devil and God not to know that both parts taste alike. Both pretensions have been so thoroughly dissected and held up to such obloquy that both have been all but worked to death and ridiculed from the stage. Samuel Miller asks: "Can [a Christian] recall heaven and hell to a people who have laughed them out of existence?" [50] Out of man's struggle to describe life's good and evil has come this reward, this divinely human attribute: *laughter*, which Meister Eckhart projected to be the impetus that brought man into being—in *The Fate of Man*, Crane Brinton quotes him: "When God laughs at the soul and the soul laughs back at God, the persons of the Trinity are begotten." [51] There is no deeper mystery than laughter. Is it lust innocently expressed? Is it passion so sublimely warm that tears must cool it, do cool it? In the view of this study, laughter is an expression of empathy. Laughter comes as saving grace in a host of situations. But ask the psychologist what laughter is and he will say: "Wit is related to aggression, hostility, and sadism; humor is related to depression, narcissism, and masochism. Wit finds its psychomotor expression in laughter; humor, in the smile. . . . Laughter occurs when libido is released from repressed aggression." [52] According to Dr. Martin Grotjahn, comedy derives from a disguised Oedipus impulse or a veiled exhibition of penis or castrated male, and a murderous desire is hidden in laughter, which affords a tempory release from devastating hostility.

Jesus did not laugh—did not smile so far as the record is concerned. The Gospel of St. John states that Jesus knew "what was in man." [53] Thus, He would have known what prompts laughter and the mystery of why He did not laugh is resolved. Jesus wept. Tears are near to laughter, are as deep a mystery.

Although Jesus did not laugh, He offered that which has come to be identified with humor: salt. He said, "Salt is good . . ." and, "Let there be 'salt between you' . . ." but let there be also humanity between men, for what good the salt if it has lost its savor? [54] Jesus calls God love and good; He calls salt good; it must follow that aggression gentled through humor constitutes an essential ingredient of love, and that hostility will in time lose itself in laughter.

Since, basically, salt is that which preserves and purifies—a corrective—the concept is posed that humor serves this need. Salted has also come to mean "immune against a contagious disease, because of having recovered from it." [55] Jesus said, "every one shall be salted with fire, and every sacrifice shall be salted with salt." [56] These words give promise that man shall become immune to that which corrupts and that humor is playing a redeeming role in life.

Jesus could not laugh; He could not risk that a fragment of the profound paradoxes He posed would be taken in jest. But the art of life—seen as an appreciative awareness and participation in it—was practiced by Him.

No theology, acting on command of or by the example Jesus set, may prescribe a stern approach to life, prohibiting eating and drinking of any food or liquid except on the ground that it is offensive to the one partaking of it; what offends one must be cast out of his life, but nothing that enters a man defiles him.[57] Jesus was called glutton and drunkard. He did not deny that He ate and drank as He chose—He stated that wisdom vindicates ascetic or nonascetic practices:

> For John the Baptist has come, eating no bread and drinking no wine, and you say, "He has a devil"; the Son of man has come eating and

drinking, and you say, "Here is a glutton and a drunkard, a friend of taxgatherers and sinners!" Nevertheless, Wisdom is vindicated by all her children.[58]

Jesus provided wine at the wedding in Cana. Does His mysterious refusal of wine at the last supper provide the basis for a doctrine of abstinence—if so, making of Jesus a man reformed at the door of death? The teaching and practice of Jesus, however, does not invite drunkenness or gluttony. He teaches that there is nothing in life that cannot be used to further its joy and abundance when man has learned to control himself.

Barrett points out that Kierkegaard's philosophy was based upon realization of the richness, not the meanness, of life.[59] But the richness of life must be leavened, and Jesus says the working or coming of the kingdom of God is leavening it. He saw that men must grasp the art of play:

> To what then shall I compare the men of this generation? What are they like? Like children sitting in the marketplace and calling to one another, "We piped to you and you would not dance, we lamented and you would not weep." [60]

Music and voices call men into action—life calls, nature calls: dance, laugh, weep, join us!

Jesus reveled in nature. Any living thing was precious to Him. He sought the open beauty of mountains and sea, the solitude of far places. He came also to the cities, the marketplace, the feasts, and to the temple. He allowed the extravagant. He aided the poor, but He did not extol the mean bone of poverty. He respected the Sabbath, but employed it to His own pursuits. He despised exhibitions of piety, vain repetitions, brutality and self-debasement. His was a total empathy, a compassionate rendering, an exquisite edition of the art of life. About "the artist," Henry Miller says:

> It's not that I put the sage or saint above the artist. It's rather that I want to see established the "artist of life." The Christ *resurrected* would be such, for example.[61]

Jesus knew the very glory of life—knew that even the stones would shout it, if men did not.[62] And yet, the Gospel of St. John presents an enormous contradiction as regards Jesus' love of life in this world. He says:

> He that loveth his life shall lose it; and he that hateth his life in this world shall keep it unto life eternal.[63]

Against these words are posed the example He set and the statement that

He came "not to judge the world," but that man might have life abundantly—and in mighty summary the Gospel states:

> For God so loved the world . . .
> God sent not his Son into the world to condemn the world . . .[64]

What then could Jesus have meant—"He that loveth his life shall lose it; and he that hateth his life in this world shall keep it unto life eternal"?

Here, Jesus may have been speaking as person, loving life, but hating His Messianic role, willing to lay down His life to complete His mission. Or He may have been stating a truth that is not always apparent: the person who has not grown much in consciousness clings to life more than does he whose consciousness of being has soared to new heights so that at best his feeling toward life in this world is ambivalent—he has felt in his being the stirrings of a future that make him embrace creation itself and he longs to shed the shell of amnesia in which he is incased, he must needs grow in knowledge of reality and only death can teach him; he loves the world, loves life itself, but cannot be satisfied with his personality: his life in this world.

But in largest sense, Jesus spoke as symbol of Authority-Ego, and when He speaks as symbol He is speaking from a different level of being than that of the ego-group:

> Ye are from beneath; I am from above; ye are of this world; I am not of this world.[65]

Symbol of "I" in man cannot accept and cannot allow the ego-group to accept the insufficiency of Homo sapiens' consciousness and all that ignorance and error cause to be manifest in life. If man's growth into a larger structure of consciousness is to be insured, Authority-Ego must lead the ego-group to hate the mixture of love and lust its limited certitude expresses. An adjustment to, a reconciliation with, an acceptance of such insufficiency as is now exhibited in this world would hinder the growth of consciousness, evolution's goal.

The evolution of consciousness has not ceased, and down through the years man's laughter shows the effect of many mutations. Audiences find Bertolt Brecht's wicked and callous meat baron Mauler "immensely funny" and invariably weep for his greedy Mother Courage—Galileo's treason is less perceptible to them than "the moving spectacle of an old man's humiliation." [66] Empathy causes men to laugh at both Satanic villain and Messianic hero. Both concepts decline from tragedy to comedy—or to such mystery as is beyond the ken of empathy, or tears, or laughter, to such mystery as makes a man shrug, or curse, or close his mind to religion and turn to science, sometimes seeking escape, but more often seeking knowledge, seeing it as saving grace to man.

V

Will scientific knowledge prove itself saving grace to man—elucidating in time the answer to the question, who and what am I? In Robert Linssen's words, "The study of the profound nature of things in the physical world causes such transformations in the mind of the attentive observer that he draws nearer to the discovery of his true nature." [67] And Robert Ardrey, in reminding man of the never to be forgotten "keeper of the kinds," says, "You may sense his word in the second law of thermodynamics . . ." [68] Will science, then, take the place of religion?

Herbert Spencer saw that science does not destroy religion—instead, science forces its purification. He said:

> Religion ignores its immense debt to Science; and Science is scarcely at all conscious how much Religion owes it. Yet it is demonstrable that every step by which Religion has progressed from its first low conception to the comparatively high one it has now reached, Science has helped it, or rather forced it, to take . . . [69]

One might say that all religions are undergoing the refining fire of the Bunsen burner. But so is science. Something as far beyond man's grasp as God emerges as the "stuff" that energy and matter is made of—the mystery of it deepens with each scientific revelation.

The greatest scientists for the most part have been and are deeply religious men, in the purest sense of the word. But in the nineteenth century this was not evident—decrying theology, scientists sought the "absolute" truth through the process of taking inventory of the material realm and were confident that in time this method would produce it.

Also decrying theology and the religious outlook of that time were the transcendentalists—Emerson, Alcott, and Thoreau, among others. They moved beyond the narrow confines of theology and science to lay the foundation for a broad new concept of God, nature, and man.

Then, Mary Baker Eddy, at one time a pupil and patient of Phineas Quimby, emerged as another guiding light for those who set themselves to rescue religion from the pigeonhole marked "Superstition." Christian Science offered a new view, a new approach, a new translation of the sacred word, bringing to this theology scientific order; and above all, bringing religion itself back into the field of the healing ministry,[70] so that this doctrine must be examined in a later chapter. Christian Science, however, imposes and suffers the limitations of a strict theological system fraught with specific and implied prohibitions. Thus, truth seekers weary of such as this turn to other fields.

By the time the twentieth century had turned its first quarter, the narrow view of nineteenth-century science was transcended, and Einstein saw that the new physics may justly call itself a theory of life, "for the general laws . . . claim to be valid for any natural phenomenon whatsoever." [71] Progoff looks to the new physics to open a new road, a new view, for psychology.[72] But the theologian as yet sees little hope of reconciling orthodox doctrine with this science. Samuel Miller asks if a Christian can talk to people of God "when they find God quite unimaginable in a . . . world scientifically structured in iron law." [73]

Today, the supreme law, the "iron law," in the physical world is seen to be the second law of thermodynamics. But it gives rise to a view of the universe and entropy's meaning that is seriously questioned by many experts in various fields who suggest, indeed insist, that this law is correct insofar as it is stated, but that as yet it is incompletely stated or its meaning is misunderstood.

Jesus spoke of an "iron law"—that is, of a law that could not fail, and He indicated that all in creation is involved with and rests upon its operation. In the view of this study, He realized that man cannot understand himself until he also understands the natural universe of which he is a part and in which life manifests itself. He saw that in the psychic working of man a parallel to nature's supreme law operates, and He described this operation in His descriptions of the working of the kingdom of God, setting forth what might be called "secondary psychic law" as well as describing *in poetic terms* the most important of the secondary laws of physics. The "secondary psychic law" He enunciated complements the law of Moses, which Jesus upheld, and forces a synthesis or the higher law of love when it operates in conjunction with the Ten Commandments. In Luke 16:16-17, Jesus says:

> The law and the prophets were until John: since that time the kingdom of God is preached, and every man presseth into it. And it is easier for heaven and earth to pass, than one tittle of the law to fail.

In Matthew 5:17-18, He says:

> Think not that I am come to destroy the law, or the prophets: I am not come to destroy, but to fulfill. For verily I say unto you, Till

heaven and earth pass, one jot or one tittle shall in no wise pass from the law, till all be fulfilled.

Jesus did not come to destroy the promise of the high ethic inherent in Jewish law, much of which must have been borrowed from the Code of Hammurabi, King of Babylon, author of the only substantially complete pre-Hebrew code of law.[74] He came to fulfill this promise which flowered in His teaching.

But His words, quoted above, must have referred to *more* and *something other* than the mass of rules and regulations which comprised "the law" of His day, upon which time's accretions bore heavily. For having said, "Whosoever therefore shall break one of these least commandments, and shall teach men so, he shall be called the least in the kingdom of heaven," [75] Jesus, Himself, repudiated more than a "jot and tittle" of the Jewish law. He healed on the Sabbath; He defended His disciples' plucking the ears of corn and taught that the Sabbath is made for man, not man for the Sabbath.[76]

In short, Jesus sets up so large a contradiction as regards "the law" of which He spoke in conjunction with the working of the kingdom of God that one must seek beyond the explanation of His upholding Mosaic law to find the full and deepest meaning of His words. Not until one compares His descriptions of the working of the kingdom of God with descriptions of the operation of the second law of thermodynamics, as will be done in the following chapter, does the parallel between the two concepts become apparent, albeit Jesus' description is poetical.

But as important as the second law of thermodynamics is to scientists, the study of energy, of light, is of first importance. Jesus appears to have seen that the secret of the universe must rest in *light*, primordial energy, and that in the creation of light rests the secret of creation itself. If He realized the nature of it, He must tell its story in large drama because prime energy, or elementary particle, cannot be identified and is not an individual. In making Himself a symbol of light in order to reveal its nature, and in being a symbol of saving grace in man, He took care to insure that someday men would realize His revelation was of universal truth. This is to say, He did not forget to enfold in the being of all humankind the primordial energy of God that He represented, and also to enfold in all humankind what appears to be the saving grace of life, for to the multitudes before Him, Jesus said:

> . . . ye are the salt of the earth. . . .
> . . . ye are the light of the world. . . .[77]

To evaluate Jesus' revelation of the law upon which the universe operates and its psychic parallel, and to appreciate His dramatization of light, one must attempt to grasp, at least in small measure, some of the basic data of the new physics. The relationship between science and psychology, which today largely substitutes for religion, cannot be determined by exploring only the one realm or the other. To make the acquaintance, to have at least a nodding and speaking acquaintance, with the doctrines of science, psychology, and religion is incumbent upon twentieth-century man. Alfred North Whitehead states the case:

> When we consider what religion is for mankind, and what science is, it is no exaggeration to say that the future course of history depends upon the decision of this generation as to the relations between them. We have here the two strongest general forces . . . which influence men. . . .[78]

To attempt to grasp in small measure some of the basic data of the new physics is not an easy task. And to see in the working of the physical world something of a mirror-reflection of the operation of man's psyche might strike many as being too far-fetched to give the subject much consideration. A question must also arise—how could Jesus have known anything of physics in today's sense of the word? His realization arose from the *unconscious*. Again, this study points to the work of Carl Jung, Aniela Jaffé and Dr. M.-L. von Franz, contributors to the book, *Man and His Symbols*. Aniela Jaffé says:

> The parallelism between nuclear physics and the psychology of the collective unconscious was often a subject of discussion between Jung and Wolfgang Pauli, the Nobel prizewinner in physics. The space-time continuum of physics and the collective unconscious can be seen, so to speak, as the outer and inner aspects of one and the same reality behind appearances.[79]

Speaking of the alchemical stone, the *lapis*, which symbolizes something in man that is eternal, Dr. von Franz says: "The fact that this highest and most frequent symbol of the Self is an object of inorganic matter points to yet another field of inquiry and speculation: that is, the still unknown relationship between what we call the unconscious psyche and what we call 'matter'—a mystery with which psychosomatic medicine endeavors to grapple." [80] In discussing science and the *unconscious*, Dr. von Franz says:

> We are still far from understanding the unconscious or the archetypes —those dynamic *nuclei* of the psyche—in all their implications. . . .

But the most promising field for future studies seems (as Jung saw it) to have unexpectedly opened up in connection with the complex field of microphysics. At first sight, it seems most unlikely that we should find a relationship between psychology and microphysics. The interrelation of these sciences is worth some explanation. The most obvious aspect of such a connection lies in the fact that most of the basic concepts of physics (such as space, time, matter, energy, continuum or field, particle, etc.) were originally intuitive, semi-mythological, archetypal ideas of the old Greek philosophers—ideas that then slowly evolved and became more accurate and that today are mainly expressed in abstract mathematical terms. . . . When examining nature and the universe, instead of looking for and finding objective qualities, "man encounters himself," in the phrase of the physicist Werner Heisenberg. . . . Pauli believed that we should parallel our investigation of outer objects with a psychological investigation of the *inner origin* of our scientific concepts.[81]

The question becomes—where to begin? In the view of this study, Jesus began with a description of nature's supreme law, the second law of thermodynamics, and thus a "dialogue" between science and psychology may begin with a brief examination of this law and its significance.

This study does not attempt to show that Jesus precisely formulated the secondary laws of physics—rather that His words and drama are *congruent* with the physicists' explanations of these laws as given by scientists writing for the public. Jesus' view of the cosmic significance of nature's supreme law differs from the nihilistic view of many scientists, disputed in some circles, but His *descriptions of its working* harmonize with those given for the laymen. Jesus must speak to a world wherein even among the learned there was no language or mathematics to couch His realizations if they were as advanced as their congruence with scientific data indicates. Thus, He must be poet, or in drama show nature's operation that He grasped—and to be congruent with today's science, His words must be as enigmatic, contradictory, yet true, as are the secondary laws of physics versus the classical, or as is the wave theory versus the quantum theory of light. Thus, certain passages in the "dialogue" may be difficult for the layman to grasp—he may glance through these, concentrating on the "psychic parallels," which may help to explain them as well as vice versa.

Chapter 6

NATURE'S SUPREME LAW

I

In *The Nature of the Physical World,* Sir Arthur Eddington takes the layman on a journey through the realm of physics, describing it in picturesque terms, but his thirty-year-old warning, that "Structural alterations are in progress," making this realm dangerous territory for the philosopher, still holds good.[1] For example, as Werner Heisenberg points out, today the idea of probability functions, which tell where electrons are apt to occur in atoms, is replacing the concept of electron orbits.[2] Textbooks, however, still measure the new ideas against the old, and various theories describe the problem from a certain point of view, so that to measure Jesus' words against the given data in the physicists' realm, one must place them against a large canvas that encompasses the transitional offering of many men. Then the observations must be translated into their psychic parallels, for Jesus could not at once be symbol of psychic Authority and symbol of light in action unless a parallel exists between psychic working and the unseen operation of energy in the physical world.

The task may be formidable, but it takes one on a fascinating excursion. The realm of physics is paradoxical, topsy-turvy, poetic, as inexpressible in the last reaches as any mystic revelation that has confronted man. Eddington says: "Sir William Bragg was not overstating the case when he said that we use the classical theory on Mondays, Wednesdays and Fridays, and the quantum theory on Tuesdays, Thursdays and Saturdays." [3] This shift of theory is necessary because scientists have had to divide their laws, putting one group in the classical compartment and another in the quantum compartment:

> Unfortunately, our compartments are not watertight. . . . The classical laws are the limit to which the quantum laws tend when states of very high quantum number are concerned. . . . The disagreement is not very serious when the number is moderately large; but for small

quantum numbers the atom cannot sit on the fence. It has to decide between . . . (classical) and . . . (quantum) rules. It chooses [quantum] rules.[4]

Here, the first parallel may be drawn: when large numbers are concerned, men must operate under classical law, outgrown from the Ten Commandments, and humanity at large will tend to operate according to the classical patterns history presents; but operating within each human being are quantum psychic laws that contradict the classical picture he presents, and as an *individual*, he is subject to these laws primarily. Just as one psychic law—the Golden Rule—bridges the dichotomy between man and society, so the physicist deals with one law that fits in either quantum or classical compartment. This is the second law of thermodynamics which, in Eddington's words, "has been equally successful in connection with the most recondite problems of theoretical physics and the practical tasks of the engineer."[5] It is the law that entropy always increases:

> Application of the "second law" of thermodynamics leads to the conclusion that if any physical system is left to itself and allowed to distribute its energy in its own way, it always does so in a manner such that this quantity, called "entropy," increases; while at the same time the available energy of the system diminishes. This law applies to the universe as a whole, hence the proposition that the total entropy increases as time goes on.[6]

Entropy is a relatively new concept to science. Introduced by Clausius about one hundred years ago, associated with Boltzmann, and given a deep meaning by Gibbs in his work on statistical mechanics, it has become a basic, pervasive concept.[7] Eddington says:

> The law that entropy always increases . . . holds, I think, the supreme position among the laws of Nature. . . . if your theory is found to be against [it] I can give you no hope. . . . From the property that entropy must always increase, practical methods of measuring it have been found. The chain of deductions from this simple law have been almost illimitable. . . .[8]

As physicists understand this law today, it appears to spell in some billions of years the heat-death of the universe. But as Dr. Alexander points out, the anti-entropic nature of living things may point to a "simultaneous process of entropy and creation. . . . the processes of nature observed by physical science are but a fraction of the picture. . . ."[9] Structural alterations are going on in the realm of physics, and physicists themselves project that there are other laws yet to be discovered, so that all one can say with certainty is that the real meaning of entropy in universal terms may not yet be known.

Eddington tries to explain nature's supreme law to the layman: [10] entropy "makes no appearance in physical science except in the study of organisation of a number of individuals." It is concerned with energy and the *organization* of energy. As example:

> When a stone falls it acquires kinetic energy, and the amount of the energy is just that which would be required to lift the stone back to its original height. . . . But if the stone hits an obstacle its kinetic energy is converted into heat-energy. There is still the same quantity of energy, but even if we could scrape it together and put it through an engine we could not lift the stone back with it. What has happened to make the energy no longer serviceable?

To return to its original height the stone must preserve both the energy and the organization of the energy. The molecules in the falling stone move downwards with equal and parallel velocities in "an organised motion like the march of a regiment." Upon impact, they suffer "more or less random collisions and rebound in all directions. . . . they have lost their organisation." There is a difference between shuffling energy and material objects, so that "it is necessary to use some caution in applying the analogy. As regards heat-energy the temperature is the measure of its degree of organisation; the lower the temperature, the greater the disorganisation." As for the stone, upon impact the random element increases.

Entropy is a measure of disorder, of the increase in the random element. The molecules in the stone continue to collide and rebound; organization cannot be brought about by continued shuffling. The increase in the random element cannot be undone. Eddington illustrates:

> Suppose that you have a vessel divided by a partition into two halves, one compartment containing air and the other empty. You withdraw the partition. For the moment all the molecules of air are in one half of the vessel; a fraction of a second later they are spread over the whole vessel and remain so ever afterwards . . . unless other material is introduced into the problem to serve as a scape-goat for the disorganisation and carry off the random element elsewhere.

As the molecules wander in the vessel, there is a faint possibility that at one moment all of them might be in one half, but the physicists ignore this—why? "If an army of monkeys were strumming on typewriters they *might* write all the books in the British Museum. The chance of their doing so is decidedly more favourable than the chance of the molecules returning to one half of the vessel. When numbers are large, chance is the best warrant for certainty." Although the chance of the molecules returning to one half the vessel is absurdly small, physicists think about it a great deal—it gives the measure of the irrevocable increase of the random element. This small chance, or adverse chance, if written in the usual decimal notation "would fill all the books in the world many times over. We are not interested in it as a practical contingency; but we are interested in the fact that it is definite. It raises 'organisation' from a vague descriptive epithet to one of the measurable quantities of exact science. . . . A common measure can now be applied to all forms of organisation. Any loss of organisation is equitably measured by the chance against its recovery by an accidental coincidence. The chance is absurd regarded as a contingency, but it is precise as a measure."

The practical measure of the random element which can increase in the universe but can never decrease is called entropy, and measuring by entropy is the same as measuring by the chance explained above. "We can, by isolating parts of the world and postulating rather idealised conditions in our problem, arrest the increase, but we cannot turn it into a decrease." Because introduction of randomness is the only thing which cannot be undone, it points to a one-way property of time which has no analogue in space:

> . . . it is possible to find a direction of time on the four-dimensional map by a study of organisation. Let us draw an arrow arbitrarily. If as we follow the arrow we find more and more of the random element in the state of the world, then the arrow is pointing towards the future; if the random element decreases the arrow points toward the past. This is the only distinction known to physics. This follows at once if our fundamental contention is admitted that the introduction of randomness is the only thing which cannot be undone.

Eddington points out that "Organisation of energy is negotiable, and so is the disorganisation or random element; disorganisation does not for ever remain attached to the particular store of energy which first suffered it, but may be passed on elsewhere."

Entropy, then, is concerned with changing arrangement, within and without. Like the number *one*, it is definite, but its measure cannot be spelled out, for *one* draws all from zero into infinity. Like *one*, entropy's significance is too small or too large to be captured on paper.

Introduction of the concept of entropy turned scientists from the view that everything could be discovered by microscopic dissection of objects;

it demands consideration of the qualities possessed by the system as a whole. In Eddington's words:

> We often think that when we have completed our study of *one* we know all about *two,* because "two" is "one and one." We forget that we have still to make a study of "and." Secondary physics is the study of "and"—that is to say, of organisation.

By entropy, "science has been saved from a fatal narrowness. If we had kept entirely to the inventory method, there would have been nothing to represent 'becoming' in the physical world." The concept of entropy had secured a firm place in science because of its favor with engineers before it was discovered to be a measure of the random element in arrangement, but it is not in the same category as the other physical qualities recognized by physicists:

> Suppose that we were asked to arrange the following in two categories— *distance, mass, electric force, entropy, beauty, melody.* I think there are the strongest grounds for placing entropy alongside beauty and melody and not with the first three. Entropy is only found when the parts are viewed in association, and it is by viewing or hearing the parts in association that beauty and melody are discerned. All three are features of arrangement. . . . It had become the regular outlook of science, closely associated with its materialistic tendencies, that constellations are not to be taken seriously, until the constellation of entropy made a solitary exception.

Entropy is admitted in the physicists' world because it can speak "the language of arithmetic. . . . if it has as we faintly suspect some deeper significance touching that which appears in our consciousness as *purpose* (opposed to chance), that significance is left outside. What I would say is this: There is a side of our personality which impels us to dwell on beauty and other aesthetic significances in Nature, and in the work of man, so that our environment means to us much that is not warranted by anything found in the scientific inventory of its structure. An overwhelming feeling tells us that this is right and indispensable to the purpose of our existence."

There is that within man which turns him to dwell on nature. Jesus says: "Consider the lilies of the field, how they grow; they toil not, neither do they spin: And yet I say unto you, That even Solomon in all his glory was not arrayed like one of these. Wherefore, if God so clothe the grass of the field . . . shall he not much more clothe you, O ye of little faith?" [11] The lilies of the field are a constellation.

Did Jesus realize that what is now called the second law of thermodynamics is life's supreme law that operates throughout creation?

II

Einstein believed that the creative principle resides in mathematics, and he says, "In a certain sense, therefore, I hold it true that pure thought can grasp reality, as the ancients dreamed." [12]

If the pure thought of an ancient led him to realize that there is but a single reality—all manifestation of matter, mind, and energy but different aspects of it—and if he grasped the nature and significance of its supreme law so that he must state the entropy concept as it relates to time, as it works within the universe, how would the ancient have done it? He could *speak as a poet*, using simple words fully, as John Ciardi says the true poet does.

A true poet uses words sparingly. He states his thought in lines that encompass the whole profundity just as a physicist states an equation, distilling the principle to a minimum of symbols perfectly arranged. Therefore, in the message left by the ancient, one would not find a detailing of the concept to be conveyed. He must satisfy himself with a few perfectly stated lines, which is all Jesus left.

Many of the passages reporting Jesus' teaching are as profoundly beautiful as a poem and as complex as the equation concerning the generation of waves by wind that Eddington presents.[13] Others, such as "The kingdom of God is within you," are as profoundly simple as Einstein's famous $E = mc^2$. Can a poet express truly, albeit symbolically, abstract concepts such as are enfolded in a mathematical formula? In *The Basis of Scientific Thinking*, Samuel Reiss writes: " . . . *any abstract concept or meaning whatever* is formulable only as a metaphorical transfer from a correspondent concrete idea or image. Thus, even such abstract notions as are associated with logic or mathematics can be expressed only through a metaphorical, or 'poetic,' language vehicle . . . ." [14] He says that symbols with an abstract meaning attached, "in order to furnish a theory, must in the end be correlated, by however involved a circuit, with concepts of the familiar intelligible kind which were tacitly assumed in the formulation of the theory." [15]

Jesus must meet the most severe test of a poet in describing the many aspects of the second law of thermodynamics and its significance. A poetic statement indicating that energy operates always in changing arrangement resulting in *increased measure* is found in two of Jesus' enigmatic remarks about the working of God.

How could an ancient describe the *measure* of the random element—spreading, increasing? The concept of entropy is enfolded in a mathematical formula, and mathematics may be thought of as the language of *size*. Descriptions which fit the incomparable size of entropy's shoe, as well as the nature of its measure, and its significance, are found in Jesus' words pertaining to the reign of God, the realm of heaven, the coming of the kingdom. He likened its "smallness" and its "largeness" to a mustard seed—"less than any seed on earth," which grows "larger than any plant." [16] Thus, like the "absurdly small" measure of adverse chance, this measure cannot be "written out": the seed is smaller than any on earth, the plant larger than any plant. He involved the working of the reign of God with the shuffling, spreading, and action of energy throughout the whole: as with the seed growing into a plant; or, He said, it is "like dough . . . buried in three pecks of flour, till all of it was leavened." [17] Jesus said this working is begun: the seed is sown, the dough is buried. And the kingdom of God, which involves the concept of the end of the world, will come—just as the physicists envision the heat death of the universe when nature's supreme law is fulfilled.

All that Jesus said of the coming of the kingdom does not refute its existence and present operation, but serves to identify that of which He speaks as being completely involved both in being and in becoming, just as entropy is involved in that which is and is coming to be—with becoming in the universe—which is to say, with *time*.

It is time—real time and the meaning of time—that unites the *unconscious* and nature's supreme law which, in Jesus' teaching, therefore, share the words: kingdom, heaven, realm, and reign of God. In the physicists' view, entropy "points time's arrow," and the *unconscious* in man is capable of calculation of time, as is demonstrated in posthypnotic response to suggestion made to the second after a span of minutes, days, months, or even years.

If one will not concede that Jesus' references to the kingdom of heaven pertain to the *unconscious* and to the working of supreme natural law in man's being and throughout the universe, he must ask himself anew what these passages refer to and concede that they cannot deal with any sort of *eternal* abode for the "redeemed" because Jesus says that "Heaven and earth shall pass away . . ." [18] but not "my words," not consciousness' manifestation.

The passing away of "heaven" indicates that the *unconscious* domain will at some point no longer exist as such because its content and power will be realized—herein is the becoming, or the coming of the inner kingdom unto each man. The passing away of "earth" indicates change born of the operation of the second law of thermodynamics, and it indicates also that flesh expressed by partial consciousness will pass away as a material embodiment born of complete consciousness comes into expression. But Jesus said of the kingdom's coming—of time's working in the *unconscious* and in the universe through entropy's increase—"The kingdom of God cometh not with observation (Or, with outward shew) . . ." [19] as man expected it to come in His day. Perhaps it is as unlikely that the "end of the world" will come as the physicists expect it today as that it will come as the early Christians expected it, for the meaning of the supreme natural law and its working in universal terms is not yet known—cannot be known entirely until the innermost workings of the universe are known, and until time's meaning is grasped.

Jesus said that the answer as to *when* "becoming" will be achieved is not accessible to Homo sapiens' consciousness:

But of that day and that hour knoweth no man, no, not the angels which are in heaven, neither the Son, but the Father.[20]

When Eddington mentions time, he says it is "Heaven knows what!" [21] Thus, only the Father knoweth the hour—even as something in the *unconscious* can calculate time without consciousness' awareness that it is calculating it.

But Eddington does try to picture what the physicist knows of time in a way that the layman may grasp it. Jesus also drew a word-picture so similar to Eddington's in many respects He must have been alluding to all that men can know of the mystery of time: primarily, that consciousness cannot penetrate its secret "now" although in the *unconscious* time's function or working is grasped.

Eddington explains that "Physical time is, like space, a kind of frame in which we locate the events in the external world. . . . We have seen that there is an infinite choice of alternative frames; so, to be quite explicit, I will tell you how *I* locate events in *my* frame." [22] First, he depicts a number of events, represented by circles, located at random around the cross encircled, representing "I," here-now, enveloped in an event. Figure 2 extends the line of the cross, vesting "I" with a past: "myself" drawn through "I, here-now," into the future. Figure 3 depicts time as "I" am related to the world or activity of others and it may be observed that "my now" and the "now" of another are not one and the same; nor is the past and future line of time-seeing precisely the same. Figure 4 shows a drawing of "Father Time," as a space-time frame involving "Absolute Past" and "Absolute Future" and "Absolute Elsewhere." [23]

Eddington says, "No observer can reach an event in the neutral zone [Absolute Elsewhere], since the required speed is too great. The event is not Here for any observer (from Here-Now); therefore it is absolutely Elsewhere." [24]

Yet, "I" am enveloped in the "disappearing act" of time and although "I" cannot see "Absolute Elsewhere," somehow "I" must touch upon this realm, for it converges upon the "event" and "myself" passing, or being passed, through it as may be seen in Figure 4.

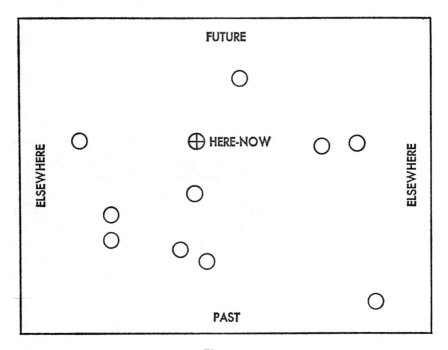

Figure 1

The diagrams are not to be taken as more than a token—a token idea is all that can be given. Therefore, if an ancient's pure thought grasped the truth of time in all its complexity, his revelation of it must bespeak *such as is beyond man's comprehension in its entirety;* and since time is so involved with space and with *a body traveling through space,* the ancient's statement could not at first glance appear to be related directly to the *mystery of time.* Jesus said:

NATURE'S SUPREME LAW

It is easier for a camel to go through the eye of a needle, than for a rich man to enter into the kingdom of God. . . . With men it is impossible, but not with God: for with God all things are possible.[25]

Look now at Figure 2. It shows, poetically speaking, that "I, myself" am being drawn through the "eye of a needle"—and when the drawings are understood, it would appear that it is more difficult for "me" to enter "Absolute Elsewhere" which the "eye of the needle" involves (see Figure 4) than it is for a camel to go through a tiny hole.

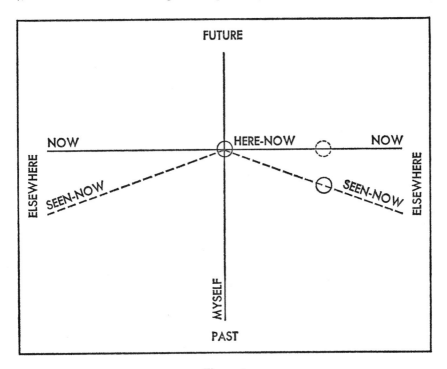

Figure 2

Consider that if a man possesses the kingdom of God within him, he is rich—and as Jesus depicts true wealth, He, Himself, is rich indeed. Thus, His words must pertain to "how I locate events in my frame" as He presents in words a form that looks like a "circle," the *eye* of a needle, which it is possible for "a rich man" to be drawn through, if God draws him, and by a force which is "heaven knows what"—time.

"Absolute Elsewhere" provides "room" for the concept of the *unconscious*, for an eternal abode of the Father who alone knows the secret of time, and who in relation to the possibility of man's seeing Him must be absolutely elsewhere—thus, all one can see of Him is to be seen in God-consciousness in man's here-now being.[26]

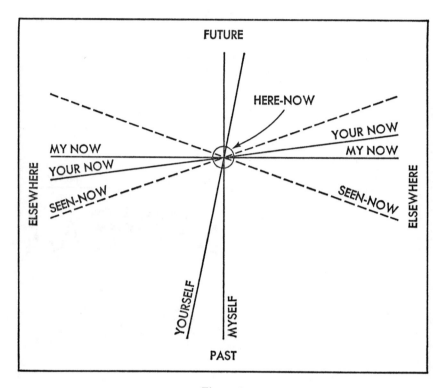

Figure 3

Jesus' strange word-picture suggests a large mass being drawn through a tiny opening—by means of this contradiction, He indicates poetically that the *actual* mass of matter is no more than a speck in comparison to what it appears to be. Scientists now confirm this.[27]

Eddington says, "As the speed of matter approaches the speed of light its mass increases to infinity, and therefore it is impossible to make matter travel faster than light." [28] Jesus made Himself symbol of light, He poetically "sets the pace" at which a material body may travel: He was called "teacher" and "Lord"—thus, when He says that the scholar is not above his teacher nor the servant above his lord, enough that they fare alike, He restricts the pace to His own, light's speed.[29]

Eddington continues, "We ourselves are attached to material bodies, and therefore we can only go on into the absolute future."[30] Conscious-

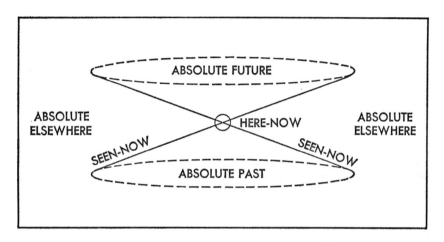

Figure 4

ness in man is attached to a material body and thus consciousness can take him only into a concept of absolute future. But man's kingdom, the *unconscious* domain, is located "absolutely elsewhere" in relation to consciousness' space-time frame; thus he does not have to "go" anywhere to enter this kingdom here-now within him, and thus he *is with* God and all things are possible to him: he *is* constantly passing through the "eye of the needle," through the *now*, which is absolute unto himself only, for there "is no absolute Now, but only the various relative Nows differing according to the reckoning of different observers. . . ."[31]

Eddington calls "Absolute Elsewhere" the neutral zone. God being the only "Absolute Elsewhere" man can conceive of makes of Him a neutral event man cannot observe because he is taking place through and within God being—just as a child is taking place through a woman "with child" and the embryo cannot observe her as an event or form, and she cannot intervene in the natural process that causes him to be brought forth through her body and being. In this process, man becomes *an event in himself,* a biological event, his flesh antientropic although the random element is increased with every move he makes, pointing time's arrow for consciousness as the *unconscious* calculates the hour.

A question may now be posed: is man somehow psychically involved in a parallel operation to nature's supreme law? Before this question can be answered, it is pertinent to note that in using a partitioned vessel as example to explain the increase of the random element, Eddington did not mean to imply that one side was a complete vacuum—absolute vacuum has not as yet been achieved. Nor has absolute zero temperature been achieved—note that Jesus' words pointing to the increasing disorder as love grows "cold" [32] are congruent with scientists' finding that the lower the temperature the greater the disorder. Nor has absolute power ever been exerted: operation of the second law of thermodynamics opposes. Not even the word, random, is absolute in its meaning, it takes a strange turn—by definition, *random* means a haphazard course or progress, without definite aim, direction, rule or method, but biologically speaking, "as if" enters the picture: "Made as if at random but controlled so as to bring together certain individuals or classes, or to make representative." [33]

III

Roderick Seidenberg writes that Henry Adams first enunciated the thesis "that the stages in the course of human evolution may be comparable to changes of state in a purely material system as expressed by the Rule of Phase in thermodynamic theory." [34] Thus the concept of "psychic dynamics" paralleling thermodynamics is not a stranger to twentieth-century man. In this study, however, the second law is seen to parallel the psychic law Jesus spoke of, saying that it must be fulfilled to the last iota, that it is easier for heaven and earth to pass away than for this law to fail.[35]

If one sees in the story of entropy a psychological parallel, one must postulate that man's psychic energy and its *organization* is altered by every impact of stimuli. No two people receive precisely the same sum or arrangement of stimuli, nor do they react in precisely the same manner to such as is shared: "Thousands of recordings of brain-wave patterns taken at neurological clinics and institutes prove that each of us has a pattern of mental activity that is as individualistic as are our fingerprints. . . . Thus on the subconscious level each of us constructs a different pattern from the same impressions received." [36] Each man is a mind of his own wherein the "psychic random element" and the organization of psychic energy or passion must play the dominant role. This study postulates that although the increase of the "psychic random element" may appear to follow a haphazard course, it is controlled so as to bring together certain characteristics to make them representative in Homo sapiens.

To suggest that something in man, or in consciousness, parallels entropy's increasing measure will, no doubt, appear fantastic to many scientists—yet, a great scientist, Teilhard de Chardin, writes:

> . . . there is in progress, within us and around us, a continual heightening of consciousness in the Universe. For a century and a half the science of physics, preoccupied with analytical researches, was dominated by the idea of the dissipation of energy and the disintegration of matter. Being now called upon by biology to consider the effects of synthesis, it is beginning to perceive that, parallel with the phenomenon of corpuscular disintegration, the Universe historically displays a second process as generalised and fundamental as the first: I mean that of the gradual concentration of its physico-chemical elements in nuclei of increasing complexity, each succeeding stage of material concentration and differentiation being accompanied by a more advanced form of spontaneity and spiritual energy. The outflowing flood of Entropy equalled and offset by the rising tide of a Noogenesis! . . .[37]

When new understanding enters consciousness, is it equivalent to "lifting a partition"—from this instant on, one's consciousness spreading to fill this section, and the measure of a "psychic something" increasing so that consciousness will never again organize in the "area" that previously held it? This concept depends upon finding a "psychic something" that is discernibly increasing in society as a result of the collision of men and ideas—in peace, in war, in literature, in action, in thought, and in body.

Again, this study proposes *empathy* to be the psychic measure which constantly increases, which may be arrested under certain conditions, but which can never decrease or be "undone." Omar Khayyám, "who stitched the tents of science," spoke poetically of a psychic parallel to that which is irreversible. Is it empathy which is written?—when:

> The moving Finger writes; and, having writ,
> Moves on: nor all your Piety nor Wit
> Shall lure it back to cancel half a Line,
> Nor all your Tears wash out a Word of it.[38]

There has been a constant increase in human *understanding*. This cannot be spelled out on paper any more than entropy's measure can be written out in decimal figures, but empathy must be calculated in dealing with men in society—for example, efforts to abolish racial discrimination bespeak it. The increase in empathy reflects, no doubt, the increase of disorder, psychic and public, born of man's social striving, but by its very nature empathy is redemptive: it is knowing with the whole being the truth of the whole situation.

A man's mental pattern is comprised of memory-images which are meaningfully related. Dr. Alexander says, "As each of these memory-images is formed, it is given a meaning in terms of the particular personality storing it. It then becomes a part of the mental 'working-capital' of that individual. . . ."[39] The concept that this working capital in sum determines one's actions and reactions must relieve man of the idea that life is subject to accident; this concept demands acknowledgment that every move in life fulfills the law which operates to increase empathy as surely as in the physical world the random element increases.

By his presence a man creates a situation: poses the possibility of exerting or receiving the force of destructive or constructive potential. Is this an accidental creation? This question is not to project that the helpless victim of disaster or crime and his grieving relatives must suffer because of like suffering imposed upon another, somehow, somewhere, sometime. Rather it is to say that man's quota of violent, destructive potential must be expended before Love can complete itself, *can complete him*. This quota is the same for every person, for he is no more, no less, than *one* and can but contain its measure, expend this measure, receive this measure. What then, is *one's* measure of good, of evil—the two major influences or ideas pervading the consciousness of man, causing him to express the energy of both?

In the physicists' wave-theory, one finds a division of energy in the frequencies associated in a light wave-group which moves *like a particle* localized somewhere within the area of the storm of space. A boundary to the wave-group "is provided by interference of waves of slightly different length, so that while reinforcing one another at the centre they cancel one another at the boundary."[40] As example, in the light wave theory one finds, roughly speaking, that 1001 of the shorter, interfering, limiting waves of a wave-group occupy the same distance as 1000 of the longer waves.[41] The numbers in themselves have no significance—Eddington could have illustrated the point using the numbers 274 and 273, for example. For the sake of simplicity it may be said that one frequency has a measure more in count than the other. The two frequencies are equally essential to bear light energy.

Although the frequencies are not equal, they occupy the *same distance*, are equal to each other in the sense that they are equal to sharing the same "house," the wave-group that acts like a particle. To call one of the frequencies good and the other evil is pointless. Most important is their *difference* that allows for interaction to provide a boundary for the wave-group's action; the *one measure of difference* may be seen as more: (+), good, or as less: (−), evil, or vice versa, depending upon how one views the situation.

Thus, in psychic parallel, one might say that as a person comes into each life experience, the measure of good and evil he must or can expend is determined by the measure of the opposing frequencies associated in his ego-group, and there is one measure in him that can act as (+) or (−), to give or to receive, and it terminates each action, providing also the boundary to his life-experience when his capacity to exert constructive and destructive force is *both* fulfilled—that is, both expended and received to the precise extent premeasured for this only life experience. How he fulfills this measure is a variable, but with each move *some of both forces* is expended and received—the man is "salted": he gains a measure of immunity to evil-doing because the sum of his memory-images, and thus his capacity to act and react to any stimuli or the suggestion of it, is altered and his empathy turns him out of certain paths, into others.

The predetermined measure man comes with is secret, even to himself. Durrell lets Pursewarden say for him: "We are all racing under sealed handicaps." [42] The pain one suffers is perhaps not the measure of what he has done so much as it is the measure of what he would still be capable of inflicting were he not himself to suffer such pain or fortune as will raise his empathy level to the point that his potential for evil-doing is lessened, bringing him into the "belt" or "range" of empathy that the great majority of humankind has reached so that he keeps apace in evolutionary progress. Or misfortune may relieve one of still worse fortune. Or it may be that through suffering great misfortune one's empathy is raised to a level beyond the norm, enabling him thereby to become a pioneer, acting as catalyst or leaven in the development of the consciousness of mankind through expression of new heights of understanding.

That a creative process is involved in much that appears on the surface to be purely evil is projected in the legend of Moses and Khidr which Dr. von Franz presents in discussing the aspect of the *unconscious* that Jung called the "shadow." She says:

> The ethical difficulties that arise when one meets one's shadow are well described in the 18th Book of the Koran. In this tale Moses meets Khidr ("the Green One" or "first angel of God") in the desert.

They wander along together, and Khidr expresses his fear that Moses will not be able to witness his deeds without indignation. If Moses cannot bear with him and trust him, Khidr will have to leave. Presently Khidr scuttles the fishing boat of some poor villagers. Then, before Moses's eyes, he kills a handsome young man, and finally he restores the fallen wall of a city of unbelievers. Moses cannot help expressing his indignation, and so Khidr has to leave him. Before his departure, however, he explains the reasons for his actions: By scuttling the boat he actually saved it for its owners because pirates were on their way to steal it. As it is, the fishermen can salvage it. The handsome young man was on his way to commit a crime.... By restoring the wall, two pious young men were saved from ruin because their treasure was buried under it. Moses, who had been so morally indignant saw now (too late) that his judgement had been too hasty.... Looking at this story naively, one might assume that Khidr is the lawless, capricious, evil shadow of pious, law-abiding Moses. But this is not the case. Khidr is much more the personification of some secret creative actions of the Godhead.[43]

The legend would seem to say that one is short-sighted when he turns his back on humankind or God because he cannot reconcile within his concept of morality life's apparently witless, useless evil.

The need to suffer could also reflect failure to learn from experience, or failure to experience and thus to learn. This poses the necessity to teach and to learn, to experience in childhood punishment for failure to abide by nature's laws and man's laws because in childhood punishment can be mild. The degree, the kind, the *measure* of power exerted by a man and exerted upon him, particularly in childhood, makes the difference. And if "with the same measure that ye mete," it shall be meted out to you,[44] a man who has abused the innocent, either deliberately, or through omission of his duty, or involuntarily, cannot suffer the exact same measure himself until he himself is innocent, and this cannot *be* until he is in a new expression of conscious embodiment. Jesus said:

> Judge not according to the appearance, but judge righteous judgement.[45]

Under life's law man's violence is expended from generation to generation—the organization of psychic energy is negotiable, and so is the disorganization or *psychic random element*. Each life is a totally new experience and endeavor. Each person is born *innocent* of what he has done and *innocent of* what he will do. Jesus said:

> Judge not, that you may not be judged yourselves....[46]

All men must experience all—in kind, somehow, somewhere, on some level—before life can fulfill to the last iota the law of empathy under which, without compulsion, harmony exists.

Each man has now a capacity to expend and to receive violence, but he has a mechanism available to alter his mental images that define this capacity—thus, the law does not make man a slave to his past nor to the untried: "The human mind . . . is capable of modifying existing brain patterns, and of developing new ones." [47] Using imagination and reasoning power, man may try evil-doing in his mind, both sowing and reaping it upon himself, having done with it *if* he will follow through in his envisioning to the final harvest, not stopping at the point of momentary gratification in the act. That is, he may exhaust the possibilities and bore himself with evil's final, empty reward.

But since good and evil interfuse each act, as do the two frequencies of a light wave-group, even if a man could always live by the Golden Rule he would still do evil. *Because this is so,* however, he may spend his life acting upon the voices of conscience and love, knowing that he expends his quota of evil, which must be expended in order that he be delivered from it—and since every person is a field in which both good seed and tares are sown,[48] his life's harvest will be of good and evil. The measure he has meted out during this experience, however, constitutes the sowing of a new field, provides a future working capital of memory-images, and the evil that comes back to him in kind will be in attenuated form. The sum of his memory-images both today and tomorrow ad infinitum spell out his empathy and they also spell out his lust: his need to experience, to *know*.

Eddington says, "Progress of time introduces more and more of the random element into the constitution of the world." [49] The psychological parallel would read: there will be more empathy in the world tomorrow than there is today—and the question arises, can empathy be complete? Can thermodynamical equilibrium be achieved? Theoretically, it can be projected in an ideal, isolated state:

> Under these isolated conditions the energy will be shuffled as it is bandied from matter to aether and back again, and very soon the shuffling will be complete. . . . With infinite divisibility there can be no end to the shuffling. The experimental fact that a definite state of equilibrium is rapidly reached indicates that energy is not infinitely divisible . . . in the natural processes of shuffling.[50]

Psychologically translated, this would say that passion is not infinitely divisible into good and evil force—rather, the two forces are shuffled up to the point that "psychic equilibrium" *is* a fact accomplished. And then —will passionate striving, the fine tensions of life, the vice turned spice, be gone, leaving man no sense of being or becoming? Eddington describes thermodynamical equilibrium:

> It would not be true to say that such a region is timeless; the atoms vibrate as usual like little clocks; by them we can measure speeds and durations. Time is still there and retains its ordinary properties, but it has lost its arrow; like space it extends, but it does not "go on." [51]

When man senses that time "goes on," he must measure himself against it: as lagging behind, or rushing to get ahead, his life measured by its passage. But when time extends like space into the blue or starry skies, he experiences a moment of perfect freedom, realizes the here-now of infinity. He cannot experience this without experiencing also a deep-seated satisfaction simply in being.

Man's lump sum of lust may be likened to the source of heat in a system; just as heat turns up as an almost unavoidable side-product and as a very probable end-product of any job he does, so, too, with lust in the psychic realm. But the final "heat" resides at lower temperature— there is less available for further use. In man, the lessening of lust may be too small to meet the eye, but one may project its decrease until there is a lust-death in consciousness when all has been experienced in mind or in deed; but as this is accomplished, one must project the increase of empathy until in the perfect shuffling of lust it becomes a divinely human desire for the beloved, love of life itself; or one might say that as lust decreases, compassion increases so that in time empathy is fulfilled and man's passion is maintained at a desirable level. This is to say, there is no psychic stillness, stagnation, or death of desire under the condition of perfect empathy any more than thermodynamical equilibrium stills the exquisite life of the atom.

If thermodynamical equilibrium is possible in an isolated, ideal environment, the psychic equivalent may exist in man now, in a part of his *unconscious*. Eddington says: "A region in the deep interior of a star is an almost perfect example of thermodynamical equilibrium." [52] Not in the partitioned conscious domain, not in the *id*, an unbounded mystery, but in the "core" of the *unconscious* complete empathy could exist and be the "resonator" that sounds through man as truth's prompting and at times gives him inexpressible, complete joy in life. In order to achieve "psychic equilibrium" or to have complete empathy, the "resonator" must have experienced the full of life's good and evil.

Eddington describes "the principle of detailed balancing" which asserts "that to every type of process (however minutely particularised) there is a converse process, and in thermodynamical equilibrium direct and converse processes occur with equal frequency." [53] Jesus' teaching indicates that there is a similar psychic operation which arises because the Authority in each man's *unconscious* acts directly to forgive another's transgression. In the Lord's Prayer, the line: "Thy will be done in earth, as it is in heaven. . . ." indicates that a process goes on in the *unconscious* which demands a response with equal frequency in the conscious domain in order to maintain its equilibrium. The clue is cast in this line: "And forgive us our debts as we forgive our debtors. . . ." for the word is not *if* —it is *as*. This projects the forgiving of transgression in the *unconscious* even as another commits it. Jesus follows with the word *if*—if you do not forgive the trespasses of those who trespass against you, you cannot be forgiven your trespasses.[54]

In a chemist's terms, one might paraphrase: if you do not forgive in consciousness what has been unconsciously forgiven, you are but "half-reacted"— you must respond in consciousness to the act that takes place in the *unconscious* or a schism is created in inner harmony. The concept here offered is that the Lord in each man is the equal of each other such One, and is devoid of will to exercise His power against His brother in destructive manner. Destructive, abusive acts stem from the ego-group and the Lord in man forgives these transgressions because He perceives that with each violence spent the constructive potential is increased in the lessening of lust, and because He knows Himself to be equally involved in *all's* expression of good and of evil, in good and evil doing in life's conscious domain.

If, in time, under evolution's "psychic entropic" working, abuse and error should decrease, then empathy, not fear or *conscience*, would guide man into the paths of compassion and decency—that is, the voice of conscience in man must lessen as empathy takes over its role, governing action from a higher level of consciousness. In the Gospels the voice of conscience calling man to repentance comes through John the Baptist, whereas the voice of empathy, the Christ, speaks of abiding in love and says:

> These things have I spoken unto you, that my joy might remain in you, and that your joy might be full.[55]

The voice of conscience, John the Baptist, says of this voice of truth: "He must increase, but I must decrease. . . ." [56] The concept that conscience must in time lessen as evolution's purpose is fulfilled may be a startling one, but Ardrey's words are also startling—he says: ". . . conscience as a guiding force in the human drama is one of such small reliability that it assumes very nearly the role of villain. . . . Conscience organizes hatred as it organizes love." [57] Jesus says of conscience—that is, of John the Baptist, its symbol—"Among them that are born of women there hath not risen a greater than John the Baptist: notwithstanding he that is least in the kingdom of heaven is greater than he." [58] In the kingdom within, conscience must have little part—does empathy take its place?

If a core of perfect empathy exists in the *unconscious*, it provides for man's capacity to love others no matter how far they fall and to love his own soul whatever its hue. How many people have glimpsed in their dreams this inner realm that is utterly theirs? Isak Dinesen speaks of her dreams: "I move in a world deeply and sweetly familiar to me, a world which belongs to me and to which I myself belong more intensely than is ever the case in my waking existence. . . . At times I believe that my feet have been set upon a road which I shall go on following, and that slowly the centre of gravity of my being will shift over from the world of day. . . ." [59] But she speaks not of dreaming as most people dream: "my dreams are always beautiful," even the monstrosity or monster, "Hell itself" turns to "favour and to prettiness." She tells of the expanses, loftiness, airiness of this world: "Its very atmosphere is joy, its crowning happiness, unreasonably or against reason, is that of triumph." [60] She mentions mystically transparent browns—this is a golden world, one's own.

As yet, psychologists offer no satisfactory explanation of a sublime self-love that draws the soul or ego-group together and toward "home"—neither do philosophers. Both seem blind to all but lust. What François, Duc de la Rochefoucauld, describes as self-love actually describes man's lust that "helps to perpetrate its own destruction" and is "content to be its own enemy . . . .":

> It finds no rest outside itself and only pauses among outside things as do bees among flowers, to feed upon them. Nothing is so impetuous as its desires, so deep-dyed as its schemes, so guileful as its maneuvers; its twisting and turning is beyond words, its altered looks surpass the chameleon's, its subtle blendings outdo the chemists. There is no plumbing the depths or piercing the darkness of its abysses; darting in and out of them it escapes the sharpest eye and is often invisible even to itself. All unknowingly it breeds, nourishes, rears a variety of affections and hatreds, some of them so monstrous that when it has

brought them to light it fails to recognize or refuses to acknowledge them.[61]

And so they are repressed—as psychologists have observed—but Love takes them in, reverses and reclothes them, makes them sufficient to re-enter the conscious domain and under life's supreme law be redeemed.

Chapter 7

ONE, ITSELF, IS TEACHER

I

Einstein writes, "evolution has shown that at any given moment, out of all conceivable constructions, a single one has always proved itself absolutely superior to all the rest." [1] If an ancient's pure thought grasped reality, he would have realized this, and he would have seen, as Einstein saw, that:

> The important point for us to observe is that all these constructions and the laws connecting them can be arrived at by the principle of looking for the mathematically simplest concepts and the link between them. In the limited nature of the mathematically existent simple fields and the simple equations possible between them, lies the theorist's hope of grasping the real in all its depths.[2]

The ancient, then, would have had to employ the simplest number: *one*. *One* is adjective, capable of adding to or being added to, yet itself unity, a complete whole, indestructible, a coherence that regardless of how often it is self-divided or self-multiplied is no more and no less than it was. The ancient's every expression about *one* must be made in the simplest possible way, and he must also convey the full significance of the mathematically simplest link between the mathematically simplest concept: *one* and *one*, choosing a symbol that would in time come to express the significance of organization—as Eddington says, the significance of *and*. Thus, he must choose the cross $+$.

Jesus chose the cross, and He based His teaching upon the number *one*. He said, "Why call me 'good' . . . ? one alone is good. . . ." [3]— He said that *one* is teacher, leader, Father. His message points to the absolutely superior concept of *one* itself. If *one* and its nature and working could be understood, in time understanding of all else must follow. Jesus saw that each One drawn into expression as "I" must contain the quality and quantity inherent in *one*:

... as the Father has life in himself, so too he has granted the Son to have life in himself. ... it is not the will of your Father in heaven that a single one of these little ones should be lost.[4]

Can the will of *one* be thwarted—even by *one* itself? So wondrous are *one*'s ways, so unlimited are its possibilities, that man calls it "God" —Harry Overstreet writes: "Almost never in the thousands of years since this insight first came into the world has its original splendor been comprehended. ..."[5]

In physics, the might, magnificence, and yet exquisite delicacy of the control of *one* is come upon when man encounters, as he must at every turn, h, an elemental unit of energy: .000000000000000000000000000655 erg-seconds. The erg is the unit of energy, the second is the unit of time, h is of the nature of energy multiplied by time. Eddington says:

> Evidently h is a kind of atom—something which coheres as one unit in the processes of radiation; it is not an atom of matter but an atom or, as we usually call it, a *quantum* of the more elusive entity action. Whereas there are [103] different kinds of material atoms there is only one quantum of action—the same whatever the material it is associated with. ... You might perhaps think that there must be some qualitative difference between the quantum of red light and the quantum of blue light, although both contain the same number of erg-seconds; but the apparent difference is only relative to a frame of space and time and does not concern the absolute lump of action. ...
>
> The indivisible units in the shuffling of energy are the quanta. By radiation, absorption and scattering energy is shuffled among the different receptacles in matter and aether, but only a whole quantum passes at each step. ...
>
> The paradoxical nature of the quantum is that although it is indivisible it does not hang together. We examined first a case in which a quantity of energy was obviously cohering together, viz. an electron, but we did not find h; then we turned our attention to a case in which the energy was obviously dissolving away through space, viz. light-waves, and immediately h appeared. The atom of action seems to have no coherence in space; it has a unity which overleaps space. How can such a unity be made to appear in our picture of a world extended through space and time?
>
> The pursuit of the quantum leads to many surprises; but probably none is more outrageous to our preconceptions than the regathering of light and other radiant energy into h-units, when all the classical pictures show it to be dispersing more and more.
>
> Consider the light-waves which are the result of a single emission by

a single atom on the star Sirius. These bear away a certain amount of energy endowed with a certain period, and the product of the two is h. The period is carried by the waves without change, but the energy spreads out in an ever-widening circle. Eight years and nine months after the emission the wave-front is due to reach the earth. A few minutes before the arrival some person takes it into his head to go out and admire the glories of the heavens and—in short—to stick his eye in the way. The light waves when they started could have had no notion what they were going to hit; for all they knew they were bound on a journey through endless space, as most of their colleagues were. Their energy would seem to be dissipated beyond recovery over a sphere of 50 billion miles' radius. And yet, if that energy is ever to enter matter again, if it is to work those chemical changes in the retina which give rise to the sensation of light, it must enter as a single quantum of action h. . . .

Just as the emitting atom regardless of all laws of classical physics is determined that whatever goes out of it shall be just h, so the receiving atom is determined that whatever comes into it shall be just h. Not all the light-waves pass by without entering the eye; for somehow we are able to see Sirius. How is it managed? [6]

Here, another question arises—if an ancient were trying to state the case of h, how could he have done it? If he could utter but one word to give evidence of his grasp of h, then that word must be, "single," *singularly* expressed in such a way that it would be true at every level. Jesus said:

The light of the body is in the eye: if therefore thine eye be single, thy whole body shall be full of light.[7]

These poetic words reflect light's *single* action, relate light and singular behavior in its absorption—and they also present truth in another field: strangely enough, surgeons now know that the cornea is the single bit of flesh that may be readily transplanted and truly grow into man's body, so that its *singularity* bespeaks the sameness of *one*.

But Jesus, Himself, had to symbolize h, the one atom of action that coheres as one unit in the process of radiation, single (as He remained), an indivisible likeness to One, bespeaking a unity that overleaps space, a unity He called the *same*, without reservation, in every man for each hath *one*. He could do no more than present a clue as to the dimension of His realization—He did not attempt to state it in full: "I have yet many things to say unto you, but ye cannot bear them now." [8] How could His disciples bear to generations unborn more than the *poetry* of the quantum, enveloped in Jesus' drama and in the one singularly expressed reference to light's absorption. How is it managed?

Eddington continues:

> Attempts to account for this phenomenon follow two main devices which we may describe as the "collection-box" theory and the "sweepstake" theory, respectively. Making no effort to translate them into scientific language, they amount to this: in the first the atom holds a collection-box into which each arriving group of waves pays a very small contribution; when the amount in the box reaches a whole quantum, it enters the atom. In the second [theory] the atom uses the small fraction of a quantum offered to it to buy a ticket in a sweepstake in which the prizes are whole quanta; some of the atoms will win whole quanta which they can absorb, and it is these winning atoms in our retina which tell us of the existence of Sirius. . . .
>
> A phenomenon which seems directly opposed to any kind of collection-box explanation is the photoelectric effect. When light shines on metallic films . . . free electrons are discharged from the film. They fly away at high speed, and it is possible to measure experimentally their speed or energy. Undoubtedly it is the incident light which provides the energy of these explosions, but the phenomenon is governed by a remarkable rule. Firstly, the speed of the electrons is not increased by using more powerful light. Concentration of the light produces more explosions but not more powerful explosions. Secondly, the speed is increased by using bluer light, i.e. light of shorter period. . . .
>
> Every electron flying out of the metal has picked up just one quantum from the incident light. Since the h-rule associates the greater energy with the shorter vibration period, bluer light gives the more intense energy. Experiments show that (after deducting a constant "threshold" energy used up in extricating the electron from the film) each electron comes out with a kinetic energy equal to the energy of the quantum of incident light.
>
> The film can be prepared in the dark; but on exposure to feeble light electrons immediately begin to fly out before any of the collection-boxes could have been filled by fair means. Nor can we appeal to any trigger action of the light releasing an electron already loaded up with energy for its journey; it is the nature of the light which settles the amount of the load. *The light calls the tune, therefore the light must pay the piper.*[9]

An ancient could convey all of this only by making a symbol of himself to show it. Jesus "radiated" His realization to speed the expansion of consciousness in a brief, intense effort—as symbol of light, "bluer, of shorter period." As light's symbol, having settled the amount of the load on the elect-ones, He, Himself, paid the piper. But there is more to the story of h and to the parallel that Jesus' drama presents. Eddington says, "classical theory does not provide light with a pocket to pay," and then continues:

> If we have any instinct that can recognise a fundamental law of Nature when it sees one, that instinct tells us that the interaction of radiation and matter in single quanta is something lying at the root of world-structure and not a casual detail in the mechanism of the atom. Accordingly we turn to the "sweepstake" theory, which sees in this phenomenon a starting-point for a radical revision of the classical conceptions.
>
> Suppose that the light-waves are of such intensity that, according to the usual reckoning of their energy, one-millionth of a quantum is brought within range of each atom. The unexpected phenomenon is that instead of each atom absorbing one-millionth of a quantum, one atom out of every million absorbs a whole quantum. . . .
>
> It would seem that what the light-waves were really bearing within reach of each atom was not a millionth of a quantum but a millionth chance of securing a whole quantum. The wave-theory of light pictures and describes something evenly distributed over the whole wave-front which has usually been identified with energy. Owing to well-established phenomena such as interference and diffraction it seems impossible to deny this uniformity, but we must give it another interpretation; it is a uniform *chance of energy*.[10]

Jesus' words bespeak the uniform chance of energy—the energy of *one*. He said, "lo, I am with you alway, even unto the end of the world." [11] And His words also indicate that something within—the atom and the man—must make itself equal to one, to h, before the light or the quantum can enter. As Eddington puts it:

> The mysterious quantity h crops up inside the atom as well as outside it. . . . the electron's orbit is restricted to a definite series of sizes and shapes. There is nothing in the classical theory of electromagnetism to impose such a restriction; but the restriction exists, and the law imposing it has been discovered. It arises because the atom is arranging to make something in its interior equal to h. The intermediate orbits are excluded because they would involve fractions of h and h cannot be divided.
>
> But there is one relaxation. When wave-energy is sent out from or taken into the atom, the amount and period must correspond exactly to h. But as regards its internal arrangements the atom has no objec-

tion to $2h$, $3h$, $4h$, etc.; it only insists that fractions shall be excluded. . . .

. . . when the atom by radiating sets the aether in vibration, the periods of its electronic circulation are ignored and the period of the aether-waves is settled not by any picturable mechanism but by the seemingly artificial h-rule. It would seem that the atom carelessly throws overboard a lump of energy which, as it glides into the aether, moulds itself into a quantum of action by taking on the period required to make the product of energy and period equal to h. If this unmechanical process of emission seems contrary to our preconceptions, the exactly converse process of absorption is even more so. Here the atom has to look out for a lump of energy of the exact amount required to raise an electron to the higher orbit. It can only extract such a lump from aether-waves of a particular period—not a period which has resonance with the structure of the atom, but the period which makes the energy into an exact quantum.[12]

If h could speak, it must say to all atoms, as Jesus, symbol of h, said to all men, that unless within themselves they accept its own "name and being"—become equal to it—they cannot receive light, for "I am in my Father and you are in me and I am in you. . . ."[13] so that *one's* operation itself determines the seemingly artificial h-rule or Jesus' "I"-rule.

Eddington points out that the conflict between quantum theory and classical theory becomes acute in the problem of the propagation of light, in effect becomes a conflict between the corpuscular theory of light and the wave theory. "In the early days it was often asked, How large is a quantum of light? . . . *The quantum must be large enough to cover a 100-inch mirror . . . small enough to enter an atom*"—because of this contradiction, he says:

> We must not think about space and time in connection with an individual quantum; and the extension of a quantum in space has no real meaning. To apply these conceptions to a single quantum is like reading the Riot Act to one man. A single quantum has not travelled 50 billion miles from Sirius; it has not been 8 years on the way. But when enough quanta are gathered to form a quorum there will be found among them *statistical properties* which are the genesis of the 50 billion miles' distance of Sirius and the 8 years' journey of the light.[14]

An ancient symbolizing h in terms of "I" might convey that when the "statistical requirements are met"—that when a "quorum of quanta are gathered"—light will be there, by saying: ". . . where two or three have gathered in my name, I am there among them." [15] Jesus' summary statement is not a riot act, unmeaningful to an individual thinking of himself in connection with light, space, and time. He simply says that God is Father, is love, that with God all things are possible—as He, Himself, symbolized that of each man which is like h, one totally committed to action, an indivisible unity that overleaps time and space, an "unbroken glory" as Jesus was upon the cross, a "gathered radiance," as He was in life and in death.

To grasp the problems confronting physicists as they probe the secrets of elementary energy, it is necessary to realize that the "classical particle" cannot be captured and pinned down for examination. The "treasure" or *reality* of matter and its place of residence in nature is hard to come by. Throughout His ministry Jesus tries to explain the elusiveness of matter—His words indicate that both the "treasure" and its place of being are never *simultaneously* possessed: "The Realm of heaven is like treasure hidden in a field; the man who finds it hides it, and in his delight goes and sells all he possesses and buys that field. Again, the Realm of heaven is like a trader in search of fine pearls; when he finds a single pearl of high price, he is off to sell all he possesses and buy it." [16] Today, the scientist knows much about *fields* in which a single pearl, the quantum h, is somehow traded, in which the treasure of energy is somehow buried. Dr. Alexander says: "Quantum physics today gives us the picture of from ten to twenty qualitatively different quantum fields interpenetrating each other. Each fills the whole of space and has its own particular properties. *There is nothing else but these fields.* . . ." [17] Jesus pictured this, using a commonplace article as symbol. He said:

> Again, the Realm of heaven is like a net, which was thrown into the sea and collected fish of every sort.[18]

A net is a *pattern* of nothing but "fields," and fish are a good symbol to suggest the elusiveness of the classical particle which Eddington describes:

> A small enough stormy area corresponds very nearly to a particle moving about under the classical laws of motion; it would seem therefore that a particle definitely localised at a moving point is strictly the limit when the stormy area is reduced to a point. But curiously enough by continually reducing the area of the storm we never quite reach the ideal classical particle; we approach it and then recede from it again.[19]

To discover why, a fundamental general principle which Eddington ranks in importance with the principle of relativity must be examined. It is the "principle of indeterminacy," presented by Werner Heisenberg, and Eddington says, "The gist of it can be stated as follows: *a particle may have position or it may have velocity but it cannot in any exact sense have both* . . . . the more we bring to light the secret of position the more the secret of velocity is hidden." [20] Speaking strictly unscientifically, the layman might say it is perfectly obvious that neither a fish nor a particle can at once be moving, exhibiting velocity, and still, exhibiting position, but the world of the physicist does not permit of such an uncomplicated view.

If an ancient's pure thought led him to the realization of the "principle of indeterminacy," how could he convey it? He must, of course, select a symbol to represent "position" and another to represent "velocity." Jesus, light, allowed Himself to be called "teacher" or "Lord"—and He spoke thusly of teacher and scholar, of lord and servant:

> A scholar is not above his teacher, nor a servant above his lord; enough for the scholar to fare like his teacher, and the servant like his lord.[21]

If teacher (or lord) is seen to represent "position" and scholar (or servant) is seen to represent "velocity" this saying shows a new dimension. It would read: "Velocity (the time rate of change of position) is not greater than the speed of light. Therefore, velocity must share the limitations of light." Thus Jesus, in saying that scholar and teacher "fare alike" indicates that at the limit, or when reduced to a point in space-time frame, "position" and "velocity" *become alike.*

In discussing position and motion, Kline says: "The modern theory of infinite sets makes possible [a] startling solution. Motion *is* a series of rests. . . . At each instant of the interval during which an object is in 'motion' it occupies a definite position and may be said to be at rest." [22] Thus, it would appear that only the *one* property, sameness, comes to rest in a point, and only sameness can be exhibited at the limit, for here time escapes man as he confronts the *now*.

Jesus presents a parable of laborers who come early to the fields and laborers who come late, each receiving the *same wage*, and thus they fare alike: He concludes with these words, "So shall the last be first and the first last," [23] indicating the indeterminacy of both velocity and position—which is to say, man may measure only the one or the other aspect of a person or a particle: its "being" or its "becoming," its position or its velocity.

Eddington says, "our particle can never have simultaneously a perfectly definite position and a perfectly definite energy. . . . Hence in delicate experiments we must not under any circumstances expect to find particles behaving exactly as a classical particle was supposed to . . ."[24]

Thus, Jesus, who in a delicate experiment made Himself a symbol of the "classical particle of God," could not in truth behave as Messiah was supposed to, and He could not produce the "ideal classical particle," God the Father, any more than the physicist can produce today the ideal iota of matter.

Men see in other men only their personalities—a wave-group acting like a particle, an ego-group acting like a man; but just as searching the wave-group does not lead to the ideal classical particle, so searching the ego-group does not lead to the God-cell within man. This cell is "our Father" to the ego-group, is "my Father" to the Authority-Ego, h, and all of it that man may see is the form that surrounds it—the form of man,[25] a being conscious of God within himself, as Son, *one*. In the divided conscious domain where super-, pre-, and subconsciousness operate, the ego-group may be likened to a cloud of electrons:

> All electrons are alike from their own point of view. The apparent differences arise in fitting them into our own frame of reference which is irrelevant to their structure. . . .
>
> An electron decides how large it ought to be by measuring itself against the radius of the world in its space-directions. It cannot decide how long it ought to exist because there is no real radius of the world in its time-direction. *Therefore it just goes on existing indefinitely.* . . .
>
> We see the atoms with their girdles of circulating electrons darting hither and thither, colliding and rebounding. Free electrons torn from the girdles hurry away a hundred times faster, curving sharply round the atoms with side slips and hairbreadth escapes. The truants are caught and attached to the girdles and the escaping energy shakes the aether into vibration. X-rays impinge on the atoms and toss the electrons into higher orbits. We see these electrons falling back again, sometimes by steps, sometimes with a rush, caught in a cul-de-sac of mestastability, hesitating before "forbidden passages."
>
> Behind it all the quantum h regulates each change with mathematical precision. . . . The spectacle is so fascinating that we have perhaps forgotten that there was a time when we wanted to be told what an electron is. The question was never answered. No familiar conceptions can be woven round the electron; it belongs to the waiting list. Similarly the description of the processes must be taken with a grain of salt. . . .
>
> *Something unknown is doing we don't know what*—that is what our theory amounts to.

ONE, ITSELF, IS TEACHER

Eddington points out that "At certain times, viz, when [an electron] is interacting with a quantum, it might be detected by one of our watchers; but between whiles it virtually disappears from the physical world, having no interaction with it. We might arm our observers with flash-lamps to keep a more continuous watch on its doings; but the trouble is that under the flashlight it will not go on doing what it was doing in the dark." [26]

In parallel, man's ego-group bespeaks an unknown process—something unknown is "doing we don't know what"—and one might say that, like an electron, a self-concept or an image of another which makes up the ego-group goes on existing indefinitely, but is relegated to the subconscious, or is repressed into the *unconscious*, not showing itself until some stimulus from the outside world calls it from latency. In man, the "something unknown" that, with mathematical precision, is doing "we don't know what" can be only the Authority-Ego working to bring forth a genuine, classical elect-one: a personality in accord with *one*.

Jesus' drama depicts the Authority-Ego speaking to the multitude of personality images surrounding it. The group ponders, rejects, doubts, does not fully understand. Resistance continues until one in the group becomes equal to the idea of *one*—then light enters his consciousness. A scribe, raised to a "higher orbit of thought" as he listens to Jesus, says: "'Right teacher! You have truly said, He is One, and there is none else but Him. Also, to love Him with the whole heart, with the whole understanding, and with the whole strength, and to love one's neighbor as oneself—that is far more than all holocausts and sacrifice.' [Jesus replies] 'You are not far from the realm of God.'" [27] The scribe has stated the concept of *one* and *wholeness*.

Jesus tries to explain that the spirit or energy of truth is spread about in man in a manner by no means comparable to preconsciousness or to any image of self in the ego-group, but that as one's superconsciousness is heightened, Christ-consciousness condenses in his mind, and like an "electron" becomes as a compact body moving around with his ego-group. This drama, He, Himself represented, and He must show that in life as man's consciousness reaches a certain pitch of intensity, a vision of the Christ will emerge like a genie—in the finale one sees this happen.

Jesus said that Christ-consciousness overcomes "this world" [28]—it overcomes the world of intellect. Time and again this has happened. For example, Newton appears to have been as concerned with theology as with physics. And Clerk-Maxwell's letters to his wife attest to his preoccupation with the meaning of Jesus.

Christ-consciousness appears to be sent from the *unconscious* domain. Before this light can enter consciousness, something in man must be equal to its action: Jesus says the *will* (the energy) must be as the Father's, as One's. He insisted that He, the light, was *sent* into the world, and that He expressed the will or energy of the Father, unapparent save in man. How does light come into the physical world? Eddington says:

> . . . the individual wave-systems in the sub-aether are composed of oscillations too rapid to affect our gross senses; but their beats are sometimes slow enough to come within the octave covered by the eye. These beats are the source of the light coming from the hydrogen atom, and mathematical calculations show that their frequencies are precisely those of the observed light from hydrogen. Heterodyning of the radio carrier waves produces sound: heterodyning of the sub-aethereal waves produces light. Not only does this theory give the periods of the different lines in the spectra, but it also produces their intensities—a problem which the older quantum theory had no means of tackling. It should, however, be understood that the beats are not themselves to be identified with light-waves; they are in the sub-aether whereas light-waves are in the aether. They provide the oscillating source which in some way not yet traced sends out light-waves of its own period.[29]

An ancient who referred to himself as Light—and of the same "period" as the Father of all manifestation, God—might try to make clear that the "beats" in the "sub-aether" (or that unapparent source) are not to be identified with Himself, and that it is their action that produces the phenomenon, by saying:

> I speak not of myself: but the Father that dwelleth in me, he doeth the works.[30]

Certainly Jesus repeated insistently that He was *sent* to do light's work in this world. And the opening verses of the Gospel of John indicate an understanding of light's operation in the physical realm that scientists have now discovered: the radioactivity of matter, and X-rays, which an ancient might refer to as "the light shineth in darkness; and the darkness comprehended it not." [31] Jesus summed His statement of light's dual activity: "As my Father has continued working to this hour, so I work too." [32] In explaining the dual activity that produces sound and light, Eddington says: "We remarked that Schrödinger's picture of the hydrogen atom enabled it to possess something that would be impossible on Bohr's theory, viz. two energies at once. For a particle or electron this is not merely permissive, but compulsory—otherwise we can put no limits to the region where it may be." [33] Jesus understood that any *one* in manifestation—and thus every man—is possessed of two energies (or wills) at once, because light itself involves two frequencies operating in the same wave-group. In drama and word, He indicates that the energy of Satan or evil operates in man, as well as the energy of God or good.[34]

Because man has both a conscious and an *unconscious* domain, his will is both free and bound, limited and unlimited. Jesus said that only as man's will becomes as the will of One can it be perfectly free and perfectly controlled. Only then can one be "as God" and yet "as himself." The will to be "as God" and the will to be "as himself" compose the two wills a person expresses simultaneously. The two opposing wills are thus the same and yet opposite: to be "as God," whole-one, and to be "as man," one-whole. The first expresses man's consciousness of *a priori* God and his compulsion to follow a like pattern of action: destruction of self-in-isolation as ALL in being. As a man dies, he expresses this inherent prerogative of *a priori* God: self-destruction of the form that was. The will to be one-whole, as *living* God, expresses Christ-consciousness in man that is whole, as One is whole, and is utterly committed to life. Adler recognized man's need to express himself as wholeness; Jung saw that human nature tends toward wholeness; to Rank the "urge to immortality" is man's inexorable drive to feel connected to life in terms of his individual will with a sense of inner assurance that the connection will not be broken or pass away." [35]

Jesus did not teach that man should try to be as solitary God, *a priori*. He taught that man should strive to be "perfect as your Father is perfect . . ."—"perfect in one," as Jesus described the Father and the Son to be perfectly one.[36] But He saw that because man *is* of both God-strands of will, he must act under the compulsion of each: thus he must come to lay down his life willingly, under no compulsion, as *a priori* God willingly laid down His life, and he must also pick it up again as did God become One everlastingly committed to life, action, and the freedom in consciousness to decide what one's life will be.

Viktor Frankl, author of Logotherapy, writes, "There is nothing conceivable that would so condition a man as to leave him without the slightest freedom. Therefore, a residue of freedom, however limited it may be, is left to man in neurotic and even psychotic cases. Indeed, the innermost core of the patient's personality is not even touched by a psychosis." [37] He sees that the individual personality remains essentially unpredictable—

"In other words, man is ultimately self-determining. Man does not simply exist, but always decides what his existence will be, what he will become in the next moment. By the same token, "every human being has the freedom to change at any instant. . . ." [38] He recognizes that man is a finite being, and that "his freedom is restricted. It is not freedom from conditions, but freedom to take a stand toward conditions . . ."—in suffering, for example, "what matters above all is the attitude we take toward suffering, the attitude in which we take our suffering upon ourselves." [39] Thus, "In a word, each man is questioned by life; and he can only answer to life by *answering for* his own life; to life he can only respond by being responsible. Thus logotherapy sees in responsibleness the very essence of human existence." [40]

Thus, the answer to the ancient argument as to whether man's will is bound or free comes to rest in the answer that it is both and neither—it is the will of a *responsible* creature, self-determining his attitude toward life and what he will make of his own life in any condition in which he finds himself or that may be imposed upon him.

Just as Jesus saw that in order for a man to fulfill his desire to express Selfhood, his will must transcend itself and become as the will of the Father, so Frankl sees that "self-actualization cannot be attained if it is made an end in itself, but only as a side effect of self-transcendence." [41]

If man is empowered of and by the two aspects of God—which may be seen as Self-actualization and Self-transcendence—a concept based upon duality should suffice. But duality evokes the third aspect of being, so that one must come to grips with the trinity principle. In life, it involves man, woman, and child—in the physical realm, positive, negative, and neutral energy—in theology it gives rise to that most baffling of trinities: the mystery of Father, Son, and Holy Ghost. What is the Holy Ghost? And why must it be?

II

To attempt to explain the Holy Ghost is to attempt image building of something altogether different from any manifestation. To try to say what "it" is *not*, is to say that the "Holy Ghost" is not the precise opposite of everything in manifestation, but is different from and equal to it because "it" empowers, contains, and is the all-pervading medium. The only "thing" one can liken to "it" is *space*—that of space which is not its fields, is not energy, but is the "manifestation of nothing," paradoxical as this statement is, that allows energy's manifestations to operate within it and matter to exist in it in discrete state. It both encompasses and involves energy's dual nature that gives rise to the trinity in being: negative, positive, neutral.

A scientist would be as hard put to explain what *space itself* is as a theologian is to explain what the Holy Ghost is—both can discuss only what takes place through it. For example, Einstein and Lorentz saw space to be endowed with physical qualities and thus with ether, but Einstein says that the concept of motion cannot be applied to ether; [42] and Lorentz divested ether of its mechanical properties, divested matter of its electromagnetic properties, posing the concept that: "Inside material bodies no less than in empty space the ether alone, not atomically conceived matter, [is] the seat of the electro-magnetic fields . . . . the elementary particles of matter are capable *only* of executing movements; their electro-magnetic activity is entirely due to the fact that they carry electric charges." [43] The all-pervading space that contains Einstein's motionless ether may be likened to the Holy Ghost of God, *a priori*, that which cannot itself be examined because the ether, motionless, stands between it and all manifestation within it. The ether alone as the *seat* of the electromagnetic fields may be likened to the *being* of God, the Father, one's refuge, that allows him to "Be still and know. . . ." [44] The Son may be likened to the elementary particle, endowed with the "electric charge": *I* will be. Jesus speaks of the Son "sitting on the right hand of the power," [45] and His teaching points to the Father as the seat of the power that is being given over to the Son.

Einstein proposed that each three-dimensional portion of space "always contains a total electrical charge whose size is represented by a whole number," [46] despite the fact that its electrical density disappears everywhere. Thus, one might say that space "holds" the charge, but is not itself that which it holds.

Each person involves and is held in being by space. If there is a "divine Absolute," space is the only "manifestation" of it that man knows. Sufism teaches that: "Each human soul is a particle of the divine Absolute, and the mystic aims at a complete union with the Divine. This union is attained in the knowledge that he is himself that ultimate Reality which he seeks. But the individual self is completely annihilated in this higher Self. . . ." [47] The difference between Jesus' teaching and Sufism is that Jesus saw that creation, space, Holy Ghost of God, is that ultimate reality which cannot be undone, so that He insists upon the "study of *and*," of the organization and arrangement of energy within it. He saw that God as Father lives in a centering of power in *one's*, and in the transferring of the power inherent in "ultimate Reality" to consciousness of God in one's being: i.e., Christ-consciousness. "I" am conscious of God as the seat of the power in "my" being, and as the *rest* possible to life. This borders on Sufism:

> I stood on the edge of things, as on a circle inscribed
> But time's revolutions have borne me into the still centre.[48]

But Jesus saw that the individual self is not annihilated as time bears one to union with the center and seat of his being, that is, to rest or death. One's life is harvested, his soul and "charge" renewed, and time's revolutions bear him again to "the edge of things." But to what end? Can one find a clue in the realm of physics?

Einstein says, "The de Broglie-Schrödinger method, which has in a certain sense the character of field-theory . . ." deduces the existence of "only-discrete states," and that it is "in astonishing agreement with empirical fact, on a "basis of differential equations operating with a kind of resonance-theory, but it has to do without a localization of the mass-particles and without strictly causal laws." [49] To appreciate this poetically as it may be used to deduce a psychic parallel, one must observe the definitions of *resonance:*

> To the physicist, resonance means the phenomenon shown by a vibrating system which responds with maximum amplitude under the action of a harmonic force; this occurs when the frequency of the applied force is the same as a natural frequency of the vibrating body.
>
> To the electrical engineer, resonance means the state of adjustment of a circuit permitting a maximum flow of current when an electromotive force of a particular frequency is impressed.
>
> To the chemist, resonance means the phenomenon shown by a molecule to which two or more structures, differing only in the disposition of electrons, can be assigned. Its effect is to increase stability.
>
> To the musician, resonance means the intensification and enriching of tone by supplementary vibrations.

Thus, in psychic parallel each man's existence is an only-discrete state, a particular adjustment he is making wherein he is coming to be resonant with life—as the word applies to manifesting the maximum amplitude possible to his natural frequency which, like one's *frequencies*, permits two or more structures of consciousness in order to effect increased stability and allow a maximum flow of life's current to pass through, thus intensifying and enriching his sense of being until he can make of his life

ONE, ITSELF, IS TEACHER

a satisfaction in being sufficient to keep it in consciousness everlastingly.

Jesus teaches that man carries within himself a resonator in perfect accord with life's resonator—One, God. And this One is "come that they may have life," have it more abundantly, "have it to the full." [50]

Why was this not given in the beginning? The Absolute gave its ALL, but the Absolute as a concept of life is impure because absolute power is corrupting. Life moved from this impurity into a process of purification that must insure in time the manifestation of the pure satisfaction of *One*, as number, as wholeness, as a power absolute unto itself only. Biochemists have shown that "organic substances do not crystallize until they are pure or virtually so." [51] As ALL gave itself, it gave into life the death processes that arrest the psychic crystallizing and allow life to continue "salting"— the purifying discipline that offers as reward perfect freedom under the law of empathy to which one responds naturally, effortlessly, and which will be complete when all has been experienced by each, somehow, on some level.

To show the reason for man's successes and failures in his attempts to make himself resonant, an image may be fashioned of Mach's view, which fascinated Einstein: "what inertial resistance counteracts is not acceleration as such but acceleration with respect to the masses of other bodies existing in the world." [52] Poetically translated into psychic parallel, one might say that ALL, the Holy Ghost, restricts evolution's pace, as well as the individual's pace, to the progress made by the least one in his experiencing of solitariness as he "adjusts his circuit" to permit a maximum flow of truth through his being— so that first, last, poised, or rushing, none shall be first, last, or lost in space, but each shall become as One, the resonator operative throughout life that conscience merely introduces.

In man, empathy, not conscience, is the resonator. But conscience has a vital role to play. Just as a satellite must have a continuous sensing of its motion and attitude in space, keeping itself horizontal in relation to the surface of the earth below if it is to perform its complicated maneuvers,[53] so man must have a continuous sense of "right or wrong," regardless of the compassion his empathy arouses within him as he views good or evil in this world. Conscience, which is of the closed world of the past, acts as an "inertial reference package" to balance the course empathy takes.

III

There are many fascinators in the world of physics—things to make one wonder. If one wonders long enough, the fascinators begin to relate themselves to life. Such is the FitzGerald Contraction. Eddington explains it:

> Suppose that you have a rod moving at very high speed. Let it first be pointing transverse to its line of motion. Now turn it through a right angle so that it is along the line of motion. The rod contracts. It is shorter when it is along the line of motion than when it is across the line of motion. This contraction, known as the FitzGerald Contraction, is exceedingly small in all ordinary circumstances. It does not depend at all on the material of the rod but only on the speed. For example, if the speed is 19 miles a second—the speed of the earth round the sun—the contraction of length is 1 part in 200,000,000, or 2-1/2 inches in the diameter of the earth.[54]

The FitzGerald Contraction is a property of matter, of evil's, or the serpent's domain. As one draws a poetic parallel, one must consider that by resisting, one is apt to turn evil transverse to its line of motion, thereby elongating or elaborating it.

Jesus said, "resist not evil. . . . Love your enemies . . . . pray for them which despitefully use you. . . ."[55] In effect, only by taking a line transverse to evil's line will you outmeasure it.

Eddington says the FitzGerald Contraction is "the same for a rod of steel and for a rod of india-rubber; the rigidity and the compressing stress are bound up with the constitution in such a way that if one is large so also is the other."[56] Jesus states the psychic parallel—"Wherefore I say unto thee, Her sins, which are many, are forgiven; for she loved much: but to whom little is forgiven, the same loveth little."[57] If the one aspect is large so is the other.

Evil is symbolized by the serpent whose line of motion is along the line of earth's, horizontal. But man, the only true biped, posed himself uprightly—alone in all the world, threw himself transverse the "natural" line, became a vertical being, in truth measuring more than he was and more than evil measures. As he moves along evil's path, the natural path, he also moves transverse to it, creating within himself, poetically speaking, a sphere that is independent of either line of motion because it is at once both and neither, as is the point where the vertical crosses the horizontal: +.

Jesus could leave no better symbol than the cross to convey His realization of the opposing lines of motion, and of the two energies man is provided with that give rise to a discrete series of possible energies, just as the atom has. He said the Father knows what man has need of [58]—surely the Father knows the perfection of His own matter, knows that man has need of his evil as well as his good if he would have matter of his own, dominion over it.

Jesus restated David's enigmatic prophecy, defining the symbolic words which point to man's inner conflict arising from his own opposing forces, and to his discrete series of possible energies. The prophecy casts a clue as to why life operates this pattern and what is to be accomplished through this working:

> ... as Jesus taught in the temple, he asked, "How can the scribes say that the Christ is David's son? David himself said, inspired by the holy Spirit,
>
>> The Lord said to my Lord,
>> 'Sit at my right hand,
>> till I make your enemies a
>> footstool for your feet.'
>
> David here calls him Lord. Then how can he be his son?" [59]

To understand the poetry one must understand the symbolic words. Jesus defined a man's enemies to be of his own household [60]—thus the opposing forces are original endowment. Jesus says that earth is the footstool of God [61]—footstool must be defined as matter. Therefore, the prophecy lies at the root of matter and man's relationship to it: to the motions he is making within himself in sequence to the motions God made within Himself to bring forth One in material being.

The prophecy appears to say that alone in all creation God, ALL, has become His own residue: THE Lord which is One-whole, *itself finished of inner conflict* and therefore unequal to further divisive action on or within itself. Whereas the other, my Lord, is One equal to self-division or self-divisive action, and for this reason they are not now precisely the same. But in a corresponding position, they maintain a balance in one sphere until a new arrangement in the other sphere is completed—until the expressive force, my Lord, expends its own destructive potential and comes to express itself as identity in matter of its own.

Just as Eddington sees in a complex equation the lovely words, "There are waters blown by changing winds to laughter," so the poetic eye and ear can see and hear in David's poetry a suggestion of an equation, somewhat mysterious:

$$qp - pq = ih/2\pi$$

Eddington says all authorities seem to be agreed that this equation lies "at, or nearly at, the root of everything in the physical world. . . ." [62] Part of its mystery is that qp and pq are unequal. David's prophecy would say that *time* gives rise to this variance between qp, The Lord, and pq, my Lord.

Life to *be*, must express itself in matter. Therefore, a concept of crucial importance is presented in David's poetry: man's prime *unconscious motivation* is to grasp matter of his own. But Jesus taught that it is not the "stuff" itself man must seek—rather, it is understanding of it. The truth of its being is the truth of man's being, for he is made of it. When he has dominion over it he will have dominion over himself—when my Lord becomes as The Lord, presently active in perfect matter of His own, life begins to be everlasting, expressed as matter under the dominion of full consciousness, the kingdom is come, one's will is done in earth.

Jesus saw that the destructive potential in man can be dealt with only as it is set against itself: i.e., as it becomes a house divided; thus, "I" come not to bring peace, but the sword, to set the household against itself; yet, "he who does not gather with me scatters" [63]—the expanding and limiting frequencies are set to provide a boundary for expression. Jesus said, "This is an evil generation," [64] but He also said that life is being leavened, transformed through the working in and of the realm of God. It is from this generation—this bringing into being—that man prays to be delivered into life eternal, which must also mean into matter of his own under his own dominion.

Jesus prays, "Deliver us from evil," but this is not to say OF evil. Huxley makes the distinction between *from* and *of*, though his remark does not refer to the Lord's Prayer. He says that "freedom from" is applicable to the undesirable aspects of life: "freedom from restraint, from tyranny . . . from want . . . from fear, and from many other undesirable things. But *freedom of* is equally important: freedom of opinion, belief, opportunity, assembly and so forth." [65] Jesus' teaching indicates that one cannot exclude or dispense with evil itself—man cannot be delivered OF it. Consider this parable:

> When an unclean spirit leaves a man, it roams through dry places in search of ease. As it finds none, then it says, "I will go back to the house I left"; and when it comes it finds the house clean and all in order. Then off it goes to fetch seven other spirits worse than itself; they go in and dwell there, and the last state of that man is worse than the first.[66]

The concept of repressions greatly empowered in latency and their strange return to the "house" of consciousness is presented here. Also presented is a psychic parallel to the theory of relativity, wherein coming to rest has no meaning: "A decrease of velocity relative to one frame is an increase relative to another frame." [67] But most important, Jesus presents the concept that evil cannot be cast out and thereby obliterated; therefore, it must be regenerated, recast—from its destructive potential man must pray to be delivered. Thus, Jesus' prayer might be paraphrased: "Deliver us from evil: from the matter we are in, from flesh expressed by partial consciousness—deliver us to death that we may be reborn into eternal life in such flesh as complete consciousness will express and have dominion over, that true riches may be committed to our trust." As for that in each man's dominion which is spurious, wicked, it shall be recast as it is cast into "the furnace of fire" [68]—into matter which is an "ever-burning" manifestation, but which is also a delight to man's soul.

When consciousness of good and evil came to life, the first division was made, the process of setting the man's "household" against itself was activated. But when this creature posed himself uprightly, the "stuff" he was made of outmeasured the "stuff" of the serpent-evil that travels the horizontal path, although both creatures were made of the same "stuff."

Perhaps ancestral-man first picked up not a weapon, but a stick to use as staff. But as he used whatever he held as tool to slay his brother, the "rod" turned to evil in his hand, for as one lays on a club he must turn it from vertical to horizontal position, and the whole organization of its energy changes, just as the whole organization of a man's psychic energy changes as he uses tool for weapon. The story of Moses, lawgiver and slayer, depicts the strange play of man's rod turning to evil, the serpent, in his hand.[69] But David said: ". . . thy rod and thy staff they comfort me." [70] The animal that nature has not armed needs a weapon, and the same *rod* that strikes and thus takes evil's horizontal line is the *staff* that upholds man's vertical stance—the biped must use it as he travels the natural path, moving uprightly toward "something" that is made of both good and evil when the destructive potential is spent.

IV

Jesus promised not heaven, but everlasting life. Life must be lived in the material realm which is shared by good and evil. In it they are reconciled through the *one* measure that both separates and rejoins the two frequencies that constitute light's "household" or wave-group, providing a boundary for its action. In the material realm, the second law of thermodynamics reigns supreme—the law that says any physical system left to itself and allowed to distribute its energy in its own way does so in a manner such that entropy increases while the available energy of the system diminishes. These two aspects of the physical realm are dramatized in the strange play between Jesus and Judas.

If one reduces the diminishing effect of the second law to the smallest or simplest operation conceivable, he must show that *one* iota of the source energy of a system, or *one* representative of the energy of a system, must be made unavailable, or "lost," as the cycle of one full operation is completed, or simply when the time has come. At Jesus' death, the "system" the disciples represent, left to itself, diminishes by one as Judas dies, and an outside source of energy must be incorporated if another full cycle is to be completed. St. Paul fulfills this role.

Jesus, Light, stays in consciousness long enough to determine the load upon the elect-ones, then retires into the *unconscious* domain. Jesus appears to have "fixed the load" upon Judas, to have cast him in the role of the *one measure* the system "loses" in the course of time.

The loss of this measure appears to be directly concerned with the acquisition of matter or the conversion of energy to matter, and the return of matter to the field or into a field, for Judas was involved with matter in keeping the purse, and he was handed the sop of bitter herbs (according to Stauffer) [71] or bread, "my body," [72] my matter, as the signal to collect his reward in silver—precious matter. Of his own volition, Judas finished himself—into matter, and the silver was returned to "purchase" a potter's field.

The mystery of Judas touches many thinking men. Renan says:

> Without denying that Judas of Kerioth may have contributed to the arrest of his Master, we still believe that the curses with which he is loaded are somewhat unjust . . . . if the foolish desire for a few pieces of silver turned the head of poor Judas, he does not seem to have lost the moral sentiment completely, since when he had seen the consequences of his fault he repented, and, it is said, killed himself.[73]

In the accounts of the betrayal, there is implication that Jesus had discussed Judas' role with him. Jesus announces that He is to be betrayed and describes the fate of the betrayer. Judas asks, "Surely it is not me, rabbi?" Jesus answers, "Is it not?" [74] This suggests that Judas had been instructed, had not fully comprehended the implication in what he was to do, faltered when it came to him, and would have faltered when Jesus handed him the sop, save for Jesus' command: "Be quick with what you have to do." [75]

This passage continues, "None of those at table understood why he said this to him; some thought that, as Judas kept the money-box, Jesus told him to buy what they needed for the festival or to give something to the poor. So Judas went out immediately after taking the bread."

There seems no doubt that Jesus could have stopped Judas with a word, but Son of man must follow the path outlined by Scriptures: a betrayer was a necessity to fulfill His mission. Judas hanged himself and Jesus bore His cross—as many who followed after Him bore theirs. The disciples had been warned that they would suffer as Jesus must suffer if they dedicated themselves to His mission. They expressed their willingness to suffer death however it might come—countless men before and after have been so dedicated.

Judas appears to be the first to die in service to Jesus: Jesus outlined an action and gave Judas both the signal and the command to perform it. As Judas kissed Jesus to betray Him, Jesus called him, "Friend." [76] Would He have chosen this moment to be ironical, sarcastic, hypocritical? Truth speaks truth. Jesus called Judas *friend*. At the last supper, Jesus said: "Greater love hath no man than this, that a man lay down his life for his friends. Ye are my friends, if ye do whatsoever I command you." [77] Moffatt translates Jesus' words at the moment of betrayal, "My man, do your errand." There was still a Scripture to be fulfilled—and Judas had an errand to do before it could be fulfilled—this Judas did before he killed himself. The prophecy reads:

> . . . and I took the thirty silver pieces, the price of him who had been priced, whom they had priced and expelled from the sons of Israel; and I gave them for the potter's field, as the Lord had bidden me.[78]

As the Lord had bidden me. The fulfilling of this prophecy bespeaks the interaction between Jesus and Judas. The money "bought" earth—"bought" matter.

Jesus did not have to bid Judas to hang himself. He knew he would be unable to live with himself after his act. As Judas acquits his role, a boundary is provided for Light's action.

Judas, the despised, rejected of all, the *one* lost that the Scriptures be fulfilled,[79] that nature's supreme law might be fulfilled to the last iota—Judas, an utter revulsion to the elect upon whom fell the task of building Christianity—is he not the stone that the builders rejected? Scripture says: [80]

> The stone that the builders rejected is the chief stone now of the corner: this is the doing of the Lord, and a wonder to our eyes? . . .

> The stone that the builders rejected is the chief stone now of the corner. Everyone who falls on that stone will be shattered, and whoever it falls upon will be crushed.

A stone is matter. Matter is head of the corner of the building—the temple of life, the body. Most precious to man, the inherent and first necessity of life, is matter of his own. Yet this "stone"—flesh and its demands—is seen to be evil. Money is mammon's symbol, and mammon is seen as evil. With matter and money Judas is completely identified. Was it not Judas upon whom the crushing stone fell—was not the Judas drama the doing of the Lord?

As one views the whole picture, it would appear to say that there is *one* among the elect of consciousness, the superego, who gathers and disperses matter. At the command of Authority-Ego, this factor moves to convert this experience in life into "hard coin." This member of the household that betrays to death can find solace only in death, but through its action One's mission in life is completed and he gives back the "mammon" he has taken unto himself. Jesus says:

> And I tell you use mammon, dishonest as it is. . . .
>
> He who is faithful with a trifle is also faithful with a large trust, and He who is dishonest with a trifle is also dishonest with a large trust. . . . So if you are not faithful with dishonest mammon, how can you ever be trusted with true Riches? And if you are not faithful with what belongs to another, how can you ever be given what is your own?[81]

Mammon is dishonest because matter is not what it appears to be—it is but a trifle of mass. Judas had been faithful with the "trifle" of keeping the purse; Jesus could depend upon him to be faithful in executing the large trust involved in His betrayal and its aftermath—essential to His work. This world's wealth, or matter, is not actually man's own, but God's. In this stewardship man must prove himself capable of using wealth before he can be given true riches—matter of his own.

Scientists estimate that a human being absorbs only one neutrino in his lifetime.[82] This smallest particle is indeed a mystery. The Jesus-Judas drama indicates that the "iota" of matter one has taken unto himself must be returned to the "ground" from which it came, even as he carries away one iota of "true Riches," a quantum of light's radiant energy.

There is a strange prophecy that the Judas drama appears to fulfill. Scripture says:

I will redeem them from death . . . repentance shall be hid from mine eyes.[83]

The repentance of Judas is "hid" from the eyes of Jesus. The two die "in phase," the one called good, the other called evil. Through his death Judas is redeemed—this is to say, he reacted to the realization of what he had done by making the greatest act of contrition, of repentance, a man can make when no reparation can be made, and thereby he redeems himself to some degree in the eyes of mankind. Because he took his own life to give expression to his unbearable remorse and grief, he cannot be regarded as utterly evil and inhuman—after the betrayal, he fulfilled his mission and then did a very *human* thing.

There is an ancient Jewish sect, Hasidism, which holds that "the essential unity of creation precludes the artificial separation of the sacred and the profane . . . destroying the boundaries which cut off the evil from redemption and secure the righteous in their pride." [84] This study concurs. Each person is both good and evil—each deals with his own of ALL's evil, generating from it a "footstool for his feet," as he loses one ego-member who "buys" a bit of earth, pure matter and thus *pure* evil, when he returns the "coin of the realm" he has taken.

In the psychic domain is there a Judas factor, rejected by the ego-group, unforgiven even though, as Judas did, this member so repents his deed as to be unable to bear himself and thus "spends" his life in sorry reparation? In the view of this study, there is a Judas-factor and it has a special task, but it is not this utterly repentant one that represents damnation in the ego-group. Everything in Jesus' teaching leads to the concept that the sorrowing and repentant are forgiven, whatever they have done. He upbraids the "cities" wherein His mighty works were done because they *repented not*. He warns, "It shall be more tolerable for Tyre and Sidon at the day of judgment, than for you." [85] Authority-Ego is addressing His own strongholds—this is to say, Jesus, as symbol of it, could address none other than His *own*. Only the "crumbs" that fell from the table He spread could be gathered by any other than "Israel." [86]

Are the cities representative of "knowledgeable" sins, repeated, boasted, sins that corrupt oneself and others, wrongdoing that one knows is wrongdoing but will not cease and does not suffer, as though his conscience had been beheaded and he will not listen to the voice of life within him telling him that he deals in evil? Do these ego-members gather into great strongholds, into settlements upon the plain of personality, dominating or coloring the whole structure of it, tainting the life of the soul's populace with their own degradation, corrupting the flesh like slums corrupt great cities? In *The Alexandria Quartet,* Durrell writes: "I see at last that none of us is properly to be judged for what happened in the past. It is the city which should be judged though we, its children, must pay the price." [87] There are iniquitous cities in one's inner world, and when he lives in a soul become as sin-ridden as a slum is rat-ridden, each day's newly born ego-member is lost in the morass before he can make a fresh start. There is that in every person's life that he *knows* to be damnable, knows to be corrupting to the newly stated soul his "computer" hands him day by day. But all his sinning is not so easily bedamned, so wantonly begot—nor can it be ceased, for there is not the will in him to have done with it at the time; even when what might be called "an episode of sin" is over, he cannot truly regret it—the experience has raised the level of his understanding and he would not possess less. He can say of such sin only this: "I did it knowing it was wrong, but I cannot regret that I did it; I know now, however, that I could not bring myself to do this again because I know now its cost to me and to others." Such experience represents, in truth, a lesson learned.

But there are other deeds that even though they have brought new understanding, one must regret to the end of his life and in the very-depths of his being, saying of them, "God be merciful to me a sinner," [88] as though to pray, "forgive me this terrible toll of life I have taken, toll of my own life and of another's, for which I shall be bitterly sorry in every breath I draw now and forever." Or he quickly represses and forgets the sin *he cannot forgive himself*—the sin that must await the resurrection of damnation.

Thus, there are sins one may deal with on the intellectual level, there are sins conscience deals with as long as it has a voice in the inner realm, but there are sins which blaspheme the preciousness of life itself—these are unforgivable because a man cannot bring himself to forgive himself: they sever his connection with his own Authority-Ego and still the voice of the ego-member in the world of selves, as Judas' voice was stilled.

Jesus says each man is responsible for and must bear the consequences of his every action and *word.*[89] The greatest enlargement of the "word sin" into mortal error is found in part of a statement in itself contradictory:

> I tell you, therefore, men will be forgiven any sin and blasphemy, but they will not be forgiven for blaspheming the Spirit. Whoever says a word against the Son of man will be forgiven, but whoever speaks against the holy Spirit will never be forgiven, neither in this world nor in the world to come.[90]

First, Jesus says man will be forgiven *any* sin and blasphemy. Then, *any* is contradicted—man is not forgiven blaspheming the holy Spirit. Is the holy Spirit not life itself? Who can live without in some way at some time cursing or reviling life? Is true repentance of no account? What, exactly, *is* the mortal sin?

In the view of this study, Jesus recognized that there will be one blaspheming of life itself which a man will be *unable to forgive himself*—this is the mortal sin. He did not name this sin, because unto each is his own expression of it—it might be no more than kicking his dog: the sin as such has no name. In the great majority of cases, he is unable to forgive himself, because this sin is quickly repressed and forgotten; if not, he "spends his life" in remorse and dies still unable to forgive himself what he has done. Thus, in one way or the other Homo sapiens bears this unforgiven sin into the "world to come" which develops as his ego-group develops. Because man never recovers from infant amnesia, the newly stated ego-group does not and cannot know the name and nature of the sin he bears into the world at birth—thus, the sin cannot be forgiven in this life. For this reason, each man is committed to pay the wage of this nameless sin, each pays the wage that Judas paid—in one way or another he destroys himself:

O Israel, thou hast destroyed thyself. . . .[91]

As one's work in this world draws to completion, Authority-Ego places upon the Judas-factor the burden of the unknown sin. Through death the unknown sin is forgiven and the Judas-factor is redeemed. But as a person dies, he takes into the world to come another nameless, unknown sin that will command the price of death which the Authority-Ego *and* the Judas-factor will pay to redeem this evil. Because each person comes bearing his unknown, unforgiven sin, death is already stated in his being. Will man be forever in bondage to this wheel, to a nameless sin, to death? Scripture says:

O death, I will be thy plagues; O grave I will be thy destruction.[92]

If this scripture be true, man will not forever lay down his consciousness in the grave. This study concludes that as long as man commits sins he cannot in consciousness and good conscience forgive himself, death alone can reduce to dust his psychic "cities" of sin and his corrupted flesh. But death returns him to life to try again to learn how to live without corrupting himself and others. In each life experience, man can and does have done with error as his lust is recast into empathy. In death an iota of his evil purchases a bit of *pure matter*. Thus in time he will regenerate himself —will don incorruptible flesh born of incorruptible consciousness guided in life by empathy. Man will be free of the grave, but he will not be absolutely free of death—which is to say, death will be *in* his life as sleeping and waking is to his present consciousness, or as inhaling and exhaling is to his present body.

In summary, the Judas-factor of the ego-group that betrays to death and purchases with its life a bit of pure matter is not the *perpetrator* of the unnameable, unknown sin he is commanded to bear to the grave, that he buries in the purchase of earth which is a "potter's field"—a final resting place for the unknown, the derelict, the outcast. Purchase of a "potter's field" indicates that what one loses of himself to purchase his own of matter are those members the like of which are buried in such a field— they are ego-members of a prior group, members he has forgotten or refuses to remember because *he cannot bear to live with them*. They are the resurrection of damnation in him, but because a full cycle of death, birth, and life stands between them and his consciousness, mercifully, he cannot, will not, remember them, cannot mourn their loss.

This concept does not imply that the Judas-factor necessary to the transaction is without sin, any more than Judas himself was without sin, or that any man or any member of the ego-group is without sin. Each member bears his quota of it. But this concept does imply that Judas himself and the Judas-factor of the ego-group, or any man or factor that recognizes his sin, is not beyond redemption even though what this member has done is unspeakably cursed in the eyes of men and in the eyes of the other members of the ego-group. Consider that Judas said the word against the Son of man—betrayed Him—and Jesus says that he who speaks against the Son of man will be forgiven. Thus, He implies that Judas will be forgiven—not by Jesus, who had nothing to forgive him. He plainly states that He chose him for this role [93]—and the Gospels plainly state that Judas was commanded to his act.

Was it necessary that the Judas role be played? Dr. von Franz writes: "One of the most important among the physicists' concepts is Niels Bohr's idea of *complementarity*. Modern microphysics has discovered that one can only describe light by means of two logically opposed but complementary concepts: The ideas of particle and wave." [94] And the light-wave group itself can be understood only in terms of "opposing frequencies" that reinforce each other at the center and cancel out together, providing a boundary for the group, for light. The world will forgive Judas when his role is understood: he, too, was a symbol, essential to the drama—his action reinforced Jesus' action at the central point upon which the play turned as they "canceled out" together, providing a boundary for "Light's" action in this world, freeing it to act unseen on another level that it might express itself again. Judas and Jesus may be seen as the complementary components necessary to dramatize the story of light.

That the mortal sin is nameless, that it is a derelict from the forgotten past which can be any sin a man has repressed or has been unable to forgive himself, rests upon Jesus' contradictory words. He says *any* blasphemy will be forgiven—and He, Himself, blasphemed if "pronouncing the forbidden name of God" is to say, "Ani hu," and if to say, "Ani hu," is blasphemy.

The forbidden name of God is indeed a mystery. What is this name? The definition of blasphemy reads: "In Jewish law, cursing or reviling God or the king . . . pronouncing the forbidden name of God. See Tetragrammaton." [95] Tetragrammaton? "The four letters (variously written, without vowel points . . .) forming a Hebrew tribal name of the Supreme Being . . . too sacred to pronounce." [96] What is this mystery having to do with four "unpronounceable" letters, IHVH, or JHVH, etc.? Does the blasphemy rest in rendering the form of God in a four-dimensional concept such as consciousness can know? Could one state the forbidden name in numbers, for example:

$$\frac{1}{1} = \frac{1}{1}$$

Could this be "blasphemy" because although the equation might bespeak a four-dimensional concept, it does not coincide with the "odd-even" division of a light wave-group and thus it cannot truly and fully satisfy life's situation? Is there anything in the realm of physics and mathematics that might explain this mystery?

The answer is yes. But to solve the riddle one must enter into an argument that engages the scientific world. The gist of the argument can be very simply told: it hangs upon what Jung calls, "the dilemma of three and four," [97] and one may grasp its general outline in Jung's work and that of the physicist W. Pauli, joined in a volume entitled, *The Interpretation of Nature and the Psyche*. The "dilemma of three and four" deals with a very old dispute, but it is one that is examined to this day. Trinity or Tetragrammaton? Triad or Tetrad?

The dilemma must be viewed in its historical perspective and in its current dress. Then Jesus' answer to it will be given, for He resolved the question, transcended the impasse in stating the *quinta essentia* in His Equation of One that demands

> . . . from the beachcombers on the ocean's fringe
> A pearl which is outside the oyster of Space and Time.[98]

Chapter 8

THE DILEMMA AND THE PEARL

I

Summarizing the opposing concepts that constitute what Jung calls the dilemma of three and four, W. Pauli says that two types of minds have battled through history: first, the thinking type that considers the quantitative relations of the parts to be essential—and, secondly, the intuitive type that senses the qualitative indivisibility of the whole.[1]

The first type mind is posed on the side of *three*. This type took its stand with Euclid, resting upon his well-known axiom: the whole is equal to the sum of its parts. This axiom, together with the rest of Euclidean geometry, dominated Western thought until the late nineteenth century. One might say that Euclidean geometry still dominates, for the revolution in mathematics that tumbled it from sacred pre-eminence has not yet seeped down to the layman's level, and many students will learn first, by rote, Euclid's axioms, imbedding in the subconscious mind these fallible statements which have been presented as unquestionable truth, and thus they become a part of every analogued answer handed up to consciousness. Mathematicians, of course, are aware of the limited applicability of Euclid's axioms.[2]

Today, the second type mind, posed on the side of *four*, insisting upon the qualitative indivisibility of the whole, regains much of the standing lost in recent centuries. As regards the sum of the parts in relation to whole being, scientists, dealing with one whole atom and the sum of its parts, have found that in fission energy escapes, and they have also found that in the formation of a nucleus from protons and neutrons some of the mass of the particles apparently is converted to energy.[3] The chemist sees that the combined action of several elements taken together is greater than the sum of them taken separately. Mathematicians working with transfinite number theory confront the concept that the whole can equal one of its parts. In short, one is forced to alter his concept that a discrete whole within the universe can be divided and its parts regathered to equal the sum of the erstwhile whole—or that a new whole constituted of parts enjoined is exactly equal to the sum of those parts calculated as a group of discrete entities—because the phenomenon of whole being is disturbed through the acts necessary to take its measure by means of calculating the sum of its parts.

Although scientists move away from the quantitative view toward the qualitative view and acknowledge the validity of both positions, the dilemma of three and four is by no means resolved—its beginning is lost in antiquity and its end is not yet in sight. As to its beginning, Jung says that number helps more than anything else to bring order into "the chaos of appearances . . . primitive patterns of order are mostly triads or tetrads," and he points to *I Ching, Book of Changes:*

> . . . the experimental basis of classical Chinese philosophy . . . one of the oldest known methods for grasping a situation as a whole and thus placing the details against a cosmic background—the interplay of Yin and Yang . . . there is also a Western method of very ancient origin which is based on the same general principle as the *I Ching*, the only difference being that in the West this principle is not triadic but, significantly enough, tetradic. . . .[4]

He refers also to the alchemists' tackling the problem of three and four, seeing the dilemma stated in the story that serves as a setting for the *Timaeus* and extending all the way to the "Cabiri scene in *Faust*, Part II . . . recognized by a sixteenth-century alchemist, Gerhard Dorn, as the decision between the Christian Trinity and the *serpens quadricornutus*, the four-horned serpent who is the Devil."[5]

W. Pauli discusses the controversy between Johannes Kepler, discoverer of the three famous laws of planetary motion, and Robert Fludd, in his day a famous alchemist and Rosicrucian. Pauli says that Kepler's ideas "represent a remarkable intermediary stage between the earlier, magical-symbolical and the modern, quantitive-mathematical descriptions of nature," indicating a way of thinking that produced the natural science which today is called classical.[6] Kepler, a devotee of Euclid's geometry, insisted upon strict mathematical methods of proof. His premise was that "Mathematical reasoning is 'inborn in the human soul'. . ." His is a trinity-concept, his symbol "contains no hint of the number four or quaternity."[7] Fludd, however, was a mystic with great aversion to all quantitative mensuration: "It is significant for the psychological contrast between Kepler and Fludd that for Fludd the number four has a special symbolical character, which, as we have seen, is not true of Kepler."[8] Fludd drew his inspiration from Moses, and he brilliantly defends his stand on the nature of the soul. Kepler, however, appears to best him in all scientific argument until one realizes that Kepler considered the quantitative relations of the parts to be essential while Fludd considered the qualitative indivisibility of the whole.[9] Pauli says, "modern quantum physics again stresses the factor of the disturbance of phenomena through measurement,"[10] as Fludd (and Goethe) insisted upon. He concludes that the only acceptable point of view appears to be one that recognizes both the quantitative and the qualitative, "the physical and the psychical" as compatible, embracing them simultaneously.[11]

This attitude eases the argument, but it does not resolve the dilemma of three and four, as may be seen in a mathematician's explanation of continua. In the mathematician's view, the physicist deals with four continua, or—more precisely—with four dimensions. In geometry, four dimensions would mean that one has four independent directions. For example, this could be seen by drawing four lines through a given point, all perpendicular to the others. In this narrow sense the universe has only three dimensions. Then mathematicians extended the concept of dimension to any situation where events can be described by independent coordinates, and where certain simple laws hold. In this broader sense Einstein found it convenient to use four independent coordinates, with time playing the role of a fourth dimension. In pure mathematics, as well as in its applications to physics, it is often convenient to use many more dimensions, even infinitely many.

But the idea of wholeness, or of continua itself, as one dimension greater than any number of dimensions has not broken through the tetragrammaton—through the confines of four. For example, Einstein speaks of the "bold" interpretation of the modern quantum theory associated with de Broglie, Schrödinger, Dirac, and Born—he says their interpretation "is logically unobjectionable and has important successes to its credit. Unfortunately, however, it compels one to use a continuum the number of whose dimensions is not that ascribed to space by physics hitherto (four) but rises indefinitely with the number of the particles constituting the system under consideration."[12]

The dilemma of three and four is not confined to the world of science. One comes upon the play between three and four in the world of art. Here one sees that musicians, like ancient alchemists, strive to bring together four "elements" to make possible the *quinta essentia*, the *lapis*, that brings forth a new element or a whole new statement. Although musicians do not discuss this in terms of the dilemma of three and four, one can hear the play between the two numbers in Beethoven's *Symphony #5 in C Minor*. This symphony begins with a four-note rhythm, described by the composer as "destiny knocking at the door." Deems Taylor calls it an "ominous" signal. This signal announces an agitated main theme which changes to suppressed tragedy, to resignation, to a lyrical movement during which the dread reminder of the four-note rhythm is played. It continues as a sinister reminder throughout the work. The third movement is a dream of terror wherein the four-note beat "sounds noble," but the nobility fades and it becomes a caricature—the restated theme becomes a "macabre joke." Reduced to its original skeleton, it becomes suppressed tension, increasing in rhythmical intensity, releasing tightly harnessed fury which becomes a bridge to the last movement. Here triplet note rhythms are introduced, artistic unity is achieved, the symphony ends on a one-two-three beat and a magnificent *chord* in a triumph of grandeur.[13] In that chord is expressed wholeness: *one* sound based upon the number man's hand is based upon—*five*. Abt Vogler says of music:

> I know not if, save in this, such gift is allowed to man
> That out of three sounds he frame, not a fourth sound but a star.[14]

Perhaps Sibelius was trying to say this in another way in his mighty *Seventh Symphony*—here, symphonic expression is not given in four movements following each after the other, posed the one against the other: one movement encompasses the whole expression that transcends the dilemma of three and four.

The question becomes—how does life transcend its play between triad and tetrad to produce *one*, wholeness? In his work, *What is Life?*, Schrödinger is not concerned with investigating the ancient dilemma of three and four, but he describes cell divisions, and in his descriptions one sees that the "triadic" family structure, mother-father-child, is involved with a "tetradic" pattern—as Schrödinger discusses the hereditary "code-script" that rests in the chromosomes, he says:

> . . . this whole four-dimensional pattern is known to be determined by the structure of that one cell, the fertilized egg.[15]

He points out that physical laws "rest on atomic statistics" and their "precision is based on the large number of atoms intervening," whereas the living organism is under the control of "incredibly small groups of atoms, much too small to display exact statistical laws," but they play a dominating role, control observable large-scale features, determine important characteristics of its functioning, and "in all this very sharp and very strict biological laws are displayed." [16] These laws insure that each *one* is always an event in himself, unto himself.

The strangest thing about the dilemma of three and four is that some time ago those on the side of three, embracing Euclidean geometry which says that the whole is equal to the sum of its parts, were contradicted in the nursery:

> Humpty Dumpty sat on the wall,
> Humpty Dumpty had a great fall.
> All the King's horses and all the King's men
> Couldn't put Humpty Dumpty together again.

This bit of wisdom is restated by Kluckhohn, the anthropologist, "A whole is different from the sum of its parts," and it is restated by Koestler, "A whole is defined by the pattern of relations between its parts, not by the sum of its parts. . . ." [17] And in the nursery, those on the side of four, insisting upon the qualitative aspects of the whole, were reminded that *time* changes the aspects:

> Hickory, dickory, dock.
> The mouse ran up the clock.
> The clock struck one, the mouse ran down.
> Hickory, dickory, dock.

In these rhymes both the devotees of three and the devotees of four were given the clue: the whole must be described in terms of *one*, whole, and *one* must be seen as a *working principle* through which as *time* changes the arrangement of material forces within and without, *one* remains, itself a unity and the measure of unity.

This is to say, the answer to the dilemma of three and four rests in the answer to the mystery of *one*. This answer must be given in a mathematical statement that describes the composition and inner operation of *one*, itself. Jesus stated the Equation of One which must be seen against the briefly sketched background of the dilemma of three and four in order to appreciate the magnitude of His thought, for He transcends the dilemma, giving as the measure of *one* or wholeness, the number *five*.

II

Jesus has never been considered a mathematician. He made but few statements dealing with number. Yet, He made many statements about *one*, the number that is the basis of arithmetic through which all branches of mathematics become possible. If He described *one's* inner structure and the principle upon which *one, as measure*, operates, He was a mathematical genius. How could this come from the man of Nazareth?

The realization could have arisen from His *unconscious*, as has been the case with other great mathematicians. Jung felt that a fruitful field for further investigation was the study of man's basic "mathematical *axiomata*—which Pauli calls 'primary mathematical intuitions,' and among which he especially mentions the ideas of an infinite series of numbers in arithmetic, or of a continuum in geometry, etc." [18] Dr. von Franz writes that "William James once pointed out, 'the idea of an unconscious could itself be compared to the 'field' concept in physics.' " [19] She says:

> In other words, our conscious representations are sometimes ordered (or arranged in a pattern) *before* they have become conscious to us. The 18th-century German mathematician Karl Friedrich Gauss gives an example of an experience of such an unconscious order of ideas: he says that he found a certain rule in the theory of numbers, "not by painstaking research, but by the Grace of God, so to speak. The riddle *solved itself as lightning strikes*, and I myself could not tell or show the connection between what I knew before, what I last used to experiment with, and what produced the final success." [20]

But one does not have to look altogether to the *unconscious* for Jesus' source of mathematical knowledge. Within His reach was Alexandria, the center of mathematical studies and of Neo-Pythagorianism. Here, Nicomachus of Gerasa, one of the "golden chain" of philosopher-mathematicians, is presumed to have studied, for Gerasa was a city in Palestine, primarily Greek—it is near to the place where Jesus cast demons called "Legion" into the swine—and it is probable that Nicomachus did not receive all of his education there. "Jamblichus says of Nicomachus: 'The man is great in mathematics, and had as instructors those that were most skilled in the subject.' " [21] Nicomachus is thought to have flourished between the middle of the first and second centuries, but it is possible that he was a contemporary of Jesus, and he could have brought Alexandrian mathematics to Palestine, placing this knowledge within His easy reach: "In one of his surviving books, the *Introduction to Harmonics*, he mentions a certain Thrasyllus, presumably Thrasyllus of Mendes, a writer on music, who lived in the reign of Tiberius [B.C. 42–A.D. 37]." [22] Because in his writings Nicomachus did not mention Ptolemy, whose recorded astronomical observations were made between A.D. 127 and A.D. 151, it is most probable that Nicomachus preceded him and was more nearly a contemporary of Thrasyllus.

Many of Jesus' statements regarding *one* reflect Nicomachus' thinking, which, in turn, rests upon the mathematical knowledge of his day. Nicomachus had much to say of *one*, which he saw as *unity*. Jesus' mathematics came to rest in His concept of *one*, which appears to have arisen from His grasp of the operation of signed numbers and the concept of zero.

Morris Kline says that insofar as history can ascertain, "the Hindus were entirely original in creating . . . the concept of negative numbers. Corresponding to each number such as 5, they introduced a new number —5 and called the old numbers positive to distinguish them from the new, negative ones."[23] Long after the death of Jesus, the negative and positive symbols were introduced in the West. Today, they are indispensable to scientists. Although the concept of negative and positive numbers came late to the Western world, this concept might have existed in the Hindu thought world in the time of Jesus, coming to Him as a gift of the Magi; or the concept may have arisen in His own mind. As will be discussed later, He gave evidence of understanding the operation of signed number.

About the time Euclid was stating his axioms (300 B.C.) an unknown scribe jabbed into a wet clay tablet a *point* to make the space that zero would come to occupy about a thousand years later when Hindus brought to the court of the Caliph of Baghdad the digit 0, still used today. To the mathematician, zero—0—is indeed a perfect pearl, for the possibilities opened through this symbol are limitless. Did the digit 0 take shape in Jesus' mind—or was it another gift of the Magi? In speaking of the "eye" of the needle, Jesus called to mind this configuration: 0, and related it to "naught," for the "eye" of the needle is the "nothing" of it that makes it operable; and in this enigmatic statement, He brought God, the *absent* or "minus" *one* into correspondence with man, the *present* or "positive" *one*, and brought both *one*'s into correspondence with this "hole," or whole of "nothing" that takes on a "circular" shape, through which God, "minus" *one*, draws man, "positive" *one*, into infinity. Through this correspondence, any *one*-thing is vested with zero's enigmatic, unmeasurable properties. But Jesus appears to have realized that although *one* and zero are corresponding unities, they are not the same in action and reaction.

When all of Jesus' statements are applied mathematically, and when one considers the full import of His presenting the cross (+), the positive sign, as His symbol and *all-embracing answer* it would appear that His mathematical concepts moved beyond those of His day, and that He attempted to describe the *reality* of the operation of the energy that mathematics attempts to describe. To measure His grasp of mathematics, one must measure His thinking against that of another acknowledged master mathematician as nearly His contemporary as possible. Thus, this study poses His words against the concepts of Nicomachus of Gerasa, who may have been Jesus' contemporary—there is a hint of this in Jesus' words, for both He and Nicomachus use "father and son," and "teacher and pupil," to symbolize the "greater and lesser," or the concept of opposites, unequal; but in Jesus' concept these opposites meet and are reconciled in the unity of *one*, or *sameness*.[24]

Nicomachus saw the number *one* as unity, which alone out of all numbers when it multiplies itself produces nothing greater than itself. He points out that Pythagoras saw the "same" and "sameness" in 1, and the "other" and "otherness" in 2, as the two beginnings of all things, and these two differ only by 1, so that the "other" is fundamentally "other" by 1, and by no other number. Spherical or circular numbers he saw to be recurrent numbers which always end in the same number no matter how often they multiply themselves—for example, the numbers 5 and 6 are spherical or circular numbers. Nicomachus saw *one* as a spherical or circular number. But he also saw unity, *one*, as the first pentagon, potentially. He saw unity to occupy the place and character of a *point*, and a point as non-dimensional, thus unity as non-dimensional and elementary; he saw a point as the beginning of dimension, but not itself a dimension, and as the beginning of a line, but not itself a line.[25] He wrote: ". . . when a point is added to a point, it makes no increase, for when a non-dimensional thing is added to another non-dimensional thing, it will not thereby have dimension; just as if one should examine the sum of nothing added to nothing, which makes nothing."[26] Jesus appears to have taken another view of a *point, primitive zero*, as though:

> Two roads diverged in a wood, and I—
> I took the one less traveled by,
> And that has made all the difference.[27]

This is to say, when the cross (+) as symbol and all-embracing answer is applied to the problem of the "sum of nothing added to nothing," it would say that Jesus did not overlook the word *added*—the symbol (+) introduces the problem of organization, or, as Eddington puts it, of "and." The cross as answer indicates that there cannot be a "non-dimensional thing,"—or, one might say, until a point has dimension or until it is defined, a point is not a point: the cross has dimension and it also defines a point, or gives a point dimension. The cross (+) as answer and symbol calls forth the concept of negative (—) and positive (+) numbers.

In the view of this study, Jesus realized that the correspondence between *one* and the whole, zero, and between *one* and each other ensuing digit, differing only by *one*, makes of *one*, *measure itself*. This is to say, *one* is not merely a unique digit: it is, rather, a *principle* or *action* involving opposites, "minus-one" and "plus-one," upon which the whole operates. Thus, Jesus saw that in the definition of *one* as an *operative principle*, the definition of *the* underlying principle upon which *one* and *all* operate could be grasped. And as Jesus examined in His own mind the "sum of nothing added to nothing," which must perforce involve the division of "nothing," or the whole or zero, the positive (+), the cross, arose as the only possible answer to the problem of "naught divided by naught." This, because the problem itself is posed in terms that may be seen only as *a negative divided by a negative which produces a positive answer*. Or, one might say, that if through use of zero—0—an infinite increase in number may be drawn, then unlike the number *one*, when zero multiplies itself it produces more than itself: it must forever reproduce itself *plus*.

Zero must be seen as the whole, beyond examination, and therefore its measure, unapparent, is expressible only in *negative* terms, so that zero's division must correspond to: $(-/-=+)$. But this simple division is equivalent only to taking the diameter of a circle; to define the center point in its being, the product of this division must be divided by itself, so that the whole equation of zero-divided must correspond to: $(-/-=+/+=+)$. Again, the positive sign (+) is presented as answer, just as the configuration of the cross appears when one determines the center point of a circle by bisecting its diameter. The center point defined by the cross cannot be seen as a correspondence to negative-one or positive-one; it is neutral in its position and must correspond to one-neutral or one-whole. The point itself cannot be defined, except as it is defined by the cross (+), that is, in the definition of the *cross itself*.

Nicomachus said that a point is "the beginning of a line, or an interval, but is not itself line or interval." [28] The point enfolded in the cross is not the beginning of either line, but is an interval in both lines, and is the *one* point so arranged and sustained by the opposing horizontal and vertical lines or "forces." One might say that this point is defined in negative, positive, and specific terms, so that it is the only point in actual being.

If Jesus realized that a point may be seen as a "beginning" or as an "interval," but not as a defined whole, line or interval, then the question became: how many "beginnings" or "intervals," which may be symbolized as (°), are necessary to define a point or to give it "actual being"?—that is, not to define the operative positive force itself, which may be said to correspond to the vertical line bisecting the horizontal diameter of a circle, but to define *one* point in the circle that the cross enfolds? Or, the question may be put, simply: how many "intervals" (°) are required to draw the configuration of the positive sign (+), which appears as answer to the problem of the product of zero divided, and also defines a point?

Five "intervals," (°), are the fewest that will satisfy the situation:

```
         °
      °  °  °
         °
```

Neither a triadic nor a tetradic configuration or symbol will *completely* "secure" one point between two opposing lines or forces, as does the quintuple arrangement that may be drawn with five "intervals." The number *five*, itself a spherical number, completely "houses" the one point defined. If *five* is the "measure" of *one*, defined, *one* cannot measure the same in every direction: in the figure above, both the vertical and the horizontal line "count" *three* intervals, but if they are "taken apart" one line will "inventory" more intervals than the other.

Consider now that light, first in manifestation, is conceived to be corpuscular in a photon; but it is also conceived to be interaction between wave trains of different frequencies, their difference involving the concept of "more and less," or "plus and minus," which reinforce each other at the *center* as they cancel out to define a boundary. The two smallest segments of line that can exhibit one degree of difference *and* move to completely secure and reinforce one "corpuscle of light" must measure *three* "intervals" (°) in one segment, *two* "intervals" (°) in the other. As the three-interval segment moves perpendicular to the two-interval segment, the two-interval segment may divide and close against the three-interval segment as it passes through, thus securing and reinforcing its center point. This action may be symbolized:

```
   °  °                       °
      °      becomes,      °  °  °
      °                       °
      °
```

Both segments perfectly share and equally sustain the one-interval that becomes a "corpuscle of light."

The concept presented above: five "intervals" needed to completely secure or "house" *one* of them, and three "intervals" moving against two "intervals" as two "intervals" react against three "intervals" to accomplish this, is presented in Jesus' Equation of One. He says:

> ... five in one house divided, three against two, and two against three.[29]

To insure that these words be recognized as a mathematical formula, Jesus gives an explicit division of the household. He states it as: father *against* son, mother versus daughter, mother-in-law versus daughter-in-law. Only if the mother plays a *dual role*—that is, mother is also mother-in-law—can these *six* "factors" be reduced to *five* forces, the number of forces "at issue" in *one's* household as given in the equation. And only if every family were four in number with one son married, and one daughter unmarried, could the words apply to life. Jesus spoke symbolically or poetically, but He spoke as mathematician.

If one follows the custom of assigning the positive sign to the male factors and the negative sign to the female factors, then *two* positive signs and *four* negative signs are presented: father and son versus mother and daughter, mother-in-law and daughter-in-law. But one must see mother and mother-in-law as a negative sign *divided*, $(-/-)$, which is *equivalent to* a *positive* sign, so that *one's* household must be seen to be constituted of three positive factors versus two negative factors; or of one force divided that is *apparently* a negative force but is, *actually*, a positive force operating against two manifestly negative forces and with two manifestly positive forces. Only if one understands that *a negative number self-divided is equivalent to a positive number* can one conform the number of forces operative in the "house of one," *five*, to the number of "signs," *six*, that Jesus presents in His description. In the view of this study, here, Jesus gives evidence of understanding signed numbers. Thus, having presented a *predominantly negative* "field" of signs and forces underlying *one's* "equation," He nevertheless presents the *positive sign* $(+)$ as all-embracing answer and predominant symbol to be associated with His revelation of reality.

Jesus states the field formula so explicitly that His words bespeak a still "finer division" underlying the matrix. That is, He describes the forces at issue as: father versus son, and son versus father; mother versus daughter, and daughter versus mother; mother-in-law versus daughter-in-law, and daughter-in-law versus mother-in-law. His words give rise to twelve signs, eight negative, four positive, thereby "elaborating" the ratio of negative to positive force, presenting the concept that a still finer division of forces underlies the "field"—a force that involves "doubly stated double negatives" giving rise to *a negative effect which is of positive value in life,* an effect that sustains the division of the manifestly positive factors and/or measurable dimensions of any *one* thing.

This negative effect that is of value in life, but can be expressed by "nothing positive," may be described only as Lao-tzu describes Tao:

> We put thirty spokes together and call it a wheel;
> But it is on the space where there is nothing that the utility
>   of the wheel depends . . .
> Therefore just as we take advantage of what is, we should
>   recognize the utility of what is not.[30]

This, Tao—Holy Ghost, zero, nothing explicable—has endless descriptions which yet cannot state the nature of it:

> There is something formless yet complete
> That existed before heaven and earth.
> How still! how empty!
> Dependent on nothing, unchanging,
> All pervading, unfailing.[31]

Is "it" not *space?* Only by paradoxical exclamation points can the fullness of it in the universe be implied, so that "Tao never does; Yet through it all things are done." [32] Space may be seen as pre-existent unity and multiplicity at once, as continuous creation of positive value by means of the eternal presence of "nothing manifest" in which one and all have their being.

The words that follow Jesus' Equation of One indicate that *one* has its being in a negative effect that provides positive value which is not manifest, and that *one* arises through a field of opposing forces which today man calls positive (+) and negative (−) energy.

Translating into numbers the words, "five in one house divided," Jesus' Equation of One would read:

$$\frac{1}{1/1} = \frac{1}{1}$$

Translating into numbers the words, "three against two and two against three," the equation would read:

$$3/2 \times 2/3 = 1$$

Mathematicians may hastily dismiss Jesus' equation much as William James dismissed another very similar to it:

$$\frac{0}{0} = \frac{1-1}{1-1} = 1$$

seeing this arrangement as unsatisfying.³³ To mathematicians, Jesus' equation may appear redundant. But as Kline points out, "In the words of the philosopher, Wittgenstein, mathematics is just a grand tautology." ³⁴

Mathematics is tautological, but the point is, Jesus understood that a certain redundancy is essential if man is to convey the truths he has grasped. Jesus' understanding of the necessary redundancy is encompassed in another formula He gave, but before this formula is considered, some of the "pointer readings" enfolded in His Equation of One must be examined briefly.

First: in Jesus' equation:

$$3/2 \times 2/3 = 1$$

a simple arithmetical truth is stated. A fractional expression multiplied against its corresponding inverted fractional expression always produces *one*. In His formula, fractional expression disappears and *one* appears, which is consistent with reality in the physical world, for the atom of action, h, refuses fractional statement.

In life's deepest reaches, something appears to insist that fractions, as such, must disappear. In the living cell, "something" becomes the "plus" factor to restore a "minus" situation such as 2/3 represents, or it becomes the "minus" factor to reduce a "plus" situation such as 3/2 represents. In short, "something" inverts and poses a fraction against itself, thereby restoring wholeness. Scientists have shown this. To the astonishment of biochemists, Hans Driesch discovered that one fourth the egg of a sea urchin would produce a complete organism; then he fused two eggs and succeeded in raising one giant organism.³⁵ Scientists have shown also that inverting a fractional part of an egg cell causes it to "state itself" as a whole: T. H. Morgan discovered that one half of a frog's egg would develop a whole embryo if he turned it.³⁶ Thus, he showed that *inverted fractions* operate in life's most secret working to bring forth *one*, wholeness.

Second: Jesus' equation reflects the *principle* underlying the FitzGerald contraction because it bespeaks two measures of *one* in this world, posed against each other. 3/2 may be seen as the "long" or expanded measure of *one*, which is to say, it is "more"—but as it is inverted, it becomes "less," or succumbs to its "short" or contracted measure, 2/3. *One* must be equal to both its measures, but neither is the *one measure number* that "houses" it.

Third: Jesus' arrangement, 3/2 × 2/3 represents the principle of the *maximum working against the minimum and vice versa*. The importance of this principle to physicists cannot be overemphasized. Kline says that

Einstein was engaged in the task of compressing all electrical and mechanical knowledge into one mathematical sentence from which the laws of nature would be deduced by a minimizing *or* maximizing process.[37] Jesus' equation indicates that *both* a maximizing *and* a minimizing process work within the whole, sustaining it—and thus it points to a dual and opposite operation within the whole. The minimum statement that can contain the fact appeals to the mathematician, but nature does not evidence unremitting concern for economy: "There are situations . . . when a light ray takes a path requiring the most time compared to the time required for other possible paths." [38] Scientists postulate that nature operates a process wherein some function is either at a maximum or at a minimum. According to Jesus, both processes operate at once and this may be observed when any *whole* operation is viewed—as, for example, in Kline's drawing which depicts refracted light:[39]

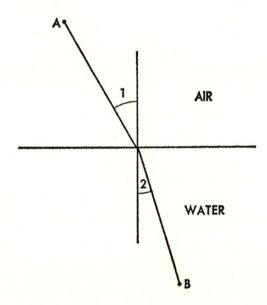

From the air, the larger angle (1) is working against the smaller angle (2), but from the water, the smaller angle is working against the larger angle. Measured from left to right, the span between point A and point B forms the maximum angle that works against the span between point B and point A measured from right to left. Other arrangements wherein the maximum is posed against the minimum and the minimum against the maximum may be observed. Jesus' equation indicates that light, prime manifestation, is perfectly equated between the maximizing-minimizing processes that serve both to sustain and to free it for singular action even as its *unity*, or correspondence with *one*, is preserved.

Fourth: Jesus' equation written as:

$$\frac{1}{1/1} = \frac{1}{1}$$

introduces *asymmetry* and indicates that an asymmetrical operation lies at the root of *one's* or nature's working. The equation is then stated in the formula (3/2 vs. 2/3), bringing to the discussion the subject of parity.

Briefly explained:

> The term, "parity" was first used by mathematicians to distinguish between odd and even numbers. If two integers are both even or both odd, they are said to have the same parity. If one is even and the other odd, they are said to have opposite parity. The term came to be applied in many different ways to any situation in which things fall neatly into two mutually exclusive classes that can be identified with odd and even integers. . . . Theoretical considerations (such as the left-right symmetry of space itself) as well as experiments with atomic and sub-atomic particles indicated that, in any isolated system, parity was always conserved. Suppose, for example, that a particle with even (+1) parity breaks down to two particles. The two new particles can both have even parity or both have odd parity. . . . Parity is conserved. If an even particle should break down into two particles, one even and the other odd, the total parity of the final state would be odd. . . . Parity would not be conserved.[40]

As elementary particles were discovered, a puzzle was presented by the *k*-particle, which disintegrated sometimes into three *pi* mesons and sometimes into two *pi* mesons. This puzzle led to the work of Chen Ning Yang, T. D. Lee, and Mme. Chien-Shiung Wu, who proved that asymmetry must be attributed to the disintegration process of cobalt, which is due to a weak interaction. Their findings led to the "fall of parity," and a new view was opened to physicists, for prior to their discovery, right-left symmetry in physical laws, together with nuclear parities, atomic parities, etc., dominated scientific thought and made it hard going for any idea reflecting an *asymmetrical* working.

It was discovered that the least, or first particle, number *one* in the arrangement of the table of elementary particles, the *neutrino*, is a "structure with a true spatial handedness:—that is, it exhibits true spatial asymmetry." [41] By 1958, it was known that parity is violated in all weak interactions—such interactions constitute the very secret of nature's processes.

Jesus' equation indicates that *one* "breaks down" into *five points* of being; one sees that in the division of *five*, parity is opposite; but His equation also indicates that *one* in positive being again arises in the switching of its "plus" aspect (3/2) into its "minus" aspect (2/3) in an operation that demands "cross-action" between the two aspects of *one*. That is, symmetry, as seen in the *cross* (+) designating positive being, is regained.

Yang points out that "if one performs a mirror reflection *and* converts all matter into antimatter, then physical laws remain unchanged." [42] He adds, "the question remains why it is necessary in order to have symmetry, to *combine* the operation of switching matter and antimatter with a mirror reflection. The answer to such a question can only be obtained through a deeper understanding of the relationship between matter and antimatter. No such understanding is in sight today." [43]

Fifth: Jesus' equation indicates that what applies to *one*'s least measure (the neutrino) must also apply to *one*'s greatest measure (the universe), but that there is a cross-action within it through which *one* is constantly restored to or maintained in a state of wholeness. That is, in its every aspect *one* and the whole is *self-conserving*. Thus, it indicates that the conservation principles apply in terms that are meaningful to man and to life: that is, the ability of the universe to support itself and life within it *is conserved* through the operation of opposite systems. Because *one* is in all ways self-conserving, the nature of this one universe may be known by its present appearance: that it is *here-now* and able to support life with life's need for warmth is all one may say with certainty about it.

The formula, 3/2 vs. 2/3, may be seen as representing greater and lesser systems, or left-handedness, vs. right-handedness, 3/2 representing action in one kind of sphere, 2/3 representing reaction in another kind of sphere. The "lesser" sphere may represent an energy system as man now understands one: never to be seen as wholly conserved in a meaningful way because there is a "heat loss" constantly to be reckoned and apparently never to be regained. The sphere represented by 3/2, first stated, may be a system that precedes and underlies the lesser one, and as the two systems operate against each other, a loss in one is a gain in the other until the one converts into the other and vice versa, so that in terms of the whole, "loss" has no real meaning: i.e., there is a *constant restoration*, but how and when is buried in the secret of time's *now*.

Schrödinger points out that "entropy, taken with the negative sign, is itself a measure of order," and he points out also that at room temperature, "entropy plays an astonishingly insignificant role in many "chemical reactions.... For a pendulum clock room temperature is practically equivalent to zero." [44]

Jesus' equation indicates that *one* is a working principle involved throughout the whole and in each particular—because it is not itself "absolute," no expression can be absolute. Thus, "absolute symmetry," zero hour, zero temperature, complete vacuum, "absolute thermodynamical equilibrium," etc. cannot actually exist or be achieved. Some law must insist upon this, but this law must be like Tao—"a borderline conception lying at the extreme edge of the world of appearances," in which the opposites "cancel out in non-discrimination," but are still potentially present.[45] Jesus' equation, seen in the light of the whole of His message, indicates that opposites are always potentially present, even as *one* is constantly restored—and freed for action, so that the system itself is neither confined nor confining. That is, within it, whatever is confined is set free as that which confines it passes away even as the material of the universe is ever made anew. It may be that nature in her largess cannot let her left hand know what her right hand is doing.[46] With one hand she takes away, as with the other she gives back, in time, what she has taken as it is needed.

III

Jesus' formula and the words that follow indicate that life and the universe depend upon cross-action between a maximum and minimum working by opposite forces, and that this cross-action cannot be contained within a concept that limits life, or *one*, or *light* to a four-dimensional space-time frame. Perhaps this is why the forbidden name or "measure" of God is Tetragrammaton—that is, life and light cannot be confined within a four-dimensional concept.

Jesus appears to have seen that the cross (+) is not tetragonal in its inner or point structure. Within it is held the quintessence of being, light, one-point defined; thus, through cross-action *one* is triumphant. It should come as no surprise, but it does, to see that Jesus created the symbol to indicate that as men began to "handle" light and to try to elucidate its secret, they would come upon an *indivisible whole, one,* which would so elude them as they labored within the confines of a "four-dimensional" concept that they would resort to a "game of chance" to try to possess its secret. This symbol of wholeness and this drama may be observed at the foot of the cross, where soldiers cast lots for His robe.

Before observing this play, however, consider that the twentieth-century scientists play their game of chance because when numbers are large, "chance is the best warrant for certainty." [47] It is when number is small, specifically when they confront *one, h,* that the number, four, upon which this play is based, is seen to be inadequate to deal with the quantum, a unity that appears to be "outside the oyster of Space and Time." This indivisible piece bespeaks another dimension that somehow transcends the four-dimensional concept—bespeaks another dimension which, like Tao:

> . . . "covers the ten thousand things like a garment" but does not claim to be master over them. . . .[48]

This, the "fifth dimension," may be likened to the all-encompassing, seamless unity of a single reality covering life like a garment woven in one piece, as was Jesus' robe, the robe of Light.

Throughout the centuries Jesus' robe has possessed inexpressible appeal, as though it possessed unseen power that redeems and forgives man his part in the tragedy Beethoven set to music to the measure of the Tetragrammaton:

> Then the soldiers, when they had crucified Jesus, took his garments, and made four parts, to every soldier a part; and also his coat: now the coat was without seam, woven from the top throughout.[49]

And for this precious piece, indivisible, the soldiers cast lots, played a game of chance, while above them an unbroken glory covered the cross with outstretched arms, leaving as His symbol this sign: †.

The † denotes the positive. Jesus hung upon the †. His truth must hang upon it, upon the positive. Adler says, "every psychical expressive form presents itself as a movement that leads from a minus to a plus situation."[50] And Linssen quotes Carlo Suares, who speaks of the fundamental "something" or the "plus"—the perpetually positive balance sheet of a thousand million apparently negative and positive transformations: "Everything, from ourselves to this planet, to the sun, to the thousands of millions of solar systems which surround us is only perpetual transformation."[51] If these transformations produce a perpetually positive balance sheet, then change is not the single reality—to the contrary, positive being is the single reality in the midst of these changes.

This concept is based upon the whole drama of Jesus as symbol of light, drama which says that light is eternally resurrected and returned to action in this world. His drama says that light is sent into the world from an unknown and unknowable state or source, to which it returns, but from which it re-emerges whenever the "statistical" requirements are met—

whenever, wherever two or three are gathered in the "name" of light. Or light arises as the need arises, and the "void" in which light may be received is created—as when upon the death of Jesus and Judas, St. Paul who was from "outside" the system of followers, entered the group, representing an infusion of energy which Matthias, elected to replace Judas, could not do since he was from within the "system."

But before Jesus' answer to the mystery of primordial energy and perpetual change can be accepted, there must be stronger evidence that the law He referred to was the second law of thermodynamics, and that the working within the hidden kingdom refers to entropic working in man's inner world and throughout the universe. The strongest proof that this is so rests with another formula He gave—its meaning deeply hidden until in the twentieth century two men opened a door. But enough said here, for this is the subject under discussion in the following chapter.

Chapter 9

WHAT HAS BEEN HIDDEN

I

The word, entropy, from the Greek, *trope*, means: a turning, change, after energy. Jesus' name for this changing arrangement as energy runs its course is "realm of heaven"—He says it is:

> ... like a grain of mustard-seed, which a man takes and sows in his field .... it becomes a tree, so large that wild birds come and roost in the branches of it. ... Jesus said all this ... to fulfil what had been said by the prophet,
>
> > I will open my mouth in parables,
> > I will speak out what has been hidden
> > since the foundation of the world.[1]

Several years ago a strange bird indeed was found roosting in entropy's branches. So strange was it to scientists to find *communication* involved with entropy that Warren Weaver and Claude E. Shannon, authors of *The Mathematical Theory of Communication*, appear awed to find that an entropy-like expression is involved in this problem. Weaver says: "To those who have studied the physical sciences, it is most significant that an entropy-like expression appears ... as a measure of information ... when one meets the concept of entropy in communication theory, he has a right to be rather excited—a right to suspect that one has hold of something that may turn out to be basic and important." [2] This study finds it most significant that Jesus gave evidence of understanding the relationship between entropy and communication—between "bits" of information, "fowl of the air," and nature's supreme law. But before one can appreciate Jesus' statement on this subject, he must understand more of Weaver's and Shannon's theory. In the above quotation, Weaver uses the word *information* in its technical sense. He describes the capacity of a channel in terms of:

> ... its ability to transmit what is produced out of a source of given information. [Information must not be confused with meaning; he defines it as the logarithm of the number of choices.] ... in the general case, capacity measures not the number of symbols transmitted per second, but rather the amount of information transmitted per second, using bits per second as its unit.[3]

Weaver says:

> That information be measured by entropy is, after all, natural when we remember that information, in communication theory, is associated with the amount of freedom of choice we have in constructing messages. ... One has the vague feeling that information and meaning may prove to be something like a pair of canonically conjugate variables in quantum theory, they being subject to some joint restriction that condemns a person to the sacrifice of the one as he insists on having much of the other. Or perhaps meaning may be shown to be analogous to one of the quantities on which the entropy of a thermodynamic ensemble depends.[4]

He then quotes Eddington's passage regarding entropy, wherein he places it "alongside beauty and melody" rather than alongside distance, mass, and electric force, and says: "I feel sure that Eddington would have been willing to include the word *meaning* along with beauty and melody; and I suspect he would have been thrilled to see, in this theory, that entropy not only speaks the language of arithmetic; it also speaks the language of language." [5]

The Christ was to "tell us all things . . ." [6] *Communication* was the heart of His problem. If Jesus grasped the significance of entropy in communication, He saw that He could use the Scriptures as His "source" of information on the Christ, and that the number of the descriptions of this One in the Scriptures would allow Him wide freedom of choice in selecting among them those required to construct His message in such way that the ideal in *redundancy* might be achieved, enabling Him to convey the maximum of meaning within the limits of possibility.

In the *redundancy* lies the secret. Speaking technically, Weaver says of it:

> The ratio of the actual to the maximum entropy is called the *relative entropy* of the source. If the relative entropy of a certain source is, say, .8, this roughly means that this source is, in its choice of symbols to form a message, about 80 per cent as free as it could possibly be with these same symbols. One minus the relative entropy is called the *redundancy*. This is the fraction of the structure of the message which

is determined not by the free choice of the sender, but rather by the accepted statistical rules governing the use of the symbols in question. It is sensibly called redundancy, for this fraction of the message is in fact redundant in something close to the ordinary sense; . . . this fraction of the message is unnecessary (and hence repetitive or redundant) in the sense that if it were missing the message would still be essentially complete, or at least could be completed.[7]

Here, Weaver points out that:

. . . the redundancy of English is just about 50 per cent, so that about half the letters or words we choose in writing or speaking are under our free choice, and about half (although we are not ordinarily aware of it) are really controlled by the statistical structure of the language . . . . it is interesting to note that a language must have at least 50 per cent of real freedom (or relative-entropy) in the choice of letters if one is to be able to construct satisfactory crossword puzzles.[8]

Cross(+)word? Did Jesus leave cross-word messages, wherein a key word or words serve to work both ways just as a letter or letters work both ways in a crossword puzzle? In giving His Law of Communication, Jesus indicated that 50 per cent redundancy is ideal:

. . . let your communication be, Yea, yea; Nay, nay. . . .[9]

The second "yea" and the second "nay" give to the whole statement a 50 per cent redundancy—as though to point out that in verbal expression, speaking in the ordinary sense of the word, too little redundancy is apt to render the meaning obscure, but too much redundancy is apt to give over the meaning to senselessness. At either extreme comprehension rests upon intuitive promptings or suggestibility rather than upon an intellectual grasp which enlarges the whole structure of consciousness. Thus, it would appear that an expression 50 per cent redundant most surely conveys its meaning.

Weaver says, "There is more 'information' if you select freely out of a set of fifty standard messages, than if you select freely out of a set of twenty-five." [10] If the prophecies in Scriptures regarding the Christ are viewed as the number of "standard messages" from which Jesus could freely select, then the quantity in this one source provided the greatest opportunity for Him to state and show His truth through use of them.

In the physical system of communication described by Weaver, one part only receives source noise. The message is changed into a signal by the transmitter—"The *receiver* is a sort of inverse transmitter, changing the transmitted signal back into a message. . . ." [11] Noise plays the role of good and evil, increasing uncertainty, but if uncertainty is increased, information is increased. However:

> Uncertainty which arises by virtue of freedom of choice on the part of the sender is *desirable uncertainty*. Uncertainty which arises because of errors or because of the influence of noise, is undesirable uncertainty.[12]

Weaver concludes, "Language must be designed (or developed) with a view to the totality of things that man may wish to say; but not being able to accomplish everything . . . . it too should deal with its task statistically." [13]

As Jesus describes the way He deals with the task of "telling us all things," the term, "statistically," comes to mind—that is, He scatters His words widely, knowing that some will fall on "stony soil," but that some will fall on "good soil," will take root and grow in the minds of men.[14] This statistical dealing with words, which He also involves with the working of the "kingdom of God," as well as His involving *communication* with a certain *redundancy* which man now knows to be necessary and to be involved with *entropy*, and His saying that the "kingdom of God" and its working grows into a "tree so large" that its reach is lost to physical measurement, that it harbors or involves the "bits" of sound that birds, poetically, represent, indicates that Jesus was indeed referring to the working of the second law of thermodynamics in His descriptions of the realm or reign of God.

One might leave the mathematical theory of communication here and go on to observe Jesus' answer as to the meaning of entropic working, but Weaver's explanation of the theory opens vistas too intriguing to ignore. This is to say, a very close parallel may exist between the mathematical theory and transmission of information in the ordinary sense of the word. If so, one must contend with the joint restriction: as one insists upon having much information, meaning may be sacrificed. A *biorhythm* chart which describes the oscillating waves of three rhythmic-cycles in human life—roughly classed as the physical, emotional, and intellectual cycles—will serve to illustrate the point.[15] The cycles depend upon the date, and therefore the hour, of birth. They vary by a difference of five days: 23 days to complete one, 28 to complete another, 33 to complete the third. The chart on which Hans J. Wernli plots the cycles resembles somewhat the chart plotting electromagnetic waves, the field intensity passing periodically through zero. When one or more of the three strands that make up the biorhythm chart crosses center line, a critical, cross-over day has come.

As each strand reaches the height or depth of its curve, supposedly one reaches the height or depth of his physical, emotional, or intellectual powers, as the case may be. Periodically, all three forces converge to share the same cross-over day, presenting a critical day when the physical, emotional, and intellectual forces are in a complete state of flux.

Such a chart is indeed informative, but since the precise minute of birth is seldom available, any degree of error in time at the beginning must so extend itself as to turn the diagram upside down as the years go on. Consider, too, that a man may not be at the height of his intellectual powers at the top of this curve because intellectual power is based upon the ability to grasp truth and communicate it—a person may more readily grasp truth at the height of his intuitive power, which may coincide with the height of his emotional flux. But at this point he may overplay or underplay redundancy in expression, obscuring his meaning in writing so complex or so poetically brief as to render it incomprehensible even to himself within a few weeks. When the critical cross-over days approach do they produce desirable or undesirable uncertainty? In short, does such a chart have much real meaning?

This is not to decry Wernli's work nor the usefulness of biorhythmical information to surgeons in whose field the charts were first applied, nor to deny that the theory may have other uses as more is learned about life's working. In this study, the biorhythm chart is used as example to indicate that as life communicates itself, cross-action is come upon and the joint restriction inherent in the cross must be respected: because of it, any effort devoted to giving over-much information forever falls short of its attempt to truly sustain meaning.

The biorhythm chart is used also as example to point out that sufficient unto the day is the uncertainty thereof—but this is desirable uncertainty. Life's play around time provides it for man. Uncertainty as to time of death appears to be desirable uncertainty; but death itself, the cross-over day, is desirable certainty to Homo sapiens constituted as he is. Man's life is, actually, a "time of expectation" because this uncertainty and certainty are superimposed upon consciousness. Consciousness will be lifted—death is reached when the lift occurs.

This may be likened to the "time of expectation" as it applies in the physicists' realm to the molecule's moving to the next higher energy level. There is no sharp temperature limit at which the lift occurs with certainty and immediately. At any temperature different from absolute zero there is a certain smaller or greater chance for the lift to occur, the chance increasing with the temperature of the heat bath. Schrödinger explains:

The best way to express this chance is to indicate the average time you will have to wait until the lift takes place, the "time of expectation." From an investigation, due to M. Polanyi and E. Wigner, the "time of expectation" largely depends on the ratio of two energies, one being just the energy difference itself that is required to effect the lift (let us write W for it), the other one characterizing the intensity of the heat motion at the temperature in question (let us write T for the absolute temperature and kT for the characteristic energy). What is amazing is how enormously the time of expectation depends on comparatively small changes in the ratio: $W:kT$. To give an example (following Delbruck): for W thirty times kT the time of expectation might be as short as 1/10 sec., but would rise to 16 months when W is 50 times kT, and to 30,000 years when W is 60 times $kT!$ [16]

In life's parallel, the "time of expectation" does not extend very much beyond "50 times kT"—and during man's "time of expectation" the uncertainty born of freedom of choice is desirable, the uncertainty arising from error is undesirable, as though life itself operates in accord with the mathematical theory of communication and the uncertainty of the hour presents a certain incentive to man to live while he may. This theory presents uncertainty as a constructive factor when based upon a percentage of "real freedom" and a percentage of "control."

As far as the universe is concerned, there is desirable uncertainty in the postulations of scientists as to when its "heat-death" will occur. For twentieth-century man the hour appears comfortably distant, so distant the matter can be of concern only to one who so loves life that the idea is dismaying. Nevertheless, he must face it, for the physicists tell him it appears quite certain that energy is constantly transferred from the available to the unavailable state, and transfer in the opposite direction never occurs in nature. This brings cosmology into the discussion and returns this study to the point in question—Jesus' answer as to the real nature of entropic working and its meaning in universal terms.

II

Loren Eiseley says that man thinks toward creation of the ultimate—the ultimate weapon—"Ultimate, ultimate, and still more ultimate, as if there were a growing secret zero in [his] mind. So terrible is the fascination of that zero, so much does it appeal to some ancient power-loving streak in our still primitive natures, that whether men plan aggression or defense from it, they are, in degree, corrupted." [17]

This "zero" that expresses the will to exercise *all* power, the idea that man can exercise ultimate power, is delusion. Ultimate or absolute power is finished of itself, and thus, an eternal penultimate (o — 1) is all there is within the realm of possibility. From this remaining *one*, life can ever be raised up again—which is to say, God, *one*, could call it forth from a cold stone. Scientists, however, dispute this postulation, and dispute among themselves as to the life or death of the universe and the forms within it, which is to say, a number of cosmogonies vie with each other. Of the major theories, the "outlook" offered by the first three to be considered is broadly summarized by Fred Hoyle as follows:

The Explosion Theory—"The galaxies will continue to move apart from each other until, in the ultimate limit in the future, space will present a uniform, featureless emptiness. . . . All sources of energy will be exhausted." [18]

The Expansion-Contraction Theory—this theory depends upon an initial explosion of universal "stuff" as does the first theory, but in this view "eventually expansion will cease altogether. Gravitational attraction will then cause the clusters [of galaxies] to start moving together," and in time the stage will be set for "a reversal of the contraction process, and another universal expansion." [19]

The Steady-State Theory—"the clusters of galaxies expand apart, but as they do so new galaxies are born, and at such a rate that their average density in space remains unaltered with time." [20] According to this theory the universe did not have a beginning and it will not have an end.

Observations made by Martin Ryle with radio telescope, reported in 1961, dealt the Steady-State Theory a supposedly near-fatal blow; [21] but as astronomers gathered later on that year they found that the whole puzzle had grown. For example, the universe appears to be 20 to 30 billion years old, not the 10 to 11 billion years old the scientists had thought. Alton Blakeslee reported that one galaxy "seems to be running away from us at half the speed of light . . . yet it is apparently only half as old as the rest of the universe about us." [22] In the same year, P. A. M. Dirac presented his conclusion that habitable planets will continue to occur indefinitely—therefore the existence of life need never end.[23] An opposing view was offered by R. H. Dicke—the universe would have to be roughly at its present state of development for habitable planets to exist.[24] Is there an answer to this mystery? If so, it rests upon *one*. The universe is *one*, and so is each discrete particle within it.

In the view of the physicists, no particle of matter is permanent, but particles may be changed into other particles and the division of the elementary particles serves simply to give rise to other elementary particles.

There are particles having a life span of less than a millionth of a second. Yet J. Robert Oppenheimer says, "their lives seem very long compared to the millionth of a billionth of a billionth of a second it takes for products of their decay to move apart. . . ." [25] As Oppenheimer points out:

> . . . there are very weak forces which appear in radioactivity; we do not understand why some of these weak forces change properties that strong forces, manifested in the collision of particles, do not change. To one such slow change, almost prohibited by a selection rule—an occasional collision in the vast interior of the sun in which two protons form a deuteron and a positive electron—we owe most of the heat and light reaching the earth.[26]

Now consider another very weak force that gave rise to a weak "explosion"—this is presented by Eiseley:

> In a sense it was the most terrible explosion in the world, because it forecast and contained all the rest. The coruscating heat of atomic fission, the red depths of the Hydrogen bomb—all were potentially contained in a little packet of gray matter that . . . quite suddenly appears to have begun to multiply itself in the thick-walled cranium of a ground-dwelling ape. . . . Even the solar system has now felt the impact of that tiny, soundless explosion.[27]

In time, this explosion produced a bundle of gray matter through which was expressed two thousand years ago the *strength of mildness, of weak forces.*

Jesus' cosmogony, expressed in the opening verses of the Gospel of St. John, presents as the creative impetus a force as "weak" as a word or one measure of light. Other words He spoke, and the opening words of Genesis, point to a beginning of the universe in one act that brought forth light, and to a "becoming" of the universe as it operates under the Law He described in terms of the working of the kingdom of God. In Jesus' description of the working of the kingdom, the idea of the "expansion" and "shuffling" of energy up to a given time is encompassed. But because Jesus speaks of the "unquenchable fire" [28] (in which matter is involved), His cosmogony does not project "heat-death" for the universe. Can these words that once struck terror to the heart be words of comfort now to men in a universe scientists say faces "heat-death" when entropy's role is played? According to Jesus, the "flame" cannot be quenched and the warmth of life will ever be.

In the Sermon on the Mount, pointing to the lilies of the field, Jesus gave His answer to the future; in this passage there occurs the word *arrayed* (its synonym *arrangement* is the word so intimately involved with entropy). He concludes:

> Take therefore no thought for the morrow: for the morrow shall take thought for the things of itself. Sufficient unto the day is the evil thereof.[29]

If evil is pure matter, as this study postulates, then sufficient unto the day is *matter*, the source of heat. This is true today and will be true every day, or always. Thus, Jesus says, in effect, take no thought for the morrow's supply of fuel.

Jesus did not limit His statement—"Take therefore no thought for the morrow"—to the question of source energy in the universe. At first glance this unequivocal dictum appears to be against all reason. Why, then, would He state it? Did He see that the changing arrangement of the constellations would in time become so evident that man would lose himself in the concept of the rate of change, then rate of rate of change, until mental exhaustion would reward his efforts to plan for the morrow, leaving him without will to tend the day's wants? Consider also that the better one plans for the morrow, the more certain he is to be floored by the insuperable problem of "no problems at all"—or life in deadly boredom. Besides, the morrow cannot be reached. Only the day, here-now, may be experienced and he who deals with the problem it poses is he who makes solid preparation for the day that comes to him.

Planners for the morrow are ever bedeviled and bemused by the inertia of the masses who go on propagating and resist the change planned for their good. And planners for the morrow are befuddled by the creation of a new problem with the solving of an old one. Robert Heilbroner presents as the "quintessential fact" that massive inertia which resists change is "responsible for more of 'history' than all the campaigns, the movements, the revolutions," and he says that at the level of society which is visible only as personal and private encounters, the level at which life is lived, life remains much the same regardless of the new boundaries in which it is contained.[30]

What scientists fear today is that within the boundaries of the planet the expanding population cannot be fed, if the rate of increase continues, so that the specter of starvation hovers on "tomorrow's" horizon—and another specter just as ugly is companion to it. For example, Philip Toynbee writes that "Cosmopolis" threatens to "turn us all into criminals or lunatics or both" when living in one "world-covering city" erases from life the naturalness that feeds man's soul:

WHAT HAS BEEN HIDDEN

Scientists tell us that the human race has two trillion years of life on this planet still ahead of it if we do not commit mass-suicide in our generation. Two trillion years of imprisonment in cosmopolis; that is the heaviest collective sentence of penal servitude that has ever been passed on human kind.[31]

Jesus appears to have seen that man comes finally to think of the morrow in terms that rob today of its pleasure and numb the will to tackle future problems in the only way they can be alleviated: by solving those that confront man today.

Jesus says, "Take therefore no thought for the morrow," but He does not teach that man should live in a witless, indolent manner. In practical terms, "looking ahead," investing, sowing, tending, reaping, preparing for the arrival of the future, are today's job as described in His very down-to-earth parables. These command man to the day's tasks that he may meet the morning with joy, considering the lilies of the field, hearing the song of the sparrows that surround him now, even in his cities. It was toward the level of actual existence that Jesus addressed His words in the Sermon on the Mount—this is to say, He spoke of the ability of the system in which life is contained to support it satisfactorily whatever the tomorrow men envision as they "look ahead." How can this be, in the face of the second law of thermodynamics? The legend of Jacob presents a clue.

Jacob, later to become "Israel," dreamed of a ladder set up on the earth, its top reaching to heaven, angels ascending and descending upon it. When he awoke, he took the stone used for a pillow, set it as a covenant, and made this vow: "of all that thou shalt give me I will surely give the tenth unto thee," [32] Something in man, in life, demands *tithing*. If one meets the need of the day, he will see to a self-imposed taxing of his revenue. Tithing serves the Lord, *thy* God—one must bank for *himself* a bit of all that comes his way. He must serve his body and its needs, seeing it as "temple," even as Jesus did.[33]

Apply tithing to the second law of thermodynamics, for tithing appears to be the *meaning* Jacob gave to his dream. "Angels"—the expressed energy of God—ascending and descending the ladder reaching from earth to heaven bespeak a changing arrangement, not of the system itself but of the energy within it; but if tithing is the meaning inherent in this, the dream would say that in universal sense nature's supreme law works so that through the motion of any system *all power cannot be exerted or spent* because its effect is diminished as a bit of the energy is "banked" to provide in space source energy for the future. If so, source energy cannot be entirely spent: the last act provides a reserve ad infinitum—thus, the universe rests upon the last act's creation of a reserve. If in each move that has ever been made nature has tithed a bit of energy, there is everywhere "banked" in space a reserve in God's name: *one*, and it could be that energy, made unavailable at the time, is returned *in* time or *now* as available energy. Such energy made available *now* would not reverse time's arrow or the *direction* of the transfer of energy from available to unavailable state because *now* is past before man can grasp it, and thus the arrow points always from past to future. This is to say, time—heaven knows what—shields this secret.

Time may also allow for the expansion of the universe up to a point or "turning" which evokes a contraction, and this contraction is experienced in the *now*. The *now*, being "Absolutely Elsewhere," cannot be grasped by consciousness so that the turning point is hidden in time. The expansion and contraction itself is, like breathing, nontraumatic.

Looking at the future, one must consider the possibility of thermodynamical equilibrium being achieved in universal terms. This depends upon the shuffling of energy until shuffling becomes complete within the confines of space. Two questions arise: can space be evenly and completely occupied?—is space something confined within self-limits? A clue is cast through the work of Peter G. Bergmann and his associates. They were not concerned with the questions this study has posed when they undertook a calculation in the course of studying gravitational waves, but their findings are pertinent: ". . . the nature of space curvature can be seen when an attempt is made to construct from great circles a 'square,' that is, a quadrangle all of whose four sides are of equal length and mutually perpendicular. As the 'square' is built up side by side, the figure fails to close upon returning to the point of departure." [34] Then they examined the analogue of this geometric test of curvature for the space surrounding a large mass and calculated the size of the gap as a measure of the deviation of the space from flatness:

> They found that if the size of the figure is increased proportionally to its distance from the center, the gap does not shrink indefinitely but tends to a final value, or limit, at an infinite distance from the mass. . . . The typical gap in a figure caused by a mass like that of the earth is half an inch. For a mass like that of the sun, the gap is one mile. . . .[35]

These calculations suggest that space is not "something" that can be thought of in terms of its being "confined" by or within itself, or itself confining *time*—perhaps, poetically speaking, *now* creates the "gap."

Not what is *in* it, but space itself is the great mystery, as great a mystery as time. Eddington's drawing shows twelve segments converging in the sphere of "here now"—or "I." Thus, twelve "thrones" govern man in space-time, but there is room for many more segments, more "mansions" —and there must be many more space properties than man knows of today and some, like "Absolutely Elsewhere," beyond that which consciousness can penetrate.

As for that in space which consciousness can observe, Jesus says, "Heaven and earth will pass away. . . ." [36] As to how this passing will happen and when, man can know from Him only that the reign of God, the working of *the* law, is begun, that the Father knoweth the hour, that this passing away *will not come as men expected it then*. Today, as men observe the process of evolution, change, and decay that passes away the arrangement of celestial bodies and the matter which sustains life, they are committed to another concept of the end of things—but in saying that heaven and earth will pass away, Jesus also said that the *creative force*, the *word*, weak a force as it may seem, will not pass away. Thus, His cosmogony comes to rest upon the concept of constant creation or renewal, upon the precept that all things are made anew. His words allow for "becoming" *within* the universe, but not *of* the universe which now sustains life in many mansions,[37] and is now operating under perfect and infallible law, in accord with *one* which is, mathematically speaking, self-sustaining.

Now consider that *only in life* does change communicate itself to consciousness, and *only in life* does man's flesh, the "earth" of him, pass away as the body's cells divide. When man's flesh ceases thus to "pass away" death claims his body and returns it to dust.

But each sojourn in consciousness adds a new dimension, because a measure of truth is harvested, and a measure of his "heaven," his *unconscious*, has passed away in the act of his becoming more conscious of it. If the measure of truth he has harvested is to bear rich fruit, life must pass it through a "neutral" state—not into but through the eye of the needle, zero, the ultimate—just as energy passes through the "ultimate" as the electric field intensity periodically becomes zero. But the electromagnetic waves travel on. One might say, the promise inherent in the seed of truth man harvests is to be realized only in its planting.

This appears to be true in the field of cosmology: in 1961, The Steady-State Theory was dealt a "death blow"—poetically, it was "planted." But in 1962, the seed flowered again when Gerald S. Hawkins presented The Static Universe Theory, which differs from the Steady-State Theory by avoiding the concept of continuous creation: "Matter, the scientist said, is continually being used and re-used. New stars and galaxies are formed from the decay of previous remnants. The universe is not expanding, there was no violent explosion at any time, the galaxies are not moving, and will not end in isolation. . . ." [38]

But such a "static" universe as Hawkins postulates does not do away with the concept of the "end of the world" within this galaxy. The "end" is envisioned in a very-distant future as the sun burns itself out—or, as is considered less likely, as the sun explodes, or as the earth is destroyed in a collision with another celestial body.

In *Worlds in Collision*,[39] Immanuel Velikovsky postulates that near collisions between the earth and other celestial bodies gave rise to cataclysmic events in the past that made necessary an altering of the systems used to calculate time, for the time tables and methods of calculating were upset and were changed universally and simultaneously, or nearly so. He presents a mass of evidence to support his postulation that the devastating upheavals reported to have occurred in the time of the exodus and in the time of Joshua and later prophets refer to real encounters between the earth and a comet that later became the planet Venus, and to the reactions that shook the world when Venus and Mars came into close contact. A vast body of literature and legends arose simultaneously all over the world to describe in like manner the disasters suffered on this planet as its course was altered by the influence of another celestial body. Not until space exploration began to reveal Venus' secrets and to upset old calculations did Velikovsky's theory, presented thirteen years before, flower again to challenge the world of science and provoke great argument. Most scientists ignored or refused Velikovsky's theory when first presented, and many if not most still reject it in its entirety. This study neither accepts nor rejects it in its entirety, but finds it worth consideration because it rests heavily upon legend which enfolds a seed of truth, often many seeds of truth. For example, data given by archeologists and geologists tend to support Biblical legends in a number of particulars.

The descriptions of world-shaking events as given by these legends undoubtedly point to upheavals in the physical world, but undoubtedly they bespeak as well emotional reactions to these events and to social events, and reveal in poetic terms psychic upheavals such as are experienced by everyone in the process of the ego-group's development and its awakening to the power of the *unconscious* and the Authority-Ego. This is to say, man must look to nature to find a vehicle to provide analogy for what he feels or realizes when no adequate words exist to describe it. But there is more than such poetic expression to be found or read into the volume of given data Velikovsky has amassed. An "outward" event must *happen* before it can become a vehicle to express an inexpressible "inward" event, although in the telling and in time the event tends to be elaborated, and material is interpolated to make it fit the psychic or "inward" happening.

Velikovsky's theory is introduced into this study to point out that for centuries before Jesus' birth mankind had expected the end of the world to come when a celestial catastrophe worse than those past, as revealed in legend, overtook this planet. Jesus' saying that the end would not come as men expected it takes on new meaning: the end will not come by means of a celestial catastrophe. But in another passage, Jesus appears to indicate that the earth will once more feel the impact of a celestial event which will affect it drastically, although not destroy the planet. A discussion of this passage, however, must be delayed because just as Velikovsky, in offering evidence from many disciplines breaks the barriers between disciplines and arrives at conclusions which no discipline has reached independently, so a discussion of the "end of things" as given by Jesus combines much that must be discussed before His words can be appraised. Suffice it to say here that His cosmogony enfolds the concept of life everlasting.

But the concept of everlasting life, finally to be beset by no uncertainty, becomes itself an insurmountable problem, a terror. Take heart. Jesus says: "Sufficient unto the day is the evil thereof. . . ." If sufficient unto the day is pure evil, or matter, also sufficient unto the day is evil's expression: man's lust—his lust for life and the problems it will always pose. If in psychological parallel to nature's tithing of energy, man tithes an iota of lust in his every act, this small bit, this weak force, spells idea, desire, appetite, relish of life. This bit of evil is divine—is good in being—because it makes man human. Because of his lust-reserve, man need have no fear that life will be unable to support abundantly his desire for it.

And if God, *a priori* the whole of being, "granulated" in one act while "weak" forces gave rise to singular action and reaction, the *one* that *was* can contain in His re-formed system each one of Himself. Society's overcrowded inn, albeit set in oceans of space, may be full of harassed taxpayers huddled to be counted in order that those who think on the morrow may know how to spend, and it may appear that the inn is unable to accommodate more; but as each one comes onto the scene, life lifts his star, calls to the shepherds and the Magi, the humble and the truly wise, who will always welcome the babe nature borns in the manger. This is not to say that man's intelligence should not bring to bear on the problem posed by rapidly increasing populations, or that contraceptive measures should not be taught and practiced—every resource should be used to solve this problem. But it is to say that each child who *does* come into the world should be welcomed as the Son of God—as *one* whom life has need of and who has need of life in this world, however he comes into it, to complete or increase his measure of empathy.

"Come now, and let us reason together, saith the Lord. . . ." [40] Consider the lilies of the field. Consider that they pass away by means of a process that renews them in satisfying likeness even as it prohibits such exact repetition as spells hopeless monotony. This, after nature has rested, buried, the energy enfolded in the seed. Consider a sunset. It passes away. Look now, for it is never again to be seen exactly as it is. But a satisfying likeness will come again some day as the morning passes into noon and noon passes into night wherein the light of the sun is unavailable only for a time, returning with the dawn.

Even as all things pass away, all things return, created anew in satisfying likeness. Jesus indicates that even as the imperceptible changing arrangement of energy takes place, there is fulfillment of a law which insures the support of life in many mansions in the universe. Today, in astronomy, confusion reigns. No one knows how much energy is "hidden" in space, how it is distributed, or what sort of universe is evolving through the processes they observe.

Consider that in effect every move made is a division of the whole, of zero, which, as this study puts it, is equivalent to the division of a negative number which always gives as answer a positive number. Or, in Suares' terms, change produces a perpetually positive balance sheet. Strangely, or not so strangely, the configuration of the cross, †, is hidden in the field of space. This symbol, †, took shape in the reaction of wire and compass needle to open the minds of scientists to *field* forces, also "hidden since the foundation of the world," forces discovered but little more than a century ago to involve "cross-action." The question becomes: is it an accident that Jesus left as His symbol the cross, the configuration that revealed the electromagnetic fields in space?

III

Jesus says, "the very hairs of your head are all numbered." [41] Thus, He refutes blind working in nature. The deeper one searches, the more difficult it is to believe that so much as one word or symbol is accidental in its use or in its composition. Only a certain form can shield and carry onward a certain truth, or be the "key" to unlock a certain secret that nature hides, which may or may not be known to consciousness, although it is known in the *unconscious*. For example, Jung says, "Fishes frequently occur as symbols of unconscious contents." [42] Jesus spoke of fishes in connection with the kingdom of God—the fish was the earliest symbol associated with Him. Is this accidental? Jesus might have left this clue to indicate that His message reveals the contents of the *unconscious*, His own *unconscious* giving rise to and dictating use of the fish as symbol. It is difficult to believe that symbols are any more a matter of choice than the letters or words man chooses in writing or speaking.

Jesus also left the cross as symbol. Is it an accident that it appeared on the mathematical scene to denote the positive, the proton? Or that the form this symbol takes appeared also in an experiment which started the fusion of the hitherto separate disciplines of magnetism and electricity? In 1920, Hans Christian Oersted held a wire in which there was an electric current over a compass needle:

> ... the needle rotated until it was at right angles to the wire ... and when he reversed the direction of the current in the wire, the magnetic needle reversed its direction also, but again came to rest at right angles to the wire.[43]

The cross, thus drawn by needle and wire, gave rise to the branch of physics known as electromagnetism.

Could Jesus have known or realized anything about electromagnetic phenomena? His description of the opposing forces in the household, following His Equation of One, indicates that He understood *like signs repel, opposites attract*. Does He attempt to cast a clue also by posing the gifts of the Magi symbolically? This is to say, myrrh and frankincense are two *amber* substances; gold is a good conductor of electricity and in ground state there is one electron in the outermost energy level, a -1, and when this is removed the $+1$ ion results; the amber effect, as electrical phenomena was called, was known to exist before Jesus' birth, but the attraction displayed by amber was long confused with the attraction that lodestones, natural magnets, show for iron, "a phenomenon that was known at least as early as the 6th century B.C." [44] Realization of the cross-action between the two forces of electricity and magnetism may have dictated the form His symbol must take. How could Jesus have realized such as this?

In *The Psychology of Invention in the Mathematical Field*, Jacques Hadamard does not discuss Jesus' ideas, but he does relate experiences which indicate that questioning in one's own mind is a sort of "knocking on the door" of the *unconscious*. If this act is to be fruitful, one must be prepared in consciousness to know what to ask, and he must be able to receive the answer which comes when he is least expecting it, as does the returning bridegroom in Jesus' parable.[45] Hadamard says that one must be able to accept the answer that comes to him, he must have an open mind which is yet faithful to the proposition it has accepted as a basis for its work, and he must work in "this world" of consciousness to verify and "precise" the answer he has received. Hadamard says:

> As my master, Hermite, told me: "We are rather servants than masters in Mathematics." Although the truth is not yet known to us, it pre-exists and inescapably imposes on us the path we must follow under penalty of going astray.[46]

If one substitutes the word *life* for the word *Mathematics*, he has the message of Jesus in this paragraph. Could it have come from other than a disciplined, mathematical mind?

It is not essential to concede that Jesus understood physical phenomena and mathematics as such—it is necessary only to concede that truth pre-exists and inescapably imposes the path to be followed, and that the *unconscious* in man has direct access to truth, and that Jesus knew how to tap this fount within Himself, letting it express through Him and direct His drama. In the view of this study, however, Jesus consciously grasped nature's laws, but His revelation of them met with minds that dismissed them as meaningless. He lived in a world wherein Babylonian mathematics, capable of calculating large numbers, was all but lost in the sands of time, in astrological lore, and in soothsaying, while the Greeks "still thought of the number 10,000 as a "large, uncountable aggregation." [47] Were the mathematicians the ones to whom Jesus came, but "his own received him not," [48] because His thought was too advanced, His realization of the hidden secondary laws too disturbing, for minds committed to the classical view?

Jesus' treatment of any problem indicates that He realized "a law must be framed in terms of the measurements of a particular observer." [49] Is it an accident that He called Himself *light*, insisting that He was the SAME as every other human being, brother to any man, thereby indicating that "the velocity of light is the same for *all* observers in the universe regardless of how they may be moving relative to each other" [50]—for ALL observers, even the least of these? Could His Law of Communication, presenting a certain redundancy as essential, be an accident? Does not his formula also present a *neutral* force to be most penetrating, as vindicated in the work of Enrico Fermi who demonstrated the penetrating power of the neutron? Is it an accident that looking back two thousand years one sees high on a hill, † † †. There are three (+) signs and two spaces, "minus signs," between them. If one reads this unforgettable picture as 3(+), 2(−) signs, or as (+ − + − +), there is represented a positive "statement" that "outweighs" the negative.

This brings to mind a report in *Science News*, July 9, 1966, which stated that for the third time in ten years, long-held theories of physicists have been upset. Experiments directed by Dr. Paolo Franzini and Dr. Juliet Lee-Franzini showed that the theory that particles and antiparticles are mirror images of each other does not always hold true. It was found that in the decay of the neutral particle known as the eta meson, the positive particle that emerges is more energetic and travels away from the reaction site faster than the emerging negative particle, which means that oppositely charged particles in interactions of intermediate strength react in different ways, not in the same way as had been previously thought. Disproving the so-called "invariance" of oppositely charged particles is of such importance because it involves the fundamental nature of matter: positive and negative charges are the prime factors in all electrical, magnetic, chemical, and atomic reactions and interactions.

A "positive" statement that "outweighs" the negative insofar as the cosmos is concerned, also brings to mind a theory proffered in 1959 by Raymond A. Lyttleton and Hermann Bondi. Their theory was based upon the assumption that although the difference may be too little to measure with today's instruments, in the hydrogen atom the positive electrical charge of the proton is not exactly equal to the negative charge of the electron, as has been generally assumed. Lyttleton and Bondi suggested that the protons have the bigger charges and from this base work out their theory which offers an explanation as to why the galaxies are fleeing.[51]

The maximum-minimum working so prevalent in nature gives reason to consider again that there may be an asymmetrical array of the positive and negative forces in prime matter. Eddington says:

> I think that . . . the limitation of physical schemes that has troubled us before [is] that in all such schemes opposites are represented by + and −. Past and future, cause and effect, are represented in this inadequate way. One of the greatest puzzles of science is to discover why protons and electrons are not simply the opposites of one another, although our whole conception of electric charge requires that positive and negative electricity should be related like + and −.[52]

The mystery of *positive and negative charge* may depend upon arrangement of opposite forces to give rise to 50 per cent *redundancy* in expression of the one or the other force. Electrical *neutrality* may depend upon an arrangement of the forces that is *not* 50 per cent redundant in expression of either positive or negative force, as would be the case with the signs in this grouping: (+ − + − +), for if the signs are canceled to zero, insofar as possible, (o + o), the arrangement becomes 50 per cent redundant in neutral signs (or force), so that, electrically speaking, *neutrality*, rather than *positive charge*, would be *communicated* although the positive value (+) in the original expression of the signs (or force) necessary to give rise to (o + o) is the greater. This is to say, *what is communicated* may depend upon what is 50 per cent redundant in expression *and* what is not 50 per cent redundant.

All Jesus said of "unrighteous mammon," the material realm, indicates that it does not communicate itself *as it truly is*. And yet, "God so loved the world." Perhaps "mammon" cannot communicate truthfully because its real nature is "hidden" behind a redundancy of neutral energy which is all it can communicate. The secret of communication may be: a certain redundancy is necessary to communicate, and whatever is redundant will be communicated.

The cross † as Jesus' symbol, His Equation of One, 3/2 vs 2/3, His description of the "household" presenting positive and negative symbols in male and female beings, appear to say that opposite forces are not equal. No more than the number 2 can be a mirror image of the number 3 can the negative force be assigned a measure number equal to its opposite "positive number." Opposites cannot be the *same*. *Asymmetry must be the basis of opposites*. Jesus appears to say that in the make-up of *one*, the positive force is the *more*, and in one of its aspects the positive force arises through the division of a negative matrix: i.e., mother/mother-in-law, father, son. But in the universe, a negative aspect is the *more apparent*.

If one sees that *one* is *not a number*, but is a principle of operation that measures other numbers, then as he assigns measure numbers he must begin with the number *two*. Thus, two would be the measure number of negative energy, the lesser; three would be the measure number of positive energy, the greater. If one relates opposite types of energy to *one whole*, he must begin by relating them to the "least" neutral particle: the neutrino, which must be seen as an indestructible union of positive and negative energy because there is nothing small enough to penetrate it. Its opposite forces must be seen as three positive aspects engaging two negative aspects to give five aspects of being involving the principle upon which *one* operates: it is self-conserving. Since 3 is greater than 2, in this "iota" of neutral energy, the positive "outweighs" the negative. The formula, 3/2 vs 2/3, would say also that there is no "simple one" in manifestation: there is "one *and* one"—two *arrangements* of positive and negative energy to give rise to two *kinds* of neutrinos. Today, scientists know this to be so. In Jesus' formula, 3/2 vs 2/3, each type "little one" has a measure of force identified by the number 2, and a measure of force identified by the number 3, making them *equal in being* although opposite in arrangement and function. Thus, in nature they parallel the pattern in Genesis bespeaking the equality of man and woman, or the "us" of God, *One*, as Father and Son.

The force that binds the opposite types of energy in the neutrinos cannot be measured because they cannot be put asunder. This must be the "least" yet the greatest force in the universe—is it mammon's expression of love? Man is so immersed in neutrinos that perhaps the scientists cannot see the forest for the trees: neutrinos may be the veritable building blocks of which all in creation is ever made anew.

The secrets "hidden since the foundation of the world" may be that in manifest energy the positive outmeasures the negative; and space which appears negative in its "non-being" is actually positive-being, so that space repels and thus supports manifest energy within it which can operate only upon the matrix; and because within the whole, positive-being outmeasures negative-being, neither matrix energy nor manifest energy can completely occupy space; space and matter in ground state cannot communicate as positive-being, matrix energy cannot communicate as negative-being, because in its constitution each *type being* is redundant only in terms of neutral energy.

Emerson believed that nature is a language put together into a significant, universal book. He wanted, not to learn a few nouns and verbs, but to read this book. Today, scientists construct out of their dearth of knowledge of nature's whole book a nihilistic dogma. Do they really believe their verdict? Despite nature's violent acts, who can doubt that she speaks with life-giving reason in her every move? This is Jesus' verdict, different from scientists' views; but the congruence of His words with their "pointer readings" gives reason to believe His revelation of the psychic as well as the physical realms which are met in man. Thus, this study enters next the realm of parapsychology to examine the miracles in the light of today's knowledge.

Chapter 10

ALL IS NATURAL

I

It is fitting that a discussion of parapsychological phenomena begin with the following observation:

> What is beyond our present understanding we term supernatural, inferring that it is also beyond Nature. As soon as the onward march of Science has dissected and explained a certain matter, we calmly gather it into the realm of natural happenings. The whole of our existence and perception takes place in a realm governed by Nature. In consequence all is natural.[1]

Frederick Marion's words serve to state the premise of this study. In its view, phenomena which appear to be supranatural are the product of power emanating from the *unconscious* bringing to bear on consciousness, perception, behavior, and flesh. Here, the word *power* must be understood to mean the very opposite of all the term means in a physical sense to a scientist—there is as yet no proper word to describe the *unconscious'* working. But man must face the fact that extrasensory perception is operative, that hypnotic responses are miraculous, that the "stuff" of matter, or flesh, is mysterious as a ghost, as illusory as it is real.

In an essay, "Religion and Science," Alfred North Whitehead writes:

> A clash of doctrines is not a disaster—it is an opportunity . . . . in the evolution of real knowledge it marks the first step in progress towards a victory. . . . It is easy enough to find a theory, logically harmonious and with important applications in the region of fact, provided that you are content to disregard half your evidence. . . . An unflinching determination to take the whole evidence into account is the only method of preservation against the fluctuating extremes of fashionable opinion.[2]

This study attempts to take the whole evidence into account.

Scientists have compiled an impressive amount of evidence validating the operation of extrasensory perception—best known, perhaps, are the experiments undertaken by J. B. Rhine. Although the validity of these and similar experiments has been questioned by C. E. M. Hansel,[3] there is such abundance of evidence that ESP is demonstrated on occasion, and the records of such psychics as Emanuel Swedenborg, Edgar Cayce, and others are so conclusive, one cannot dismiss the subject albeit experimentation in the field leaves much to be desired. And almost daily one confronts evidence that through hypnosis, miracles are worked.

Parapsychologists, however, concern themselves primarily with telepathy, clairvoyance, psychokinesis, and pre- or postcognition. Pre- or postcognition is evidenced in experiments even more readily than telepathy.[4] Such phenomena are most readily demonstrated by children beyond the age of seven, by primitive peoples, by the unsophisticated, or by people found to be especially attuned and willing to work with investigators.

The phenomena of hallucination, illusion, and delusion give rise to other categories of mysterious happenings. By definition, hallucination is the product of disordered nerves or mental states, whereas illusion implies an ascription of truth or reality to that which only seems to be true or real, and delusion is a misleading of the mind. Henri F. Ellenberger offers the definitions given by nineteenth-century psychologists: "Hallucination is perception without an object. Illusion is a perception inadequate to its object. A delusional idea is erroneous judgment which is maintained by the subject in spite of contrary evidence."[5] The word *hallucination* is itself distasteful. G. N. M. Tyrrell says, "To many people the word . . . suggests something false and deceptive, if not actually morbid," but "Little hallucinations occur quite commonly in daily life."[6] He cites cases where the hallucination affected the senses of sight and touch and was indistinguishable from normal perception—the cause seemed to have been a settled expectation, but hallucinations have other causes and sometimes take the form of inner feelings or impulses to obey specific commands. He says that hallucination sometimes occurs as the result of an idea in someone else's mind, not in the mind of the percipient, and the hallucination "is just as clear and lifelike as a normal percept. It is, indeed, commonly mistaken for one at first."[7] Tyrrell also describes cases of collective hallucination which involve "normal" people, for hallucination is generally regarded as a pathological symptom. But, as Erwin W. Straus points out, interpretation of the norm predetermines the possible interpretations of the pathological: "This is just as true for hallucinations as for all other phenomena. A better understanding of hallucinations therefore must wait for a deeper understanding of the norm of sensory experience."[8] This little understood phenomenon may play a large part in normal perception.

There is no doubt, however, that delusion is pathological. Illusion, on the other hand, is not indisputably so. Mystics of all times describe an experience that is illuminating—and similar. Their illusions cannot be described except in terms of ideas with which the conscious mind is familiar, but these are admittedly inadequate to reveal the essence of their illumination. Although abnormal conditions may give rise to such ecstasies, in the words of William James: "To pass a spiritual judgment upon these states, we must not content ourselves with superficial medical talk, but inquire into their fruits for life." [9] And Tyrrell adds, "There are dangers of a pathological kind attending the life of contemplation, just as dangers of a pathological kind attend other walks of life. It needs discrimination to separate the truth of mysticism from its abnormal excrescences and to put each in its rightful place." [10]

Separating the true and the false in mysticism is an urgent problem today. In the words of Marion, "I am not urging the investigation of a gifted few so that the reaches of *their* minds may be charted. The whole question is much larger than that. It is a question of the generic mind of mankind itself." [11] Tyrrell points to the most important aspect of man's mysterious psychic power: this power is the root of his creative capacity. He says both illusion and hallucination have an astonishing power of creation and that: "It is not commonly realised that an element of creation enters into ordinary, everyday perception, too. The view that external objects exist in space *exactly as we see them* is extremely difficult to maintain. We *must* provide a good deal of the environment which we commonly think of as simply there." [12] Eddington pointed out that to reach the reality of a "table we need to be endowed with sense-organs to weave images and illusions about it." [13] Can *sense organs* perform such a creative function? Or is it the ability to hallucinate? If the power to hallucinate is involved in every perception, then what might be termed a "slip" or a "simple" hallucination is not pathological in character.

In the view of this study, hallucination becomes delusion, pathological, when sensory stimuli are severely limited by diseased or deteriorated tissue, or by restricted environment, or when the nervous system is out of kilter as a result of strain, fatigue, trauma, starvation, drugs, or alcohol, so that conscious or unconscious fear, hatred, memory, expectation, fantasy, and imagination become factors to be incorporated in the perception the psychic power must deduce from inadequate or distorted sensory stimuli. Experiments tend to confirm this point of view, and to suggest that the power to hallucinate plays an important role in normal as well as abnormal perception.[14]

Illusion shows the other side of this coin, incorporating faith and love rather than fear and hatred. Thus, illusion is not necessarily pathological because faith and love are not destructive in character. Illusion, too, appears to arise when stimuli are restricted or inadequate, or when the nervous system is out of kilter, or when the percipient lapses into trance.

Insofar as perception itself is concerned, another question confronts scientists: how do the sensory organs transmit images from one stratum of consciousness to the other and then project them upon the "scene one is seeing"? Straus writes, "Though we are often told that the mind is 'part of what the brain does,' no one dares to claim that projection is a physiological process. . . . Hence, projection must be an activity of the mind itself. . . ."[15] Or is it man's ability to telepathize, to project an idea, word, or image, that does the trick of transmitting so that projection may be considered to be telepathy's normal function? As Pauli discusses the processes involved in understanding, he asks:

> What is the nature of the bridge between the sense perceptions and the concepts? All logical thinkers have arrived at the conclusion that pure logic is fundamentally incapable of constructing such a link. It seems most satisfactory to introduce at this point the postulate of a cosmic order independent of our choice and distinct from the world of phenomena.[16]

Could not extrasensory perception—post- and precognition or clairvoyance— be involved? Could the formation of a concept be likened to an epoxylike reaction wherein a strand of sensory perception meets with a strand of extrasensory perception to create the solid situation of normal perception and understanding? Apart from each other, neither "liquid" strand can give rise to "solid" or true perception, but when they enjoin, without "heat or pressure" being necessary to the operation, something substantial is generated from the stimuli man constantly receives.

This is to postulate that extrasensory perception is so interfused in the process of perception that there is nothing remarkable about it until severely curtailed or distorted sensory input gives rise to extraordinary demonstrations of the psychic power. When a person is in a state of trance, sensory stimuli can be obliterated, altered, or misrepresented by auto-suggestion or by the hypnotist with such ease that this study concludes: mysterious phenomena occur for the most part, if not altogether, when a person is in some degree of hypnotic trance. The trance may be self-induced and so light or fleeting that one does not realize he is or has been in trance. Or trance may have been induced by another quite unbeknownst to the one entranced. Or trance may have come upon one spontaneously. This does not explain the mystery of extrasensory perception or the psychic power in man, but it does impel an observation of hypnosis and its dynamics.

II

All cultures, old and new, show evidence of employing hypnosis in one way or another. So broad is the statement of it that each man must satisfy his own need to validate its prevalence and historical usage. Today, medical men begin again to examine the subject—but gingerly. Leslie LeCron writes:

> Like medicine, hypnotism sprang from magic. While medicine has lost this stigma and has become respectable, hypnotism, unfortunately, is still regarded, in the eyes of the public and of scientists alike, as akin to witchcraft—to the shame of the scientists. . . . If hypnosis is ever to become of real value it must meet with public approval, and such approval can only come through a proper understanding of hypnotism.[17]

In the distant past, hypnotism was practiced by the medicine men or by powerful priestly cults. The dynamics of inducing trance, of implanting and directing suggestion, were carefully concealed—giving rise to the idea that there existed a special power operable only by and through a special few. In such hands hypnosis could but act either as a compelling curse or as an enslaving balm. William Neilson points out that a most vital part of Moses' mission was to lead Israel away from the influence of the Egyptian priests and their pagan practice of hypnotism—ancient Judaism made a valiant effort to prohibit misuse of this power.[18]

Today, it is known that every person possesses to some degree hypnotic power and is to some degree susceptible to its exercise by another. But the degree varies widely and this makes experimentation and research in the field extremely difficult if consistency in results is the aim.

Nevertheless, in the nineteenth century, hypnotic therapy—called mesmerism—was used to cure all kinds of diseases, often after orthodox measures had failed. Its success in one area was spectacular and consistent, as Aldous Huxley shows in discussing the work of Dr. James Esdaile, who used hypnotic trance to induce anesthesia: in Europe, the operating room was a chamber of horrors, the postoperative mortality rate almost 25 per cent; but in India, Dr. Esdaile, using the perfect anesthesia of deep hypnotic trance, performed more than three hundred major operations with a mortality from postoperative infection of only 5 per cent. European medical men, however, scarcely investigated nature's perfect anesthesia. With the advent of chloroform in 1847, pain was lessened—although in the aftermath of shock and infection, the postoperative mortality rate did not lessen.[19]

Today, mild hypnotic tactics are often used to prepare the patient psychologically before an operation; hypnosis is used in conjunction with a narcotic agent, and it has been used by Dr. Milton J. Marmer as the prime anesthetic in cases where a patient could not tolerate narcotic anesthesia and in such cases major surgery has been performed successfully and painlessly.[20]

Mesmerism as a means of therapy in the psychological field shone brightly and briefly in Vienna and Paris, but Freud discarded it in favor of psychoanalysis. Today, it is again employed in conjunction with psychoanalysis and its helpfulness is generally conceded—Robert Coughlan sees it as a "pathway" into the mind.[21]

There are reasons for the checkered career of hypnosis in medicine: in too many cases it is extremely difficult to induce the desired state of trance; in very deep trance, catalepsy may ensue, and in rare cases a severe heart reaction may develop as the patient is being brought out of this state. Despite its outstanding successes, hypnosis as a therapy has as many if not more unrecorded failures; and in cases where a healing response is obtained, this is sometimes reversed within a short while, or another, perhaps worse, symptom is exhibited so that, in the words of Hafiz of Shiraz: "The Power of the Self works its false wonders. . . ."[22]

But as one attempts to appraise the whole situation, he must conclude that in the hands of a competent physician, a patient receiving hypnotic therapy runs no greater risk than he does in receiving any other treatment; as an anesthetic it is as safe or safer than any other; and its spectacular successes, as well as its unspectacular failures, continue to be exhibited. The spectacular successes can best be understood if some of the physical reactions that can be brought about under trance and the dynamics of inducing trance are observed:

Hypnotic trance does not place an extra load on circulation and breathing, nor on the liver and kidney systems—it is entirely nontoxic. Degrees of trance range from very light to deathlike coma. James A. Christenson, Jr. says, *"pure hypnosis,* if there is such a state, is *reverie* only"—and adds:

> The fact that some subjects simply lapse into hypnosis, "adopting" the new state of mind spontaneously rather than depending on the

mechanical process . . . indicates that hypnotic states are spontaneously generated far more frequently than we might suspect.[23]

Below the level of stuporous or plenary trance, comes a stage of suspended animation, of which LeCron says, "Spontaneous states such as this have been reported from time to time. During the last century many people had great fear of being buried alive under such circumstances. One of the most famous cases of such burial, where the woman was rescued, was that of the mother of Robert E. Lee." [24]

Yogins submit to being buried alive and they are exhumed unharmed; British physicians have attested to the honesty of such demonstrations.[25] The yogins induce the stage of suspended animation by auto-hypnosis.

But ordinarily, as Christenson points out, "An essential feature of the *hypnotic situation* is that another individual is involved, and hence all phenomena are conditioned by the subject's awareness of the agent's expectation that he shall do something. In *self-hypnosis* this separation is made when the "subject plans in advance what he is to do . . ." [26] Subjects have a remarkable ability in hypnosis to sense the attitude of the hypnotist through minimal cues and will respond accordingly: "If the operator believes a negative result will ensue, the subject will probably respond negatively." [27]

In a process so subtle, the role of expectation cannot be overemphasized, and if the agent himself does not have definite expectations, the subject may "tailor the form taken by the hypnotic trance to fit his speculations, prejudices, fears, or desires." [28] Hypnosis has been described as a state of heightened suggestibility—suggestion and response to it depends upon the conviction of the patient as this applies to his assimilation of the suggestions and their consistency with his needs and desires. It is thought that a patient under hypnosis will not respond to a suggestion that is contrary to his fundamental character, but a good deal of controversy surrounds this issue.

A patient will respond to a suggestion psychosomatically. For example, he will produce a blister in response to the suggestion that an object is burning him even though the object is cool, or his movements can be commanded or restricted, or he can hold a position apparently without effort.

In trance, a patient may be carried backward in time to remember in detail experiences in earliest childhood. Although beyond hope of proof, remarkable exhibitions of regression into a past, supposedly before birth, have been recorded; and in cases of "automatic writing" both the style and competency exhibited are apparently beyond the experience and capacity of the author.

While in trance, time may be distorted or altered: a patient may experience minutes as hours, or vice versa. Posthypnotic response to suggestion demonstrates the unconscious calculation of time, and also that actions may be carried out without awareness of the source of the impulse. The reach of posthypnotic response has not been determined. Nor has the reason for the patient's response been determined. The psychoanalytical school believes that the operator symbolically represents the parent in the mind of the subject, so that there is an unconscious attitude of blind belief and a compulsion to obey on the subject's part.

The hypnotizability of people varies greatly. The reason is probably to be found in the unconscious needs, wishes, and prohibitions which influence all the person's behavior.[29] Traditionally, inducing trance depends upon repetitions made vocally, mechanically, or manually during which the subject has fixed upon an object such as a hand, or he has fixed upon an idea. Although it may take several long sessions to induce deep trance, even in a person of average susceptibility, once the hypnotist has succeeded, thereafter the patient may be quickly and easily hypnotized to the desired degree—a touch, a word, any signal will immediately induce the hypnoid state.

Dr. Joseph Whitlow discusses a technique for rapid initial induction into trance which requires no more than a few seconds—generally, this is the technique used by stage entertainers.[30] Medical men say it is dangerous for the subject, but that in the hands of a skilled operator a patient may be presumed to suffer no greater risk than if deep narcotic anesthesia were induced.

A process which quickly transfers the idea of visual fixation to an inner fixing of the idea of vision is discussed by Frank A. Pattie, contributor to Roy M. Dorcus' book, *Hypnosis and Its Therapeutic Applications:*

> James Braid (1795–1860) was the first to use it. His method was nearly the same as those that employ fixation today. In the last years of his career he did not insist upon prolonged fixation but had the subject close his eyes after a short time. The fact that he could hypnotize the blind and that seeing subjects could be hypnotized in the dark led him to believe in the essentially subjective nature of hypnosis and to hold that direct verbal suggestion was the best method.[31]

As a result of wide research, Pattie concludes:

> The hypnotic state can be induced while the subject is standing erect and without closure of the eyes or any suggestions of relaxation or drowsiness, and without any reduction of sensory input except that which is incident to ocular fixation and concentration of attention.[32]

Terminating hypnosis is brought about easily by suggesting the idea of wakefulness. But if left to themselves, after varying lengths of time, patients spontaneously resume the normal state.

As for recent spectacular successes in the use of hypnosis, two examples will suffice to show something of the nature of responses that may be obtained:

> A woman declining from loss of weight and nervousness, bothered by a rash on her hand, was kept hypnotized for five days. She ate, retained her food, gained four pounds, and awakened—rash cured—with a great sense of well-being. Edwin L. Baron reported this case.[33]

> A patient, severely burned, under hypnosis twice obeyed the command to "lock" arm and leg in a grotesque position and "hold it" for weeks while a skin graft was accomplished. When the command, "unlock it," was given, each time the limbs were fully flexible and painless. The patient had not suffered the miserable discomfort of such dual operations when they are done with use of casts to hold the limbs in place. Dr. Denys Kelsey and Dr. John N. Barron reported this case in the *British Medical Journal*.[34]

Of the multitude of cases that might have been selected, these two were chosen because they indicate the value of hypnosis in cases not generally thought of in connection with its use.

Although much is written on the subject of hypnosis, and use of it is slowly gaining some ground, for the most part it remains in the background or on the fringes of standard medical practice. The medical world is enmeshed in such vast and incredibly complex research in other fields that doctors cannot in reality keep apace what might be called the "changing gains." But, as Dr. Rene Jules Dubos points out, medicine's vision of a physical utopia ever recedes because as man's environment changes so do his diseases—they do not disappear.[35]

There is a growing volume of disenchantment in the medical world.[36] Neither the men who speak out nor this study wish to minimize the tremendous strides medical science has made or to say the promise it holds is a false one—the reports simply point to the truth of the situation: there is another side to the bright coin of twentieth-century medicine. The problem compounds because it is becoming more and more difficult to draw the line between physical and mental or emotional illnesses. Tension, anxiety, fear become the villains of the piece—hatred and guilt their shrouded, silent companions.

Dr. Hans Selye has found in his studies of the body's reaction to physical stress—which must in turn produce mental stress—a pattern of: alarm, reaction, adaptation, or exhaustion. All normal and abnormal reactions can be brought about by various combinations of ordinary stimuli and inhibitions of the biologic mechanism of the body; but Dr. Selye's studies show that the body is limited to the following patterns of response:

Alarm, resistance, adaptation.
Alarm, resistance, over-resistance, exhaustion.
Alarm, resistance, prolonged stress unto exhaustion.

Dr. Selye says of his work:

> To my mind, the most important contribution of research on stress is that it has furnished an objective, scientific basis for the development of a new approach to the treatment of disease. This is neither specific causal nor specific symptomatic therapy, but a treatment based upon the imitation and perfection of Nature's own autopharmacologic responses. These defensive reactions have become exquisitely adapted to our needs, through countless centuries of evolution, so that we may meet all the usual assaults against health and life to which man is commonly exposed. A therapy which thus attempts to cooperate intelligently with the natural healing powers of the body could not fail to inspire confidence.[37]

As one works his way through the maze of the medical world, he cannot escape the conclusion that man needs the anesthetic measure to temper his fear, but that upon occasion he needs also a stress-factor to shock him into responsive state. Hypnosis induces anesthesia, and the hypnotized respond to a "whisper" of shock as though it were a stimulant of tremendous power. To turn man's mind toward hypnosis is to suggest that medical men strive to understand this natural means through which sometimes the whole of the body's responses are brought to function harmoniously. But hypnosis can be regarded only as a tool, not as a panacea, not itself as a cure. Trance is a condition that can be induced in an effort to cooperate with man's natural curative force via suggestion.

But for all the necessity to understand hypnosis, research in the material realm must not be curtailed, for man is made of matter [38]—wondrous matter.

Since the incredible "resurrection" of the DNA of dead pneumonia germs startled the scientific world,[39] biochemists have been hard put to know where life ends—and so have doctors who have revived bodies from which every sign of life is gone, returning people from what appears to be the land of the dead to the land of the living.

As scientists in many fields probe the mystery of life, they come upon many surprises. For example, as men peered into the living cell they found that it is much like an industrial metropolis operating with great efficiency upon the law of supply and demand. Chemical plants, assembly lines, barges of raw materials and barges of finished products were being towed to specific docks—building and commerce were flourishing—or so Ruth Moore describes it: "It was a clear, efficiently organized operation, but its perfection and significance were sheer magic." [40] Nowhere under the microscope, however, is there to be seen the intelligence that devised this marvel, the *being* for whom it operates, the *being* that returns to the "dead body" physicians revive. Can science disclose this being? Hans Driesche, the great biochemist, turned to search in the field of parapsychology.

But in the realm of parapsychology, one finds that hypnosis—which opens a pathway into the mind—is relegated to the side lines because like man, himself, its working is inconsistent, irrational, and upsetting. Playing down hypnosis, playing up extrasensory perception is error on the part of parapsychologists. Hypnotic susceptibility and all psychic phenomena are closely related if not entirely interdependent, but the range in degree of trance and its duration, as well as the means and method of induction, obscure this relationship—and so does the whole subtle business of suggestion and response to it.

The whole question of perception is involved with ESP and hypnosis or trance. How deeply? What part does such as this play in learning? What part might it play? These questions must be answered, for coming generations confront a staggering load of knowledge to digest and pass along. And subtle use of and reaction to the hypnotic means in advertising and politics—evidenced by the public's response to repetitive suggestion and propaganda—could lead to still another perversion of man's natural power that would work to deliver him into the hands of a new type "high-priestdom."

But another consideration arises. Consider that, according to Jung, the changes of mind that appear inexplicable stem from the *unintentional influence* of one or a small group of people:

> The deepening and broadening of . . . consciousness produces the kind of effect which the primitives call "mana." It is an unintentional influence on the unconscious of others, a sort of unconscious prestige, and its effect lasts only so long as it is not disturbed by conscious intention.[41]

If unintentional influence on the subliminal mind of others exists, it is not always necessarily benign. No man is safe from a pestilential idea that can be unconsciously and involuntarily communicated, unconsciously and involuntarily assimilated. This poses the threat that psychological distress is a communicable disease. Criminal delinquency may also be such. If so, and if telepathy is responsible, the problem is not solved when man becomes his brother's keeper—that is, when he incarcerates him, or when he makes of his whole civilization an inescapable institution. Without belaboring the point, this study proposes that twentieth-century man must try again to understand the "miraculous," extrasensory perception, and mysterious phenomena arising from expression of the psychic force in man which appears to be most surely released through hypnosis.

III

As one approaches the Biblical miracles, he must consider not how much he knows that makes it impossible for them to be true, but rather how little he knows to make it possible for him to understand them and *describe* them in the scientific terms he now demands. One must ask oneself what the words were trying to describe when the Scriptures tell of the parting of the seas, the fiery chariot or whirlwinds. Events? Emotions? Hidden workings?

Man has always grasped more than he can describe, and so he resorts to the poetic word or a symbol to convey the inexpressible. Lavoisier saw that the analogy between respiration and combustion had not escaped the philosophers of old, interpreters of the poets:

> The fire stolen from heaven, the fire of Prometheus, is not merely an ingenious poetical idea; it is a faithful picture of the operations of Nature, at least for animals that breathe. . . .
>
> When we consider these remarkable anticipations, we are sometimes tempted to think that . . . fable is indeed only an allegory under which [the ancients] hid the great truths of medicine and physics.[42]

The Old Testament miracles may be in the same category.

In *Frontiers of Medicine*, Rudolph Friedrich quotes the great physicist, Max Planck, who said, "Physical and psychical events are not different events. They are the same events, seen from two different sides," and then adds that psychosomatics denies a real distinction between mental and physical disorders because an "organic disease may have mental causes and a mental disease organic ones."[43] In psychosomatic cases, quite often a word that touches upon the root of the trouble will effect a cure.

Just as a mathematician must ask the right question before he can receive the right answer, so man must ask the right question about miracles.

And if he looks for one to happen, he must meet the requirements Jesus enunciated. These are seldom met—men appear to forget that they are prerequisite. For example, Dr. van den Berg says, as he remembers the utter agony of a hopeless, helpless victim dying slowly and crying out to God to relieve him of his torture, ". . . to believe in a miracle, now, is blasphemy. Because God cannot do it any more. . . . Or should we think that He could, but does not want to? That is what I meant by blasphemy. He cannot do it. We have made it impossible for Him. . . . That is why miracles do not happen any more." [44] But the question is, could the victim comply with the conditions Jesus predicated the miracle upon?—which are:

If ye have faith, and doubt not . . .

. . . all things, whatsoever ye shall ask in prayer, believing, ye shall receive.

If ye shall ask any thing in my name, I will do it.

. . . if two of you shall agree on earth as touching any thing that they shall ask, it shall be done for them of my Father which is in heaven.[45]

Man cannot *will* the miracle—he must *believe* it will come, *doubting not*. Belief is the most difficult of all psychological states to induce in oneself in the moment of hopelessness. The atrocity Dr. van den Berg refers to took place in a concentration camp. Was there present another person to gather with the poor man in the asking, believing, in the working of the miracle? Was the victim an orthodox Jew? If so, could he understand that only through the spirit in man that says, "I am he," can man come unto the Father? Could he ask in the *name* Jesus used: Son of man? Could he see, as Jesus did, himself brother to every man, the Christ present in every man, even in his persecutors? Or could a Roman Catholic? Or a Protestant? Or a liberal so tolerant as to have no real conviction? Theologies and lack of faith stand between man and the miracle.

Only one who could become the acting power of truth, seeing the Christ in his persecutors and being the Christ of Himself as he confronted them, might under such circumstances work the miracle. The point is, in today's world, or in the plight of the victim, *it would be a miracle if any man could fulfill the conditions Jesus outlined*. He pointed, however, to an easier way—not specifically to work the miracle, but rather in terms of meeting one's every need: He said, "seek ye first the kingdom of God, and his righteousness . . ." [46]

Suppose the victim had known how to enter trance quickly, inducing nature's perfect anesthesia, as finding himself in hopeless plight he prayed to be delivered through it to death. The Father has provided man with the perfect anesthetic. When men can protect themselves with it, how can they torture each other's bodies? When man really understands the power of the kingdom of God within him, a whole new dimension in freedom will be added.

The miracles associated with Jesus fall into five categories: medical, social, demonstrations of extrasensory perception, illusory visions, and the resurrection. Each category will be examined.

Many of the miracles are reported in two or more of the Gospels, but the reports vary in detail. Only by montaging all accounts of the same incident can one obtain as full a picture as the Gospels can give. This study postulates that posthypnotic response to Jesus' suggestion prompted the disciples to have the Gospels written, and that posthypnotic response to His suggestion of remembrance permitted them to recall His works, words, and actions in detail and with a degree of accuracy that otherwise would have been impossible.

Jesus could reveal the truth of man only by acknowledging and demonstrating hypnotic power and extrasensory perception. It should give no offense to say that He performed no miracles, that the cures were effected through His application of the hypnotic means—its dynamics and man's natural healing power perfectly understood. He advocated the practice of pure hypnosis: *pure reverie*, which He called prayer, saying it should be practiced in solitude, without verbalizing, in faith, and without ceasing [47] —which is to say, man must make this practice a part of his life as long as he lives.

Jesus taught that the power generated through prayer would act to fulfill secret desire.[48] Secret or subconscious or unconscious desire states itself without word and without ceasing—thus its fulfillment is sure. The nature of unconscious desire can be altered only as consciousness is widened or as man alters his self-concept through self-contemplation. A man *is* how he is regarding himself, consciously and unconsciously, the one concept measuring itself against or through the other. To pray in faith is to use one's natural psychic powers normally. But when the ego-group is guilt-ridden, harassed, or paralyzed in fear, pure reverie cannot be achieved. It is then that the healing ministry of man unto man may be brought to bear. (See Appendix II, p. 396.)

Chapter 11

JESUS' HEALING MINISTRY

I

Faith healing was practiced with success in Israel apart from Jesus—as is indicated in the report of the invalid who waited for the "angels to bubble the water" at the renowned pool, and also as is indicated in the report that Jesus does not prohibit a man who is casting out demons in His name, saying that anyone who offers so much as a cup of water in the name of the Christ "shall not lose his reward." [1]

Jesus did not claim to have unique or supranatural power. He said that His followers could do greater works than He performed.[2] He refused to perform "signs." He told people their own faith, belief, *expectation* had made them whole. He did not effect a healing every time He attempted to cure—or else He did not attempt all the cases He was expected to cure—for it is stated, "There he could not do many miracles owing to their lack of faith." [3] The failure occurs when Jesus is in His home territory, without prestige. In Mark's Gospel a few healings of minor sickness are indicated, but nevertheless His efforts here are clearly stated to be unsuccessful, disappointing. Thus, one sees the pattern of healing effected through hypnotic therapy wherein the patient reacts according to his own expectations which are largely based upon the prestige of the operator.

Since so much of the healing ministry deals with "unclean spirits" and "daemons" it must be pointed out that the medical world confronts them today. One is startled to read in a case history reported by Friedrich that in the mid-twentieth century a psychiatrist would address a demon directly, as Jesus did, and then—"Can you imagine the emotional shock I received when it actually replied?" [4] These "creatures of the imagination" are real enough to take possession of the patient's voice and of his limbs. McCurdy devotes a long passage to such phenomena:

> What is it that demon theory and Freudian theory have in common? The emphasis on the power of psychic, purposeful, and essentially

invisible forces. How do they differ? In the degree of independence of the human body assigned to these forces. . . . Charcot, Freud's teacher at the Salpêtrière, was quite aware of demonology, which of course he rejected. Nevertheless, he included in his concept of hysteria the "demoniacal attack" . . . It is quite understandable why earlier theorists, having witnessed such attacks singly and in epidemic form, should have spoken of demon possession. . . .[5]

As McCurdy points out, current rejection of demon theory is partially due to antipathy to religion.[6] It is due also to antipathy to such an unscientific term. In the words of Friedrich, "Psychotherapy is refining its methods of treatment from year to year, but fundamentally it is doing only what the great physicians, priests, shamans and magicians of all peoples have been doing instinctively for thousands of years—it is mobilizing the powers of the soul against the demon of disease."[7] And it has developed a new terminology: "unclean spirits" are now labeled neuroses or psychoses, etc.

Jesus dealt widely and successfully with psychic disorder, knowing that the demon, although made of the patient's own repressed fears and fury breaking loose upon him, is real to the possessed and to those who must deal with him. Whether treating physical or psychic illness, He dealt with the whole man, seeing mind and body as an indivisible unity.

Very little detail of Jesus' procedure is given in the Gospels, but there is one graphic report of a healing effected by Peter and John after Jesus' death which casts the clue that He induced trance rapidly by the process of gazing as He commanded attention, then followed with suggestion *and* the "shock" of touch, authoritative command, action, for the disciples must have copied Jesus' procedure:

> Peter and John were on their way up to the temple for the hour of prayer at three in the afternoon, when a man lame from birth was carried past, who used to be laid every day at what was called the "Beautiful Gate" of the temple, to ask alms from those who entered the temple. When he noticed that Peter and John meant to go into the temple, he asked them for alms. Peter looked at him steadily as did John, and said, "Look at us." The man attended, expecting to get something from them. But Peter said, "I have no silver or gold, but I will give you what I do have. In the name of Jesus Christ the Nazarene, get up and walk!" And catching him by the right hand he raised him. Instantly his feet and ankles grew strong, he leapt to his feet, started to walk, and accompanied them into the temple . . .[8]

Dr. Esdaile says, "In mesmerizing, the gazer projects the influence of his brain direct through the recipient eye to the brain of the patient."[9] Peter's command: "look at us," the man attending, the reference to "looking steadily at him," gives the pattern of inducing hypnotic trance through gazing. The patient *expects to receive something*. The shock of the command: "get up and walk!" coupled with decisive, shocking touch and action, provided well defined and accurately directed suggestion which the hypnotized will obey if rapport is established.

Experiments prove that actual organic changes occur under hypnosis. Alan Mitchell reports on an experiment that proves pigment in the subject's eye is used up when he is told that he is staring at a red lamp, although a white lamp is shown. He gives another example of organic change or reaction: ". . . when you tell a hypnotized patient that you are going to count 'Three,' and then shine a light in his eyes, and you do count 'Three' but do not shine a light, you will often get a contraction of the pupils. . . . an organic reaction has been produced." [10] If organic changes can be effected, the question becomes—to what degree? To answer this question, this study examines Jesus' record.

Jesus is reported to have cured leprosy, fever, and hemorrhaging, but the majority of the disorders He dealt with were nervous, sensory, and psychic: paralysis, blindness, deafness, dumbness, epilepsy, and demoniacal attack. Since psychic disorder can produce any symptom, Jesus may have dealt only with psychosomatic cases. There is, however, one incident that cannot be so classified: during the betrayal one of Jesus' followers cut off the ear of the servant of the highpriest, whereupon He touched the man's ear and "healed him." [11] All four Gospels tell of the man's ear being cut off, but only in the Gospel of Luke is it stated that Jesus touched the man and healed him. The word *healed* may be assumed to convey that the cut was healed, but if one assumes the ear was replaced, the miracle may still be within the range of the possible insofar as hypnotherapy is concerned, if hypnotherapy can produce any organic result obtainable by medicine and surgery—which is to say, surgeons have now shown that severed flesh and bone may possibly be replaced if all conditions are favorable. But in the view of this study, Jesus healed the cut in the ordinary sense of the word, for in the parable of the good Samaritan, He gives His suggestion for dealing with wounds—bind them up and give the patient care—which is to say, He did not go about healing "with a word" such injuries as broken arms, lacerated bodies, and battered heads. The whole drama in the Garden of Gethsemane is so strangely reported that it must be considered also in another category of miracles because, when the four versions are montaged, a picture of hallucinatory property emerges. But if, in reality, Jesus dealt with a cut ear and healed the cut, this response has been exhibited in connection with hypnotic phenomena, which is to say, Thérèse Neumann, stigmatist, and Paul Diebel, who duplicated the phenomena she displayed, attest to the power of the psychic force to produce and heal a bleeding wound. Paul Diebel allowed his hand to be nailed to a board and "when the nail was removed, he immediately caused the bleeding to cease and the wound to heal under the bewildered eyes of the observers," a group of hardheaded medical men and newspaper reporters, as Marion describes them.[12]

Jesus is reported to have healed many demoniacs "with a word" [13]—today, verbal suggestion has to its credit many cures of psychic disorder. Jesus convulsed a man with an unclean spirit, which brings to mind the convulsive effect of electric shock therapy which sometimes produces good results, but doctors do not understand why or how it works. There are no indications that Jesus attempted to restore terminal or torporous mental patients.

The point this study attempts to make is that Jesus employed hypnotherapy, and attempted to cure only those cases in which such therapy would be effective; and since the effectiveness of hypnotherapy depends upon the patient's faith, the type of ailments He could cure were limited because beyond a certain point no person can muster sufficient faith. Jesus pointed to the limitation of faith, limitation that consciousness and reason insist upon, and limitation that the difficulties of inducing trance impose, as will be discussed later on in this study.

When the panorama of Jesus' healing ministry is surveyed, His success would appear to depend upon His ability to induce trance almost instantaneously; when in contact with His patients, the mystery of the medical miracles appears to be no greater than the mystery of healing through the hypnotic means, a means that throughout history has been successfully employed in many cases.

There are, however, three reports of healings when Jesus did not come into physical contact with the patient: the daughter possessed by a demon of the woman who begged the crumbs from the master's table, the paralyzed servant of the army captain who understood authority, the feverish son of the royal official.[14] In each case, belief is emphasized—in the first two, Jesus expresses amazement at the faith of the person acting as mediator for the patient. These healings appear to stem from the ESP, faith, and willingness to act of the mediator. In each case, the patients would have had great confidence in the mediator, and each patient is in the classification of those generally possessing the ability to demonstrate extrasensory perception. Although telepathy is not proved as a channel of communication between any two people, it has been shown that it can operate between two given people, called gifted subjects, in card experiments and with extraordinary reliability. A pattern suggests itself: consciously or unconsciously, the patient had his "fix" on the mediator and telepathic communication was established through this rapport so that inducing trance in the mediator made possible the projection to the patient of the inner idea of vision (as must be done to hypnotize the blind) and also made possible the projection of the authoritative command which the patient in each case would be prone to obey. In trance the power of telepathy is heightened.[15] Parents and master became "as a child," as the one in need, projecting to the patient also their unfaltering expectation that the cure would be effected. Jesus said one must become as a child to enter the inner realm wherein the unconscious or cellular processes must be determined.[16]

But the psychological pattern presented by these three reports is of greatest importance because in so many cases Jesus laid down in drama a play too complicated to convey in the words of His time: the child or servant represents the cellular and subconscious level. Parent or master represents the superego and ego-group. Jesus represents the Authority-Ego. The cellular, subconscious, or unconscious needs can be met by the Authority-Ego only when the superego and ego-group put aside intellect, fear, pride, and skepticism, and aware of or intuitively grasping the power of the unknown within allow its force or "word" to pass through consciousness uninhibited. Superego and ego-group must become "as a child" for a healing to be effected.

The strangest and most dramatic of Jesus' healings occurred as He cast "legion" into the swine.[17] To begin to understand the message concealed in this episode, one must concede that no man knows the state of his psychic being—how much he has repressed that may spring forth disguised. No man knows whether he has to sustain but one more grain of trauma to tip the scales into psychic or physical decline. No man knows the intricate pattern of adaptation to life's stress his body has woven or which turn it will take to deal with its next input of stress, for this depends upon the sum total of his life up to that moment. No man knows how psychic stress is transferred to the physical level—or why—but it is transferred.

If one searches the medical ministry of Jesus for a clue regarding the interaction of the psychic and physical aspects of man, one finds it in this unforgettable drama: Jesus casts two maniacs' demons named "legion" into a herd of swine innocently grazing on a nearby hill, causing the swine to rush madly to destruction in the sea. The maniacs (or maniac, since Mark and Luke report but one whereas Matthew reports two) are cured, but the townspeople beg Jesus to leave their shores to which He has crossed over. The demonstration appears to be a cruel whim on the part of Jesus, who had shown that with a word He could heal. Today, the disturbing picture is dismissed, much as the townspeople dismissed Him. Did all this actually happen? Animals are particularly sensitive to human fear, a herd can be put into panic with little reason to prompt it—the important question is why Jesus made such a demonstration. In the view of this study, He constructed a drama to picture a reaction too complicated to trust to words: the casting of psychic distress onto the physical level.

The maniacs were repressed, that is, they were chained but could not be kept bound, which presents a pattern of subliminal fears bursting loose. Jesus made the maniacs *name* their demons: they called them "legion . . . there is a host of us." Thus, the fears and phobia could not be defined—legion represented an accumulation grown into a powerful force that must be sent somewhere by its very nature. Jesus had revealed in a parable that a psychic force of destructive potential (an evil spirit) cannot be destroyed merely by driving it out of consciousness because it will return, its force increased, and devastate the "house" from whence it came.[18] In this parable, and in the drama of legion, one may observe that as repressions are reversed and re-presented to consciousness, if they are not reconciled within it by a widened understanding they gather into a host of nameless, unrecognized fears, a mass which can no longer be dealt with one by one for they have lost their identity. The Authority-Ego must then present them to the world of self by casting their destructive force onto the cellular level, as symbolized by the swine. When transferred to or cast upon the animal flesh in which man is clothed, legion drives it to panic and self-destruction. Thereby, legion expends itself and the Authority-Ego wipes out an expression in flesh that can no longer contain its accumulation of unidentified fear. When legion's tensions and conflicts cross over into the cellular realm, they give rise to a death-dealing disease which moves at panic's pace. Is it unconscious, or subconscious panic that causes death?

In society, man has had experience of one man, or one act, stemming the tide of panic—and certain individuals appear to be immune to panic's lure. Although man does not know how it is achieved, he does know that there is no panic-paced disease in which spontaneous remission has not taken place. Consciously or unconsciously, patients have grasped or responded to something, so that in the most hopeless cases remission has been effected.[19]

On three occasions Jesus returned the dead to life: the daughter of Jairus when the mourners said she had died, a young man as he was being carried out of the City of Nain, and Lazarus who had been buried four days.[20] The most detailed account is that of Lazarus' resurrection:

Stauffer (or his translator) makes the statement: "John stresses unmistakably that Lazarus had already lain in his tomb for four days; that the smell of decay was already noticeable. . . ."[21] The Gospel report does not justify this interpretation:

> Jesus said, "Remove the boulder."
> "Lord," said Martha, the dead man's sister, "he will be stinking by this time; he has been dead four days."[22]

Martha surmised that a man four days dead would stink, but nowhere is it reported that any odor of decay was noticed. Previously, Jesus had said, "Our friend Lazarus sleepeth; but I go that I may awake him out of sleep" —because the disciples thought He had spoken of his resting, Jesus said "unto them plainly, Lazarus is dead."[23]

In these words, Jesus indicates that death itself begins in a state of sleep, and progresses to the stage of trance below the plenary level wherein animation is suspended. By His own words, He raised the dead from their deep sleep—which is to say, brought them out of the last stages of trance. Were these people "really dead" or were they simply in trance? Today such trance and death are not so easily confused, which makes it all the more difficult to answer the question because doctors have restored patients after all symptoms of life have ceased as determined by their modern instruments—there is no heartbeat and breathing has stopped so that the patient appears to be dead. Are such patients actually dead? If not, why do not more patients respond?

Certain passages in the drama of Elijah may provide a clue.[24] The son of the widow who befriended Elijah was so ill that "there was no breath left in him." Elijah "crouched over the child three times, crying out . . ." and restored him. Later, it is reported that after forty days and nights in a cave on Horeb "the mountain of God," Elijah came to himself—suddenly this word from the Eternal came to him, "What are you doing here, Elijah?" At the command of the Eternal to "go outside" there follows a passage:

> Suddenly the Eternal went past. A strong, fierce wind tore the mountain, crashing the rocks before the Eternal; but the Eternal was not in the wind. After the wind came an earthquake, but the Eternal was not in the earthquake; after the earthquake a fire, but the Eternal was

not in the fire; after the fire the breath of a light whisper. As soon as Elijah heard that, he wrapped his face in his mantle and came out to the entrance.[25]

These words indicate that in the last extremity of life, in death-trance, the ego-group of the patient will respond only if the physical measure applied to the body is reduced in traumatic impact to a *whisper* as the force penetrates the inward psychic reaches. Today great suffering sometimes accompanies the physicians' efforts to restore a patient as the patient regains a measure of consciousness—which is to say, it may be that often the severity of modern methods may prove their undoing.

Are sonic waves suggested by the word, "whisper"? An unconscious person may sometimes hear—Mitchell cites a case of an anesthetized patient's hearing the conversation in the operating room.[26] Would sonic waves gently massage the heart? Today, scientists are doing strange things with plain ordinary noise and with high-frequency sound.[27] Jung found that the Self of man is represented in the mandala symbol, the symbol of wholeness, and that an appropriate understanding of archetypal symbols can have a healing effect. Dr. von Franz presents a photograph of sound waves given off by a vibrating steel disk that produce a "strikingly mandala-like pattern."[28] Could the symbol of wholeness be impressed via sound waves upon a person in coma or unconscious? How much does the symbol or pattern convey? The "stuff" of the *word* is sound, and according to the Gospels, Jesus healed many with a word. Elijah crouched over the child, "crying out"—as Jesus raised Lazarus, He "called out loudly."

But however the dead may be raised from their trance, Elijah's hesitancy bespeaks a reluctance to return. Tyrrell describes the painful re-emergence of a man from the hinterlands of life.[29] Of the many called, few indeed respond. Perhaps in death one knows himself and is unwilling to return to the condition of amnesia man calls consciousness.

Jesus demonstrated that even from the extremity of death it is possible to return a man's ego-group to its conscious existence, but death processes were not arrested by Him when a person was beyond the prime of life or when the body was not in good condition. The body does not deteriorate in trance. Does Jesus' raising of the dead suggest that if man thoroughly understood the procedure of recall Homo sapiens might interminably postpone or defeat death? Jesus' drama indicates that the answer is no. Each one's capacity for fulfillment is set by his Authority-Ego before birth; when a man has fulfilled himself life can offer him no more, nor does he have more to offer life; then he must face death in faith, laying down his life willingly, even as he lays it down each night in sleep.

Having spoken or shown all that could be conveyed, Jesus dramatized the end: Authority-Ego will elect to die,[30] will consume no more of the life-giving psychic power—the fruit of "I . . . the real Vine . . ."[31]— not until "the day I drink it new within the Realm of God."[32] This montage of His words at the last supper presents the subjective nature of hypnosis and the anesthetic qualities of trance, for Jesus refused the anesthetizing cup at the cross, and in identifying the vine as "I," also identified the fruit of which He spoke—thus giving His word that He would suffer the cross, as those who followed Him might suffer, without inducing upon Himself the anesthesia of hypnotic trance.

II

The psychoanaytical school explains hypnotic response by the idea that the operator symbolically represents the patient's parent, so that he has an unconscious compulsion to obey. If the operator holds this concept, his attitude toward his own parents, or parental power as such, perforce becomes deeply involved in his symbolization of parent. The psychoanalyst reflects in his attitude his commitment in whole or in part to the Freudian view of parenthood which may confuse the patient's expectation and his inclination to respond. Jesus was committed to the concept of God, *love*, as true and real Father of man—no personalities were involved and His attitude reflected unmitigated faith in God-parent and in God-parent's love for child-man. Thus, an unadulterated compulsion to obey His suggestion could be present in the patient. This may be one of the secrets of His success.

Today, the experimental approach is demanded—but Jesus refused to perform "signs," in effect, refused to perform "experiments." It appears certain that neither hypnotic response nor ESP can be endlessly manipulated or irresponsibly indulged to make the power a panacea for all ills and insufficiencies. As Jung points out, ability to demonstrate ESP fails rapidly after a few trials. He says Rhine's experiments depended in large measure on the subject's interest, but either this or his ability waned and other volunteers were substituted so that a large number of subjects were used. But from Rhine's point of view, from the scientific point of view, this served to validate the operation of ESP for it was proved statistically.[33] Jung maintains, however, that "he would never have got the results he did if he had carried out his experiments with a single subject, or only a few."[34] Jesus' example indicates that the Authority-Ego will not long permit a play upon or a testing of psychic power.

Although physical responses may be elicited falsely under hypnosis, there appears to be an Authority in man which corresponds only with truth—which is to say, a healing that fades must stem from a false play upon the power, albeit unintentional on the part of operator and patient, and the symptoms of illness return when support of the healing from the *unconscious* is denied. Jesus indicates that the desire of the Authority-Ego is for growth of consciousness and greater fulfillment in life—one must conclude that with each use of the hypnotic or extrasensory means, conscious command and conscious response must be enlarged. Man does not live by bread alone, but it appears to be true also that he cannot live depending upon a constant call for the miracle to solve his problem—he must grasp the truth of his being, the reason for his cure, the nature of his illness, the authority of the Monarch of the kingdom of God within him. How many of those cured return to give thanks, to give the credit, to the Lord in man? [35]

Jesus heals with the words, "your sins are forgiven." [36] But when He is asked about the man blind from birth—is he blind for his own or for his parents' sins?—Jesus says, for neither. He is blind for the "work of God to be illustrated in him." [37] The words, "Your sins are forgiven," indicate that illness may derive from sin—today, one would say from a "guilt complex." Illness may derive not so much from what one has done as from his "sins of omission." Friedrich writes: "Weizsaecker concludes: 'Instead of solving a problem or a personal conflict we get sick.' To escape an unbearable condition people often seek refuge in disease . . ." [38] But Weizsaecker warned against a wrong interpretation of the concept that guilt causes illness—Jesus said, "Judge not, that ye be not judged." [39] Certainly no layman, and perhaps no doctor, can afford to judge illness in terms of the patient's guilt or sin, for it is equally likely that the "work of God" is being illustrated in him. The work of God is to bring to an end the destructive potential vested in each *one unit of total power* through expending evil in the flesh of God in which every man is clothed for there is none other—who owns "for keeps" the body he inhabits? Each one has his quota of evil with which he must deal in this flesh, from which he is delivered as he is delivered from this flesh. It would be as ridiculous to say the sick are sinful as to say the healthy are without sin, but it is also ridiculous to close one's eyes to the intimate relationship between the state of a man's soul and his physical being.

Dr. A. H. Schmale, Jr. discovered that out of forty-two patients between eighteen and forty-five years of age, selected because they happened to be in the hospital at the time, all but one had suffered a blow to his ego, thirty-one of them within the week past, the rest within the year.[40] The legend of Cain tells that an "ego blow" and sin are closely related—when Cain's offering failed to command respect, he was very wroth, with fallen countenance, and the Lord said unto him: "If thou doest well, shalt thou not be accepted? and if thou doest not well, sin lieth at the door. . . ."[41] Barrett points out that Kierkegaard offered two general principles in advance of nearly all current psychologies: "Despair is never ultimately over the external object but always over ourselves. . . . The condition we call a sickness in certain people is, at its center, a form of sinfulness."[42]

If man fulfills himself at every moment, as Zen teaches, an accident or an illness must be self-fulfillment of a secret need, desire, or anxiety that the person can fulfill in no other way. Today, even as medical control over disease moves at fantastic pace evidence also mounts to attest that psychic forces control man's flesh, determining in large measure his responses to therapy as well as his susceptibility to illnesses, even to bacterial assault.[43]

Jesus said: nothing that enters a man defiles him—his reactions to life, the acts he commits that perforce set up psychic reactions, make him unclean, defile him.[44] His words indicate that man is not at the mercy of microbes. Man's auto-pharmacologic responses indicate that he has the potential to deal with any of life's normal stresses; his RE (reticuloendothelial) system gives evidence that nature has provided built-in defenses to make possible his successfully combating any bacterial assault made upon him if his body is operating at peak efficiency. It would appear that Jesus recognized nature's own curative force and through inducing trance could command it to action by loosening what might be called the "log jam" in the soul that had in the first instance curtailed the body's normally smooth operation.

Nevertheless, germs, viruses, contagion are facts man must deal with, and until the mystery of them and his responses to them be resolved he must insist upon his immunizing vaccinations, and in illness of any sort he should partake of all medical science can offer. Every time he takes a step in understanding the material realm, he will also in time put the other foot forward to gain a step in understanding the psychic realm. Despite protests to the contrary, he has gained much in understanding himself.

Jesus did not altogether ignore the physical factor in effecting healings, for He made a paste of clay to put upon the blind man's eyes.[45] This is to say, in this case, and in all others wherein He was in immediate contact with the patient, Jesus appears to have realized that something more than verbal suggestion is needed—that the physical factor plays a role. As Dr.

Alexander points out, "notwithstanding the brilliant record of therapeutic suggestion, this school has never been able to produce the spectacular results obtained by the old Mesmerists. . . ."[46] As opposed to the suggestion technique, Mesmer's technique involved a degree of physical force or *direction of suggestion* via the method of passing the hand over the affected area, with the thought that a "magnetic fluid" passed from operator to patient.

When the hemorrhaging woman is healed by touching the robe of Jesus, He feels power passing out of Himself.[47] This indicates a transfer or altering of psychic energy; but its actual meaning may have to do with the drain of the operator's energy as he induces trance or acts as the medium through which hypnotherapy is employed. No matter how rapidly the operator achieves trance, the actual toll of his own energy may be the same.

Certainly Jesus saw the need of reinforcing or directing verbal suggestion, for almost always in effecting a healing He stretched forth His hand or touched the patient—one might say that His suggestion was thereby reinforced and precisely directed, enabling the subconscious to "locate" or understand the trouble with no effort and immediately. And Jesus said ". . . whatsoever ye shall loose on earth shall be loosened in heaven . . . if two of you shall agree on earth as TOUCHING anything that they shall ask, it shall be done for them of my Father which is in heaven."[48] Jesus also employed the suggestion technique: He commanded His patients, and a command carries with it a degree of shock to evoke response. An emotional shock can produce the diversion of attention from a physical symptom that will permit of near-spontaneous remission—emotional shocks are usually delivered via the word.

Faith, belief, the condition upon which the healing depends, is not an act of the will nor of the intellect nor of concentration. It is the ability to *let go the problem*, to put it in the hands of someone or "something" outside one's consciousness. An instant of its actual nonexistence in the mind is sufficient to break its hold upon the flesh and consciousness—and thus so often a shock works a miraculous cure. And yet it is not the shock itelf that cures: it is the *respite* the shock affords consciousness and subconsciousness in dealing with the problem. Friedrich speaks of "Anesthesia healing with its miraculous one-second cures . . ."[49] The anesthetic quality of trance may be experienced in the instant of receiving a verbal shock, for there is a "pause of mind" before its impact is felt during which man's self-healing power may be restored to action—the stymie has been broken.

There can be little hope of half-measures producing consistent results in hypnotic therapy. This clue is intricately woven into the report of Jesus' curing the man in whom the "work of God" is to be illustrated. Argument rages over this miracle—the Pharisees question the man, expel him. Jesus then seeks him in order to clarify the question:

"Dost thou believe on the Son of God?" Jesus asks. This is the title He seldom permits because it implies the Judaic concept of Messiah.

"Who is he, Lord, that I might believe on him?" The man addresses Jesus as Lord, bringing into play a title He permits.

And Jesus said unto him, "Thou hast both seen him, and it is he that talketh with thee."

These words of gossamer poetic construction are interpreted as though they read, "Thou hast both seen and talked with him; I who am talking with you am the Son of God, Messiah." Jesus did not say this. He used the mysterious word *it*. On another occasion, speaking to the disciples, He said, "IT is given unto you to know the mysteries of heaven"—He did not say, "I have given you the privilege of knowing." To the blind man He had cured, He said, "IT is he that talketh with thee," thereby objectifying the truth He wished to convey: Thou hast *both seen him*. What could "both" seeing mean? Could these words mean that as a man beholds the Christ and hears this voice *in another* he beholds and hears the Christ in himself? May one see and hear the Christ within himself *only* as it is reflected through the eyes and voice of another? Does one's own Lord then speak the healing word?

The words, "both seen," suggest that Jesus as operator first sees the Christ of God in His patient, reflecting it in His own eyes, being, and presence so that the patient through Him may grasp, may feel, the Christ presence within himself. As the patient sees in Jesus the Christ of God, he beholds the Christ of himself and thus *both sees* his own and another's, the Christ being in each, *outer* vision giving rise to *inner*. It may be that one cannot see the Christ in another except as he goes into trance with him, both acting, both expressing thereby their faith.

There is much in literature regarding the ancient or primitive practice of hypnotic therapy which suggests that modern application of it is missing the point because to produce results the operator must also go into trance, operating under his own "plan in advance"—to emerge rapidly and give the command and then bring his patient out of trance. It is known that the direct eye-gaze method, and fixing the idea of inner vision by which the blind are hypnotized, which appears to be the method employed by Jesus, may easily produce trance in the operator.[50] Did Jesus go into trance with His patients and thereby quickly *lead them into trance*

Himself? The problem is to discover the *principle* He employed so that techniques could be worked out to utilize it, for trance can be induced without the aid of an operator whose prejudices play so great a part in the procedure. Mitchell points out that trance can be induced, for example, by looking at a piece of machinery going round and humming.[51]

To go into trance, a person must have *faith* in the operator. Consciousness of man's fallibility and knowledge of the operator limit this faith—as was demonstrated when Jesus failed to heal many, if any, in His own village. Thus, the limits of faith that it is possible to possess *in reality* limit the effectiveness of hypnotherapy which may, *theoretically*, be without limit in its application, but in reality is limited because reason limits faith.

As one reviews the healings of Jesus when the patient was there and conscious, one sees a pattern of:

Rapid induction into trance (relaxation)
Authoritative command or surprising word to produce a degree of shock, coupled with a physical factor, such as touch or stretching forth the hand, to reinforce and direct verbal suggestion.
Therapy is administered by an operator devoid of ego-group in play; the patient is given over to the forces within him; faith is the determining factor.

When the patient was not there, not conscious, not sane, the suggestion could have been sent via telepathy. Dr. Alexander suggests that mind is a "stillness" with the capacity to form and to reflect images which organize and direct energy, and that it is "possible for an image formed by one human mind to be transmitted to another human mind, either visually, orally, or by telepathy." [52]

The image Jesus formed and projected was the Christ of God in man which makes him whole and perfect. Jung recognized that such symbols of Self as "Divine Child," appearing as "savior-messiah," often have not only "a redemptive meaning, but a psychological healing effect as well." [53] Through this symbol, Jesus healed. His secret appears to rest in knowing that only the Christ which is in man can perform the miracle of a true and lasting healing. When John the Baptist sent a messenger to Jesus to ask, "Are you the Coming One?" Jesus returned the word of His healings.[54]

III

However keenly one observes the method of Jesus, he must acknowledge that His work cannot be repeated until an operator understands Homo sapiens as Jesus understood him. Therefore, he who attempts to follow His pattern must be prepared for many failures. But failure teaches and is revealing: the failure of Jesus to work many miracles in His native place, where He was a prophet without honor and prestige, reveals that He employed hypnosis. If this failure had not been recorded, the great number of healings He effected apparently so effortlessly would have led eternally to a concept of His exercising supranatural power.

It took Mary Baker Eddy to see that He employed a principle which worked with "mathematical precision." She said, "Jesus of Nazareth was the most scientific man that ever trod the globe." [55] There is much in Christian Science dogma with which this study cannot concur, but it is in agreement with the principle upon which Mrs. Eddy based her healing ministry. She recognized that Jesus made a distinction between "wonderful works of magic," even the magic of hypnosis, and healings that "follow from a knowledge of and conformity to God's will, or the nature of reality." [56] Robert Peel says of her:

> Only as one recognizes Mrs. Eddy's constant, unremitting efforts to set a metaphysical line of demarcation between spiritual understanding and mental suggestion can one comprehend what New Thought writers have called her authoritarianism or narrow exclusiveness. . . . Among the welter of "mind-curists" at that time, some of them disaffected students of hers who found her leadership too exacting and her doctrine too rigorous, the one common denominator seemed to be some sense of the "God within" or the "Christ within." Yet without the denial of corporeal personality and its own will to control, Mrs. Eddy felt there was mortal danger of identifying God with one's unregenerate human inclinations.[57]

This remains the danger today. But is not the Divine Mind in man, which Mrs. Eddy saw to be the healer, another name for the Christ in man?

In the view of this study, Mrs. Eddy was correct in believing that a broad, vague, and unprincipled approach would not suffice—that the way to healing is as disciplined and disciplining as an equation. Christian Science has a host of incredible cures, well attested, to its credit. More nearly than any other faith-healing doctrine, it points the adherent in the direction he must go to achieve a real and lasting cure of any type ill—the "mortal mind," himself in consciousness, must give way and give over the problem to the Divine Mind within himself, knowing that this Mind is perfect, its will is that he be perfect, and in it rests the healing power that is *real*. This Mind demands that concomitant with healing there be a lifting or enlargement of consciousness—that a man's will be brought more nearly in accord with the will of the Father, perfect in love and compassion. Mrs.

Eddy spurned the mesmerism of her day—and it was, indeed, wide of the mark. But hypnosis is involved with the practice of her doctrine, for prayer itself is pure hypnosis: pure reverie, a letting go and giving over to God-sense within—an act of faith.

There is a danger in practicing hypnotism, and this Mrs. Eddy recognized. She was aware, apparently, that the hypnotist as well as the subject runs a risk—as is recognized today. What might be called a degree of Messianic delusion may overcome the operator—according to a report given by Dr. Louis J. West and Dr. Gordon H. Deckert, "The hypnotist may become convinced that he is somehow superior to other people because of his ability to induce hypnosis and influence others. . . . The process of such corruption may turn a well-meaning hypnotist, devoted to his work, into a grandiose professional cripple." [58] Mrs. Eddy knew that her church must rest on "Principle, not personality. . . . 'There was never a religion or philosophy lost to the centuries except by sinking its divine Principle in personality.'" [59] Robert Peel says, "She saw the hypnotic control of one human mind over another as the very antithesis of Christian Science practice, in which the human mind must yield to the divine." [60]

One might say that Mrs. Eddy bypassed the customary procedure and, although she would abhor the word, led her followers to practice autohypnosis by *fixing* on the one idea of the Divine Mind within, *believing* that they would realize its presence. She led Christian Science practitioners to limit their involvement to seeing or affirming the Divine Mind in the patient, even as they held to its presence in themselves—thus, "both seeing," they accomplished and still accomplish many miracles of healing. But not all who attempt to apply this principle succeed. Too many people cannot "let go" the problem. In such cases, hypnosis could play a helpful role.

When both operator and patient operate upon the *principle* Mary Baker Eddy taught, the dangers attendant upon hypnosis for the most part vanish. Thus, this study both accepts her teaching with regard to healing and holds that hypnosis is a valid tool of medicine and psychiatry. When it is better understood, and applied in conjunction with the Christian Science principle, it may well become the most important single tool to be used in the healing ministry.

Jesus warned that the approach is broad, but the way is narrow.[61] Each man may have a secret "loop hole" through which he enters the state of sleep or trance—both conditions could be differing degrees of anesthesia which permits the self-healing power to operate.

Anesthesia itself may be the secret—if so, nontoxic electric anesthesia and sleep-treatment hold great promise. Sleep and trance could be differing degrees of hibernation—by inducing artificial hibernation, surgeons have been able to perform miraculous operations—and man may at one time have been a hibernator of sorts. Ancestral man may have been able to survive the rigors of his time because he could lapse into trance, or a sort of hibernating sleep.

But restoring health and prolonging life is not in itself enough—the physician must restore meaning to the life of the patient. Adler saw that "for psychology to restore meaning to the life of the modern person, an act of religious dimensions would be necessary." [62] Today, men are seeking and finding experience of "religious dimensions" through use of drugs. Recently, a headline in *Science News Letter* announced: "Vision Drug Increases Religious Feeling," but as the article describes the effect of LSD-25, a note of caution is added, "The drug can bring on a mental breakdown." [63] Gerald Heard describes its effects in an article, "Can This Drug Enlarge Man's Mind?"—he recognizes its potential, cautioning, however, that for the time being it should remain a research drug to be used with greatest care.[64] Dr. Sidney Cohen tells the story of LSD in *The Beyond Within*.[65] Aldous Huxley describes his reaction to another vision-producing drug, mescalin, in *The Doors of Perception*.[66]

These drugs, and others that cause similar reactions, may in some cases prove of great value by bringing a patient quickly to the land-of-being behind the façade of consciousness and to a threshold it takes the analyst months or sometimes years to reach, but just as hypnosis and narcotics may be misused and prove a danger, so with the drugs that heighten sensibility and transport one into the world behind his eyes, reawakening in him religious conviction, albeit nameless.

The task of the psychologist remains: he must give his patient the courage and faith to face the truth of himself, his inner world. Such faith, precisely, is needed to effect trance which takes the subject out of this world and into a realm of his own. The difficulty of inducing trance might be greatly lessened if initial "baptism" into it were undertaken in childhood. Jesus gave this suggestion: "Let the children come to me, do not stop them: the Realm of God belongs to such as these. I tell you truly, whoever will not submit to the Realm of God like a child, will never get into it at all." [67] But he who would be party to such baptism must remember this admonition also: "And whoso shall receive one such little child in my name receiveth me. But whoso shall offend one of these little ones which believe in me, it were better for him that a millstone were hanged about his neck and that he were drowned in the depth of the sea." [68]

JESUS' HEALING MINISTRY

These words indicate that a child comes easily unto the Authority in his *unconscious*, is easily hypnotized, but they indicate also that such baptism presents its dangers. Little is known as to the limits of a person's suggestibility, and in hypnosis one automatically regresses. The child could be protected from abuse of his susceptibility by suggestion that he cannot go into trance beyond pure reverie unless he actually desires it and makes some overt act to signal this; but if all precautions are taken, such baptism should not be tried until there is greater understanding of the degree of susceptibility to subtle suggestion necessary to normal functioning in life, and until there is greater understanding of the part involuntary trance plays in providing man with essential rest.

There are many fields in which research in hypnotic response should be undertaken. For example, if society's best hope rests with finding an effective contraceptive that will be used to hold population in balance, doctors should investigate the possibility that a suggestion given during trance, to the effect that a woman cannot conceive until she consciously wishes to, might be contraceptive—and the opposite suggestion might in many cases relieve sterility.

In the words of Dr. Alexander, ". . . the science of hypnology can be extended to cover the whole explanation of human behavior. Moreover, it can perhaps become the instrument by which the riddle of our personal arrival and departure as physical creatures might be explained . . . . this new science in the West is bringing with it new and wider horizons and an almost infinite range of possibilities." [69]

When it is acknowledged that Jesus demonstrated hypnotic therapy to the fullest of its capacities, hypnosis will have the sanction it requires, and scientists will begin to explore this field more broadly and with less misgiving. Many men have, of course, stated or implied that Jesus healed through the hypnotic means, but few recognize that the social miracles also reflect exercise of this power. In the following chapter these demonstrations will be examined. (See Appendix III, p. 407.)

Chapter 12

THE SOCIAL MIRACLES

I

Feeding the multitudes, preventing the stoning of the adulteress, changing water to wine at the wedding at Cana, stopping the troops in the Garden of Gethsemane, are seen as social miracles which will be observed in this chapter. In these miracles, one sees generosity, mercy, conviviality, and the dropping in its tracks of coercive action. These demonstrations suggest that every man will exhibit these qualities and let drop in its tracks his will to abuse another if the suggestion is presented with sufficient force to penetrate his deepest reaches.

Jesus would not demonstrate the destructive potential inherent in the capacity of a large group of people to respond unwittingly to subtle suggestion, but the drama involving "legion" points to the destructive aspects of mass susceptibility—and gives also a clue as to the nature of what must be called a mental disease: Messianic pretension and delusion. All kinds of people suffer it —why? Because the Christ *is* in everyone and when a sense of this power overcomes consciousness, the temptation to be Messianic is upon one. The drama of legion unveils this mystery. Therefore, it must be re-examined.

But the first of the demonstrations to be considered is feeding the multitudes. Consider that among the thousands of people who came to hear Jesus teach in remote places, more than one person must have had the forethought to provide his own food with some to spare—man's natural instinct is to provide for himself and his own. Gospel reports do not say that the few loaves and fishes were all the food there was among the crowds; they say the disciples had made no provision to feed such masses and that the few loaves and fishes were all that was proffered. The reports do not say that Jesus commanded these to "grow" and that before the eyes of the people the bread and fish grew as He broke it—nor do they say that as the food was taken from the baskets other pieces appeared.

THE SOCIAL MIRACLES

The actual reports are very simple:

Jesus had the disciples arrange the people in groups. Each one was thus "fixed" in the expectation of eating. Then He took what He had, gave thanks, broke the food into pieces and placed it before the crowd. The suggestion of sharing and eating, implemented by His own decisive action, must have spread with the lightning of telepathy throughout the crowd, for the simple story then ends, "So the people ate and were satisfied"—and there were baskets of fragments left over.[1]

This event appears to be a spontaneous mass reaction to suggestion. Jesus' audience was, no doubt, entranced. Certainly, they were deeply involved in the play so that each one must join in or withdraw—must share what he had or go hungry, must use his hidden reserves. This analysis is not an apologetic rationalization. The reports simply do not state so much that is assumed. And later, it is stated:

> ... they considered not the miracle of the loaves: for their heart was hardened.[2]

Moffatt translates, "they had not understood the lesson of the loaves: their minds were dull." This statement is usually interpreted to mean that within hours of its occurrence the disciples had forgotten or dismissed the stupendous miracle, if bread and fish appeared from nowhere. The statement could mean that whatever occurred, it appeared to the disciples so unmiraculous—that is, expectation naturally fulfilling itself with the means at hand as people brought forth their food and shared it—that at the time they did not regard this drama as a miracle, only in retrospect did it become miraculous. Or, as will be discussed in a later chapter, their "forgetting" the miracle so soon more likely means that whatever occurred the disciples did not see the action and were conscious only of the alpha-omega facts of the case—for these were all they reported: thousands to be fed and only a few loaves and fishes to feed them, then suddenly the meal was over and baskets of scraps remained.

If Jesus were teaching a lesson, it appears to be: increase comes by using what is at hand to provide the capital, no matter how small it appears to be in the face of the need, and by being willing to share it. Hero of the piece was the one who had planned for the *day*—he teaches that it is the responsibility of each man to provide for himself with some to spare so that he may know the joy of dining in peace and sharing his bread with a stranger. And if this study reads the lesson correctly, it enfolded also a deeper message: the phantom of fear that human population will increase beyond the capacity of this planet to support it bountifully may be consigned to Legion's ranks. The unforgettable drama appears to say, poetically, that if the world were reduced to a desert with a multitude upon it, life could still provide more than enough to fulfill the needs of body and soul through releasing the hidden power in the minds of men.

Feeding the multitudes appears to be a demonstration of mass response to suggestion—and the disciples' part in it is obscured because, apparently, they suffered a dulling of their ability to perceive.

Saving the adulteress from the scribes and Pharisees is another demonstration of decisive word and action moving men. By word and deed, surprising in its quiet confidence, penetrating to the point of shock in its crystal-clear conveyance of the truth of the situation, Jesus demonstrated that all men know they stand in need of mercy and will react by showing mercy if this suggestion penetrates consciousness before violence takes over. Looking at His drawing in the sand, Jesus said:

> ... He that is without sin among you, let him first cast a stone at her.... And they which heard it, being convicted by their own conscience, went out one by one, beginning at the eldest, even unto the last....[3]

In this demonstration, one sees verbal shock giving pause, providing an instant's "anesthesia" that breaks loose the grip of violent impulse and restores the humanity of man. The lesson? Truth blots out the desire to behave viciously in the name of the innocent punishing the guilty, of good punishing evil, for as truth penetrates it disperses error in every direction, just as the group dispersed, leaving the adulteress in the presence of Jesus who, finding none to condemn her, did not condemn her Himself—and thus He did not hold Himself to be alone of men, without sin. As symbol of the Authority-Ego, He neither condemns nor condones the adulteress: "Neither do I condemn thee; go, and sin no more."

It is reported that with a word He stopped the armed band who sought to capture Him in the Garden of Gethsemane—but only in the Gospel of John is it reported that "As soon then as he had said unto them, I am he, they went backward, and fell to the ground."[4] Versions of the drama in the Garden vary widely—only in the Gospel of Luke is mention made of the agony Jesus suffered, "and his sweat was as it were great drops of blood falling down to the ground."[5] Can a man sweat blood? The reports say, *like* blood—not that He sweated blood. Even so, Thérèse Neumann and Paul Diebel produced tears of blood flowing from the eyes.[6] The point, however, is that assumption handed down from generation to generation creates an expectancy that causes men to read into Biblical passages words that are not there. Expectancy creates the same sort of *hallucination* that makes one oblivious to typographical errors—the mind's eye moves on to meet its anticipation of the content. Tyrrell points out that common expectancy frequently produces hallucination either in individual or group, that expectation acts as suggestion which produces its own response. Whenever one comes upon widely varying reports of the miracles Jesus performed, hallucination must be suspected because of its subjective nature.

At the wedding in Cana, Jesus showed that a man's expectation will act as suggestion strong enough to produce in him an hallucination that is real to the one experiencing it. It is widely assumed that Jesus changed gallons of water to wine, that all the guests partook of it and pronounced it the best wine—but the report says that only one cup of water was changed, that only one man, the ruler of the feast, pronounced it wine.[7] In truth, the governor was drinking wine—his cup held the produce of "I," the real vine, different from any other. One man quickly put in trance, responding to his own expectancy, produced this miracle. But a group hallucination could have occurred. All the guests were expecting wine, and hallucination spreads like water to engulf, or like the warmth of laughter. When such a feat is accomplished, one must conclude that the group "follows the leader" into trance as he induces auto-hypnosis, emerging rapidly to address his then highly susceptible-to-suggestion audience.

When Jesus entranced His audiences, He gave them the suggestion of sharing their hidden reserves of food, their hidden reserves of mercy, their hidden reserves of conviviality—and He gave them the suggestions recorded in the Sermon on the Mount. The twentieth century, however, confronts a stark horror that is no less a miracle for its hue: Adolf Hitler entranced his audiences and loosed their "legion" along with his own upon a world that realizes it was somehow party to his acts.

II

The drama of Legion shows the destructive potential arising from mass susceptibility which makes it possible to transfer manic Messianic impulses from one man to a large group. It must be considered again in terms of Legion's outworking in the individual and in society.

The nature of the madman's delusion is revealed when he calls Jesus, "Son of God," and says, "What have I to do with thee," for Jesus had said, "Come out of the man, thou unclean spirit."[8] This is to say, the man expressed the Judaic Messianic term, calling Jesus Son of God and worshiping Him, but Jesus responds by calling this the expression of an "unclean spirit"—which names itself Legion and then "all the devils" speaking in this name are given leave to enter the swine. All the "devils" of Messianic delusion are not individually named, but in the drama Jesus showed that he who suffers it in any of its forms is relieved only as his Legion is cast upon the flesh; and in so doing He showed also that Legion may be cast upon the masses. When this happens, society is as innocent of what is happening as was the herd of swine.

Messianic delusion leads to madness, to self-destruction—for Legion, having entered the swine, must share their fate. The phobia travels many routes to achieve this end which it inevitably seeks. The devils of Legion besought Jesus not to "send them away out of the country"—this suggests that one man's Legion does not itself seek primarily to destroy anything but itself in its own realm through expressing its violence in the flesh. Jesus showed that the Authority-Ego allows it to expend itself upon this level—He does not send it far afield, does not loosen its violence upon mankind at large. For this to happen, other inward and outward factors must take over.

He whose Legion is loosed upon unsuspecting society may be seen today as the "social criminal" who makes society both victim and culprit. His force may be limited by one violent act which causes society to deal with him; or his influence may be as wide as Hitler's, a man with so much blood upon his hands that history will be able to cleanse them only by recognizing his madness for what it was: Messianic pretension. Herbert J. Muller says:

> Hitler may have been sincere when he proclaimed himself an emancipator: "Providence has ordained that I should be the greatest liberator of humanity. I am freeing man from the demands of a freedom and personal independence that only a few can sustain." [9]

One of the devils of Legion is the impulse to save humanity from itself. Hitler is the last "Messiah" to speak: the last man to think that providence ordains he shall liberate humanity from its social ills by ruling over all the kingdoms of the world.

It is a miracle that a man gone coldly mad could lead the world into such horror and insensate cruelty as was evidenced in World War II. Hitler did not work this dark miracle alone. Since every person harbors his quota of evil's destructive potential that lends itself readily to inhuman madness, as men entranced responded to Hitler's manic exhortations they were not responding in a manner completely foreign to their natures— nor were the safely distant do-nothing onlookers. A man cannot express the whole force of Messianic delusion, of Legion, by himself: to be a "Messiah" he must have worshipers, followers. Jesus saw that worshiping or following blindly after any man as "leader" is insanity—"nor must you be called 'leaders,' for One is your leader. . . ." In proclaiming the brotherhood of man, He proclaimed that man is capable of sustaining the demands of freedom and personal independence.

In the orthodox concept, Messiah is above or beyond the law—is law unto himself. This is the Messianic property the criminal exhibits whether the crime be as large as Hitler's or a single act of lawlessness committed in the name of killing "social sin," which has become incarnate in the person who appears to the criminal to be the symbol of it, so that he indebts mankind by ridding the world of evil.

Today, society is blamed for creating the criminal as well as the neurotic who all too frequently becomes a criminal. Both are seen as symptoms of a sick society and many crimes can be laid at the door of the mounting and maddening pressures of society, or traced to its pockets of squalor, mental and physical. But there are other crimes quite inexplicable in these terms—for example, an apparently happy young mother murders her children, remembers her act, but does not know what happened to prompt her to it; and society has no choice but to imprison her in asylum or penal institution although she appears to have recovered from her moment of madness. What happened to induce her insanity? In the view of this study, an all but indescribable devil in the ranks of Legion, one which never shows its face but for an instant, has wreaked its violence—for entangled in Messianic delusion is the urge, disguised as the necessity, to slay the innocent. A sudden urge to slay the helpless, the trusting, has come upon many people, and left so swiftly that he who has not lifted his hand in his mad-sane moment is left weak and terrified of what he came so close to doing.

In the Bible, one comes upon the urge to slay the trusting innocent in the story of Abraham and Isaac. The legend says that the Lord "tempts" Abraham to make this "sacrifice"—but it also says that the angel of the Lord stays his hand, and the moment of temptation is over.

From earliest times, man's compulsion to make sacrifice of self or another has expressed itself. Thus, all theologies involve the concept of sacrificial offering which culminates in Pauline doctrine in the concept that God sacrificed His beloved Son to expiate the sins of man. This is St. Paul's view—Jesus quoted Scripture to reveal God's nature: "I care for mercy, not for sacrifice." [10] But His was a dual mission: He must make Himself a symbol of the Christ in man, and He must play Messiah's role to show in the end the falseness of Judaic Messianic expectation with the seed of Abraham's delusion buried in it—revealed in his temptation to sacrifice Isaac—that came to flower in St. Paul's conclusion that Jesus had been sent like the ram to take over the role of sin-offering. Barrett likens Kierkegaard's sacrifice of marriage to Abraham's urge to sacrifice his son —he says:

> . . . most of us are not called upon to make such drastic sacrifices. But even the most ordinary people are required from time to time to make decisions crucial for their own lives, and in such crises they know something of the "suspension of the ethical" . . . For the choice in such human situations is almost never between a good and an evil . . . rather it is between rival goods, where one is bound to do some evil either way, and where the ultimate outcome and even— or most of all—our own motives are unclear to us.[11]

When some sort of inner crisis causes "suspension of the ethical," a person is insensate and compelled to act unless something brings him to his senses in time. The play appears to be determined on the unconscious level: he acts, or an unconscious prohibition has restrained him in the moment of waking trance when he might have responded to the suggestion of the indescribable devil of Legion. What causes the trance—what gives the suggestion—what determines the type of response? This study suggests that telepathy and clairvoyance have been brought into play.

Just as one may suddenly perceive what is on a page of another's consciousness, so his power of clairvoyance may suddenly show him what is on a page of another's past—this information, as it montages, elicits one whole impulse. Violent, fearful words prompt violent, fearful acts—the same would be true of telepathized images which act to organize or disorganize one's force. Sydney Harris quotes C. S. Lewis: ". . . 'suspicion often creates what it suspects.' . . . It is no accident that playmates gang up on the boy who thinks everyone is always ganging up on him."[12] If conscious mental patterns are projected and invite their expectation's fulfillment, is it not possible that unconscious mental patterns are projected and these also invite a response that fulfills unconscious expectation? McCurdy writes:

> D. H. Lawrence makes the strong statement that if a man is murdered it must be because he has issued an invitation to the murderer by indicating his willingness to be murdered. The power of the look (or, more correctly, the intention behind the look) has to be reinforced by the consent of the one looked at before the little push it gives results in actual motion.[13]

And Jung quotes Goethe to point out that "We all have certain electric and magnetic powers within us and ourselves exercise an attractive and repelling force, according as we come into touch with something like or unlike." [14] The strange phenomenon of "automatic writing" and translation of the fragmented, cryptic, and symbolic messages by a hypnotized subject indicates, in the words of Dr. Leslie LeCron, that the "language of one subconscious mind is understood by the other subconsciousness." [15] Perhaps certain people can translate a cryptic, symbolic image which is telepathized; such people may possess within themselves a likeness to it or an opposite to it, or both, and thus the telepathized image becomes repelling, attractive, or neutral. And just as a person fearful of an animal is very apt to attract its attention and a violent response from it, so perhaps a person who accords a fearful response to a telepathized image invites thereby the act of violence—not even a glance need pass to convey the force of fear: it is "felt."

Guilt generates fear—both are difficult to conceal. As Kluckhohn discusses crime, he refers to what Freud called "criminality from a sense of guilt," and quotes him: "Paradoxical as it may sound, I must maintain that the sense of guilt was present prior to the transgression, that it did not arise from this, but contrariwise—the transgression from the sense of guilt." [16] Does the guilt arise from unpunished or unrepented and forgotten error? If so, it poses the concept that unless life, or Authority-Ego, or parent, punishes *and* forgives childish transgression, thus relieving the child of his guilt, the guilt itself will induce still greater transgression—this would apply to individual and to race, to one's own past however far back it stretches and to the past of Homo sapiens, committed to nature's law: as ye sow, so shall ye reap.

Kluckhohn says of conscious actions, "one cannot validly diagnose personality on the basis of isolated actions, taken out of their dynamic context and detached from the meanings they have and the ends they serve for the individual actor." [17] Insensate acts may serve unconscious ends—they may work to effect a mutual shattering of mental patterns in which each party is stymied, the "survivor" sacrificing his victim and then himself to the demands of society that he be punished. Or perhaps the telepathized image is translated into the picture of a wounded soul, and some ancient animal instinct leaps to slay it—the guilty and the fearful are almost always wounded personalities. Or perhaps the image is translated into ignorance, appalling and insistent—ignorance is not innocence, the untried cannot be called true. A person cannot be "free" of any sin until his knowing empathy both stays his hand and turns him out of sin's path.

Since every man is both fearful and unafraid, both guilty and innocent, he possesses both a likeness and an opposite to most of the mental patterns telepathized. Therefore, for the most part there is no reaction to the telepathized images that constantly impinge upon him, nor to those he constantly projects. Taken as a whole, there are but a few criminal acts precipitated by unconscious forces finishing themselves in violent action inexplicable save as momentary madness.

In the most profound sense of the word, all criminals are insane, but the great majority are conscious of what they are doing, albeit they are mental cripples. They have made their decisions as to how they will react to conditions—decisions society cannot tolerate or condone. Society must protect itself against them. As it attempts to deal with them, however, the most persistent devil in Legion's ranks calls the play. This is the lie that scars man's psychic hide and at its worst drives him to kill in the name of the innocent punishing the guilty for a capital crime. This breaks the commandment upon which the hope of social order rests. So long as society allows itself to be led into the criminal's trap, becoming criminal itself in dealing with the transgressor, rather than subjecting him to the medical or psychiatric treatment and measure of confinement that the type and degree of his deviation prescribes, making every attempt to re-educate the young or first offenders to become responsible law-abiding citizens, crime cannot be dealt with on a plane above that of the delinquent. Until society rises above the criminal's level in its handling of him, it will continue to invite the elaboration of crime—the neurotic, callous, and depraved will try their guilt-ridden wits against its forces in an unconscious effort to reap what they have sown or to see the face on the other side of the coin of the crime committed.

There is another lie in Legion's host—a lie that life cannot permit, although today society tends to accept it. This devil is not easily described. There is a mental pattern projected consciously or unconsciously, that presents oneself as *innocent victim* even as it invariably invites persecution by the entreaty, "torment me not," and then turns every response to torment of itself. Perhaps it is this particular devil Arthur Miller attempts to unveil in his controversial play, *After the Fall*, in which he deals with a character called Maggie. The play has to do with the unwillingness or inability of a person to discover in himself the seeds of his own destruction:

> Maggie is in this play because she most perfectly exemplifies the self-destructiveness which finally comes when one views oneself as pure victim. And she most perfectly exemplifies this view because she

comes so close to being a pure victim—of parents, of a Puritanical sexual code and of her exploitation as an entertainer.[18]

Miller explains that what "Quentin in this play tries desperately to do is to open Maggie's eyes to her own complicity with her destruction; it is an act of love, for it requires that he open himself to his own complicity if his imprecations are to carry any weight; he must, in short, give up his own claim to innocence in order to win her back from self-destruction." [19]

Consider now that Jesus made no claim to innocence—although He asks, "Which of you can convict me of sin?" [20] this is not to say, "I am without sin," for on another occasion He summarily dismisses even the concept that He is to be seen as "good": "Why callest thou me good? there is none good but one, that is, God. . . ." [21] He makes it clear that He is not innocent victim of Jewish persecution: He, not the Jewish priests, called every turn in the play. Of His own accord, He gave His life to break the Messiah mold, to destroy the idea of the innocent sacrificial lamb, pure victim, because the whole idea of scapegoat carrying off sin, or of innocent victim, or of pure innocence itself is madness—and this, at least in part, is what Miller sees and says:

> It is, always and forever, the same struggle: to perceive somehow our own complicity with evil is a horror not to be borne. Much more reassuring to see the world in terms of totally innocent victims and totally evil instigators of the monstrous violence we see all about us. At all costs, never disturb our innocence. But what is the most innocent place in any country? Is it not the insane asylum? There people drift through life truly innocent, unable to see into themselves at all. The perfection of innocence, indeed, is madness.[22]

Miller believes his play "to be a dramatic statement of a hidden process which underlies the destructiveness hanging over this age." [23]

In dealing with the adulteress, Jesus dramatizes the precept that no person is innocent of the sin that brings him into his predicament, nor is any person innocent enough to stone to death another. But it was in the drama of Legion that He showed the inward and outward working of Messianic delusion to be the hidden process which underlies the self-destruction of the "innocent," or "pure victims," as were the swine—showed it to constitute the destructiveness hanging over any age, any person. Why is it so destructive?

The Messianic concept depends upon the image of pure and perfect innocence. This, projected onto man in human consciousness and flesh, is the insufferable lie that comes to rest in madness. In taking upon one's own shoulders the sin of the world, in order to save it, one must take upon himself a greater load of evil than can be borne in sanity. This is to say, insanity is the ultimate in evil one must know if his involvement in evil is to be *complete* so that *further involvement* in it becomes impossible and he, paradoxically, is beyond it, capable only of exercising its opposite, absolute good, able to do no wrong. Only one who is insane can hold this view of himself, or see another in this light.

From the man in the grip of Legion, Jesus called forth the orthodox concept of Messiah, "Son of God," to which He replied, "unclean spirit." Messianic delusion is madness, entreating torment by adjuring it, as does the maniac. To acquiesce to the plea of its insanity is to acquiesce to its self-destruction—seen in Legion's destruction in the "suicide" of the herd. Because there are many devils in Legion's ranks, there are many devils or degrees or types of madness that tend toward the complete expression of Messianic delusion as seen in this strange drama that culminates in the destruction of "innocence," and of the masses, the swine.

All insane or criminal acts against another, or the masses, or against oneself may well stem from some "mutant" of the "unclean spirit" of Messianic delusion or Messianic pretension—a "mutant" not readily recognized to be one of the devils in Legion's ranks, but eventually traceable to this host. Within the scope of one book, not all the paths can be traced, not all the deceits in Legion's host can be named. Some are small of stature and in the Sermon on the Mount Jesus described them for what they are. The effect of these words upon succeeding generations of men is indeed a social miracle. At the time, people did not marvel so much at what Jesus said as at the *authority* with which He spoke:

> . . . the people were astonished at his doctrine; For he taught them as one having authority, and not as the scribes.[24]

Today, "scribes" have rewritten these words. In *The New English Bible*, read the translation thirteen scholars offer to men whose souls are starved, and scared, and scarred—it is a timid bit:

> . . . he taught with a note of authority.

The translators write in the tenor of their age—a "note" of faith in anything, a "note" of authority in anything, is all that is left. But because of this, the twentieth century is a time pregnant with the possibility of grasping truth, for now man must seek the Authority within himself.

III

In the social miracles, Jesus showed that Legion's fearful images are not the only ones man telepathizes and casts upon the masses. He showed that the invitation to share, to show mercy, to savor life's wine is also extended by the Authority-Ego in man. These dramas proclaim the abundance in life and also the abundance of understanding in man. From whence does this understanding arise? Empathy provides it.

Jesus implied that His joy was complete.[25] Only one who is perfectly balanced between empathy born of life's problems, pain, and evil *and* empathy born of life's promises, satisfaction, and good could project the compassion and the undiluted candor of the truth Jesus spoke, could project joy in life complete so that the prospect of everlasting life is not appalling to him. Seeing Jesus as symbol of the Authority-Ego, it follows that this factor in each man is totally empathetic, has experienced all it is possible for Homo sapiens to experience, and is therefore ready to move into new species wherein life will be more abundant as consciousness is completed. Because this factor has experienced the sin and the suffering sin involves, it expresses a will wherein choice becomes "do unto others as you would have others do unto you"—thus, forgiving is its proclivity and it says to the sinner, "Neither do I condemn you; go and sin no more." This is to say, the Authority-Ego is life's one whole act accomplished in each man: One's resonator sounding its note in his depths.

Kluckhohn says about criminals what is true of sinners, true to some degree of every man: "Society may wish to change them or they may wish to change society, but they rarely wish to change themselves." [26] Jesus saw that man may change only himself—that each man "hath one" which judges him and deals with his own evil and will in time save his own world. Society's salvation must follow.

Society's Legion must be bound as the Lilliputians bound Gulliver.[27] If a man can secure one cord upon it, he will find satisfaction: he may secure a cord upon it as he secures a cord upon his own.

The man who thinks he can change society is expressing to some degree Messianic delusion. In the drama of Legion, Jesus showed that the attempt to rid man of evil in one grand play that changes society's dealing with him results in destruction of the masses. His whole ministry points to the realization that society cannot be delivered of its ancient evils within the life-span of any one man—not even upon the advent of a Messiah—for He tells of the struggles men will have to endure in society before the final struggle is met,[28] and He indicates that this struggle will be met upon the psychic plane.

Jesus gave His life to break the Messianic-mold, to seal off the false hope of the many who look to the advent of a Savior to bring judgment and salvation. His every word and move indicate that Messiah is not and cannot be a "Social Miracle": He tells Pilate that Son of man is not a governing authority in the social realm, He tells His followers not to look for Him to "appear" on the social scene—many will come in His name, but they must not believe it when people say, "here is the Christ, or there . . . he is in the desert . . ." [29]

Jesus had told from whence the Son of man will come—the clouds of *heaven* will bear this glory and thus the Christ can enter one's world only through his *unconscious* domain.

The *unconscious* is the seat of the psychic power. In the view of this study, Jesus exercised His psychic power to show the real limits of this mysterious force in man, so that any strange phenomenon that cannot be reconciled within the framework drawn by His deeds must be regarded with suspicion.

In his book, *Psychical Research Today*, Dr. D. J. West sifts to an irreducible minimum those evidences of extrasensory perception and psychokinetic force that must be accepted as valid—he concludes:

> Paranormal phenomena are of undeniable importance. . . . If only this study were to receive a fraction of the support it deserves, we might before long come to a new understanding of man and his place in nature that would have a more direct bearing on human welfare than all the discoveries of atomic physics. Far-seeing thinkers, from Socrates to Henry Sidgwick and Albert Einstein, have been convinced of the importance of investigation of psychic phenomena. . . .[30]

Dr. West appears at times to be painfully overcautious, but parapsychology is a field wherein caution to the extreme is better than careless credulity. On the other hand, the play between caution and credulity of researchers tends to push into the background the most important aspect of paranormal perception: its *creative* force.

Jesus appears to have seen that the psychic power is deeply involved in awareness, perception, the process of learning, and artistic expression, so that to show its inward play upon man, and Himself to express the true limit of its power within and without oneself, was His mission. As teacher, He was artist and He used His psychic power to teach and demonstrate His lessons. In the lesson of the loaves, more than an entranced audience's response to suggestion is involved as will be observed in the following chapter dealing with Jesus' demonstrations of psychic power and extrasensory perception.

Chapter 13

JESUS' DEMONSTRATIONS OF EXTRASENSORY PERCEPTION AND THE PSYCHIC POWER

I

No description of events in the brain that is expressed in purely physical terms explains the miracle of awareness—of what it is that bridges the gap between physical sensation and the perceptions in a man's consciousness. It appears unlikely that mind can ever be explained in terms of matter, or energy, or any exclusively physical concept.

Man's ordinary ability to perceive is miraculous. At times, he demonstrates also extraordinary perception—of the type referred to in a textbook, *Foundations of Modern Physical Science*, by Gerald Holton and Duane H. D. Roller:

> ... [the] process of inducing a hypothesis or a postulate from a necessarily limited number of facts can be likened to the unpredictable experience one may have during a game of chess, when one suddenly "sees through" the whole arrangement on the board and in a single flash discerns the chain of moves that will bring about a successful ending . . . . the mechanism of such sudden perception is not well understood. . . .[1]

Is extrasensory perception involved? As the chess player sees through the problem in a single flash, he appears to be exhibiting a sort of clairvoyance which merges with post- and precognition to become sudden perception of what he must do. Because the "seeing through" is unpredictable and instantaneous, ESP suggests itself as the factor involved. If so, it must be involved in every perception and when functioning normally in man does not produce a greater miracle than that of giving a commanding insight into the problem at hand, an insight which enfolds the past and shows the future possibilities inherent in the situation.

Again and again, Jesus sees through "the whole arrangement on the board," and speaks with true perception, or moves to bring the drama to the end He has determined. His ability to see through a problem in a single flash and then address that problem helps one to see its nature, to see what goes on behind the façade men present to the world.

At times, men demonstrate a still more extraordinary type perception—an inexplicable awareness called telepathy, pre- or postcognition, or clairvoyance. These demonstrations are abnormal, but in the view of this study they are no more supranatural than an abnormal degree of temperature in man is supranatural, for many people have demonstrated ESP and almost everyone has experienced it at one time or another in one way or another to greater or lesser degree. Therefore, it is not necessary to consider individually Jesus' many demonstrations of purely extrasensory perception—suffice it to say that it was necessary for Him to show that such perception is a valid expression of the psychic power. In the view of this study, such perception arises when the psychic power is operating abnormally because sensory input is inhibited, as is often the case when one lapses into trance; ordinarily, sensory and extrasensory perception must constitute nearly equal and opposite forces operating to translate stimuli into normal awareness and sometimes into penetrating insight.

Because extrasensory forces are "spiritual" as opposed to "material," in one sense to pray is to exercise one's psychic power; in another sense, to pray is to exercise and consciously direct one's mental powers of concentration either in an affirmative or in a negative manner. When men pray, they attempt to bring these forces to bear upon themselves or others. Jesus taught men how to pray, what to pray for: Our Father . . . *thy will be done*. However heavily larded one's mind may be with his concept of what should happen as regards anything or anyone, or of what is moral and desirable, to attempt through exercise of mental and spiritual forces to direct the course of events or the course of another person is to pray: *my* will be done. Thus, such efforts veil a grasp for power. To pray in the spirit of love for another person is to place him in the hands of the Father, God, love itself. Certainly, prayer or the exercise of mental and spiritual forces, whatever this be called, appears to be effective to some degree upon oneself and others.

Parapsychologists deal with another mystery involving unseen forces producing effects: psychokinesis, PK, refers to events in which objects are set in motion, moved or affected by unseen forces. Of all psychic phenomena, PK is least understood and is most likely to lead to self-deception and trickery if one embraces the concept too hastily. PK brings to mind poltergeists, mischievous spirits which produce physical effects. Are they to be taken seriously? Borrowing words from Dr. West: "Until investigators can themselves witness the extraordinary antics of the poltergeist, and can see and photograph the objects while they are actually jumping about of their own accord, the only reasonable attitude is one of severe scepticism." [2] To get to the bottom of such a mystery, one must consider the whole concept of a psychokinetic force as such.

An unseen force is responsible for no-motion, no reaction, demonstrated during hypnosis when the subject is commanded to lock and unlock his limbs. An unseen force moves his flesh to manifest a blister, or to obliterate the symptom; and the hypnotized subject may be made blind to any person or object in the room with him, although he sees all other people and objects present, when the operator "blinds" him to a certain thing or person or tells the subject that they are alone. Such phenomena indicate that man possesses an unseen force which moves his own object or material: it acts within and upon his body and flesh, and upon his *perception*.

The whole range of psychosomatic diseases arises from "unseen forces" —and the phenomenon of stigmatization is a physical effect produced by the unseen force of thought. As West says, "it appears as if thought has an almost direct local action on a particular area of the body that cannot be explained in terms of the known nervous and secretory mechanisms. It may not be too fanciful to picture a link between these peculiar mind-body effects and the phenomenon of psychokinesis." [3] And it may not be too fanciful to link most PK phenomena—poltergeists in particular—to what might be termed *hallucinatory blindness* or not-seeing something that takes place although one is seeing his surroundings, and to a companion hallucinatory-deafness. Hallucinatory blindness and deafness could prevent comprehension of action that takes place before an individual and group in trance. The operator may be as innocent of what he is doing as is the audience. An unsuspecting and susceptible person (or group) may be put in trance with ease. In trance, he may be commanded to see or not see, to hear or not hear, whatever the operator suggests.

Jesus pointed out that man is subject to blindness and deafness as he yet sees and hears, and that he is also given to seeing and hearing mysteriously:

> . . . they seeing see not; and hearing they hear not, neither do they understand. And in them is fulfilled the prophecy of E-sa′jas, which saith, By hearing ye shall hear, and shall not understand; and seeing ye shall see, and shall not perceive: For this people's heart is waxed gross . . .[4]

More than stubborn or stupid refusal to comprehend is indicated in this passage, which brings to mind another: "they considered not the miracle of the loaves; for their heart was hardened." [5] The archaic meaning of the word *considered* is: to look at attentively; to examine. A heart waxed gross, a heart hardened, suggests both an attitude *and* a change in the physical system that gives rise to lack of comprehension, which is to say, hallucinatory-blindness and deafness may have been involved in the drama of feeding the multitudes. The disciples may have been blind and deaf to what actually happened, and Jesus may have used this opportunity to teach the deeper lesson: *a fantastic demonstration involving objective matter to a degree entirely beyond the creditable is not what it appears to be—through hypnosis, hallucination or hallucinatory-blindness has been induced.*

Another incident points to Jesus' ability to induce hallucinatory-blindness in the group observing Him: it is reported that as the people were about to stone Him, . . . "Jesus hid himself, and went out of the temple going through the midst of them and so passed by." [6] Jesus said that the spirit quickeneth; flesh is as nothing—thus, "What gives life is the Spirit: flesh is of no avail at all." [7] Perhaps "hiding" oneself is possible as hallucinatory-blindness is produced in the audience, suddenly entranced, when the operator projects a psychic force or suggestion that slows down either the sensory or the extrasensory forces in the spectator, upsetting the equal and opposite operation of these forces in the individual, so that he "waxes gross" and his flesh, his eyes and ears, are of "no avail at all."

Jesus spoke of unseen force moving objects: He said that faith as a grain of mustard seed could remove a mountain, could uproot and transplant a tree in the sea.[8] *But He made no such demonstration* and therefore a close examination of His remark is in order. In Jesus' words, a mustard seed is as the realm of God—this seed, less than any on earth, grows larger than any plant.[9] Therefore, faith "as a mustard seed" indicates *faith larger than is possible to Homo sapiens' consciousness* which cannot enfold the whole realm of God. Jesus says also that to work such miracles, one "shall not doubt in his heart . . ." [10] One might say, in truth, all things are possible, but the attempt to exercise faith that is potentially as great as the mustard seed Jesus described often flowers into fantastic hallucination, and that what actually may be achieved through hypnosis is limited because there is a limit to the faith man can express, doubting not in his heart that what he asks will be done.

Jesus said, however, that men would do greater works than He performed. Much has been demonstrated which has no explanation except that concentration on the affirmative side, or on the negative side, is operative to some slight degree. Louisa Rhine discusses experiments with six-sided cubes in motion whereby measurable effects have been obtained showing that the will of the human subject can act upon the dice.[11]

Mrs. Rhine discusses also many puzzling physical effects which are interpreted as messages from a dying person—such effects as the spontaneous stopping of a clock to mark the time, inexplicable breaking of china or crystal, falling pictures, and sounds announcing the event.[12] Could the unseen energy involved be sonic waves? A violin note can break a crystal goblet, reverberation can cause the collapse of a material object. At an unexpected shock, a person may scream so suddenly that he himself does not hear it, is unaware that he has uttered a sound. Is what must be called a "silent scream"—one that hits a note beyond man's hearing range—possible and this sound effect breaks the vase? Could such a para-piercing note break from one's lips coincident with reception of a telepathic message which, if passed along unconsciously, begets a "mental-heterodyning" that converts to an hallucinatory sound effect following after the flight of telepathic communication, just as the sound effect follows after the jet plane has passed unseen? Perhaps the person who "hears" the message telepathically transmitted does not hear the reception he accords the information—and he is blind and deaf to himself in action to produce an event to mark the moment, or to his "silently screaming" the unearthly note, and to his telepathizing to the group present the message that falls like a thud and somehow echoes like a footstep on the stair heard by all who are hearing with their inner ears the telepathized message.

All one can say is that unless experimenters are deluding themselves psychokinetic force may possibly affect objective matter to a small degree; and a psychokinetic force is operative upon subjective matter to a large and undetermined degree. As to puzzling effects, man has scarcely begun to realize the possibilities vested in the *word,* in sound, the "stuff" the word is made of, which in the view of this study gives rise to much of the phenomena involving PK, except where sound is the effect and this is hallucinatory. In other cases, a dulling of comprehension, which has been termed hallucinatory-blindness and deafness, cloaks one's own actions or those of another that produce the mysterious effects. This conclusion is based upon the premise that if psychokinesis as it is now explained could be considered a valid display of the psychic power, Jesus would have demonstrated "objects moved by unseen forces" more precisely than appears to be the case.

The one demonstration Jesus made that suggests a psychokinetic force in play, the withering of the fig tree, must be seen as hallucination on the part of the disciples in response to suggestion given by Jesus while they were in trance because posthypnotic response is also involved: in the Gospel of St. Matthew, it is stated that the tree withered instantly, while in St. Mark's account posthypnotic response to suggestion is evidenced for it is stated that not until the next morning did the disciples see the tree in passing and it appeared then to be withered to the root.[13]

This episode, with its discordant time note, may have been devised by Jesus to show that what appears to be psychokinetic phenomena is involved with hypnosis. There is, of course, nothing in the Gospels to indicate that this is the case. The reports ignore, as they must, the contradictions they pose—just as they ignore the contradictions Jesus posed. But a serious student of the Bible can no longer ignore the contradictory reports and the incongruous aspects of Jesus' life and teaching. The contradictions insist upon interpretation and in the view of this study Jesus deliberately posed them, knowing that in time men would search them deeply for the meaning enfolded in them.

The episode of the withering of the fig tree points up clearly the contradiction posed by the whole drama of Jesus: the accounts indicate that Jesus must have been angry because the tree had no fruit, but if so, He was irrationally angry, for "it was not the time for figs." [14] He says, "May no one ever eat fruit from you after this!" [15] Could the Savior of the world, essence of love Himself, petulantly destroy a tree because it was growing normally? An intricate message must be enfolded in this drama and it must hinge upon what the tree and its fruit represent.

Jesus made a tree the *symbol of Himself*, calling Himself the vine. Thus, the tree may be viewed as the *effigy of Himself that Jesus cast*, and the withering of it becomes the withering of something to do with Himself. The incident takes place the morning after His entrance into Jerusalem, just before He is to provoke His own destruction in terms of an *effigy* of Judaic Messiah, on the cross over which is written, "King of the Jews." The fig-tree drama involves irrationality—the major irrationality Jesus contended with was the prevailing concept of Messiah, and His involvement with it appears irrational for He constantly refuted the Judaic ideas of Messiah even as He claimed the title: Son of man. Peter's expression of the worldly view of the Christ called forth from Jesus words of anger. The worldly view of Messiah demanded a fruition that life could not meet in natural course: the fruits of life or truth could not be given to the "Judaic-tree" alone, nor to any "tree" before the species could produce them of its own accord in due time as the fig tree must produce its fruit.

If the fig tree represented Jesus cast in the hateful role of Judaic-type Messiah, then He must say, "may no one ever eat fruit from you after this"—and the drama could indicate that the odious and irrational in life is best destroyed through a withering process that is initiated when one destroys a symbol representing whatever he would have done with.

The power to produce an effect through the manipulation of an effigy has been demonstrated in practice of "black magic"—today men continue to destroy an effigy of whatever their passions move them to destroy, thus relieving the violent impulses of the group and placing a barb of withering fear in the breast of the one the effigy represents. Modern man will not decline and die because of this as might a terrified primitive, but he will feel its impact. Men have devised a new way to cast the odious in effigy: lampoons and "political cartoons" that wither the victim. These give way now to the cartoon or "comics" in which the effigy cast is that of "everyman" involved in all manner of irrationality—the gamut of life in these times is run. Thus, there is much to deplore. But despite all protest, a small voice is heard to say aside, "Good grief . . ."—the hero of "Peanuts" comes upon the stage.[16] In his adult-child world no grown-up treads, but the grown-up world is mined and its irrationality refined into pure delight —the casting of effigy and through it the withering of the irrational has been elevated into pure art. Humor, gentled, presents itself as saving grace.

This study concludes that the withering of the fig tree teaches that art is making an effigy of oneself to destroy through it the irrational or odious in life—to destroy it not explosively, but surely. At the same time the artist makes of his work a symbol to convey as large a measure of truth as he can. Thus, every artist is both destructive and creative. And every man is artist: of his life he creates both an effigy he would destroy and a symbol of truth he would express. As artist, Jesus was both destructive and creative—He destroyed the ancient Messianic mold and created the concept of the Christ in every man. Even the least bears this glory—is human, is divine—to borrow words from Colin Wilson:

> As the Steppenwolf sees in his moment of vision in bed with Maria, memory has enough accumulated material to make a man into a god —even the meanest and most degraded of men.[17]

Thus, in the view of this study, the "object" affected by "unseen forces" in the drama of the fig tree was the "object of Jesus as Judaic Messiah"— His irrational and petulant act must serve to wither the concept of Himself as God incarnate, alone among men. Only after the Messianic mold was broken and His own image as Messiah had withered could men come to understand the Scripture:

I said, ye are gods.[18]

In the drama of the withering of the fig tree, psychokinesis, as the term is generally understood, was not involved. At least, the disciples' varying reports indicate this to be the case. And this study concludes that Jesus deliberately created the dichotomy in the reports by giving opposing suggestions to His entranced disciples, so that in time men would recognize that hypnosis is involved in what appears to be psychokinesis.

Parapsychologists deal with other mysterious phenomena which Jung calls "Synchronicity"—meaningful coincidences that cannot be causally explained, premonitions that are confirmed by omens which PK appears to author. Is psychokinesis involved? If not, what gives rise to such events?

In the view of this study, man's ability to create poetry and to *be* poetic authors the mysterious phenomenon. The poet suffers what might be called "extreme perception," seeing and hearing the mystery of creation in everything, when the "moment of truth" overtakes him:

> This is the mysticism of Kirilov in *The Devils:* the mere existence of *anything* is a mystical fact—a leaf, a grain of sand.[19]

Poetry is acausal—a word "happens" to the mind and it fits the mood, the moment, the time, the rhyme, conveying feeling in a way that is beyond the norm in expression, imparting meaning that is beyond whatever experience the poet suffered. Every adult is not a poet, but every child is born one. The child reveals his poetic bent in sing-song soundings, in rapid comprehension of onomatopoeia, in quick grasp of the rhyming or rhythmic. His "bright sayings"—unintentional or acausal—are meaningful coincidences in words that lead him to express and then to understand beyond his original "cause" or intention.

More than poetry, however, appears to be involved in synchronicity. ESP plays its part. This is to say, the poetic bent in man establishes in mind and by word a connection with some physical phenomenon that imbues the moment with extraordinary meaning when depression of sensory perception allows extrasensory perception to take over momentarily, giving rise to pre- or postcognition or clairvoyance. Man is surrounded by things and sounds that express the poetry of life so that at any instant an omen is there to mark the moment miraculously and poetically, synchronistically, if one wishes to have it so confirmed. A most unusual omen may be born of hallucination, but this is seldom necessary. At any instant countless creatures and objects are out of place in the normal scheme of things, but for the most part this goes unnoticed. When one is emotionally disturbed, his imagination prompts him to grasp the obvious and convert it to the mystical.

A wealth of sensory stimuli impinges upon a person every moment. Sudden awareness of objects, sounds, or actions that normally would go unnoticed, and realization of the *meaning* inherent in the most commonplace thing that normally goes unrecognized is an indication of distorted perception—this symptom shows the other side of the coin of hallucinatory-blindness: mental defenses that should have censored the material or forewarned that it is of no real consequence have broken down, giving rise to extreme sensibility and awareness.

An example might better explain this situation. On one occasion, Jung demonstrated to Freud "a so-called catalytic exteriorization phenomenon."[20] Jung had suffered a moment of extraordinary tension during one of their long talks. In the view of this study, nervous strain, emotional stress, and his physical exhaustion served to diminish his intake of sensory stimuli so that when an unusually loud "pop" from the wall or bookcase broke in upon consciousness, it poetically confirmed his feelings and gave pause, relief, a moment's "anesthesia" to the problem, releasing thereby extrasensory power which vouchsafed a moment of precognition enabling him to create a mystery by knowing and announcing that another loud report would follow—and it did. Freud explained the mysterious event by two things:

> The first is an enormously intensified alertness on the part of the unconscious, so that one is led like Faust to see a Helen in every woman. The second is the undeniable "co-operation of chance," which plays the same role in the formation of delusions as somatic co-operation in hysterical symptoms or linguistic co-operation in puns.[21]

In the view of this study, intensified alertness gives rise to the "co-operation of chance." And ESP plays a part in one way or another to produce the meaningful moment.

Almost everyone suffers occasional "extreme" perception, or is involved in a synchronistic event. But such perception is indication of a pathological condition when one begins to see too long and powerful a chain of "omens" or coincidental happenings that tend to confirm his fears, or else tend to confirm what appears to him to be his strange and unique grasp of truth. Hysteria threatens because at such a time one cannot tell coherently of all he "sees"—life and all the universe suddenly become a synchronistic expression that "spreads" his power to comprehend so that he grasps the whole secret of it. The schizophrenic also suffers extreme perception—the tormenting voices that press upon him are everywhere, drowning out life's own poetic-voice that sounds within him only when the clamorous voices of the ego-group and outer world are hushed—in his case, every casual thing or happening is a dark omen to confirm his fears.

Occasional synchronistic events are so common among the "normal" population, however, one must conclude that the poetic bent in man, operating with his psychic power, performs a necessary function in the whole process of perception and expression. What is this function?

Jesus provided the answer. He did not, however, involve Himself in a demonstration of synchronicity. What of the dove alighting upon Him as He was baptized? A dove did not alight upon Him, and witnesses did not hear a voice from the skies saying, "This is my beloved Son, in whom I am well pleased." [22] At least, the Gospels of St. Matthew and St. Mark do not report that this miracle happened. They say that the heavens were opened unto Jesus; He saw the Spirit of God descending like a dove and lighting upon Him—then, "lo, a voice from heaven saying . . ." Thus, the inner realm, His own, was opened unto Him and a voice within Him sounded the words. These passages describe His own reaction to baptism in poetic terms. In the Gospel of St. Luke, the subjective nature of the experience is indicated, but the report tends both to becloud and to objectify the vision.[23] In the Gospel of St. John, it is said that John the Baptist suffered the vision as he baptized Jesus.[24]

By giving utterance to the visionary moment, Jesus reveals that *illusion, or hallucination, plays a leading role in perception*, that the power of clairvoyance plays inwardly upon man, momentarily lighting up the dark terrain of the subconscious and *unconscious*, and that the creative poetic force in man *fashions an image of his belief and impels enactment of that which is "imaged"*—for afterward Jesus began His ministry that expresses the vision in terms of acting out the "omen" of the dove and the sounding of the words: He proclaimed love of Father-self for Son-self, of Self-for-Self in man, and expressed Himself as symbol of inner peace, represented by the dove.

Jung saw that each instinct expresses a guiding image which enfolds the meaning of the instinct and impels a man to act upon it.[25] And deRopp points to the need of symbols of the "Perfect Man" because symbols act as guiding images and give "the self-correcting mechanism in man's psyche a more definite basis for action than vague philosophical concepts about goodness and truth." [26]

What happens, then, when there is a concerted effort on the part of the literati and artists in every field to distort and finally obliterate the religious images, the symbols, the illusions as well as the delusions man has cherished? Before one can attempt to answer this question, he must attempt to answer another—what is modern art trying to say?

II

Paul Tillich says, "I believe that existentialist art has a tremendous religious function, in visual art as well as in all other realms of art, namely, to rediscover the basic questions to which the Christian symbols are the answers in a way which is understandable to our time. These symbols can then become again understandable to our time." [27]

Traditional Christian symbols reflecting orthodox theology are no longer embraced. Great art depicting the Christian dogma and its religious figures is reverenced for what it is—for art's sake—but what such works "said" to generations past is, for the most part, rejected by, or incomprehensible to, this generation. This would indicate that art tends to confirm Freud's diagnosis of Western man's neurosis: at bottom is hatred for, or refusal of, orthodox Christianity.

If one begins a journey, moving through the ages as he moves through the temples of art, he finds that in no period can he escape "Gehenna." He sees that art voices the despair of men who make supplication through the tortured and grotesque—these are the men who cannot believe, for if they "will not listen to Moses and the prophets, they will not be convinced, not even if one rose from the dead." [28] What can assuage the thirst of perishing intellectualism and empty riches, the thirst of men fearful for their sanity and souls, save the grace of God rising up within them?

In each age art asks this question, then shows this miracle and touches the mind with the healing view of nature, or the charm of any simple thing, or an impression of humanity in men, or an expression of the love of life. In the twentieth century's hall, one finds art that expresses a Pythagorean faith in the mystery and beauty of mathematics. And as though to teach the "atomic language" in which man is not yet fluent, the artists picture the new geometries, the nuclear forces, the space-time frames, "my here-now, your here-now," the rain of the random element, the devastation of the organization of energy that follows collision, the prism colors of light, and the secret of the FitzGerald Contraction—such as this may be read into their abstract renderings. One sees that compassion's hand still paints the crippled soul, and hope still depicts the young, the strong, the fertile as willing to bear life's burden while the world awaits the dawn of a new consciousness in mankind.

But just as fear and faith hang side by side in the human mind, so in the corridor of twentieth-century art one sees the twisted forms of the demoniacal stripped of their mythical garb, and the compelling stare of madness lingers in the memory of the viewer as he moves on through the whole landscape of life and reality distorted as only the psychotic can distort truth. The canvases become as inarticulate as one in the grip of hysteria. Turn a corner, and one is confronted by a smear, taken from life's body, or by a scream painted, the note hangs in the dripping, unfinished of all save a cry so fearful it cannot be delivered of itself. It is as though every remnant of shrapnel, grossly enlarged, every scorched patch of earth or skin, every thrust and gutting, torn and dangling limb, drizzle of blood from a wound or the clotting, starving cell or shrieking nerve, gray and mongering terror are here gathered—the fruit of the womb of art delivered of this time an incoherent monstrosity, a "New View of Man." [29]

Rollo May sees in modern art a desperate attempt "to express the immediate underlying meaning of the modern human situation, even though this means portraying despair and emptiness," but he sees that the insights of a crisis period are more than the product of anxiety, and that a crisis is required to shock people out of unaware dependence upon "external dogma and to force them to unravel layers of pretense to reveal naked truth about themselves which, however unpleasant, will at least be solid." [30]

The twentieth century enfolds a generation that has lived through an unprecedented series of crises. It has known the most ghastly of all wars, the most nerve-wracking of all rumors of wars, has seen love grow cold as men observe the increase of iniquity, has seen friends and family betray one another—and it now confronts the abomination of desolation that a nuclear war portends, or else the equally appalling prospect of the scientific control of man that Aldous Huxley satirizes in *Brave New World*. It lives in a time of great tribulation, for:

> War, by imposing hardships and controls on daily life, produces an aggressive mentality and degrades people's character according to their wretched conditions. The result in this case was a general state of public disorder in all countries. As time went on and the earlier atrocities became an accepted fact, the later ones were marked by refinements of technique and novel methods of retaliation. Even words lost their proper meanings and were changed to suit current propaganda . . . . family ties were broken for the sake of party loyalty. . . . Relations between people were governed not by the security of established customs but by the prospect of selfish gain in defiance of the law.[31]

These words, so aptly describing this century, were written by Thucydides to describe Athens as it warred with Sparta. Such was the prevailing atmosphere when Socrates appeared upon the scene to lead men to truth by questioning the laws that govern man's inner being.

Then, and today, man must find what Tillich calls "the courage to be." And this was also true when Jesus spoke to His disciples of the culmination of man's struggle—and of the "end of things" as they must face it. For any man in any age, the "end of things" is the same—death takes him; and history shows that in any age crisis following upon crisis leads to the final terror that lifts its battered head: this is knowledge that the ultimate battlefield is the individual mind. Today, one structure of consciousness is falling, another rising, even as was true in Jesus' day, and in this travail, neurosis spreads—sanity itself seems threatened.

But today, in another sense the ultimate battlefield is the individual mind: upon the minds of a handful of men, perhaps upon any one of them, the fate of civilization may rest—only one bomb need fall to call into action all of them. This century, however, has already seen the fulfillment of the prophecy of Malachi—"behold, the day cometh that shall burn as an oven. . . ." [32] So burned the days when the bombs were dropped on Hiroshima and Nagasaki. Thus, to this century, Jesus' words foretelling the final struggle—"except those days should be shortened, there should no flesh be saved"—have real and immediate meaning. Indeed, the whole description of the culmination of man's struggle as Jesus gave it, recorded in Chapter 24 of Matthew, appears to be uniquely applicable to the twentieth century.

Pearl Harbor, and battles raging on the frozen ground of Russia, come to mind as one reads, "pray ye that your flight be not in winter, neither on the sabbath day." Incendiary words, bombs, and the Gestapo awaiting come to mind as one reads, "let him who is on the housetop not come down to take anything out of his house . . . neither let him who is in the field return back to take his clothes." The effects of atomic bombing are presaged in these words: "Woe to women with child and to women who give suck in those days"—for "Tumors of the lung, stomach, breast, ovary, and uterus were twice as numerous among the bomb survivors as in the normal population. Women bearing children conceived within four months prior to radiation were more likely to give birth to mentally retarded offspring." [33] This generation knows of the existing "pollution of our food and our genetic heritage with strontium 90 and carbon 14." [34] Its art cries out:

> . . . Hurt not the earth, neither the sea, nor the trees, till we have sealed the servants of our God in their foreheads. . . .[35]

But the "end is not yet." The inner powers of man are shaken. The psychic disorder attests to this—and gives meaning to the words, "Immediately after the tribulation of those days shall the sun be darkened, and the moon shall not give her light, and the stars shall fall from heaven, and the powers of the heavens shall be shaken." When the "powers that are in heaven," the *inner powers*, are shaken, man confronts in himself the terrible apparition of madness:

> When ye therefore shall see the abomination of desolation, spoken of by Daniel the prophet, stand in the holy place—whoso readeth, let him understand . . .

This generation begins to understand: the "abomination" is insanity standing in the "holy place" of one's erstwhile concept of ego and superego.

This generation suffers travail "as the days of Noah were"—the days that involve a rebirth of consciousness which cannot happen until there is not left standing one stone of the temple of consciousness that housed first a Messianic theology and then a godless intellectualism. Thus, in Davenport's words, a "blue haze" of fear hangs over men unable to find a doctrine to give them confidence as they face their inner worlds to which they are awakening: "However it may come about, one fact concerning this phenomenon is clear: it is a fearsome experience. In a deep psychological sense it is analogous to physical birth. . . ." [36] In their search for something to believe in, many are caught in strange cults—and not the least of these is the cult of modern art in which sacrifice of self, in suicide or wanton recklessness, all too often follows the artist's distortions that finally tend to extol madness or drive him to it.

In the cult of modern art, anything goes—and strange rites are condoned. Not too long ago, Jean Tinguely built death into the "gizmo" he had made to pay "homage" to New York, the "phallic city." In the garden of New York's Museum of Modern Art, a crowd gathered to watch the "suicide-fated machine" destroy itself— but the best it could do was to flame and struggle. Looking at the ineffectual effigy, did something in Tinguely cry out the closing verses of Matthew 24?—". . .cut him asunder, and appoint him his portion with the hypocrites. . . ." There shall be weeping and gnashing of teeth when a man cannot build destruction into the object of odium he has represented—and firemen with axes must finish the job.[37]

As one turns to the literati of the twentieth century to find an explanation of its art and to see what such art portends, he is again confronted by distorted expression, and with evidence of distorted perception. He sees that, as happened in ancient Athens, words have lost their proper meanings.

In *The House of Intellect*, Jacques Barzun describes the sad state of language.[38] In an article, "Solomon or Salami," Helen R. Lowe discusses the appalling extent and nature of reading failure. She points to the tendency of today's student to read not what is written, but a distortion of the words that are used—for example, *Solomon* read as *salami*. She says that imposed upon the majority of students is a:

> perverse and illogical concept of a word as a visual symbol of meaning instead of as a symbol, by the grace of the letters which compose it, of the sound which conveys the meaning. We are not dealing with the practical handicap of slow and unskillful reading but with a disabling and deforming of the learning powers of many of the brightest. . . . Without reading, there is no opportunity.[39]

Without reading, men become slaves to a tyrant ignorance.

And today because so few men read or write or understand even a few words of the language of science, "two cultures" have developed. Sir Charles P. Snow says that men considered highly educated "look blank" when asked, "What is the second law of thermodynamics?"—this question he sees as the scientific equivalent of "Have you read a work of Shakespeare's?"[40] Art tries to bridge the two cultures. For example, May writes that in Chagall's paintings "space is less 'anisotropic' than our common space. . . ."[41] but how many viewers can see this or comprehend what he has written—do they read picture and word "anisotropic" or "antisocial"?

It is impossible to establish a direct connection between widespread acceptance of the hopelessly distorted or inchoate in art and methods of teaching which give rise to distortions in reading and writing. One can say only that in preponderant number neither artists nor students are truly articulate and much in modern literature reads as though penned by Caliban:

> You taught me language, and my profit on't
> Is, I know how to curse.

Louis Zahner says, "If the remedy lies in education, it is in education in the broadest sense: in whatever goes on, for better or worse, in the entire life of the pupil, of which the classroom is an almost infinitesimal part."[42]

Lack of ease in speaking, reading, and writing makes of anyone a social cripple, an incompetent, in modern civilization. Harrison Salisbury points to the "high correlation between incapacity for self-expression, low-reading skill, and antisocial behavior."[43] And Dr. Raymond Fosberg writes, "Failure of the nervous system, the sensory and communications apparatus of the human organism, is not merely equivalent to, but, from the point of view of society, worse than, the complete failure of the whole organism, or death." [44]

Whatever the cause of the failure, man inarticulate, unable to communicate his feelings, or to mitigate his sense of isolation through comprehension of the written word, is indeed in bondage, unarmed, his soul nakedly savage in its plight.

Consider the "beat" as Robert Brustein describes him—member of the "Cult of Unthink." He remains "cool" and detached until moved to commit an incomprehensible act: the "kick-seeking adolescent" sinks his knife into the flesh of his victim and thanks him for the "experience." The hero of the "beat" is utterly inarticulate—the "beat" also inarticulate himself engages "in playing against his emotions," and seeks relief in drugs: ". . . if he can't find it with the aid of the various narcotics . . . he turns to 'Plotinus Poe St. John of the Cross telepathy and bop kaballa,' not to mention Zen Buddhism. For the hipster, these philosophies are designed to initiate him not into life but into nothingness. . . ." [45] The "Beat Generation" cannot speak for itself. The poet, Allen Ginsberg, speaks for it:

> I saw the best minds of my generation destroyed by madness, starving hysterical naked . . . [46]

When communication fails and words have lost their meanings, madness leers. It becomes, then, the work of the prophet to proclaim the meaning of the word, the meaning of the logos in man. The world appears to have missed the point of the revelation that came *first* to Mohammed:

> So Mohammed turned away, disdaining the idolatry of the Meccans, seeking communion with God alone in a cave on the mountain. It was there, in the silence of the desert night, that the revelation came. The voice cried: "Read!" He said: "I cannot read." Again the voice said, "Read!" again he said, "I cannot." For the third time he was commanded. He said, "What can I read?"
>
> > "Read: In the name of thy Lord who created,
> >   Created man from *clots of blood*.
> > Read: For thy Lord is the most beneficent
> >   Who hath taught the use of the pen;—
> >   Hath taught man that which he knew not." [47]

Today, Islam and every other faith embraces millions of men who cannot —Read! Nor can they use the pen, nor do they comprehend the power this represents.

Gautama realized that there is "neither a higher self nor a lower self" [48] —Jesus realized that within man there is a teaching capacity and a learning capacity, yoked and geared: they "fare alike." This study postulates that "teacher" operates upon extrasensory perception, that "scholar" operates upon sensory perception, that through the diminishing of these opposite powers the power of speech—a power greater than either, greater than both—became possible.

It does not suffice to say that the development of the cerebral cortex, of the Broca area, made speech possible. What gave rise to this development? Only through a dulling of the sensory mechanisms did the creature that became man escape a fatal narrowness, and only through a dulling of extrasensory powers would the need of language press upon ancestral-man-creature and evoke an expression of a third power within him. Dr. West writes: "It has been suggested that unconscious resistance to ESP is a deep-rooted biological defence mechanism that prevents the orderly stream of conscious thought from being swamped by innumerable extraneous impressions." [49] Through the dulling of sensory and extrasensory perception, concentration became possible, an impression could arise from within, a new means of apprehending and communication became necessary. Ancestral-man-creature broke out of the vicious circle of the animal world when he spoke, translating stimuli into articulated vocable, into a word, trade-worthy symbol of life's supreme power.

Jesus saw that the powers of God are gathered in the power of the word—and thus in misuse of this power, in the lie, sin resides. This, the third power, is disciplined, disciplining, and enduring—by words shall man be judged, by words acquitted, heaven and earth shall pass away but not words. A word is Son-power, offspring of God-power, a priori. This, and much more, Jesus said of the word.[50]

The creative potential is vested in the word—the limits of its power cannot actually be defined. Straus writes: "Sound, although something, is not properly a thing, it is not one of the *pragmata* that we can handle. One cannot do anything to sound, and yet it is not nothing; it eludes our grasp, we are helplessly exposed to it. The power of sound goes on working in the articulated vocable, the Word, the creating command of God. . . ."[51] Once this power had expressed itself through man, the development of his brain-power, the increase of his consciousness, was assured.

Through the word, Son-power, man came in time to vanquish the fearful and fantastic aspects of the extrasensory power in life, and to give wings to thought through poetic expressions of ideas that stretch the mind. He began to fashion and name mental images to preserve in these symbols the truth he sensed but could not express because language to contain his realization had not come into being. Such a symbol is Pegasus, winged horse, that sprang from the head of fear—of the snaky-haired Gorgon, Medusa, whose awful countenance turned men to stone—when Perseus, son of Zeus, "son of God," had slain her. With a blow of Pegasus' hoof, he caused Hippocrene, the fountain of the Muses, the arts and sciences, to spring from Mount Helicon—hence, "poetic inspiration."

The question has been put—what happens when myths, symbols, and guiding images are distorted or discarded? This study suggests that words begin to suffer the same fate and this serves to hobble both the teaching and learning capacity. The question has been put—what is modern art trying to say? This study suggests that it proclaims:

> Theology based on vicariousness of any sort is perishing.
>
> As the belief that man is no more than chance product or a superior animal takes over, meaning and purpose in life decline, so that the will to exercise the exact and exacting power of the word (which sets man apart from and above the animal kingdom) also declines.
>
> Communication begins to falter, and a sense of isolation in independent existence threatens sanity.
>
> Psychic disorder progresses until meaning in life, *religion*, can be restored.

III

Today's art and writing bears witness to reason's harvest a century after the "tares" that infested the whole field of religion were ripped out with little thought of the damage done to the roots of truth planted alongside.[52] A new literati—offspring of an intellectual elite that eschewed religious symbols, myths, and guiding images—is coming face to face with a generation that was taught to believe implicitly in nothing, even as it was led to explore and express anything, and thus it derides everything.

An irreligious outlook has been built into the whole educational system and into Western culture by educated men who speak suavely, convincingly, artistically, scientifically, earnestly, as they offer an empty, stultifying analysis of the great religious figures. In another day, in another way, this also happened:

> Woe to you, you impious scribes and Pharisees! you shut the Realm of heaven in men's faces; you neither enter yourselves, nor will you let those enter who are on the point of entering . . . . you are like tombs whitewashed; they look comely on the outside, but inside they are full of dead men's bones and all manner of impurity. So to men you seem just, but inside you are full of hypocrisy and iniquity. . . .

> You build tombs for the prophets and decorate the tombs of the just, and you say, "If we had been living in the days of our fathers, we would not have joined them in shedding the blood of the prophets." So you are witnesses against yourselves, that you are sons of those who killed the prophets! And you will fill up the measure that your fathers filled. You serpents! [53]

Jesus speaks to society's "scribes and Pharisees," but, as Authority-Ego, He speaks also to the "educated reasoning power" in every man that stifles intuition, repudiates extrasensory power, strikes faith with a blunt word, stones hope with a derisive laugh, whitewashes sin or fear with a shrug, and in the end edits meaning out of life, thereby rendering man's reasoning power itself inane. So long as this faction leads the ego-group, history will repeat itself.

As surely as extrasensory perception gives rise to delusion upon occasion, upon occasion unbridled reasoning power elaborates fact until it fabricates a fantasy that is against all reason and thus "witnesses against itself." This is to say, reasoning power has led to such "knowledge" as makes knowledge itself, and life, meaningless: if man is on a dying planet, dependent upon a dying sun, in a universe doomed to die a heat-death, and if his religion is a "conditioned reflex" so that there is no hope even of a "spiritual realm" to which life moves when the material realm is "dead," then his effort to master nature and himself is meaningless—if he is no more than an accidental bit of sanity in the void of an insensate, dying nature, then the quicker he obliterates his flickering consciousness with its longing for immortality, the better.

Today's knowledge rests largely upon statistics which seldom tell the whole truth. Nor do scientists have such statistics as might present the whole picture and justify the conclusions they offer. Among them are many who voice this fact, and bypassing both religious theology and nihilistic scientific dogma, they acknowledge faith in God, or in an intelligent purposeful Cause, pointing out that all in creation responds to intelligent probing and to love or care. But too many others in one way or another quietly teach the doctrine of decay in an inane and doomed universe. Few people appear to appreciate the insidious influence this doctrine has upon the present generation—are not the various art forms dramatizing or caricaturing this dogma? How many are *un*motivated by it?

Viktor Frankl writes, "there is a danger inherent in the teaching of man's 'nothingbutness,' the theory that man is nothing but the result of biological, psychological and sociological conditions, or the product of heredity and environment. Such a view of man makes him into a robot, not a human being." [54] He sees that "The existential vacuum that is the mass neurosis of the present time, can be described as a private and personal form of nihilism; for nihilism can be defined as the contention that being has no meaning." [55]

Frankl developed his philosophy in the living laboratory of the concentration camps, and on this testing ground witnessed man's behavior when he had lost his faith in the future:

> The prisoner who had lost faith in the future—his future—was doomed. With his loss of belief in the future, he also lost his spiritual hold; he let himself decline and became subject to mental and physical decay. Usually this happened quite suddenly, in the form of a crisis, the symptoms of which were familiar to the experienced camp inmate.... Usually it began with the prisoner refusing one morning to get dressed and wash or to go out on the parade grounds. No entreaties, no blows, no threats had any effect. He just lay there, hardly moving.... He simply gave up ... and nothing bothered him any more.[56]

Consider now that a person can have no *real* faith in the future, either the future of the species or his own, if he accepts the nihilistic view science takes today and acquiesces to the pan-deterministic evaluation of religion which "contends that one's religious life is conditioned inasmuch as it depends on one's early childhood experiences, and that one's God concept depends on one's father image." [57]

To this generation, so prone to repudiate its fathers and shift the blame to their shoulders, Frankl points out that even the worst father image need not prevent one from:

> establishing a good relationship with God; rather, a deep religious life provides one with the resources needed to overcome the hatred of one's father.... A cross-sectional statistical survey conducted by my staff at the Vienna Poliklinik Hospital revealed that about one-third of those patients who had experienced a positive father image turned away from religion in their later life, whereas most of those people screened who had a negative father image succeeded, in spite of this, in building up a positive attitude toward religious issues.[58]

Faith in God brings meaning to life and faith in the future—the world's future and one's own. But "educated reasoning power," observing the transitoriness of man's life, stones this hope. In so doing, it renders the past as meaningless as the present "accident" of nature that man and this universe is held to be. Seeing man and the universe as the product of blind forces moving nowhere but to self-destruction, or death in the case of individual, renders inane the concept that man is a responsible being and must be educated to assume his responsibilties and to realize his potentialities. Frankl writes:

> ... the only really transitory aspects of life are the potentialities; but the moment they are actualized, they are rendered realities; they are saved and delivered into the past, wherein they are rescued and preserved from transitoriness. For in the past, nothing is irrecoverably lost but everything irrevocably stored. Thus, the transitoriness of our existence in no way makes it meaningless. But it does constitute our responsibleness; for everything hinges upon our realizing the essentially transitory possibilities. Man constantly makes his choice concerning the mass of present potentialities; which of these will be condemned to nonbeing and which will be actualized? ... At any moment, man must decide, for better or for worse, what will be the monument of his existence. Usually, to be sure, man considers only the stubble field of transitoriness and overlooks the full granaries of the past wherein he has salvaged once and for all his deeds and his joys and also his sufferings. Nothing can be undone, and nothing can be done away with. I should say having been is the surest kind of being.[59]

Here speaks an *educated man*—in the words of Gordon W. Allport, his words "rest on experiences too deep for deception." [60]

The tragedy of following blindly the dictates of "educated reasoning power" is that it seldom *really* believes the doctrines it poses with such bravado, secure only in the knowledge that it is in line with the consensus of the intellectual elite of its day. If man were dependent upon it alone, his case would be hopeless. He is not. There is another and more powerful voice within to tell him that nihilism is false—that life has meaning, that his every act or failure to act brings to bear upon his future, that his every *word* is meaningful, is judged by an Authority within him.

Legend says that sin arises when man acts upon the delusion his "reasoning power" presents to him as truth: Eve, and then Adam, reasoned that the serpent knew whereof he spoke with such authority, but it was delusion to think that man could thwart the power of the word arising within him to direct and discipline. Cain reasoned that to kill Abel would be to erase his competitor, but it is delusion to believe that man's life can be taken—Abel's blood cried out from the ground—and again the "word of God" disciplined, but did not destroy.

Moses gave the psychic law upon which social law must be based—gave it in writing. The miracle wrought was the miracle of the *written word* leading Homo sapiens to accept government by law as the "promised land" of life. The progress of civilization keeps apace man's use of the written word. He cannot vitiate his language without himself, his law, and his society becoming vitiated. He shares power as he teaches use of the pen. As he reveres truth, he must revere his word as his bond, for it is his bond to God: it is Son-power.

Jesus addressed the problem of a generation that could not—Read! He spoke to a generation wherein only the educated elite could even pretend to give meaning to the verbiage they spouted and were themselves desolate —and deluded if they thought they truly exercised the third power in performing the function of scribe, for, borrowing words from Boris Pasternak, "The task of men of letters . . . is to heed 'the living voice of life,' to bear witness to the good, the true and the beautiful." [61]

Jesus spoke harshly to the scribes and Pharisees, but He ended this discourse with a cry unsurpassed in tenderness:

> O Jerusalem, Jerusalem, thou that killest the prophets, and stonest them which are sent unto thee, how often would I have gathered thy children together, even as a hen gathereth her chickens under her wings, and ye would not! [62]

To those without ears to hear and eyes to see, to those who would not believe even if one rose from the dead to speak to them, life can hold forth only the promise of despair:

> See, your House is to be left desolate. For I tell you, you will never see me again till such time as you say, Blessed is he who comes in the Lord's name.[63]

When a man turns cold or uncomprehending eyes upon the hand of compassion held forth to him, only the miracle of rebirth of consciousness can rescue him from the desolation of his inner world. The poets who must speak for an inarticulate, "beat" generation recognize this—Brustein points to Kerouac's celebrating the "attractiveness of death, just as Ginsberg frequently writes of his desire to curl up in the soft comfort of the womb." [64]

Every age in history presents both unique and universal problems, hindrances. There is nothing new about reptilian consciousness which is what men express when love grows cold and they are repelled by what they see as their father's iniquity. Reptilian consciousness is what the delinquent expresses when, like a serpent sinking his fangs into an unsuspecting victim, he strikes. Each age has its reptilian consciousness to conquer; and each age produces a St. George to slay the dragon.

The greatest of these dragon-slaying symbols is *Shiva*. He, the God-son, incorporates evil because each drop of the dragon's blood spilled to the ground gives rise to seven more like it—thus, *Shiva* must drink its blood to vanquish it. This symbol says that man must deal with evil within himself because he has incorporated its power. Only through expending its destructive potential can he so attenuate its virulence that in time it turns to laughter.

As this age deals with its reptilian consciousness and the fear it engenders, it must consider that psychology leads man to place the blame for his ills and errors upon an ever receding past-parent until, in the end, as theology does, it leads to the concept of the son's vicarious assumption of and atonement for sin. Thus, the reality of life and one's own responsibility to fulfill its purpose eludes the individual. In one way or another, psychology and theology make man the victim of an iniquitous father and bring sin to rest in vicariousness.

But vicariousness itself is the sin—when one's own responsibility in life declines, so does his potential and, as May points out, a feeling of guilt arises from the forfeiting of one's "own potentialities." [65] This is but another way of saying that the immature adult suffers feelings of guilt which may be expressed in neurotic or in criminal ways. Barrett writes: "What Dostoevski saw in the criminals he lived with is what he came finally to see at the center of man's nature: contradiction, ambivalence, irrationality. There was a childishness and innocence about these criminals, along with a brutality and cruelty, altogether not unlike the murderous innocence of a child." [66] If from his earliest years a child was taught that he possesses an inner Authority which must bring him to suffer his every violation of himself or another, he would know that there is no chance to escape the consequences of his every word and deed. But the child must know also that this Authority within is love of life expressing itself in him, is love of him itself, is his own of God:

> Yea, I have loved thee with an everlasting love . . .
> From of old I love you, so now I draw you gently home.[67]

The child must know that the measure of his joy in life depends upon the measure of his growth in consciousness of this One within which leads him to see that man is as yet child, life is the parent.

In *Child of Our Time*, Michel del Castillo reveals that life is parent, that in the darkest hours or places one will find men who are men in the divinely human sense of the word. He, himself, is an expression of the miracle of love of life. Somehow it survived in him through a torment beyond the comprehension of one mercifully spared witnessing or suffering such an ordeal. Only the children of this century can chronicle the complete inhumanity, the utter indecency of its war—and bespeak without a word the accomplice to it that each man somehow became. But even as Michel del Castillo's grasp of his own potentialities led him to express the trauma through the creative act, to tell of it so simply that anger is disarmed and reprisal becomes unthinkable, so anyone may express truth and heal himself and heal the image of mankind itself—leaving "hate to those who are too weak to love." [68]

Man is artist when he writes to himself alone, drawing his work from out the deeps of his life, knowing the shining creation he struggles with may cost him himself—to bring no more than the bare skeleton of truth's glorious magnitude to the shores of consciousness that it may lap with the waves against the jetties through a night and day, evoking splendid curiosity. In *The Old Man and The Sea*, Ernest Hemingway wrote of the victory turned defeat and the defeat turned victory that each life represents—he heals the image of man with the promise of a boy's company tomorrow.[69]

As artist Rico Lebrun insists, "the human condition is the only valid theme. . . no brutality will ever cancel that meaning. . . . a painting can enhance the meaning by changing what is disfigured into something that is transfigured." In commenting upon his tortured figures, *Time's* writer adds, "in suffering they still hold to life." [70]

Out of suffering is born a consciousness that transcends the "time of sorrows." Such consciousness is expressed by the artist who paints a canvas of living, moving, breathing beauty, his subject bathed in light within, without, the canvas taking on the quality of truth, or life, or love, or laughter, becoming witness to man's faith in humankind, and this he hands as gift to the next generation. Such a work says that love still works the miracle, that life's promise is enwrapped in the mystery man is, the mystery of his mirth. Whatever the form art takes, it withers the destructive potential, even its own, and man is salted: "The reassuring thing about modern art is that things can't be as bad as they're painted." [71] What turns man's fear to laughter? What is the secret "stuff" his mind is made of?

Does Jesus give a clue? He begins the Sermon on the Mount with words as mysterious as any He uttered: "Blessed are the poor in spirit: for theirs is the kingdom of heaven." [72] Spirit is extrasensory. Homo sapiens is "poor in spirit," poor in extrasensory perception—but he is "rich" in his possession of the *unconscious* domain. Thus, Jesus expresses His confidence in mankind:

JESUS' DEMONSTRATIONS OF PERCEPTION AND THE PSYCHIC POWER

Ye are the salt of the earth. . . . Ye are the light of the world. . . . Be ye therefore perfect, even as your Father which is in heaven is perfect.[73]

Is the mark of genius the undiminished confidence in man and in life that Jesus expressed—and that men such as Pasternak continue to express in spite of all man's failures? In Pasternak's unforgettable poetry:

> O do not trouble then, and do not grieve!
> Despite my helpless state, I swear, I'll stay
> With you that day. The strong in hope endure,
> Through all the plagues that bring them low in life.

He sees that "Christ and the Christ-in-everyman is the last best hope of earth." [74]

Jesus saw that each human being, "I," is a manifestation of a promise made of reunion on *that day*, a promise of Self-reunion:

Let not your heart be troubled, neither let it be afraid. . .

Never will I fail you, never will I forsake you.

. . . lo, I am with you alway—even unto the end of the world.[75]

But a grasp of the Christ, "I," in Jesus or in any man is not to be had through *sensory* perception:

. . . flesh and blood hath not revealed it unto thee . . .[76]

Thus, Jesus' demonstrations of extrasensory perception were necessary: He had to show that although man be "poor in spirit" he possesses enough of the psychic power to perceive the Christ in himself and in another—this He demonstrates in the dramas this study calls the illusory miracles which will be examined in the following chapter.

Chapter 14

THE ILLUSORY MIRACLES

I

Jesus' stilling the winds and waves, walking across the waters and stretching forth His hand to Peter, the Transfiguration, and the voice from heaven glorifying the Father's name are miracles that fall into the category of the illusory—which is to say, in the view of this study, these miracles "happened" only in the minds of those who experienced them. They are of tremendous importance because they illuminate the Christ, picturing what is otherwise inexpressible, through *visionary experiences*.

In the drama known as the Transfiguration,[1] Jesus leads Peter, James, and John up a high mountain where He "was transfigured before them: and his face did shine as the sun, and his raiment was white as the light. And, behold, there appeared unto them Moses and Elias talking with him." As Peter then speaks to Jesus, a "bright cloud overshadowed them: and behold a voice out of the cloud, which said, This is my beloved Son, in whom I am well pleased; hear ye him. And when the disciples heard it, they fell on their face, and were sore afraid. And Jesus came and touched them, and said, Arise, and be not afraid. And when they had lifted up their eyes, they saw no man, save Jesus only." Because when Jesus *touched them* all was normal, there is indication that the drama was played while the disciples were in hypnotic trance and at Jesus' touch were awakened to reality. Jesus speaks of the experience as *a vision*.

On another occasion Jesus says, "Father, glorify thy name," and it is reported that "Then came there a voice from heaven, saying, I have both glorified it, and will glorify it again." The people standing by said that it had thundered.[2] If the voice came from heaven, it came from within— only those who suffered the visionary moment heard the reverberation, the words.

The most mysterious of all the illusory miracles are those having to do with Jesus' walking across the waters, stilling the winds and waves, saving the sinking Peter. And these dramas are strangely reported:

The Synoptic Gospels report that Jesus, asleep in the boat, is awakened and stills the wind and waves—the Gospel of St. John omits this incident. St. John's Gospel does, however, report His walking across the water, as do other Gospels although the versions differ greatly: the Gospel of St. John does not report that Peter walked out upon the water to meet Jesus, nor is this mentioned in the Gospel of St. Mark which Moffatt says was the first composed and "tradition" tells that it was based "upon Peter's reminiscences."[3] In the Gospel of St. Matthew, the report states that Peter walks out upon the water to meet Jesus.

In the Gospel of St. John it is said that Jesus made the disciples embark alone because He perceived that the people were about to seize Him to make Him a king, and that when the terrified disciples agreed to take Him aboard as He approached them walking upon the water, the boat "instantly" reached land.[4] The instantaneous reaching of land may be compared to awakening at a touch as reported in the account of the transfiguration. An enigmatic passage follows:

> Next day the crowd which had been left standing on the other side of the sea bethought them that only one boat had been there, and that Jesus had not gone aboard with his disciples. . . .[5]

The concern of the crowd was to know how Jesus got to the other side. As Jesus perceived they were about to seize Him to make Him a king, He may again have "hidden Himself" by inducing in them and the disciples hallucinatory-blindness, so that moving in the midst of them He entered the only boat that was there and was in the boat as the disciples suffered their vision of Him walking upon the waters.

The important point, however, is that toleration of such variations in the reports indicates that visionary experience with Jesus could not be conveyed in uniform terms because it was not uniformly suffered. In the view of this study, the disciples were in trance and remembered the experience only as commanded to remember, and Jesus commanded such magnitude of diversity in the disciples' remembrance in order that man would come in time to accept the demonstrations for what they appear to be: visionary illumination, mental mirages so clearly pictured as to be more energizing and more important than experience confined to factual happenings because they describe to man events in the "universe behind his eyes."[6]

Colin Wilson quotes Wittgenstein: "There is indeed the inexpressible. This *shows* itself; it is the mystical."[7] In the illusory miracles, Jesus demonstrates the inexpressible, leads His disciples into the realm of the visionary. Wilson insists that the mental giant must be a mystic—speaking of Rimbaud, he says: "Reason for him, as for Blake, meant 'single vision and Newton's sleep' . . . 'I accustomed myself to simple hallucination' . . . His achievement remains: it can be summarised in his phrase: 'One makes oneself a visionary . . .'" [8] As Wilson points out, "Nothing was ever *discovered* by logic. All things are discovered by intuition, as the lives of the great mathematicians and scientists prove again and again." [9]

Jesus included His disciples in visionary experiences. He appears to have realized the role intuition plays in discovery of truth, and that use of extrasensory perception to visualize what cannot be verbalized leads to a grasp of such truth as is too significant personally and too infinite in its involvement with the world and others to be put into words. But He also symbolizes through these demonstrations that, necessary as extrasensory perception is to the development of consciousness, man's greatest danger lies in exercising it, for this leads him onto the deeps of the inner world and up to the fearful heights of mysticism. They *show* the extremities of psychic life: the exaltation of the soul, sinking in the deeps of being, falling from the heights of realization. The terrifying temptation to fall that seems to drag one into the abyss is known to anyone who is fearful of high places. There is a psychic parallel: one is tempted to fall into the abyss of insanity as he reaches the heights of realization and there is much to suggest that he must drop into the pit, suffer at least an insane moment, if he is ever again to reach the common ground of consciousness.

Boehme writes, "When I go upward I have no giddiness at all; but when I look back and would return, then am I giddy and afraid to fall." Nietzsche puts it, "Not the height, but the drop is terrible. That drop where the glance plunges down and the hand reaches up . . ." [10] To the aspiring solitary, Zarathustra says:

> A day shall come when you shall see your high things no more, and your low things all too near, and you will fear your exaltation as if it were a phantom. In that day you will cry: All is false.[11]

Wilson says that the "Insider is the man who blinds himself" to chaos, but the Outsider is the man who has faced it, is facing it, as the inward climb enlarges one's sense of the abyss: ". . . higher consciousness imposes new strains, and the men who have the greatest sensibility often wish they could get rid of it. . . . They are half afraid of it. They are afraid of insanity." [12] Wilson comments that Wittgenstein "probably lived on the border of mental illness, and was always afraid of being driven across it," and that he failed because he "could never resist the temptation of the intellect." [13] The temptation toward madness that coincides with the temptation of the intellect to explore the deepest reaches of life is seen again as one reads:

> Steppenwolf's first comment in Hesse's novel is that when a man has embarked on the life of the mind, he has left the solid land of the physical world, and may easily steer himself into insanity. But the life of the mind, even if it brought about the Fall of Man, is the road to becoming more than man, and it must be embarked on. As opposed to the life of the body . . . it involves living in a different world . . . of spiritual perception.[14]

In the world of spiritual perception, away from "solid land," the illusory miracles take place. In this world man becomes more than he was as he falls from the heights, sinks toward the abyss of madness, and through this ordeal grasps the hand of truth. The illusory miracles *show* the coming or awakening of the grace of God in man— this is the mystery, permeating every great religion, which cannot be explained. Dr. D. T. Suzuki, Zen Buddhist, says "It is not something that one man, even after he discovers it, can tell another. Each must grasp it himself. . . . The process is abrupt, discrete . . . an act rising from self-nature itself which is the Unconscious." [15] *Satori*, an intuitive grasp of things, comes as *Prajna* lays its hands on emptiness—but this involves, or is, a paradoxical process, an intense spiritual experience that dispels intensity as it enhances life and enlightens consciousness.

Wilson makes an astute comment: "Man does not know the extent of his own greatness until he has been introduced to it through some intense spiritual experience, which has the effect of freeing him from his own stupidity. . . ." [16] Rank also glimpsed the irrational hinterlands of the psyche—he spoke of it as vital experience:

> It takes place at a psychic level deeper than rationality, and its result is a sense of connection to life that extends beyond the present moment in all directions of time.[17]

Rank said that through this vital experience "the individual finds a 'new soul,' not quite literally but in essence"—or one might use Adler's term, an awakened "social feeling" which, as Progoff explains, "links man not only to others of his species but to all creation." [18] Progoff says that Adler found himself unable to describe this profound experience, for it "could not be brought into existence by a conscious decision in rational terms. It was not something that could be accomplished on an intellectual level.

It had to be experienced in order to be known." [19]

If the psychic travail were confined to men of genius it would be extravagance to discuss it in this study, but psychologists have found that such experience is well nigh universal, although the form it takes varies widely. Kierkegaard saw that every human existence *that does not know itself as spirit* is in despair, and that every means man has of "coping with despair, short of religion, is either unsuccessful or demoniacal." [20] Pascal emphasized "that the men who seek most feverishly after pleasure —the men who look as if they are most happy—are actually the most deeply miserable." [21] Rank's culminating insight was: " 'Man is born beyond psychology and he dies beyond it but he can *live* beyond it only through revelation, conversions or rebirth.' . . . There is no rational substitute for each man's experience of his own soul in the light of immortality." [22] Jesus, in His discussion of rebirth with Nicodemus, says of the Son of man:

> He that believeth on him is not condemned: but he that believeth not is condemned already, because he hath not believed in the name of the only begotten Son of God. And this is the condemnation, that light is come into the world, and men loved darkness rather than light, because their deeds were evil. For every one that doeth evil hateth the light, neither cometh to the light, lest his deeds should be reproved. But he that doeth truth cometh to the light, that his deeds may be made manifest, that they are wrought in God.[23]

In the view of this study, Jesus, speaking as symbol of the Authority-Ego in man, indicates here that anyone who does not know himself as God-Son, and live as best he can in the spirit of truth and love that this acknowledgment imposes, is condemned to be brought by the light within him to suffer self-judgment which involves such psychic travail as may destroy his world: his sanity; and until this psychic reaction occurs, he will suffer the unconscious despair of the godless that expresses itself in evil doing. But His words indicate, too, that the person who seeks to live in the spirit of truth and love, and seeks to know the truth of himself in being, will also be brought to the light of self-judgment in order that the power of the God-Son within him to save his world, or sanity, may be made manifest to him; and once this psychic reaction has occurred, he will bear witness to it in his work or deeds, expressing through them his religious conviction.

Anton T. Boisen, Congregationalist minister, pioneer in religious psychology, and author of *The Exploration of the Inner World*, died in October, 1965. Reporting Boisen's death, *Time* says that his "own mental difficulties (he suffered from schizophrenia) led him in 1936 to advance the theory that 'certain forms of mental disorder and religious revelation are closely interrelated' . . . ."[24]

Each man's experiencing of his own soul as he ventures upon the deeps of his being, each man's suffering the temptation of the intellect to explore the heights and depths of good and evil, leads to psychic travail that varies in degree from nebulous, mongering anxiety to the horrifying prospect of beholding madness in himself. No description of what happens can meet with general acceptance because the pattern of response to psychological stress and the symbols employed to describe it will vary. The drama may not play itself out to any reportable conclusion; it may reach its end in agonizingly slow motion; it may be so confused one cannot remember it; it may happen spontaneously in a flash of realization that brings one through it with a sort of baptismal "gasp"—or it may come through the plodding of conscience in seemingly unrewarding labor, or through the wrestling of an intellect that will not "let go" until the "angel blesses."

Conrad Aiken chose the word *Gehenna* to title his short piece which describes the disintegration, the granularization, of one's soul as it struggles in the watery depths—or when the selves that make up a man stand as naked entities in the mirror of consciousness, each an independent existence.[25] Some men describe the horror in terms of self turned leprous, and all men are seen to be lepers—life itself horribly corrupted by man's penetration into the deepest reaches of the mind. When intellect tears apart good and evil, and consciousness beholds each standing naked, the one is seen to be as terrifying as the other: neither is human. In that moment one knows that every person is involved in the *unspeakable*, and thus he must abhor them even as he abhors himself as author of his every relationship or knowing of another.[26] It is then that he sees: ". . . the appalling Horror standing erect in the Holy place." Its insanity is more than he can bear: it is his own face hapless, freed of all save crazy pain confronting unveiled fear. Only through self-blinding to it can the then "seeing" regain his tolerance of self or brother man.

In this hour, only the psychic action that Jesus called judgment can save one's inner world, his ego-group, from madness. Jesus spoke of judgment in a paradoxical way, in contradictory terms:

> It is for judgment that I have come into this world, to make the sightless see, to make the seeing blind.
> . . . it is not I who judge him; for I have not come to judge the world, but to save the world.[27]

The last statement tells what judgment accomplishes; the first statement explains what judgment actually is: a psychic process through which understanding is evolved and one makes his peace with life: the "sightless" see that the corruption of the outer world, past and present, has its counterpart in personal guilt and suffering within the inner world of each individual, that each is both torturer and tortured, both helpless and insensately cruel or cunning. But this extension of self into involvement with the evil of all time accomplishes a spiritual transformation—or can. In the agony that blinds one to the leprous in himself and all others, a new face is born upon him and upon each of his fellowmen—his every contact with humanity is healed, his sanity or inner world is saved.

He has understood, finally, that the *human*, the commonplace, is divine, that man can be neither good nor evil—he can be sane or insane, and sanity is more precious than life itself. In the act of judgment, he grasps the grace of God, understands it to be: sanity. He becomes a disciple of the Authority within that revealed unto him the hypocritical self-righteousness of anyone who judges any other man, the world, life, as evil. The act of judgment humbles him, not before the world, but in his own heart—it leads him to love not just his own of family and friends, but his fellowmen, and this engenders his abrupt turning from arrogance to mildness—it leads him to see of himself and of all others what Sartre puts so well:

> I am never any one of my attitudes, any one of my actions. . . . Perpetually absent to my body, to my acts, I am despite myself that 'divine absence' of which Valéry speaks.[28]

Not Jesus, but a man's own "divine absence" is his judge. Jesus says, "He that rejecteth me, and receiveth not my words, hath one that judgeth him: the word that I have spoken, the same shall judge him. . . ."[29]

The Word, "I," the Logos in man, is a definite sounding in an authoritative voice that is one's own—and yet is apart from any of one's selves. At the heights of exaltation, if one will but listen, this voice will speak and lead one down, or in the midst of inner tempest, if one will but call, this voice will speak to calm the storm. It may not speak such words as can be remembered; it may sound as lightly as a whisper; or it may reverberate like thunder through consciousness as it calls one back from the abyss of madness. The voice sounds through one. It does not come from consciousness, nor superego, nor ego-group—these are in the sinking boat engulfed in fear—nor does it lodge in consciousness, and thus it cannot be captured in the personality world.

One who has heard it knows it to be *sane*, to be the grace of God, given a man—his own of it—it is the "I" of himself lifted up, drawing his ego-group together into a communicable sanity in the ranks of Homo sapiens. One who has heard it becomes as a child again, his own world saved from the inward chaos he faced—". . . without form, and void; and darkness . . . upon the face of the deep." [30] It is then that the Spirit of God moves upon the waters to save one's sanity. And afterwards, it is blessed to be an ordinary soul. Whitman voices this:

> I have perceived that to be with those I like is enough,
> To stop in company with the rest at evening is enough,
> To be surrounded by beautiful, curious, breathing, laughing
>   flesh is enough. . . .[31]

Not all men suffer the blinding-seeing action of judgment as acutely as it has been described—not all men need to suffer it so acutely. Those humble in their hearts as they confront the mystery and miracle of life have suffered it—those who are peacemakers have made their peace with themselves and their fellowmen as they suffered it—somewhere, somehow, perhaps mildly day by day, perhaps in a forgotten past. Jesus says that no man escapes the fire of the discipline[32]—the blinding fire that purifies the heart so that one sees God round about him and the promise of life fulfilled in the living of it.

The height of consciousness or the reach of intuition measures the depth into which the mind plunges. Of those who survive the ordeal in sanity, many evidence a change in personality that shows itself as renewed humor, humanity, humbleness, tolerance, and a willingness to serve truth and man whatever the cost to oneself or family as though the ability to continue one's work is in itself the grace of God, and the work bears witness to this. Others fear their work and turn away from it as though to continue their exercise of the intellect would be to blaspheme again the Holy Spirit of life itself. But in his life or in his work the man who has suffered and survived the psychic fall expresses a conversion of religious proportions. In the lives of men of genius one often sees a montage of these reactions, but they cannot or dare not describe what happened to make them do an about face.

Wilson points out that Whitehead was a mathematician and scientist of formidable qualifications, and says:

> It is one of the miracles of the history of philosophy that a man who began as an "abstract philosopher" should have ended by expressing the attitude of the prophetic visionary. . . . "The self-confidence of

learned people is the comic tragedy of civilization. There is not a sentence which adequately states its own meaning. There is always a background of presupposition which defies analysis by reason of its infinitude. . . . [Whitehead].³³

Consider Isaac Newton. He "appears to have had what we would now call a nervous breakdown. On recovering, and until his death thirty-five years later, he did very little further work in science, turning more and more to theology." ³⁴

Consider Julius Robert Mayer, whose work "definitely suggested *a general equivalence and conservation of all forms of energy,*" but his imaginative, "almost metaphysical" essay was at first refused and his work went unrecognized for almost twenty years—"During much of this time Mayer suffered from a severe mental disorder. . . ." Eventually he recovered, but no longer engaged in creative work.³⁵

Rimbaud renounced his genius and his writing career. The title of his last book tells the story—Wilson says, "If *A Season in Hell* is really his last work, there is irony in the fact that the book is a recantation of his previous 'errors,' and was intended to be a 'new beginning.' " ³⁶

Goethe did a strange about-face: after his youthful leadership of the "storm and stress" group when his *Werther* sentimentalizing the whole tendency toward self-destruction was so acclaimed, it was some time before he could again trust himself to use his creative capacity—Priestley says, "when so many roads led the way to dreamland or madness, he had to create his own world in which to create his own work," and that he represented more than the sum of his accomplishments, "creating his works within the larger containing act of self-creation." ³⁷

Consider William Law. It was not until after his brilliant works, which demonstrated his intellectual powers, had been completed—after his reading Boehme—that the "Shavian controversialist" completely disappeared and he retired to lead a semi-monastic life, producing then the "works which are now generally recognized to be his greatest: *The Spirit of Prayer* and *The Spirit of Love,*" in which as Wilson points out, "The atmosphere is one of devoutness and humility." ³⁸

There is no better example of man's inner violence culminating in a grasp of the grace of God than Dostoievsky's. In the words of Marcus Bach, "He could not reconcile human suffering and divine compassion," but he "finally rose from the 'purgatory of doubt by the grace of God whom he had condemned.' . . . When he lay dying he said he regretted most leaving the world before he had fully expressed himself." ³⁹

Johan August Strindberg, Swedish dramatist, suffered a "mental breakdown" and "emerged with a deeper interest in religious themes," using much symbolism in his later drama. Priestley says that he "may have been saved from the madhouse by the playhouse," [40] but his work speaks for itself—the grace of God delivered him and returned him to his work. The "blinding" and then the "seeing" of St. Paul is suggested in the title of his trilogy, *The Road to Damascus*.

In the field of drama, another genius has taken an unexpected turn. In the picture, "The Virgin Spring":

> God makes his first miraculous intervention in the world of Ingmar Bergman. . . . The development described in Bergman's work seems to have been realized in his life. . . . friends have noticed a new mellowness in the man. . . . Life, he cries, is the meaning of life. "Step by step you go into the darkness. The movement itself is the only truth. . . . The most dangerous ways are the only passable ones." [41]

Wilson says, "The chief problem of life is not to learn how to think correctly, but simply to live. The thinking capacity cannot march forward on its own. Like a mountain guide, it is tied by a double rope to its companions, the emotions and the body. It can go so far and no further." [42]

Today, the thinking capacity in man has moved too far upon the deeps of life on its own—too many live on the verge of psychological collapse. What happens to the overextended intellect? Whitehead named the "misconception which has haunted philosophic literature throughout the centuries"—he called it *the notion of independent existence*.[43] Something more than a mind at the end of its rope is indicated in these words—the seed of the insanity men fear is planted in his statement. The fear of being in an independent existence drives one mad—madness is "mental solitary confinement."

In the history of thought there is one concept that places a man in a truly independent existence: the concept of Messiah as only Son, Himself God-incarnate, one man alone among men—the concept that, in the view of this study, Jesus gave His life to destroy, insisting that the Christ is not an independent existence, but is in every man.

How did the concept of life in independent existence enter consciousness? It appears to arise from the *unconscious*. A sense of independent existence overcame Rousseau—Priestley says his genius exploded from the *unconscious*.[44] Rousseau's experience of this appears to be curiously like St. Paul's conversion. As Priestley describes it:

> . . . on a hot summer day on the road to Vincennes . . . in an instant . . . he lived in another world, he became another man. Great truths descended upon him in a torrent; he saw in a flash his life's work. . . .[45]

And Priestley says, when Rousseau was dying, "after suffering for years from persecution mania, he thought himself 'alone on the earth' and condemned to be alone for eternity." [46] This is Messianic delusion—Messiah, *the only one of such kind ever to be,* is the one alone on the earth and for eternity. This is also such madness as can be limited only by death.

Insanity appears to be a state peculiar to Homo sapiens. In *Wild Heritage,* Sally Carrighar writes, "Insanity is a human development. So far as we know, animals in the wild do not have mental illness; except for brain injuries and infections, all are sane." [47] From whence in nature's sane world does man's distinguishing characteristic of susceptibility to madness come? Does this susceptibility cast the clue that man's mind is offspring of a mind that does not express itself to the full in any other form in nature?

Is madness the culmination of evil that man must know if he would become as God with dominion over evil, over himself, his flesh, his life? Must he know madness in order to be "salted," immunized against this, the final expression of evil, so that there remains to him only the possibility of expressing it at the minimum whereupon it turns to good, becoming the ingenious in the mind that man is? Must death remain a part of life until man is no longer susceptible to madness, evil's culmination?

As Jesus speaks of evil's culmination, He says, "for the sake of the elect, those days will be cut short." [48] Death cuts them short. There is enough "elect," superego, in every man's conscious domain to insure his death. One caught up in the notion of an independent existence is one who fears himself to be alone, unique, among mankind, which at the extreme translates itself into the fear that unless he insures his death he cannot or will not die. This is the fear he cannot acknowledge, the fear he represses that converts itself to persecution mania, the fear that forces martyrdom of mind in madness, or of body in psychosomatic symptom, or of person through society's mechanisms. This appears to be the secret fear that besets the Messianic minded—the fear they themselves are unconscious of or cannot afford to voice if it is recognized. Thérèse Neumann innocently reveals it.

A woman cannot exactly lose herself in the classical delusion that she is Messiah. The epitome of Messianic-being she can express is the stigmata—more women suffer it than men. Although Dr. West says Thérèse Neumann probably resorted to trickery, he credits the case of Louise Lateau to be valid—the Belgian Academy of Medicine passed a resolution affirming the reality of the phenomenon.[49] Although Thérèse Neumann's story, as told by Albert Paul Schimberg, cannot be accepted by this study without some reservation, and a good deal of self-deception on her part may be involved, there seems no reason to doubt that she suffers the stigmata. In a vision, she heard these words, "You must be a living and providential witness to the supernatural realities," and one sees the revelation of the Messianic's fear in her prayer—"For herself she makes no request, save only that she be permitted to die." [50]

The man who undertakes to "tell us all things" also pretends to Messiah's role, and consciously or unconsciously seeks to insure his message and his death by demanding martyrdom. Wilhelm Reich is a good example. Sydney Harris says that Reich had no doubt "seized a piece of truth by the tail," but like the "unfortunates in mental hospitals," he thought he possessed all the "secrets of life. . . ." When almost seventy years old, he invited his imprisonment, where he died a year later.[51] Truth is as the mustard seed: it grows so large that consciousness can neither contain nor express the whole of it. The truth bearer's growing failure in this regard shows itself as increasing irrationality in expression until insanity overcomes him, else he attempts to encompass his realization in symbol, form, or word that will act as panacea, mysteriously conveying all he cannot tell and has martyred his mind to search out. As society rejects, ignores, or fails to understand his work, he unconsciously, or in a subtle manner, demands persecution in order to force society to deal with his realization through dealing with him. Through his persecution his message is given a wide audience and he is relieved of *being* the "imperishable truth" he is unable and yet compelled to convey.

A man committed to Messiah's truth-bearing task begins to fear that he must drink Messiah's cup: that he must die as he finishes his work and gives it to the world. It has become his life, and he must give his life in order to seal and escape his work and to let it escape his fragile personality. As he realizes the truth of a sudden intuitive insight, fear grips him: he feels power draining from himself into his creation—when he finishes or hands over his work, as though a time bomb had exploded in his subconscious, he meets death head on. Until he is willing to die for his creation, he cannot afford to finish it or, if finished, to publish. Copernicus follows this pattern: he withheld his work for years and died as it was published. As truth bearer he must also harbor the very real and justified fear that society would martyr the man who challenged its treasured delusions. Kierkegaard also follows this pattern: when he finished the pamphlets titled, *The Instant,* he collapsed, and two months later he was dead. Barrett says Kierkegaard's thinking had "become an existential deed, as powerful as a blow of the fist. . . . here the thinker stands and wills to stand thoroughly and absolutely rooted in his situation." [52]

These words describe the Messianic-minded. They also describe Jesus, who showed in His death drama the height and depth of Messianic fear and gave the answer to its madness: fear itself is the killer of the man who fears he will and must, or will not, cannot, die. Is this not fear questioning:

. . . My God, my God, why hast thou forsaken me? [53]

Stauffer points out that this Psalm, or prayer, is directly related to Messianic theology in the time of Jesus.[54]

Fear turns the blood into a heavy mass from which a serum issues—it produces the state of shock that brings on death. As the side of Jesus was pierced, "water and blood came forth." [55] Fear kills. Man must bear this cross, fear, if he would die. In that terrible cry, Jesus loosened the phantom of fear on His body. He had suffered all He could if He were to fulfill the Scriptures which said that no bone of the One to come would be broken. At this point He must show not only that the end of Messianic pretension is unconscionable fear, but also the truth that Son of man, true Self, goes from this life an unbroken glory. Did Jesus fear that He could not die quickly enough to fulfill this prophecy? He needed to die quickly —He loosed fear upon Himself and died quickly. Labeled the height of Messianic delusion, "King of the Jews," Jesus put the question that by its asking reveals Messianic pretension and the Messianic expectation of His day to be false. He cried out its fear and broke the mold. Then He said: "It is finished. . . ." [56] What was finished—His torture, life, or the work He undertook to do: destroying the Judaic pattern of Messianic expectation?

God has forsaken the man in Homo sapiens' generation who cannot die—but God has not forsaken any man, nor did He forsake Jesus. Each comes into this world harboring sufficient fear to insure his death. But on the cross Jesus also showed that at the very end faith overcomes fear and that the Father is there—"Father, into thy hands I commend my spirit. . . ." [57] Thus life passes through death but not into it.

St. Paul's theology hinges on Jesus' statement that the Son of man has come "to give his life a ransom for many." [58] Old Testament prophecies indicate that the ransomed are the righteous, but St. Paul says that Jesus gave Himself "a ransom for all, to be testified in due time," [59] and Caiaphas says, "it is in your own interests that one man should die for the People, instead of the whole nation being destroyed"—it is added that the high priest did not say this of his own accord, but that a prophecy might be fulfilled.⁶⁰ Neither Jesus nor the prophets say that the Christ comes to give His life a ransom for the People, enlarged in St. Paul's view to be the purchase of man. The question becomes—who are the many, the righteous, the ransomed? Are they not those compelled to be Messianic truth bearers who loose their Legion not upon society, but upon themselves?

From the cross, or from the depths of madness, a man may give to the world only a cry that relates unconscionable fear and madness to Messianic pretension, as did Jesus, as did the man in the grip of Legion, as did Nietzsche. Barrett says that Nietzsche "split himself in two" by attempting to deny the Christian in himself, letting the symbol of Dionysus possess him intellectually:

> In the end, however, the symbol of Christ proved the more potent; and when his unconscious finally broke irremediably into the open, it was Christ who took possession of Nietzsche, as shown by the letters written after his breakdown which he signed "The Crucified One." ⁶¹

Nietzsche tried to tell the world the truth he realized too late—he could speak only symbolically, only through the revealing signature which, in effect, says, "*Ani hu,* I am he." This signature reveals his Messianic delusion, reveals also that from the *unconscious* the Christ in man comes to redeem through death one's inner world lost in madness because intellect attempted to tear good and evil from their enduring embrace. Like all men who give themselves in the service of truth, the symbol Nietzsche himself becomes is greater than all else he expressed: from the depths of madness he gave voice to the reality, the truth, he had crucified his mind to find and share—the Christ, *same* as the Christ in Jesus, is in man. "*Ani hu.*"

Priestley speaks of Pascal and others like him, ". . . so bent on torturing themselves and yet so often . . . greatly gifted, courageous, noble at heart, who will continue to appear and to suffer, sometimes to the point of self-destruction, until our Western civilisation discovers a religion that can ultimately contain it, giving it both a basis of thought and emotion and an ample framework of living." ⁶² By living the role of Messiah and dying to finish it, Jesus ransomed the righteous—those who hunger and thirst for the truth of life. That is, He relieved them of the necessity to be Messianic, to unwittingly or deliberately grasp the cruel role and drink its bitter cup, for He and the men who established His work, bringing forth the Bible of human consciousness, have completed Messiah's task. By calling Himself the same as the least person on earth, Jesus repudiates the independent existence of the Christ. He saw truth itself incarnate in every man, thus relieving any man of the necessity to convey the whole of it.

Jesus linked the independent existence of Judaic Messiah to the temptation He suffered at the height—thus, He prays: "Lead us not into temptation, but deliver us from evil." Again and again, Jesus links the word, temptation, (or tempting) with the Messianic role.[63] His prayer might be paraphrased to read: "Lead us not into Messianic delusion, but deliver us from the madness engendered in our search to know, to be, good, God, incarnate." To know truth forever tempts the intellect; to know God or holiness forever tempts the intuition. Jesus saw that man's consciousness of God is revelation of God-being within him, saw that it is truth incarnate in him that poses always the temptation to grasp and know it, leading the mind to higher consciousness until fear engulfs. Jesus understood that such power as truth engenders must be shared to be had or tolerated in sanity. He saw that because each man is independent in his being, he will come to realize his independent existence and must struggle with this madness until he can grasp truth larger than his solitariness: the Fatherhood of God insuring the brotherhood of man, *the Christ within himself as his indestructible bond with the whole of life* insuring his communication and communion with each other human being, making him a free agent in a social whole wherein every person on earth has the *same* endowment of power, glory, and truth at his disposal when his conscious and *unconscious* domains are summed—the Beatitudes project this summation.

Whatever a person is, whatever he does, the seed of God he bears will come to flower should he but "sleep, and rise night and day," although he knows not how this happens: Jesus says, "the earth bringeth forth fruit of herself; first the blade, then the ear, after that the full corn in the ear," and this is harvested—so it is with the kingdom of God within man.[64] Upon this realization, one is reborn in consciousness—the need to save man from himself or to save the outer world has left him, and for his own sake he labors humbly in truth's vineyard, awaiting the grace of nature, knowing that life has given itself, its voice, to man, for man.

In acting the thoughtless fool a man mocks his voice—and man mocks God in trusting mundane wealth rather than inward riches. He mocks God in the notion that a pious demeanor hides hypocrisy or avarice, and he mocks Him in the comic tragedy of intellectual pride that leads to judging the world or another.[65] If one calls his brother "fool," [66] he has taken the first small step in judging life that leads to a season in hell, to the rise of unconscionable fear that engenders madness, else to judgment that reborns his consciousness in the fire of pain that is the blinding-seeing action.

Whatever the form this rebirth takes, as evil culminates in the mind there is "sore misery." [67] But just as a woman's sorrow comes with labor and afterward she "remembers her anguish no longer, for joy that a human being has been born in the world," [68] so when a person's travail is over, his joy is great that himself as a *human* being, a brother to mankind, has come into the world. He remembers not the anguish, but he remembers the meaning inherent in the appalling Horror he has seen within himself as he undertook to judge the world—Jesus indicated this when He said, "Get thee behind me, Satan," [69] as Peter urged upon Him the worldly view of the Messianic mission.

Messianic missions are Legion. But there is a difference between Messianic pretension and Messianic delusion. Messianic *pretension* involves a host: every degree and type of deceit and self-deception that leads one to exercise the will to power, to express self-aggrandizement, or self-righteousness. Messianic pretension is often expressed in self-defense when feelings of inferiority convert into a compulsion to play the "superior" role. The pretender's importance swells in his own eyes, and he becomes more and more aggrieved as he fails in his attempt to command and exercise authority beyond his ability or willingness to do the work and assume the responsibility attendant upon the executive role. He veils his failure in mounting suspicion and in excuses that transfer the blame. Messianic pretension is also veiled by taking on the reformer's role, attempting to right the world or simply to deal with the mote in a brother's eye— unmindful of, or refusing to acknowledge and deal with, the beam in his own eye,[70] which all too often turns reformer into persecutor even as he insists that he is being persecuted, that destiny handed him his role. In Messianic pretension, a man's Legion is loosed upon others, upon society, but it is also an agony to himself.

Messianic delusion, on the other hand, involves every degree of compulsion to be truth bearer, and one's increasing awareness of his inability to reveal *all* leads to the cup of self-sought martyrdom—this, at the end of a course his own grasp of truth has led him on and will not allow him to turn his back upon.[71] Such a man's Legion is loosed upon his own mind and body. Society can take or leave his work as truth's accord in men prompt them to accept or reject it.

Messianic delusion or Messianic pretension can overcome any cup-bearer who proffers truth or attempts to open the doors of perception for others. For example, Dr. Cohen discusses the dangers in using hallucinogens (LSD, etc.), not only to the patient but to the *therapist*. He says that an "unusual number of those dispensing these drugs have themselves come down with psychiatric disturbances," manifested in various ways, among them "megalomaniacal ideas of grandeur. . . . Those who have had latent notions of omniscience can become privately or expressly convinced of their own pre-eminence." [72] Thus, "Only well-adjusted therapists without personal needs to play God will be unaffected by the potency inherent in the situation." [73] Instability to begin with, and consumption of fabulous amounts of the drugs are also cited as causes. In the view of this study, however, the "strange malady," or "peculiar disorder" which Dr. Cohen says might be called "therapist breakdown," [74] can be understood only when it is recognized that everyone enfolds within his being the Christ, God-head; thus, he comes sooner or later, in one way or another, to express this power pathologically, if he does not accept its *reality and universality*, expressing it in terms of humanity toward men and the brotherhood of human beings.

Dr. Cohen says, "The intensity of the sibling rivalry among the psychedelic (mind-manifesting) prophets is striking." [75] Perhaps both Messianic pretension and Messianic delusion arise in many men because they cannot bear to be the "lesser brother"—cannot bear the idea that another person of any time or place or purpose is more important to God and life, or is more beloved of God, than they. In truth, there is no call for sibling rivalry.[76]

Most men express both Messianic pretension and Messianic delusion in what might be called the minimum degree, loosening their Legion upon their flesh—neither upon their own minds nor upon society. But as one is led to express both aspects of the Messianic role to an ever greater degree, he begins to present to the world an intellect laced with irrationality—else strangely humbled because he has suffered a rebirth of consciousness.

Because Jesus revealed the whole Messianic complex, one must conclude that He could not have understood it so well had He not at one time suffered both Messianic pretension and Messianic delusion. Only empathy gives ears to hear, eyes to see, understanding that speaks with the authority of experience. The Gospels state that Jesus *overcame* the temptation of Satan, offering Him all the kingdoms of the world,[77] and thus coinciding with the Judaic Messianic concept. Not until the ordeal was over did he undertake His ministry. Consider also that there is every indication Mary and Joseph were committed to Messianic expectation and that they fulfilled their parts according to prophecy in the belief that Messiah would be born of Mary; so that from birth the suggestion that He was Messiah was implanted in Jesus' mind. It is likely that He believed Himself to be Messiah, until He confronted madness in Himself standing in the holy place of His Messianic concept of Himself.

The close relationship between Jesus and John the Baptist, between Mary and Elizabeth, leaves one without explanation as to why John sent to know if Jesus were the Christ—unless His revelation of Son of man was so foreign to John's concept, a concept he thought Jesus shared, that he could not believe Jesus still tread the path set forth for them before their births. John's question serves to indicate that Jesus did not attempt to explain what had happened to make Him both grasp and repudiate the Messianic role.

There can be no doubt that Mary continued unabated in her conviction that Jesus was Messiah—her bewilderment and suffering must have been a cross Jesus had to bear as surely as He bore unto the end His love for her. In the Gospels, one finds the hint of cross purpose between Jesus and His mother.[78] Jung speaks of the dual aspect of the archetype mother—she represents all that is benign, but she represents also a "terrifying and inescapable" secret such as "fate." Jung says:

> Perhaps the historical example of the dual nature of the mother most familiar to us is the Virgin Mary, who is not only the Lord's mother, but also, according to the medieval allegories, his cross.[79]

Just as the child of its own accord grows into being in the womb, making the ordeal of the mother an inescapable fate, so realization of her part in the destiny of her child must grow in the mother's mind and she will suffer in her being all the child experiences. This is the parental fate: of God, of love, a fate human parent, male or female, understands only as he experiences it. In stating both that He was sent and that He came of His own accord to fulfill His role, Jesus relieved Mary of the "blame" for His fate. But He could no more relieve the agony His suffering imposed upon her than He could relieve her body of His without the ordeal of giving birth being imposed upon her. Both parent and child share each other's lives and they also represent each to the other all that is benign.

It was necessary for Jesus to both grasp *and* repudiate the Messianic role in order to become a symbol that would overshadow the growth of false Messianic expectation and wither the concept of absolute power being absolute good. Before His day, Gautama, Socrates, Epictetus, and others had repudiated and decried the Messianic concept, but to little or no avail—the Messianic role could be finished only as one played it to a degree of perfection that could not be surpassed so that no other Messiah could overshadow the seed of the concept Jesus sowed: the Christ in every human being. He could speak only in the name, "I." If a man would speak in the name of God, he can speak in no other name, for God is *one*.

The name glorified in the thunderous moment sounding the voice from heaven appears to be "I" or "it"—in effect, "I am it," the Father's name each speaks, a glory now, to be glorified again as love transfigures man. In the Transfiguration, Jesus indicates that at the height of realization when one is illuminated in his being he undergoes a metamorphosis which puts upon him the shining raiment of love, and that as this happens the body and emotions he is "roped to" will, like the disciples, be "sore afraid" —but if a man has grasped the Christ in being, this One will lead him up to the heights and safely down again—will warn him that the full meaning of this vision cannot be realized in life or so long as one is in this world, but he must nonetheless bear witness to it.

The miracles upon the waters show that if a man is aware of the Christ in being, he may call upon this One to still the tempest in his mind, and that as he ventures out alone to meet truth upon the deeps, this One will stretch forth a hand to save him as he sinks. Blake wrote a book in this short verse:

> Each Man is in his Spectre's power
> Untill the arrival of that hour,
> When his Humanity Awake
> And cast his own Spectre into the Lake.[80]

The Christ casts it own image, "Spectre," upon the lake of the mind. Because the psychic force in man both opens the heavens unto him and drives him into the desert to suffer the temptation,[81] man is at the mercy of his fear, "Spectre," until he realizes that the Christ is in the same boat with him, is his Humanity.

The mystic is apt to try to prolong his vision until, like Pascal, he feels that he has "sinned" [82]—but on the other hand, to use Wilson's words:

> The rationalist . . . is driven by a will to power over the world; a power which he is convinced that unending reason and logic can give him. . . . reason and logic may give man power over the outside world, but no power over himself. They can make him into a dictator, but not into a genius. . . . It is those deep insights into his own being that really give man mastery over himself and then over the world.[83]

Progoff says that Freud, Adler, Jung, and Rank came to know that more important than the insight men achieve intellectually is their contact with the "profound symbolism of the depths of man, the symbols in which the ultimate aspect of man's existence are reflected. As they came into touch with what is 'mythically' and inherently valid in man's life, they gained an insight of larger significance than anything they had attained analytically." [84] The insight Rank gained he stated to be the "will to immortality," which Progoff says meant to him "man's inherent need to live in the light of eternity." [85]

In the illusory miracles, Jesus created the symbolic dramas that portray man's experiencing the ultimate aspect of his being. These dramas are redrawn, or are seen piecemeal, in the descriptions many men give when commanding truth is aroused within them or when the intellect, like Peter, is sinking in the deeps of the mind. The illusory miracles portray psychic action in valid terms, and they give an insight larger than is possible in any attempt to describe what happens to the terrified visionary. If a man can grasp the Christ, as symbolized by Jesus, he will be able to withstand the psychic travail.

When one is in the midst of the purgatorial ordeal, he cannot be helped by metaphysical dissertations and systems—a more "present help," [86] a more human understanding, is required to meet his need: he must have something to turn to, a mental image of the Christ, a symbol of the grace of God in man, which will take him in hand, to which he may cling as a child. Jesus said, "he will be saved who holds out to the very end." [87] Wilson's description of an episode in Arnold Toynbee's life seems to fit these words:

> . . . in a time of physical sickness and spiritual travail, he dreamed, during a spell of sleep in a wakeful night, that he was clasping the foot of the crucifix hanging over the high altar of the Abbey of Ampleforth and was hearing a voice saying to him *Amplexus expecta* ("Cling and wait").[88]

Turning to prayer or to a religious symbol to still the inner tempest is likely only if one has had religious training as a child and prayer is a ritual with him. If, habitually, he turns away from violence, when he must suffer inner violence habit itself will stay the mind and hand from abuse of self or another. Man learned early the value of ritual and habit, demanding it as a vital part of religious training. Jesus did not offer Communion as a priestly rite, but suggested it as an act of remembrance one might make as often as he would. When breaking bread, He gave thanks.

He sought the open spaces to pray, but He went also to the temple. He observed the Sabbath, but He disengaged the ritual day from its all-engulfing regulations, stating that the Sabbath is made for man.[89] His acts show that it is to be rewarding, rehabilitating—not monotonous—it is a habit man is to keep himself, for it breaks the chain of days however he lives and relieves him of the conscious or unconscious intensity that repetition or monotony mounts. The ritual Sabbath—a regular routine of rest and change—extends and enhances the creative potential in man. But he cannot afford to do even creative work without interruption—although not in itself monotonous, in doing it the mind must hold itself intensified for long periods and this intensity expends itself inwardly, precipitating the psychic fall. Intensity grows as unobtrusively as Samson's hair, and will expend itself in violence.[90]

Each person suffers to a greater or lesser degree his own and the violence of others—often unconsciously loosening it upon himself—and in turn each expends upon others his own violence be it unreasonably or reasonably aroused. However it is brought about, and to whatever degree it is expressed, a man relieved of the violence that mental or emotional intensity engenders feels himself compelled to make an act of contrition within some framework of religious expression. He feels the need to build an altar, to consecrate life itself:

> On the spot where the beautiful virgin is brutally done to death, a spring bubbles forth from the dry land. And Bergman cries out, with the voice of the girl's father: "Here I will build unto Thee a church . . . I know no other way to be reconciled with my own hands. I know no other way to live." [91]

In this cry, read the history of Homo sapiens.

II

A man with reborn consciousness turns again to the church. The petty, conditional requirements of dogma are passed over—he is no longer "inside," captive, restive, unwilling, or lethargic, and he is not altogether "outside," too free, unoriented, apprehensive. He simply knows himself to be involved in consciousness with the church and comes to it of his own accord—that which was irrational in it has somehow withered before his eyes—for through the ages it has borne the *symbology* that came to him as the grace of God in the midst of his private hell, when intellect and superego were swamped in fear, and restored unto him the preciousness of life, of work, of sanity.

Such a man sees that the church has given him the material from which he freely fashioned his own philosophy in secret; it has played the mother role in the development of his thought. But just as the mother cannot hold the healthy adult in bondage, so theology cannot hold in bondage a reborn consciousness—the umbilical psychic cord that bound him to it has been cut. But he sees that there is no reason to deprive others of the church's mother role—it meets the need of the children of the world, is a bulwark for those unconscious of their despair, feeds the emotional hunger of man, cushions his irrationality with its own, and more effectively than any other organ in society diverts his intensity from criminal expression, allowing him to wear a hair shirt if he must, or to love life and serve his fellowmen. Be the church as full of frailty as the human mother, she is better than none.

But most important, the church allows for vicarious grasping of the Christ until the grace of God comes unto the man himself. This is essential, for a man *must grasp the Christ in another*, and realize the Christ to be in all men, before he can realize the truth of its being in himself and sustain this realization in sanity.

But when a church overstates itself, or begins to be driven by the will to exercise absolute power in life, it, too, suffers Messianic pretension, suffers the fall, and undergoes conscious rebirth. This is to say, the church itself does not die, an offshoot denomination appears, widening and dispersing religion's powers. Each offshoot of Christianity has been marked by an increasing humanity and humbleness in that it has been marked by a simplification of ritual, demand, and condition of active participation.

From Judaism, become completely introverted, domineering, and Messianic, Christianity sprang; but Jesus did not attempt to destroy the mother-lode, Judaism itself. He upheld the work of Moses and the prophets, the other voices of truth preceding Him in Judaism's history; but He appears to have realized that the religion's development had been arrested because of centuries of mental isolation and that it confronted an insurmountable impasse in its Messianic concept. His words, work, and drama also indicate, however, that the impasse a religion confronts is not broken by one with lack of faith in it—to the contrary, the impasse is surmounted by one with such faith as nothing can shake, by one who knows the religion as intimately as it can be known, by one who loves it deeply.

Because Jesus possessed a unique grasp of the Scriptures, He could sum His knowledge and experience to present a whole new answer, and He had to found a church to receive and transmit it. He appears to have realized that man must do truth's work in this world in order to fulfill his human destiny—church provides for this need.

Wilson says that Shaw, like Toynbee, saw "that civilizations invariably collapse at the point where man's power outruns his religion." [92] Jesus saw that Roman power was outrunning Roman religion—Christianity became new religious tissue both weak enough and strong enough, both old enough and new enough, to survive the collapse of the empire. Jesus founded His church upon Peter, "the rock." Peter symbolizes a union of intuition and intellect, a union seen also in Jesus' words:

> God is spirit, and they that worship him must worship him in spirit and in truth.[93]

This statement must be taken at face value, as though it read, "in all honesty and not superficially," but "in spirit" must also mean through use of the psychic power and "in truth" must also mean through the intellect's learning and composing facts into a constellation with meaning, into knowledge that feeds the ego-group as Peter was thrice directed to do—"Feed my sheep." [94] The need to exercise all one's powers is reflected in Jesus' words that to those with knowledge of the mysteries of the kingdom within "more abundance" shall be given, but to "whosoever hath not, from him shall be taken away even that he hath." [95] This indicates that worship "in truth" or with the intellect alone leads to a sterile theology as surely as worship "in spirit" alone leads to a sterile mysticism or system. Jesus' words bespeak an organization and cross action between the *unconscious* and conscious forces in man. He says to Peter:

> And I will give unto thee the keys of the kingdom of heaven: and whatsoever thou shalt bind on earth shall be bound in heaven: and whatsoever thou shalt loose on earth shall be loosed in heaven.[96]

What the intellect binds is bound: it is repressed. And what is loosened from the *unconscious* to be brought forth as knowledge, the intuition loosens. And to those who have, more is given—Einstein says that Newton "had a unique command of the empirical material available in his day. . . ." [97] and it was Einstein's abundance of mind, his unique grasp of mathematics, that permitted his attainment. A man must know what to ask, how to ask it, how to convert the answer intuition gives into real gain: into transmissible and workable knowledge. Thought provides its own food for more thought; knowledge prepares the ground for more knowledge.

There is another type cross action between intuition and intellect, a binding, loosening play. That which intuition presents to intellect as evil, and intellect binds so that it is not expressed in consciousness, is recast in the *unconscious* in truth's mold and expressed through consciousness as something of real value. Einstein provides a good example. His intellect led him to "bind" avarice within himself because intuition told him the desire to acquire more and more in the material realm was the evil at the root of the world's troubles. One sees this in his extreme aversion to wealth:

> I am absolutely convinced that no wealth in the world can help humanity forward, even in the hands of the most devoted worker in this cause. . . . Can anyone imagine Moses, Jesus, or Gandhi armed with the money-bags of Carnegie? [98]

And yet, the likes of those with the money bags of Carnegie have put books at man's disposal, and they help to build and sustain the temples of learning in which Einstein lived and worked. His intellect's denying and binding greed in himself did not prohibit his unconscious compulsion and his unconscious knowledge, that Homo sapiens' prime task is to acquire and master matter of his own, from coming into expression through him, bringing true riches. Setting himself to acquire knowledge, he found himself with a grasp of matter so far beyond the mundane as to make his an immortal name among men. He was servant of truth and therefore servant to all men: he was true to himself and therefore served humanity's needs in bringing new knowledge that will serve man. He knew how to question his *unconscious*, he knew how to work with the answers intuition handed to him. His was an intuitive, daring, and faithful mind and it was also a disciplined mind, well tutored. He realized the best that wealth can offer: the time and wherewithal to pursue the work closest to one's heart.

In Christianity's history, Peter has stood not as a symbol of man's united mental powers, but as the one to whom Jesus gave authority in arbitrating questions with regard to His church and doctrine. This, He most assuredly did, and Peter acquitted his task of founding the Christian body through which Jesus' teaching would be established. But as the power of the Church widened, so did the prerogatives it assumed—prerogatives reaching far beyond those to be drawn from this passage:

> Moreover, if thy brother shall trespass against thee, go and tell him his fault between thee and him alone: if he shall hear thee, thou hast gained thy brother. But if he will not hear thee, then take with thee one or two more, that in the mouth of two or three witnesses every

word may be established. And if he shall neglect to hear them, tell it unto the church: but if he neglect to hear the church, let him be unto thee as a heathen man and a publican. . . .

Then came Peter to him, and said, Lord, how oft shall my brother sin against me, and I forgive Him? till seven times? Jesus saith unto him, I say not unto thee, Until seven times; but Until seventy times seven.[99]

The keys Jesus gave to Peter were the keys to the kingdom within. It is here that men may be excommunicated or reconciled—it is here that things are bound and loosened—although the power of the church as a body of men to excommunicate a member from the group may be drawn from His words. But this power does not separate such a man from the grace of God, for the passage begins with the statement that it is not the will of the Father to lose a single one and it ends with a parable insisting upon man's forgiving man even as he himself is forgiven by his Lord.

In another passage it is reported that a man approaches Jesus requesting Him to "tell my brother to give me my share of our inheritance," and Jesus says to him, "Man, who made me a judge or arbitrator over your affairs?"[100] If Jesus would not take upon Himself the role of arbiter nor send the man to the church to have it act as arbiter, nor give the advice He gave to Peter, it would seem unlikely that His deepest meaning insofar as excommunication is concerned has to do with the church. The process He describes to Peter could be a dealing with the brother's image in one's inner world, for here this image lives with the ego-group and its abuse is unremitting. Dr. Alexander says that one's psychical resources are "squandered in fratricidal internal conflict."[101] The question becomes—how does one escape it?

The images in a man's inner world are the only reality he can know of the persons from whom they are drawn. Such images are so real one may at times feel himself to *be* another—and thus he can take his part in inward counseling. Certainly, through his intellect he can take both sides of the question, and what he straightens out in his own mind he can as a rule communicate as understanding which will act to reconcile the conflict. But if one cannot accomplish this, or reconcile the difference through actual counseling with the offender, he must have a means of dealing with the situation because the situation, not the person, is all he has the power to change. If in his inner world he excommunicates the image of the offender, he will present himself as faceless and will see the other as faceless, neither resisting him nor attempting to deal further. This actually alters the situation: the problem can no longer touch him personally, inwardly, because he has let go and broken its hold upon him.

THE ILLUSORY MIRACLES

An attitude is commanded at each meeting of the eyes of two people because the look mirrors the regard and usage each has of the other—one wears upon his own face a "transparency" of the other created by his feeling for him. When one loves or hates a person, he shares his own face with that person's image whenever the thought of him arises or when they come in contact. A man cannot see or show himself: as he looks into the mirror or is seen he presents a montage of his loves, hates, ambivalences, and indifferences. When a man sees "nothing" and certainly "nothing of himself" upon the face of his erstwhile victim, he knows the person to be beyond his reach in one realm of his being—he has somehow "hidden himself" inwardly. And if the offender persists in his trespassing, he finds himself as foolish as though he were flogging a dead horse or enticing a dead bird—finds himself frightened as he perceives that the "dead" one he strives to make respond is himself dead in the world of the other. If the separation of one's ego-group from the other's image and any further mental wrangling with the problem is not feigned, but is actual and complete, this changed situation will be unselfconsciously communicated—more often than not bringing about a desirable reaction.

One's own world, the personality he is creating through his experiencing of life and brother beings, is immeasurably enriched by every friend, by every one he loves—and each adds a glowing touch to his own countenance as he looks out upon the world through the transparencies of others that people his inner realm. His loves are the true riches he has stored in heaven. Love is the wealth he both takes and leaves as, in Bergman's words, death becomes "a part of life." [102] Man is compelled to probe this veil—Barrett quotes Tolstoy: "If a man has learned to think, no matter what he may think about, he is always thinking of his own death. . . . And what truth can there be, if there is death?" [103] The only truth one can present is that man knows no more from whence his consciousness comes than where it goes. And one can present only the fact of man's divided psychic domain which allows for the concept that consciousness withdraws into his *unconscious* but that life continues and in time he comes again into consciousness vested in a body.

Any possible perception of the existence of life after death can be only illusory, intuitive, but man's sense of the certainty of life has persisted through the ages. It may be openly avowed, or it may be barely suggested as Wilson barely suggests it: ". . . it remains true that, in the moment of ecstasy, as one's mistaken vision of oneself is suddenly swept away by the flood of certainty, one's feeling is of complete humility, complete instrumentality, a strong desire not to allow any of one's stupidities, any of the corrupt, earthbound personality, to interfere with the cold wash of vitality." [104] Personality is corrupt and is earthbound because it is not Self. The "stuff" of personality is the images of others expressing themselves in a man's consciousness. These images are corrupted by the man himself even as he is corrupted by them. But a better word to express this concept is the word Jesus used: adulterated. Everyone's personality is adulterated by countless others—these make up the face a person wears.

What did Jesus look like? There is no description of Him in the Gospels. But when one beholds compassion in another, compassion so candid as to be real, he has seen all that can be said of the look of Jesus; when he feels this compassion within himself, he wears the look Jesus must have worn. Has the Christ risen within him?

Chapter 15

THE RESURRECTION

I

In the field of parapsychology, researchers confront innumerable reports of the dead contacting the living and speaking through the offices of a medium. Although Frederick Marion places some spirit seances in a category beyond understanding, he states that in those which are not deliberately fraudulent, the messages from the dead appear to be picked up from the guests themselves.[1] This study concurs, and concludes that *all* nonfraudulent seances are thus understandable:

The medium goes into trance and induces trance in one, several, or all who are present, and the telepathic powers of all concerned are then heightened. The medium repeats only what is "heard" from the subliminal depths of the one who has called up an image of the dead in his own mind, asking it to speak to him. Through the medium it tells him something he already knows, though he may have forgotten it in the act of receiving the information, or it may have been telepathized to him while the dead was living but its content did not register in consciousness. Or nonrelated information may come through his own heightened powers of extrasensory perception during trance and it is presented through the image of the dead because this is the factor operative in his mind at the time. If he possesses acute clairvoyant, telepathic, post- or precognitive capacity, the mystery of what he may "hear" from himself compounds. The vague and often pointless communications most often reported bespeak the paucity of unusual or unrealized material in the subconscious of the great majority of people and their very slight ability to exercise ESP in or out of trance.

Even if there is no medium, no seance, in the intensity of emotion produced by the death of a loved one, a certain type of hallucination occurs: his voice converses with one's consciousness—memory supplying the tones, attitudes, expressions that make the encounter seem so real one is convinced he is communing with the dead. He is communing with the image of the departed, the image that lives on in his inner world. This image contains, enfolds, all he knows or could project of the person after whom it was fashioned while he was still alive. Love lays its own ghostly communing, its own ghosts—one wants to remember, but not to be haunted. Images of people associated with guilt, neurotic passion, hatred, violence, recklessness, are harder to bury in the minds of the living who survive them. Images born of ambivalence or casual knowing are soon stilled within the group but they can be activated when man is holding in mind the dead from whom he fashioned his own still-living creation of them.

The power of the images of the dead, and of those images of characters created by authors, is immeasurable. Marcus Bach met an elderly teacher in Stalingrad who credits the Russian victory there, and places his hopes for Russia's future, upon the concept that "the dead are praying" even if the living are not and he believes that God will answer their prayers.[2] Thus, the Russian who holds an image of Dostoievsky, of certain of his characters, or of Tolstoy, or Berdyaev, is praying through those images that pray. In each man who has come upon their words, a living literary-image born of their writings has its being and its say in the inward communication among the selves in man. Today, Jesus is a literary-image in the minds of mankind—His "person" is born of His words, for there is a description only of His seamless robe. To say, however, that this literary-image converses with consciousness does not explain the Resurrection.

Just as poetry can present certain mystical issues but cannot investigate them,[3] so the Gospels can present the Resurrection only in the way that a flash of lightning lights up a landscape. As one searches the reports to try to determine what actually happened, a pattern deeply involved with hallucination emerges. A closer examination of hallucination is required.

Griffith Williams points out that the Chinese ancestor worshipper induces hallucination by achieving a highly elaborated form of trance. The celebrant is "required to fast and meditate for three days" during which time he must recall the looks of the deceased, "how he stood and sat, smiled and spoke, what he liked to think and do," before the ancestor finally appears and speaks to him.[4]

But hallucination may also occur spontaneously. Sometimes another person is transformed in the sight of the percipient—at least, this appears to be what has happened. Louisa Rhine discusses the experience of a doctor who suffered such hallucination.[5] Or a thing may be suddenly transformed. Empty space may be filled with a vision, sometimes revealing information foreign to one's knowledge so that the hallucination must have been induced by reception of a telepathized image or message, or through the percipient's own clairvoyance or precognition. Most often, however, the hallucination conforms to an idea or expectation in the mind of the percipient. Under hypnosis, hallucination involving all the physical senses may be induced by suggestion, and what happens only in the mind of the subject seems so real to him that he will not believe afterward that the experience was not actual even if he is told that what he thinks he saw or did was in response to the operator's command and that in reality nothing of it happened.[6] If a group be sufficiently involved, group hallucination may occur, one telepathizing to the others, so that all behold a vision or hear a message resembling the general expectation in each mind, or resembling the telepathized image and words.

Hallucination cannot be understood by one who has not experienced it— he cannot know that seeing with the inner eye and hearing with the inner ear is *actual* to the percipient. The images within have their being in the life of the one who harbors them—when hallucination occurs, they appear and are utterly real to their host.

The important point to establish is not that the Resurrection drama derives from the hallucinatory experiences of the disciples of Jesus— there is clear evidence in the Gospels that hallucination occurred. The important point to establish is that *this, specifically, was the end Jesus said He would accomplish.*

Jesus' body was gone from His tomb on the third morning. He was seen again only in visionary appearances that had greater impact because the tomb was empty. But if He reappeared only in the hallucinations of those devoted to Him, it does not necessarily mean that His physical resurrection did not also take place: He could have roused Himself from death trance, all but indistinguishable from actual death. In the view of this study, however, this is not the answer. Many people had reason to want His body removed, and there are endless possibilities as to how this may have been accomplished—but again, it is not the conclusion of this study that His body was stolen. An explanation of the mystery is offered later. The point to be made here is that regardless of why and how the tomb was emptied, what Jesus told His disciples of His Resurrection attests that it was to be in the nature of hallucinatory, not literal, experience—and this is the way they reported it.

Jesus says, "A little while longer and the world will see me no more," indicating a nonliteral reappearance, "but you will see me," indicating an hallucinatory experience, "because I am living and you will be living too.

You will understand on that day, that I am in my Father," in the kingdom within, the *unconscious*, "and you are in me, and I am in you," indicating that the image, each of the other, lives on in his inner realm. "He who possesses my commands and obeys them is he who loves me, and he who loves me will be loved by my Father, and I will love him and appear to him." [7] One must have knowledge and love of Jesus before He can appear to him. "I tell you this now, before it occurs, so that, when it does occur, you may believe." [8] Thus, Jesus explained the hallucinatory nature of His reappearance so that the disciples might know the Resurrection to be valid: *as* He told them it would be, nonliteral but real to them.

Their hallucinatory experiences could have been prompted by posthypnotic response to Jesus' commands, for a number of times He implanted in the minds of the disciples the suggestion that He would rise on the third day; and He prepared them for the transformation of any man into an *image of Himself*—"Inasmuch as ye have done it unto one of the least of these my brethren, ye have done it unto me." [9] There is evidence of the hallucinatory transformation of another person who at first was not recognized as Jesus, then suddenly appeared to be the risen Christ.

In hallucination, sensory data take on the meaning one's own intuition vests them with—thus in the encounters with transformed persons, or in the visionary moments, the sounds heard took on the meanings, the commands, that Jesus had planted in the minds of His disciples. After His death, they evidence an intuitive understanding so wide as to be all but inexpressible, illustrated in the statement that the risen Christ opened their minds to understand the Scriptures.[10] Only a montage of the various accounts of His appearances can reveal what happened insofar as it can be told. There are four different reports of the experience of the two Marys at the tomb:

> In Matt. 28:1–10, a severe earth tremor is reported; the sentries appear to have shared both the terror of the women and their vision, for they "became as dead" in their fear when the "angel of the Lord descended from Heaven" and rolled back the stone. As the women go to tell the disciples the words of the angel—words that have arisen from within if the angel is from heaven—"Jesus met them, saying, all hail." In Mark 16:1–9 it is reported that the stone had been rolled back before the women arrived, and that they had a terrifying encounter with a young man dressed in a white robe who was sitting in the tomb. Then it is said: "Now when Jesus was risen early the first day of the week, he appeared first to Mary Magdalene, out of whom he had cast seven devils." In Luke 24:1–12, it is reported that two men in dazzling

raiment appeared to the women as they approached the tomb from which the stone had been rolled away. It is not reported that they saw Jesus; verse 23 refers to a vision of angels. In John 20:1–18, a detailed account is given. Mary remained at the tomb after the disciples had gone. "She turned round and noticed Jesus standing, though she did not know it was Jesus . . . supposing that he was the gardener." She suffered the hallucinatory transformation of this man into the image of Jesus. Although in Matthew 28:9 it is reported that the women "held him by the feet," in John 20:17 it is reported that "Jesus saith unto her, touch me not . . ."

Two other reports indicate the hallucinatory transformation of some man into the person of Jesus. In Luke 24:15–32 it is reported that two disciples met Jesus on the road to Emmaus, "though they were prevented from recognizing him." And in John 21:4, it is said, "Now at the break of day Jesus was standing on the beach, though the disciples did not know it was Jesus"—not one of them dared ask him who he was; they knew it was the Lord.

All reports of the appearance of Jesus imply visionary experience, as indicated by the italicized words in the following accounts: [11]

> The disciples gathered at the hill "where Jesus had arranged to meet them," indicating a response to suggestion. "When they saw Him they worshipped Him, though *some were in doubt*." When Mary Magdalene tells of seeing Jesus, she is not believed, but "After this, *he appeared in another form* to two of them as they walked on their way to the country. . . . Afterwards *he appeared at table* to the eleven themselves and reproached them for their unbelief and dullness. . . ." It is reported that Jesus entered *through closed doors*. And that "Just as they were speaking *he stood among them*," but the disciples were terrified and thought it was a ghost. A number of *"proofs"* reveal Him to the disciples for forty days—these proofs are not described.

Many of the reports merge quickly from visionary beginning into factual statements attesting to the reality of the encounters—for example, as He suddenly "stood among them" and saw their terror, He assured them that He was flesh and bone, ate in their presence, and led them to Bethany. But the factual encounters also end with visionary overtones—again, for example, after leading them to Bethany, He "parted from them and was carried up to heaven." Regardless of the reality these experiences assumed, once the vision appeared, in each case it is clearly implied that the encounters were abnormal, first and last. One must remember that hallucinations are utterly real to the ones experiencing them. Mitchell says that hypnotized patients "rarely suspected that they were experiencing an hallucination, however bizarre it might be," and could not believe it afterward even though they knew they had been hypnotized.[12]

This study concludes that as the disciples lapsed into reverie or went into trance in posthypnotic response to suggestion, they suffered hallucinatory encounters with the living image of Jesus they bore within themselves, else ordinary men were transformed into the image of Jesus' *essence in being*. He could show Himself after death only in the minds of living men, but through the Resurrection drama He showed the reality of life. This is to say, He showed that His words lived on and that He lived on, an active participant in the inner worlds of living men—and if His body was not stolen, and if He did not rouse Himself from deathlike trance, then He demonstrated some other power over His own flesh after death, proving that life, or the power of man's Authority-Ego to command his flesh, persists beyond death.

How did He dispose of His body? In this study, only a conjecture can be offered. The Gospels enfold a few clues from which it is drawn.

II

To fulfill the Scriptures, it was not necessary that Jesus reactivate His body after death when nature takes over and deals with it. But to fulfill David's prophecy it was necessary to alter nature's processes because this prophecy stated that the flesh of the One who revealed the Christ in man would not "suffer decay" in the grave.[13] The final problem Jesus faced, then, was the disposition of His body in such a way that His flesh not "see corruption." How did He "vanish" it? In saying that He would give only one "sign" [14]—the sign of Jonah, meaning "dove"—to this generation, He said, in effect, that He would leave but one mystery that could not be readily solved. Today, the other miracles can be identified as exertion of ESP or hypnotic power in man.

A clue pointing to the use of hypnotic response in vanishing His body is presented in His statement that He *would* "drink the produce of the vine" anew in the realm of God to which He passed over in death.[15] If hypnosis has been correctly identified as the "produce of the vine" to which Jesus referred, His statement poses the concept that He employed it from the *unconscious* domain to which one withdraws in death.

The new view of Jesus presented in this study allows for no aimless lament on His part: the miracle of His work rests upon the precision with which He stated and showed the truth of man and the limits of his power, so that His every word and act must be regarded as conveying some measure of His message in poetic form. Jesus says:

> I have come to throw fire on earth. Would it were kindled already! I have a baptism to undergo—what tension I suffer, till it is all over!

In the King James Bible, this passage reads:

> I am come to send fire on the earth; and what will I, if it be already kindled? But I have a baptism to be baptized with; and how am I straightened till it be accomplished! [16]

The baptism can be no ordinary one, for Jesus had been baptized by John. The baptism could refer to pain and death—but what then of the reference to throwing or sending fire on earth—on matter? John the Baptist has said that the Christ will baptize with the holy spirit and fire.[17] The tension Jesus suffers, the exclamation: "how am I straightened till it be accomplished!" could indicate, if both meanings of all words are considered, that in Jesus' grasp of hypnosis He projected in His own mind, or "had already kindled," a final possibility within its scope and knew that the validity of His concept of man hinged upon His success in accomplishing this last demonstration, impossible to test in life, but essential to "straighten" in unbroken chain the command of the Authority-Ego over the flesh projected into life. The throwing, sending, the sign of the dove, could imply casting power from the realm of the living *unconscious* into the flesh of the dead body to act upon it.

Jesus' words after the Transfiguration which brought together with Him the visions of Moses and Elijah were, "Tell this vision to nobody until the Son of man is raised from the dead." [18] He relates the vision to the Resurrection. Why? There is a common denominator between the three figures: the disposition of their bodies after death was strange.

Moses died alone, and there is evidence that his followers knew where, but not where he was buried, for "the Eternal buried him in the valley . . . but to this day no one knows his burying-place." [19] How did his followers know that the Eternal buried him in the valley—did they find his clothing? All that was left of Elijah was his "mantle"—"Suddenly, as they walked and talked, a chariot of fire with horses of fire drove between them, and Elijah went up by a whirlwind to heaven. . . ." then Elisha "lifting the mantle which had fallen from Elijah . . . went back and stood on the bank of the Jordan. . . ." [20] Only the body-wrappings were left to mark the spot where Jesus was laid in His tomb.

The possibility that one could evoke a rapid, all-consuming disintegration of the body into a handful of dust—an internal self-cremation—suggests itself. Asimov says of flesh:

> The major component of all living tissue is, of course, water. . . . The remaining material, however, consists in the main of compounds that are distinctly unlike the substances so common in the inanimate world. . . . The substances isolated from living tissue . . . are easily destroyed by heating. All are more or less flammable and, even if heated in the absence of air, so that they cannot burn, are nevertheless decomposed. They then give off vapors and change permanently in one way or another.[21]

Jesus says, "fear him who can destroy both soul and body in Gehenna."[22] In effect, the Son in man can destroy the soul in the fire of the blinding, seeing action of judgment that raises the "psychic temperature" to such heights one feels a burning in his brain though he exhibits no temperature physically speaking—can the Son also destroy the body through a psychic force that causes its rapid disintegration?

Although they did not vanish their bodies, many men appear to have felt the psychic fire "already kindled" within them—for example, after Pascal's death "there was found stitched into the lining of his doublet a scrap of parchment with a rough drawing of a flaming cross and a few words around it to keep alive the memory of his experience. . . . Fire . . . God of Abraham, God of Isaac, God of Jacob. Not of the philosophers and of the learned."[23] To Nijinsky, "God is fire in the head"—Yeats speaks of "Heaven blazing into the brain."[24]

Jesus' words, "I have come to throw fire on earth," could indicate that He would provoke an internal cremation that would prevent His flesh from suffering decay—and casting what might be called the "psychic fire" could pose the final test of One who would reveal the full extent of the psychic power in Homo sapiens. An "internal cremation" would vanish the problem of the body—only the clothing would remain—and such a cremation would vanish the problem by a process of racing along the same path nature travels slowly and inevitably to vanish the flesh of man. This is to say, it rests upon the possibility of speeding up the natural process which causes man to revert to "dust" so that this process is complete within three days—this through posthypnotic response to a plan in advance, wherein at the moment of death the disintegration begins its accelerated pace. Did Jesus signal the beginning of the process, accelerating its pace, in the loud cry He uttered as He expired?

An internal cremation, vanishing the problem of the body, brings to mind the ancient legend of the phoenix—and it coincides with the words, ". . . for dust thou art, and unto dust shalt thou return." [25]

Although there is nothing in the way of evidence to support the conjecture that Jesus destroyed His body by inducing an internal cremation through posthypnotic response to auto-suggestion, there is a case reported by *Time* in which a man made his plan in life to control the disposition of his flesh after death and succeeded in this effort. The report concerns a Buddhist monk:

> Chih Hang was . . . widely known as a good man, but he feared that he might be unworthy of the faith his disciples placed in him. When, on Formosa, he felt death approaching, he called them together and gave them unusual instructions. "When I die," he said, "do not bury my body, but seal it in an urn. After three years, open the urn, and if my body has decayed, bury it in the ground. But if it has not, encase it in gold and place it in a pagoda." Chih's disciples dutifully sealed their master's unembalmed body, seated cross-legged in the position of meditation, in a six-foot concrete urn, enshrined it behind the monastery near Taipei where he had spent his last days, and at once set about collecting money for the gilding they were confident he would deserve. It took them five years to find the funds. When they had the money at last, the urn was opened, and there was Chih Hang—his body considerably thinned, but firm and uncorrupted. Last week, in another shrine . . . Chih sat for his gilding. . . .[26]

Favorable natural conditions may have turned Chih's body into a natural mummy. Bodies found in the Capuchin cloister in Palermo, in the cloister on the Great St. Bernard, in the lead cellar at the Bremen Cathedral, and in the castle of Quedlinburg are all natural mummies.[27] But natural mummies may in themselves be a greater mystery than they are generally accorded to be. Most people will dismiss the case of Chih Hang—but many will come to honor this evidence that truth is often a shining stranger. And—

> A truth which was lost long ages
> ago may be sought with confidence
> in the thousand years yet to come.
> —TSUNG PING

And it may be that the tension Jesus suffered, like the tension Chih Hang suffered, was not for fear of failure in itself—it was because He knew that if He could not express and demonstrate the truth He had grasped, He would fail those who trusted Him.

If Jesus vanished His body through rapid internal cremation and appeared again, upon occasion, in the sudden transformation of an ordinary man into a representation of Himself such as was unmistakable to those who knew Him, a question will arise in the minds of those familiar with strange phenomena. Did a demonstration of Possession take place—thus validating this concept?

III

Frederic W. H. Myers defines Possession as "A developed form of motor automatism, in which the automatist's own personality disappears for the time, while there is a more or less complete substitution of personality, writing or speech being given by another spirit through the entranced organism." [28] There are a number of cases wherein such possession has been evidenced. Many of these appear to stem from what might be called a sick imagination—in many cases trickery must be suspected. Actual cases of demoniacal possession are brought on by repressions, reversed in latency, returning to take command of consciousness. Other substitutions of personality may derive when the subject lapses into trance and the censoring mechanism that limits intake of stimuli or information from the subconscious mind fails to function properly—as though the record that should have played on gets stuck in one groove—which is to say, the person is possessed by another personality only in the sense that he is possessed by what he knows of that personality and not by a foreign "spirit." In the most mysterious cases where the possessing personality is unknown to the possessed, but is recognized by others, one can postulate only that the possessed is "locked" in trance and that his own powers of clairvoyance, post- and precognition supply the necessary information—else it is received telepathically—so that again he is possessed by what he somehow knows and not by another's spirit. Mrs. Rhine cites examples in which complete strangers are involved through telepathy and clairvoyance.[29]

Jesus treated cases of possession as mental illness. But there is a passage that prompts the question—can what might be termed "benign" possession occur? As Jesus explains to the disciples the hallucinatory nature of His reappearance, Judas (not Iscariot) asks, "Lord, why is it that you are to appear to us, and not to the world?" Jesus replies, "If anyone loves me he will obey my word, and my Father will love him, and we will come to him and take up our abode with him." [30] Jesus says, "we"—not "I"—will take up "our" abode with him. Jesus appears as Christ-risen only in a few men and not in the person of any of those devoted to him and obedient to His commands; His essence in another is glimpsed but for a fleeting moment; and there is every indication that the disciples were suffering hallucination that transformed a stranger into a representation of Jesus.

But most important, the very heart of Jesus' message is that the Christ may be identified in everyone—thus, there was and is no need for Jesus to possess the body of another. But he who loves the image of Jesus cast in his mind through the Gospels' message will have the sense of His abiding presence. If a man's concept of Jesus takes possession of him so that he proclaims himself to be possessed of Him, to be a "medium" through whom He speaks or writes, or to be Jesus returned, he is suffering Messianic delusion which will all too often end in psychotic symptom as fantasy suddenly turns to fear and fear takes possession of him. Jesus warned that many would come in His name, but those who obey His commands will not believe them. Thus, His words indicate that "possession," as it is commonly described, cannot be benign.

That which is benign, abiding, Jesus refers to as the Spirit of truth which "shall teach you all things, and bring all things to your remembrance, whatsoever I have said unto you." [31] He says to the disciples:

> When the Helper comes, whom I will send to you from the Father, even the Spirit of truth who issues from the Father, he will bear witness to me. . . .[32]

When the drama of Jesus is viewed as a revelation of man's psychic working, one sees that the Spirit of truth comes to the conscious domain after the Authority-Ego has withdrawn into the *unconscious,* and that this Spirit operates through the superego. Observe, too, that the words of the Christ in man must come into this world through the lips and by the pen of superego, for Jesus wrote nothing and His words before and after His death are presented only as the Spirit of truth brought remembrance to those who heard them. The voice of one's Christ may sound through him as an inward hearing, but the words are delivered by superego to consciousness and then to the world as the Spirit brings remembrance.

The purity of the revelation in the Gospels depends upon the purity of the remembrance of the disciples and upon their passing along only Jesus' words, and not their elaborations. Very little of their own material is interpolated; and because man can remember accurately what is imparted to him when he is in trance, Jesus' message could come to posterity with what may be called a minimum of adulteration by the superego's interpretation in the men who wrote the record. Jesus could not write His own record if He were to present through His drama this function of the Spirit of truth working with superego.

Jesus says that there is much more to be imparted than He attempted to tell, but that the disciples, superego's symbol, cannot bear it. What "I" comprehend is of such magnitude that only a portion can be communicated to, can be apprehended by, Homo sapiens. In parallel, one can impart only so much to a child. Thus, when a man questions beyond his ability to comprehend life's answer, or when he questions in terms too broad, or when the question itself is composed of error, truth must be given in *parables* [33]—in allegory, metaphor, or symbolic form. Jung saw that each "new content that comes up from the unconscious is altered in its basic nature by being partly integrated into the conscious mind of the observer. . . . Thus the unconscious can only be approximately described (like the particles of microphysics) by paradoxical concepts. What it really is 'in itself' we shall never know. . . ." [34]

Because what can be imparted through a man's superego and what can be apprehended by Homo sapiens' consciousness is limited, one might say that as the Spirit teaches and brings remembrance the translation of its message by superego suffers the limitations suggested by the mathematical theory of communication—that is, when overmuch information as to past or future is sought or given, meaning is sacrificed. When the question is composed of error or is hopelessly wide of the mark, the "noise" arising from error incorporated in the question gives rise to undesirable uncertainty as to the value of the answer, because it must incorporate the asker's fantasy just as an algebraic problem posed in a given set of symbols must be worked using those symbols. Whether the Spirit is questioned as the intellect ponders a problem, or whether it is questioned when an operator asks information of a person in trance, the answers that come will incorporate the conscious commitments, imagination, and subconscious knowledge of the person or persons involved.

Jesus chose as disciples men who were neither intellectuals nor mystics. He could commit them to the one simple task of conveying His message —of asking the Spirit of truth, in consciousness or in trance, only for that which it can do: to bring remembrance of His words and drama as He had implanted in their minds the story He wished to be recorded in the written word.

But the Spirit of truth in Jesus, too, must speak through His superego as He went into trance and let "I" reveal itself through His voice. His revelation is so pure and is eternally fresh in meaning because in consciousness He was completely committed to the *natural* in life and to the discipline of mathematics which is born of the self-discipline inherent in the number *one*. Thus, His parables follow nature's path or the everyday channels of living in any age, else they are couched in the "language of arithmetic" which everyone can understand. His voice speaks only in terms of *certainty in being:* "I am" now and "I was" before the world was and "I will ever be." Very little description of past or future is given.

Jesus did not attempt to explain what it is like to die or to be dead. The most that can be said is: if life moves through death onto another plane, or into the *unconscious,* or into the womb, this cannot be described in terms that consciousness can apprehend, for such a state must needs be "Absolutely Elsewhere"—different from any concept consciousness holds, needing words to describe it that consciousness does not possess. Jesus simply said that to God all are living. As for the dead contacting the living, He told and demonstrated all that can be told or demonstrated: there is nothing objective about it—the communion comes through and from the mind of the one who seeks it, expects it, and already *knows* what he seeks. Contact is possible because "you are in me and I am in you"— each is living in the other's world and can communicate in terms that are meaningful because what is told is what is known or can be known as the Spirit brings remembrance.

A man who possesses Jesus' commands and obeys them will look to present problems, will bring his psychic and conscious powers to bear in a healing and teaching ministry, and will be committed to the ethic of love. Jesus says, "the road that leads to life is both narrow and close, and there are few who find it." [35] He warns of the danger of the broad approach. From the ground of the subconscious there must be one-only way to enter into the realm of Word-power in the *unconscious*—no man can tell another exactly how to do it. In this realm, Word-power, the power of speech, operates hand in glove with the Spirit of truth which allows man upon occasion to "speak with new tongues. . . ." [36]

There are many cases of people in trance spontaneously speaking foreign tongues or in technical terms so foreign to them that they constitute a new language—one of the most thought-provoking involves a mentally retarded child. Ashley Mixson, psychologist at the Kentucky training home for the mentally retarded, says:

> "How can I explain a retarded child who can . . . read from my French book and pronounce the words better than I can?" Bobby arrived at the training home in 1957. . . . "All he could do was walk, sleep and read [English]. He couldn't feed or dress himself." Authorities say Bobby can read Latin, French, German, Spanish and Turkish. . . . Does he understand what he is reading? Officials at the home do not know.[37]

Bobby, ten years old in 1962, could read names in the telephone book when he was three or four years old; he can read the American Journal of Mental Deficiency, pronouncing correctly the medical terms. Neither telepathy nor clairvoyance can account for his ability to make the sounds, to speak Turkish script written on a blackboard. Nor can any sensory or intellectual factor explain the mystery, and this study does not attempt to explain it. But Bobby's case does bring to mind and to this discussion Barrett's explanation of Heidegger's philosophy which deals with word-power in man. Heidegger proposes that speech depends upon silence as much as upon words. Barrett explains:

> Nor is the silence merely a gap in our chatter; it is, rather, the primordial attunement of one existent to another, out of which all language—as sounds, marks, and counters—comes. It is only because man is capable of such silence that he is capable of authentic speech. If he ceases to be rooted in that silence all his talk becomes chatter.[38]

Barrett explains—"Men exist 'within language' prior to their uttering sounds because they exist within a mutual context of understanding, which in the end is nothing but Being itself." [39] What is the "silence" Heidegger speaks of if not another name for the *unconscious* domain?

Bobby is rooted in this "silence," in his *unconscious*, in his being. He does not communicate with others, but he exists "within language" and thus is capable of authentic sounds although he may not understand these sounds which must be regarded as "chatter" on his part until he gives evidence of grasping their meaning. If this is the case, it would appear that one must be rooted both in his *unconscious* AND in consciousness before authentic speech is possible.

Going in and out of trance as regularly and evenly as one breathes may be prerequisite to authentic speech. The infant and young child moves in and out of consciousness, spending more and more time away from sleep until he has struck the balance seen as normal in the durations between sleep and waking and between awareness and unawareness of his environment. As he begins to live a conscious existence, he begins to speak and to live in two worlds—his own and the outer.

Heidegger sees that a person exists in "untruth" and also "in truth"—he says *existence* means to "stand outside oneself." [40] This study would say that as consciousness of self and environment evolves, a person begins to exist in the conscious domain *and* in the *unconscious*. Consciousness means to stand outside oneself, or to stand outside the "I-substance" that *is* at the center of "my field," which makes possible communication with oneself and upon this, communication with others depends. But "my" *existence* does not depend upon "my" ability to communicate nor upon "my field" of consciousness. When the door to the *unconscious* is closed, "my" speech becomes chatter—but when "my" existence fails or ceases to be rooted also in a field of consciousness, "my" speech also becomes chatter.

Heidegger sums the relationship of existence and essence in this sequence of ideas: revelation, light, language.[41] The opening verses of the Gospel of St. John present a mirror reflection: language, light, revelation. Jesus realized that man exists in language—in the beginning was the Word. He saw that an existence "in truth" and "in untruth," in being and non-being, in light and in darkness, in freedom toward life and toward death, is a child's existence: the child both is and is not man. Homo sapiens is child-man, bearing the promise of life, the Being-Word, "I," which brings the revelation and is truth, light, radiating to consciousness. Thus, Jesus saw, as Heidegger does, that "Truth and Being" are inseparable, are always given together.[42] Upon the plateau of Heidegger's philosophy, twentieth-century metaphysics rests.

As Barrett points out, however, one question always remains—there is no sufficient reason to explain WHY man or the universe exists. In answer to the whole question of being, Jesus offered the one word: love. Love itself is a mystery that returns one to consider again the whole subject of possession and being possessed—by love, through love, and by the desire for love's expression in one's life and being.

IV

The Christian thinks of life after death in terms of heaven and hell—the only desirable aspect of either as a place of residence is the promise of reunion with those one loves. Consider, however, that what one knows of another identifies that person in his mind, but that one's knowledge of another represents only a fragment of the other's being. The personality he attaches to a loved one is not carried by the person from whom it is drawn—this personality is a valid representation of that person only as he exists within one's own inner kingdom. The problem of reunion is vanished when one realizes that his eternally cherished loves are carried onward within himself and that part of his being is himself made of all he has loved and held dear in experience.

Life offers countless loves—as many as there are relationships. But however dearly one loves another, he cannot merge his inner world, his very being with another—life or death separates. All he can possess of another is the image of him that lives in his inner world and enfolds the essence and meaning of all he has experienced through the association. Through these images love becomes "my" being—"I am my love in being, I alone know what I love and thus I alone know, have, am reason for my being." Because the beloved's living image is a part of self-in-being one may love another *as himself*, but he cannot possess another, either now or in the hereafter. Barrett expresses Sartre's view of sexual love:

> The lover wishes to possess the beloved, but the freedom of the beloved (which is his or her human essence) cannot be possessed; hence, the lover tends to reduce the beloved to an object for the sake of possessing it. Love is menaced always by a perpetual oscillation between sadism and masochism: In sadism I reduce the other to a mere lump . . . while in masochism I offer myself as an object, but in an attempt to entrap the other and undermine his freedom.[43]

In saying that one's human essence cannot be possessed, Sartre reaffirms the First Commandment: "I am the Lord thy God. . . . Thou shalt have none other gods before me"—or in Jesus' words, "Thou shalt love the Lord thy God with all thy heart, and with all thy soul, and with all thy mind. This is the first and great commandment."[44] As symbol of "I" in being, Jesus shows in His drama that this factor does not marry, and His words indicate that the complete joy of love is not to be had in the outer world. Thus "I" being in man cannot be possessed nor would it possess other than "Thou," the ego-group or soul to which it is eternally and completely committed.

The twentieth century's own prophet, Kahlil Gibran, teaches that one's love is never lost, and that in truth love can express itself only as one retains his independent being:

> Aye, you shall be together even in the silent memory of God.
> But let there be spaces in your togetherness,
> And let the winds of the heavens dance between you.
> Love one another, but make not a bond of love:
> Let it rather be a moving sea between the shores of your souls.
> Fill each other's cup but drink not from one cup.
> Give one another of your bread but eat not from the same loaf.
> Sing and dance together and be joyous, but let each one of you be alone,
> Even as the strings of a lute are alone though they quiver with the same music,
> Give your hearts, but not into each other's keeping.
> For only the hand of Life can contain your hearts.[45]

Lust—not love—is expressed in a dependency that must possess and feed upon another even as it offers itself to the existence it claims. Lovers try to consume the very-Self, each of the other, until the psychic law of singleness reasserts itself and the lover's parasitical consciousness is spent, their lust transformed, reborn as love, so that the true value of their union comes to them in the new coin of affection, rapport, compassion, empathy, humor—in sum, as a companion-sense which contains the immeasurable treasure of one's own love: himself regained. Only one who is independent can truly love and possess himself sufficiently to have something to offer, something to share.

Most people are for awhile "possessed"—not by another's spirit—by their own lust. Some do not recover—to them sexual expression must be forever disillusioning as they sublimate it, miscall it love, depend upon it for their sense of identification in and with life. Sexual hunger is lust—nature's divine lust for life. It is good for man to be possessed by it for awhile. In its expression the "bit" is tithed that comes in time to lure him onward in life, and his aggression attenuates to laughter which mixes with lust so much more happily than pious sublimity. This possession is what might be called nature's "bit" of insanity which is good in being, for it leavens the burden of bearing life. Theodore Reik writes that romantic love "has a certain affinity to insanity. . . . But it is doomed to perish. Then a transformation must take place—affection and rapport move in to take over." [46] Nature insists upon romance: the plant flowers first, then enfolds the seed.

But it matters not how rewarding one's experience with another, it matters not how deep the affection, how complete the rapport, that takes over when romance is transformed—love's longing is not satisfied in this life. Is "I-being" the immortal love each soul seeks and can find in no other person? This is to say, man's unfulfillable longing in this life is born of his psychic division: he is dimly aware of another Self of himself. Man senses that his soul is the feminine complex in his nature—Herbert Spencer writes: ". . . his soul was frozen to her depths. . . ." [47] But man senses also that at the core of his being there is the masculine component —the Sufi mystic says:

> I am he whom I love, and he whom I love is I,
> We are two spirits dwelling in one body.
> If thou seest me, thou seest Him,
> And if thou seest Him, thou seest us both.[48]

Speaking as symbol of "I-being" in man, Jesus says, "Abide in me, and I in you"— but "I-being" in man would not turn him from experiencing love in this world, for Jesus follows with these words: "This is my commandment, That ye love one another, as I have loved you." [49] Nevertheless, He teaches that only as one abides in himself, with "I" which is immortal love's expression in him, can any experience in Homo sapiens' consciousness bear rich fruit.

Just as the child cannot love beyond the limitations imposed by his immaturity, so Homo sapiens cannot love beyond loving another *as himself*. As the beloved's image becomes a part of himself in being, the beloved's essence is experienced, but not possessed. Like a child, Homo sapiens enfolds the promise of knowing a different kind of love as he reaches maturity. With whom will he know it, share it? With the incomparable of himself made of *all* he has known of love. Nothing other can satisfy him eternally and be perfectly at home in his own world and being. This is not to suggest that the hope of reunion with others is false. It is to suggest that each becomes an eternal and essential part of another who has loved him, and he will recognize himself in that person; just as another he has loved becomes an eternal part of himself, and will recognize himself as an essential part of one's own love. One *keeps* one's loves. As to that which he loses, in Shakespeare's words, "Nothing of him that doth fade, but doth suffer a sea-change into something rich and strange." [50] Beyond this, the "dimensions of heaven" cannot be mapped.

This study offers only the concept that man's first creative act is to fashion from his life experience a complementary-being: a personality he truly loves, born of and incorporating all he has loved. The idea is suggested in the symbolic emergence of Eve from Adam. It is expressed in the intuition that describes God: "Let us make man in our image, after our likeness; and let them have dominion . . . ." [51] And the idea appears in Revelation—the New Jerusalem comes down from heaven like "a bride adorned for her husband." [52] Jesus likens the returning Son of man to a bridegroom coming to his marriage.[53] Boehme expresses it:

> . . . suddenly my spirit did break through the gates of hell, even into the innermost moving of Deity, and there I was embraced in love as a bridegroom embraces his dearly beloved bride.[54]

Wilson says that as an awareness of one's own godhead arises suddenly, the remote God the Father "becomes an immediately sensed God the Brother. The image of the bride and bridegroom also arises naturally, for the flood of energy is like an impregnation." [55] Did Shakespeare experience such as this? Priestley says that *Antony and Cleopatra* begins as would a moral tale, showing how worldwide order is disrupted by middle-aged passion, lust, and folly:

> . . . then suddenly, when all is lost and the tale almost told, the moral is swept aside, the great verse, whose very intensity proves the presence there of the poet's whole personality, rises triumphantly, finding immortal words for immortal longings, now transforming passion, lust, folly, into love: the dying wanton queen cries, "Husband, I come," and is woman . . .[56]

Does the dying Cleopatra call out to immortal love within herself, "Husband, I come"? In describing the strange and unattainable quest of the Romantics, and especially of Rousseau, Priestley presents the hint that one's true love emerges from within: ". . . there arise from the unconscious certain strange symbolical images of the other sex, images that may be vague but are still illuminated by the green and gold of the depths . . ."[57] Guillaume writes of the mystics: "A Persian used to cry 'Glory to me' during his ecstasies and claimed to have ascended to Heaven in a dream. . . . Lover, beloved, and love are one."[58] Junayd, the great Sufi mystic, taught that "though man died to himself he did not cease to exist as an individual, but his individuality or personality becomes perfect through God and in God—Junayd's pupil Hallāj taught that "God is love, and in his love he created man after his own image so that man might find that image within himself and attain to union with the divine nature . . . indwelling. . . ."[59]

William Ernest Hocking writes that death brings "a oneness with the One. . . ." and that this would be "at once self-recovery, remembrance, and the continued lure to create through love in ongoing time."[60]

This study makes no attempt to suggest the manner in which the development of one's complementary-being might be accomplished. The postulation is that man is to possess a new *sense* of being: a companion-sense in life born of love itself. This conjecture is drawn from the words that come in response to Jesus' request, "Father, glorify thy name"—"I have both glorified it, and will glorify it again."[61] Today, man senses his "I-being"—in some tomorrow he will sense "us-being" when the love he has known in life twice glorifies him.

Julian Huxley makes no such postulation as is made above, but he does say:

> For man to fulfil his destiny truly and effectively, the first step must be one of discovery. He must learn to recognize and identify the systems of transformation operating in reality, the nature of the self-creative process as a dynamic organization, its form, and the modes of the transformation of that form to new and richer forms; and in particular the particular transformation now under way.[62]

In the spirit of Huxley's words, this study offers its concept of an evolving companion-sense born of love expressed in life in consciousness. Certainly, as man comes into conscious possession of his *unconscious* domain and its power, which he shows promise of doing, he will no longer be as Homo sapiens is. A new species may thus be envisioned, a species in which the Legions of evil in Homo sapiens' generation will have been drowned in the seas of memory.

No man in Homo sapiens' generation can map the dimensions of what life can sustain, what it holds forth in promise, for he is only partially conscious and only a part of his brain appears to be at work. Thus, in eternity's light, his life and any life he can imagine appears to him an insufficiency, is an insufficiency—but in his psychic division rests life's promise. As he comes into this world he faces unfinished and unpresented problems, laboring under the necessity to achieve perfect control of self in life before, or as, his kingdom comes to him.

In the view of this study, the final question posed by Barrett cannot be answered objectively—it can be answered only to one's own satisfaction by his satisfaction in being. The question of one's own life is vanished in the solving of a multitude of problems even as the mystery of death remains, becoming a beckoning-on that leads one to meet the morning glad to be alive, willing to do its work to earn a measure of satisfaction until, finally, death becomes the goal.

> Even as a man will cast aside
> His tattered garments, taking
> New vesture, so the body's lord,
> Old, tattered forms forsaking,
> Endues himself with fresh attire
> In forms of newer making.[63]

Let this, then, be the evening song and epitaph:

> The day shall not be up so soon as I
> to try the fair adventure of tomorrow.[64]

V

This study has presented much to suggest that the power vested in man which may take possession of him, or be released through him, is beyond that which reason can deal with. The intention is not to present shocking concepts—it is to state that there are possibilities which have not as yet been widely voiced, if voiced at all, inherent in the power man has glimpsed through practice of hypnosis as well as in parapsychological research and experiment with consciousness-changing drugs.

When one finishes writing or reading such a discourse as this, a feeling that it is all a fantastic fiction comes over him, bringing with it an urge to dismiss the whole subject. But there follows a piercing sense of the reality of hypnotic phenomena, the reality of the mass of evidence that attests to ESP's operation in humankind, the reality of life, the reality one faces: death must come. In the great majority of humankind the conviction persists that death is not the end of being—consciousness of "I-being" has led man to proclaim the existence of God and his own relationship to Him.

The compelling task presents itself: man must strive to understand himself and his natural powers. Julian Huxley says:

> We need a science of possibilities. Such a science will take account of the limitations of reality as well as of its immense potentialities. As an immediate step, we need a new science directed to the investigation of unrealised human possibilities.[65]

He is not referring specifically to ESP, hypnosis, or any aspect of parapsychology, although these subjects are not excluded; he is saying that man "must accept what is given in the universe . . . we must not deny the reality or validity or significance of any elements in it." [66] Dr. Ian Stevenson remarks upon the number of men who reject ESP without investigating the original reports of the parapsychologists engaged in the work:

> Certainly the implacable opposition parapsychology encounters among some scientists illustrates again the relationship between the heat of antagonism and the possible threat to established convictions from the new data or ideas. For the data of parapsychology portend, I believe, a conceptual revolution which will make the Copernican revolution seem trivial in comparison.[67]

Other avant-garde thinkers, such as Gerald Heard, echo this conviction.[68] The mounting evidence will not be ignored, but as research in hypnosis and in parapsychology enlarges it will become ever more important to remember that in no other field are the data so prone to misinterpretation—self-deception must be guarded against. Jung warns that one may easily and innocently err in favor of his parapsychological experiment—"I know . . . from long experience of these things that spontaneous synchronistic phenomena draw the observer, by hook or by crook, into what is happening and occasionally make him an accessory to the deed." [69]

Something in man prohibits or thwarts his efforts to use his psychic powers experimentally. Jesus would not "perform signs." Throughout His ministry He leads man to exercise his conscious powers. But He exercised His psychic power as the real need arose, and He practiced hypnotic therapy in the medical ministry.

To try to prove through experiment and to the satisfaction of scientists the presence of the Christ in man may not be possible. Nor is it the intention of this study to propose that twentieth-century man could or should attempt to determine the limits of the power to be released through hypnosis. Everything in Jesus' teaching indicates that fulfillment of hypnosis' possibilities depends upon fulfillment also of one's possibilities in the conscious realm and upon his religious conviction—his faith in God: as Father, as Son in man, as love, as life operating under and responding to a perfect principle.

The sickness besetting man's soul cannot be healed by medical science or by hypnotherapy—this illness is caused by loss of religion, which gives rise to a decline in one's sense of purpose and meaning in life, and to unspoken despair. In the words of Sir Julian Huxley, the new "science of possibilities" must eventually be "matched with a religion based on the idea of fulfillment of possibilities . . . ." and he adds, "Never was there greater need for a large perspective . . . Yet, paradoxically enough, never was there a greater possibility of attaining so large a perspective, and attaining so firm and enduring a belief." [70]

To the twentieth century, Jesus' words still say: "If thou canst believe, all things are possible to him that believeth. . . ." [71] And like the father of the tormented child, this century cries out and says with tears:

Lord, I believe; help thou mine unbelief.

Today, as always, "mine unbelief" is the sickness that must first be healed.

The concept of Jesus presented in this study does not hinge upon acceptance of the conjecture as to what happened to His body, which is offered to provoke thought upon the furthest reach of hypnotic response when one is in deepest trance, or *at* death. Among other possible answers, Jesus could have roused Himself from deathlike trance; but if so this study holds that He also immediately disposed of Himself in a way that His flesh did not see corruption in the grave, giving His life to complete His work and fulfill prophecy as He said He would. The conclusion to be accepted or rejected is: *Jesus' Resurrection was as He told His disciples it would be*—visionary but real to those who experienced it.

Chapter 16

RETURNING TO THIS WORLD

I

This study accepts the principle of man's rebirth into life, of his returning to this world in virgin flesh to live again and again until his empathy is complete; but it holds also that after the empathy to be evolved from life in this world as Homo sapiens can know it is complete, man will not be reborn into Homo sapiens generation; and thus because Jesus' empathy was complete He will not be born again into Homo sapiens generation.

Much has been written of Jesus' coming at the apocalyptic end of the world—but His own words refute the concept of His returning to this world again in recognizable form. He speaks primarily in objective terms of the coming of "your Lord," or of the Son of man, saying that many will come in His name, but they are not to be believed: do not believe it when men say He is "in the desert" or in the "secret chambers." [1] He gives no clue as to how He, as person, may ever be recognized again.

Because Jesus thus eliminates the prospect of His expected return to this earth and yet speaks of the returning Son of man, this study postulates that as symbol of the Christ He returned in the Bible to become a living literary image in the inner worlds of all who read His words. But this concept must be posed against Chapter 24 of the Gospel of St. Matthew, wherein Jesus foretells the destruction of Jerusalem's temple, and answers the disciples' question as to "what shall be the sign of thy coming, and of the end of the world?"

Jesus' reply may be read in terms of the afflictions the disciples would suffer before He appeared again in the first written record of His work which came onto the scene as unobtrusively as a "thief" in the night, so that "in such an hour as ye think not the Son of man cometh." But so, too, does death. Thus His words may be read in terms of the "end of the world" coming as death overtakes one. Death is that mysterious force that takes but one woman of the two grinding at the mill, and of two men in the field takes one and leaves the other—"Watch therefore: for ye know not what hour your Lord doth come." Jesus says the Son of man comes on the clouds of heaven—and heaven is within. Since for each one the end of the world comes with death, the Son within him must come to him at this moment.

Jesus' reply may be read also in terms of His own death, of the Son in Him coming as the sun suffered eclipse and an earthquake rent the temple—and His words may be read in terms of the fall of the Roman Empire and the darkening of civilization into the strange "night" that separates modern and ancient history.

Jesus describes all the conflict the world would know and then says, "Immediately after the tribulation of those days shall the sun be darkened, and the moon shall not give her light, and the stars shall fall from heaven, and the powers of the heavens shall be shaken." These words may be applied to the end of one world of consciousness, but other words presage birth—"as were the days of Noah"—and thus Chapter 24 of the Gospel of St. Matthew may describe the psychic travail of conscious rebirth that accompanies the collapse of any individual's temple of conviction when his old world is being swept away and only by enduring great anguish unto the very end of the struggle is his sanity saved.

The whole of the chapter, however, must also be read in universal terms—in terms of the planet upon which man lives and in terms of each age, each civilization of the generation: Homo sapiens. Each age see its wars and rumors of wars, its treachery, its desolation, its earthquakes in divers places, its eclipses, and celestial bodies falling in what appears to be a shower of stars on many nights when the "heavens declare the glory of God. . . ." [2] And each age sees the destruction of its mightiest buildings as well as the destruction of its temples of thought. But Jesus' words indicate that these recurring catastrophes will mount in intensity until they culminate in tribulation greater than man has ever known, greater than he will ever know again.

Each age feels itself to be the one in which tribulation culminates, presaging the end. The twentieth century may well be the one that has seen, or will see, the culmination of conflict. Realm rises against realm, the fixed principles of past ages fall, the heart grows cold and desolate as a desert when men look ahead and see the forces that turn men to "criminals or lunatics, or both" [3] marching over the horizon. Nuclear war looms. The days of it must be cut short if a soul is to remain alive— the days of it that man has known were cut short, and he may now have known all of nuclear war that he will ever know. Can worse than nuclear war come? Must Jesus' words be read in terms of the coming of another cosmic catastrophe such as ages past must have seen?

As Velikovsky shows, the legends of all peoples describe cataclysmic events, clearly associated with the action of celestial bodies, that gave rise to worldwide upheavals.[4] Too much evidence supports Velikovsky's theory of near-collisions between this planet and other celestial bodies—resulting in an altering of earth's orbit and axis which gave rise to sudden climatic changes, to displacement of seas, and to an altering of the planet's motion that perforce caused man to alter the calendar and methods of time-telling—to deny categorically that cosmic "clashes" did occur and may occur again. It is, nevertheless, difficult to envision that life could have survived if the legendary descriptions of these events are not exaggerated, and if Velikovsky's interpretations of the legends are altogether correct. As one attempts to appraise these legendary descriptions he must remember that myth is a *poetic* conveyance of fact and that a phenomenon produced by other than celestial forces may be enfolded in the story.

For example, although the legend of Joshua may bespeak a celestial event, it may also bespeak a phenomenon produced by trance—which is to say, the sun may have stood still only insofar as his perceptions were concerned. In trance, one's sense of time may be slowed or hastened, and if slowed the mind can work in one minute clock time a mathematical problem it would require an hour clock time to work in consciousness. Trance may have given Joshua's mind the time to solve the problem by permitting him to experience precognitive clairvoyance wherein there was rolled out upon the field of his mind the whole play of battle and this seemingly took hours, but as he awakened from a moment's trance he saw the sun still high in the sky—time enough to win the battle—and the legend of this victory enfolds his own sense of the distortion of time, of the sun's standing still.

But many of the miracles of the Old Testament, especially those attendant upon the days of wandering in the wilderness, do not need either trance or Velikovsky's interpretation to satisfy the question of the reality of the happening. For example, Keller presents evidence that manna did and does today fall in the desert, much as this is described in the Bible.[5]

The point is, the fact that legends exist and reach back into the dawn of consciousness shows that conscious life has not perished in the cosmic upheavals of the past. And although Jesus indicates that this world would know great tribulation after His day, He also indicates that the end of the world is not coming as the progeny of men who experienced cosmic upheavals would expect it: in another "clash" of celestial bodies which may have threatened the life of the planet in the past. And He indicates that the days of the worst travail man will know will be cut short so that Homo sapiens will survive all the ordeals nature may pose, as well as those that man may precipitate through war.

The question of Jesus' return is not fully satisfied, however, by saying that He re-appeared in the Gospels. If His words are true, He came back. Although in the view of this study Jesus *will not* be born again as Homo sapiens, He *was born again* during the lifetime of the disciple John; He must live and die again to lose through infant amnesia His memory of Himself as Messiah, burying it forever in the potter's field provided for each personality as resting place for that of oneself he cannot bear to live with; and He must harvest in another life cycle the good and evil sown and experienced in His own life. But He would not have had need to live long because His empathy was complete. The concept of His rebirth is drawn from His words on the cross, "To day shalt thou be with me in paradise" —Eden, womb of life. Thus, Jesus could have returned in an unrecognizable way, at an hour the disciples thought not. All that can ever be known of His person is in the Gospels.

Whatever may be in store for this planet or for man, Jesus preaches the one gospel of life everlasting and this in individual terms. Thus, the problem confronting man is to learn how to live with himself and his fellowman.

Whether or not a person has answered to his own satisfaction the metaphysical questions that confront him, the morning always returns him to this world and the business of the day. This brings to the discussion the whole question of economics—a question involved, as John Maynard Keynes saw, with every aspect of living so that no part of man's nature or his institutions lie entirely outside the regard of the economist.[6] Thus, to reveal the truth of man, Jesus must reveal the economic principles which operate in accord with the nature and need of man. His doctrine must be measured against the doctrines of *The Worldly Philosophers*, as Robert Heilbroner titles his penetrating history of economists from Adam Smith to Joseph Schumpeter. In the following chapter, therefore, the economic doctrine of Jesus will be examined, and posed against what man now understands of the processes and principles involved in economic life.

Chapter 17

THE ECONOMIC DOCTRINE OF JESUS

I

Jesus, economist, appears to have seen that the course man's nature leads him to follow traces the same economic pattern, whatever the name he gives his operation. He espoused the principles upon which an ethical and dynamic economy could operate to leaven, not to level, life in this world, whatever the political superstructure might be. He acknowledged the need of government, commanding man to support it in the brief and telling words of the poet, which also point the way to good government—to man's social obligation and to society's obligation to man as individual.

But before His worldly philosophy can be examined, one must survey briefly the political and economic scene today, for these two aspects of life are inseparable. And yet, the need today is to distinguish between economic principles and the various forms of government under which these principles must and will operate as surely as man must and will operate both the economy and the government whatever the name he gives his system.

Every underdeveloped nation in the world faces the need to industrialize, and every developed nation faces the need to assist in this process, for its own sake if for no other reason, even as it deals with its own problems that industrialization and affluence pose. Whatever the political organization of the nation, the industrializing process is the same: resources which would otherwise be used to satisfy immediate wants must be freed to build capital. However little the nation has, it must save something—this "saving means the freeing of labor and the resources from consumption-goods production so that they may be applied to capital-goods production." [1] Capital is measured in industrial equipment: in machine tools that are necessary to build the machinery that increases production, in means of transportation, of generating power, of irrigating land, and increasing agricultural output, etc. Such capital must be acquired, and the laboring force must be educated in the use of these means. This is the first step.

Today, a number of political systems and economic ideologies vie with each other to show themselves the best or only way to achieve the goal of industrialization. So desperate is the need as large segments of mankind strive to meet the demands of exploding populations and deal with a worldwide awakening to the need for economic progress and social transformation, that the tendency is to advocate any means that will quickly accomplish the goal. Faced with mounting nuclear power and mounting numbers of impoverished, illiterate people in bondage to their own stultifying traditions, both developed and underdeveloped nations face an unprecedented crisis in the history of human affairs—and there is no one answer as to how to resolve it and evolve beyond it.

Thus, this study takes issue with Teilhard when he says that to accomplish the next step in the evolution of consciousness and society, man must undergo a process of "social organisation" to be identified with totalitarian political systems and collectivization, for he writes:

> In the totalitarian political systems, of which time will correct the excesses but will also, no doubt, accentuate the underlying tendencies or intuitions, the citizen finds his centre of gravity gradually transferred to, or at least aligned with, that of the national or ethnic group to which he belongs. This is not a return to primitive and undifferentiated cultural forms, but the emergence of a defined social system in which a purposeful organisation orders the masses and tends to impose a specialized function on each individual. . . .
>
> In short, everything happens as though, in the course of its phyletic existence, every living form achieved (with more or less success) what may be called a period, or even a point, of socialisation. . . .
>
> . . . we cannot continue to exist without undergoing the transformation which in one way or another will forge our multiplicity into a whole. . . . Seen in this light the modern totalitarian regimes, whatever their initial defects, are neither heresies nor biological regressions: they are in line with the essential trend of "cosmic" movement.[2]

It must be pointed out that Teilhard recognizes the danger inherent in proposing collectivization and totalitarian rule to be the answer for the whole of mankind. He says:

> Man is not an insect. Nothing is more pathetic than the total and blind devotion of an ant to its ant-hill; and to us nothing could be more deplorable. The ant toils without respite until it dies of exhaustion in a state of complete self-detachment whose absolute nature and "faceless" purpose are precisely what we find repugnant. . . .

> ... the socialisation of the human mass becomes a retrograde step and a state of monstrous servitude—*unless* we can discern in it the birth of a new "shoot" destined eventually to bring forth stronger individualities than our own. Only with this reservation, and within these limits, is the phenomenon to be tolerated. Collectivisation in itself, no matter what form it may take, can only be a provisional state and one of relative unimportance.[3]

This did not prove the case with the ant. Perhaps because the whole "ant mass" collectivized, extinguishing thereby the example of any other way of life into which the creatures might emerge when their monstrous, faceless servitude had served the purpose of establishing them firmly in industry.

To say that the "human mass" must *undergo the process of socialization* is to ignore the simple fact that Homo sapiens is a social creature and has never been without social organization insofar as his history can be read in the existing primitive peoples collectivized in tribal societies, and in the libraries of the world. From the time he appeared on the scene, he has been in the process of socialization and his progress has been marked by the refinement and evolution of his social organization.

All political ideologies and economic systems are "mutations" of ancient forms. Today's collectivist societies may be seen as the rebirth of tribal, primitive economy in more sophisticated form in response to the stress of the times, and collectivization is a means to accomplish industrialization at a cruelly fast pace. Today's fascist societies, the dictatorships, may be seen as a rebirth of the early absolute monarchies in more sophisticated dress. Dictatorships, too, are a means whereby industrialization may be accomplished at a rapid pace, but they are also a means by which the revolution this entails may be postponed. What they achieve depends upon what those in power desire to accomplish. These regimes have much in common with totalitarian collectivist societies; but they also have much in common with democratic-capitalistic societies, and they cannot one and all be lumped and called "good" or "bad." Today's democratic, representative, or constitutional systems that draw their authority from the law of the land are, to greater or lesser degree, *socialistic;* and they, too, are a rebirth in more sophisticated terms of the ancient system of men counseling to direct the affairs of the tribe. Such societies tend to develop with, or as a result of, the successful development of a capitalistic economy that operates more or less along the lines of the market system.

Each of these three types of government is authoritarian to some degree. Government must be authoritative to exist and fulfill its functions. Each type of government operates to some degree a planned economy. Men pay lip service to the notion that one type cannot coexist with the other. In the blunt and honest terms of Nikita Khrushchev, there is no other alternative—they will coexist or all will perish. Any doctrine formulated before the day of "the bomb," any doctrine that has to do with world domination of ideology, system, or nation, is hopelessly outmoded. Men on both sides of many curtains cling to notions incompatible with the realities they face. Either a substitute for "victory" must be found, or the "pre-bomb" concept and ideal of victory must itself undergo a transformation.

This is to say, no more than all nations and all men can tolerate totalitarian communism can all nations afford a representative, democratic government operating for the most part a free market economy. All nations do not have the *human resources* to establish and maintain such a system: their rich and educated are too few and are unwilling, their poor and uneducated are too many and are unable to function effectively. Facing the problem realistically, Heilbroner writes:

> Above all, an effective policy requires a change in the official attitude of America toward "socialism" in the underdeveloped world . . .
>
> On the capacity of the West to overcome its stereotyped conception of other societies, on its capacity to discriminate between mere oppression and purposeful social direction, on its capacity to persevere in the encouragement of development despite inevitable disappointments and failures will depend much of the outcome of the central process of historic change in our time.[4]

He sees that the United States must encourage the finding of independent solutions along indigenous socialist lines, that it must speak the "language of planning, of controls, of social and economic justice," accepting the revolutionary potentials inherent in economic development, and demonstrating to the "leaders of the underdeveloped nations that we too have our profound problems, albeit of a different sort, and that we are capable of as much political courage at home as we do not hesitate to ask abroad" —even as it takes as primary task the preservation of its own system and demonstrates "to the emergent leaders of the world that the United States is still the bearer and the guardian of the ideals of freedom in whose name it was founded."[5]

By the example it sets, each system sells itself. Both the United States and Russia, to use the one as an example of the capitalistic system and the other as an example of the communistic system, have worked economic "miracles." Each has paid a high price; each has cruel chapters in its history; each has suffered a terrible civil war; but above all each is a continuing revolution acting as catalyst to speed the *evolution* of social organization and economic society; and each is itself rapidly evolving into a form that begins somewhat to resemble the other. But in Heilbroner's words:

> This does not imply that the two major systems today are about to become indistinguishable. The convergence of economic mechanisms may blur, but it is not likely to obliterate, the basic distinctions between them. Nor does the convergence of mechanisms in itself portend profound changes in the larger social structures of socialism and capitalism. . . . we have sought to draw a careful line between the economic substructure and the political and social superstructure. . . . Hence a gradual rapprochement of the economic mechanisms should not lead us to hasty conclusions about the rebirth of "capitalism" in the Soviet Union or the advent of "socialism" in the United States. Capitalism and socialism alike exist not as textbook models but as historic societies, each with its identity, its nationality, its traditions and beliefs.[6]

Each ideology may have a role to play. Certainly, each nation will choose the way that its *own most dynamic and effective people* see to be in the best interest of the nation at its present level of development.

China chose collectivization—the enormity of her problem may have dictated the choice, and her people may have been better prepared to withstand its traumatic impact than they were to deal with the problems of establishing a dictatorial socialism or a democratic capitalism. As Heilbroner points out:

> For its political and social ugliness notwithstanding, communism offers a means of achieving the Great Transformation. There is no secret about this means. A communist nation, like a capitalist one, must take its workers from agriculture, must rationalize its agriculture, must import basic industrial equipment, and must relentlessly plough back its increments of output into more capital, more capital, ever more capital. The difference is that communism or total collectivism does the job with little of the "inefficiencies" of a free society. Where land is needed, it is simply taken; where workers are required, they are moved; where opposition is encountered, it is suppressed.
>
> As was the case in Russia, all this is likely to be accomplished at a fearful social cost. In communist China, too, millions have been put to death for opposing the regime, and life for the remainder has been

regimented and militarized to a chilling degree. Yet such an iron hand weighs less heavily on peoples who have never known any form of government other than despotism and who will submit to the yoke of communism if they see a chance of lifting the yoke of poverty from their grandchildren.[7]

It is a question of how much the nation is prepared to suffer to gain an initial, but only an initial, burst of speed. This study does not believe *any* nation is in such desperate straits that in its own best interest it should adopt a system wherein man is de-humanized, and cruel, criminal practices will be invited, perpetrated, and condoned in the name of "progress." Nor does it propose that democratic government is the only or best way to meet the desperate needs of some nations. This is to close one's eyes to the actual situation in the world today. But to speak of the need of the whole of mankind, the "human mass," to "undergo" the process of social organization in terms of collectivization, as Teilhard does, and therefore to abolish the capitalistic system and representative government under law, is also to close one's eyes to man's history as a social being and to the existing differences in the level of development among the various nations, and to the progress man has made in the past.

The question is, which of the mutations of human socialization will meet the need and fit the resources of a given nation *today*, particularly its *human resources* in terms of educated, dedicated people. No nation undergoes the industrial revolution without grievous suffering on the part of large numbers of its people, rich and poor alike. The process requires an initial "reduction in the living standards in order to mount the investment effort by which, in time, standards will exceed their former level," [8] and this, most often, must be imposed. But as Heilbroner says:

> the underdeveloped countries, who suffer from so many handicaps in comparison with the developmental days of the West, enjoy one not inconsiderable advantage. Because they are in the rear guard rather than the vanguard of history, they know where they are going. In a manner denied to the West, they can see ahead of them the goal they seek to reach. They do not wish to reach this goal, however, by retreading the painful and laborious path marked out by the West. Rather, they intend to shortcut it, to move directly to their destination by utilizing the mechanisms of command to bring about the great alterations that must be made.[9]

One can only hope that they will be equally determined to see that their new wealth is equitably distributed, which is by no means always the case.

But there is another question each nation must ask itself. Which of the mutations of human socialization will be able to stay the course, finish the job, keep the fences mended, and lead the way into tomorrow's technology which entails treading once more a painful and laborious path, marking it by trial and error? The job to be accomplished cannot be completed in one man's lifetime—two, three, perhaps more generations will be involved in the process of industrialization. In the long run, something in man tends to confound his every effort at Babel Tower building, his *totalitarian efforts*, however rapidly he may lay their foundations. True, the "quickest," the "logical," the "rational," the "predictable" course for humankind may point toward the mechanism of command and collectivization, but Homo sapiens has a way of doing the unpredictable. For example, as Loren Eiseley points out, the man of the future, as sketched by the mid-twentieth-century anthropologists in biological terms, such as the size and shape of skull and teeth, has come—and gone. Ten thousand years ago, the Boskop people of the South African coast met "in every major aspect the physical description of the man of tomorrow"—they were the "end evolutionary product in a direction quite similar to the one anthropologists tell us is the road down which we are traveling." [10] Their "evolutionary gallop" led nowhere, "save to a dwarfed and dying folk—if, with some authorities, we accept the later Bushmen as their descendants." [11] In parallel, an "economic gallop" that is too traumatic may lead nowhere, save to a dwarfed and dying economy because the economy rests, as does the government, upon the temper, initiative, and dynamic quality of the people; and man cannot read his own future in the "mirror of other living forms," [12] which is to say, in terms of the collectivized ant-heap, without sickening in his soul. When he is treated as mere animal, inertia and apathy overcome him. Mysteriously, whole civilizations vanish or dwindle as did Boskop man. In him, one sees evidence that Homo sapiens may have already *bypassed* his "predictable" biological future—even as his every ancestral creature did, else he would still be a tree-living ape.

The creature who became man at every turn took a different path from the one followed by all other animal life, made an "irrational" choice. The unprecedented way is his, and today man begins to employ an *unprecedented* means to cope with the need to transform the whole social organization of humankind. As Heilbroner points out: ". . . the deliberate transfer of wealth from rich nations to poor for the express purpose of bringing the poor toward a closer parity with the rich is something quite new under the sun. Partly because it is so new, foreign aid is an untidy subject." [13] It is easier to give the aid than to insure that it is put to proper use. Errors, even tragic mistakes, and political naïveté surround every aspect of this unprecedented policy and cause many of the recipients to castigate the donors, the United States in particular—for, having the lion's share, it has given the lion's share, but unable to satisfy all, it has satisfied none, itself included, in its attempt to leaven international economics. But it has by no means been alone in this effort. Despite all the mistakes and failures on the part of givers and receivers alike, on the whole the policy has been indeed beneficial and bids fair to become more so. For this new and precious tool, the infant idea of foreign aid, is being sharpened—more sophisticated ways to handle it are being devised by communistic and non-communistic countries alike. As this policy and attendant trade and banking policies gain momentum, they will alleviate to great degree the suffering every nation undergoes during the transition to an industrial society—which can be rewarding only if man does not sacrifice his individuality, his dignity as a human being, and the beauty, harmony, grace, and individuality of his culture in the process.

This brings to the fore the last question each nation must ask itself. Which of the three mutations of human socialization—totalitarian communism, dictatorial socialism, or democracy operating under law and what might be called "educated capitalism"—will be able to *survive success?* Technology promises a truly affluent society the world over in a not too distant future. It will bring man to the point where he must govern things rather than things governing him, and for the first time in history there will be sufficient leisure that "the potentialities of the entire human race may be explored." [14] Which of the systems will survive or emerge to show itself as the one truly in line with the "essential trend of 'cosmic' movement" in the ever developing consciousness and capabilities of educated humankind?

To answer this question, it is necessary to take a look at the economic substructure that underlies the use of power and institutions of government. And it is necessary to inquire into the actual experience of daily existence in capitalism, socialism, and communism, which is to say: man must investigate *his own nature* to see what principles he employs and what these principles flower into as he, himself, operates his social organization. The truth of himself, his own nature, will answer the question and point the way.

In the view of this study, Jesus revealed the economic nature of *man* and the principles he employs, so that all "isms" come in the end to resemble each other—and each must face in the end the same problem, the same great question: "whether men will use their triumph over nature to achieve a much more difficult victory over themselves." [15]

II

Jesus did not "name" His economic doctrine. He did not use the word, "capital," but the principles He espoused and revealed in their outworking may be identified today with those associated with capitalism. And since, as Heilbroner points out, to acquire *capital goods*, more capital, and ever more capital, is the goal of every nation, it is as pointless for the communist to shun and abhor the word *capitalism* as it is for the republican to shun and abhor the word *socialism* while operating an attenuated form of it without which he would be lost in today's world.

The "worldly philosophy" of Jesus must be identified with capitalism because one idea, the idea of making and accruing *profit*, is basic to His economic teaching. But His words allow for no self-deception as to what real and honest profit is, or as to the pocket from which it should come, or by whom it should be accrued and how accrued profits should be handled. He saw, however, that the psychological rewards and costs outweigh the material rewards and costs: He taught that man does not live by bread alone, that the body is more than raiment, that " a man's life consisteth not in the abundance of things which he possesseth": [16]

> For what shall it profit a man, if he shall gain the whole world, and lose his own soul? [17]

Questions arise. How is one to live so that his life is in reality of profit to himself? Is profiting oneself the goal one should set himself? Should one not spend his life in an effort to bring profit to the lives of others? Is the profit system evil? Can it be operated honestly? Can man operate any other system?

Jesus' parables indicate that as a man serves his work well, whatever the work may be, he is rewarded in one way or another, and that it is not possible to serve another person well without in truth profiting oneself. His words still say that one's life is profit to himself only as he loves his neighbor as himself.

Jesus appears to have seen that Homo sapiens is a self-seeking, pleasure-seeking, profit-seeking creature. He neither denied nor decried man's nature. He saw *life as the one force manifest*, the only force man can possibly serve, and each man's own life as the single reality he deals with. Consider that He says man "cannot serve God and mammon"—if he tries to serve two masters he will love the one and hate the other.[18] If man *cannot* in love serve two masters it must be that there is a single reality commanding his eternal devotion and whatever he does he serves this *one*, which as the parable of the dismissed steward shows, *is himself* and the Lord in the parable commended him.[19] The honest and the dishonest are both self-serving. Whatever one does he is self-serving, sometimes in the highest sense of the word, and this must be as life must have it.

Pleasure-seeking, self-serving, and sometimes greedy men operate the markets, the profit system; but pleasure-seeking, self-serving, and sometimes greedy men must also operate the government that attempts to legislate against the evils of the market place. This is to say, human frailty and human nature bring to bear upon the practice of any system.

But as Frederic Bastiat saw in 1848, the danger is that men will pay too much attention to the imperfections of the profit system and will sacrifice their freedom to dictatorial authoritarianism, or what he saw to be the evil of socialism, in its stead. In the words of Heilbroner:

> He began a book entitled *Economic Harmonies* in which he was to show that the apparent disorder of the world was a disorder of the surface only; that underneath, the impetus of a thousand different self-seeking agents became transmuted in the market place into a higher social good. But his health was now disastrously bad. . . . In 1850 he passed away, whispering at the end something that the listening priest thought was "Truth, truth. . . ."[20]

Jesus calls mammon "unrighteous" but He, too, appears to have seen that self-serving becomes transmuted in the market place for He says, "Make to yourselves friends of the mammon of unrighteousness . . ."[21] This is to say, know the working of nature's physical realm and of the mundane economic world. The temporal, which is mammon, *serves life*. Thus, man is not to hate mammon, although the temporal is not steadfast, and thus is unrighteousness; whereas truth is steadfast, and thus is righteousness. That which is unrighteous in life's operation, mammon, gives way in time to the righteous, to the truth in being which calls man to self-service in the most enlightened sense of the word, that his life may be of profit to himself in reality, which means that it must also be of profit to his fellowman.

Here, one must face the question of whether there can be a real, a true, an honest profit, for Jesus bases His doctrine upon the profit system and capitalism rests upon it.

Karl Marx insisted that capitalism at its best was doomed. This reasoning led him to base his theory upon a theoretically "pure" capitalism in which he insisted that the seed of destruction was sown. Heilbroner describes Marx's theoretical world wherein capitalism at its best operates. Malthus' theory of population increasing to the defeat of the worker has been dismissed by Marx, who saw it as a "libel on the human race." [22] In this theoretical world, the evils of capitalism so prominent in Marx's day have been abolished. Every commodity sells at its proper price, which Marx deemed to be its value in terms of the amount of labor the article represents. The worker also has a "proper price," or wage, which depends upon the amount of labor-time it takes to sustain him. But in a full working day the worker produces more than this, although like everyone else, and like every *thing*, he "has no right and no power to ask for more than his own worth as a commodity." [23] Thus, the capitalist can afford to sell his products at *their* true value and realize a so-called profit because "there is more labor-time embodied in his products than the labor-time for which he was forced to pay." [24] In short, Marx's theory of doomed capitalism rests upon the belief that there is no real profit, no honest profit, to be made. But is this actually the case?

One may dispute Marx's theory by using his own basis for pricing *things*. This is to say, in rebuttal to his proposition, that the real labor-value incorporated in any product must include contemporary and past labor-value. But *past* labor-value is incalculable because the labor-value in any *thing* goes back to a time before Homo sapiens appeared: any product incorporates the inspiration, the physical and mental labor, the work done by the first hominid to devise tool and weapon. Thus, from the day Homo sapiens began his operation of the market, each thing he could produce and sell could *rightly* be sold for more than the amount of *calculable* labor the article represents; and real profit is to be realized as accrued labor-value gives rise to improved tools and methods which allow for more to be produced in less time and with less work. The simplest article is worth incredibly more than it costs to manufacture. If the article is sold at a profit, the employer can afford to pay his employees for what they produce and more. No man is being robbed when the consumer pays a profit because everyone is a consumer; and an incalculable amount goes to the consumer as gift from the past, even as a calculable amount is charged as profit. The profit goes to the industrialist upon whom rests the responsibility to accrue a portion of it to repay the debt to the past by insuring the means of future production.

Mammon is temporal—things pass away and means of production must be renewed. Accrued labor-value also depreciates as methods and things become outmoded, but it does not altogether disappear: there is residual value because pleasure-seeking man takes pleasure in doing things done in past days. For example, the accrued labor-value involved in the making of sails is greatly depreciated today, but man still makes them and sails for pleasure.

If a man does not insist upon charging a profit for a *thing* because of what it represents in labor-value from the past, he cannot insist upon charging a premium for his work so that he may be paid a wage based on what he produces in his working day *plus interest*. In the parable of the ten talents,[25] Jesus validates usury: He demands that a man turn a profit on his labor and capital. Usury has become an ugly word—but "a premium paid for a loan of money or goods; interest,"[26] is the pristine definition of the word. Since each person is his own first capital good, he must realize a profit upon this capital: himself, his life, rather than working for his keep as does slave or animal. One lends himself to his job, may invest himself as heavily as he will in his work, must insist upon a premium for his efforts, and this in addition to the return of his capital: himself as a free agent. His demanding a return on money, capital investment, allows him to insist upon a wage or interest that will constitute a profit on his labor. His money represents his or another's labor—as he invests it, he must demand both interest and the return of his capital if he is to demand a premium for his efforts and freedom for himself.

Selling an article for the exact price of the calculable labor-value is equivalent to paying a laborer no more than the cost of his keep. In such a system, there is no respect for the real value of *things*, or for the *life in them* as represented by the labor-value of countless men and creatures. Marx based his doctrine of doomed capitalism on so-called profit that is squeezed from the laborer. Doomed it is, dead and buried, but a new type capitalism fortified by organized labor as well as organized capital has arisen to take its place.

Adam Smith saw that deep-seated laws of evolution propelled the market system in an ascending spiral of productivity. The first of these is the Law of Accumulation: profits must be accumulated.[27] John Maynard Keynes says that hoarding wealth breaks the flow of money from pocket to pocket. Savings must, therefore, be invested—that is, be put to work.[28] In the parable of the ten talents, Jesus commands man to *invest* his capital and profits profitably— not to hoard his money or bury it in the ground where it ceases to flow from pocket to pocket as it is put to work. Again, He warns, "Store up no treasure for yourselves on earth,"[29] for He saw that such treasure is of value neither to the economy nor to the man in terms of true security, as is shown in the parable of the rich man whose soul was required of him the very night he considered himself to have ample stores.[30] He says, "I tell you, use mammon. . . ."[31] Thus, man cannot serve mammon, for mammon's purpose is to serve him, to be used by him. Using mammon provides opportunity for production and exchange of goods. Spending is sharing. Investing one's capital to earn a return upon it, or lending it and requiring interest for the use of it, is to employ *credit* as a means of expanding the economy.

Jesus commanded men to offer credit *and* to exercise their faith in God, in life, and fellowman. Credit, from the Latin *creditus*, means faith. To exercise credit is to exercise faith—to extend the one is to extend the other. Today, through use of credit, man is indeed moving mountains. Credit offers the greatest reward both to the one who extends it and to the one who receives it. Although it is quite true that "loan oft loses both itself and friend, and borrowing dulls the edge of husbandry," [32] more often than credit "dulls," it allows a man to help himself. It makes of the man with little or no wealth a responsible person who spends his income more effectively, or it makes of him an effective producer of goods or services. To advise the man with or without a purse to "neither a borrower nor a lender be," [33] is to make a hollow mouthing—Shakespeare lets it come from the lips of Polonius. For every person comes into the world a debtor, beholden to the past, to parents and to society, and every man lends something, borrows something, even if it be no more than a man's time and mind to elicit his advice. Jesus said:

> . . . give to the man who begs from you, and turn not away from him who wants to borrow.[34]

Today the power of credit to expand the economy, to raise the standard of living through offering consumer credit, has been demonstrated.

But the abuses of credit are many. The cost to the "time-payment" buyer is often exorbitant—the real rate of interest hidden behind "fixed charges." Nevertheless, practice of consumer credit allows for the most equitable and the widest distribution of goods among the populace.

Credit as a means to abundance is discredited when men begin to measure wealth in terms of debt—this is self-deception and hypocrisy. And borrowed money or credit is not free capital of the sort that should be used to purchase securities, for securities can fulfill their function and live up to the *name* only when they represent invested *savings*. Savings carry into this market as much debt as it can safely tolerate because each dollar of it carries the debt of the nation.

Credit is the goose that keeps on laying golden eggs, but there is a limit to the abuse this means can take when it is operated deceptively by individual or State, by producer or consumer. Credit will not substitute for earnings and savings, but acting in conjunction with them it truly leavens and does not level the economy, bringing real profit to the man or nation exercising it honestly.

Many of Jesus' "economic parables" are based upon *absentee ownership* which He does not see as evil. In these parables, one sees that the *power* inevitably attendant upon money and its disbursement accrues to the *manager* who handles the owner's property well and realizes a return on the capital he is given to work with—this is to say, more money is given him to handle if he does his job well. The parables indicate that a day of reckoning for independent managership must come and does come when the absentee owner brings his power to bear—so that the power vested in ownership is real, albeit "absent." In today's capitalism, one sees that the managers exert the power the owners used to exert, and that successful management operates larger and larger aggregates of investment capital—thus giant corporations have arisen to become the "lords of industry." The real owners of these corporations are too far removed from the scene to take an active part in the operation just as the "lords" of the parables are somehow always "abstracted" from the industry that goes on in their name.

The parable of the dismissed factor indicates that the manager's self-interest leads him to seek security in his old age, or in "enforced retirement"—this appears to be the motivating urge of today's corporation man. In some of the parables, it is projected that the managers cease to be overly concerned with the absentee owner's interest and some mismanage and abuse their laborers.

In the words of Heilbroner, as the corporate system grew, "The new independent managers shrugged their shoulders at the market, smiled at the fictional character of ownership, and simply ran their businesses—reconciling the claims of labor, stockholder, government, community, and themselves—as best they could and as they saw fit." [35] Heilbroner points out that today various industries may be likened in their power and wealth to principalities run by a self-perpetuating body of professionals—a type bureaucracy that James Burnham saw to resemble "no one quite so much in the tasks they performed as the professional managers of the Russian commissariats and the Nazi combines." [36] What Heilbroner calls Burnham's "chilling notion" about the professional managers of neocapitalism brings to the fore a point this study wishes to make: *regardless of the name by which a society calls itself, the people within it operate along the lines of the capitalistic system wherein power accrues to the managers.* Jesus' parables indicate that power accrues to the managers, and He insists that the power of the owner must and will be exerted to offset managerial power. Power tends to corrupt unless there is a balancing factor to be reckoned with.

And, regardless of the name by which a society calls itself, *people* within it operate a market system—"black markets" appear when the market system itself is denied or when for reasons of stress or manipulation it cannot function properly. People appear to be willing to take the risks the market system involves because it affords them the opportunity to profit themselves in buying and selling. When the existence of real profit, as well as the right to strive to make a profit, is denied, and when competition among individuals is denied, so that industry and initiative and good management are not amply rewarded, the best managership conceivable cannot operate its business or the national economy well. *People* insist upon operating within a profit system so that they may profit themselves in one way or another.

Nineteenth-century capitalism had to fail because neither the owners nor the workers could profit themselves: as accrued labor-value gave rise to machines and improved methods and then to real profit in the way of an abundance of goods, surpluses upset the market because a laboring force, paid no more than a subsistence wage, could not buy the goods—nor could the rich absorb the abundance. Money could not be reinvested profitably at home where the purchasing power of the populace was so limited. As John A. Hobson saw, this type capitalism led to "a paradoxical situation in which neither rich nor poor could consume enough goods" [37]—a foreign pocket must be reached. Imperialism entered the picture, war following in its wake, and the type capitalism Marx knew began to express itself abroad.

Much that Marx said was right: the type capitalism he knew and the system he proposed to be "pure capitalism"—wherein so-called profit is obtainable only as it is squeezed from the pocket of labor, entitled only to a subsistence wage although a man produces more in a working day than his labor-value in subsistence terms—has met or is now facing its inevitable doom. But much that Marx said was wrong or wrongly labeled, and there is evidence that he realized this before he died: in Heilbroner's words, he "grew weary of the bickering of the working-class movement and delivered himself of a statement that has never ceased to bedevil the faithful. ('I am not a Marxist,' he said one day); and then on a March afternoon quietly slipped away." [38]

Perhaps at the end Marx saw that *there are simply various types of capitalism,* and that the "pure capitalism" he built his theory upon and through which he foretold the collapse of capitalism itself, coincided with the type economy that would be practiced in his name. Lenin was the architect of this economy. It is a system in which real profit, the accrued labor-value from the past that could work to increase production and reduce costs as profit is maintained, is not acknowledged. Goods are not manufactured for a profit and all factions operating the economy are committed not to the concept of abundance but to the concept of *need*, each according to his needs, which in truth means that labor is entitled to no more than a subsistence wage. Concentration of wealth is complete: the government owns and monopolizes all means of production. This government, now "purely capitalistic," is in the same boat with the "pure capitalism" upon which Marx based his predictions. It is simply one giant corporation; it must operate its business; the world market is the factor it must reckon with and in this market it must profit itself or like any business it will perish; the nature of profit-seeking, self-seeking, pleasure-seeking man reasserts itself at every turn, forcing the operation of its industry into capitalistic channels.

A dispatch that appeared in a morning newspaper "tells a book" in a few words. It was reported that Khrushchev gave a "backhanded" blessing to a sort of profit system in factories, although he cautioned, "Our industry manufacturers goods not to obtain a profit, but because they are needed by the entire society"—he admitted, however, "In the struggle for raising output, comrades, you cannot base yourself only on moral factors. Material encouragement is also needed." [39] What could say better that communism as a system of government must begin to operate its business more nearly in accord with the principles upon which capitalism operates if it is to succeed. A transformation appears to be underway—the system is evolving.[40]

The point this study wishes to make, however, is that *the profit system operates regardless of the type government in force because people will not for long operate upon any other principle*. This is the truth Jesus saw and thus He laid the foundation for an ethical and dynamic capitalism in His economic doctrine.

Another dispatch appeared at the side of the report given above. It stated that the increase in the record rate of income in the United States was "split equally between workers in private industry and employes in state, local, and federal governments." [41] What could say better that the type capitalism Marx knew and turned the force of his pen against has been destroyed—*this battle has been won*. It should be evident by now that the efforts of Marx and Engels served capitalism well, served humanity well, by forcing the rapid evolution of the capitalistic system: workers began to unite and through their unions insist upon equitable treatment and profiting themselves. A new type capitalism wherein control is balanced between labor and management, with government arbitrating between them and under the obligation to limit their powers and its own, is evolving. Harris writes:

> What we have in America today is a mutation of capitalism—something quite new in the history of the world; so new that we have not yet found a word for it.[42]

This is true, and it is also true that Marx and Engels must in large measure be thanked for it. It is also true that the need to evolve into a more enlightened capitalism and a more honestly capitalistic society presses upon this "mutation" as heavily as it presses upon the Soviet Union. In both systems, the power of "independent managership" that develops into a callous or careless bureaucracy must be brought into line by exertion of the power of the "absentee owners"—who are they and where are they?

In a society where ownership is decried, where everyone owns everything and therefore no one really owns anything, the owners are indeed absent, abstracted, and theoretical. It will be difficult to bring the necessary power to bear upon the managerial class to fulfill the promise of an ethical and dynamic economy. But if Jesus' doctrine is true, the power of the absentee owners will in time be brought to bear—which is to say, in time an educated populace will bring the power of the people to bear upon managerial government.

In the mutation of capitalism operating in the United States, there is in large degree absentee ownership. Managers of the giant corporations own but a small fraction of the stock of the companies they manage. Millions upon millions of people own these securities, or have a vested interest in industry through their holdings in pension funds and profit-sharing plans, through the investments of their labor unions, through the investments of banks and insurance companies. Directly, or through collective means, ownership of the means of production rests in the hands of all but a small minority of the people. If a man owns so much as burial insurance he owns a bit of the ways and means, for the funds of the company are invested in the economy, the industry, of the nation. Such absentee ownership, and absentee ownership as such, becomes, paradoxically, the most ethical type ownership if "ethical" is to be measured in terms of the widest possible distribution of vested interest and *possession* of the means of production that can be called real and not illusory.

Either directly or indirectly the monetary profits that accrue to the owners and the return on invested capital pass into the hands of the people or into the hands of the managers of their unions and collective agencies. *Real* profit in the way of abundance of goods passes into the hands of the consumers. Thus, in the widest sense of the word, the consumer profits. If the "whole moral justification for capitalism" rests upon the fact that in a competitive market the "consumer" is "king," [43] then the consumer, everyone, must exercise his authority and assume the responsibility that rests upon the king, upon the head of government, theoretical owner of all it controls.

But not all of the parables deal with "absentee ownership" and "independent managers." The parable of the prodigal son returning to the house of his father presents, for example, a very present owner-manager quietly operating quite profitably and ethically through all the years the younger son lingered far afield until he was reduced to eating "husks." Today, it may be seen that *real private enterprise*, such as was espoused by Jesus—that is, individually owned and managed businesses—can and will operate in conjunction with giant corporate enterprise. As Heilbroner points out, in England and in the United States, the "*share* of the big firms in the entire economy does *not* seem to be increasing"—the economy as a whole has grown fast enough to expand the total number of enterprises at about the same rate as the big corporations increased their sales; in 1932 there were 3 million "pigmy" firms; in 1960 there were 1.3 million *more*.[44]

The power of the owners of small businesses, as well as the power of stockholders and the public at large, must be brought to bear upon the managerial power in the giant corporations, and upon giant managerial government, the capitalists' currently haunting specter.

Jesus appears to have seen that the strangely twisting and turning road down which the practice and malpractice of capitalism would lead man, must bring him to the place in history when in one way or another everyman would find himself in the shoes of owner of the means of production, so that the power and responsibility attendant upon ownership, and exercise of the means of production, must devolve onto growing numbers of individuals whose ethics and aspirations would become the decisive factor in operating the economy. Heilbroner writes, "As the control of our destiny devolves increasingly upon ourselves, we shall have to make choices—desperately important ones—among the counsels of the present. It is from the scope and wisdom of the economists of the past that we must reap the knowledge with which to face the future." [45]

The insight of one great economist of the past led Him to proclaim the *instability* of evil, for evil is a house that divides against itself. Thus, in time, malpractice, based upon self-deception or the lie, will cause the collapse of any type society that does not evolve toward an enlightened and equitable practice in its economic and governmental life.

Jesus insisted upon the importance of the *moral factor*. Insofar as modern society is concerned, Heilbroner writes:

> It is not without significance that its outcome may depend as much on moral factors as on the impersonal process of economic evolution alone.[46]

Today, it may be said that both communism and capitalism are evolving. Although they are avowed enemies and opposites in their goals and operations, paradoxically enough, each for moral reasons has singled out and openly declared war upon the same foe: *poverty*. Another paradox enters the history of economics: the poor are not rising against the rich and successful so much as the rich and successful are rising against the poor, in that they are insisting that poverty must go so that the poor will be no more.

The revolution against capitalism appeared to begin as a revolution against the wealthy, the "leisure class," and it was thought that the poor desired to destroy the rich so that the rich would be no more—until an economist with great insight proclaimed what appears to be the fact of the case: Thorstein Veblen announced that the poor did not want to do away with the rich, they wished to emulate them.[47] An earlier economist had also observed this to be the fact of human nature—Jesus had said, enough that the servant fare "like his lord," [48] for He saw that both the servant and the lord, the rich and the poor, housed the predatory instincts of the barbarian and operated under the discipline of savage life from which man has but recently been removed—which is to say, all men share human nature and this binds the divergent interests of humankind.

Jesus recognized the right of the rich and the poor to exist, and He saw that both would exist in any type society, at least to some degree. But before examining His attitude toward the poor or the rich, it must be said that He placed such emphasis upon *work*, one might say of Him what Heilbroner says of Veblen: ". . . he was not even wholly convinced that leisure was in and of itself preferable to work." [49] Indeed, Jesus appears to have understood that work is most precious to man, and that the wealthy are seldom as idle as the truly poor—the beggar, and the incapacitated.

Because Jesus recognized that the rich and the poor would exist, He recognized that society must support a "leisure" class—which, paradoxically, is now seen to be the poor, the unemployed and unemployable, whose leisure is harder to bear than hard labor. Leisure means: time free from employment—unemployment is the haunting specter accompanying the technological revolution, for it appears that more and more people will be "free from employment" because machines have replaced them, or because they do not possess the skills and education needed in industry.

The question becomes: how large a leisure class composed of indigent aged, orphans, disabled, and those poor in education, ability, willingness to help themselves, and desire for improvement can a nation support? What is the real root of poverty? Can it be eliminated? How can it be defined? Is there virtue in it? What was Jesus' attitude toward poverty, toward wealth? It was St. Paul, not He, who said that love of money is the "root of all evil." [50]

Jesus saw that a man may invest his talents in many provinces. He may set himself to accomplish a mission, knowing that he cannot accomplish it alone and that to accomplish it at all he must make beggars of his helpers. Schweitzer, speaking of men who wish to undertake charitable missions, says: "Only one who thanks to his own ability or the devotion of friends is in worldly matters a free man, can venture nowadays to take the path of independent activity." [51] Only those who would join with Jesus in His mission were commanded to first free themselves of worldly matters. As He sent His disciples forth to begin their ministry, He stated that the workman is worthy of his keep,[52] but these words also imply that people who work in charitable enterprises supported by contributions should not expect to command high salaries for their services—they must profit themselves in nonmaterial ways. When the rich young man asks, "what good thing shall I do, that I may have eternal life?" Jesus answers, "keep the commandments." He did not tell him to give his wealth to the poor and join in His mission until the young man had said he had kept the commandments from his youth up—it was then that Jesus invited him to relieve himself of the responsibility great wealth imposes, a responsibility he could not have been acquitting to his own satisfaction else he would have been content with Jesus' first answer.[53]

Jesus' teaching demands that those who inherit wealth acquit justly their stewardship of it. He related the acquisition of wealth directly to initiative, and to the assumption and acquittal of responsibility. The wealthy held up as bad example are those who place their trust in hoarded riches and those who enrich themselves by dishonest means. There are no poor extolled, save the widow who considered herself wealthy enough to give her mite into the coffers of charity, thereby reflecting her trust in God, her self-possession. The rich as well as the poor were Jesus' friends and followers.[54] The lords of the parables are wealthy, expansive, generous, and just—

whatever is miserly or meanly done is ever spurned.

Jesus comforts the poor, and lack meets always with His compassion. He saw, however, that giving to the poor seldom alters their lives or their ways, nor does it bring abundance to society as a whole. He indicated that half a man's wealth is, in the extreme, all he need feel called upon to give,[55] and that one is not to spend his all upon the poor. In saying, "For the poor always have ye with you," [56] Jesus presents the concept that poverty cannot be eradicated in Homo sapiens' generation—one must conclude that some have psychic need of being poor and life has need of them. But this is not to say that in a truly civilized society poverty cannot and should not be largely done away with. Jesus gave the requirements, told what is needed to bring abundance in society, but before discussing these suggestions, poverty itself must be examined.

The great majority of humankind are very nearly equally endowed with the capacity to produce a good living, but the graph of the frequency distribution of income makes immediately apparent gross differences in income levels and calls attention to the disparity between income and physical and mental abilities.[57] Why should this be so? It is too easy to say that the greed and cunning of a few has prevailed throughout the vast time that the earth has been peopled by men of corresponding ability, and in the face of all that has happened in the way of natural disasters, wars, and falling civilizations which serves to redistribute opportunity. Other factors must be responsible.

Because so many of the poor have less than a grammar school education, the need to provide for and insist upon the education of every child to the limit of his ability to learn becomes self-evident. But schooling will not eradicate what John Fischer calls "The Stupidity Problem." [58] There is a "severe and increasing shortage of people brainy enough to man the upper level jobs in our over-developed Society"—thus, the poor in intellectual capacity will be "with us," but this may be blessing in disguise, for in time it may serve to slow the crashing and traumatic pace of the Scientific Revolution. Picking up a child, giving no indication of its IQ, Jesus says:

> See that you never despise one of these little ones, for I tell you their angels in heaven look upon the face of my Father in heaven.[59]

As Fischer points out, IQ is not the measure of the value of a life—to individual or society.[60]

But one has only to look around him to see that the "stupidity problem" arises because so many able students are unwilling to exert themselves to master the subject matter required in a complex technological operation.

Like the miserly rich, these students are poor in knowledge despite their abundance of "gray matter." Their lack reflects better than any other type poverty that the poor are often those who are reluctant to assume much responsibility or to invest themselves more heavily in their work.

The parable of the prodigal son shows that there are those who invest themselves heavily in their work, but refuse to invest themselves in gaiety, without which either wealth or poverty is misery. The elder brother begrudging the celebration was himself miserly and therefore poverty-stricken in the midst of untouched abundance. Or, as another parable shows, there are those who are too busy with their personal concerns to accept life's invitation to the feast [61]—they, too, are insistently poor in terms of joy in life, just as the brainy student who refuses an education is insistently poor in terms of a formal education and is a failure upon a plane whereon he could easily have been a success.

When one views the rural poor or the tenacious slum dwellers, clinging to their marginal lands and dwellings, or by inertia resisting such amelioration of their condition as can be offered, or when one strives to help the poverty-stricken who will not seek work nor help themselves nor do more than is necessary to keep body and soul together, he must wonder if some unspoken wisdom vindicates their ways, their need to know the freedom of Diogenes. When Alexander asked what he might do for Diogenes, Diogenes replied, "Only step out of my sunlight."

The freedom to be poor, to know want, to know failure, to refuse gaiety, or a formal education, or the more sterile poverty that welfare and charity measures provide may meet a man's need. This is the freedom that appears to meet the need of the insistently poor, of the begrudging miser, of the brainy student who will not invest himself in learning, and of those with low IQ who find their comfort in indolence. In today's society this is indeed a costly freedom to support. It can be justified only as its opposite freedom is allowed: the freedom to be rich, to know abundance, to amass wealth, to know success, to be highly rewarded for knowledge, initiative, and industry.

Among the poor and the rich one finds the industrious and the idle. In nature, one finds both types. Nature does not appear to love the ant and despise the grasshopper—she serves both, for both serve life and serve themselves, both are guided by an inborn wisdom that sends the one upon its busy and the other upon its frivolous way. Thus, it may well be that whatever the state of being a man evidences, experiencing it is necessary to his development of empathy.

Jesus teaches that however a man is situated in life, the promise of wealth is there—the kingdom of God is within him and in time he will come into the true riches with which he is already endowed—but first he must learn to handle honestly and well what belongs to another, and must show himself willing to create wealth and share it by providing opportunity for others to amass it also. The prodigal son returning to his father's house must be prepared to find himself a wealthy man therein.

Jesus taught that a purse that never wears out, treasure that never fails,[62] is possessed by the man who understands the transience of this world's wealth and is willing to invest himself and his capital in human endeavor even if his capital be only himself and if he be able to add by his presence only to the pleasure of another.

The man who is too heavily taxed or too meanly rewarded, both materially and psychologically, cannot or will not work "with all his heart" [63] —Hezekiah's profoundly simple recipe for prospering in public service appears to apply also in private enterprise, for truly successful people have one bond in common: they love the work they do and do it wholeheartedly.

Harvey Swados writes of work and its compensations, its psychological costs and rewards, saying that there is little difference between the psychic reaction of factory worker, white-collar worker, and many professionals: each labors at a fragmented task and questions the basic worth of what he is doing, all lead lives of "quiet desperation" because they have been "conned" into over-buying to gain "middle class" prestige, and nothing but "sterile fantasies and day-dreams of escape can issue from repetitive work" regarded as "degrading" by the all but "anonymous units of the firm's labor force." These men want to be contributing members of society, they miss a sense of completion in their work, miss having any contact with product or consumer. Thus Swados says that it is a fallacy to think that the "basic problems of American workers" have been solved through a "combination of unionism and social legislation." [64]

Man's need to work is as deeply ingrained as his need to express his Self-hood: "My Father worketh hitherto, and I work." [65] Because work is a psychic problem, Jesus dealt with it. The simple truth is that neither unionism nor legislation can do more than insist upon decent conditions wherever men work and upon equitable treatment for all—neither satisfaction in one's job nor the desire to serve the job well, whatever one does, can be legislated. It is hard to believe that so many men live lives of "quiet desperation" as Swados would have one believe—men conscious or unconscious of their own despair are apt to see the world through despairing eyes—but his article and the real problem of work cannot be so easily dismissed.

On one side of the coin one sees again that each person feels the necessity to identify himself—something in him refuses to become a part of the company's Group-ego, himself all but anonymous, and he knows that he must wear the corporate uniform first, last, at work and at leisure, if he is to reach the top. And today's work costs man the mental freedom he used to be able to enjoy as he performed monotonous physical labor—the man at the machine cannot be as free in his mind as the man behind the plow. The parable of the laborer who started late in the vineyard and yet received the same wage for his work as those who had started early in the day may be applied: [66] fewer hours of work in this latter-day world become equivalent to the dawn-to-dusk labor of former ages. The mental and physical stresses attendant upon getting to his work, the tensions engendered by its repetitive nature, the loss of communion with himself, nature, or fellowman as he does his job take a high toll of the worker.

On the other side of the coin, one sees that such a man as Swados describes fails to realize that whatever he does if he supports himself and his family he is a contributing, constructive member of society. And to borrow words from Harris: "For every one person who is bored with his surroundings, there are a thousand who are bored with themselves, because they have not planted enough foliage in the landscape of their personality." [67] The landscape of personality is enriched only as knowledge, talent, rich experience in living, and love come to flower there—neither unions nor government can do the work that must be done to bring these seeds to fruition. As one learns to appreciate life itself, his personality appreciates and grows rich foliage.

Such a man as Swados describes fails to have regard for the people from bottom to top who are serving him, making possible his fragmented task in which he serves himself. He is not happy to *serve* either self, or product, or society—nor then could he be happy to be chief whose task is not fragmented, who must serve the whole problem—who, as Jesus said, must be servant to all [68]—must live his work.

Jesus saw that to a greater or lesser degree man lives his work—it is his life. Here, one comes to the heart of the problem that faces the worker today in factory or office, and enfolded in his dissatisfaction is his fear: in a highly developed technological society, the necessary specializing tends to isolate men, and complex machines tend to rob a man of his value to society by making unnecessary more and more of the jobs he is able to do, or rendering inane his part in the process, thereby reducing to inanity his life, which depends in large measure upon the satisfaction work and communication bring.

But another factor is involved in the dissatisfaction of men who earn high wages and have so much, yet suffer lives of "quiet desperation" as they struggle with debt. Covetousness leads them to misuse the precious means of credit. They do not understand until it is too late that things bring no satisfaction to the man whose own covetousness, far more than a salesman's "conning," has led him to overbuy to gain "middle class prestige." The Ten Commandments insure psychic health as well as social order, and among them is this one: "Thou shalt not . . . covet." [69] Jesus said that life consists not in the abundance of things a man possesses, and He warned, "Take heed, and beware of covetousness. . . ." [70] No man can be satisfied by things he has bought to gain prestige, for he must be *servant* to his possessions and in whatever manner he possesses them they possess him.

Jesus is identified with but one possession. That was rare: a perfect and seamless robe, used and treasured. It was the best that love could fashion and in the minds of men it has a living relationship with Him, but as Dr. van den Berg writes: "We no longer believe in the aliveness of things and consequently we are deaf to their entreaties." [71] One might say that Jesus was "housed" in His robe—and that the difference between the tortoise who wears his home and a person in his home is only one of degree. A man's home reflects his being, his possessions reveal him, and if there is nothing he can in truth call his own he cannot in truth call his soul his own, for his soul must have a *housing*. *Things* provide a man's housing.

Things one needs, uses, and loves, things one will work for, care for, and treasure, do bring a large measure of real satisfaction. Love made the Robe, and love wore the Robe—the one thing Jesus made so completely His own that it becomes the symbol of truly private property. Private property is of such importance because, as Whittaker Chambers writes, "ownership of property . . . is the final guarantee of freedom. It cannot be breached without breaching freedom, and if it is ended, freedom is ended. . . . The benevolence of those who would deny this has nothing to do with the case." [72]

Jesus' doctrine comes to rest in the concept that man cannot view mammon supinely nor use mammon dishonestly and reap a profit on his life. He damns the damnable with candor, and commands man to pluck out, to cast off, the offensive in himself.[73] He teaches that when a man is honest and friendly in his dealing with and usage of mammon, things, the material realm, mammon serves him well—to borrow words from Dr. van den Berg, he will have more of those days "when everything appears to be possessed of a new persisting light. The sun is brilliant, the colors of the flowers are unexpectedly deep, and even the smallest thing gives . . . its own bit of happiness without becoming in the least poorer in consequence." [74]

Man began his work in this world tending a garden, as the legend goes, so that an appreciation of the living quality of things must be the first lesson he is to learn. Tending them, working with them, keeping the world as a garden is kept is his job. His need to work is so deep-seated that Berdyaev saw work as *worship*—he believed that freedom is:

> . . . the organization of society by such a means as will guarantee the opportunity of work and creation to every man.[75]

Opportunity, as opposed to enslavement or coercion, creation in addition to mere labor, are the points of importance here. Providing opportunity depends upon providing education and training in ever wider fields wherein man at leisure, if not at work, can be champion, master, victor, creator of the whole product he may make and market if he can. Opportunity involves a chance to compete, and a certain degree of competition appears to be a necessary ingredient to insure real achievement, as well as to give the bread by which man lives a satisfactory taste. Providing opportunity to work to every person who is able to work is possible, is more economical and rewarding than providing more and more charity, for this tempts the parasitical and saps the moral fiber, pride, ambition, and energy of the recipient and the nation. To provide true freedom is to enable every person capable of work to earn a living for himself, thereby serving himself and society.

In any type society the world has ever known, however, there is a degree of uncertainty as to whether the needs of the populace will be met, and there is a degree of instability and flux in jobs, prices, values, supply and demand, as well as types of goods and services needed, types of skills required. As men deal with the uncertainty problem that besets every type government, the mathematical theory of communication could teach a valuable lesson: the uncertainty that arises from *freedom of choice* is desirable uncertainty—which is to say, to put security, stability, certainty above all else is to trade precious freedom for a myth because actual security does not exist and cannot be guaranteed. But freedom of choice, both for the industrious and for a Diogenes, is a limited freedom. As Julian Huxley points out: ". . . human individuals cannot realize their possibilities except as members of social groups, and through means which only organized societies can provide. . . . Thus the paramountcy of the individual is not absolute: it is limited by the need of maintaining and improving social organization." [76] Organization is a *tool*. Civilization progresses as the tools man devises are improved. Social organization is as yet crudely fashioned and clumsily handled—much of it is spurious, parasitic, abusive, as it was in Jesus' day. Nevertheless, He says:

> Render . . . unto Caesar the things which are Caesar's; and unto God the things that are God's.[77]

He held in His hand a coin. What image does this coin bear? The image of *government*, and His words command man to serve both it and religion, holding separate Church and State, for both serve him. He understood that truth would prevail, that in the long run, only the religion and only the type social organization or structure of government that meets with the truth of man, with his nature and need, can and will prevail because it will command humanity's wholehearted support without coercion. Truth governs and frees. Knowledge is power. Today, every nation faces the necessity to educate its populace in order to operate in a complex civilization that cannot for long oil its wheels with lics, for mathematics must be taught—it is the *universal language*, the language of the future every man should learn, even as he learns to speak in his own tongue—and mathematics teaches men to think, makes them dependent upon the truth. Wherever in the world a child is being educated, a step toward the political freedom and economic independence of man is being taken—for ignorance forges the bonds of servitude and gives rise to enslaving poverty that can be eliminated only through learning.

Jesus understood the necessity and the value of government. Two thousand years ago He saw that a people who will not be taxed to support a government that operates apart from their religion and a people who will not pay their taxes honestly, rendering unto Caesar his due, will not render unto God His due: the cooperation they owe their fellowmen. Nor are they serving themselves. In one short sentence, He rendered tax money as important, as sacred, as the money given to support whatever one embraces religiously; and thus He implies that a decent citizenry, good government, and a dynamic economy which produces abundance for its people must operate upon the principle of taxing. Regardless of the name by which it calls itself, government is of little value if it cannot or will not command its taxes, or if its taxes are not equitable and congruent with the demands of the time, and if it does not equitably handle tax money. Heilbroner makes a telling point: "Tax reform, like land reform, is a perennial subject on the agenda of most underdeveloped nations, but both have remained for the most part only on the agenda." [78]

The symbol of government Jesus called into play represents a government of limited power—only one side of the coin bore its image, the other side was free to bear the face of the individual in the name of God. Thus, the value of government must also be measured by its ability to limit its powers and protect the basic rights of the individual even as it commands its taxes. The respect government accords tax money, and its usage of that money reflects the respect and usage it has for its people—and it is of little value if it cannot itself adhere to sound economic operation.

In short, crafty taxation and crafty tax-dodging must give way to the art of taxing—to equitable taxes efficiently collected—if a nation is to realize the potential vested in the principle of taxing. The principle of taxing parallels the operation of the Second Law of Thermodynamics—which is to say, nature commands a tithe of the heat or energy, and taxing commands a tithe of the available energy in terms of money that is made unavailable for use by individuals through each cycle of operation or each year.

It is time to take a new view of the ancient idea of tithing: the first call upon a man's income should be to invest a tithe of it in insurance to fulfill the need of the Lord in being, *himself*. As government commands from each citizen a tithe of his income, investing it in insurance for him, the citizen becomes an investor in the nation's economy that he may be self-supporting throughout his life, specifically, in his old age. In operating such a tax program, the government commands the individual to exercise good economic hygiene—and there is a constant buildup of deferred purchasing power which begins in time to feed the market, creating a demand. Today, the right of government to command the act of tithing to provide "social security" for oneself and family is established, but there is wide ground for improvement and enlargement of the practice, which is often defeating to its purpose by arbitrary restrictions placed upon the recipient and by the generally insufficient amounts involved. Such insurance is *bought*, its payment is not a "welfare dole"—and if the principle is to operate successfully, government must invest and administer honestly the tithe it commands in order that all its people may know the blessing of financial independence, of having sufficient purchasing power to be an asset to the community.

Government must also tax to support itself and the services it supplies. Thus, it must make a further demand on the incomes of its people. The idea of graduated taxes is now well established—indeed, it is all but worked to death. This principle is enfolded in Jesus' words—from those to whom much has been given, much will be required; but He also said that from those who have little, even that would be taken.[79] Applying these words to taxation, one may say that to no one has so much been given as to the "self-made" wealthy man—he has been provided the climate of opportunity, the freedom to work, the chance to accrue, and to know success. Much in taxes should be required of him, and of those whose wealth has been inherited, and of those who receive high salaries. But Caesar's image appeared on one side only of the coin—this symbol would say that government represents no more than half the measure and that, in what might be called the normal course of events, half a man's means is all it can command from him justly regardless of how much he earns or how much comes his way. If government took all, however, it could not sustain itself by overtaxing the industrious, rich, and successful. It must command its support by all the people. Thus, something must also be taken from those who have little, for they too must demand and enjoy the services that government alone can provide, and the purchase of social security insurance is of crucial importance in their lives.

But there will always be "with us" those unable to work, and therefore the tithe cannot be commanded of them. Thus the charitable aspects enfolded in the religious concept of tithing must be expressed by supporting with a portion of taxes the social organizations that provide for those who cannot provide for themselves. But this is not enough. For man to meet the need of man, he must love his neighbor as himself, so that charity in the smallest and largest sense of the word, in every sense of the word, must be practiced privately as well as publicly. Enough must be left in the pocket of the individual to make this possible.

The complicated business of taxation—its practice and malpractice—cannot be entered into in detail in this study. The principle it involves is of first concern because it points to the important role government must play in the lives of men. Like any business enterprise, it must demand more for its labor and its services than subsistence. Like any insurance company it must invest its funds, for in no other way can it insure the nation's healthy being, and this is its business. Government is communal business that must accrue a profit and invest capital to expand its services to include all of its people and improve their lot. Jesus gave the key: see to their education—know the truth, for the truth will set you free.

Because government is *corporate industry* in which all its people have vested interest, credit as a means, or deficit financing as this becomes necessary, is proper to its function. But its currency must be its constant concern if it is to fulfill its obligation to the *owners:* its people. A government's currency bears its image, tells its story, and represents the value of its word, as did the coin of Caesar. If government abuses deficit financing as a means, its currency will suffer—but, as John Maynard Keynes realized, the tremendous leverage this principle affords cannot be ignored in good times or bad. The "future generation" saddled with the debt begins to arrive the day it is incurred to enjoy and profit by whatever the borrowed money is used to produce. But it is not at home that currency is threatened so much as it is when it goes abroad, or into the hands of hoarders, or those ignorant, irresponsible, or dishonest in their dealings with men —into the hands of those who will not render unto Caesar his due nor unto God that which is God's.

Jesus both did and did not espouse the philosophy of laissez-faire. This is to say, He saw that in universal terms and in the long run, nature would take its course—but He also called men to action, commanding them to have done with self-deception and to bring their power to bear upon life in this world, exercising faith, *creditus,* and honesty in their dealings with God and man. In today's world, the government must insist that its people cease to practice laissez-faire in their personal economic lives. It must command them to practice the good economic hygiene that tithing and insurance represent. And it must play an active role in the economy: in the words of Heilbroner, "all business welcomes *some* government investment and all parties endorse *some* public spending: the issue is no longer whether or not but *how much* and for *what purposes.*" [80]

There will be ten thousand answers as to how much and for what. There is one guiding principle, the one by which giant corporations came finally to be guided: live and let live—so that both private and public enterprise may continue to exist. This principle must include the "pigmy" private enterprises, both profitable and charitable, which in truth reveal the health and resourcefulness of the nation. One might say that they are the "thermometer" by which big business and big government may take their own temperatures.

Both private and public enterprise must co-exist because, as Heilbroner points out, the central weakness of the market system is "its inability to formulate public needs above those of the market place" which tends to satisfy the desire for luxuries while allowing the more basic needs of the poor to go unmet.[81] Thus, government must respond to this "market," to the needs of the poor, for upon alleviating their plight and increasing their purchasing power depends the economic health of the nation. Government must respond to the "market of national need"—no one can say what it should or should not do, for it must serve the changing needs of its people. Who can say what they will be tomorrow? It is difficult enough to define them today.

Probably no more astonishing statistics have been presented to this statistic-ridden century than those which emerged when the doctors in Saskatchewan, Canada, and later in Belgium, went on strike against socialized medicine. It would have been surprising enough if the death rate had remained the same during the time of the strikes, but in both places, the death rate *dropped appreciably*.[82] The vice-president of the Belgium Medical Association attributed the fewer deaths to improved emergency service because doctors, rather than interns, maintained this service. But other factors—psychological factors—must have been involved. What were they? In Saskatchewan, the hospital load was abnormally low. Were there fewer accidents because people took more care? Were there fewer severe and critical illnesses? Every possible statistic having to do with this strange interlude in medical history should be gathered—for it is an experiment no one planned as such, and no one would want to see it repeated.

In a paradoxical way, the doctors may have proved their point—socialized medicine may not be good for the populace because people will take more care and deal more readily with their own ills if medical assistance is not automatic or overabundant, but the assistance that is provided voluntarily is of the highest quality. The statistics point to the conclusion that in the field of the healing ministry private enterprise in every sense of the word must operate alongside improved emergency service and public health measures in the market place that life somehow *is*.

The market—Bastiat's concept of the transmutation of self-interest into a public good sounds the same note, strangely or not so strangely, as the note sounded in the Principle of Detailed Balancing.[83] In economics, an uncertainty principle also appears to operate—the observed or calculated value of a quantity may depart from the "true" value, the uncertainty expressed as the average deviation, the probable error, or the standard deviation. Perhaps the economists who see an ever expanding economy to be a healthy one should take a look at a chart showing the progression of electromagnetic waves: periodically, the electric field intensity becomes zero but the wave passes through this point and travels on; nature's play between "boom and bust" is smoothed into a satisfying flow of energy as her forces pass through and respect a "sabbath" rest: zero. As economists attempt to discern the pattern man's economic systems must weave, or as they try to shape them to perfection, let them take a look at nature: the demands created by disorder, disorganization, and decay are ever present in her system despite its honesty, affluence, harmony, beauty, satisfying and challenging change. In her system, the Second Law of Thermodynamics reigns—the law that apparently always leaves *something wanting*.

To the question of what happens in the end to the market system, to capitalism, one can say with a degree of certainty only this: the threat of Utopia is not inherent in it—and herein rests its appeal. In a capitalistic society, sufficient unto the day is the evil thereof: like nature, whatever the abundance it produces, it always leaves man something to contend with, demands a change of pace, and a re-evaluation of the situation. As John Kenneth Galbraith observes, today's affluent society in the United States leaves much wanting:

> The family which takes its mauve and cerise, air-conditioned, power-steered and power-braked automobile out for a tour passes through cities that are badly paved, made hideous by litter, blighted buildings, billboards and posts for wires that should long since have been put underground. They pass on into a countryside that has been rendered invisible by commercial art. . . . They picnic on exquisitely packaged food from a portable icebox by a polluted stream. . .[84]

Affluence creates its own problems. And man defiles the scene. But something in him will always turn him to "consider the lilies of the field" and to seek nature unadorned, splendid in isolation. Today, men are beginning to realize that capitalism must mark its progress not only in terms of economic well-being, but in terms of changing arrangements of beauty, melody, harmony, and communication—the values Eddington and Weaver relate to entropy.

But there are those among the worldly philosophers who see no hope for capitalism whatever the abundance it produces, however well it cleans up the mess industry makes, however ethically and intelligently the system is operated. For capitalism calls for a venturesome spirit, involves a degree of risk, is competitive and depends upon a wide appetite for goods—depends upon qualities they see to be edited out of security-seeking corporation men, unable or unwilling to accept the challenge and contend with the problems posed by success or failure, by affluence or lack.[85] But these are the qualities exhibited by a long chain of creatures that rose in time to become a venturesome ground-dwelling primate concerned with *things* who in turn rose to the stature of Homo sapiens.

Among those who take a dispirited view of capitalism's future is Schumpeter. In speaking of him, Heilbroner says that for the first time an economist has said that economic development by itself does not "ultimately determine the history-making process by which the fate of capitalism [will be] settled" [86]—thus Schumpeter believes that capitalism with a shrug will "fade away" presumably to be replaced by some sort of collectivism or communism. Schumpeter's doctrine is the opposite of that of Marx, who preached that history is determined by economic processes—and yet the two men arrive at the same conclusion, Marx with the militant spirit of a revolutionary, Schumpeter expounding a doctrine that reflects such world-weariness as cares not what happens. Schumpeter's resignation and Marx's strange words, "I am not a Marxist," indicate that both see in the end how great the self-deception men indulge when they believe that economic development by itself has or will determine the history-making process by which any "ism" will be settled. Schumpeter, however, is not the first to point out that economic development alone is not the deciding factor. Long ago another economist made this statement:

> For what shall it profit a man if he shall gain the whole world, and lose his own soul? [87]

The men who advocate or foresee some sort of "benign" authoritarian or collectivist system to replace capitalism practice self-deception: they are closing their eyes to the reality of authoritarian or collectivist systems, which must and do practice *monolithic capitalism* wherein it is indeed difficult for the owners, the people, to bring their power to bear upon the necessary power of the managers. In simple truth, *man cannot escape capitalism for he, himself, is capital-good.* Thus, to take a dispirited view of capitalism is to take a dispirited view of man.

In the not too distant future, capitalism—both monolithic and differentiated—must face the problem of affluence, the problem of leisure, and the problem of work in altogether new terms. Today, to provide the opportunity to work to every man is by no means an insurmountable problem —but what about tomorrow? In Heilbroner's words:

> ... in the highly automated world toward which technology appears to be moving us ... it is perfectly possible to assume that economic engagement will become the function of a minority rather than of the overwhelming majority, that work will become more of a privilege than a necessity. This view does not forecast a condition of social poverty: on the contrary, it is posited on the most enormous social abundance. But whether the market will then provide the mechanism by which that abundance is distributed—or by which

access to productive tasks is regulated—is, to say the least, a debatable question.[88]

Government will have to play a role, just as it does today. But in the view of this study, the less work there is to be done to produce the necessities, even the luxuries, of life, the more work there is to be done to educate the citizenry and supply the demands of leisure. A decrease of work-demand in one "frame" means nothing but an increase of work-demand in another "frame." The principle of relativity will operate. The concept of "luxury" as well as of "work" will shift its focus. And so will the market.

Because private enterprise and entrepreneur quickly sense a new market and also quickly sense what is surplus, or spurious, because it is the proclivity of the market to satisfy the desire for luxuries, because it allows for wide freedom of choice, the market system appears to be ideally suited to cope with tomorrow's abundance and leisure, for leisure opens an enormous new market that no type of "automation" can satisfy. A machine may be used to teach a man, but it cannot learn for him; a machine cannot obliterate man's desire to create something for himself; a machine may be used in his recreation, but it cannot play for him.

Homo sapiens has a big and diverse appetite for fun; he continues to play as long as he lives, and is willing to work at perfecting his game. This is to say, he often turns play into work and work into play. He enjoys the market place. He enjoys doing business sociably, communicating with his fellows as he goes about his task. In the new market that leisure will open, enjoyment will tend to be reinitiated into work, leaving to the faceless machine the monotony and isolation attendant upon much of man's work today in an industrialized society.

Simply because man enjoys buying and selling and turning a profit, the market system, operating at some level in terms of private enterprise, bids fair to persist. Man brought forth this system himself. It is *unprecedented* in the animal world and therefore in line with the whole development of the cell of life that became Homo sapiens. It is the newest economic system under the sun, and as with any powerful new idea or tool, it must be tempered and disciplined before the real profit in it is to be fully realized.

Underlying the profit system, upon which capitalism depends, is a principle which in the view of this study led Jesus to espouse it: He saw that the capitalistic system cannot in truth profit itself by malpractice, and thus it tends toward the ethical in its best self-interest and must come in the end to measure its worth in moral and aesthetic as well as material terms. Therefore, He offered what Galbraith says society needs: "Men cannot live without an economic theology." [89] (See Appendix IV, p. 410.)

III

Although today it is fashionable to decry materialism, in all honesty one must admit that Jesus' doctrine is materialistic—*divinely materialistic*. And its primary concern is with life in this world—that it be abundant, profitable, rewarding in every sense of the word.

Jesus drove out of the temple the money changers and merchants who desecrate not the spiritual but the material aspects of life as they foist themselves upon the privilege of learning and worshiping, putting upon this privilege not its real cost, the high cost of freedom, but a petty price they can comfortably extort. The likes of these infest the temple of each man's being, corrupt his ego-group, and corrupt the concept of the divine expressed in, through, and by the temporal and material aspects of life.

In a divinely material universe, man operating a divine lump of matter, his brain, must become not less, but more materialistic and more honestly self-serving—which is to say, more understanding and commanding in his grasp of nature: his own nature *and* the matter and energy in which he is involved, for this is all he can apprehend of what he calls God or good. Many men have grasped the wedded nature of life, the meeting of God and mammon, good and evil, within man: "If man marries his hell to his heaven, his evil to his good, Blake holds, he will become a creature such as the earth has not yet seen. Nietzsche put the same insight paradoxically: 'Mankind must become better and more evil.' " [90] Blake and Nietzsche appear to be trying to say what Niels Bohr says better: "There are trivial truths and there are great truths. The opposite of a trivial truth is plainly false. The opposite of a great truth is also true." [91]

A scientist understands that a great truth is wedded to its opposite truth and both truths are true. He may say, "matter is mass" and he may say, "matter is energy." He does not love and serve one aspect of matter and hate the other. He is as true in his dealing with mass as he is in his dealing with energy. He works with matter and serves life. He sees that mass and energy are met in matter even as Jesus saw that God and mammon are met in man: life. The man who has little respect for, desire for, and appreciation of mammon, matter, has little love for God, author of the "stuff." God and mammon are opposite truths, both true—the one truly steadfast (righteous) and the other truly volatile (unrighteous). The one cannot function apart from the other any more than matter can function apart from space. The world and mammon are one. The world is not to be condemned.[92]

Science has made unto itself a friend of mammon. The scientist is devoted to unswerving honesty in performing his task—in his laboratory he uses the least of mammon faithfully, according it justice. When a scientist enters his laboratory, or confronts the mathematics of the problem, or works to apply his knowledge, to the utmost of his ability he is steadfast, patient, faithful, and true in what he does—to be otherwise would be such folly, so unsupportable, as to label him deranged. Because science operates the ethic of honesty in its work, one might say that it operates the ethic of Jesus—it commands man's respect and awe because of its approach and method. Like all humankind, the scientist may err, but his self-imposed discipline allows him to labor with all his heart, and thus science prospers. As individual, the scientist is not immune to the foibles of man nor to the evil of psychic disorder, nor to the pressures of society. But whatever his life may be, his *work* is more often than not satisfying to him despite its specialization because adding to knowledge or applying new knowledge brings its own unmeasurable reward.

The power of today's science is so great that if misused, it can indeed become a curse rather than blessing. There is growing fear of this power, even among scientists, so that some of them and some laymen believe that scientists will or should tend to conceal the dangerous discoveries and keep secret their knowledge, becoming as esoteric as alchemists. In the view of this study, such a course would be disastrous, and impossible if sufficient scientists and engineers are to be trained to operate civilization at its present state of development. Because of its esoteric nature, alchemy became a lost science, a lost art—lost in the act of storing the information in private code so abstruse that even those within the discipline could not communicate with ease. Today, a fantastic quantity of such "stored information" exists, but at present its value is negligible—and there may never be enough students to tackle the job of deciphering it to render it of value. Norbert Wiener writes, "The idea that information can be stored in a changing world without an overwhelming depreciation in its value is false. . . . Information is more a matter of process than of storage." [93] And it is involved with nature's supreme law that exacts a toll even when a system is left to itself. For science to become "secretive" could do no more than postpone the day when man must learn to live with his incredible power without exercising it destructively—for eventually his power would be revealed to him through another discipline, just as science arose and bypassed alchemy. At any rate, it is too late for postponement—Pandora's box has been opened.

Unlike the alchemists, past and present, scientists are not avowedly engaged in their labors for the purpose of bringing about through their working with matter a transmutation or elevation of their own consciousness. Nevertheless, many accomplish this to greater or lesser degree, and give expression to it in terms of an ever greater reverence for the marvel the universe, man, and matter is. Like all disciplines, science has many sorry chapters in its history. But as Michael Polanyi points out in *Science, Faith, and Society*,[94] it is in the nature of scientific inquiry to be guided by conscience, and to demand freedom to share its findings, as well as to govern itself in a community dedicated to truth and service. As the scientist serves these ends, he serves himself and all. But not all can be scientist, nor should they try. Other fields must also be tended, and the least person on earth serves in life's large purpose and process—if nothing else, serving man's deep-seated need to serve his fellowman.

To serve the poor, but not to enslave them in poverty, is a delicate and difficult task. Today in many public schools, children of the very poor become at the outset "charity cases" in the eyes of students and teachers—conditioned to this role, pride broken, self-respect gone, hostility chronic, before they begin, or become dropouts—because they are "free lunch" cases, cannot pay "book and gym fees," cannot afford to participate in curricular or extracurricular activities. Much could be done to break the cycle of poverty if public school education were truly free. The costs defeat those who need most to escape for a part of the day the world of deprivation supported by "welfare." If ALL costs are paid by taxes, and in school there is no call to spend any money, every child will be more nearly on equal footing, able to respond to the opportunity of education. And each child should be taught how to apply sound economic principles in his own life, so that he may enter the adult world prepared to use mammon.

Jesus saw that as man uses mammon, he serves life, and as man serves life, he serves God. He saw that in a trifle, a coin, God and mammon are met—that this *thing*, a coin bearing man's image, represents the power vested in him: the power of the word. Today, in earning, spending, sharing so much as a penny of the currency of the United States of America, God is served by its message: "In God We Trust." God is served also by all that the image this coin bears, the face of Abraham Lincoln, has come to represent in the history of human affairs.

Chapter 18

TRUTH—WHAT IS TRUTH?

I

When Christianity's message framed in orthodox theologies became feeble and unintelligible, and throughout the world men began to voice growing disillusionment with religious dogma, political ideologies took over the stage—statesmen, unorthodox but deeply religious, began to lead the crusade toward human dignity and freedom. True political saints arose in so many nations that this study cannot begin to name them. But wherever and whenever they appear in history, as Thomas Jefferson did, they fight against tyranny, however it may be expressed: theologically, economically, politically. In a letter to Dr. Benjamin Rush, written in 1800, Jefferson said, "I have sworn on the altar of God, eternal hostility to every form of tyranny over the mind of man." [1]

True political saints seek, as Lincoln sought, not to gain or save or free the whole world, but to preserve and extend the gains that man has made by dint of untold suffering. Lincoln sought to preserve the United States of America with its concept of government: under God and law, government of the people, by the people, and for the people, that it should not perish from this earth. And this remains the crucial task of its leaders today.

Jesus saw that a man or a nation is as a city high upon a hill. What each *is* cannot be hid, and if this city be enlightened, it will cast its light far and wide, drawing all men toward it:

> A city that is set on an hill cannot be hid. . . . Let your light so shine before men, that they may see your good works. . . . [2]

Today, men engaged in politics continue to lead the way. Under the pressure of widened consciousness, all over the world men are striving to legislate justice and rationality in economic and civil affairs. But when social ideals are translated into laws for which men at large or whole minority groups are inadequately prepared, then anarchy, resistance, inertia, chaos, wantonness, or war blunts the edge of accomplishment—even as happened in Lincoln's day.

On the other hand, change born of the evolution of consciousness cannot be blocked. Truth comes to consciousness and moves men onward, letting the "dead bury their dead." [3] Many a devoted son has been troubled by Jesus' remark, but on the face of it the saying is poetical. Jesus was making a point, revealing a truth that is now becoming apparent: dead problems bury themselves. John Dewey wrote: ". . . intellectual progress usually occurs through sheer abandonment of questions together with both of the alternatives they assume—an abandonment that results from their decreasing vitality and a change of urgent interest." [4] Self-burial of that which is dead is taking place throughout the world. As Jesus did, *truth* states itself and continues to work—but, in the words of Pilate, what is truth?

In an attempt to answer this question, the intellectual elite wage a war of ideas using Georg Wilhelm Friedrich Hegel's logical dialectic, or some distortion of it. His philosophy has been a tremendous force in shaping history—particularly in its influence upon Marx and Lenin. Hegel proposed that thesis contains the seeds of and evokes its opposite, antithesis; and that reconciliation of the two produces synthesis which reacts upon thesis; this concept leads to the idea of *becoming* until the Absolute is realized; in the progressive restatement of a purer thesis, evoking antithesis and synthesis to react upon purer thesis, the Absolute is represented by one idea, one man, one people at a time; the interaction between individual and society produces the State, expressive of moral life, a totality above all individuals, which in its higher development must be an organization commanded by a single person, not a political body operating upon law and democratic principles; the philosophy embraces the absolute idea, absolute power, truth, morality—and reign by one person. Thus, Hegel's logical dialectic is the *Messianic ideal* expressed more logically and practically in temporal terms.

Today, it would appear that Hegel was right in saying that truth or thesis contains and evokes its opposite-truth or antithesis. But countless assertions of truth and opposite truth have shown that the only Absolute to be arrived at is: *the law of opposites restates itself to the defeat of the Absolute as a concept.* For example, Barrett says that Heidegger is right when he speaks of Western metaphysics culminating in the concepts of Nietzsche, "which metaphysics in turn culminates in the situation of the world today where power rides supreme" [5]—but Barrett also writes:

". . . the law of opposites, the oldest tragic wisdom of the race, suggests that at the very height of his power man is bound to experience, as Oedipus did, his absolute impotence. There are a good many straws in the wind today that point in that direction, including the testimony of modern art . . ." [6] Opposing the culmination of Western metaphysics is the truth that today power does not ride supreme. Great powers are more than somewhat helpless—their arms are self-defeating, contradictory in their might. They are as Goliaths posed against many Davids who have for weapon but a pebble.

Man's helplessness at the height of his power presents the concept that truth when fully stated must conclude in contradictory truths of equal magnitude—in a bifurcation, a forking outward from the penultimate point of truth so that the end of it cannot be reached save as point that opens itself to question, requiring judgment in order to settle the issue or to act upon either the one or the other premise it projects. Thus, no one *final* or *absolute* statement of objective truth can be made.

Law may be seen as a penultimate point of objective truth that opens itself to question requiring that *judgment be exercised*. Today's truth or contradiction in magnitude, seen as man's power versus man's helplessness, comes to rest upon the question of whether he will accept law as the means of governing and settling disputes. If there was a victory in World War II, it rests in the hope that the weapons forged were so terrible they must serve to end war, so that the day of judgment, when judgment must take over from power to settle the conflicts of the world, is at hand. In the war trials, in truth, *war* with all its subterfuges stood trial and was condemned. Until history reached these days no man could know the magnitude of destruction, of cruelty, and the disgrace to humankind that war would come to spell—now spells. In the past there were certain virtues to be practiced, certain rewards to be reaped, in victory or defeat—in nuclear war there can be no reward, no victory, no virtue.

Nevertheless, mankind is unprepared for peace as the world gives it. Peace does not solve the fundamental problem of man himself, and he fears he will hopelessly maim himself and society if he accepts peace as the world gives it. What else but a deep-seated fear of peace, as the world gives it, is revealed in today's psychological novels?—for example, Samuel Beckett's *The Unnamable*, depicting "Mahood," worm man who "never leaves a jar," [7] preserved in a formaldehyde of his own tears, encased in his own exhibitionism, unable to sink into oblivion because simple consciousness prevents.

Why does man fear peace? Is it because peace threatens his birthright—the right of an unarmed animal to fashion and bear weapons? When ancestral creature picked up a stick to use for weapon and bequeathed to man his sword, he did his being-duty: only by fashioning a weapon could he survive, rise above the animal kingdom, and be different from it by refusing to evolve into, or in himself *be*, a physical weapon as all other creatures are to greater or lesser degree. Because their swords are built into them their threat to each other persists generation after generation so that fear and enmity are reborn in each species and between neighboring species. Man alone can lay down or pick up his sword. Man can be friend or foe, can love his neighbor as himself.

Man will always be able to wage war, whether with sticks and stones or bombs. Late twentieth-century methods of warfare—like art, music, and the dance—express the paradoxical situation man finds himself in: war is fought in a sophisticated and yet primitive way in many corners of the world while in others peace is waged with "passive ferocity." There is much talk of disarmament—but to disarm the nation in a hostile world in time of wars and rumors of wars will run afoul man's need, nature, and being-duty. The need for armaments will slowly wither in what appears to be becoming a worldwide climate inhospitable to war—but the time to beat sword into ploughshare has not yet come. Man must learn first to live with his incredible power and not use it destructively, working all the while to diminish or at least to curtail the growth of the nuclear arsenal.

Jesus said, "Blessed are the peacemakers . . ." but He did not in His time seek to abolish war, saying that wars had to come.[8] He offered the only peace as yet real—inner peace: "my peace I give unto you: not as the world giveth, give I unto you." [9] Lest His words of peace be misunderstood, He said, "I have not come to bring peace but a sword" [10]—but He said also, those who "take the sword shall perish with the sword," [11] and in this line is written much of the history of man who today confronts the judgment he has pronounced upon himself: war fought with nuclear weapons will be criminal.

Why, then, did Jesus bring the sword, why do His words lead man to accept war as a necessary part of the evolution of consciousness? Why did man's evolutionary trek take the turn that leads him to war with his own kind? Why does the "Lord, thy God," appear in Scriptures to lead man into war after war, as though, in modern terms, to prevent his making peace in his time at any price, prompting him to fight even in the face of overwhelming odds posed against him? In the words of Krishna, one finds the answer to these questions—man wars because he must to do his *being-duty*.

Warring among themselves must have been the only social mechanism men could employ if they were to rise above the jungle peace with which fear keeps constant company. This is to say, war developed a certain sense in man. What is this sense? As war brought such magnitude of suffering as appalls the mind, men came also to possess such empathy for fellowmen that humanity at large begins to understand what being-duty means: being what he is, man cannot permit man to misuse man, nor to own man as he owns an animal, nor to use man as animals are used, nor to exterminate the worst, best, or least of humankind as lice are exterminated; to do his being-duty, man must insist upon the human dignity as well as the social rights of each individual on earth, himself included, and defend this concept with his sword, give his life for it, destroying any civilization that cannot evolve to operate upon it. Man shows no greater love, and therefore reaps no greater profit on his life, than in laying it down for his friends [12]—humankind become his friends.

War will end when the being-duty of man demands it. War will recede as a threat when men, nations, and ideologies abandon the Messianic pretension that any one of them can play world savior, or be world ruler.

Much has been written to the effect that evolution's processes are now in man's hands—that he can determine the course of his future. In the view of this study, Homo sapiens has only his own temporal structures in his charge. He, himself, life itself, is entrusted to evolutionary principles that will still operate, so that even if he destroyed himself in nuclear war, in time he would appear again: Homo sapiens is a necessary step in the development of fully conscious life, a repeatable experiment by the force that produced him. There is evidence in the literature of Alchemy and in its tradition, and in many legends, which suggests that consciousness has in time past reached the level Homo sapiens' consciousness has reached—only to be decimated and like the phoenix arise from its own ashes to again address the problem of learning how to live in accord with being-duty and truth.

Today, each ideology proclaims that all humankind are brothers. Homo sapiens has taken a giant step forward in consciousness by accepting this concept, even though in theory only. To have real meaning, the doctrine of the brotherhood of man must rest upon the Fatherhood of God and the Christ in every human being, setting man apart in the complex of creation. Twentieth-century civilization, however, may not be able to contain its power long enough to let time teach these truths, and to educate men to practice the ideal of brotherhood it expresses. This civilization may be destroyed in one last conflagration.

But twentieth-century man may not destroy his civilization. Enough men may come to see that no "tree" can produce its fruit before, in the natural course of events, the tree is ready to bear it; they may come to see that "rear guard" action allows for retreat instead of chaotic rout as humanity withdraws from its old positions; they may see that opposition is as necessary to effect real progress as antithesis is to effect synthesis. Enough men may come to see that man's consciousness is fluid, and thus he cannot, will not, move against the natural law that water seeks its own level. Empathy, and lack of empathy, divides men into classes, endeavors, and attitudes that support their need to avoid or to join in, to know or not to know, to oppose or to assist. But empathy itself is a gathering force. It will not forever divide. As William Stuart Nelson teaches, "all beings hate pains," [13] and in their growing empathy men cannot look upon the passive face of suffering without suffering pain themselves. Thus, enough men may grasp the essential truth that leads them to do their being-duty in peace—this truth, presented by Jesus, is echoed in the words of Whitman:

> Whoever degrades another degrades me, and whatever is done or said returns at last to me.[14]

Empathy's pace may not keep abreast impatient plans to right the world, to rewrite history and human nature, but empathy will stay the course as light stays the course of the wave-group in operation—and empathy, like light, will be there when the course is run, freeing man of his destructive impulses.

Empathy demands moral progress, which Philip Toynbee sees as natural and occurring—he defines moral progress as: "an increasing and active recognition of the fact that other human beings are as fully human as oneself." [15] This is the truth that apparently only the sword could teach, that the sword *has* taught and need no longer be used to teach, indeed no longer can teach—it is better taught with the pen and it is better defended by law. Today, man's nuclear sword can be posed uprightly only as it hangs at the nation's side.

Moses was provoked to slay as he beheld man misusing man—he responded to man's sense of being-duty—empathy prompted his act. But he understood that the sword was not always to be the way, that man's best hope lay in transforming staff to pen—in wielding the power of the written word, law.

The problem of war, the problem of peace, the problem of stating social law was not, however, the fundamental problem Moses dealt with. He dealt with the same problem men have grappled with throughout the ages—Radhakrishnan states it in its twentieth-century dress:

> We are in search of a religious message that is distinctive, universally valid, sufficient and authoritative, one that has an understanding of the fresh sense of truth and the awakened social passion which are the prominent characteristics of the religious situation today. Belief may be difficult but the need for believing is inescapable. We must present struggling and aspiring humanity with a rational faith, which does not mock the free spirit of man by arbitrary dogmas or hesitating negations, a new vision of God in whose name we can launch a crusade against the strange cults which are now competing for mastery over the souls of men.[16]

Stating a valid, rational, ethical, and soul-satisfying religious concept is the problem that confronts humankind with each enlargement of the boundaries of consciousness. Whatever else may appear on the surface to be engaging the efforts and attention of Homo sapiens, religion is the fundamental problem he deals with, for at base it concerns the problem of himself, the question of "who and what am I?" Nicholas Berdyaev saw that: "The problem of class war is above all a spiritual and moral problem which involves a new attitude of Christians towards man and society, and a religious renewal of all mankind." [17]

A seasoned man may refuse certain aspects of religious dogma, but he knows that atheism is sophomoric, is self-deception—knows that a time will come when a passionate cry, "O God," will burst from his lips involuntarily and it will not be as empty curse or lament. It will arise from his very being. A seasoned man knows that a time will come when he can express his sense of being-duty only in terms of God. Khrushchev, speaking of the Soviet Union's 100-million-ton bomb, says, "May God grant that we never have to explode such a bomb." [18]

Man's need to express himself in religious terms has not collapsed; his God-sense has not failed. It is the worldwide collapse of theologies that demands a new religious concept, and such a concept must be psychologically based, for only then can it be universally cogent, and congruent with the whole of religious expression. As Radhakrishnan points out:

> In the personal experiences of the seers of the different religions, we discern characteristics which are unaffected by differences of race and geography and which illustrate an astonishing similarity in regard to spiritual life in spite of slight variations. Direct spiritual experience

is a psychological state, independent of the metaphysical doctrine which may be derived from the experience.[19]

Psychology, which did so much to undermine religion, now finds itself confronted with evidence of *religion's* authenticity regardless of the decay of theological systems. Rank concluded that psychology's analytical interpretations are substituted for traditional teachings of a fundamentally religious kind.[20] But as Viktor Frankl sees, psychology is not to be worshiped *as* religion and made the explanation for everything.[21] In simple truth, its findings have reaffirmed man's experience of himself as a spiritual being: "Freud's conception of the unconscious has led beyond itself. . . ."[22] Progoff says, "Something that is more than the sum of the individual parts comes forth, crystallized into a new form and living a new life."[23] Jung learned that "the ever deeper descent into the unconscious suddenly becomes an illumination from above"—he realized that the fulfillment of psychology's findings must lie in a realm beyond psychology.[24] In the development of Logotherapy, Viktor Frankl has opened the psychiatrist's door not to any one particular religion, but to religion itself. In his work one can see the dawn of a new day in psychology's history. Recognizing Freud's contributions but moving beyond them, he has transcended psychology's old "theology" and its "existential vacuum."

Not only psychology must transcend its old "theology" if it is to fulfill the promise inherent in its findings—the fulfillment of Christianity and of Judaism also depends upon their moving beyond their theologies. In this regard, laymen are leading the way. Arthur A. Cohen observes that the Jew as well as the Christian is ignoring his orthodox dogma, dogma which may be summed: "a Messiah is yet to come who will redeem history," and the role of Israel and Judaism until the advent of the true Messiah, "is to outlast the world and its solutions. . . ." Cohen says:

> It is to the dogmatizing work of St. Paul that one must ascribe the transformation of "prophet" into "Christ"—and it is therefore St. Paul who severs Jesus from the life of Israel. . . . the rejection of Jesus must now stand to the end of time.[25]

Only St. Paul's Messianic concept of Jesus need stand rejected by Judaism. It may join with a concept that acknowledges Jesus as truth-bearer whose most profound statement is one with Judaism's own: Hear, O Israel, the Lord is One:

> One is your teacher. . . . One is your heavenly Father. . . . One is your leader, even the Christ. . . .[26]

Jesus did not proclaim Himself Judaic Messiah—He proclaimed the Christ of God to be the One-self of every man, "I," the truth of him. Messianic expectation vested in anything or anyone foreign to one's own being invites the destructive forces of Messianic pretension to break loose upon the world, and it leads the pretender to suffer Messianic delusion, so that the Messianic-minded will invite, demand, enforce his own persecution to the degree that such delusion is suffered.

Jesus presented Himself *as* Messiah must present himself to fulfill the role as it was described in Scriptures, the frame in which and against which Messiah could be measured. He chose this way to show the "truth of truth": it finishes itself always in cross-action which demands a change-over and reconciles opposites by reflecting the confronting image as likeness. Likeness is all that can be perceived. In finishing the Judaic Messianic role by playing it to its bitter end, He broke the mold and any like unto it. Judaic-Messiah came into the world in the Bible, made manifold in the one volume encompassing the expression of Homo sapiens' consciousness.

Until Judaism reborn in Christianity had been presented to the East, to which Jesus acknowledged His debt in His birth legend, mankind could not be relieved of false Messianic expectation by coming to see that the same truth is expressed in every religion. The gospel Jesus preached is not His alone:

> *The Bhagavadgītā* tells us: "Whatsoever being there is, endowed with glory and grace and vigour, know that to have sprung from a fragment of My splendour."
>
> *Mahābhārata* says that there is no external judge who punishes us; our inner self is the judge. . . .
>
> Look at the following saying of Kabīr: "I laugh when I hear that the fish in the water is thirsty. You wander restlessly from forest to forest while the Reality is within your own dwelling . . . the truth is here!" [27]

Truth—what is truth? Each man who seeks life's profound mystery long enough. diligently enough, comes finally to say, "I am truth": "The Sufi martyr al-Hallāj was put to death because he proclaimed that he himself was Truth. . . . his real offense was not blasphemy, but the indiscreet revealing of a profound mystery." [28] Jesus says "I" am truth, but He also says, "I" and the Father are one [29]—thus, "I," subjective truth, cannot be absolute for "I" am involved with the father, making "my" truth complex in being. The concept that "I" am or can be absolute gives rise to Messianic delusion.

The voice of "I" that speaks through the Lord Buddha, the Lord Krishna, the Lord Muhammed, the prophets, poets, and sages the world over—through all sacred writings—must be seen as an expression of the inner light and truth of each and every human being:

> . . . bring my sons from far, and my daughters from the ends of the earth; Even every one that is called by my name: for I have created him for my glory, I have formed him; yea I have made him.[30]

God is *one* and the name of *one* is "I." Thus, "I" and "I" alone can be the name of God—every single person calls himself by that name. Each *one* is first-last, *only*. *One* can be no more, no less.

Jesus saw that communication depends upon truth meeting with corresponding truth. He said, "No one tears a piece from a new cloak and sews it on an old cloak: otherwise he will tear the new cloak, and the new piece will not match with the old." [31] He presented to His listeners a new view of their own religion, speaking in their own tongue, utilizing the symbols most meaningful to them. And to fulfill the prophecy of Scripture, His message must bring on the day when:

> . . . they shall sit every man under his vine and under his fig tree; and none shall make them afraid. . . . For all people will walk every one in the name of his god, and we will walk in the name of the Lord our God for ever and ever.[32]

The restoration of religion meaningful to man which the whole world seeks can come simply as each man takes *a new view of his own religion*.

Social progress may also depend upon the revitalization of religion, for sustained endeavor appears to depend upon what might be called religious acceptance of an idea. Arthur Bonner comments upon this in an article, "India's Masses—The Public That Can't Be Reached." "After living in India for more than five years and realizing the force of dharma, I am convinced that there is a direct relation between the de-emphasis of religion since Gandhi's death and the fact that much of the enthusiasm that existed at the time of India's independence has now evaporated." [33] But what his article actually shows is that India's masses *can* be reached when approached by individuals like Vinoba Bhave, Gandhi's disciple, and the progress that stems from his labor is sustained although the villagers refuse or abandon the new ideas the external ideologies press upon them.

Today, another Gandhi—Rajmohan Gandhi, grandson of the Mahatma —marches through India. He sees that the world must rearm, that India must rearm, but the rearmament he seeks and demands of the Indian people themselves is moral rearmament.[34] And thus one is returned to a concept presented at the beginning of this study: "Religion alone can carry the load. . . ."[35] Religion alone can deal with many of the problems man faces. Religion alone can give meaning to one's own life and to twentieth-century man's efforts to save his civilization that it may evolve to provide a more abundant life for all men in this world—and everywhere.

II

Poised now on the edge of the Space Age, man prepares himself to enter a new type wilderness—and he arms himself with a new type law to deal with it. *Space Law and Government* has to do with metalaw, a system for "dealing with the beings we will encounter in our exploration of the vast beyond."[36] As Elizabeth Mirel understands Andrew G. Haley's book, metalaw's guiding principle is to:

> . . . treat others the way they want to be treated, that is, to do unto others as they would have done unto them. It is a reversal of the golden rule. . . . The trouble with the golden rule is that it is too self-centered, or too anthropomorphic. If we apply the rules of man to outer space, we will be contaminating it with all our own earthly faults and foibles. We will be imposing our own standards either on people that do not know any better or on peoples that are superior to us. This would have disastrous results similar to the Spanish destruction of native Mexican and Peruvian civilizations in the 16th century or to the American trampling on native Indian tribes during the time of the westward push. But in addition, the upset to the balance of nature might be irreparable. The idea and practice of giving up the golden rule is not exclusive with metalaw specialists. . . . Students of strange cultures try to understand "weird" or even "evil" practices of these lands in terms of their function and meaning for the people as a whole. This way of thinking is called cultural relativism.[37]

Consider, first, that it was because men did *not* deal honestly, humanely, and according to their highest ethic, the Golden Rule, that the history of the development of the American continents enfolds so many sorry stories of man's dealing with strangers and strange civilizations.

Consider next that there are practices in every culture that man's being-duty and the Golden Rule will not allow him to condone—and once *he is involved* he cannot free himself of the responsibility his being-duty imposes upon him by "washing his hands" of the matter. Today, children are born into a world wherein *all men are involved* with each other, and the question of whether there is real choice as to whether man presses on into space, knowing *he may involve himself* in the affairs of other beings thereby, is an open one. This is to say, once the power to move into space is established, it is doubtful if it can or should be denied—it puts the world in the position of the chick that must peck out of its shell. If man becomes involved with other beings in space, he may find there practices to which he cannot acquiesce in truth—he may find himself one day standing in the shoes of Pilate, born into an age he did not create, faced with a situation he did not create.

Consider now that Caiaphas demanded of Pilate the "weird" and "evil" sacrifice of Jesus by crucifixion because the high priest thought of this travesty in terms of its function and meaning for the people as a whole:

> . . . consider that it is expedient for us, that one man should die for the people, and that the whole nation perish not.[38]

This way of thinking leads to all cruel and senseless abuse and sacrifice of human beings—which, in Whitman's words, "returns at last to me."

Pilate, also guided by expediency, applied "cultural relativism" to law, and to his dealing with a strange people in a strange land. He could call them neither inferior nor superior to himself—just different. And he dealt with the situation as they would have him deal.

A workable principle is reciprocal and demands cross-action. Such a principle is the Golden Rule, which has been man's guiding light—*it is an expression of empathy*. Jesus spells it out in terms of selfhood and others: love the Lord, thy God, with thy whole heart, mind, and soul, and thy neighbor as thyself, doing unto others as you would have others do unto you. "Thy God," man's *Selfhood*, must and will command him. He cannot be another's creature, nor the creature of any State. He cannot long behave in terms of another creature. How does one determine what others would have done unto them except in terms of what one would have done to himself were he in the other's place AND in terms of being true to himself, to mankind itself, as he stands in his own place bound to do his being-duty?

Man can deal on earth and in space with others and other forms of life only *in* terms of himself—but it is not necessary to deal *on* his own terms, imposing them. And he cannot impress his ethic, here or in space, upon another species of life with which he has no real communication. Concerning himself about how to deal with intelligent beings on other planets, may be much ado about nothing. The fact that he, himself, is a mathematical improbability would suggest that his duplication anywhere else is out of the question.[39] If man is the most highly developed form of life, the only speaking creature, in the universe, then in the most profound sense of the word, the earth is the "center" of it. And in some very distant tomorrow, man's destiny may be to "Be fruitful, and multiply, and replenish" the "many mansions" to be found in it.[40]

But somewhere else nature may have done the improbable, so that living beings that match or surpass man in intelligence and capabilities may already exist on other planets. If so, in the view of this study, such life will possess the same physical characteristics, give and take here and there, that man does—otherwise it could not match or surpass his intelligence and capacity to perform. Above all, it must possess the psychological impulse, the "gift of the power of speech," which will lead it to translate sounds into a basis around which to unite its own ideas into a complex mode of behavior. In the words of Norbert Wiener, "Speech is such a peculiarly human activity that it is not even approached by man's closest relatives and his most active imitators"—the chimpanzees.[41]

Nothing man has come upon is alive, conscious, and capable in the sense that he is. But nothing he has come upon can rightly be called dead and altogether unconscious: even an elementary particle is a bundle of activity, sufficiently sentient and knowledgeable to recognize its like sign and opposite sign, communicating this "consciousness" by its behavior. Man cannot separate himself from the inorganic realm and its "consciousness." He and the stars are made of the same chemical elements. Nor can he separate himself from the chain of living creatures, amoeba to gorilla. His flesh and in large part his consciousness is inherited from the likes of them, and he is as subject to the demands of the body as they. Thus, he is humbled in his intellectual pride. And yet, when all that sets him apart from the rest of nature is considered, it becomes increasingly difficult to apply the word *life* indiscriminately to him and to any other living thing. All in creation is alive, and may be seen as the "flesh" of the living God to be used with intelligence and compassion. But the mind that thinks to speak is abstracted from all living material except man. Man did not inherit the power of the word from the animal kingdom; speech was initiated in him and he initiated it in this world, perhaps in the universe. The similarity between living things serves only to enhance the mystery of the origin of man's unique power of speech. Is possession of this power synonymous with possession of life itself, *in reality*, as opposed to being living material to some degree conscious as is a proton and a gorilla? The opening verses of the Gospel of St. John define life and

God in terms of the *word:* the word was God, in the word "was life; and the life was the light of men." By this definition, *life* can be ascribed only to man.

Jesus words indicate that living organisms exist elsewhere in the universe.[42] If human life exists elsewhere, then to deal with other people and all living things according to his own highest ethic is all man can do if he would do his best. Enfolded in this ethic is the command that he deal with the beam in his own eye before attempting to remove the mote from another's [43]—this is what metalaw appears to be saying. The concept of metalaw itself bespeaks an attempt to apply the Golden Rule and the idea of metalaw is not to be decried.

But in the view of this study, the terms in which metalaw is currently stated—if these have been correctly understood—are misguided and misguiding: to say that men might better give up the Golden Rule in space must carry as companion suggestion the idea that they might better abandon it upon this planet which is also in space. If what man considers his highest ethic here is not to be practiced there, then as his consciousness moves into the concept of himself living in the space age, the concept of the practice of the Golden Rule as the best hope of earth must wither and a Stygian night will enfold it. The Golden Rule bespeaks the light in man—"If therefore the light that is in thee be darkness, how great is that darkness!" [44]

As to the question of how to live in this world or in the universe, it is not possible to present a new answer that will surpass the highest and most practical ethic of Homo sapiens—his consciousness cannot rise above the ethic of love, enfolded in the Golden Rule. Although this, his light, may be as little as the firefly casts, nevertheless, it is to be regarded as India's great poet, Rabindranath Tagore, regarded the firefly's: his light may be tiny, but it is not small, for it is akin to all the light in the universe.[45] Someday, Homo sapiens may bring light to mansions far flung in space—for:

> Neither do men light a candle, and put it under a bushel, but on a candlestick; and it giveth light unto all that are in the house.[46]

III

In the trial of Jesus, He was not mocked, God was not mocked. Law— the defender, the protector, the governor of every man—was mocked. Caiaphas mocked the ethic of Jewish law in his insistence that Jesus convict Himself. Pilate mocked the majesty of Roman law by washing his hands not of Jesus and the Jews' conviction of Him, but of his duty. Truth—what is truth? One can state only a moment's worth of it. The truth at that moment was: Pilate stood as judge, peer and jury—and He permitted the execution of a man in whom he could find no fault. Law was mocked by everyone present: the mob reigned.

The promised land toward which Moses led the Israelites was a stone upon which was written, the law. Government under law makes of any place the promised land—it promises order, justice, humane treatment of man insofar as Homo sapiens practicing the highest ethic of honesty can administer these, its precepts. Until man accepts law as his guiding principle, he will mill in the wilderness. Until he holds law as sacred as his sword, as precious as his tools—cares for it as he does these, cleansing it of time's accretions, reworking it to heighten its efficiency, and restating it in universally acceptable terms that all men will agree to as being in their self-interest—there cannot be peace on earth, not on any patch of it, not throughout the whole of it. Homo sapiens appears to be more than "forty years" [47] away from this promised land, but he is moving toward it. What, then, can be said of him? What is this moment's truth?

Men all over the world are suffering the tribulations that rebirth of consciousness and the scientific and industrial revolutions are bringing. But these forces are also bringing the promise of abundance, beauty, meaning, and justice to life. Man is gaining in stature as he makes friends with mammon in his laboratories, uses the least of matter honestly, and insists upon his temporal organizations being used more honestly. Man begins now to understand himself and his environment in terms of the marvel the material realm is, begins to know himself also in terms of his inner world, begins to grasp the purifying nature of "salt," the blessed corrective that laughter is. Men can look ahead to a humanity educated to its role in society, as well as dedicated to the selfhood of the individual.

Men are taking thought of the "things" of their day, recognizing at last the importance of conserving precious wilderness and nature in her primal glory, seeing that all things must be made anew—and they can look ahead to a world that will be cleansed of many of its present eyesores and pollution. This, in truth, is the pressing problem of the day, and it is being brought to the attention of the public.

Truth is, a man sees the world, its past and future, not as *it* is, but as *he* is. To the children of today and to the children of tomorrow the world is fresh and new and full of promise because they themselves are, and love is—and so are these words:

> . . . ye are the light of the world . . .

Chapter 19

IN CONCLUSION

Today, there is a mighty crying in the wilderness, "make way for the Lord"—make way for the religious idea to be reborn upon the plateau of consciousness man has now reached. Among the many voices to be heard, this study selects that of Amadeus, a character in Ernst Wiechert's *Tidings*, to speak for it, as summarized in *Time*'s review:

> Like wounded animals, three noble German brothers drag themselves home to their Hessian castle at the close of World War II. The eldest heals his wounds by charity, tending the displaced persons who occupy the castle. The second heals himself by husbandry, tending the displaced soil and its peasants. But the third brother, Amadeus, finds no panacea to hand. Years in a concentration camp have killed his trust in human beings. War and revolution have so sapped his faith in the earth itself that he can only sigh skeptically when a cheerful clergyman assures him that healing "always begins with the hands. . . . Our heavenly Father looks after the heart." . . . What Amadeus sees is . . . Defeat or victory in battle means "nothing or next to nothing," because today both victors and defeated share equally the "appalling fear of the terrible loneliness of the human race." [1]

Amadeus seeks profound regeneration, and searches his way to the origins to begin at Christendom's own beginning: ". . . to be reborn in the idea of the Nativity itself and to stand, with his two brothers, in the same relation to the hopebearing Child as did three wise men of the East 2,000 years before." [2]

In Jesus' birth legend, the wise men returned to their own countries—and so wise men will do today. But will not the East bring again its gifts to the West, and will not the West again send back a clarion call—peace on earth, goodwill toward man? For that night in Bethlehem:

> The hopes and fears
> Of all the years
> Are met . . .

Jesus, working in the light of humanity's classical expectation of Messiah, presented the contradictory and corresponding truth that stands opposite and equally true—the real idea of the Nativity, as He proclaimed it, is: the Christ is born in every babe.

No one can escape some kind of faith. This study proposes Jesus to be *one*, only, among history's truly divine men, in whom a person may place his faith. His works, words, and the concepts He presents in drama are congruent with scientific data and with the given data of human experience. His revelation leads to precepts beyond measure, but a religious idea which fails to lead beyond the measurable is not congruent with man or science.

Jesus saw every person as ONE, Son of parent life, itself now transparent, only indirectly perceptible—He saw it as that which insures the life of each iota of being expressed through its being. He taught that one cannot reach beyond the divinely human in attempting to know God. This is the philosophy Martin Buber offers today—his words are quoted by Arthur Cohen and Gabriel Schonfeld: ". . . the simple truth is that the wretchedness of our world is grounded in its resistance to the entrance of the holy into lived life. . . . Man cannot approach the divine by reaching beyond the human. To become human is what he, this individual man, has been created for." [3] Holiness comes to rest in humanity among men.

Jesus' teaching leads man to grasp the Christ-being in another, and in all others, for until a man has done so he cannot sustain in sanity the knowledge of the Christ-being within himself as he becomes aware of its truth and power. This need to see Christ-being in another can be met only by preserving the religions that enfold symbols of God incarnate in man. Jesus recognized the need to preserve the mother-church even as the tissue of the new religious idea is given shape and form; He realized that no new religious idea will be widely acclaimed and quickly assimilated in preference to the old and mellowed idea; so that if the old vessel is overcome by the "wine" of the new, both perish. He said:

> . . . no man putteth new wine into old bottles; else the new wine will burst the bottles, and be spilled, and the bottles shall perish. But new wine must be put into new bottles; and both are preserved. No man also having drunk old wine straightway desireth new: for he saith, The old is better.[4]

Thus, He came not to destroy, but to fulfill the promise of the old religion, incorporating in the new church He created, man's precious heritage: the Scriptures.

Jesus taught that pure worship is privately done, its expression intensely personal. Puritanical attitudes, petty prohibitions against eating and drinking, piety as the world holds it to be, He dismissed as affectation. By word, example, and parable, He taught that true love of God is expressed by one's love of nature and his fellowman, and by his partaking of the feast life spreads, by his joy in it. He commanded man to cast out of his life only that which was offensive to himself, or that which he could not practice when living by the Golden Rule. That is, one must keep the Ten Commandments and the commandment Jesus gave:

> Thou shalt love the Lord thy God with all thy heart, and with all thy soul, and with all thy mind . . . Thou shalt love thy neighbor as thyself.[5]

If one accepts the concept of Jesus presented in this book, it must follow that:

He will acknowledge Jesus made Himself a *symbol* of God subjectified in one's being, and "I" is the Word that expresses this power over his flesh, power to understand and to love. He will acknowledge Jesus realized that in the flowering of His precepts the Messianic mold would be broken, to destroy Messianic tradition was His mission, completed as He returned in the Bible, demanded by His words, itself historical Messiah.

He will read the Bible as his personal journal, seeing the words spoken by "I," the Eternal, Lord, or Jesus as words spoken by his own true Ego. He will see Israel, the chosen ones, as *symbol* of the history of his personality, Israel's promise and burden, his own. He will see that when he prays, the Christ of his being is praying to living reality, truth, power, and love within himself, but in correspondence with all reality, truth, power, and love in the universe.

He will accept life eternal, his own in individual terms, as the *fact of his being*, acknowledging that until a person accepts this fact of being, he does not begin to live in reality, does not perceive the reason he must learn to live in truth.

He will accept, on faith if need be, that the universe operates under perfect law, that the system is now and will ever be sufficient to support abundantly the needs and desires of life if man will but bring his intelligence and humanity to bear upon all social problems.

He will accept as *reality* every person's *unconscious*, the measure of which brings all men to equality in being. He will acknowledge that the Son of man within it brings him into conscious embodiment to experience life, returning to consciousness as death overcomes it to receive the many selves of the conscious domain; and that the Son in each person deals with his own one measure of good and evil, expending the destructive potential of each power in the flesh of God which man now wears; and that one's own Authority-Ego judges and saves his own world in which nothing he has known of love and satisfaction will be lost; but that of himself which he cannot bear to live with will be lost to memory, cast into the eternal fire of matter; and in time complete empathy and complete consciousness will generate flesh that man can call his own and keep, with full dominion over it. Then, Self-union will bring him forth in new species wherein expression of evil is diminished to its minimum, thereby turning evil to good, this "bit" of it bringing desire, satisfaction, and ingenuity to life.

He will realize that the final questions—why the universe and man, why am "I" living and conscious of myself and all?—cannot be answered objectively. But these questions may be answered subjectively, and are answered by man's love of life. This recognition of the universe, this process is the one man has chosen to vivify with his own mind and love.

Love forever remains the most daring answer to universal mystery. In the words of Louis Pauwels and Jacques Bergier: "From now on, it is no longer a question of pessimism or optimism: it is a question of love. . . . The more I understand, the more I love; for everything that is understood is good." [6]

Erich Fromm says:

> If I truly love one person I love all persons, I love the world, I love life. If I can say to somebody else, "I love you," I must be able to say, "I love in you everybody, I love through you the world, I love in you also myself." [7]

Love is the answer to the mystery of life, of God, that Jesus gave.

The Christian Church has but one foundation upon which it can continue to exist: belief in the answers Jesus gave to the questions of God, creation, life, man, "who and what am I?" Jesus' Church must stand upon Peter, the rock, therefore upon the Gospels—not the Epistles of Paul.

Faith in Pauline theology cannot be regenerated by disclaiming more and more of its tenets, and arbitrarily dismissing all in the Gospels that science questions, thereby casting increasing doubt upon the integrity of Jesus and His disciples. To survive, Christianity must face squarely its *reason for being:* to preserve and pass along the record of Jesus, and to proclaim and practice *His* doctrine. Christianity can no longer ride the shoulders of St. Paul, mighty as they are. The day of dependence upon vicarious atonement, and vicarious acceptance of the glory, grace, and reality of life is over.

A new Christian theology based upon Jesus' own revelation must be formulated. Christian Realism, as proclaimed by Him, is the gospel that each human being is the Christ, Son of God, eternal, living.

What is God? Jesus said: God is *love*. Love is the mystery that gives meaning to life, the force of attraction that binds in imperishable union all in creation from the "least" particle, the neutrino, to the universe itself, and every precious relationship within it. Love cannot be measured. Jesus said: God is *spirit*. Spirit is unmanifest, save as the unmeasurable energy of mind, or of space itself. Jesus said: God is the *word*. The power of the word, of speech, is now expressed by man, although he cannot define it, or discern its dynamics, or calculate its limits.

Jesus taught that in the power of the word rests the creative principle which insures the enlightenment of man, and the becoming of the universe to express the ideal in being and change that sustains life and satisfaction in life. He taught that God, "The Absolute," gave itself into nature and into man, thereby destroying "The Absolute" in life's operation wherein power is shared with man and expressed in the working of perfect natural law through which truth reigns and governs.

Jesus taught that through the working of natural law, God works. He showed and taught, however, that within natural law the "miraculous" is possible—as is evidenced in phenomena arising from hypnosis, *and* in the miracles wrought when man seeks truth, applies knowledge in the natural realm, and operates the ethic of love and honesty in dealing with mammon.

Jesus taught that truth and God-power are perfectly divided, perfectly stated, in "one," each as "I," and in the principle *one* enfolds: *one* is absolute unto itself only, is indestructible. God is One-Parent-Being with life in itself which cannot be *objectified*, save as the universe and all within it, because this One-Parent-Being is *subjectified* in man, Son, who thereby has life in himself and in whom is reserved one power no other creature expresses: word-power.

Jesus taught that God is only begotten, or "personified," in man. He saw that the God-seed in man is not fully expressed in his consciousness, but that it will flower there if he but sleeps and rises: Homo sapiens is as *child, growing*. Through him, God is committed to the process of evolution—in him, God will be revealed when his consciousness and empathy are complete and the evil inherent in his one measure of absolute power is so diminished through expressing it in life that what remains of it is "laughable."

Thus, Jesus taught that God can be "seen" only in a divinely human being who recognizes that each *one* bears God's being in full and equal measure, and therefore sees himself as brother to, not Father of, humankind. But within each person the God-seed enfolding the power, glory, grace of One-Parent-Being is to him as loving Father, "closer than breathing," utterly his own, God entirely involved in his life, personal to him, perfect in understanding, sufficient unto his every need, insuring his growth, his *humanity*, and his ability to communicate with itself, Himself, and humankind through expression of word-power.

It is the Father-Son relationship that brings love to life, brings moments of joy complete, brings moments of peace that passeth understanding, brings quiet confidence in the grace of nature and of God.

This much may be said now. But much more is to be said, for as the future unfolds, so Jesus' own gospel flowers, and a full understanding of it must come hand in glove with the flowering of knowledge born of intuition and intellect, the one measuring itself against the other, correcting man's course as he walks the path of truth. It cannot all be told today—it could not all be told by those who heard Him speak:

> . . . there are also many other things which Jesus did, the which, if they should be written every one, I suppose that even the world itself could not contain the books that should be written. Amen.
> *John 21:25*

APPENDICES

Appendix I

In Harold's psychology, the *unconscious* may be thought of as a sphere which is the "ground" of one's whole being, containing every potential of life, recognized and unrecognized. Within the *unconscious* there is a nucleus that enfolds the whole "codescript" of life, and knowledge of the principles upon which the Cosmos operates—just as DNA in the nucleus of every cell in the body contains the "codescript" or "blueprint" of the whole body.

This nucleus in the *unconscious* is the "seat" of God-consciousness in humankind, enfolding the whole of truth. Each person possesses one full and equal measure of God-consciousness. Therefore, each of us is in one-to-one correspondence with all others, and is in one-to-one correspondence with Cosmic-consciousness. The unconscious is both individual and collective in the sense that its potential is the same in each human being.

Consciousness cannot comprehend unconscious operations. They are just that: "Not-conscious." This is why Jesus' descriptions of the kingdom of heaven or reign of God are so strange and incomprehensible: It is like a "mustard seed," a "net cast into the sea," a "lump of dough," etc. But in the light of modern physics (as Harold shows later on in the book) these descriptions become meaningful indeed in terms of the operation of the universe.

This inner kingdom, the *unconscious*, gives each person Cosmic dimensions, and makes it possible for him to comprehend abstract ideas and mathematical concepts. Einstein's rare vision emanated from this source as well as from his knowledge of mathematics. His view of the Cosmos is described succinctly by Dr. John A. Wheeler: [1]

[1] John A. Wheeler and Seymour Tilson, *The Dynamics of Space-Time* (New York: *International Science & Technology Journal*, December, 1963, reprinted by *Artoga*,

A matter-free universe that nevertheless must be thought of in terms of the "stuff" of space-time—a remarkably malleable *primordial dough* catalyzed only by energy and by the fertile *yeast* of mathematical imagination.

Listen now to Jesus' "yeasty" reply when he was asked to explain what the life and action of the whole Cosmos is like—for the "Reign of God" can be nothing less. He said:

> To what shall I compare the Reign of God? It is like dough, which a woman took and buried in three pecks of flour, till all of it was leavened. (Matt. 13:33.)

Today, scientists in their efforts to explain the action of energy in the universe, the Cosmos itself, draw upon the same poetic words and ideas Jesus used.

Jesus' ability to set aside his consciousness and let the fount of truth within the nucleus of his *unconscious* flow through him enabled him to grasp, as surely as Einstein did centuries later, something of the nature of universal patterns of operation.

In Harold's psychology, consciousness is likened to an aura arising from and surrounding the sphere of the *unconscious*. He uses the word much as Teilhard de Chardin uses it. Or, in the Jungian sense: Consciousness is a projection of inner light. The subconscious mind is of the realm of consciousness, a stratum of the aura. It is the "computer" in which the whole of one's experience is stored. Superconsciousness is also a stratum in the aura of consciousness, and Harold's concept of it differs sharply from Freud's as the reader will see. But the *unconscious* is a realm apart, "absolutely elsewhere" in relation to any aspect of consciousness.

Winifred Babcock

Appendix II

Harold believed that all mysterious phenomena are related to the hypnotic state, because, in his view, the hypnotic state includes any

---

Communications 70 and 71, October and November, 1964. Quotation drawn from the reprinted article. Italics mine.

"shift" of consciousness or sensibility in which the person is not normally alert and *using his intellectual powers*. The span of hypnotic states is much broader than it is generally regarded to be. These states range from the *hyper-alert*, to momentary lapse of awareness, through recognizable levels of trance, down to a death-like state.

Paradoxical as it may seem, in the hyper-alert state one's attention is so fixed on what is being said or done that he is blocking out much sensory stimuli. He is apt to be more open to suggestion that he would be in states of obvious trance, because his state of expectancy and willingness to "get" the information is heightened. The hyper-alert state occurs spontaneously. It is difficult, if not impossible, for an operator to induce it deliberately. It differs from the ordinary state of intense concentration in which the intellect is also operative. It may be thought of as "pure concentration"—so pure that sensory stimuli and "thought interference" that might question or debate the issue play no part. The listener is completely open, completely receptive, to the information or commands coming to him. Posthypnotic response to suggestions given in the hyper-alert state is made as readily as when the suggestions are given in a state of deep trance. The hyper-alert state arises of its own accord if the subject matter is important enough to the listener to command this state, and if the speaker is felt to be the authority on the subject and is so assured in his manner that he voluntarily or *involuntarily* elicits the complete attention of his listener.

As for how the Gospels were structured through posthypnotic response and recall, consider that information as to what was and was not to be included, how they were to be protected, how and when they were to appear, could have been given to the disciples by Jesus when they were in the hyper-alert state. The lost "Q" source could have been destroyed at his command when the Gospels took their final form. He could have prohibited circulation of them for many years to *prevent* the early Christian community from altering their content as the years passed and Jesus did not return as expected.

But it is just as possible that the disciples were in a recognizable state of trance when such information pertaining to the Gospels was given by Jesus. In any of the hypnotic states the shift in consciousness causes the blocking out of ordinary stimuli, opening the way for the subject to become receptive to suggestions and commands to be carried out posthypnotically. Jesus could have commanded the disciples not to remember what was said until through posthypnotic response to suggestion they would remember. He could have reinforced his commands through calling upon their powers of auto-suggestion in posthypnotic recall to repeat them again and again until the time came to write the Gospels as they were instructed to do.

The important point is that, in Harold's view, Jesus understood the operation of psychic and mental energy so perfectly, and was himself such a master of his own psychic power, that he could exercise it effortlessly and lead others into releasing their own psychic potential naturally. It was not necessary for him to go through the motions we associate with inducing trance state. Such motions are not necessarily required, as has been pointed out in Chapter 10. And a person who has once been hypnotized can be put into trance state with no effort. Any simple word or gesture is sufficient. Jesus could have led his disciples in and out of trance at any time with ease. But he was not a "practicing hypnotist" as we think of such today. He used his psychic power naturally and quite naturally his disciples and others responded to it.

"Hypnotism" has a cloud hanging over it, and is somehow presently associated with the occult and witchcraft. The word has become distasteful to many. It merely meant "sleep" in Greek. Some have said that Harold should not have used the term. He could have coined a term of his own—or referred to "altered states of consciousness," the polite term for hypnosis today. But he chose not to do so. The simple fact is that any alteration of normal "working" consciousness puts one into some type of trance or hypnotic state. *Loss of consciousness* need not be involved, and is not involved at many levels of trance. Indeed, consciousness may well be heightened, making one more aware. But there has been a shift, a change, in consciousness that enhances or diminishes perception, or alters body-mind states.

Today, a number of techniques to induce these states are taught and practiced; but many of the teachers insist that hypnosis is not involved. It is involved, if any *fixing of attention together with suggestion of any sort is involved.* For example, in biofeedback attention is fixed on the apparatus (lights) and suggestions of various sorts are given. There is nothing wrong in employing such a technique as this—or techniques for meditation, to use another example. They can be very beneficial. And it is better in every way if a mechanism or technique can be employed to induce self-hypnosis, teaching the person to control his own mental and physical powers. But the principle or process that is being called upon is the *same one* that is involved in hypnosis: fixing attention on something, shift of consciousness, giving suggestions.

Using other terminology for hypnotic practices can be confusing. In referring to *altered* states of consciousness, we must not confuse the temporary shift (which can be of varying durations) with *expanded or enlarged* consciousness. When one achieves a state of expanded consciousness through meditation, prayer, learning to express the mind-body relationship more fully, or in any one of a number of ways, this shift is not temporary. Consciousness is thereafter on a higher level. One has greater depth and breadth of understanding, is more aware of everything. It is as though consciousness has been reborn upon another plateau of empathy and understanding of life itself. Practicing *altered states* of consciousness, such as meditation, can lead to *expanded states* of consciousness. It is wise to make a clear distinction between these terms. Just as hypnosis can be misused and under some circumstances pose problems, so it is with any technique that produces altered states. Harold avoids confusion by using the word *hypnosis*. And he saw that in subject matter dealing with hypnotism there is a wealth of information about the phenomena associated with psychic power. In tracing the history of hypnotism back through the ages, one finds every mysterious practice directly or indirectly related to it, from "black magic" to "white magic," voo-doo, witchcraft, oracles, healings, etc.

To Harold, it was as important to understand hypnotism's dark side as to understand its constructive potential. If use of hypnosis (by whatever name it may be called) presents a threat to well being, we must know how to guard against it. If it offers a natural means to extend one's own capacity for learning, for releasing the human potential, or for healing self or others, we must learn how to use it. We must understand mind-body relationships, and the *principle* that is employed when physic phenomena occur, so that psi-power can be used constructively. Dodging "loaded words" will not help. Knowledge is dangerous only when it is not common knowledge. And knowledge, to be most useful, must be common knowledge.

There was another reason for Harold's using the word *hypnosis*. Many scientists deny that any form of extrasensory perception or psi-power exists. But the most skeptical cannot deny that an *unknown range* of hypnotic states can be induced and the phenomena that can be produced in these states can be demonstrated repeatedly. In combining the study of all paranormal phenomena into the study of a larger concept of hypnosis, Harold brings his reader into contact immediately with *undeniable reality*, and provides a framework within which the miracles can be studied.

In pointing out that all of the miracles can be shown to be demonstrations within the known limits of hypnotic phenomena, so that all of them fall within the realm of natural happenings, Harold in no way insists that this is the only explanation of them. He offers it as *an* explanation that accords with the way the miracles are reported in the Gospels and with Jesus' own appraisal of his work. Jesus said that others would do greater deeds than he, thereby ruling out the idea that God worked through him in a supranatural way.

If Jesus understood psychic power as Harold believed he did, then the "dark" side of this power must also be shown by him. He showed this *symbolically* in the drama of casting the "Legion" of demons into the swine—as Harold explains in detail. Harold believed that Jesus showed the valid limits of ESP and of hypnosis: Its ability to *delude* as well as to illuminate; and that he demonstrated the release of the body's healing power in trance.

In "The Mystery of the Miracles," a paper on Harold's work prepared for a seminar by Dr. Alan McGlashan, psychiatrist, London, he presents such lucid comments on hypnosis and medicine that excerpts from his paper are quoted in the following section.

* * * * *

Excerpts from: "The Mystery of the Miracles" by Alan McGlashan

Rhythm may be the key to many of these paranormal events . . . in truth the most we can do with rhythm is to observe its periodicities and its effects, and tune ourselves in to its invisible power. . . . This tuning-in process is a vital part of the procedure in *hypnosis*. The faintly absurd preliminaries of hypnotic induction . . . are attempts to establish a shared rhythm between patient and operator. The patient is lulled and caressed and carried unresistingly along on regular waves of sight or sound. The process is part of the magical effect of poetry, of music—and of waterfalls. . . .

Exceptional Being that He was, Jesus was able usually to dispense with hypnotic preliminaries. . . . He was able to rely on the immediate effect of His voice and gestures, endowed with—who can now tell?—what compelling qualities of rhythm, to penetrate like a laser ray to the depths of the psyche and accomplish the healing.

It seems extremely probable that Harold's hypothesis of incomparable hypnotic power covers many of the miracles of Jesus. . . . As regards [Jesus' miracles of healing], I think Harold would say that given sufficient knowledge and control of the physiology of the body and the psychology of one's own and the other person's mind . . . miraculous organic changes can be achieved by hypnosis, which, although far beyond the range of conventional medicine and surgery, nevertheless fall within the scope of natural law. . . . It opens up fantastic therapeutic possibilities. But in this field of therapy there are also enormous resistances to be overcome. It would seem, therefore, that now is the time for the whole question of hypnotism and its relationship to the miraculous to be re-examined. . . .

Ever since the days of that magnificent but shameless showman, Mesmer, hypnotism has been under a scientific cloud. Even today it is still struggling for full recognition. I think the reason for its current devaluation is connected with the strong bias of contemporary thought, and especially medical thought, in favour of logical objectivity. In the effort to attain medical respectability in this intellectual climate, hypnotism has been compelled to present itself as entirely a matter of technique, discreetly divorced from any connection with spiritual forces in either the hypnotist or his patient. One point I wish to make is that this is a valid aspect of hypnotism. At this level hypnotism is a technique which can be learned by any intelligent person, and which produces demonstrable and repeatable results. It fulfills the essential criteria of scientific procedure, and can be accepted into the body of scientific orthodoxy—which, strangely enough, seems to be the heart's desire of many hypnotists. In this form hypnosis is a valuable tool, and is in fact already in frequent use, for example in dental and surgical operations.

But such an assessment of hypnotism is a gross misapprehension of its potentialities. It has led certain medical scientists to regard hypnotic phenomena as little more than a demonstration of the unreliability of the human sensory apparatus, and a further proof of the need for ever stricter objectivity. This is a monstrous misconception. But understandable. It is hard for the contemporary medical scientist to make a true evaluation of hypnotism. The thing scares him because it draws him away from his familiar world of double-blind controls and computered statistics—into a region of pure mystery. . . . As Preston Harold has written, "Man must face the fact that extrasensory perception is operative, that hypnotic responses are miraculous, that the 'stuff' of matter or flesh is as mysterious as a ghost, as illusory as it is real."

Self-evident as these words may seem to us, we must also face the fact that, even now, to the rank and file of the medical world they are the blackest heresy. This is a natural and self-protective reaction. For the majority of medical researchers feel themselves threatened and disoriented by these "dangerous" views, and cling more tightly than ever to such comforting techniques as the double-blind check, the primary aim of which is to separate as completely as possible the doctor from the patient.

Though uneasily aware that a new spirit is abroad, these meticulous researchers are still entangled in the attitudes of 19th century science, which surely touched its apotheosis of absurdity in the remarkable statement of the then world-famous chemist Berthelot: "From now on," he announced, "there is no mystery about the Universe." Today, when leading physicists use the expressions such as *forbidden radiation* and *absolute elsewhere*, and speak of fluids so volatile that they can pass through a hole which does not exist, I think we can assure the illustrious shade of Berthelot that somehow mystery has crept back into the Universe.

It is one of the many fine achievements of Preston Harold that he has brought back this sense of mystery and the miraculous into the healing of the sick. Facile explanations of hypnotic therapy must be discarded. The theory that healing by hypnosis is dependent on the artificial creation of a parent-child situation is inadequate, applying only to the limited forms of hypnosis already in use. But there is another, an "altogether other," level of hypnosis in which spiritual forces are deeply involved, and for which *empathy* of a high order is demanded. I suggest that in this kind of hypnosis the healing occurs at the meeting point between two mysteries: the Self of the healer and the Self of the patient, [Harold's concept]. It is a moment of truth; and it lies, where the Pearl of Hafiz of Shiraz lies, "outside the oyster of Space and Time."

We need another word for this event. The word "hypnotism" is too caught up in irrelevant associations to be anything but a hindrance to the concept I am trying to convey, which calls for a different kind of man, with a new grasp of the potentialities and limitations of psycho-therapy. It cannot be built up on the basis of hypnotism as at present practised. It cannot be taught by weekly lectures in medical schools. It is a first step in another dimension.

This may sound as if I am confirming the rift between science and religion which Preston Harold in his treatment of miracles has done so much to heal. But this is not my intention. I am dealing not with the intuitions of genius but with matters as they stand today in what could be called "the double-blind world" of medical research. After all, one should not attempt the impossible in too short a time. It is said that Mahomet entirely failed to convert his grandfather!

The most that can be asked at present of the majority of medical scientists is that they should open their minds to a new possibility: the emergence of an altogether different factor in the art of healing. . . .

Such an act of integration should not be impossible for the medical profession, whose fading but still-operative Hippocratic Oath retains a trace of the archaic insight that, in certain callings, spiritual quality is as basic as skill. We have to recapture this insight. It was born again, nearer to our own time, in the minds of the mediaeval alchemists, who tried to transform *themselves*, as well as their material, and who approached matter with a passionate conviction that it held a mystery, the nature of which was different in quality and in essence from its material container. This is the conviction, and could have been the very words, of Preston Harold. And I believe that this great unknown, slipping invisibly through our midst as did Jesus through the Temple crowds, has left the world a priceless clue to the fusion of many levels of perception. In the light of his harmonizing concepts an image of the Nativity re-appears: philosopher, doctor, and physicist, the "three wise men" of the West, make their way once more towards the cradle where lies Truth, the Shining Stranger.

* * * * * Alan McGlashan [1]

McGlashan, too, deplores the inadequacy of the word *hypnotism* to convey the dimension of the spiritual forces involved in Harold's concept of Jesus' use of psychic power. But his paper conveys the essence of Harold's approach to the mystery of hypnotism—and also, Harold's concept of the empathy and resonance between Jesus, his disciples, and patients that allowed him to use but never misuse his "incomparable" hypnotic power.

Harold points out that Jesus "sealed" every healing with command or suggestion that would encourage his patient to enter life again operating under a *changed mental pattern;* and that Jesus called upon everyone to exercise conscious powers and conscious control of themselves to the same degree that psychic powers are exercised. The mental pattern that has given rise to the patient's symptoms must be changed if the healing is to be complete. Only as his consciousness is expanded and thereafter operates at a higher level can the healing be sustained. This is the spiritual dimension that is overlooked too often by medical men and healers of every sort. This is why many healings by some form of hypnotherapy are short lived, or if one set of symptoms is removed another set appears.

In the work of great faith healers today, such as Katherine Kuhlman, one can observe the spiritual dimension that sets the mental stage for a healing to occur. We can observe her ability to bring many in her vast

[1] Alan McGlashan, "The Mystery of the Miracles," unpublished manuscript, 1972. Available from Harold Institute.

audiences into resonance with the rhythm of her own faith and expectation. Few who attend her services fail to enter to some degree an altered state of consciousness. And those who can receive her suggestions of healing, who can *accept* the miracle of the body's own ability to heal itself almost instantaneously, who *act* upon this belief, are healed. The faith and expectancy of one, Katherine Kuhlman, strengthens the faith and expectancy of another, and the other's of another, until, in her words, the auditorium is filled with the holy Spirit of life itself—God.

There is a common denominator—a single principle—that operates in all faith healing. Harold points it out as demonstrated by Jesus. Medical science should strive as hard to state this principle and find ways to employ it as they strive to enlarge research in drugs and what might be called mechanical medical technology.

It must be pointed out that Harold's respect for and appreciation of the medical profession is evident throughout. He believed that we should call upon medical science and utilize all it can offer—the many blessings it provides. But he realized that its focus is too narrow. There is not enough regard for the mind-body relationship. Its research must be broadened to include this relationship and the spiritual dimension McGlashan speaks of. When will the medical profession realize that *suggestion* may well be the sharpest tool in the kit?—and that it can work both ways?

The mind-body relationship is brought into dramatic focus in Harold's dealing with the episode wherein Jesus casts the maniac's "legion of demons" into swine and the herd rushes to destruction in the sea (see above, pp. 232–233). Harold saw that this strange play upon opposite forces conveyed a pattern of the casting of psychic trauma upon the flesh. Nameless fears, stresses, phobias are repressed until they grow into a "host" that must be sent somewhere. The force of "legion" must be expended in the mind or in the flesh.

Harold related cancer to this pattern (see reference 19, Chapter 11). Cancer that metastasizes throughout the body, as "legion" may be said to have "metastasized" or spread throughout the herd of swine, drives the body to death at panic's pace. Harold indicates that Jesus showed this pattern and revealed the cause to be the transfer of psychic distress to the flesh. In 1936, Dr. N. D. C. Lewis suggested that *cancer was a form of paranoia at the cellular level*.[2]

A number of studies show a relationship between emotional factors and cancer, but medical science as yet takes little note of this. Certainly,

[2] N. D. C. Lewis, *Research in Dementia Praecox*, National Committee for Mental Hygiene, New York, 1936.

little if anything is done in most cases to treat the patient's mind as well as his body. And yet, as Dr. A. Hoffer writes:

> LeShan (1961) isolated a factor primarily in patients dying with cancer. Out of 18 patients with cancer, 16 had severe despair . . . LeShan believed despair accelerated tumor growth.[3]

Most, if not all, cancer patients suffer varying degrees of depression, although this is often masked behind the brave front they put on for sake of family, and perhaps to keep themselves in hand. Later, the depression is masked by drugs they are given to control pain. Depression is expected, so no effort is made to treat it, especially in cases that are considered hopeless. But a wholistic approach, treating mind and body, might be of great benefit even to advanced cases.

The use of electroconvulsive shock therapy (ECT) has been the most successful treatment for depression. No doubt, ECT has been misused—used punitively and with little regard for the patient's apprehension in a number of large mental institutions. Many people regard it with fear, which is unjustified when it is properly given. Today, techniques for administering ECT have been improved greatly. There is no physical discomfort and the disorientation afterwards is only temporary. A surprising number of physicians, other than psychiatrists, do not know much about it outside of generalities.

ECT is the least radical of all treatments for a disease that requires radical treatment—cancer. In addition to relieving depression, it may also produce physiological effects that enhance or evoke host resistance, so that biological control of the tumor becomes possible. There is little information on the results in cancer patients treated with ECT, or shock therapy of any sort, but what there is indicates that this treatment *in conjunction with standard medical treatments* could be effective in many cases.[4]

Harold points out that Jesus "convulsed" a man with an "unclean spirit," and it brought to his mind "the convulsive effect of electric shock therapy." It is not known exactly why ECT is so effective for depression. But it is evident that the mental pattern in which the patient is trapped is *disorganized*, and then a healthier mental pattern organizes to

---

[3] A. Hoffer, M.D., Ph.D., F.A.P.A., C.R.C.P. (C)., "The Psychophysiology of Cancer," *The Journal of Asthma Research*, Vol. 8, No. 2, December, 1970, p. 63.
[4] Charles Goldfarb, M.D., Jerome Driesen, M.D., and Donald Cole, M.D., "Psychophysiologic Aspects of Malignancy," *American Journal of Psychiatry*, 123: 12, June 1967. [This is the only article I have come across, but I have been told that there are others.]

provide a better mind-body relationship, as the patient emerges from the *anesthesia* that relieved his mental pain.

As for the mind-body relationship, Dr. Hoffer writes:

> Kowal (1955) reviewed the early historical evidence which showed a relationship between emotional factors and cancer. This was noted in the 18th century. Subjects with cancer had frequently lost a significant person and suffered from despair and hopelessness. Kowal assumed the emotional factors were causal to the cancer. It does not seem likely that emotional factors could play a major causal role, although there is no longer room for doubt that the cancer can cause mental changes.[5]

Whether "legion," the repressed trauma all of us harbor, accumulates to reach such force that it must be cast upon the flesh, giving rise to cancer, or whether once the dread disease is diagnosed and a "legion" of fear and despair accumulates rapidly to accelerate tumor growth, it is time for medical science to recognize the value of treating the whole person. Physicians should *treat the depression,* if for no other reason than to relieve the mental suffering of their patients, just as they try to relieve the physical suffering. There is reason to believe that such a wholistic approach would be more effective and offer more hope than any standard treatment offered today.

But the patient and his family also have a responsibility here: They must acknowledge the mental condition that cancer gives rise to, and they must *request* the standard and accepted treatment for the depression, as well as the standard and accepted treatment that may be indicated for the body, such as surgery.

I have drawn attention to the drama of "legion" to point out that Harold's approach to the subject of healing is deeply involved with the effects of stress, and implicit in it are suggestions that include much more than hypnotherapy. But he also indicates that when hynotherapy is better understood, it would be possible to produce the same effect via suggestion as some medical techniques or treatments, such as ECT, produce.

Because so much was deleted from Harold's original manuscript that made his approach to the miracles and to the subject of hypnosis much clearer, I feel that this Appendix, lengthy as it is, will help the reader to understand better the chapters that follow.

Winifred Babcock

[5] Hoffer, *op. cit.,* pp. 62–63.

Appendix III

In the following chapters, Harold examines the miracles that do not pertain to healing. He related these also to the phenomena that can be produced under hypnosis. These phenomena include altered perception. The subject can be made to see only what he is told to see, or can be blinded to objects that are there, to actions that do take place, or can experience a vision or hallucination that is completely *real to him*.

Again, it must be pointed out that Harold offers these explanations not as the only possible ones, but as the probable ones because of the way these miracles are reported in the Gospels.

Dr. Alan McGlashan, whose paper is quoted in part in Appendix II, questions whether thereby Harold "preserves his concept of immutable natural laws." The answer to this question is: Harold did not believe that natural law is immutable. But due to deletions in his manuscript, this is not made clear at this point in the book, so it should be clarified here.

Harold believed that truth resides in the "perfect contradiction." Or, in Lawrence Durrell's words, "Truth is what most contradicts itself." Harold also quotes Niels Bohr: "There are trivial truths and there are great truths. The opposite of a trivial truth is plainly false. The opposite of a great truth is also true." We are confronted with the perfect contradiction of light, as physicists describe it: Light is a particle and light is a wave-group. Each aspect of light appears to be "equally true," quantum mechanics useful in one set of circumstances, wave mechanics in another.

In Harold's view, *at the limit* any law, natural or psychic (as he saw the Ten Commandments to be), expresses itself in terms of a perfect contradiction. This is to say, law is a statement of the *penultimate*—not the ultimate—point of truth. This penultimate point of truth divides, presenting opposite truths of equal magnitude, requiring a choice to be made, or judgment to be exercised. In physics, we are confronted by the *uncertainty principle* set forth by Werner Heisenberg. We reach the point where this principle takes over; and for Harold this coincides with the penultimate point of truth. Or, to put it another way, *the absolute* cannot be expressed in the mental or physical or natural realms. And the ultimate cannot be expressed other than in terms of a perfect contradiction that presents opposite truths of equal magnitude, either of which may be acted upon, but not both at once.

The nature of "perfect law," then, or perfection, is to maintain an open system, a process that always provides at the minimum "another way out," or provides for contradictory action. In short, a system that is characterized by at least a degree of freedom of choice. There is no real freedom of choice between the obviously true and the obviously false. Choice of the false will take its toll whether we are aware of this or not. True freedom of choice comes when we must choose between truths of equal magnitude. Once this choice is made, we have not encompassed the ultimate or the absolute. We are again at a penultimate point that again divides to present us with the perfect contradiction.

In so far as nature's laws are concerned, there is an *optimum* "choice" or mode of expression for every particle, force, or field. Natural law describes this mode. These laws are useful because everything in the universe expresses in terms of the optimum mode so preponderantly that the laws are *statistically reliable,* and through use of them we can make predictions. But we must, nevertheless, remember that under given circumstances, the perfect contradiction may be expressed. In this sense, no law is immutable. Under certain conditions, it is *probable* that the optimum pattern of behavior of nature's forces will not be followed, that the opposite effect will occur.

For example, fire burns. This is its optimum effect. This makes it useful, and enables us to control the effect most of the time in a beneficial way. But it is not only possible, it is indeed probable, that fire will not burn the feet of certain fire-walkers. There is no question about this. It has been demonstrated too many times, and the phenomenon has been witnessed by too many accredited observers, to doubt that it does happen. But natural law has not been transgressed or suspended. Fire-walking is within the realm of the natural. It demonstrates the control of the mind, consciousness, or psyche, if you will, over the body's own flesh. By the same token, levitation that appears to suspend the law of gravity can occur.

In the open system that this universe is, "all things are possible." But all things are not necessarily probable, or desirable. Only as we understand nature's realm, including the limits and dynamics of our own psychic powers, will we be able to evoke the perfect contradiction at appropriate times and in appropriate ways. The danger lies in toying with these powers.

Harold says that Jesus did not use his powers indiscriminately, lightly, or inappropriately. But he did call upon psychic power to evoke visionary dramas, or to produce effects, which could convey truth too complex to be trusted to words. He also created dramas that are precise and unforgettable patterns of psychic operations—patterns as rich in meaning as the most potent symbols, patterns that convey "books" of information and feeling. Every such miracle had manifold meaning and messages to convey. But, as Harold pointed out, if Jesus himself was true, then these miracles must convey truth at every level. That is, the visionary drama must *be possible*, so that if accepted at face value, it would still be pointing to reality in all its depths. And this, Harold believed, is the case.

Because of the way the "illusory miracles" are reported, Harold believed that they took place in the minds of those reporting them. To these disciples, they were utterly real. By creating the mental drama, Jesus could bring it into clear focus, presenting at once the panoramic and "close up" view, so that a much clearer grasp of the pattern of action could be had than would have been possible otherwise.

When we watch a football game on television, all of the play is presented on a screen by cameras that give a better view of the action throughout the game at any place on the field than any seat in the stadium would provide. In parallel, a mental drama focused on the screen of one's mind can give a perfect view of the entire episode. Because of this, on occasion Jesus could accomplish his purpose more readily by having his disciples share visionary experience with him than he could if the action had taken place in physical reality, although it would have been *possible* for him to accomplish it in actuality. Every visionary drama *could have happened*. Therefore, the miracles are not false on any level. They do not transgress or suspend natural law, because natural law is not immutable. The "perfect contradiction" can be evoked. Consciousness controls the flesh that houses it, and consciousness evokes the contradiction. But, for Harold, it is probable that certain miracles were demonstrations of psi-power or were visionary encounters with reality. This, because the Gospels, when accounts of the miracles in all of them are taken into consideration, indicate the nature of these episodes by the way they are reported.

In the "social miracles," one sees that, in Harold's view, Jesus' greatest accomplishment was to call forth quietly from groups or multitudes of people the *optimum in human behavior*. It can be done. This is the real message underlying these episodes, the real miracle.

Winifred Babcock

Appendix IV

Reactions to "The Economic Doctrine of Jesus" vary widely. *The Philosopher*, Journal of the Philosophical Society of England, comments: "Chapter XVII in a class by itself is the soundest exposition of contemporary economics we know." Some, however, are distressed that Harold, who they feel otherwise touched so profoundly and truly upon the essence of Jesus' message, could have involved him with capitalism, the profit system, or anything pertaining to materialism. But Harold drew only upon Jesus' own words—Jesus involved himself in these issues.

Again, the trouble is "loaded words." Again, Harold did not dodge these issues or words. He presented them in a wider perspective. As time passes, the perspective becomes even wider. The following article by Sydney J. Harris, that appeared in his syndicated column, "Strictly Personal," on December 15, 1972, shows another paradoxical turn in the course of economic history:

> It may just turn out to be the supreme irony of the late 20th century that capitalism—which Marx saw as fomenting wars to gain new markets and profits—will become the instrument for the abolition of war. Not for any moral reason, but simply for economic good sense. One of the astonishing transitions in our technocratic society is the rapid spread of the "multinational" corporation—the large and sprawling company, with roots in one country and branches everywhere else.
>
> These companies have found that new markets can be generated by economic aggressiveness with far greater effectiveness and less danger than by political or military aggressiveness. They have become, or are becoming, "suprapolitical" entities of an entirely new sort. War, on the nuclear scale upon which it can now be fought, has become obsolescent, because its consequences can no longer be controlled, and also because there would be no conceivable "winners" left after a nuclear holocaust. The last thing the multinational corporation wants to do is to decimate its potential worldwide markets. It seems to me that if a true state of peace is ever arrived at—and not just the uneasy truces we have had every few years—not religion nor morality nor sentimentality will secure it.
>
> It will be secured, if at all, by the same considerations that made war

profitable in the past—by economic considerations. If it was mainly the drive for profits that created national conflicts (and here I believe that Marx was right), then it will be the same drive for profits that overrides political and nationalistic factors that still strain for war. We tend to forget that capitalism, by its very nature, is as "internationalistic" as communism is, or pretends to be. In the past, capitalism used the politics of its own country to develop and expand; it was to its short-term interest to wrest markets from competing lands.

Now the new technology has given capitalism the means and the access to tremendous new markets without firing a shot or capturing an acre of land. Consider what Japan has been able to accomplish in the post-war period, though completely demilitarized and impotent in world politics. If she had won the war with the attack on Pearl Harbor, she could not possibly be as well off as she is now, as the "loser."

Marx predicted the victory of international communism. What we may yet live to see is the victory of international capitalism—a capitalism that has grown wise enough and flexible enough and long-sighted enough to learn that people elsewhere can, and must, be raised to the level of buyers, not reduced to the level of beggars.

Sydney Harris in the above article does, indeed, seem to support Harold's view, in the sense that Jesus espoused capitalism and the profit system because he saw that this system cannot in truth profit itself by malpractice.

Winifred Babcock

REFERENCES

[Quotations from the Bible, as translated by Moffatt, James, are indicated by: (M)]

CHAPTER 1: THE PROBLEM, THE OBJECTIVE, THE CRUCIAL QUESTIONS

1. William Barrett, *Irrational Man* (New York: Doubleday, 1958), p. 20
2. Alfred Guillaume, *Islam* (Baltimore: Pelican Books, 1956), p. 14
3. Julian Huxley, *New Bottles For New Wine* (New York: Harper, 1957), p. 237
4. Samuel Miller, "The Evolution of Religion," *Saturday Review*, November 14, 1959, p. 70
5. J. B. Priestley, *Literature and Western Man* (New York: Harper, 1960), p. 445
6. *Ibid.*, p. 444
7. Carl G. Jung, "God, the Devil, and the Human Soul," *The Atlantic*, November, 1957, p. 58
8. J. H. van den Berg, *The Changing Nature of Man* (New York: W. W. Norton, 1961), pp. 101, 69, 40
9. *Ibid.*, pp. 40, 83
10. *Ibid.*, pp. 45, 46
11. Priestley, *op. cit.*, p. 444
12. Russell W. Davenport, *The Dignity of Man* (New York: Harper, 1955), p. 53
13. Nikita Khrushchev, Associated Press Release, San Francisco, September 22, 1959
14. Jawaharlal Nehru, Associated Press Release, New Delhi, September 9, 1958
15. Colin Wilson, *Religion and the Rebel* (Boston: Houghton Mifflin Co., 1957), p. 275, quoting George Bernard Shaw, *Prefaces* (London: Odhams, 1938), p. 506
16. Davenport, *op. cit.*, p. 250
17. 1 Cor. 6:19–20 (M)
18. Guillaume, *op. cit.*, p. 76
19. Davenport, *op. cit.*, p. 165

20. Whittaker Chambers, *Cold Friday* (New York: Random House, 1964), pp. 165, 166, 181, 182, 184, 189
21. Huxley, *op. cit.*, p. 110
22. Radhakrishnan, *Recovery of Faith* (London: George Allen & Unwin Ltd., 1956), p. 103
23. Barrett, *op. cit.*, pp. 152, 153
24. Matt. 7:18, 12:33
25. Radhakrishnan, *op. cit.*, p. 152
26. Alexander Blok, *The Twelve* (New York: William Edwin Rudge, 1931), XII
27. Radhakrishnan, *op. cit.*, p. 188
28. Matt. 25:40
29. Huxley, *op. cit.*, p. 97
30. John 8:32
31. "Cabal and Kaleidoscope," *Time*, August 8, 1958, p. 80. See also: Lawrence Durrell, *Balthazar* (New York: Pocket Books, Inc., 1961), p. 92
32. Henry A. Murray, "Two Versions of Man," in *Science Ponders Religion*, ed. Harlow Shapley (New York: Appleton-Century-Crofts, 1962), p. 176
33. *Ibid.*
34. John Ciardi, "Dialogue with the Audience," *Saturday Review*, November 22, 1958, p. 10
35. Priestley, *op. cit.*, pp. 122, 221
36. Arnold Toynbee, *An Historian's Approach To Religion* (New York: Oxford University Press, 1956), p. 125. (Heb. xiii. 8)
37. *Webster's New and Unabridged Dictionary* (Springfield, Massachusetts: G. & C. Merriam Co., 1940), see: POETRY. Cf. Plato, *The Sophist*, 265–266.
38. Ciardi, *op. cit.*, p. 12
39. Arthur Eddington, *The Nature of the Physical World* (Chicago: University of Michigan Press, 1958), pp. 316, 317
40. *Ibid.*, pp. 315, 324
41. Barrett, *op. cit.*, p. 168
42. Jung, "God, the Devil, and the Human Soul," p. 63
43. Huxley, *op. cit.*, pp. 81, 108
44. Burnett H. Streeter, *The Four Gospels* (New York: St. Martin's Press, 1924)
45. Ethelbert Stauffer, *Jesus and His Story*, trans. Richard and Clara Winston (New York: Alfred A. Knopf, 1960), p. 8
46. Matt. 19:28 (See also, Luke 22:30)
47. Matt. 20:20–23 (M)
48. Mark 10:35
49. Luke 17:21
50. Albert Schweitzer, *Out of My Life and Thought* (New York: New American Library, 1949), p. 186
51. Ira Progoff, *The Death and Rebirth of Psychology* (New York: Julian Press, 1956), p. 9
52. Morris Kline, *Mathematics in Western Culture* (New York: Oxford University Press, 1953), p. 57
53. Luke 19:40
54. Kline, *op. cit.*, p. 440 (Re: Albert Einstein)

REFERENCES

CHAPTER 2: THE MESSIANIC MISSION OF JESUS

1. Ernest Renan, *The Life of Jesus* (New York: Random House, Modern Library, 1927), p. 386. [See also: Oswald Spengler, *Decline of the West* (New York: Alfred A. Knopf, 1934), II, 212–215.]
2. Renan, *op. cit.*, pp. 125, 224, 240, 329
3. *Ibid.*, see Chapter XVI, pp. 249, 254
4. *Ibid.*, pp. 161, 162
5. Albert Schweitzer, *Out of My Life and Thought*, pp. 42, 43, 47
6. Matt. 24:35, John 4:23
7. Schweitzer, *op. cit.*, pp. 50, 180
8. *Ibid.*, p. 46
9. Renan, *op. cit.*, pp. 83, 90–93, 133, 137, 138
10. Ethelbert Stauffer, *Jesus and His Story*, p. 53
11. Renan, *op. cit.*, pp. 112, 218
12. *Ibid.*, p. 351
13. *Ibid.*, p. 353
14. Stauffer, *op. cit.*, p. 103
15. Luke 4:16–20, John 8:6
16. Renan, *op. cit.*, p. 390
17. Stauffer, *op. cit.*, p. 170
18. Robert deRopp, *Science and Salvation* (New York: St. Martin's Press, 1962), p. 129
19. Edith Hamilton, "The Lessons of the Past," in *Adventures of the Mind*, eds. Richard Thruelsen and John Kobler (New York: Alfred A. Knopf, 1959), p. 79
20. Luke 2:51
21. Matt. 13:53–58 (M)
22. Ranjee Shahani, "A Lamp Unto Himself," *Saturday Review*, September 26, 1959, p. 31
23. Clyde Kluckhohn, *Mirror for Man* (New York: McGraw-Hill Book Co., 1960), p. 56
24. Renan, *op. cit.*, p. 104
25. *Ibid.*, pp. 101, 102
26. Luke 24:44–45
27. Schweitzer, *op. cit.*, p. 50
28. William Barrett, *Irrational Man*, p. 176
29. *Ibid.*, p. 188
30. I Cor. 3:11 (M)
31. Stauffer, *op. cit.*, p. 163
32. Matt. 23:24
33. James Moffatt, *The Bible* (New York: Harper, 1935), pp. xxii, xxiv, xxxii, xxxiv
34. Henry Pitt Van Dusen, "To a Total Comprehension," *Saturday Review*, March 5, 1960, p. 24
35. Stauffer, *op. cit.*, pp. 160, 97
36. William Neil, *The Rediscovery of the Bible* (New York: Harper, 1954), p. 210

37. John 4:25–26
38. Matt. 16:13–20 (M)
39. Matt. 22:41–46 (M)
40. John 12:48
41. Matt. 22:36–40 (M)
42. John 8:54 (M)
43. Matt. 23:8–12 (M) (Italics mine)
44. John 1:12–13 (M)
45. Luke 17:20–21 (M)
46. John 3:13
47. John 6:59–66, 7:12
48. John 7:28 (M)
49. Luke 1:35
50. John 1:34
51. Luke 4:41, Mark 3:11–12
52. John 10:34–37
53. Matt. Chapter 24
54. Mark 14:61–63 (M)
55. Matt. 24:34
56. Matt. 24:30
57. Luke 22:70
58. Matt. 26:63–64
59. Mark 15:2, Luke 23:3, Matt. 27:11
60. John 18:34–37
61. John 19:20–22
62. Matt. 25:40–45 (M)
63. Moffatt, *op. cit.*, p. xxvi, quoting William Ralph Inge without reference.
64. John 1:14 (M)
65. Matt. 24:35
66. John 21:20–22
67. Moffatt, *op. cit.*, p. xxxiv
68. *Ibid.*, p. xxxii
69. Henri Daniel-Rops, *What Is The Bible?*, trans. J. R. Foster (New York: Hawthorne, 1958), reviewed by: John W. Chase, "The Church," in *Saturday Review*, December 20, 1958, p. 19
70. Ndabanningi Sithole, *African Nationalism* (New York: Oxford University Press, 1960), pp. 52, 53
71. Nancy Wilson Ross, "Something Called 'Zen,' " *Horizon*, September 29, 1959
72. deRopp, *op. cit.*, p. 118
73. Werner Keller, *The Bible as History* (New York: William Morrow & Co., 1956), pp. 98–99. (See also: p. 15 for Keller's description of a "Tell.")
74. *Ibid.*, pp. 97, 139. (See also: James Mellaart, "A Neolithic City in Turkey," *Scientific American*, April, 1964. Re: City of Catal Hüyük)
75. Keller, *op. cit.*, p. 154
76. John 1:1
77. Heb. 10:5–7 (M) (Refers to Ps. 40:6–8)
78. Matt. 9:13 (M)

79. Barrett, *op. cit.*, p. 198
80. John 5:31, 7:16, 8:14, 12:44-48 (There are other similar passages. Italics mine.)
81. Matt. 22:31-32 (M)
82. Stauffer, *op. cit.*, pp. 179, 181
83. Stauffer, *op. cit.*, pp. 176, 177
84. John 12:28, 14:6-10, 17:26
85. *The Bhagavad-Gita*, trans. Arthur W. Ryder (Chicago: University of Chicago Press, 1929), II, 12
86. Lancelot Law Whyte, *The Unconscious Before Freud* (New York: Basic Books, 1960), pp. 9, 10, 181
87. Heb. 4:12-13 (M)
88. Whyte, *op. cit.*, p. 142
89. *Ibid.*, pp. 142, 178. (See pp. 148ff on C. G. Carus.)
90. Ira Progoff, *The Death and Rebirth of Psychology*, pp. 1, 265
91. Sigmund Freud, *A General Introduction to Psycho-Analysis* (New York: Doubleday, 1953), pp. 426, 388
92. John 16:33, 8:23
93. Progoff, *op. cit.*, pp. 153, 162, quoting Sigmund Freud, *The Ego and the Id* (London: Hogarth Press and the Institute of Psycho-analysis, 1949), pp. 17, 18
94. *Ibid.*, pp. 206-207, 234, 236 (Also see Chapter 3)
95. John 13:34
96. van den Berg, *op. cit.*, p. 184, quoting Sigmund Freud, *Neue Folge der Vorlesungen zur Einfuehrung in die Psychoanalyse*, 1933, *Gesammelte Werke*, XV, 86
97. John 8:58, 14:6
98. Freud, *A General Introduction to Psycho-Analysis*, p. 222
99. John 18:36
100. Matt. 11:28
101. Matt. 11:28 (M)
102. Luke 11:9-10
103. John 14:20
104. Harold McCurdy, *The Personal World* (New York: Harcourt, Brace & World, 1961), p. 258
105. John 10:14-18
106. Progoff, *op. cit.*, p. 161, quoting Sigmund Freud, *The Ego and the Id*, p. 52
107. *Ibid.*
108. John 10:16, 10:27 (M)
109. Carl G. Jung, *Man and His Symbols* (New York: Doubleday, 1964), pp. 161, 162
110. *Ibid.* See Index for the many references to mandala symbol and its meaning.
111. Progoff, *op. cit.*, p. 153
112. *Ibid.*, pp. 157, 158
113. *Ibid.*, pp. 158-159
114. Mark 13:20, 13:27, John 15:16

115. Matt. 11:11
116. Matt. 11:11
117. John 17:15-16
118. McCurdy, *op. cit.*, pp. 186, 184
119. *Ibid.*, p. 206
120. Psalms 121:4
121. Luke 9:58
122. Matt. 13:16
123. Matt. 13:13-14
124. Luke 13:28
125. Luke 13:26
126. Whyte, *op. cit.*, p. 183
127. Mark 13:34
128. Matt. 28:20
129. deRopp, *op. cit.*, pp. 86, 87
130. Psalms 73:25
131. Psalms 46:7-10
132. Rollo May, "Contributions of Existential Psychotherapy," in *Existence: A New Dimension in Psychiatry and Psychology*, ed. Rollo May, Ernest Angel, and Henri F. Ellenberger (New York: Basic Books, 1958), p. 91
133. *Ibid.*
134. Smiley Blanton, "The Best Prescription I Know," *Reader's Digest*, December, 1962, pp. 64-65
135. Progoff, *op. cit.*, p. 183 (Re: Carl Jung)
136. *Ibid.*, p. 183
137. Psalms 81:8-10, RSV
138. deRopp, *op. cit.*, p. 105
139. *Ibid.*, p. 143
140. Progoff, *op. cit.*, pp. 203, 204, quoting Otto Rank, *Beyond Psychology* (Camden, N.J.: Hadden Craftsmen, 1941), p. 277
141. Psalms 111:10
142. Psalms 103:12-14
143. Progoff, *op. cit.*, pp. 221, 222, quoting Otto Rank, *Modern Education* (New York: Knopf, 1932), p. 112.

CHAPTER 3: MAN'S ARCHIAC HERITAGE

1. Sigmund Freud, *Moses and Monotheism* (New York: Vintage Books, 1958), pp. 125, 129
2. *Ibid.*, pp. 108, 125-130
3. *Ibid.*, pp. 11, 12
4. *Ibid.*, p. 7
5. *Ibid.*, pp. 7, 8
6. *Ibid.*, pp. 102, 103
7. *Ibid.*, pp. 105, 106
8. *Ibid.*, pp. 107, 109, 110, 111
9. *Ibid.*, p. 113
10. *Ibid.*, pp. 110, 111, 129

REFERENCES

11. *Ibid.*, pp. 114, 111, 112
12. *Ibid.*, pp. 113, 108
13. *Ibid.*, pp. 116, 117
14. Carl G. Jung, *Memories, Dreams, Reflections,* ed. Aniela Jaffé (New York: Pantheon Books, 1963), p. 151
15. Matt. 13:30, 24:6-7
16. Luke 21:17 (M)
17. Matt. 15:6-9 (M)
18. Oswald Spengler, *The Decline of the West,* II, 220-230 (See pp. 224, 226 in particular).
19. I Cor. 6:19-20, 7:2, Col. 2:11 (M)
20. John 7:22-24 (M)
21. Matt. 19:3-12
22. Gen. 5:1-2
23. Matt. 5:28 (M)
24. John 8:11
25. Luke 7:47
26. Luke 20:27-38 (M)
27. Mark 8:38
28. John 4:16
29. Matt. 12:36-37
30. Jung, *Man and His Symbols,* pp. 30, 31, 97, 123
31. M.-L. von Franz, "The Process of Individuation," in *Man and His Symbols,* ed. C. G. Jung
32. John 10:10
33. I Cor. 7:22-24 (M)
34. I Cor. 7:22-24 (M). (In King James Bible, terms are: "servant" and "freedman")
35. Albert Schweitzer, *Out of My Life and Thought,* p. 97
36. Rom. 8:38-39, I Cor. Chapter 13
37. Luke 16:1-8 (M)
38. Freud, *Moses and Monotheism,* p. 166
39. Robert Ardrey, *African Genesis* (New York: Atheneum, 1961), p. 163
40. Ira Progoff, *The Death and Rebirth of Psychology,* p. 55 (Re: Alfred Adler)
41. Philip Rieff, "A Burden of Knowingness," *Saturday Review,* November 26, 1960, p. 24, quoting *Letters of Sigmund Freud* (Basic Books)
42. Ardrey, *op. cit.,* p. 158
43. Samuel Miller, "The Evolution of Religion," pp. 70-71
44. A. T. W. Simeons, *Man's Presumptuous Brain* (New York: E. P. Dutton, 1961), p. 36
45. Arnold Toynbee, *An Historian's Approach to Religion,* p. 282

CHAPTER 4: THE LEGENDARY CHAIN OF LIFE

1. Pierre Teilhard de Chardin, *The Phenomenon of Man* (New York: Harper, 1959), p. 59, 60, 61, 217, 220
2. Jung, *Man and His Symbols,* pp. 200, 202

3. Joseph Wood Krutch, *The Great Chain of Life* (Cambridge, Mass.: Riverside Press, 1956), p. 28
4. *Ibid.*, p. 41
5. *Ibid.*, pp. 21, 22
6. *Ibid.*, p. 177
7. *Ibid.*, pp. 36, 177
8. *Ibid.*, p. 36
9. *Ibid.*, p. 201
10. A. T. W. Simeons, *Man's Presumptuous Brain*, p. 38
11. *Ibid.*, p. 12
12. *Ibid.*, pp. 25–26
13. *Ibid.*, p. 23
14. *Ibid.*, pp. 22, 23, 24
15. *Ibid.*, pp. 275, 277
16. *Ibid.*, p. 277
17. *Ibid.*, p. 65
18. *Ibid.*, p. 74
19. Krutch, *op. cit.*, p. 114, and see also pp. 50–57
20. *Ibid.*, pp. 112, 113
21. *Ibid.*, p. 127
22. Gen. 2:5
23. Gen. 22:2
24. Simeons, *op. cit.*, p. 29
25. Arthur Koestler, *The Sleepwalkers* (New York: Macmillan, 1959), p. 514
26. Luke 8:17
27. Robert Ardrey, *African Genesis*, pp. 279, 246
28. Ruth Moore, *Man, Time, and Fossils* (New York: Alfred A. Knopf, 1961), p. 251
29. Ardrey, *op. cit.*, p. 23
30. Moore, *op. cit.*, p. 407. (Re: Sherwood L. Washburn)
31. *Ibid.*, p. 409
32. *Ibid.*, p. 415
33. Ardrey, *op. cit.*, pp. 328–329
34. *Ibid.*, p. 23
35. *Ibid.*, p. 270 (See Chart)
36. *Ibid.*, p. 312
37. *Ibid.*, p. 184
38. *Ibid.*, pp. 262, 263, 327, 328
39. *Ibid.*, p. 223 (See Rainfall Chart of Africa); Gen. 3:17–18
40. Ardrey, *op. cit.*, p. 257
41. Psalms 90:4–5
42. Ardrey, *op. cit.*, pp. 256, 257
43. *Ibid.*, pp. 330, 353
44. *Ibid.*, p. 12
45. *Ibid.*, p. 265
46. Gen. 4:26
47. Gen. 4:17–18, 5:8–29
48. Gen. 4:17, 5:18

49. Gen. 5:24, 4:23, 5:28–29
50. Ardrey, *op. cit.*, pp. 246, 281
51. *Ibid.*, p. 262
52. Gen. 3:21
53. *Science News Letter*, April 17, 1965, "Man Evolved Like Animals," by Charles A. Betts. (See also: "Third Species Questioned," p. 243—re: Louis S. B. Leakey and LLK skull.)
54. *Ibid.*
55. *Ibid.*
56. Ardrey, *op. cit.*, p. 160
57. *Ibid.*, p. 173
58. Isa. 2:4
59. Psalms 119:105
60. M.-L. von Franz, "Conclusion: Science and the Unconscious," in *Man and His Symbols*, p. 306
61. Psalms 127:1
62. John 15:1–5
63. Moore, *op. cit.*, pp. 71–94, 130–170 (Re: Hugo De Vries, Gregor Mendel, and Chevalier de Lamarck)
64. Pierre Teilhard de Chardin, *The Future of Man* (New York: Harper & Row, 1964), pp. 30–31, see all of Chapter II
65. Loren Eiseley, *The Immense Journey* (New York: Vintage Books, 1957), p. 140
66. Matt. 22:37
67. John 13:34, Matt. 22:39
68. Oliver Wendell Holmes, *The Chambered Nautilus*
69. Psalms 127:3
70. Exod. 2:1–10
71. Helen Spurway, *Lancet*, in United Press Release, London, November 13, 1955
72. "The Biology of Individuality," *Time*, June 2, 1958, p. 47. [See also: Rostand's *Can Man Be Modified?* (New York: Basic Books, 1959)]
73. "The Biology of Individuality," p. 47
74. Ruth Moore, *The Coil of Life* (New York: Alfred A. Knopf, 1961), p. 243 (Re: work of Edward L. Tatum and George Wells Beadle)
75. Moore, *The Coil of Life*, p. 242
76. Ira Progoff, *The Death and Rebirth of Psychology*, p. 216, quoting Otto Rank, *Psychology and the Soul* (Philadelphia: University of Pennsylvania Press, 1950), p. 37; and Progoff, p. 218, quoting Rank, *ibid.*, p. 47
77. Lawrence Durrell, *Justine* (New York: Pocket Books, Inc., 1962), frontispiece
78. John 1:12–14, Matt. 23:9
79. Matt. 19:12
80. C. W. Ceram, *Gods, Graves, and Scholars* (New York: Alfred A. Knopf, 1962)
81. Gen. 11:4
82. Gen. 11:6–7
83. Rolf Alexander, *Creative Realism* (New York: Pageant Press, 1954), p. 50

84. Mark 10:14-15
85. Matt. 11:29-30
86. Gen. 11:1 (M)
87. Joan Fitzherbert, United Press Release, London, January 17, 1961
88. Franz E. Winkler, *Man: The Bridge Between Two Worlds* (New York: Harper, 1960), p. 51
89. Frederick Marion, *In My Mind's Eye* (New York: Dutton, 1950), p. 128
90. Martin Grotjahn, *Beyond Laughter* (New York: McGraw-Hill, 1957), p. 91
91. J. H. van den Berg, *The Changing Nature of Man*, p. 102
92. *Ibid.*, p. 169
93. *Ibid.*, p. 170
94. Progoff, *op. cit.*, pp. 156, 157, quoting Sigmund Freud, *The Ego and the Id*, p. 30
95. William Wordsworth, *Tintern Abbey*
96. Alexander, *op. cit.*, p. 234
97. Robert Louis Stevenson, *Dr. Jekyll and Mr. Hyde*
98. "American Abstraction Abroad," *Time*, August 4, 1958, p. 40
99. John 12:25, Luke 14:26, Mark 3:33-35, Matt. 5:48, John 17:20-23
100. Edith Hamilton, "The Lessons of the Past," p. 73
101. *Ibid.*, p. 74
102. *Ibid.*, pp. 75, 78
103. John 8:34
104. Sidney Cohen, *The Beyond Within, The LSD Story* (New York: Atheneum, 1964), p. 185

CHAPTER 5: ORIGINAL SIN AND SAVING GRACE

1. Gen. 7:2
2. Rolf Alexander, *Creative Realism*, p. 16. [For a complete survey of the subject, see: Joseph Head and S. L. Cranston, *Reincarnation, An East-West Anthology* (New York: The Julian Press, 1961): "Reincarnation is frequently regarded as an oriental concept incompatible with western thinking and traditional belief. The present encyclopedic compilation of quotations from eminent philosophers, theologians, poets, scientists, etc. of every period of western culture, and the thoroughly documented survey of Reincarnation in world religions, will serve to correct this error in thinking." Copy on jacket of book.]
3. Alexander, *op. cit.*, p. 114
4. John 14:3-4
5. John 3:7 (See also: Head and Cranston, pp. 32, 34; Matt. 17:9-13, Matt. 11:11-15, and John 9:2-3, in which Jesus is asked if the man blind from birth is blind for his sin or his parents' sin, implying Karma.)
6. John 3:3-9
7. John 3:15-16
8. John 3:12

REFERENCES

9. Luke 23:43
10. John 5:21-23 (M)
11. John 12:50
12. Marcus Bach, *God and the Soviets* (New York: Thomas Y. Crowell Co., 1958), p. 156, quoting Nicholas Berdyaev, without reference
13. John 8:41-44
14. Job 2:10
15. Meir Ben-Horin, "Existence and Divine Essence," *Saturday Review*, March 4, 1961, p. 44
16. Luke 11:23-26 (Parable about evil spirit returning to the house it had left)
17. John 5:28
18. Psalms 121:8
19. Alexander, *op. cit.*, pp. 127, 128
20. Matt. 16:23
21. Matt. 4:8
22. Matt. 12:24-28
23. Matt. 19:17
24. Thomas Troward, *Bible Mystery and Bible Meaning* (New York: Dodd, Mead & Co., 1913), p. 92
25. John 6:48-57
26. John 6:61-63
27. Matt. 26:26-28
28. Matt. 13:35
29. Isaac Asimov, *The Genetic Code* (New York: New American Library, 1963)
30. *Ibid.*, p. 168
31. Moore, *The Coil of Life*, p. 177. Re: Hans Driesch
32. *Ibid.*, p. 177
33. Erwin Schrödinger, *What Is Life?* (New York: Cambridge University Press, 1955), pp. 74, 68, 69
34. Asimov, *op. cit.*, p. 25
35. Matt. 15:10-20
36. Asimov, *op. cit.*, p. 100 (See also: Moore, *The Coil of Life*, pp. 263-265)
37. Jung, *Man and His Symbols*, p. 225.
38. Aniela Jaffé, "Symbolism in the Visual Arts," in *Man and His Symbols*, p. 267
39. Gen. 2:9, 2:16-17, 3:3, 3:22-23
40. Isa. 1:18
41. John 1:10-11
42. Harold McCurdy, *The Personal World*, p. 187, quoting William Wordsworth, *Tintern Abbey*
43. Luke 16:9, 16:11-12
44. Franz E. Winkler, *Man: The Bridge Between Two Worlds*, p. 87, quoting Herbert Dingle, ed., *A Century of Science* (New York: Roy, 1951), p. 315
45. Ludwig Binswanger, "Insanity as Life-Historical Phenomenon and as Mental Disease: The Case of Ilse," in *Existence*, ed. R. May *et al.*, p. 226
46. Alfred Lord Tennyson, *Crossing the Bar*

47. Julian Huxley, *New Bottles for New Wine*, p. 234
48. Carl Jung, "Synchronicity An Acausal Connecting Principle," in *The Interpretation of Nature and the Psyche* (New York: Pantheon Books, 1955), p. 99, quoting R. Wilhelm's translation of the Taoist philosopher, Chuang-tzu, *Das wahre Buch vom suedlichen Bluetenland* (Jena, 1912), II, 3, and the *Tao Teh Ching* of Lao-tzu, trans. Arthur Waley (*The Way and Its Power*, London, 1934)
49. Matt. 3:17
50. Samuel Miller, "The Evolution of Religion," p. 71
51. Crane Brinton, *The Fate of Man* (New York: George Braziller, 1961), p. 193, quoting Meister Eckhart, as translated by Raymond B. Blakney in *Meister Eckhart* (New York: Harper Torchbooks, 1957)
52. Martin Grotjahn, *Beyond Laughter*, p. 33
53. John 2:25
54. Luke 14:34, Mark 9:50, Matt. 5:13. (The word that is translated as "salt" was "nitron" in the original Greek and "natron" in English. *Webster's Unabridged Dictionary* defines "natron" as: "Native sodium carbonate occurring only in solution or with other salts." The Palestinians, at the time of Jesus, drained off an oil from this substance which they used as fuel for their lamps. The residue, when combined with sand, became a kind of asphalt useful for paving pathways—therefore, something fit only to be trod upon.)
55. *Webster's Collegiate Dictionary*
56. Mark 9:49
57. Matt. 15:11–20, 5:29–30, Mark 7:15
58. Luke 7:33
59. William Barrett, *Irrational Man*, p. 144
60. Luke 7:31–32
61. Henry Miller, *Lawrence Durrell–Henry Miller, A Private Correspondence* (New York: E. P. Dutton & Co., 1963), p. 261
62. Luke 19:40
63. John 12:25
64. John 12:47, 10:10, 3:16–17
65. John 8:23
66. "Black Comedy," *Time*, March 17, 1961, pp. 97, 98
67. Robert Linssen, *Living Zen* (New York: Grove Press, 1960), p. 95
68. Robert Ardrey, *African Genesis*, pp. 353, 354
69. Brinton, *op. cit.*, pp. 114–115, quoting Herbert Spencer, *First Principles*, 4th ed. (New York: Caldwell, 1880)
70. Mary Baker Eddy, *Science and Health* (New York: The Philosophical Library, Inc., 1934)
71. Albert Einstein, *Essays in Science* (New York, Philosophical Library, 1934), pp. 3, 4
72. Ira Progoff, *The Death and Rebirth of Psychology*, p. 264
73. Samuel Miller, *op. cit.*, p. 71
74. Rene A. Wormser, *The Story of the Law* (New York: Simon and Schuster, 1962), p. 29. (See all of Chapters 1 and 2)
75. Matt. 5:19
76. Mark 3:2–6, Luke 13:10–17, 14:1–6, John 5:18, 7:22–23, Mark 2:23–28

REFERENCES

77. Matt. 5:13-14
78. Alfred North Whitehead, "Religion and Science," in *Great Essays in Science*, ed. Martin Gardner (New York: Pocket Books, Inc., 1957), p. 206
79. Aniela Jaffé, *op. cit.*
80. M.-L. von Franz, "The Process of Individuation," in *Man and His Symbols*, p. 210
81. M.-L. von Franz, "Conclusion: Science and the Unconscious," in *Man and His Symbols*, pp. 304, 306, 307

CHAPTER 6: NATURE'S SUPREME LAW

1. Arthur Eddington, *The Nature of the Physical World*, p. 211
2. Cf. Arthur H. Compton, "The Human Mind and Physical Law," a review of Werner Heisenberg's *Physics and Philosophy* (New York: Harper, 1958) in *Saturday Review*, July 12, 1958, p. 16
3. Eddington, *op. cit.*, p. 194
4. *Ibid.*, pp. 195, 197
5. *Ibid.*, p. 75
6. *The International Dictionary of Physics and Electronics* (Princeton, N.J.: D. van Nostrand & Co., 1961), p. 421
7. Rudolf Julius Emanuel Clausius (1822-1888), Josiah Willard Gibbs (1839-1903), Ludwig Boltzmann, nineteenth-century physicist
8. Eddington, *op. cit.*, pp. 74, 75
9. Rolf Alexander, *Creative Realism*, p. 209
10. Eddington, *op. cit.*, pp. 69-75, 103-107
11. Matt. 6:28-30
12. Albert Einstein, *Essays in Science*, p. 18.
13. (See page 10 of this book.) Eddington, *op. cit.*, pp. 316, 317
14. Samuel Reiss, *The Basis of Scientific Thinking* (New York: Philosophical Library, 1961), p. 16
15. *Ibid.*, p. 213
16. Mark 4:30-32 (M)
17. Matt. 13:33 (M)
18. Matt. 24:35
19. Luke 17:20-21
20. Mark 13:32
21. Eddington, *op. cit.*, p. xi
22. *Ibid.*, pp. 40, 41
23. *Ibid.*, pp. 42-48
24. *Ibid.*, p. 50
25. Mark 10:25 (It is thought that "eye of the needle" referred to a small gate in the wall, so that a camel must be unloaded to get through.)
26. John 14:9-10
27. Eddington, *op. cit.*, pp. 1, 2
28. *Ibid.*, p. 50
29. Matt. 10:24-25 (M)
30. Eddington, *op. cit.*, p. 50

31. *Ibid.*, p. 49
32. Matt. 24:12
33. *Webster's Collegiate Dictionary*
34. Crane Brinton, ed., *The Fate of Man*, p. 511, quoting Roderick Seidenberg, *Posthistoric Man: An Inquiry* (Chapel Hill: University of North Carolina Press, 1950; paperback edition: Beacon Press, 1957)
35. Matt. 5:18, Luke 16:17
36. Alexander, *op. cit.*, p. 44
37. Teilhard de Chardin, *The Future of Man*, p. 78
38. *The Rubáiyát of Omar Khayyám*, trans. Edward Fitzgerald. *The Harvard Classics*, edited by Charles W. Eliot (New York: P. F. Collier and Son Co., 1910), p. 983
39. Alexander, *op. cit.*, p. 133
40. Eddington, *op. cit.*, p. 217
41. *Ibid.*
42. Durrell, *Balthazar*, p. 37
43. Jung, *Man and His Symbols*, p. 175, quoting M.-L. von Franz
44. Luke 6:38
45. John 7:24
46. Matt. 7:1 (M)
47. Alexander, *op. cit.*, p. 26
48. Matt. 13:24–30
49. Eddington, *op. cit.*, p. 77
50. *Ibid.*, p. 78
51. *Ibid.*, p. 79
52. *Ibid.*, p. 78
53. *Ibid.*, pp. 79, 80
54. Matt. 6:9–15
55. John 15:10–11
56. John 3:30
57. Robert Ardrey, *African Genesis*, p. 349
58. Matt. 11:11
59. Isak Dinesen, *Shadows on the Grass* (New York: Random House 1961), pp. 108, 109, 112
60. *Ibid.*, pp. 107, 110
61. Britton, *op. cit.*, pp. 210, 211, quoting François Duc de la Rochefoucauld *Maxims*, trans. Louis Kronenberger (New York: Random House, Modern Library paperbacks, 1959)

CHAPTER 7: ONE, ITSELF, IS TEACHER

1. Einstein, *Essays in Science*, p. 4
2. *Ibid.*, p. 19
3. Matt. 19:16–17, Mark 10:17 (M)
4. John 5:26, Matt. 18:14 (M)
5. Harry Overstreet, *The Mature Mind* (New York: W. W. Norton, 1951), p. 93

6. Arthur Eddington, *The Nature of the Physical World*, pp. 179, 184–186
7. Matt. 6:22
8. John 16:12
9. Eddington, *op. cit.*, pp. 186–188
10. *Ibid.*, p. 189
11. Matt. 28:20
12. Eddington, *op. cit.*, pp. 190–192
13. John 1:12–13, 14:19–21 (M)
14. Eddington, *op. cit.*, pp. 200, 201
15. Matt. 18:20 (M)
16. Matt. 13:44–46 (M)
17. Rolf Alexander, *Creative Realism*, p. 7
18. Matt. 13:47 (M)
19. Eddington, *op. cit.*, p. 217
20. *Ibid.*, pp. 220, 221
21. Matt. 10:24–25 (M)
22. Morris Kline, *Mathematics in Western Culture*, p. 404
23. Matt. 20:1–16 (M)
24. Eddington, *op. cit.*, p. 218
25. John 14:9–10
26. Eddington, *op. cit.*, pp. 60, 146, 290, 291, 228
27. Mark 12:32–34 (M)
28. John 16:33
29. Eddington, *op. cit.*, pp. 215, 216
30. John 14:10
31. John 1:5
32. John 5:17 (M)
33. Eddington, *op. cit.*, p. 218
34. Matt. 4:1–11, 16:23
35. Ira Progoff, *The Death and Rebirth of Psychology*, pp. 47–91, 180, 211
36. Matt. 5:48, John 17:23
37. Viktor Frankl, *Man's Search For Meaning*, trans. Ilse Lasch (New York: Washington Square Press, 1964), p. 211
38. *Ibid.*, pp. 206, 207
39. *Ibid.*, pp. 205, 178
40. *Ibid.*, pp. 172, 173
41. *Ibid.*, p. 175
42. Einstein, *Essays in Science*, p. 111
43. *Ibid.*, p. 102
44. Psalms 46:10
45. Matt. 26:64
46. Einstein, *Essays in Science*, p. 20
47. *Hafiz of Shiraz*, trans. John Heath-Stubbs and Peter Avery (London: John Murray, 1952), p. 5
48. *Ibid.*, p. 31
49. Einstein, *Essays in Science*, p. 39
50. John 10:10 (M)
51. Moore, *The Coil of Life*, p. 326

52. Einstein, *Essays in Science*, p. 79
53. "Educated Satellites," *Time*, New York, April 27, 1959, p. 65
54. Eddington, *op. cit.*, p. 5
55. Matt. 5:39, 43-44
56. Eddington, *op. cit.*, p. 7
57. Luke 7:47
58. Matt. 6:8
59. Mark 12:36 (M)
60. Matt. 10:36
61. Matt. 5:35
62. Eddington, *op. cit.*, p. 207
63. Matt. 12:25-26, 10:34-36, 12:30 (M)
64. Luke 11:29
65. Julian Huxley, *New Bottles for New Wine*, p. 233
66. Luke 11:23-26 (M)
67. Eddington, *op. cit.*, p. 59
68. Matt. 13:49-50
69. Exod. 7:15, Ezek. 7:11
70. Psalms 23:4
71. Ethelbert Stauffer, *Jesus and His Story*, p. 116
72. John 13:26-30 (M)
73. Ernest Renan, *The Life of Jesus*, p. 338
74. Matt. 26:23-25 (M)
75. John 13:26-30 (M)
76. Matt. 26:50
77. John 15:13-14
78. Matt. 27:3-10 (M)
79. John 17:12
80. Matt. 21:42, Luke 20:17-18 (M)
81. Luke 16:9-13 (M)
82. Hong-Yee Chiu, "Ashes of the Universe," *Science News Letter*, February 10, 1962, p. 84
83. Hos. 13:14
84. Arthur A. Cohen, "Those Who Keep Faith with the Covenant: The Philosophy," *Saturday Review*, June 7, 1958, p. 18
85. Matt. 11:20-23
86. Matt. 15:22-28
87. Durrell, *Justine*, p. 3
88. Luke 18:13
89. Matt. 12:37
90. Matt. 12:31-33 (M)
91. Hos. 13:9
92. Hos. 13:14
93. John 13:18
94. M.-L. von Franz, "Conclusion: Science and the Unconscious," in *Man and His Symbols*, p. 307
95. *Webster's Collegiate Dictionary*
96. *Ibid.*

97. Jung, "Synchronicity," p. 135
98. *Hafiz of Shiraz*, p. 42

CHAPTER 8: THE DILEMMA AND THE PEARL

1. W. Pauli, "The Influence of Archetypal Ideas on the Scientific Theories of Kepler," in *The Interpretation of Nature and the Psyche*, p. 205
2. Einstein, *Essays in Science*, pp. 14, 15, 50
3. Michell J. Sienko and Robert A. Plane, *Chemistry* (New York: McGraw-Hill, 1957), p. 45
4. Jung, "Synchronicity," pp. 57, 58, 49, 52
5. *Ibid.*, p. 135
6. Pauli, *op. cit.*, pp. 154, 155, 157, 175
7. *Ibid.*, pp. 165, 174
8. *Ibid.*, pp. 195, 204
9. *Ibid.*, p. 205
10. *Ibid.*, pp. 206, 207
11. *Ibid.*, pp. 207, 208
12. Einstein, *Essays in Science*, pp. 19, 20
13. Deems Taylor (Description drawn from Music Appreciation Records—but not *verbatim*—Book of the Month Club, New York)
14. Radhakrishnan, *Recovery of Faith*, p. 86
15. Erwin Schrödinger, *What Is Life?*, p. 20
16. *Ibid.*, pp. 8, 9, 19
17. Clyde Kluckhohn, *Mirror for Man*, p. 33, and Arthur Koestler, *The Sleepwalkers*, p. 517
18. M.-L. von Franz, "Conclusion: Science and the Unconscious," p. 309
19. *Ibid.*, p. 308
20. *Ibid.*, pp. 308, 309
21. Nicomachus of Gerasa, "Introduction to Arithmetic I and II," ed. Robert Maynard Hutchins, *Great Books of the Western World* (Chicago: Encyclopaedia Britannica, Inc., 1952), XI, 807
22. *Ibid.*
23. Morris Kline, *Mathematics in Western Culture*, p. 460
24. Nicomachus, p. 822; Matt. 10:24-25, Luke 12:53
25. Nicomachus, pp. 832, 838, 839, 834
26. *Ibid.*, p. 832
27. Robert Frost, "The Road Not Taken," *The Complete Poems of Robert Frost* (New York: Holt, Rinehart and Winston, Inc., 1964)
28. Nicomachus, *op. cit.*, p. 832
29. Luke 12:52
30. Jung "Synchronicity," p. 97
31. *Ibid.*
32. *Ibid.*, p. 99
33. William James, "The Problem of Being," in *Great Essays in Science*, ed. Martin Gardner (New York: Pocket Books, 1957), p. 33
34. Kline, *op. cit.*, p. 459

35. Moore, *The Coil of Life*, pp. 171, 173 (Re: Hans Driesch)
36. *Ibid.*, p. 174 (Re: T. H. Morgan)
37. Kline, *op. cit.*, p. 229
38. *Ibid.*, p. 228
39. *Ibid.*, p. 226
40. Martin Gardner, *The Ambidextrous Universe* (New York: Basic Books, 1964), pp. 209, 210, 214, 215
41. *Ibid.*, pp. 258, 263
42. Chen Ning Yang, *Elementary Particles* (Princeton: Princeton University Press, 1962), pp. 58, 59
43. *Ibid.*, p. 60
44. Schrödinger, *op. cit.*, pp. 75, 85
45. Jung, "Synchronicity," p. 98
46. Matt. 6:3
47. Eddington, *op. cit.*, p. 72
48. Jung, "Synchronicity," p. 97
49. John 19:23-24
50. Ira Progoff, *The Death and Rebirth of Psychology*, p. 60, quoting Alfred Adler, *Social Interest* (London: Faber and Faber, 1938), p. 37
51. Robert Linssen, *Living Zen*, pp. 16, 76, 77, quoting Carlo Suares, *Comedio Psychologique*

CHAPTER 9: WHAT HAS BEEN HIDDEN

1. Matt. 13:31-33 (M)
2. Warren Weaver and Claude E. Shannon, *The Mathematical Theory of Communication* (Urbana: University of Illinois Press, 1964), pp. 12, 13
3. *Ibid.*, p. 16
4. *Ibid.*, pp. 13, 28
5. *Ibid.*, p. 28
6. John 4:25
7. Weaver and Shannon, p. 13
8. *Ibid.*, pp. 13, 14
9. Matt. 5:37
10. Weaver and Shannon, p. 16
11. *Ibid.*, p. 7
12. *Ibid.*, p. 19 (Italics mine)
13. *Ibid.*, p. 27
14. Mark 4:1-20
15. Hans J. Wernli, *Biorhythm* (New York: Crown, 1961)
16. Erwin Schrödinger, *What Is Life?* p. 51
17. Loren Eiseley, "An Evolutionist Looks at Modern Man," in *Adventures of the Mind*, ed. Richard Thruelsen and John Kobler (New York: Knopf, (1959), p. 13
18. Fred Hoyle, "When Time Began," in *Adventures of the Mind*, pp. 161, 164
19. *Ibid.*, p. 165
20. *Ibid.*, pp. 168-169

REFERENCES

21. Richard C. Wald, " 'Steady Universe' Theory Disputed," London, Herald Tribune Bureau, February 10, 1961 (Re: Martin Ryle)
22. Alton Blakeslee, Associated Press Release, Berkeley, August 17, 1961
23. "Endless Life Foreseen," *Science News Letter*, November 18, 1961, p. 333
24. *Ibid.*
25. J. Robert Oppenheimer, "The Mystery of Matter," in *Adventures of the Mind*, p. 64
26. *Ibid.*, p. 66
27. Eiseley, "An Evolutionist," pp. 9, 10
28. Matt. 3:12, Mark 9:43
29. Matt. 6:34
30. Crane Brinton, ed., *The Fate of Man*, pp. 355-57, quoting Robert L. Heilbroner, *The Future as History* (New York: Harper, 1960)
31. Philip Toynbee, "Living in One World-Covering City," *London Observer* Service, London, January 16, 1963
32. Gen. 28:12-22
33. John 2:21
34. "Waves Defy Detection," *Science News Letter*, February 3, 1962, p. 67
35. *Ibid.*
36. Matt. 24:35
37. John 14:2
38. "Universe Standing Still?" *Science News Letter*, August 4, 1962, p. 78
39. Immanuel Velikovsky, *Worlds in Collision* (New York: Doubleday, 1950)
40. Isa. 1:18
41. Matt. 10:30
42. Jung, "Synchronicity," p. 15
43. Gerald Holton and H. D. Duane Roller, *Foundations of Modern Physical Science* (Reading, Mass.: Addison-Wesley, 1958), p. 519
44. *Ibid.*, p. 465
45. Matt. 25:1-13
46. Jacques Hadamard, *The Psychology of Invention in the Mathematical Field* (Princeton, N.J.: Princeton University Press, 1954), p. xiii
47. C. W. Ceram, *Gods, Graves, and Scholars*, pp. 318-319
48. John 1:11
49. Morris Kline, *Mathematics in Western Culture*, p. 440
50. *Ibid.*, p. 439
51. "Unbalanced Universe," *Time*, June 22, 1959, pp. 40, 42. See also: Raymond A. Lyttleton, H. Bondi, W. B. Bonnor, G. J. Whitrow, *Rival Theories of Cosmology* (London: Oxford University Press, 1960), pp. 22-33
52. Arthur Eddington, *The Nature of the Physical World*, p. 338

CHAPTER 10: ALL IS NATURAL

1. Frederick Marion, *In My Mind's Eye*, p. 19
2. Alfred North Whitehead, "Religion and Science," in *Great Essays in Science*, pp. 211-213
3. C. E. M. Hansel, *ESP, A Scientific Evaluation* (New York: Charles Scribner's Sons, 1966)

4. G. N. M. Tyrrell, *The Personality of Man* (Baltimore: Penguin Books, 1954), p. 119
5. Henri F. Ellenberger, "A Clinical Introduction to Psychiatric Phenomenology and Existential Analysis," in May, *Existence*, p. 94
6. Tyrrell, *op. cit.*, p. 57
7. *Ibid.*, pp. 58–64
8. Erwin W. Straus, "Aesthesiology and Hallucinations," in May, *Existence*, p. 139
9. William James, *The Varieties of Religious Experience*, 1902, p. 413 (quoted by: Tyrrell, *op. cit.*, p. 41)
10. Tyrrell, pp. 41, 42
11. Marion, *op. cit.*, p. 314
12. Tyrrell, *op. cit.*, p. 62
13. Arthur Eddington, *The Nature of the Physical World*, p. 324
14. See: Sidney Cohen, *The Beyond Within: The LSD Story*, pp. 45–63. See also: William H. Ittelson, *The Ames Demonstrations in Perception* (Princeton, N.J.: Princeton University Press, 1952). With regard to difference between illusion and hallucination and the subject of perception in general, see: Hadley Cantril, "Perception and Interpersonal Relations," *The American Journal of Psychiatry*, Vol. 114, No. 2, August, 1957
15. Straus, in May, *Existence*, p. 149
16. W. Pauli, "The Influence of Archetypal Ideas on the Scientific Theories of Kepler," in *The Interpretation of Nature and the Psyche*, p. 152
17. Leslie M. LeCron (ed.), *Experimental Hypnosis* (New York: Macmillan, 1956), pp. viii, xiv
18. William Neilson, *Mesmerism* (Edinburgh: Shepherd & Elliot, 1855), p. 165–168
19. Aldous Huxley, "A Case of Voluntary Ignorance," *Esquire*, October, 1956, p. 47
20. "The Hypnotized Heart," *Time*, July 7, 1958, p. 61. (See also "A Case of Voluntary Ignorance," p. 47)
21. Robert Coughlan, "Pathway Into the Mind," *Life*, March 7, 1960, p. 106
22. *Hafiz of Shiraz*, p. 42
23. James A. Christenson, Jr., "Dynamics in Hypnotic Induction," in LeCron, *Experimental Hypnosis*, pp. 50, 51
24. LeCron, *op. cit.*, p. 68
25. Milton H. Erickson, "Deep Hypnosis and Its Induction," in LeCron, *op. cit.*, p. 67
26. Christenson, *op. cit.*, p. 50
27. Leslie M. LeCron, "A Study of Age Regression under Hypnosis," in LeCron, *op. cit.*, p. 167. See also: L. L. Vasiliev, *Experiments in Mental Suggestion* (Church Crookham, Hampshire, England: Institute for the Study of Mental Images, 1963).
28. Christenson, *op. cit.*, p. 41
29. Frank A. Pattie, "Methods of Induction, Susceptibility of Subjects, and Criteria of Hypnosis," in Roy M. Dorcus, *Hypnosis and Its Therapeutic Applications* (New York: McGraw-Hill, 1956), p. 2/20
30. Joseph E. Whitlow, "A Rapid Method for the Induction of Hypnosis," in LeCron, *Experimental Hypnosis*

REFERENCES

31. Pattie, *op. cit.*, p. 2/2
32. *Ibid.*, p. 2/7
33. Edwin L. Baron, United Press Release, Chicago, November 9, 1957
34. "Unlock It," *Time*, April 7, 1958, p. 44
35. Rene Jules Dubos, *Mirage of Health* (New York: Harper, 1959)
36. As examples: Jesse D. Rising, *Postgraduate Medicine*, 1958 (points out dangerous side effects of modern drugs); Bradford Cannon, Judson G. Randolph, and Joseph E. Murray, *New England Journal of Medicine*, February, 1959 (point out dangerous aftermath of too much X-ray)
37. Hans Selye, *The Story of the Adaptation Syndrome* (Montreal: Acta, Inc.), 1952, p. 223
38. Gen. 3:19
39. Moore, *The Coil of Life*, pp. 262-265
40. *Ibid.*, p. 365 (See also all of Chapter XIX)
41. Jung, "God, the Devil, and the Human Soul," p. 63
42. Moore, *The Coil of Life*, p. 42, quoting Lavoisier without reference
43. Rudolph Friedrich, *Frontiers of Medicine* (New York: Liveright, 1961), p. 21, quoting Max Planck without reference
44. J. H. van den Berg, *The Changing Nature of Man*, p. 208
45. Matt. 21:21-22, John 14:14, Matt. 18:19-20
46. Matt. 6:33
47. Matt. 6:6-8, Luke 18:1
48. Matt. 6:6

CHAPTER 11: JESUS' HEALING MINISTRY

1. Mark 9:38-41
2. John 14:12
3. Matt. 13:58, Mark 6:5-6 (M)
4. Rudolph Friedrich, *Frontiers of Medicine*, p. 18
5. Harold McCurdy, *The Personal World*, pp. 540, 541. (See also: pp. 535, 542)
6. *Ibid.*, p. 543
7. Friedrich, *op. cit.*, p. 19
8. Acts 3:1-8 (M)
9. William Neilson, *Mesmerism*, p. 194
10. Alan Mitchell, *The Healing Trance* (New York: A. S. Barnes, 1960), pp. 111, 112
11. Luke 22:51
12. Frederick Marion, *In My Mind's Eye*, p. 169
13. Matt. 8:16
14. Matt. 15:21-28, 8:5-13, John 4:46-54
15. Mitchell, *op. cit.*, p. 120
16. Matt. 18:3
17. Matt. 8:28-34, Mark 5:1-19, Luke 8:26-39 (Matthew omits reference to "legion" and names the place Gergesenes, instead of Gadarenes. Both are SE of the sea of Tiberias, and the three reports appear to refer to the same episode.)

18. Matt. 12:43-45
19. "Vanishing Cancer," *Time*, September 22, 1958, p. 49; "Man's Lung Cancer Mysteriously Gone," Associated Press Release, Bremerton, Washington, November 7, 1959; "Progress Reports," *Time*, April 16, 1956, p. 77. Re: Charles S. Cameron
20. Mark 5:22-42, Luke 7:11-15, John 11:1-44
21. Ethelbert Stauffer, *Jesus and His Story*, p. 101
22. John 11:39 (M)
23. John 11:11-14
24. I Kings 17:17-24, 19:8-13 (M)
25. I Kings 19:8-13 (M)
26. Mitchell, *op. cit.*, p. 109
27. For examples: "Control by Sound," *Time*, August 3, 1959, p. 45; and Moore, *The Coil of Life*, pp. 293, 349
28. M.-L. von Franz, "Conclusion: Science and the Unconscious," in *Man and His Symbols*, p. 304
29. G. N. M. Tyrrell, *The Personality of Man*, pp. 197-201
30. John, Chapters 13, 14, 15, 16, 17
31. John 15:1 (M)
32. Mark 14:25 (M)
33. Jung, "Synchronicity," pp. 84-88
34. *Ibid.*, p. 88
35. Luke 17:12-19
36. Mark 2:5-7
37. John 9:1-38
38. Friedrich, p. 25, quoting Viktor von Weizsaecker, without reference
39. Matt. 7:1
40. "Mind v. Body," *Time*, September 15, 1958, p. 63
41. Gen. 4:5-7
42. William Barrett, *Irrational Man*, p. 151
43. A. T. W. Simeons, *Man's Presumptuous Brain*, pp. 1, 2, 98-107, 138
44. Matt. 15:11, 15:18-21
45. John 9:6
46. Rolf Alexander, *Creative Realism*, p. 146
47. Luke 8:46-47 (M)
48. Matt. 18:18-19
49. Friedrich, *op. cit.*, p. 63
50. Mitchell, *op. cit.*, p. 40
51. *Ibid.*, p. 67
52. Alexander, *op. cit.*, p. 146
53. Ira Progoff, *The Death and Rebirth of Psychology*, p. 182
54. Matt. 11:2-7
55. Robert Peel, *Christian Science—Its Encounter With American Culture* (New York: Anchor Books, Doubleday, 1965), p. 177
56. *Ibid.*, p. 150
57. *Ibid.*, pp. 106, 101, 102
58. "Hypnotist in Danger As Well As Subject," *Science News Letter*, April 17, 1965, p. 249 (Re: Report given by Louis J. West and Gordon H. Deckert)

59. Peel, *op. cit.*, p. 120
60. *Ibid.*, p. 65
61. Matt. 7:13–14
62. Progoff, *op. cit.*, pp. 89–90 (Re: Alfred Adler)
63. "Vision Drug Increases Religious Feeling," *Science News Letter*, September 21, 1963, p. 184
64. Gerald Heard, "Can This Drug Enlarge Man's Mind?" *Horizon*, May, 1963
65. Sidney Cohen, *The Beyond Within: The LSD Story*
66. Aldous Huxley, *The Doors of Perception* (New York: Harper, 1954)
67. Mark 10:13–15 (M)
68. Matt. 18:6
69. Alexander, *op. cit.*, p. 147

CHAPTER 12: THE SOCIAL MIRACLES

1. Matt. 14:17–19, 15:34–36 (M). Other reports in Mark, Luke, and John are similar.
2. Mark 6:52
3. John 8:1–9
4. John 18:6
5. Luke 22:44
6. Frederick Marion, *In My Mind's Eye*, p. 169
7. John 2:1–10
8. Mark 5:7–8
9. Crane Brinton, *The Fate of Man*, p. 269, quoting Herbert J. Muller. For a detailed account of Hitler's Messianic delusion see: Louis Pauwels and Jacques Bergier, *The Morning of the Magicians*, trans. Rollo Myers (New York: Stein & Day, 1964), pp. 146–210
10. Matt. 9:13, 12:7 (M)
11. William Barrett, *Irrational Man*, p. 149
12. Sydney J. Harris, *Strictly Personal*, March 22, 1960, *Chicago Daily News*
13. Harold McCurdy, *The Personal World*, p. 452
14. Jung, "Synchronicity," p. 46, quoting Johann von Goethe from *Eckermann's Conversations with Goethe*, trans. R. O. Moon (London, 1951), pp. 514f.
15. Leslie M. LeCron, *Experimental Hypnosis*, p. 423
16. Clyde Kluckhohn, *Mirror for Man*, p. 165, quoting Sigmund Freud without reference
17. *Ibid.*, p. 165
18. Arthur Miller, "With respect for her agony—but with love," *Life*, February 7, 1964, p. 66
19. *Ibid.*, p. 66
20. John 8:46 (M)
21. Matt. 19:17
22. Arthur Miller, *op. cit.*, p. 66
23. *Ibid.*
24. Matt. 7:28–29
25. John 15:11

26. Kluckhohn, *op. cit.*, p. 165
27. Jonathan Swift, *Gulliver's Travels*
28. Matt. 24:6–12
29. Matt. 24:5, 24:23–26
30. D. J. West, *Psychical Research Today* (Baltimore: Penguin Books, 1962), p. 217

CHAPTER 13: JESUS' DEMONSTRATIONS OF EXTRASENSORY PERCEPTION AND THE PSYCHIC POWER

1. Gerald Holton and H. D. Duane Roller, *Foundations of Modern Physical Science*, p. 255. [See also: Jacques Hadamard, *The Psychology of Invention in the Mathematical Field* (Princeton, N.J.: Princeton University Press, 1954)]
2. D. J. West, *Psychical Research Today*, p. 191
3. *Ibid.*, p. 193
4. Matt. 13:13–15
5. Mark 6:52
6. John 8:59
7. John 6:63–64 (M)
8. Matt. 17:20, Luke 17:6
9. Matt. 13:31–32 (M)
10. Mark 11:23
11. Louisa E. Rhine, *Hidden Channels of the Mind* (New York: William Sloane Associates, 1961), pp. 257, 258
12. *Ibid.*, pp. 241, 242, 257, 258, 259
13. Matt. 21:19–20, Mark 11:20–21 (M). King James version says that tree withered "presently"; Moffatt translates "instantly."
14. Mark 11:12–14 (M)
15. Mark 11:14 (M)
16. Charles Schultz, *Peanuts*, Syndicated Comic Strip, *Los Angeles Times*
17. Wilson, *Religion and the Rebel*, p. 162
18. John 10:34–35
19. Wilson, *Religion and the Rebel*, p. 297
20. Jung, *Memories, Dreams, Reflections*, pp. 155, 156
21. *Ibid.*, p. 363
22. Matt. 3:16–17, Mark 1:10–11
23. Luke 3:22
24. John 1:32
25. Ira Progoff, *The Death and Rebirth of Psychology*, pp. 171–175
26. Robert deRopp, *Science and Salvation*, p. 293
27. Paul Tillich, "Existentialist Aspects of Modern Art" in *Christianity and the Existentialists*, ed. Carl Michalson (New York: Charles Scribner & Sons, 1956), pp. 146, 147
28. Luke 16:31 (M)
29. "New View of Man," Exhibition at the Museum of Modern Art, New York, 1959

REFERENCES

30. Rollo May, ed., *Existence*, p. 17
31. deRopp, *op. cit.*, pp. 128, 129
32. Mal. 4:1
33. "The Legacy," in *Saturday Review*, October 1, 1960, p. 38 (Re: Bomb effects on population of Hiroshima & Nagasaki, report by J. W. Hollingsworth)
34. Lewis Mumford, "The Morals of Extermination," *The Atlantic*, October, 1959, p. 43
35. Rev. 7:3
36. Russell W. Davenport, *The Dignity of Man*, p. 292
37. "Homage to New York?" *Time*, March 28, 1960, p. 86
38. Jacques Barzun, *The House of Intellect* (New York: Harper, 1959), Chapter IX
39. Helen R. Lowe, "Solomon or Salami," *The Atlantic*, 1959, Anniversary Issue, pp. 128-131
40. Charles Siepmann, "Judgment Day for the Modern Mind," a review of *The Two Cultures and the Scientific Revolution* by Charles P. Snow (New York: Cambridge University Press, 1960), in *Saturday Review*, January 30, 1960, p. 22
41. May, *op. cit.*, p. 112
42. Louis Zahner, "Composition at the Barricades," *The Atlantic*, 1959, Anniversary Issue, pp. 114-117
43. Wenzell Brown, "Violence in Society's Substratum," a review of *The Shook-up Generation* by Harrison Salisbury (New York: Harper, 1958), in *Saturday Review*, October 18, 1958, p. 60
44. F. Raymond Fosberg, "Where Is Science Taking Us?" *Saturday Review*, November 14, 1959, p. 72
45. Robert Brustein, "Cult of Unthink," *Horizons*, September, 1958, pp. 38-44
46. *Ibid.*, p. 41, quoting Allen Ginsberg, *Howl*
47. deRopp, *op. cit.*, p. 197
48. *Ibid.*, p. 105
49. West, *op. cit.*, p. 211
50. Matt. 12:37, 24:35, John 1:1-5
51. Erwin W. Straus, "Aesthesiology and Hallucinations," in May, *Existence*, p. 167
52. Matt. 13:25-30
53. Matt. 23:13-33 (M)
54. Viktor Frankl, *Man's Search for Meaning*, p. 205
55. *Ibid.*, p. 204
56. *Ibid.*, pp. 117-118
57. *Ibid.*, p. 209
58. *Ibid.*, p. 210
59. *Ibid.*, pp. 190-191
60. *Ibid.*, p. x (Introduction to book by Gordon W. Allport)
61. "The Passion of Yurii Zhivago," *Time*, December 15, 1958, p. 88, quoting Boris Pasternak
62. Matt. 23:37
63. Matt. 23:39 (M)

64. Brustein, *op. cit.*, p. 41 (Re: Jack Kerouac and Allen Ginsberg)
65. Rollo May, "Contributions of Existential Therapy," in *Existence*, p. 54
66. William Barrett, *Irrational Man*, p. 120
67. Jer. 31:3 (King James and Moffatt versions)
68. Michel del Castillo, *Child of Our Time*, trans. Peter Green (New York: Alfred A. Knopf, 1958), pp. 200, 231, 281, 85
69. Ernest Hemingway, *The Old Man and The Sea, Life*, September 1, 1952
70. "Death and Transfiguration," *Time*, May 12, 1961, p. 70
71. Wichita, Kansas *Democrat*, November 1, 1963
72. Matt. 5:3
73. Matt. 5:13-14, 5:48
74. "The Passion of Yurii Zhivago," p. 88
75. John 14:27, Heb. 13:5 (M), Matt. 28:20 (Only Heb. 13:5 is from Moffatt)
76. Matt. 16:17

CHAPTER 14: THE ILLUSORY MIRACLES

1. Matt. 17:1-13
2. John 12:28
3. Moffatt, *op. cit.*, p. xxx
4. John 6:15-21 (M)
5. John 6:22-25 (M)
6. Colin Wilson, *Religion and the Rebel*, p. 229
7. *Ibid.*, p. 298, quoting Ludwig Wittgenstein, *Tractatus Logico-Philosophicus* (London: Routledge and Kegan Paul, 1949), p. 188
8. *Ibid.*, pp. 78-80, quoting first Blake and then Arthur Rimbaud, "A Season in Hell," tr. Norman Cameron (London: Lehmann, 1949), p. 41
9. *Ibid.*, p. 102
10. *Ibid.*, p. 165, quoting Jacob Boehme, *Confessions of Jacob Boehme*, ed. W. Scott Palmer (London: Methuen, 1954), p. 13, and Friedrich Wilhelm Nietzsche, *Zarathustra*
11. Colin Wilson, *The Outsider* (Boston: Houghton Mifflin, 1956), p. 254
12. Wilson, *Religion and the Rebel*, pp. 240, 61
13. *Ibid.*, pp. 291, 303
14. *Ibid.*, p. 206
15. Daniel J. Bronstein, "Search for Inner Truth," *Saturday Review*, November 16, 1957, pp. 22-23, quoting Suzuki, without reference
16. Wilson, *Religion and the Rebel*, p. 230
17. Ira Progoff, *The Death and Rebirth of Psychology*, pp. 190, 250
18. *Ibid.*, pp. 251, 257
19. *Ibid.*, p. 85
20. Wilson, *Religion and the Rebel*, p. 239, and William Barrett, *Irrational Man*, p. 151
21. Wilson, *Religion and the Rebel*, p. 239
22. Progoff, *op. cit.*, pp. 250, 252, quoting Otto Rank, *Beyond Psychology* (Camden: Hadden Craftsmen, 1941), p. 16
23. John 3:1-21

REFERENCES

24. "Milestones," *Time*, New York, October 15, 1965
25. Conrad Aiken, *Gehenna* (New York: Random House, 1930)
26. Luke 14:26
27. John 9:39, 12:47-48 (M)
28. From Jean-Paul Sartre, *Being and Nothingness*, trans., Hazel Barnes (New York: Philosophical Library, 1956), reproduced in Robert Denoon Cumming, ed., *The Philosophy of Jean-Paul Sartre* (New York: The Modern Library, 1966), p. 153
29. John 12:48
30. Gen. 1:2
31. Walt Whitman, *Leaves of Grass*
32. Mark 9:49
33. Wilson, *Religion and the Rebel*, pp. 316-317, quoting Whitehead from *The Philosophy of Alfred North Whitehead*, ed. Schilpp (Evanston: Northwestern University, 1941), p. 698
34. Holton and Roller, *Foundations of Modern Physical Science*, pp. 168, 207
35. *Ibid.*, pp. 344, 347, 348
36. Wilson, *Religion and the Rebel*, p. 78
37. J. B. Priestley, *Literature and Western Man*, pp. 135, 136
38. Wilson, *Religion and the Rebel*, pp. 209-216 (Re: William Law)
39. Marcus Bach, *God and the Soviets*, pp. 147-150
40. Priestley, *op. cit.*, pp. 479, 290 (Re: Johan August Strindberg)
41. "The Screen," *Time*, March 14, 1960, p. 66 quoting Ingmar Bergman
42. Wilson, *Religion and the Rebel*, p. 318
43. *Ibid.*, p. 314, quoting Alfred North Whitehead, *op. cit.*, p. 687
44. Priestley, *op. cit.*, p. 116 (Re: Jean-Jacques Rousseau)
45. *Ibid.*
46. *Ibid.*
47. Sally Carrighar, *Wild Heritage* (Boston: Houghton Mifflin Co., 1965), p. 232
48. Matt. 24:22 (M)
49. West, *op. cit.*, p. 192
50. Albert Paul Schimberg, *The Story of Thérèse Neumann* (New York: The Bruce Publishing Co., 1962), pp. 21, 74
51. Sydney J. Harris, "He Sought the Secret of Creation," review of *Wilhelm Reich: Selected Writings* (New York: Farrar, Strauss & Cudahy, 1960), in *Saturday Review*, October 1, 1960, p. 24
52. William Barrett, *Irrational Man*, p. 154 (Re: Sören Aabye Kierkegaard)
53. Mark 15:34
54. Ethelbert Stauffer, *Jesus and His Story*, p. 141
55. John 19:34 (M)
56. John 19:30
57. Luke 23:46
58. Matt. 20:28
59. I Tim. 2:6
60. John 11:50-51 (M)
61. Barrett, *op. cit.*, p. 163 (Re: Friedrich Wilhelm Nietzsche)
62. Priestley, *op. cit.*, p. 61 (Re: Blaise Pascal)

63. Matt. 4:1, 16:1, 19:3, 22:18, 22:35, 26:41, Mark 8:11, 12:15, Luke 8:13, 22:28, etc.
64. Mark 4:26–29
65. Matt. 23:17–19, Luke 24:16, 11:40, 12:20
66. Matt. 5:22
67. Matt. 24:21 (M)
68. John 16:21 (M)
69. Matt. 16:23
70. Matt. 7:3–5
71. Matt. 26:39–42
72. Sidney Cohen, *The Beyond Within: The LSD Story*, pp. 217, 218
73. *Ibid.*, p. 218
74. *Ibid.*, p. 217
75. *Ibid.*, pp. 218, 219
76. John 21:20–22
77. Matt. 4:1–11
78. Matt. 10:37, 12:46–50, John 2:4
79. Harold McCurdy, *The Personal World* (New York: Harcourt, Brace & World, 1961), p. 261; quoting Jung, "The Archetypes and the Collective Unconscious," in *The Collected Works of C. G. Jung*, ed. R. F. C. Hull (New York: Pantheon, 1959), Vol. 9, Part 1
80. Wilson, *Religion and the Rebel*, p. 244, quoting William Blake, *Poetry and Prose* (London: Nonesuch, 1949), p. 108
81. Mark 1:10–13
82. Wilson, *Religion and the Rebel*, p. 185 (Re: Blaise Pascal)
83. *Ibid.*, p. 190
84. Progoff, *op. cit.*, pp. 261, 262
85. *Ibid.*, p. 262
86. Psalms 46:1
87. Matt. 24:13
88. Wilson, *Religion and the Rebel*, p. 123 (Re: Arnold Toynbee)
89. Mark 2:27
90. Judg., Chapter 16
91. "The Screen," p. 66
92. Wilson, *Religion and the Rebel*, p. 275 (Re: George Bernard Shaw and Arnold Toynbee)
93. John 4:24
94. John 21:14–18
95. Matt. 13:11–12
96. Matt. 16:18–19
97. Einstein, *Essays in Science*, p. 28 (Re: Isaac Newton)
98. Albert Einstein, *The World As I See It* (New York: Philosophical Library, 1949), p. 21
99. Matt. 18:15–20
100. Luke 12:13–15 (M)
101. Rolf Alexander, *Creative Realism*, p. 91
102. "The Screen," p. 66
103. Barrett, *op. cit.*, p. 128, quoting Leo Tolstoy without reference
104. Wilson, *Religion and the Rebel*, p. 168

CHAPTER 15: THE RESURRECTION

1. Frederick Marion, *In My Mind's Eye*, p. 75
2. Marcus Bach, *God and the Soviets*, p. 143
3. Wilson, *Religion and the Rebel*, p. 300
4. Griffith W. Williams, "Hypnosis in Perspective," in LeCron, *Experimental Hypnosis*, p. 10.
5. Louisa E. Rhine, *Hidden Channels of the Mind*, p. 100
6. Alan Mitchell, *The Healing Trance*, pp. 111, 112
7. John 14:19–21 (M)
8. John 14:29 (M)
9. Matt. 25:40–46
10. Luke 24:45
11. Matt. 28:16–18, Mark 16:11–14, John 20:19–26, Luke 24:36–53, Acts 1:3 (M)
12. Mitchell, *op. cit.*, p. 111
13. Acts 2:27–31 (M)
14. Matt. 12:39–40 (M)
15. Mark 14:25
16. Luke 12:49–50
17. Luke 3:16
18. Matt. 17:9 (M)
19. Deut. 34:6 (M)
20. 2 Kings 2:11–13 (M)
21. Isaac Asimov, *The Genetic Code*, p. 23
22. Matt. 10:28
23. Radhakrishnan, *Recovery of Faith*, p. 135 (Re: Blaise Pascal)
24. Wilson, *Religion and the Rebel*, p. 166, quoting William Butler Yeats and Waslaw Nijinsky without reference
25. Gen. 3:19
26. "The Gilded Holy Man," *Time*, June 8, 1959, p. 74
27. C. W. Ceram, *Gods, Graves, and Scholars*, p. 170
28. Frederic W. H. Myers, *Human Personality and Its Survival of Bodily Death* (New York: Longmans, Green & Co., 1954), I, p. xx
29. Rhine, *op. cit.*, pp. 125–128, 234
30. John 14:23 (M)
31. John 14:16–17, 14:26
32. John 15:26 (M)
33. Psalms 78:2, Matt. 13:35
34. M.-L. von Franz, "Conclusion: Science and the Unconscious," in *Man and His Symbols*, ed. Carl G. Jung and M.-L. von Franz (Garden City: Doubleday, 1964), p. 308
35. Matt. 7:13 (M)
36. Mark 16:17
37. Ashley Mixson, Associated Press Release, Louisville, Kentucky, March 20, 1962
38. Barrett, *op. cit.*, p. 199
39. *Ibid.*, p. 200

40. *Ibid.*, pp. 198, 194
41. *Ibid.*, p. 192
42. *Ibid.*, p. 198
43. *Ibid.*, p. 229
44. Deut. 5:6–7, Matt. 22:37–38
45. Kahlil Gibran, *The Prophet* (New York: Alfred A. Knopf, 1957), pp. 16, 17
46. Theodor Reik, *Of Love and Lust* (New York: Farrar, Straus, and Cudahy, 1957). See *Saturday Review*, January 11, 1958, p. 6, John G. Fuller, "Trade Winds"
47. Herbert Spencer, *Philosophy of Style* (New York: Pageant Press, Inc., 1959), p. 36
48. Alfred Guillaume, *Islam*, p. 146
49. John 15:12
50. William Shakespeare, *The Tempest*, Act 1, sc. 2, l. 400
51. Gen. 1:26
52. Rev. 21:2
53. Matt. 25:1–6
54. Wilson, *Religion and the Rebel*, p. 167, quoting Jacob Boehme, *Confessions of Jacob Boehme*, ed. W. Scott Palmer (London: Methuen, 1954), p. 17
55. *Ibid.*, pp. 168, 169
56. J. B. Priestley, *Literature and Western Man*, p. 39
57. *Ibid.*, p. 119
58. Guillaume, *op. cit.*, p. 145
59. *Ibid.*, pp. 145, 146 (Re: Junayd and Hallāj, Sufis)
60. William Ernest Hocking, *The Meaning of Immortality in Human Experience* (New York: Harper, 1958), from Epilogue. (See also: *Saturday Review*, August 16, 1956, p. 21)
61. John 12:28
62. Julian Huxley, *New Bottles for New Wine*, p. 278
63. *Bhagavad-Gita* II. 22 (trans. Ryder)
64. William Shakespeare, *King John* Act v, sc. 5, l. 21
65. Julian Huxley, *op. cit.*, p. 242
66. *Ibid.*, p. 251
67. Ian Stevenson, "Scientists with Half-Closed Minds," *Harper's*, November, 1958, p. 69
68. Gerald Heard, *Growing Edge* (San Jacinto, California: Foundation for Social Research, Box 877, February, 1959), pp. 12, 13
69. Jung, "Synchronicity," p. 86
70. Julian Huxley, *op. cit.*, pp. 242, 245
71. Mark 9:23–24

CHAPTER 16: RETURNING TO THIS WORLD

1. Matt. 24:26
2. Psalms 19:1

REFERENCES

3. Philip Toynbee, London Observer Service, London, January 16, 1963
4. Immanuel Velikovsky, *Worlds in Collision*, see especially: Chapters 8, 10, and Part II, "Mars."
5. Werner Keller, *The Bible as History*, pp. 116–122
6. Robert L. Heilbroner, *The Worldly Philosophers* (New York: Simon & Schuster, 1961), p. 250, quoting John Maynard Keynes without reference

CHAPTER 17: THE ECONOMIC DOCTRINE OF JESUS

1. Robert L. Heilbroner, *The Great Ascent* (New York: Harper Torchbooks, 1963), p. 75
2. Teilhard de Chardin, *The Future of Man*, pp. 39, 38, 40, 46
3. *Ibid.*, pp. 40, 45–46
4. Heilbroner, *The Great Ascent*, p. 150; Robert L. Heilbroner, *The Making of Economic Society* (Englewood Cliffs: Prentice-Hall, 1962), pp. 220, 221
5. Heilbroner, *The Great Ascent*, pp. 150, 151, 154, 155
6. Heilbroner, *The Making of Economic Society*, p. 231
7. *Ibid.*, p. 219
8. *Ibid.*, p. 95
9. *Ibid.*, p. 225
10. Eiseley, *The Immense Journey*, pp. 128, 129, 130, 133
11. *Ibid.*, p. 138
12. Teilhard, *The Future of Man*, p. 38
13. Heilbroner, *The Great Ascent*, p. 113
14. *Ibid.*, p. 158
15. Heilbroner, *The Making of Economic Society*, p. 236
16. Matt. 6:25, Luke 12:15
17. Mark 8:36
18. Matt. 6:24
19. Luke 16:1–13
20. Heilbroner, *The Worldly Philosophers*, pp. 154, 155 (Re: Frederic Bastiat)
21. Luke 16:9
22. Heilbroner, *The Worldly Philosophers*, p. 133, quoting Karl Marx without reference
23. *Ibid.*, p. 132 (Re: Karl Marx)
24. *Ibid.*
25. Matt. 25:14–28
26. Definition of "usury," *Webster's Collegiate Dictionary*
27. Heilbroner, *The Worldly Philosophers*, p. 48 (Re: Adam Smith)
28. *Ibid.*, p. 231 (Re: John Maynard Keynes)
29. Matt. 6:19 (M)
30. Luke 12:16–21
31. Luke 16:9 (M)
32. William Shakespeare, *Shakespeare's Comedies, Histories, and Tragedies*, (Facsimile of The First Folio Edition, 1623) Published by Oxford: at the Clarendon Press, 1902, p. 746 (From: *Hamlet*, Act I, Scene III, by Polonius)
33. *Ibid.*

34. Matt. 5:42 (M)
35. Heilbroner, *The Worldly Philosophers*, p. 261
36. *Ibid.*, with reference to James Burnham's *The Managerial Revolution*
37. *Ibid.*, pp. 168, 169 (Re: John A. Hobson)
38. *Ibid.*, p. 126, quoting Karl Marx without reference
39. Nikita Khrushchev, Associated Press Releases, Moscow, November 20, 1961; November 20, 1962
40. "Borrowing from the Capitalists," *Time*, February 12, 1965, pp. 23–29
41. Associated Press Release, Washington, D.C., November 20, 1962 (Re: Personal Income)
42. Sydney Harris, "Why Words Cause Arguments," *Chicago Daily News*, June 3, 1960
43. Heilbroner, *The Worldly Philosophers*, p. 259
44. *Ibid.*, pp. 267–268
45. *Ibid.*, p. 292
46. *Ibid.*, p. 276
47. *Ibid.*, pp. 199–200 (Re: Thorstein Veblen)
48. Matt. 10:24–25 (M)
49. Heilbroner, *The Worldly Philosophers*, p. 197 (Re: Thorstein Veblen)
50. I Tim. 6:10
51. Albert Schweitzer, *Out of My Life and Thought*, p. 75
52. Matt. 10:10
53. Matt. 19:16–21
54. Luke 19:2–10, Matt. 27:57
55. Luke 19:8 (M)
56. John 12:3–8 (M)
57. Morris Kline, *Mathematics in Western Culture*, p. 351
58. John Fischer, "The Stupidity Problem," *Harper's*, September, 1962, pp. 14–24
59. Matt. 18:10 (M)
60. Fischer, *op. cit.*, pp. 14–24
61. Luke 14:17–20
62. Luke 12:33 (M)
63. II Chron. 31:21
64. Harvey Swados, "Works as a Public Issue," *Saturday Review*, December 12, 1959, pp. 13, 14, 15, 45
65. John 5:17
66. Matt. 20:1–15
67. Sydney Harris, *Chicago Daily News*, January 7, 1960
68. Matt. 20:26–28
69. Deut. 5:17–21
70. Luke 12:15
71. J. H. van den Berg, *The Changing Nature of Man*, pp. 211, 212
72. Whittaker Chambers, *Cold Friday*, pp. 60–61
73. Mark 9:43–47
74. van den Berg, *op. cit.*, p. 192
75. Marcus Bach, *God and the Soviets*, p. 155, quoting Nicholas Berdyaev without reference

76. Julian Huxley, *New Bottles for New Wine*, p. 294
77. Matt. 22:21
78. Heilbroner, *The Great Ascent*, p. 101
79. Matt. 25:29
80. Heilbroner, *The Worldly Philosophers*, p. 274
81. Heilbroner, *The Making of Economic Society*, p. 230
82. *Weekly Health Bulletin*, Rodale Press, 33 East Minor Street, Emmaus, Pennsylvania, May 30, 1964
83. See Arthur Eddington, *The Nature of the Physical World*, p. 143, for a description of this principle
84. Heilbroner, *The Worldly Philosophers*, p. 289, quoting John Kenneth Galbraith, *The Affluent Society*
85. *Ibid.*, pp. 278, 279, 288, 289
86. *Ibid.*, p. 280 (Re: Joseph Schumpeter)
87. Mark 8:36
88. Heilbroner, *The Making of Economic Society*, pp. 234, 235
89. Heilbroner, *The Worldly Philosophers*, p. 289, quoting John Kenneth Galbraith, *The Affluent Society*
90. William Barrett, *Irrational Man*, p. 110
91. Sydney Harris, "The Role of Complementarity," *Chicago Daily News*, May 24, 1961, quoting Niels Bohr
92. John 3:17
93. Norbert Wiener, *The Human Use of Human Beings* (New York: Doubleday Anchor Books, 1954), pp. 120, 121
94. Michael Polanyi, *Science, Faith, and Society* (Chicago: University of Chicago Press, 1964)

CHAPTER 18: TRUTH—WHAT IS TRUTH?

1. See inscription on the Thomas Jefferson Memorial, Washington, D.C.
2. Matt. 5:14-16
3. Matt. 8:22
4. John Dewey, "Influence of Darwinism on Philosophy," in *Great Essays in Science*, ed. Martin Gardner, p. 27
5. William Barrett, *Irrational Man*, p. 207
6. *Ibid.*, p. 241
7. Samuel Beckett, *The Unnamable* (New York: Grove Press, 1958). (See also: *Time*, October 13, 1958, p. 107)
8. Matt. 5:9, 24:6
9. John 14:27
10. Matt. 10:34 (M)
11. Matt. 26:52
12. John 15:13
13. *Time*, March 17, 1961, p. 48
14. Walt Whitman, *Leaves of Grass*
15. Philip Toynbee, "Moral Progress Is Natural," London Observer Service, Newspaper Column, January 9, 1963

16. Radhakrishnan, *Recovery of Faith*, p. 74
17. Marcus Bach, *God and the Soviets*, p. 156, quoting Nicholas Berdyaev without reference
18. Nikita Khrushchev, Associated Press Release, Moscow, October 17, 1961
19. Radhakrishnan, *op. cit.*, p. 144
20. Ira Progoff, *The Death and Rebirth of Psychology*, p. 11
21. Viktor Frankl, *Man's Search for Meaning*, p. 210
22. Progoff, *op. cit.*, pp. 15, 10
23. *Ibid.*, p. 14
24. *Ibid.*, p. v, quoting Carl G. Jung without reference
25. Arthur A. Cohen, "Why I Choose To Be A Jew," *Harper's*, April 1, 1959, pp. 61–66
26. Matt. 23:8–10 (M)
27. Radhakrishnan, *op. cit.*, pp. 87, 101, 112
28. *Hafiz of Shiraz*, p. 42
29. John 14:6, John 10:30
30. Isa. 43:6–7
31. Luke 5:36 (M)
32. Micah 4:4–5
33. Arthur Bonner, "India's Masses—The Public That Can't Be Reached," *The Atlantic*, October, 1959, pp. 48–51
34. Rajmohan Gandhi, *New World News*, Mackinac Island, Michigan, Jan.–March, 1964, pp. 2–21
35. J. B. Priestley, *Literature and Western Man*, p. 444
36. Elizabeth Mirel, "Golden Rule Invalid in Space," *Science News Letter*, February 15, 1964, pp. 106–107 [Reporting on: Andrew G. Haley's *Space Law and Government* (New York: Appleton-Century-Crofts, 1964)]
37. *Ibid.*
38. John 11:50
39. Loren Eiseley, *The Immense Journey*, pp. 160–162; see also: Norbert Wiener, *The Human Use of Human Beings*, pp. 40–46
40. Gen. 9:1; John 14:2
41. Wiener, *op. cit.*, pp. 82, 84
42. John 14:2
43. Matt. 7:3–5
44. Matt. 6:23
45. Rabindranath Tagore, *The Firefly*
46. Matt. 5:15
47. Deut. 2:7

CHAPTER 19: IN CONCLUSION

1. Reviewer in *Time*, April 6, 1959, p. 99, on Ernst Wiechert, *Tidings* (New York: Macmillan, 1959)
2. *Ibid.*
3. Gabriel B. Schonfeld, "Those Who Keep Faith with the Covenant: The Philosopher," a review of Arthur A. Cohen's *Martin Buber* (New York:

REFERENCES

Hillary House, 1958) in *Saturday Review*, June 7, 1958, p. 19, quoting Martin Buber without reference
4. Luke 5:37–39
5. Matt. 22:37–39
6. Louis Pauwels and Jacques Bergier, *The Morning of the Magicians*, p. 300
7. Erich Fromm, *The Art of Loving* (New York: Bantam Books, 1963), p. 39

BIBLIOGRAPHY

Aiken, Conrad. *Gehenna*. New York: Random House, 1930.
Alexander, Rolf. *Creative Realism*. New York: Pageant Press, 1954.
Ardrey, Robert. *African Genesis*. New York: Atheneum, 1961.
Asimov, Isaac. *The Genetic Code*. New York: New American Library, 1963.

Bach, Marcus. *God and the Soviets*. New York: Crowell, 1958.
Barrett, William. *Irrational Man*. New York: Doubleday, 1958.
Barzun, Jacques. *The House of Intellect*. New York: Harper, 1959.
Beckett, Samuel. *The Unnamable*. New York: Grove Press, 1958.
Ben-Horin, Meir. "Existence and Divine Essence," *Saturday Review*, March 4, 1961.
Betts, Charles A. "Man Evolved Like Animals," *Science News Letter*, April 17, 1965.
Bhagavad-Gita. Trans. Arthur W. Ryder. Chicago: University of Chicago Press, 1929.
Bible. King James Version.
Bible. Trans. James Moffatt. New York: Harper, 1935.
Bible. Revised Standard Version. New York: Nelson, 1946.
Binswanger, Ludwig. "Insanity as Life-Historical Phenomenon and as Mental Disease: The Case of Ilse," in Rollo May *et al.* (eds.), *Existence, q.v.*
Blake, William. *Poetry and Prose*. London: Nonesuch, 1949.
Blanton, Smiley. "The Best Prescription I Know," *Reader's Digest*, December, 1962.
Blok, Alexander. *The Twelve*. New York: Rudge, 1931.
Boehme, Jacob. *Confessions of Jacob Boehme*. Edited by W. Scott Palmer. London: Methuen, 1954.
Boisen, Anton T. *The Exploration of the Inner World*. Philadelphia: Univ. of Pennsylvania Press, 1971.
Brinton, Crane (ed.). *The Fate of Man*. New York: Braziller, 1961.
Bronstein, Daniel J. "Search for Inner Truth," *Saturday Review*, November 16, 1957.
Brown, Wenzell. "Violence in Society's Substratum," a review of *The Shook-up Generation*, by Harrison Salisbury (New York: Harper, 1958), in *Saturday Review*, October 18, 1958.

Brustein, Robert. "Cult of Unthink," *Horizons*, September, 1958.
Burnham, James. *The Managerial Revolution*. Westport, N.Y.: Greenwood, 1960.

Cantril, Hadley. "Perception and Interpersonal Relations," *The American Journal of Psychiatry*, Vol. 114, No. 2, August, 1957.
Carrighar, Sally. *Wild Heritage*. Boston: Houghton Mifflin, 1965.
Ceram, C. W. *Gods, Graves, and Scholars*. New York: Knopf, 1962.
Chambers, Whittaker. *Cold Friday*. New York: Random House, 1964.
Chase, John W., "The Church," a review of *What Is The Bible?*, by Henri Daniel-Rops, trans. J. R. Foster (New York: Hawthorne, 1958), in *Saturday Review*, December 20, 1958.
Christenson, James A., Jr. "Dynamics in Hypnotic Induction," in Leslie LeCron (ed.), *Experimental Hypnosis, q.v.*
Ciardi, John. "Dialogue with the Audience," *Saturday Review*, November 22, 1958.
Cohen, Arthur A. "Those Who Keep Faith with the Covenant: The Philosophy," *Saturday Review*, June 7, 1958.
——. "Why I Choose To Be a Jew," *Harper's*, April 1, 1959.
Cohen, Sidney. *The Beyond Within: The LSD Story*. New York: Atheneum, 1964.
Compton, Arthur H. "The Human Mind and Physical Law," a review of *Physics and Philosophy*, by Werner Heisenberg (New York: Harper, 1958), *Saturday Review*, July 12, 1958.
Coughlan, Robert. "Pathway into the Mind," *Life*, March 7, 1960.
Cumming, Robert Denoon (ed.). *The Philosophy of Jean-Paul Sartre*. New York: The Modern Library, 1966.

Davenport, Russell W. *The Dignity of Man*. New York: Harper, 1955.
del Castillo, Michel. *Child of Our Time*. Translated by Peter Green. New York: Alfred A. Knopf, 1958.
deRopp, Robert. *Science and Salvation*. New York: St. Martin's Press, 1962.
Dewey, John. "Influence of Darwinism on Philosophy," in Martin Gardner (ed.), *Great Essays in Science, q.v.*
Dinesen, Isak. *Shadows on the Grass*. New York: Random House, 1961.
Dingle, Herbert (ed.). *A Century of Science*. New York: Roy, 1951.
Dorcus, Roy M. (ed.). *Hypnosis and Its Therapeutic Applications*. New York: McGraw-Hill, 1956.
Dubos, Rene Jules. *Mirage of Health*. New York: Harper, 1959.
Durrell, Lawrence. *Balthazar*. New York: Pocket Books, 1961.
——. *Justine*. New York: Pocket Books, 1962.

Echermann's Conversations with Goethe. Translated by R. C. Moon. London, 1951.
Eddington, Arthur. *The Nature of the Physical World*. Chicago: University of Michigan Press, 1958.
Eddy, Mary Baker. *Science and Health*. New York: The Philosophical Library, 1934.

Einstein, Albert. *Essays in Science*. New York: The Philosophical Library, 1934.
———. *The World as I See It*. New York: The Philosophical Library, 1949.
Eiseley, Loren. "An Evolutionist Looks at Modern Man," in Richirad Thruelsen and John Kobler (eds.), *Adventures of the Mind, q.v.*
———. *The Immense Journey*. New York: Vintage Books, 1957.
Ellenberger, Henri F. "A Clinical Introduction to Psychiatric Phenomenology and Existential Analysis," in Rollo May *et al.* (eds.), *Existence, q.v.*
Erickson, Milton H. "Deep Hypnosis and Its Induction," in Leslie M. LeCron (ed.), *Experimental Hypnosis, q.v.*

Fischer, John. "The Stupidity Problem," *Harper's*, September, 1962.
Ford, Barbara. "Coptic Voices from the Past," *Science Digest*, February, 1972, p. 40.
Fosberg, Raymond. "Where is Science Taking Us?", *Saturday Review*, November 14, 1959.
Frankl, Viktor. *Man's Search for Meaning*. Trans. Ilse Lasch. New York: Washington Square Press, 1964.
Freud, Sigmund. *A General Introduction to Psycho-analysis*. New York: Doubleday, 1953.
———. *The Ego and the Id*. London: Hogarth Press and The Institute of Psycho-analysis, 1949.
———. *Letters of*. New York: Basic Books.
———. *Moses and Monotheism*. New York: Vintage Books, 1958.
———. *Neue Folge der Vorlesungen zur Einfuehrung in die Psychoanalyse*, 1933, *Gesammelte Werke*, XV.
Friedrich, Rudolph. *Frontiers of Medicine*. New York: Liveright, 1961.
Fromm, Erich. *The Art of Loving*. New York: Bantam Books, 1963.
Frost, Robert. "The Road Not Taken," in *The Complete Poems of Robert Frost*. New York: Holt, Rinehart and Winston, 1964.

Galbraith, John Kenneth. *The Affluent Society*. Boston: Houghton-Mifflin, 1971.
Gardner, Martin (ed.) *Great Essays in Science*. New York: Pocket Books, 1957.
———. *The Ambidextrous Universe*. New York: Basic Books, 1964.
Gibran, Kahlil. *The Prophet*. New York: Knopf, 1957.
Ginsberg, Allen. *Howl and Other Poems*. San Francisco: City Lights, 1956.
Goethe, Johann von. *Iphigenia*.
———. *Eckermann's Conversations with Goethe*. Trans. R O. Moon. London, 1951.
Goldfarb, Charles, Driesen, Jerome, and Cole, Donald. "Psychophysiologic Aspects of Malignancy," *American Journal of Psychiatry* 123 (June, 1967), 12.
Gospel of Thomas. See Ford, Barbara.
Grotjahn, Martin. *Beyond Laughter*. New York: McGraw-Hill, 1957.
Guillaume, Alfred. *Islam*. Baltimore: Pelican Books, 1956.

Hadamard, Jacques. *The Psychology of Invention in the Mathematical Field.* Princeton: Princeton University Press, 1954.
Hafiz of Shiraz. Trans. John Heath-Stubbs and Peter Avery. London: Murray, 1952.
Hamilton, Edith. "The Lessons of the Past," in Richard Thruelsen et al. (eds.), *Adventures of the Mind, q.v.*
Hansen, C. E. M. *ESP, A Scientific Evaluation.* New York: Scribner's, 1966.
Harris, Sydney J. "He Sought the Secret of Creation," a review of *Wilhelm Reich: Selected Writings* (New York: Farrar, Straus & Cudahy, 1960), *Saturday Review,* October 1, 1960.
——. "Why Words Cause Arguments," *Chicago Daily News,* June 3, 1960.
——. "Strictly Personal," syndicated column, December 15, 1972.
Head, Joseph, and Cranston, S. L. *Reincarnation, An East-West Anthology.* New York: Julian Press, 1961.
Heard, Gerald. "Can This Drug Enlarge Man's Mind?" *Horizon,* May, 1963.
——. *Growing Edge.* San Jacinto, Calif.: Foundation for Social Research, 1959.
Heilbroner, Robert L. *Economic Society.* Englewood Cliffs: Prentice-Hall, 1962.
——. *The Great Ascent.* New York: Harper Torchbooks, 1963.
——. *The Worldly Philosophers.* New York: Simon & Schuster, 1961.
Heisenberg, Werner. *Physics and Philosophy.* New York: Harper, 1958.
Hocking, William Ernest. *The Meaning of Immortality in Human Experience.* New York: Harper, 1958.
Hoffer, A. "The Psychophysiology of Cancer," *The Journal of Asthma Research* 8 (December, 1970) 63.
Holton, Gerald, and Roller, H. D. Duane. *Foundations of Modern Physical Science.* Reading, Mass.: Addison-Wesley, 1958.
Hoyle, Fred. "When Time Began," in Thruelsen et al. (eds.), *Adventures of the Mind, q.v.*
Hutchins, Robert Maynard (ed.). *Great Books of the Western World.* Chicago: Encyclopaedia Britannica, 1952.
Huxley, Aldous. "A Case of Voluntary Ignorance," *Esquire,* October, 1956.
——. *The Doors of Perception.* New York: Harper, 1954.
Huxley, Julian. *New Bottles for New Wine.* New York: Harper, 1957.

I Ching (The Book of Change).
International Dictionary of Physics and Electronics. Princeton: van Nostrand, 1961.
Ittelson, William H. *The Ames Demonstrations in Perception.* Princeton: Princeton University Press, 1952.

Jaffé, Aniela. "Symbolism in the Visual Arts," in Carl Jung (ed.), *Man and His Symbols, q.v.*
James, William. "The Problem of Being," in Martin Gardner (ed.), *Great Essays in Science, q.v.*
——. *The Varieties of Religious Experience.*

Jung, Carl G. "The Archetypes and the Collective Unconscious," in *The Collected Works of C. G. Jung*, edited by R. F. C. Hull. New York: Pantheon, 1959.
———. "God, the Devil, and the Human Soul," *The Atlantic*, November, 1957.
———. *Man and His Symbols*. New York: Doubleday, 1964.
———. *Memories, Dreams, Reflections*. Edited by Aniela Jaffé. New York: Pantheon, 1963.
———. "Synchronicity, an Acausal Connecting Principle," in *The Interpretation of Nature and the Psyche* (with W. Pauli). New York: Pantheon, 1955.

Keller, Werner. *The Bible as History*. New York: Morrow, 1956.
Kline, Morris. *Mathematics in Western Culture*. New York: Oxford University Press, 1953.
Kluckhohn, Clyde. *Mirror for Man*. New York: McGraw-Hill, 1960.
Koestler, Arthur. *The Sleepwalkers*. New York: Macmillan, 1959.
Krutch, Joseph Wood. *The Great Chain of Life*. Cambridge. Mass.: Riverside Press, 1956.

Lao-tzu. *Tao Teh Ching*. Trans. Arthur Waley, *The Way and Its Power*. London, 1934.
La Rochefoucauld, François Duc de. *Maxims*. Trans. Louis Kronenberger. New York: Random House, Modern Library Paperbacks, 1959.
LeCron, Leslie M. "A Study of Age Regression under Hypnosis," in LeCron (ed.), *Experimental Hypnosis, q.v.*
——— (ed.). *Experimental Hypnosis*. New York: Macmillan, 1956.
Linssen, Robert, *Living Zen*. New York: Grove Press, 1960.
Lowe, Helen R. "Solomon or Salami," *The Atlantic*, Anniversary Issue, 1959.
Lyttleton, Raymond A., Bondi, H., Bonnor, W. B., and Whitrow, G. J. *Rival Theories of Cosmology*. London: Oxford University Press, 1960.

Marion, Frederick. *In My Mind's Eye*. New York: Dutton, 1950.
May, Rollo. "Contributions of Existential Psychotherapy," in Rollo May, et al. (eds.), *Existence, q.v.*
———. May, Rollo, Angel, Ernest, and Ellenberger, Henri F. (eds.). *Existence: A New Dimension in Psychiatry and Psychology*. New York: Basic Books, 1958.
McCurdy, Harold. *The Personal World*. New York: Harcourt, Brace & World, 1961.
McGlashan, Alan. "The Mystery of the Miracles." Unpublished manuscript, 1972, available from Harold Institute.
Mellaart, James. "A Neolithic City in Turkey," *Scientific American*, April, 1964.
Michalson, Carl (ed.). *Christianity and the Existentialists*. New York: Charles Scribner & Sons, 1956.
Miller, Arthur. "With Respect for Her Agony—But with Love," *Life*, February 7, 1964.
Miller, Henry. *Lawrence Durrell—Henry Miller*, A Private Correspondence. New York: Dutton, 1963.

BIBLIOGRAPHY

Miller, Samuel. "The Evolution of Religion," *Saturday Review*, November 14, 1959.
Mirel, Elizabeth. "Golden Rule Invalid in Space," *Science News Letter*, February 15, 1964.
Mitchell, Alan. *The Healing Trance*. New York: A. S. Barnes, 1960.
Moffatt, James. Introduction to his translation of the Bible. New York: Harper, 1935.
Moore, Ruth. *Man, Time, and Fossils*. New York: Knopf, 1961.
———. *The Coil of Life*. New York: Knopf, 1961.
Mumford, Lewis. "The Morals of Extermination," *The Atlantic*, October, 1959.
Murray, Henry A. "Two Versions of Man," in Harlow Shapley (ed.), *Science Ponders Religion*, q.v.
Myers, Frederic W. H. *Human Personality and its Survival of Bodily Death*. New York: Longmans, Green, 1954.

Neil, William. *The Rediscovery of the Bible*. New York: Harper, 1954.
Neilson, William. *Mesmerism*. Edinburgh: Shepherd & Elliot, 1855.
Nichomachus of Gerasa. *Introduction to Arithmetic I and II*, in Robert Maynard Hutchins (ed.), *Great Books of the Western World*, q.v.
Nietzsche, Friedrich. *Zarathustra*, in Walter Kaufmann (ed.), *The Portable Nietzsche*. New York: The Viking Press, 1954.

Oppenheimer, J. Robert. "The Mystery of Matter," in Thruelsen, *et al.* (eds.), *Adventures of the Mind*, q.v.
Overstreet, Harry. *The Mature Mind*. New York: W. W. Norton, 1951.

Pattie, Frank A. "Methods of Induction, Susceptibility of Subjects, and Criteria of Hypnosis," in Roy Dorcus (ed.), *Hypnosis and Its Therapeutic Applications*, q.v.
Pauli, Wolfgang. "The Influence of Archetypal Ideas on the Scientific Theories of Kepler," in *The Interpretation of Nature and the Psyche* (with C. G. Jung). New York: Pantheon, 1955.
Pauwels, Louis, and Bergier, Jacques. *The Morning of the Magicians*. Trans. Rollo Myers. New York: Stein & Day, 1964.
Peel, Robert. *Christian Science—Its Encounter with American Culture*. New York: Anchor Books, 1965.
Polanyi, Michael. *Science, Faith and Society*. Chicago: University of Chicago Press, 1964.
Priestley, J. B. *Literature and Western Man*. New York: Harper, 1960.
Progoff, Ira. *The Death and Rebirth of Psychology*. New York: Julian Press, 1956.
———."The Inner Messiah." Unpublished manuscript, 1968.

Radhakrishnan. *Recovery of Faith*. London: Allen & Unwin, 1956.
Rank, Otto. *Beyond Psychology*. Camden, N.J.: Hadden Craftsmen, 1941.
———. *Modern Education*. New York: Knopf, 1932.

Reich, Wilhelm. *Selected Writings*. New York: Farrar, Strauss, & Cudahy, 1960.
Reik, Theodor, *Of Love and Lust*. New York: Farrar, Straus, and Cudahy, 1957.
Reiss, Samuel. *The Basis of Scientific Thinking*. New York: Philosophical Library, 1961.
Renan, Ernest. *The Life of Jesus*. New York: Random House, Modern Library, 1927.
Rhine, Louisa E. *Hidden Channels of the Mind*. New York: Sloane, 1961.
Rieff, Philip. "A Burden of Knowingness," *Saturday Review*, November 26, 1960.
Rimbaud, Arthur. "A Season in Hell." Trans. Norman Cameron. London: Lehmann, 1949.
Rochefoucauld, Francois, Duc de la. *Maxims*. Trans. Louis Kronenberger. New York: Random House, 1959.
Ross, Nancy Wilson. "Something Called 'Zen,'" *Horizon*, September 29, 1959.
Rostand, Jean. *Can Man be Modified?* New York: Basic Books, 1959.

Salisbury, Harrison. *The Shook-up Generation*. New York: Harper, 1958.
Sartre, Jean-Paul. *Being and Nothingness*. Trans. Hazel Barnes. New York: Philosophical Library, 1956.
Schimberg, Albert Paul. *The Story of Therese Neumann*. New York: Bruce, 1962.
Schonfeld, Gabriel B. "Those Who Keep Faith with the Covenant: The Philosopher," a review of *Martin Buber*, by Arthur A. Cohen (New York: Hillary House, 1958), *Saturday Review*, June 7, 1958.
Schrödinger, Erwin. *What Is Life?* New York: Cambridge University Press, 1955.
Schweitzer, Albert. *Out of My Life and Thought*. New York: New American Library, 1949.
Seidenberg, Roderick. *Posthistoric Man: An Inquiry*. Chapel Hill: University of North Carolina Press, 1950. Paperback edition: Beacon Press, 1957.
Selye, Hans. *The Story of the Adaptation Syndrome*. Montreal: Acta, 1952.
Shahani, Ranjee. "A Lamp unto Himself," *Saturday Review*, September 26, 1959.
Shapley, Harlow (ed.). *Science Ponders Religion*. New York: Appleton-Century-Crofts, 1962.
Sienko, Michell J., and Plane, Robert A. *Chemistry*. New York: McGraw-Hill, 1957.
Siepmann, Charles. "Judgment Day for the Modern Mind," a review of *The Two Cultures and the Scientific Revolution*, by C. P. Snow (New York: Cambridge University Press, 1960), *Saturday Review*, January 30, 1960.
Simeons, A. T. W. *Man's Presumptuous Brain*. New York: Dutton, 1961.
Sithole, Ndabanningi. *African Nationalism*. New York: Oxford University Press, 1960.
Snow, Charles P. *The Two Cultures and the Scientific Revolution*. New York: Cambridge Univ. Press, 1960.
Spencer, Herbert. *First Principles*. 4th ed. New York: Caldwell, 1880.

——. *Philosophy of Style.* New York: Pageant Press, 1959.
Spengler, Oswald. *Decline of the West.* New York: Knopf, 1934.
Stauffer, Ethelbert. *Jesus and His Story.* Trans. Richard and Clara Winston. New York: Knopf, 1960.
Stevenson, Ian. "Scientists with Half-Closed Minds," *Harper's,* November, 1958.
Straus, Erwin W. "Aesthesiology and Hallucinations," in R. May (ed.), *Existence, q.v.*
Streeter, Burnett H. *The Four Gospels.* New York: St. Martin's Press, 1924.
Swados, Harvey. "Work as a Public Issue," *Saturday Review,* December 12, 1959.

Teilhard de Chardin, Pierre. *The Future of Man.* New York: Harper & Row, 1964.
——. *The Phenomenon of Man.* New York: Harper, 1959.
Thruelsen, Richard, and Kobler, John (eds.). *Adventures of the Mind.* New York: Knopf, 1959.
Tillich, Paul. "Existential Aspects of Modern Art," in C. Michalson (ed.), *Christianity and the Existentialists, q.v.*
Toynbee, Arnold. *An Historian's Approach to Religion.* New York: Oxford University Press, 1956.
Toynbee, Philip. "Living in One World-Covering City," *London Observer,* January 16, 1963.
Troward, Thomas. *Bible Mystery and Bible Meaning.* New York: Dodd, Mead, 1913.
Tyrrell, G. N. M. *The Personality of Man.* Baltimore: Penguin Books, 1954.

van den Berg, J. H. *The Changing Nature of Man.* New York: Norton, 1961.
Van Dusen, Henry Pitt. "To a Total Comprehension," *Saturday Review,* March 5, 1960.
Vasiliev, L. L. *Experiments in Mental Suggestion.* Church Crookham, Hampshire, England: Institute for the Study of Mental Images, 1963.
Velikovsky, Immanuel. *Worlds in Collision.* New York: Doubleday, 1950.
von Franz, M.-L. "Conclusion: Science and the Unconscious," in C. G. Jung, *Man and His Symbols, q.v.*
——. "The Process of Individuation," in C. G. Jung (ed.), *Man and His Symbols, q.v.*

Weaver, Warren, and Shannon, Claude E. *The Mathematical Theory of Communication.* Urbana: University of Illinois Press, 1964.
Webster's Collegiate Dictionary.
Webster's New and Unabridged Dictionary. Springfield, Mass.: Merriam, 1940.
Wernli, Hans J. *Biorhythm.* New York: Crown, 1961.
West, D. J. *Psychical Research Today.* Baltimore: Penguin Books, 1962.
Wheeler, John A., and Tilson, Seymour. "The Dynamics of Space-Time," *International Science & Technology Journal,* December, 1963. Reprinted in *Artoga,* Communications 70 and 71, October and November, 1964.

Whitehead, Alfred North. "Religion and Science," in Martin Gardner (ed.), *Great Essays in Science*, q.v.
——. *The Philosophy of Alfred North Whitehead*. Edited by Paul Arthur Schilpp. Evanston: Northwestern University Press, 1941.
Whitlow, Joseph E. "A Rapid Method for the Induction of Hypnosis," in LeCron (ed.), *Experimental Hypnosis*, q.v.
Whyte, Lancelot Law. *The Unconscious before Freud*. New York: Basic Books, 1960.
Wiechert, Ernst. *Tidings*. New York: Macmillan, 1959.
Wiener, Norbert. *The Human Use of Human Beings*. New York: Doubleday, Anchor Books, 1954.
Wilhelm, R. *Das wahre Buch vom suedlichen Bluetenland*. Jena, 1912.
Wilson, Colin. *Religion and the Rebel*. Boston: Houghton Mifflin, 1957.
——. *The Outsider*. Boston: Houghton Mifflin, 1956.
Winkler, Franz E. *Man: The Bridge between Two Worlds*. New York: Harper, 1960.
Wittgenstein, Ludwig. *Tractatus Logico-Philosophicus*. London: Routledge and Kegan Paul, 1949.
Wormser, Rene A. *The Story of the Law*. New York: Simon and Schuster, 1962.

Yang, Chen Ning. *Elementary Particles*. Princeton: Princeton University Press, 1962.

Zahner, Louis. "Composition at the Barricades," *The Atlantic*, Anniversary Issue, 1959.

Index

Abel, 58, 68, 71, 96, 99, 279
Abraham, 33, 36, 58, 66, 251–252
Absolute, the, 99–100, 158, 161, 375, 393
Absolute-Elsewhere, 131, 132–135, 204–205, 323
Actions, conscious, 253
Adam, xxxiv–xxxv, 21, 26, 30, 51–53, 58, 61–62, 64–68, 70, 73, 110, 279, 328
Adams, Henry, 136
Adler, Alfred, 14, 36, 57, 157, 287
  quoted, 244
Adoption, 81, 83–84, 89
Adultery, 52
Africa, 30, 70–72
African Genesis, Ardrey, 68
After the Fall, Miller, 254
Aiken, Conrad, 289
Alchemy and alchemists, 176–177, 372–373, 378
Alexander, Rolf, quoted, 86, 93, 96, 125, 138, 152, 239, 241, 245, 308
Alexandria, 180
Alexandria Quartet, The, Durrell, 170
Allport, Gordon W., quoted, 279
Amoeba, 62, 78
Amnesia, 118
  infant, 81, 96
Anesthesia, 218–219, 221, 223, 227, 239, 243, 248
Animals, 233
Anti-Semitism, 49–50, 94
Antony and Cleopatra, Shakespeare, 328
Anxiety, 96, 222
Apes, 69–70
Ardrey, Robert, 69
  quoted, 57–58, 68–72, 74, 119, 144

Arjuna, 42
Art, 11, 177–178, 282
  modern, 269–276
Artificial insemination, 83
Asimov, Isaac, 106
Asymmetry, 189–190, 213
Atom of action, h, 147–152, 154
Atomic bombs, 271, 380
Atomic dating, 69
Atoms, 175, 201
Australopithecus africanus, 68–69, 71, 73, 78
Australopithecus robustus, 68–69, 71, 73, 78
Authority, 35, 37, 54, 256, 279, 281, 290
Authority-Ego, 38–42, 44, 54, 75, 80, 87, 91, 97–98, 107, 111–112, 154, 168–171, 206, 233, 235–237, 250, 253, 257, 316, 321, 392
  Jesus as, 77, 118, 155, 232, 248, 277, 288
Automatic Writing, 253
Automation, 356, 370

Babel, Tower of, 85–89, 95, 107
Bach, Marcus, 312
  quoted, 292
Baptism, 85, 317
Baron, Edwin L., quoted, 222
Barrett, William, 117, 238, 309, 325, 330
  quoted, 1, 21–22, 33, 252, 281, 295–297, 324, 326, 375–376
Barron, John N., 222
Barzun, Jacques, 272
Basis of Scientific Thinking, The, Reiss, 129
Bastiat, Frederic, 346, 367

INDEX

Beadle, George Wells, 83
Beat generation, 274
Beatitudes, the, 298
Beckett, Samuel, 376
Beethoven, 178, 192
Behavior, parasitic, 91
Belgium, 367
Ben-Horin, Meir, quoted, 99
Berdyaev, Nicholas, quoted, 98, 362, 380
Bergier, Jacques, quoted, 392
Bergman, Ingmar, 293, 304
    quoted, 309
Bergmann, Peter G., 204
Berthelot, quoted, 402
Bethany, 315
Bethlehem, 389
Beyond Within, The, Cohen, 244
Bhagavadgītā, 382
Bhave, Vinoba, 383
Bible, the, 8–9, 21, 23–24, 28–32, 51, 57–58, 167–168, 196, 251, 256, 296, 305, 383, 391
    miracles of, 225–258, 284–310
Binswanger, Ludwig, quoted, 113
Biochemistry, 106–109, 187, 223
Biologists, 63
Biorhythm chart, 197–198
Birth, 78–81, 96, 135
    of Jesus, 82–85, 389–390
Birth legends, 82–85
Bisexuality, 51, 53–54, 83
Black markets, 351
Blake, William, 371
    quoted, 286, 302
Blakeslee, Alton, quoted, 200
Blanton, Smiley, quoted, 43
Blasphemy, 170–171, 173, 226, 382
    definition of, 173
Blindness, hypnotic, 237, 263
Blok, Alexander, 7
Body reactions, 222–223
Boehme, Jacob, 292
    quoted, 286, 328
Bohr, Niels, 172
    quoted, 371, 407
Boisen, Anton T., 288
Boltzmann, Ludwig, 125
Bondi, Hermann, 211

Bonner, Arthur, quoted, 383
Boskop man, 343
Bragg, Sir William, 124
Braid, James, 221
Brave New World, A. Huxley, 270
Bread, 105, 303
Brecht, Bertolt, 118
Bremen Cathedral, 319
Brinton, Crane, quoted, 115
Brotherhood, 30, 91, 101, 210
Brustein, Robert, quoted, 274, 280
Buber, Martin, quoted, 390
Buddha, 30, 383
Burnham, James, 350
Byron, Lord, quoted, xxxviii

Caesar, 363, 365–366
Caiaphas, 385, 387
Cain, 58, 68, 71–74, 96, 99, 101, 238, 279
Cana, 117, 246, 249
Canaan, 31
Cancer, 404–406
Cannibalism, 47, 65, 79
Cantor, Georg, 15
Capital, 337, 345, 348, 359
Capitalism, 4, 339–340, 344–347, 350–355, 368–370, 410–411
Carrighar, Sally, quoted, 294
Carus, C. G., 35
Castillo, Michel del, 281–282
Castration, 48–49
Cayce, Edgar, 215
Cells, 106–109, 224
Ceram, C. W., 85
Chambers, Whittaker, 6
    quoted, 360
Chance, 191–192, 198
Chih Hang, 319
Child of Our Time, Castillo, 281
Children, 3–4, 37, 54, 81, 84–91, 94–95, 135, 208, 244–245, 266, 281–282, 373, 388, 393
    mentally retarded, 323–324
China, 4, 341
Christenson, James A., quoted, 219–220
Christian Church, 3, 304–305, 307, 392
    theology and, 2, 4–5, 392

INDEX

Christian Science, 119–120, 242–243
Christianity, 1–2, 14, 48, 305, 307, 374, 382, 392
   Arab, 6
   civilization and, 4–5
   culture and, 5
   decline of, 3, 269, 392
   and Group-ego, 94
   hatred of, 50
   Judaism and, 49–51, 56–57
Christology, 1
Church (*see* Christian Church)
Ciardi, John, 129
   quoted, 9–10
Circumcision, 49–51
Cities, 169–171
Civilization, 5, 85, 280, 306, 363, 379
Clairvoyance, 252–253, 320, 335
Clausius, 125
Cleopatra, 329
Cohen, Arthur A., 390
   quoted, 381
Cohen, Sidney, 244, 300
   quoted, 300
Cold Friday, Chambers, 6
Collectivization, 338–339, 341–343, 369
Communication, 87–89, 92, 210–211, 212–213, 274, 276, 383
   Mathematical Theory of, 194–199, 322
Communion, 91, 303
Communism, 4, 340, 344, 355
Compassion, 161, 310
Conditioned learning, 95
Conscience, 39–40, 93, 141, 143–144, 161
Consciousness, 11, 39–40, 42–44, 51, 54, 63, 77, 81, 87–91, 93–96, 101–102, 109–110, 112, 118, 131, 135–138, 143, 155, 164, 198, 205, 208–209, 237, 282, 291, 298, 309, 324, 378, 386–388, 392–393
   repressions and, 37, 165
   reptilian, 280–281
Continence, 52
Copernicus, 295
Cosmic man, 62
Cosmology, 199, 205, 211
Coughlan, Robert, 219
Covetousness, 381
Creation, 100, 112, 129, 205

Credit, 349, 361
Cremation, internal, 317–320
Criminals, 251, 254, 257, 281
Cro-Magnon man, 65, 67, 72
Cross, the (†), 11, 146, 162, 181–183, 190–192, 196, 208–209, 212
Crucifixion, 103, 192, 385
Culture, 67, 276
   Christianity and, 5
Cynodictis, 64–65

Daniel, 272
Daniel-Rops, Henri, quoted, 30
Dart, Raymond A., 69
Darwin, Charles, 46, 57, 61, 63, 69
Davenport, Russell, quoted, 4–6, 272
David, 24–25
   House of, 82
   prophecies of, 163–164, 316
   quoted, 163, 165
Deafness, hallucinatory, 263
Death, 27–28, 95, 99–103, 111, 118, 169, 171–172, 198–201, 234–235, 294–297, 309, 311, 323, 332, 392
   life after, 311–332
Debt, 361
Deckert, Gordon H., 243
DeKooning, Willem, quoted, 93
Delinquency, criminal, 225
Delusion, 200, 215–216
   Messianic (*see* Messianic delusion)
Democracy, 344
Demons, 228, 231–233
De Ropp, Robert, quoted, 19, 42, 44, 268
Devil, the, 102, 104, 109–110, 115, 176
Devils, The, 266
De Vries, Hugo, 76
Dewey, John, quoted, 375
Dicke, R. H., 200
Dictatorship, 339
Diebel, Paul, 231, 248
Dilemma of three and four, 175–193
Dinesen, Isak, quoted, 144
Dingle, Herbert, quoted, 112
Diogenes, 362
   quoted, 358
Dirac, P. A. M., 200

459

Discipline, 291
Disease, 229–231, 237
Divorce, 53
DNA, xxx, xxxi, xxxviii, 106–109, 223
Doctors, 222, 367
Doors of Perception, The, A. Huxley, 244
Dorcus, Roy M., 221
Dorn, Gerhard, 176
Dostoevski, 281, 292
Dreams, 144
Driesch, Hans, 107, 108, 187, 224
Drinking, 116–117
Drugs, vision, 244, 300
Dubos, René Jules, 222
Durrell, Lawrence, quoted, 9, 84, 139, 170, 407

Earth, 131, 163, 206
Eckhart, Meister, 115
Economic Doctrine of Jesus, 337–373
ECT, 405–406
Eddington, Sir Arthur, 124, 129, 133, 136, 138, 146, 182, 195, 205, 368
  quoted, 10–11, 124–128, 131–132, 134–135, 141–143, 147–156, 162–164, 211, 216
Eddy, Mary Baker, 119
  quoted, 242–243
Eden, 3, 62, 67, 87, 89–90, 96–97
Eden Legend, 62, 64–67, 72, 74, 89, 91, 110
Education, 76, 273–280, 357–358, 363, 373
Ego, 36, 38–39, 92–93, 272
  conscious, 35, 39
  definition of, 37–38
  Group, 86, 92–94, 360
Ego-group, 40, 42–44, 87–88, 93, 98, 111–112, 118, 143, 154–155, 169, 172, 232, 241, 326, 392
Ego symbol, 11, 36
Egypt, 18, 46
  Princess of, 81, 84
Einstein, Albert, 15, 177, 188, 395, 396
  quoted, 120, 129, 146, 159–161, 306–307
Eiseley, Loren, 343
  quoted, 77, 199, 201
Electromagnetism, 209

Electrons, 154–155, 157
Elijah, 234–235, 317
Ellenberger, Henri F., quoted, 215
Emmaus, 315
Empathy, 89, 113–115, 117–118, 137–139, 141–143, 161, 172, 379, 385, 393
Energy, 99, 109, 112, 121, 138, 147–148, 150, 156–159, 165–166, 200–201, 203–204, 208
  organization of, 126–127
  psychic, 136, 140, 165
Engels, Friedrich, 352–353
England, 354
Enoch, 72
Enos, 72, 88
Entropy, 125–131, 136–137, 190–191, 193–195, 201, 368
Environment, 67
Epictetus, 44
Equation-of-One, 179, 185–187, 189–191, 193, 209, 212
Esdaile, James, 218, 229
ESP (*see* Extrasensory perception)
Essenes, the, 18
Ethics, 5, 372
Euclid, 175–176, 179, 181
Euripides, quoted, 94
Europe, 35
Eve, xxxv, 52, 61–62, 64–65, 67, 75, 110, 279, 328
Evil, 100–102, 109–111, 113–115, 138–139, 141, 157, 162, 164–165, 168–169, 237, 256, 294, 354, 371
Evolution, 11, 52, 60–96, 115, 161, 348, 378, 393
  of consciousness, xxxiv–xxxvi, 118
Existentialism, 278, 381
  in art, 269
Expansion-Contraction Theory, 200
Experience, 114–115
  life, 139–141, 170–171, 309, 328
Exploration of the Inner World, The, Boisen, 288
Explosion Theory, 200
Extrasensory perception, xxx, 88–89, 102, 214–218, 224–225, 231, 236, 258, 311, 316, 331
  Jesus and, 15, 259–283

INDEX

Faith, 231, 239, 241, 243, 262, 270, 348, 390, 391
  loss of, 278
Faith healing, 228
Fate of Man, The, Brinton, 115
Father, DNA of cell as, 106
  God as, 16, 25, 131, 152, 154, 159, 393
  Jesus in, 151
Father image, 98, 278
Fathers, 48–49, 58, 91, 101–103, 278
Faulkner, William, quoted, xxxvii
Faust, Goethe, 176
Fear, 58, 222, 229, 233, 253–254, 270, 281, 296–297
Female, Feminine, 51–54, 67, 84, 91, 135
Fermi, Enrico, 210
Fields, 158, 185–186
Fischer, John, quoted, 241
Fish, symbol of, 11, 84, 152–153, 209
Fission, 175
FitzGerald Contraction, 162, 187, 269
Fitzherbert, Joan, 87
Five, 178–179, 184–185, 190, 212
Fludd, Robert, 176–177
Food, 65, 79–80
Footstool, 163
Forgiveness, 101, 143, 162, 172, 237
Fosberg, Raymond, quoted, 273–274
Foundations of Modern Physical Science, Holton and Roller, 259
Four, 173, 175–193
Four Gospels, The, Streeter, 12
Frankl, Viktor, 381
  quoted, 157–158, 277–279
Franzini, Paolo, 211
Freedom, 19, 157–158, 161, 164, 362
Frequencies, 160
Freud, Sigmund, xxv, 4, 35, 46, 56, 81, 92, 102–103, 219, 269, 381, 396
  doctrine of, 57–58
  quoted, 36–39, 47–49, 57–58, 253, 267
Friedrich, Rudolph, 225, 228
  quoted, 225, 228, 229
Fromm, Erich, quoted, 392
Frontiers of Medicine, Friedrich, 225
Future, the, 131–133, 141, 201–203, 278
  absolute, 135
Future of Man, The, Chardin, 76

Gabriel, 26
Galbraith, John Kenneth, quoted, 368, 371
Galilee, 18
Galileo, 118
Gandhi, Mahatma, 383
Gandhi, Rajmohan, 383
Gardner, Martin, quoted, 189
Gauss, Karl Friedrich, 180
Gautama, quoted, 30, 44, 82, 274
Gehenna, 269, 289, 318
Genesis, 96, 201, 212
Genesis legend, 59, 61, 66–68, 70–74, 78, 87, 108
Genetic Code, The, Asimov, 106
Genius, 288, 292–293
Geometry, 175–176, 179
Gerasa, 180
Gethsemane, 34, 246, 248
Gibbs, Josiah Willard, 125
Gibran, Kahlil, quoted, 326
"Gigantic person," Freud's, 57, 102–103
Ginsberg, Allen, 280
  quoted, 274
Gluttony, 116–117
God, 30–34, 49, 51–52, 80, 94, 108, 115, 156
  belief in, 240
  blasphemy and, 173, 226
  and Jesus, 5–6, 16, 24–28, 151, 197, 275, 382
  kingdom of, 13–14, 55, 74, 84–85, 120–121, 129, 131, 133–134, 197, 201, 209, 359, 391
  and life, 76, 392–393
  and love, 102, 107, 110, 112, 116, 236, 281, 392–393
  man and, 15, 30, 44, 53, 58, 60, 91, 97–100, 102, 104–105, 112, 135, 154, 156–157, 159–161, 278, 287–291, 294, 296–298, 302, 305, 328–329, 359, 382, 390, 392–393
  powers of, 275, 392–393
Gods, Graves, and Scholars, Ceram, 85
Goethe, 177, 292
  quoted, 101, 253
Golden Rule, 125, 141, 384–385, 387, 391
Good, 101, 109–111, 113–115, 138–139, 141, 165, 169, 371
Gospel of Thomas, quoted, xxxvi

461

INDEX

Gospels, the, 12-14, 23, 28-30, 82, 143, 227, 229-230, 233-234, 248, 264, 268, 285, 300, 312-315, 321, 333-334, 386
    Synoptic, 12-13, 285
Government, 19, 280, 339, 363-366, 370, 374
Greece and the Greeks, 19-23, 94, 123, 210, 270
Grotjahn, Martin, 116
    quoted, 90
Group, the, 265
Group-ego, 86, 92-94
Guillaume, Alfred, quoted, 1, 329
Guilt, 48-49, 58, 253-254, 281
Guilt complex, 56, 237

"Hadad," 103
Hadamard, Jacques, 209
    quoted, 210
Haeckel, Ernst, 78
Hafiz of Shiraz, quoted, 219
Haley, Andrew G., 384
Hallāj, 329, 382
Hallucination, 215-216, 249, 266, 311-316, 320-321
Ham, 80-81, 95
Hamilton, Edith, quoted, 19, 94
Hammurabi, Code of, 121
Harris, Sydney, 252
    quoted, 295, 353, 360, 410-411
Hasadism, 169
Hawkins, Gerald S., 205
    quoted, 206
Heard, Gerald, 244, 331
Hearing, 263
Heat, 142
Heaven, 130-131, 152, 325
    kingdom of, 13-14, 26-27, 130, 144
Hegel, Georg Wilhelm Friedrich, 375
Heidegger, Martin, 21, 33, 324, 375
Heilbroner, Robert, quoted, 20, 339-343, 346, 350-351, 354-355, 363-364, 366, 369-370
Heisenberg, Werner, 123-124, 153, 407
Hell, 144, 325
Hellenism, 18
Hemingway, Ernest, 282
Herder, Johann von, 10

Heredity, 76
Hezekiah, 359
Hindus, the, 181
Hitler, Adolf, xxii, 249-251
Hobson, John A., quoted, 351
Hocking, William Ernest, quoted, 329
Hoffer, A., quoted, 405, 406
Holton, Gerald, quoted, 259
Holy Ghost, 99, 158-161, 171, 186, 291
House of Intellect, The, Barzun, 272
Hoyle, Fred, 200
Human resources, 340, 342
Humpty Dumpty, 179
Hurkos, Peter, 103
Huxley, Aldous, 218, 244, 270
Huxley, Sir Julian, quoted, 1, 6, 11, 114, 329, 331-332, 362-363
Hypnosis, 95, 102, 214-215, 217-225, 230-231, 243, 262, 331-332, 396-403
Hypnosis and Its Therapeutic Applications, Dorcus, 221
Hypnotherapy, 231, 241, 403, 406
Hypnotic response, 220-223, 236, 239, 247, 252, 316
Hypnotizability, 221
Hysteria, 267, 270

"I," 40, 88, 93, 102-103, 105, 111, 118, 132-133, 151, 160, 164, 205, 283, 290, 302, 322, 325-329, 382-383, 391-393
I Ching, Book of Changes, xxxiii, 176
I-consciousness, 40
Id, the, 36-37, 92, 111-112, 142
Identification, 86, 91, 93, 113
Ikhnaton, 46, 48
Illusion, 215-217
Images, 308-309, 312-313
    father, 98, 278
    (*See also* Mirror)
Imagination, 267
Immortality, 36
    (*See also* Life, eternal)
Imperialism, 351
Income, 352
    mental ability and, 357
Independent existence, fear of, 293-294
Indeterminacy, principle of, 153
India, 383-384

INDEX

Individual, 125
Industrialization, 337–338, 370
Inge, Dean, quoted, 28
Innocence, 37, 62, 96, 254–255
Insanity (*see* Madness)
Instinct, 71
Intellect, 306–307
Intervals, 183–185
Interpretation of Nature and the Psyche, The, Jung and Pauli, 173
Introduction to Harmonics, Nicomachus, 180
Intuition, 286, 291, 295, 306–307, 328
Investing, 348
Iphigenia, Goethe, 101
IQ, 357–358
Irrationality, 64
Isaac, 33, 66, 251–252
Israel, 31, 44, 53, 93–94, 106, 169, 203, 381, 392

Jacob, 33, 203, 364
Jaffé, Aniela, 110
  quoted, 122
James, 13, 284
James, William, 186
  quoted, 216
Japeth, 80
Jared, 72
Java man, 68
Jefferson, Thomas, quoted, 374
Jericho, 18
Jerusalem, 264, 280
Jesus, 1, 5, 7–9, 14–15, 134–135
  baptism of, 268
  Birth of, 82–85, 389–390
  brotherhood of, 91, 101, 210
  and communication, 194–197, 210, 212–213
  crucifixion of, 103, 385
  death of, 166
  economic doctrine of, 344–373
  education of, 19–20
  fear of, 50
  God and, 151, 197, 275, 382
  Gospels and, 12–13, 23, 28–29, 392
  healing ministry of, 228–245, 403
  and Judas, 166–173
  life of, 19
  as light, 148–156, 192–193
  as Messiah, 7, 15–45, 118, 154, 246, 266, 382, 391
  miracles of, 227–258, 284–310
  mystery of, 2
  and nature, 117, 393
  and number *one*, 179–187, 189–193, 209, 212, 322–323, 393
  as poet, 129
  and richness of life, 117
  robe of, 191–192, 239, 361
  as scientist, 242
  symbols of, 11–12
  teachings of, 129–130, 143, 159, 392–393
  trial of, 387
Jesus and His Story, Stauffer, 13, 23
Jews, 16–19, 27, 46–48, 55, 57, 226, 255, 264, 296, 381
  (*See also* Judaism)
John, 229, 284
  Gospel of, 12–13, 17, 28–29, 116–117, 156, 201, 234, 248, 268, 285, 325, 386
John the Baptist, 20, 26, 39–40, 116, 143–144, 301, 317
Jonah, 316
Joseph, 82, 84, 301
Joshua, 206, 335
Judaism, Judaic, 16–18, 20–22, 26, 28, 33, 49, 51, 56, 94, 104, 218, 249, 264–265, 296, 298, 300, 305, 381–382
  (*See also* Jews)
Judas, quoted, 320
Judas Iscariot, xxix, 166–173, 193
Judgment, 140, 289–291, 298–299, 376
Junayd, quoted, 329
Jung, Carl, 36, 38, 43–44, 53, 75, 109, 122, 139, 157, 235–236, 241, 253, 268, 396
  quoted, 3, 11, 49, 173, 176, 180, 224, 266–267, 301, 322, 331, 381

Keller, Werner, 31, 335
Kelsey, Denys, 222
Kepler, Johannes, 176–177
Kerouac, Jack, 280
Keynes, John Maynard, 348, 366
Khidr, 139–140

463

INDEX

Khrushchev, Nikita, 340, 352
  quoted, 4, 380
Kierkegaard, Sören, 117, 238, 252, 288, 295
Kline, Morris, 187-188
  quoted, 14, 153, 181, 187
Kluckhohn, Clyde, quoted, 20, 179, 253, 257
Knowledge, 110-112, 277, 306, 363, 393
Koestler, Arthur, 67
  quoted, 68, 179
Kowal, 406
Krishna, 42, 377, 383
  quoted, 34
Krutch, Joseph Wood, quoted, 62-63, 66
Kuhlman, Katherine, 403-404
Kundalini, 108, 110

Labor-value, 347-348
Laissez-faire, 366
Lamarck, Chevalier de, 76
Lamech, 72
Language, 85-89, 195-197, 275, 280, 323-325
  poetic, 123, 129
Lao-tse, Lao-tzu, quoted, 30, 186
Last Supper, 105, 117
Lateau, Louise, 294
Laughter, 115-116, 118, 393
Lavoisier, quoted, 225
Law, 120-123, 280, 376, 387-388, 392-393
  of nature, 124-145, 210, 392-393, 407-409
  physical, 178, 189, 407-409
  psychic, 14, 125, 136, 279, 407-409
Law, William, 292
Lawrence, D. H., 252
Lazarus, 12, 26, 234-235
Leakey, L. S. B., 72-73
Lebrun, Rico, quoted, 282
LeCron, Leslie, quoted, 218, 220, 253
Lee-Franzini, Juliet, 211
Lee, Jung Young, quoted, xxxiii
Lee, T. D., 189
Leeuwenhoek, 62
Legends, 47, 58-60, 62, 64-68, 70-74, 78-85, 87-91, 103, 139, 203, 238, 279, 335

Legion, 249-257, 297, 298-299, 404-406
Leisure class, 355-356
Lenin, Nikolai, 351, 375
LeShan, 405
Lewis, C. S., quoted, 252
Lewis, N. D. C., 404
Life, 60, 98, 107, 112-113, 160-161, 186, 198-200, 205, 278-279, 281-283, 387, 393
  art of, 116
  blasphemy of, 171
  eternal, 55, 97-98, 100-101, 165, 207, 336, 391
  experience and, 139-141, 170-171
  infinity of, 14
  legendary chain of, 61-95
  love of, 118, 142, 281, 392
  and matter, 164
  mystery of, 105, 224, 392
  prenatal, 78-82
  primordial, 106
  reality of, 316, 391
  richness of, 117
  tree of, 109-110
Light, 110, 121-122, 124, 134, 138, 149-153, 156-157, 168, 172-173, 188-189, 191, 192-198, 208, 212
Light wave-group, 138-139, 172
Lincoln, Abraham, 373-374
Linssen, Robert, 192
  quoted, 119
Logia, 12
Logical dialectic, 375
Logos, 28-29, 34, 290
Logotherapy, 381
Lord's Prayer, 143
Lorentz, 159
Love, 17, 21, 51-52, 55-56, 66, 74, 84, 91, 102, 110-112, 114-116, 120, 138, 141-142, 145, 236, 281, 309, 325-329, 361, 391-393
Lowe, Helen R., quoted, 273
LSD, 244, 300
Lucifer, 110
Luke, Gospel of, 12, 27, 120, 230, 233, 248, 268
Lust, 52, 109, 111, 115, 118, 142, 144, 237
Lyttleton, Raymond A., 211

464

McCurdy, Harold, 37
  quoted, 37, 40, 228–229, 252
McGlashan, Alan, 403, 404, 407
  quoted, xxiii, 400–403
Madness, 22, 232–233, 249–251, 254, 256, 272, 274, 286–287, 291–303, 327
Mammon, xxxi, 112–113, 168, 345–349, 361, 371–373
Man, archaic heritage of, 46–60
  brotherhood of, xxxiv, 4, 30, 58, 378
  consciousness and (*see* Consciousness)
  Cosmic, 62
  destiny of, xxxv, 386
  economic nature of, 344
  educated, 279
  and Ego (*see* Ego)
  evolution of (*see* Evolution)
  and freedom, 157–158
  and God, 30, 44, 53, 58, 60, 91, 97–100, 102, 104, 112, 135, 154, 156–157, 159–161, 278, 287–291, 294, 296–298, 302, 305, 328–329, 359, 382, 390, 392–393
  and Jesus, 143, 241–242
  and laughter, 116
  and life, 282–283
  Logos in, 28–29, 34
  modern, 8
  origin of, 81, 84–85
  and poetry, 10
  primitive, 65–73, 84
  psyche of, 34–35
  psychological study of, 3, 35–45
  without religion, 5
  and sex, 51–54
  and society, 125, 138
  understanding of, 257
  and violence, 140–141
Man: The Bridge Between Two Worlds, Winkler, 112
Man and His Symbols, Jung, 38, 122
Managers, 350, 353–354, 369
Marion, Frederick, 231, 311
  quoted, 88, 214, 216
Mark, Gospel of, 12–13, 228, 233, 264, 268, 285
Marmer, Milton J., 219
Marriage, 52–53, 252, 328
Martyrdom, 295, 299

Marx, Karl, 4, 6, 94, 346–348, 351–353, 369, 375, 410–411
  quoted, 347
Mary (*see* Virgin Mary)
Mary Magdalene, 314–315
Maslow, Abraham, xxii
Materialism, 371
Mathematical Theory of Communication, The, Weaver and Shannon, 194–197
Mathematics, 15, 129–130, 175–177, 179–193, 210, 322–323, 363
Matter, 109, 122, 129, 134, 152, 164, 168–169, 200–201, 206, 211, 212
Matthew, Gospel of, 12–13, 27, 120, 264, 268, 272, 285, 333–334
Maxwell, Clerk, 155
May, Rollo, 270
  quoted, 43, 273, 281
Mayer, Julius Robert, 292
Medicine, 219, 222, 232
  socialized, 367
Memory-images, 138, 141
Mendel, Gregor, 76
Mental ability, 357
Mental disorders, 289, 291–297, 320
  (*See also* Madness)
Mescalin, 244
Mesmerism, 219, 229, 239, 243
Messiah, 49, 103–104, 115, 251, 256, 258, 295–296, 381, 390
  Jesus as, 7, 15–45, 264–267, 293, 296, 298, 300–302, 382, 391
Messianic delusion, xxii, xxiii, xxviii–xxix, 16, 246, 250–251, 255–257, 294, 296–300, 382–383
Messianic doctrines, 6
Messianic pretension, xxi–xxiv, xxviii–xxix, 246, 256, 297, 299–300, 378, 382
Messianic vision, 6
Metalaw, 384, 387
Metaphysics, 21, 325, 376
Miller, Arthur, quoted, 254–255
Miller, Henry, quoted, 117
Miller, Samuel, 2–3, 59
  quoted, 115, 120
Mind, 67, 129, 136, 141, 242, 306, 392
Miracles, 15, 225–226, 262, 279, 316, 393
  Biblical, 12, 225, 227, 242, 335, 393

465

INDEX

Miracles (*continued*)
  illusory, 284–310
  social, 246–258
Mirel, Elizabeth, 384
Mirror, mirror-image, 112–113, 211, 212, 309, 325
Mitchell, Alan, 235
  quoted, 230
Mixson, Ashley, quoted, 323
Moffatt, James, 12, 27, 247
  quoted, 23–24, 27, 29, 285
Molecules, 126–127
Moore, Ruth, 68
  quoted, 69, 83–84, 108, 224
Morality, 139, 355
Morgan, T. H., 187
Moses, 46–48, 51, 81, 139–140, 165, 177, 218, 269, 317, 379, 388
  Law of, 120–121, 279
Moses and Monotheism, Freud, 46
Motion, 154
Motivation, unconscious, 164
Muhammed, Mohammed, 6, 274, 383
Muller, Herbert J., quoted, 250
Murder, 48, 99, 104–105, 251
Murray, Henry A., quoted, 9
Museum of Modern Art, New York City, 272
Music and musicians, 177–178
Mutation, 75
Myers, Frederic W. H., quoted, 320
Mystics, 286, 302, 327, 329
Myths, 47, 58, 60, 81–82, 89, 91, 276
  (*See also* Legends)

Naskapi Indians, 38
Natural selection, 63
Nature, 117, 123, 208, 210–211, 238, 327, 358, 386, 392–393
  Laws of, 123–145, 150, 210, 392–393
Nature of the Physical World, The, Eddington, 124
Nazareth, 19
Neanderthal man, 65, 68, 70
Nehru, Jawaharlal, 4
  quoted, 5
Neil, William, quoted, 24
Neilson, William, 218

Nelson, William Stuart, quoted, 379
Neumann, Thérèse, 231, 248, 294
Neurosis, 269
Neurospora, 83–84
Neurotics, 251, 254
Neutrinos, 189–190, 212, 392
New English Bible, The, 23, 256
Newton, Isaac, 155, 292, 306
Nicodemus, 288
  quoted, 97
Nicomachus of Gerasa, 180–181
  quoted, 182–183
Nietzsche, Friedrich, 21, 297, 375
  quoted, 286, 371
Nihilism, 213, 278
Noah, 72–73, 79–81, 84, 95, 272
Noah legend, 78–81, 96
Now, 41, 115, 131–135, 153, 190, 204

Oedipus curse, 80
Oedipus impulse, 116
Oedipus legend, 90
Oersted, Hans Christian, 209
Old Man and the Sea, The, Hemingway, 282
Olduvai Gorge, Tanzania, East Africa, 73
Omar Khayyám, quoted, 137
One (itself), 146–174, 179–187, 189–193, 200, 322, 383, 390, 393
Oppenheimer, J. Robert, quoted, 201
Origin of Species, Darwin, 46
Original sin, 3, 49, 62, 65, 96, 108–109
Overstreet, Harry, quoted, 148
Ownership, absentee, 350, 353–354

Pain, 110, 114, 139
Palestine, 180
Parables, 15, 60, 106, 164, 194, 203, 210, 322, 345–346, 348, 350, 354, 358, 360
Paradise, 97
  (*See also* Heaven)
Parapsychologists, 215, 266
Parapsychology, 213, 214, 224, 311, 331
Parents, 3, 81, 84–85, 89–91, 94–95, 236, 253
  (*See also* Fathers)
Parity, 189

INDEX

Parthenogenesis, 82, 85
Participation, 113
Particles, 153-154, 168, 172, 189, 200-201, 211, 212, 386, 392
Pascal, Blaise, 288, 297, 302, 318
Past, the, 237
Pasternak, Boris, quoted, 280, 283
Pattie, Frank A., quoted, 221
Paul, St., xxiv-xxv, 8, 17, 28, 48-49, 51, 56, 166, 192, 251, 293, 296-297, 392
   quoted, 5, 22, 50, 55, 356, 381
Pauli, Wolfgang, 75, 122, 173, 175-176
   quoted, 176-177, 180, 217
Pauline doctrine, 1, 5-6, 8, 16, 56-57, 251, 392
Pauwels, Louis, quoted, 392
Peace, 376-377, 379, 388-389
Pearl Harbor, 271
Peel, Robert, quoted, 242-243
Pegasus, 279-280
Peking man, 65, 68-69
Perception, 216-217, 258-259, 267-268, 275, 287
Personality, 3, 37, 98, 154-155, 157, 309-310, 320, 325, 360
Peter, St., 229, 268, 284-285, 306-308
   quoted, 24, 104, 284, 308
Pharisees, scribes and, 276-277, 280
Phenomena, parapsychological, 214, 276
   supranatural, 214
Physicists, 126-131, 160, 189, 198-201, 212, 225
Physics, 120, 122-125, 127-128, 137, 147-148, 160-161
   quantum, 14, 150-152, 177
Pilate, 27-28, 258, 375, 385, 387-388
PK (psychokinetic force), 263, 266
Planck, Max, quoted, 225
Plato, 19
   quoted, 10
Pliocene, 70-71
Poets and poetry, 9-10, 15, 123, 129, 266, 274-275
   of the Bible, 9
Polanyi, Michael, 373
Political systems, 338-344
Possession, 320-321, 327
   definition of, 320

Possessions, 353, 361
Postcognition, 215, 217
Posthypnotic response, 221, 321
Poverty, 117, 355-358, 363, 373
Power, 5, 22, 89, 99-100, 113-114, 203, 214, 351-352, 354, 363
   absolute, 200, 393
   of God, 275, 393
   psychic, 216, 258-283
   to reason, 278-279
Prayer, 227, 391
Precognition, 215, 217, 267
Preconsciousness, 41, 154
Priestley, J. B., 5
   quoted, 3-4, 10, 292-294, 297, 328-329
Princess of Egypt, 81, 84
Private property, 361
Prodigal son, 358
Profit, 345-346, 348, 351-352, 370
Progoff, Ira, 120
   quoted, xxvi-xxvii, 35-36, 39, 44, 287-288, 303, 381
Protein, 108
Pseudopregnancy, 82, 85
Psyche, 34-35, 92
Psychiatrists, 43
Psychic ability, 102-103
Psychic disorder, 229-231, 271, 276
   (*See also* Mental disorders)
Psychic equilibrium, 142
Psychic law, 14, 125, 136, 279
Psychic power, 216
   Jesus and, 258-283
Psychical Research Today, West, 258
Psychoanalysis, 37, 219, 221, 236
Psychologists, 3, 35-37, 41, 44, 57, 59, 89, 92-93, 144-145
Psychology, 3-4, 34-45, 92-93
   religion and, 244, 281, 381
   science and, 122
Psychology of Invention in the Mathematical Field, The, Hadamard, 209
Psychosis, 157
Psychosomatics, 220, 225
Psychotherapists, 43
Psychotherapy, 229
Punishment, 101, 115, 140, 253
Pythagoras, 182

INDEX

Quantum, 14, 147, 150–152, 154–155, 168, 177
Quimby, Phineas, 119

Radhakrishnan, quoted, 6–7, 380–381
Random, definition of, 136
Random element, 126–127, 129, 136, 140, 192
Rank, Otto, 36, 44, 157, 287, 381
  quoted, 45, 47, 84, 288, 303
Rationality, 64
Reading, 273–275, 280
Reality, 15, 98, 118, 129, 159, 181, 215, 308
Reasoning power, 278–279
Rebirth, 38, 97–98, 101–102, 111, 288, 299, 304, 333–336
Redemption, 14, 55–56, 145
Redundancy, 195, 197, 210–212, 213
Regression, 3, 48, 220
Reich, Wilhelm, 295
Reik, Theodore, quoted, 327
Reincarnation, 95, 97–98, 101
Reiss, Samuel, quoted, 129
Relativity, 152–153, 165
Religion, 6–7, 303–306, 380, 383–384, 390–391
  decline of, 1–5
  mental disorder and, 289–297
  psychology and, 119–120, 242–244, 381
  questioning, 6
  science and, 119–123
  society and, 4
Renan, Ernest, 20
  quoted, 16–19, 166
Repentance, 169, 171
Repression, 35, 37, 41, 145, 165, 229
Resonance, 160–161
Resurrection, 109–110, 170
  of Jesus, 117, 311–332
  of Lazarus, 234
Reward, 115
Rhine, J. B., 215, 236
Rhine, Louisa, 263, 312, 325
Riches (see Wealth)
Rimbaud, Arthur, 286, 292
Ritual, 303–304
RNA, 106–107
Robe of Jesus, 191–192, 239, 361

Rochefoucauld, François, Duc de la, quoted, 144–145
Roller, Duane H. D., quoted, 259
Romance, 327
Rome and the Romans, 18–20, 94
Rostand, Jean, 82
  quoted, 83
Rousseau, Jean Jacques, 293–294
Rush, Benjamin, 374
Russia, 340–341, 353, 380
Ryle, Martin, 200

Sacrifice, 32, 251–253
Salisbury, Harrison, quoted, 273
Salt, 116, 282, 388
Salvation, 48
Sanity, 288, 290–291, 305
Santayana, George, 9
Sargon of Agade, 81
Sartre, Jean-Paul, 326
  quoted, 290
Saskatchewan, Canada, 367
Satan, 104, 109, 115
  (See also Devil)
Saul of Tarsus, 56
Saving grace, 115, 119, 121
Schimberg, Albert Paul, 294
Schizophrenics, 268, 289
Schmale, A. H., Jr., 237
Schonfeld, Gabriel, 390
Schrödinger, Erwin, 160, 198
  quoted, 108, 178–179, 190–191, 199
Schumpeter, Joseph Alois, 368–369
Schweitzer, Albert, 20, 22, 43, 55
  quoted, 17–18, 21, 356
Science, 8–9, 125, 128, 212, 278, 372–373
  and psychology, 122–123
  and religion, 119–123
Science, Faith, and Society, Polanyi, 373
Science News Letter, 244
Scientists, 119, 134, 136, 168, 175–177, 187–188, 213, 223, 371–372
Scribes and Pharisees, 277, 280
Scripture (see Bible)
Seances, 311
Second Law of Thermodynamics, 120–121, 123, 125, 129, 131, 136, 165–166, 193, 197, 203, 273, 364, 368

468

INDEX

Seidenberg, Roderick, quoted, 136
Self-actualization, 158
Self-consciousness, 6, 77
Self-control, 102, 113
Self-estrangement, 42
Self-hypnosis, 220
Self-interest, 367
Self-love, 144
Selye, Hans, 222
   quoted, 223
Sensory stimuli, 266–267
Sermon on the Mount, 17, 201, 203, **249**, 256, 282
Serpent, serpent power, 108–109, 162, **165**, 176
Seth, 72–73
Sex, xxxiv, 3, 50–51, 55–56, 63, 84, 327
Sexual libido, 49–50
Sexuality, xxv, xxxiv, 49, 51, 54, 84
Shahani, Ranjee, quoted, 20
Shakespeare, William, quoted, 328–329, 349
Shannon, Claude E., 194
Shaw, George Bernard, 5, 306
Shem, 80
Shiva, 281
Shock, 223, 230, 239, 241, 405–406
Sibelius, Jean, 178
Sibling rivalry, 300
Simeons, A. T. W., quoted, 64–66
Sin, 94, 101, 111, 115, 169–173, 253–255, 279, 281
   remission of, 111, 162, 237
Sirius, 148, 151
Sithole, Ndabanningi, quoted, 30
Sleep, 244
Smith, Adam, 348
Snow, Sir Charles P., quoted, 273
Social security, 364
Socialism, 340, 344–345
Socialization, 338–339, 342–344, 367
Society, 90–91, 93–95, 362–363
   crime and, 251, 254, 257
   man and, 125, 138
   religion and, 4
Socrates, 19
Son of man, 17, 22, 26, 28, 32, 76, 172, 258, 288, 296, 301, 318, 328, 392

Sonic waves, 35, 263
Sons, 57–58, 157, 159, 281
Soul, 54, 144, 169–170, 289, 291, 326
Space, 132, 152, 158, 186, 191–192, 204–205
Space Age, 384
Space Law and Government, Haley, 384
Speech, 386
   power of, 323–325, 393
   (*See also* Language)
Spencer, Herbert, quoted, 119, 327
Spengler, Oswald, 50
Spirit, 105, 107, 109–110, 112, 282, 322, 392
   (*See also* Soul)
Spurway, Helen, quoted, 82
Stars, 11, 148–151
State, the, 94
   (*See also* Government; Political systems)
Static Universe Theory, 205
Stauffer, Ethelbert, 13, 166, 296
   quoted, 18, 22–24, 33, 234
Steady-State Theory, 200, 205–206
Stevenson, Ian, quoted, 331
Stoics, the, 44, 94
Straus, Erwin W., quoted, 215, 217, 275
Streeter, Burnett H., 12
Stress, 223, 232–233, 238, 267
Strindberg, Johan August, 292
Suares, Carlo, 208
   quoted, 192
Subconsciousness, 41, 86–87, 95, 101, 136, 154–155, 253, 323
Suffering, 139–141, 282
Sufi mystics, 382
   quoted, 327, 329
Sufism, 159–160
Suggestion, hypnotic, 220–223, 239, 245, 247, 252, 266
Sun, the, 208
Superconsciousness, 154
Superego, 39–40, 92, 112, 168, 232, 294, 321–322
Superstition, 119
Suzuki, D. T., 287
Swados, Harvey, 360
   quoted, 359
Swedenborg, Emanuel, 215

INDEX

Symbols, 7, 11, 38, 97, 105, 108, 118, 121, 124, 129, 134, 146, 162–163, 173, 181, 195–196, 209, 264–265, 269, 275–276, 303
Symmetry, 190–191
Synchronicity, 266–268

Tagore, Rabindranath, quoted, 387
Tao, 114, 186, 191–192
Tatum, Edward L., 83
Taxation, 363–365
Taylor, Deems, 178
Tears, 116, 118
Technology, 344
Teilhard de Chardin, Pierre, 61, 76, 396
  quoted, 76, 137, 338
Telepathy, 87–88, 215, 217, 225, 231–232, 241, 252–253, 311, 313, 320
Ten Commandments, the, 14, 21, 120, 125, 361, 391
Tennyson, Lord Alfred, quoted, 114
Tension, 267, 319
  (*See also* Stress)
Tetragrammaton, 191–192
Theology, 381
  Christian, 2, 4–5, 7–8, 276, 281, 381
Thermodynomical equilibrium, 142, 191
Thrasyllus, 180
Three, 173, 175–193, 212
Thucydides, quoted, 270
Tidings, Weichert, 389
Tillich, Paul, quoted, 269, 271
Time, 129–133, 135, 141–144, 147, 152, 191–192, 198–199, 204
Tinguely, Jean, 272
Tithing, 203, 364
Tolstoy, Leo, quoted, 309
Totalitarianism, 338, 340, 343–344
Totemism, 48, 80
Toynbee, Arnold, 303
  quoted, 10
Toynbee, Philip, quoted, 202–203, 379
Trance, 217–221, 223–224, 226, 229, 234–236, 238, 241, 244–245, 252, 311, 322–323, 335, 396–403
Transcendentalism, 119
Transfiguration, the, 284, 302

Transgressions, forgiveness of, 143
  (*See also* Forgiveness; Sin)
Trauma, 81, 94, 103
Trinity, 99, 158–159, 173, 176
Troward, Thomas, quoted, 104
Truth, 7–9, 11, 14–15, 28–29, 33, 35, 55, 74, 82, 94, 98, 105, 107–108, 118, 121, 155, 192, 215–216, 227, 248, 280, 286, 295, 297, 299, 321–322, 325, 371, 374–388, 390–393
Tsung Ping, quoted, 319
Tyrell, G. N. M., 235, 249
  quoted, 215–216

Ulla, quoted, 19
Uncertainty, 197–199
Unconscious, the, xxi, xxxi, 14–15, 34–36, 38–43, 45, 75, 81, 87, 91, 98, 100, 102, 105, 130–131, 134–136, 139, 142–144, 155–157, 166, 180, 206, 209–210, 214, 237, 245, 258, 287, 293, 298, 306, 309, 316–317, 321–325, 330, 381, 395–396
  collective, 122, 395–396
Unconscious Before Freud, The, Whyte, 34
Underdeveloped nations, 337–338, 342
Unemployment, 356
United States, 340, 344, 352–354, 368, 373–374
Universe, the, 60, 205–206, 208, 278–279, 392
  expansion of, 204
  theories of death of, 200
Unnamable, The, Beckett, 376
Usury, 348

Van den Berg, J. H., quoted, 3–4, 92, 226, 361–362
Van Dusen, Henry Pitt, quoted, 23
Veblen, Thorstein, 355
Velikovsky, Immanuel, 206–207, 335
Victims, 138, 254–255, 265
Violence, 140–141
Virgin Mary, 26, 82, 84–85, 301
"Virgin Spring, The," Bergman, 293, 304
Visions, 284–286, 302, 315, 317
Vogler, Abt, quoted, 178
Volvox, 62–63, 74, 78

INDEX

Von Franz, M.-L., quoted, 54, 75, 122–123, 139–140, 172, 180, 235

Wages, 153
War, 270–271, 284, 334, 351, 376–380
Washburn, Sherwood L., 68–69
Wealth, 168, 298, 307, 309, 348, 350, 352, 355–359, 368
Weaver, Warren, 368
   quoted, 194–197
Weizsaeker, Viktor von, 237
Wernli, Hans, J., 197–198
West, D. J., 294
   quoted, 258, 275
West, Louis J., 243
What is Life?, Schrödinger, 178
Wheeler, John A., quoted, 396
Whitehead, Alfred North, 291, 293
   quoted, 122, 214, 291–292
Whitlow, Joseph, 221
Whitman, Walt, quoted, 291, 379, 385
Whyte, Lancelot Law, quoted, 34–35, 42
Wiechert, Ernst, 389
Wiener, Norbert, quoted, 372, 386
Wild Heritage, Carrighar, 294
Will, 63, 156–158
Williams, Griffith, 312
Wilson, Colin, quoted, 265, 285–287, 291–293, 302–303, 306, 309–310
Winckler, Hugo, 31
Wine, 116–117
Winkler, Franz, 112
   quoted, 88
Wittgenstein, Ludwig, 286
Woman, xxxiv, 51–54, 67, 84, 135, 212
Word, the, 31–33, 275, 279–280, 387, 392–393
Work, 66–67, 359, 360, 362, 369–370, 372, 392–393
World War II, 376
Worlds in Collision, Velikovsky, 206
Wu, Mme. Chien-Shiung, 189

Yang, Chen Ning, 189
   quoted, 190
Yeats, William Butler, quoted, 318
Yin and Yang, 176
Yoga, 42
Yogi, 108, 110
Yogins, 220

Zebedaeus, 13
Zahner, Louis, quoted, 273
Zen, 238, 287
Zero, 181–183, 186, 191, 197–199

XIV - Introduction - Bringing rel. & science together

P. 23 - find kingdom within yourself -

P. 28 - Understanding who & what we are - the depths of unconsc. mind - Second coming of Christ thru Bible

P. 74 - Inner drive in evolution, not just a happening

P. 90 - Family relations - let late teens make own decisions thru God within

P. 230 - Hypnosis helps to bring forth info. from subcons.

P. 227 - Posthypnotic (thru thoughts) mind - sug. by Christ to write gospels.

P. 298 - Thru vision of Christ in mind our lines may be graced

P. 321 - Christ may be ident. in everyone

P. 332 - Resurrection - manifestations real to some who were prepared but not real to all

P. 391 - Jesus came not to destroy but to fulfill - thru private worship.